Lotus Notes® R6 Professional Projects

Lotus Notes® R6 Professional Projects

Nilima Agarwal
and
Sanjeev Sreedharan
with
NIIT

Premier Press™

ISBN: 1-931841-38-1

Library of Congress Catalog Card Number: 2002116164

Printed in the United States of America

03 04 05 06 07 BH 10 9 8 7 6 5 4 3 2 1

Premier Press, a division of Course Technology
2645 Erie Avenue, Suite 41
Cincinnati, Ohio 45208

Publisher
Stacy L. Hiquet

Marketing Manager
Heather Hurley

Manager of Editorial Services
Heather Talbot

Project Editor
Argosy

Copy Editor
Ginny Kaczmarek

Interior Layout
Argosy

Cover Designer
Mike Tanamachi

Indexer
Sharon Shock

About NIIT

NIIT is a global IT solutions corporation with a presence in 38 countries. With its unique business model and technology-creation capabilities, NIIT delivers software and learning solutions to more than 1,000 clients across the world.

The success of NIIT's training solutions lies in its unique approach to education. NIIT's Knowledge Solutions Business conceives, researches, and develops all of its course material. A rigorous instructional design methodology is followed to create engaging and compelling course content.

NIIT trains over 200,000 executives and learners each year in information technology areas using stand-up training, video-aided instruction, computer-based training (CBT), and Internet-based training (IBT). NIIT has been featured in the *Guinness Book of World Records* for the largest number of learners trained in one year!

NIIT has developed over 10,000 hours of instructor-led training (ILT) and over 3,000 hours of Internet-based training and computer-based training. IDC ranked NIIT among the Top 15 IT training providers globally for the year 2000. Through the innovative use of training methods and its commitment to research and development, NIIT has been in the forefront of computer education and training for the past 20 years.

Quality has been the prime focus at NIIT. Most of the processes are ISO-9001 certified. It was the 12th company in the world to be assessed at Level 5 of SEI-CMM. NIIT's Content (Learning Material) Development facility is the first in the world to be assessed at this highest maturity level. NIIT has strategic partnerships with companies such as Computer Associates, IBM, Microsoft, Oracle, and Sun Microsystems.

Acknowledgments

We owe many thanks to our families and friends for being patient with us while we were authoring this book. Not only this, they also motivated and inspired us at all times to bring out our best in the book. Thank you all for this!

We would also want to thank Mridula Parihar and Sripriya for showing complete trust in us. Their valuable inputs while reviewing the book and constant guidance helped us a lot in successfully completing the book. A very special thanks to both of you!

We also extend our sincere thanks to Kathleen Byrne and Ginny Kaczmarek for editing the chapters so well. Without their help, the book would not have been in its present form.

Our special thanks to Stacy Hiquet for entrusting NIIT with this project.

About the Authors

Nilima Agarwal is a Principal Certified Lotus Professional for Release 4 and a Certified Lotus Professional for Release 5 in both Application Development and System Administration. She is also a Certified Lotus Instructor in both Application Development and System Administration. Nilima's career with Domino began when she was employed with a Lotus Authorized Education Centre in New Delhi, and for the past four years, she has enhanced her expertise as a freelance Lotus Notes consultant. She has conducted numerous training sessions on various topics in Domino and has also been actively developing applications for Lotus Notes. She has provided Subject Matter Expertise (SME) for various books, CBTs, and Web-based training materials on Lotus Notes for NIIT.

Sanjeev Sreedharan is a seasoned entrepreneurial technologist with over ten years of experience in the IT industry. He has expertise in E-business, Web development technologies, product development, system architecture, system integration, and project management. During his career, he has held various positions that have augmented his Lotus Notes expertise, including his tenure as director of technology and operations for an IT consultancy and solutions company, his time as a consultant in close association with Lotus Corporation, India Operations, his participation as designer and developer of a Knowledge Management Solution for McKinsey, India, and his time as a System Analyst and Software Specialist.

Sanjeev has executed numerous projects based on Lotus Notes. He conceived, designed, and developed various software solutions including Retail Business Management System, Distribution Management System, and HR Consultancy Management System, on various platforms such as Lotus Notes, Oracle, and FoxPro. He implemented the Lotus Notes Network with gateway connectivity across India, and he also implemented JP Morgan's worldwide Lotus Notes and Messaging Network. In addition, he designed and developed the software product "Harmony," a comprehensive Human Resource Management System with workflow automation capabilities in Lotus Notes, which was first of its kind of product in India on Lotus Notes.

Contents at a Glance

Contents

Introduction

This book provides you with a comprehensive knowledge about the Domino Designer. This book is aimed at readers who have been end users of Lotus Notes. The book does not require any extensive programming background as a prerequisite, but expects the reader to have some experience developing applications using other tools and languages. The book also assumes that the reader has working knowledge of word processing packages and is familiar with the concepts of formatting a document.

Part I of this book provides you with an overview of Domino Designer R6. This part contains chapters that walk you through the basic concepts of designing an application in Domino. You will be introduced to creating a database and creating design elements such as forms, pages, views, agents, and navigation structures. You will also be introduced to the various programming options available in Domino Designer such as formula language, LotusScript, JavaScript, and Java. The later chapters in this part introduce you to securing a Domino application and creating and deploying database templates. The concepts learned in these chapters are implemented in later parts of the book.

Parts II through VI of the book cover several projects that include creating, testing, and deploying Domino applications. The types of applications demonstrated in this book include a reference application, a discussion database, a workflow and tracking application, an application to access non-Notes databases, and a Web-enabled application. These projects use the concepts discussed in Part I of the book to build projects that can be used in everyday scenarios. In addition, readers learn advanced programming concepts to enhance these projects to create real-life business solutions. After developing the projects in the Professional Projects parts of the book, the readers will be able to appreciate the ease of creating and deploying the applications created using Domino Designer R6. The reader will also be able apply the knowledge gained to create customized applications using Domino Designer in real-life scenarios.

The next section of the book, Part VII: Beyond the Lab, covers some useful programming concepts that can be implemented in any Domino application. Chapter 26 introduces you to the implementation of XML in a Domino application. Chapter 27 explains creating help for an application. Chapter 28 provides detailed knowledge on working with lists and multi-value fields. Chapter 29 covers implementing calendar and scheduling feature in a Domino application.

The Appendices provide information for reference. There are appendices providing a list of LotusScript classes, Java classes for Domino, Domino URL reference and the features to be avoided in a Web application. Also included is an introduction to the fundamentals of JavaScript that lists the JavaScript objects for use in a Notes application.

PART I

Introducing Domino Designer R6

Chapter 1

Overview of Domino Applications

Domino is a groupware platform that provides messaging, calendaring, and scheduling tightly integrated with application development framework that enables people to communicate, collaborate, and coordinate irrespective of their locations. Domino provides the environment and necessary tools for development and deployment of applications that can be used to achieve business process and workflow automation in a secure and scalable way.

Take an example of a simple task, such as applying for leave. An employee fills out a leave application, which is presented to his boss for approval. Filling out the leave application and presenting it to the boss is communication. The boss evaluates the application and decides whether or not the application should be approved. When evaluating, the boss accesses the leave application and shares her comments with the employee. This is collaboration. After the application is approved, an HR executive updates the employee's leave record and also organizes for the available facilities, such as leave travel allowance or hotel bookings. This is coordination. If this process were manual, it would have led to a waste of a lot of time and energy at all levels: employee, supervisor, and HR executive. With Domino, you can automate business processes and, therefore, save time and effort that would be wasted in physical movement and manual processing.

In this chapter, you'll learn about the complete Domino family. The chapter will identify the various types of applications that can be created using the Domino Designer client and the various components of the Domino Designer interface. You'll also learn about different methods to create a database. Finally, you'll learn to generate a design synopsis for a database.

Introduction to the Domino Family

Domino is based on the client/server architecture, where the server serves clients by providing services like messaging, scheduling, and access to shared applications. The Domino family includes various servers and clients, which are described in the following sections.

Domino R6 Servers

A Domino server is a powerful software platform used to perform tasks such as routing messages to Notes and the Internet; allowing users to browse the Web; hosting applications for Notes, Web, and mobile users; and providing real-time integration with enterprise data.

Based on their functionality, Domino servers can be categorized as follows:

- **Domino Messaging server.** This server is used only for messaging and supports Notes mail in addition to Internet standards for mail, such as SMTP (Simple Mail Transfer Protocol), POP3 (Post Office Protocol Version 3), IMAP (Internet Message Access Protocol), and Web mail.
- **Domino Utility server.** This server provides application services only. This server does not include support for messaging services but supports Domino clusters.
- **Domino Enterprise server.** This server has the built-in features of the Mail and Utility servers. Additionally, it provides features such as clustering for failover and load balancing.

Domino R6 Clients

Domino clients access the Domino server to perform functions such as sending e-mail, accessing databases, and Web browsing. Various Domino clients are as follows:

- **Notes client.** This client is for end users. It can be used for tasks such as messaging, Web browsing, organizing schedules, and accessing applications.
- **Administrator client.** This client is for administrators. It is used for all types of administrative tasks, such as registering the Domino server, registering users, and setting up and managing the Domino infrastructure.
- **Domino Designer client.** This client is for application developers. It provides an integrated development environment that allows you to develop Domino applications for various purposes.

Besides these three clients, some other clients that can access a Domino server include:

- Web browsers, such as Internet Explorer and Netscape Navigator
- Internet mail clients, such as Outlook Express
- Mobile clients, such as WAP-enabled cellular phones and PDA
- iNotes

Types of Domino Applications

You develop Domino applications in the Domino Designer client. Domino Designer allows you to create applications that can be used by Notes clients, Web browsers, or mobile clients. The different types of Domino applications that can be created are as follows:

- **Workflow.** This type of application allows users to communicate, collaborate, and coordinate business activities. Some common examples of workflow applications are leave approval, loan approval, and purchase requisition.
- **Reference.** This type of application is used to store online references, such as company policies or ISO documentation. Since Domino allows you to share information, these applications are available to all users.
- **Collaborations.** This type of application is typically used for discussions. A discussion application is used as a forum for exchanging thoughts and inviting feedback from other users.
- **Tracking.** This type of application is used to track the status of any item, such as a customer complaint, a credit card number, or a document life cycle.
- **Broadcasting.** This type of application is used to send newsletters to users over e-mail.

Domino Designer allows you to create common applications for use on both Notes and Web clients and mobile platforms. Additionally, Domino Designer provides you with specialized Web development features, such as an HTML editor, JavaScript libraries, embedding Applets and Java agents. For more information on these Web-related features, refer to Chapter 6, "Working with HTML and JavaScript," and Chapter 7, "Working with Java."

Domino Designer allows you to create applications that interact with enterprise data, such as RDBMS (Relational Database Management Systems) like Oracle and Syabase, TP (Transaction Processing) systems like IBM MQSeries and IMS, and ERP (Enterprise Resource Planning) systems like SAP and Peoplesoft, and unstructured data. You can create applications that process data in Notes and then post the data to a back-end database. You can also create applications that provide real-time access to enterprise data. To create such applications, Domino Designer provides tools such as DECS (*Domino Enterprise Connection Services*), DCR (*Data Connection Resources*), LEI (*Lotus Enterprise Integrator*), and Domino connectors. You can connect to enterprise data from a Domino application by using LotusScript and Java classes. For more information on connecting to enterprise data refer to Chapter 19, "Accessing Non-Notes Databases from Domino"

Domino Designer also allows you to create multilingual applications that can be translated to the local language of users. To translate Domino applications to different languages, Domino Global Workbench is used, which is a translation tool integrated with Domino Designer. This feature helps develop international applications for users worldwide.

Introduction to Domino Designer

Domino Designer provides you with an integrated development environment that allows you to write programs using several languages, such as formula language, LotusScript, JavaScript, and Java.

The Welcome Page

When you start Domino Designer, the first screen displayed is the Welcome page as shown in Figure 1.1.

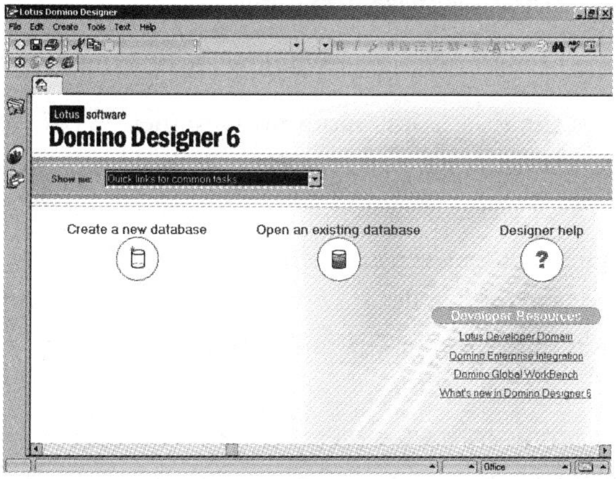

FIGURE 1.1 *The Welcome page*

The Welcome page displays a Show me list that offers a user several options. By default, Quick links for common tasks is selected. This option displays links for opening a database, creating a new database, and accessing Domino Designer Help. It also contains links to various developer resources on the Web, such as Notes.net.

You can customize the Welcome page by selecting any other option from the Show me list to display one of the following pages:

- **Domino Objects for LotusScript and OLE.** This page displays a hierarchical representation of LotusScript classes that are used to access Domino objects programmatically. For more information on LotusScript classes, refer to Chapter 5, "Working with LotusScript."
- **Domino Objects for DXL Support.** This page displays Domino objects as represented in XML. DXL is the XML representation of Domino objects, such as forms, views, and documents.
- **JavaScript Object Model.** This page displays the JavaScript objects that are used to access Domino objects. For more information on JavaScript objects, refer to Chapter 6.

Components of the Domino Designer Window

The Domino Designer window contains elements such as a menu bar, a toolbar, and preview buttons, as shown in Figure 1.2. These elements are used for different purposes at various stages during database designing.

The various components of the Domino Designer window are described as follows:

- **Title bar.** This displays the title Lotus Domino Designer. When you open any database element, the name of the element is added to the title bar.
- **Menu bar.** This contains context-sensitive commands, such as Save or Close. The menu bar is customizable. It contains a Tools menu option that can be used to add new tools or customize the tools on the Tools menu.
- **Toolbar.** This contains tools for faster access to commands, such as creating a new design element or saving an element in a database. If the toolbar is not displayed, choose File/Preferences/Toolbar Preferences. Then in the Toolbar Preferences dialog box, check Show Toolbars. You can also display multiple toolbars.

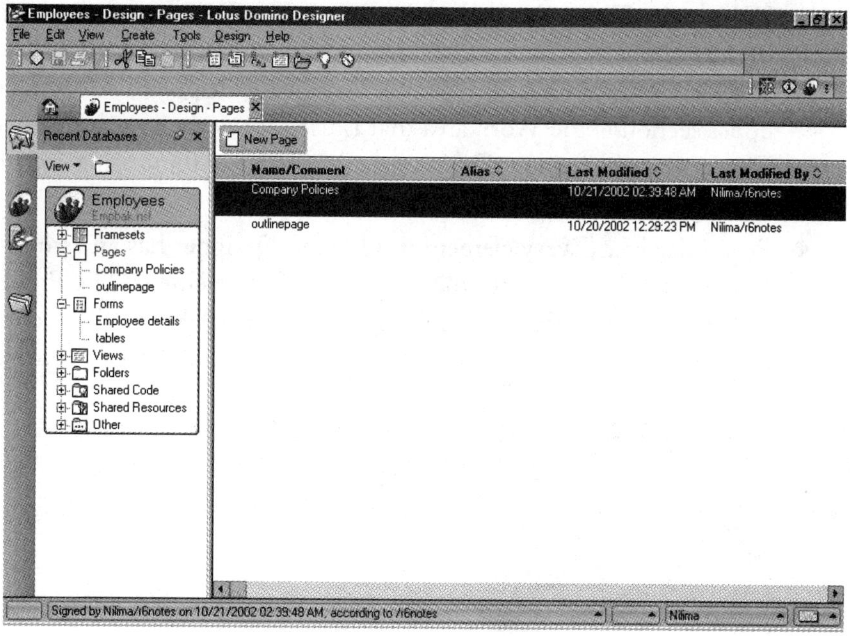

FIGURE 1.2 *Components of the Domino Designer window*

- **Preview buttons.** These are used to launch a Notes client or a browser to preview an element that you've designed while working on a database. Domino Designer adds a preview button for every browser that is installed on your computer.
- **Tabbed windows.** These tabs allow you to navigate from one open window to another. You can also close a window without navigating to it.
- **Bookmark bar.** This is located to the extreme left of the Welcome page and contains bookmarks for databases. Bookmarks help you quickly access databases and organize them. The default bookmark is called Recent Databases and contains links to the databases recently opened in Domino Designer. You can create additional bookmarks on the Bookmark bar.
- **Design pane.** This displays a list of design elements and resources that a database can contain.
- **Design list.** This displays a list of elements that exist in the current database. For example, when you click Pages in the Design pane, the Design list of pages is displayed to the right.

- **Work pane.** This is located to the right of the Design pane and contains the Design list for the selected design element. When you double-click any element in the Design list, the Work pane displays two sections. The upper section is the Work area that is used for designing the element. The lower section is the Programmer's pane used for writing code for the element.
- **Properties box.** Every element in Domino Designer has an associated Properties box used to set the properties of the element. The Properties box can be accessed from the Design menu or the Properties tool on the toolbar. Figure 1.3 shows the Properties box for a database.

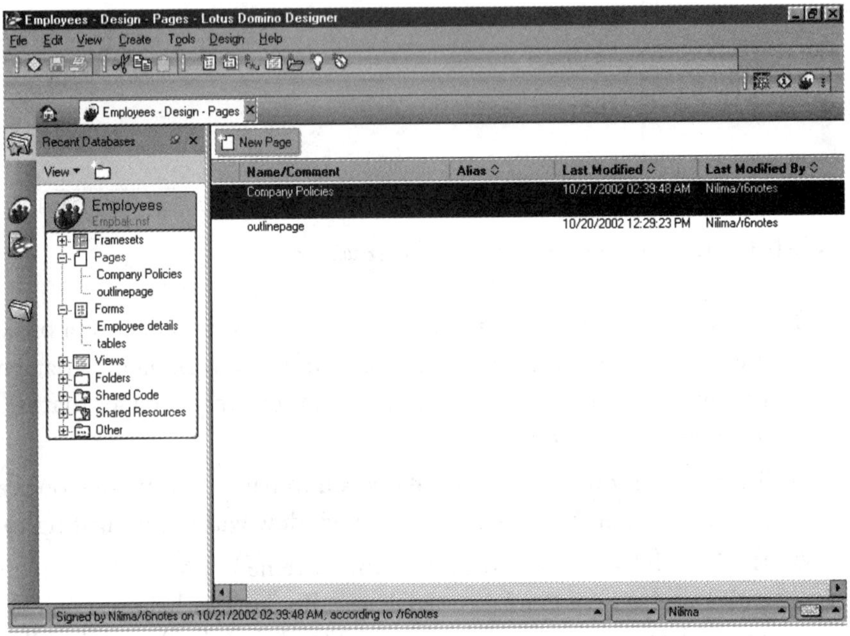

FIGURE 1.3 *A database Properties box*

Database Design Elements

All Domino applications consist of one or more databases. A database is a collection of related documents. For example, the Domino directory is a database that contains documents for every person, server, or group in an organization. Similarly, a user's Mail database contains incoming mail documents, sent mail documents, and drafts.

Each database has an ACL (*Access Control List*) associated with it. ACL is used to define the access level for various persons, servers, and groups to the database. There are seven access levels, which are described below:

- **No Access.** Indicates no access to the database
- **Depositor.** Indicates access to create documents but not read them
- **Reader.** Indicates access to read documents in a database, but not create them
- **Author.** Indicates access to create a document in the database
- **Editor.** Indicates access to modify any document in the database
- **Designer.** Indicates access to modify the design of a database
- **Manager.** Indicates full access, including access to change the ACL of a database

For more information on ACLs, refer to Chapter 8, "Securing Your Application."

A database contains various design elements, such as forms, pages, views, the data stored as a document, the logic for the application, and security settings. The various design elements in a database are:

- **Framesets.** These are used to provide a multipane interface for the user. A frameset consists of multiple frames.
- **Pages.** These are used to display information to users.
- **Forms.** These are used to collect information from users and as a template to display documents. A form contains fields, and users enter data in these fields to create documents.
- **Views.** A view provides a table of content, which lists selected documents and are the entry points to a database for users for accessing documents. Database should contain at least one view.
- **Folders.** These are structurally similar to views but display documents that are manually moved into them by users.
- **Shared code.** This contains a list of code that can be shared among databases. The elements included in the list are agents, outlines, subforms, fields, actions, and script libraries.
- **Shared resources.** This is a list of design elements that can be shared among databases. The elements include images, files, applets, style sheets, and data connections. For information about these shared resources, refer to Chapter 3, "Working with Shared Resources."

- **Other.** This list contains database resources, including icons, the "Using Database" document, the "About Database" document, database scripts, navigators, and a synopsis of the database.

The above-mentioned design elements are explained in the Chapter 2, "Basics of a Notes Application."

Creating a Database

Creating a database is the first step toward the development of a Domino application. You can create a database from scratch or based on an existing database or template.

A database may be stored on the server if it needs to be shared among groups of users. If a database has been created for personal use, it can also be stored on the local hard disk of the user's computer. A database stored on the server is a *shared database*, while the one on the local hard disk is called a *local database*. A database file has the extension .NSF. The following sections explain the three ways of creating a database.

Creating a Database from a Template

Templates are database designs that can be used to create functional databases. Template files have the extension .NTF. You can create a database from a template if you want to create a database based on a standard design. For example, you can use the Notes Doc Library template (doclbw6.ntf) to create a document reference library database. You can also use templates to create a system database that may have been corrupted or deleted accidentally. For example, you can recreate a user's mail file by using the Mail R6 (mail6.ntf) template.

Notes has several templates that are shipped with Domino software. You can use one of these templates to create a database. You can then modify the database design, if required, to suit your needs. The Domino server and client software ship with their own sets of templates. Some of these templates may be common to both. Therefore, when creating a database, you need to know the location (server or client) where the template exists. Domino also allows you to create your own templates. For information on creating templates, refer to Chapter 9, "Working with Templates."

Suppose you need to create a discussion database for the IT team in your company to help it discuss IT-related issues. You can use the default Discussion template to create this database. Perform the following steps:

1. Click the Create a new database link on the Domino Designer Welcome page. The New Database dialog box appears, as shown in Figure 1.4.

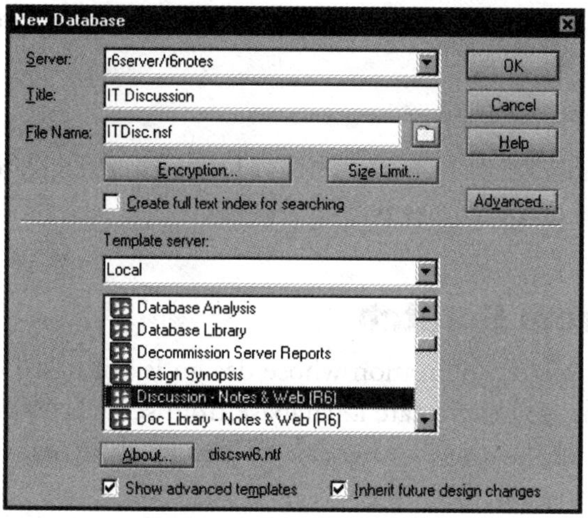

FIGURE 1.4 *The New Database dialog box*

TIP

You can also choose File/Database/New to open the New Database dialog box.

2. From the Server list, select the name of the server where you want to store the database.
3. In the Title field, enter the title for the database as **IT Discussion**. The title of a database can be up to 96 characters long. The File Name field automatically displays the file name for the database.
4. Edit the File Name field to read **ITDisc.nsf**. The file name must be in accordance with the operating system file-naming conventions.
5. From the Template server list, select the location of the template as **Local**. Check the **Show advanced templates** option to view additional templates.

NOTE

The Discussion template ships with both the Domino server and client. You can also select the server as the location of the template.

6. From the list of templates, select the template as **Discussion—Notes & Web (R6) (discsw6.ntf)**.
7. Click OK to create the database.

This creates an IT Discussion database based on the Discussion template. The database is added to the Recent Databases Bookmark pane.

Creating a Database from Scratch

If you need to create a customized application whose design is not based on any existing template or database, you can create a database from scratch. When you create a database from scratch, you need to create all design elements, such as forms, views, and navigators, manually.

Suppose you need to create a database to store employee data in your company. To create a blank database named Employees.nsf, you need to perform the following steps:

1. Open the New Database dialog box.
2. From the Server list, select the name of the server where you want to store the database.

TIP

You can create a database on the local hard disk and copy it to the server after it is successfully tested.

3. In the Title field, enter the title for the database as **Employees**.
4. In the File Name field, enter the file name as **employees.nsf**.
5. Select **Blank** from the Template list to create a blank database.
6. Click OK to create the database.

Creating a Database by Copying an Existing Database

Sometimes you may need to create a database based on an existing database. For example, to archive the details of all employees who have retired or left an organization, you'll need to create a database based on the design of the Employees database.

When you copy a database, both the design and documents in the database are copied by default. To create a new database, you must copy only the design of an existing database. If the new database will have different users or security settings than those of the source database, you must choose not to copy the ACL.

To create a database with the design of the Employees database, perform the following steps:

1. In the Bookmark pane of Domino Designer or Notes client, select the Employees database.
2. Choose File/Database/New Copy. The Copy Database dialog box appears, as shown in Figure 1.5.

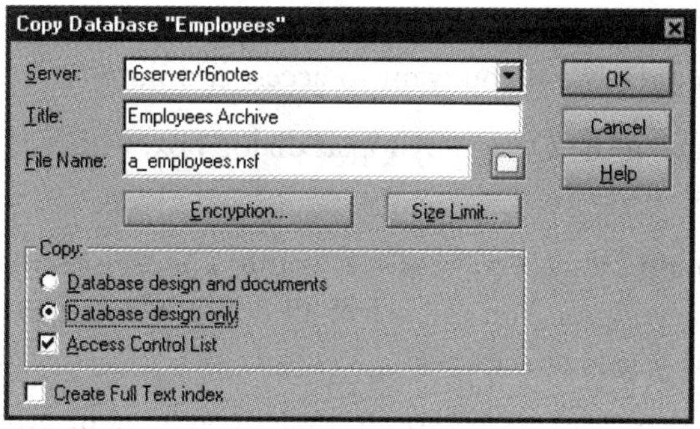

FIGURE 1.5 *The Copy Database dialog box*

3. From the Server list, select the name of the server for the archive database.
4. Modify the title of the database to Employees Archive.
5. Modify the file name to a_employees.nsf.
6. From the Copy section, select Database design only. This ensures that only the design of the database is copied.
7. Click OK to close the dialog box and create a copy of the database.

Instead of creating a copy of a database, you can copy individual design elements, such as forms and views, from another database or template. To copy individual design elements, you must open both the source and the target databases in Domino Designer. Select the design element to be copied from the source database, and copy it to clipboard. Then navigate to the target database and paste the element. This helps you to design a database by using existing elements from one or more databases.

Design Synopsis

A person who creates a database may not always be present to maintain it. It is a good practice to create documentation for any application you develop so that maintaining the application becomes easy for other users.

Design synopsis is a tool used by a developer to create a detailed report for a specific database. It contains information about every element in the database, such as the element properties, the programming logic used, and the security settings. You can specify details for as many elements as you want in the design synopsis. The synopsis can be created as a document that you can export to a word processor. It can also be stored in a database if you want to access it online.

A design synopsis is created using the Design Synopsis dialog box, which contains four main sections as follows:

- **Choose Design Element.** This section allows you to choose specific design elements for a synopsis. You can select all design elements or specific elements, such as forms or outlines.
- **Choose DB Info.** This section allows you to include general information about a database, such as its title and location. Other information that you can include is information about space usage, such as the size of the database, the number of documents in the database, replication settings of the database, and the access list for the database.
- **Define Content:** This section allows you to specify content for each element that you have selected in the Choose Design Element section.
- **Format Output:** This section is used to specify whether you want to send synopsis output to a document or a database. You can also specify if you want the design elements in the synopsis to be separated by a blank line or a page break.

To generate a design synopsis for a database, perform the following steps:

1. Open the database for which you want to create a synopsis in Designer.
2. In the Design pane, Click Other and then click Synopsis. The Design Synopsis dialog box appears as shown in Figure 1.6.

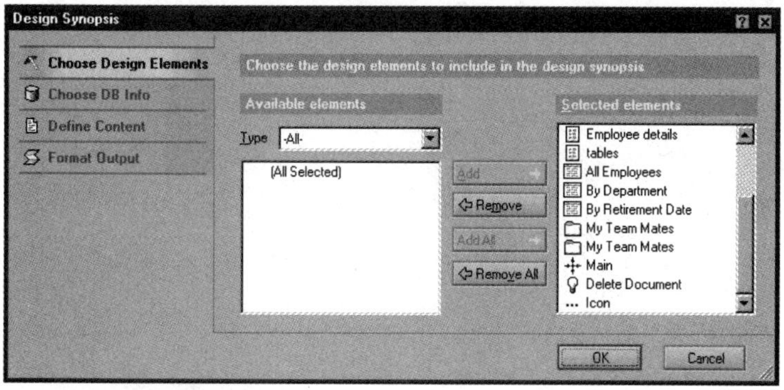

FIGURE 1.6 *The Design Synopsis dialog box*

3. In the Choose Design Elements section, select the type as All to include all types of design elements and click the Add All button to add all design elements of all types to the selected elements list.
4. In the Choose DB info section, check the General Information option to include database title and location information.
5. In the Format Output section, select Direct output to: Page.
6. Click OK to generate the synopsis as shown in Figure 1.7.

Lotus Notes Database Synopsis - Generated at 01:35:50 AM on 10/28/2002

Form Information

Name:	**Employee details**
Alias:	emp
Last Modification:	10/21/2002 12:31:55 PM
Comment:	[Not Assigned]
Type:	Document
Include in Compose Menu:	Yes
Include in Query by Form:	Yes
Default Database Form:	No
Automatically Refresh Fields:	No
Mail New Documents When Saving:	No
Store Form In Documents:	No
Inherit Default Field Values:	No
Updates Become Responses:	No
Retain Prior Versions As Responses:	No
Activate Objects When Composing:	No
Activate Objects When Editing:	No
Activate Objects When Reading:	No
Document Encryption Keys:	[None Assigned]
Composed Documents May Be Read By:	All Users
Form May Be Composed By:	All Users

FIGURE 1.7 *A sample design synopsis (continues)*

Subcomponents:	
Field:	**ecode**
Datatype:	Number
Number Format:	General
Percentage (value * 100)%:	No
Parentheses on Negative Numbers:	No
Punctuated at Thousands:	No
Help Description:	[Not Assigned]
Field Type:	Editable
Sign When Mailing/In Section:	No
Encryption:	Disabled
Update Requires Editor Access:	No
Is Scripted:	No
Field:	**ename**
Datatype:	Names
Help Description:	[Not Assigned]
Field Type:	Editable
Sign When Mailing/In Section:	No
Encryption:	Disabled
Update Requires Editor Access:	No
Is Scripted:	No
Field:	**Department**
Datatype:	Keywords
Help Description:	[Not Assigned]
Field Type:	Editable
Keyword User Interface:	Standard
Allow Values Not In List:	No
Allowable Keywords:	IT
	HR
	ACCTS
	MKTG
Sign When Mailing/In Section:	No
Encryption:	Disabled
Update Requires Editor Access:	No
Is Scripted:	No
Field:	**birthdate**
Datatype:	Time
Time Format:	10/28/2002
Help Description:	[Not Assigned]
Field Type:	Editable
Sign When Mailing/In Section:	No
Encryption:	Disabled
Update Requires Editor Access:	No
Is Scripted:	No
Field:	**rdate**
Datatype:	Time
Time Format:	10/28/2002
Help Description:	[Not Assigned]
Field Type:	Editable
Sign When Mailing/In Section:	No
Encryption:	Disabled
Update Requires Editor Access:	No
Is Scripted:	No
Field:	**jobhistory**
Datatype:	Rich Text
Help Description:	[Not Assigned]
Field Type:	Editable
Sign When Mailing/In Section:	No
Encryption:	Disabled
Update Requires Editor Access:	No
Is Scripted:	No
Action:	**Save Document**

FIGURE 1.7 *A sample design synopsis (continues)*

JavaScript & HTML Code:	
[None]	
LotusScript Code:	
[None]	
Name:	**tables**
Last Modification:	10/21/2002 10:00:21 AM
Comment:	[Not Assigned]
Type:	Document
Include in Compose Menu:	Yes
Include in Query by Form:	Yes
Default Database Form:	No
Automatically Refresh Fields:	No
Mail New Documents When Saving:	No
Store Form In Documents:	No
Inherit Default Field Values:	No
Updates Become Responses:	No
Retain Prior Versions As Responses:	No
Activate Objects When Composing:	No
Activate Objects When Editing:	No
Activate Objects When Reading:	No
Document Encryption Keys:	[None Assigned]
Composed Documents May Be Read By:	All Users
Form May Be Composed By:	All Users
Subcomponents:	
Field:	**Untitled**
Datatype:	Text
Help Description:	[Not Assigned]
Field Type:	Editable
Sign When Mailing/In Section:	No
Encryption:	Disabled
Update Requires Editor Access:	No
Is Scripted:	No
JavaScript & HTML Code:	
[None]	
LotusScript Code:	
[None]	

View Information

Name:	All

FIGURE 1.7 *A sample design synopsis*

Summary

In this chapter, you identified the complete Domino family. You learned about the different types of applications that can be created using Domino Designer and identified the Designer interface. You also learned about the various methods to create a database. Finally, you learned to create a design synopsis for a database. In the subsequent chapters, you'll learn about database elements in detail.

Chapter 2

Basics of a Notes Application

An application in Domino consists of one or more databases. A database contains various design elements, such as pages, forms, views, folders, framesets, and outlines. To create these design elements in a database, you must have Designer access to the database.

In this chapter, you'll learn to design various database design elements, including pages, forms, views, folders, framesets, outlines, navigators, and agents. You'll also learn to create different types of objects in a page or a form, such as tables, computed text, sections, and links. Finally, you'll learn to create database resources, such as a database icon, an About Database document, and a Using Database document.

Pages

A *page* is used to display information to users. It can contain objects like text, links, tables, sections, graphics, and attachments. However, a page cannot contain fields. Therefore, a page cannot be used to accept data from users.

A page can be displayed within a frameset, or it can be viewed independently within the application window by accessing it using a link, an outline entry, or an action. You'll learn about these design elements and objects in the later sections of this chapter. You can also launch a page from a database as soon as the database is opened.

Creating a Page

Suppose you want to create an Employees database to store employees' data. Employees will also use this database to perform various activities, such as applying for leave, claiming certain expenses, and filling out vouchers. Currently, the HR policies of your company are stored as PDF files. You want to create a Company Policies page in the Employees database that will give users access to all the company policy PDF files. To create a Company Policies page in the Employees database, perform the following steps:

1. Open the Employees database in Domino Designer.
2. In the Design pane, click Pages. The Pages work pane, displaying the list of all the pages in the database, appears to the right of the Design pane.
3. In the Pages work pane, click the New Page button. The work pane for the new page appears.

4. Design the page by typing the required text. Use Text menu options to format the text on the page. Insert graphics if required. Refer to the sample page in Figure 2.2.
5. To add an attachment to the page, place the cursor at the location where you want to add the attachment.
6. Choose File/Attach. The Create Attachment(s) dialog box appears.
7. Select the PDF file to be attached from the directory and click Create.
8. Choose Design/Page Properties to open the Page dialog box, as shown in Figure 2.1.

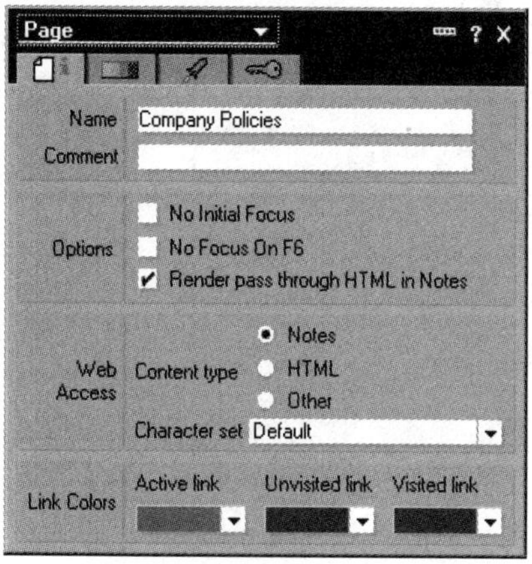

FIGURE 2.1 *The Page dialog box used to set the properties of a page*

9. In the Name field, enter Company Policies.

> **NOTE**
>
> When you design a page in Notes, the default content type is Notes. You can select the content type as HTML if you're designing the page in HTML.

10. Activate the Background tab of the Page dialog box.
11. From the Color list, select a background color for the page. If you want to have a graphic in the background, copy the graphic to the clipboard and click Paste in this dialog box. You can also specify the name of an

image resource stored in a database in the Resource field to use it in the background. For more information on image resources, refer to the section "Image Resources" in Chapter 3, "Working with Shared Resources."

12. Close the Page dialog box.
13. Choose File/Save to save the page and then choose File/Close to close the page.

Figure 2.2 shows a sample Company Policies page.

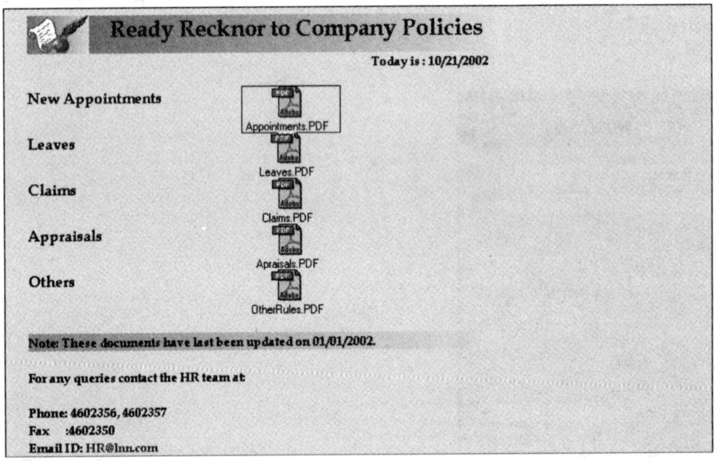

FIGURE 2.2 *A sample Company Policies page*

Creating Objects on a Page

As mentioned in the previous section, a page can contain objects such as text, graphics, attachments, tables, links, and sections. A page can also contain computed text used to display dynamic information, such as a user's name or the current date.

In the following sections, you'll learn how to create some commonly used objects on a page.

Creating Tables

A table can be inserted into a page, a form, or a subform to organize content. Tables are especially useful when you design Web applications because each browser has its own display properties. When a form or a page is displayed in the browser, the text properties such as font, font size, style are altered according to the fonts and styles supported by the browser. The size of an image may also be altered accordingly. The use of a table to design a page or a form ensures that the formatting of the page is not lost when the page or the form is viewed in a browser because a table aligns these objects correctly within the cell in which they are located.

Types of Tables

You can create five types of tables in Domino Designer: basic, tabbed, animated, caption, and programmed.

- **Basic table.** This table displays all rows and columns simultaneously.
- **Tabbed table.** This type displays each row as a tab at the top of the table. Users can access a specific row by activating the specific tab. Figure 2.3 shows a sample tabbed table.

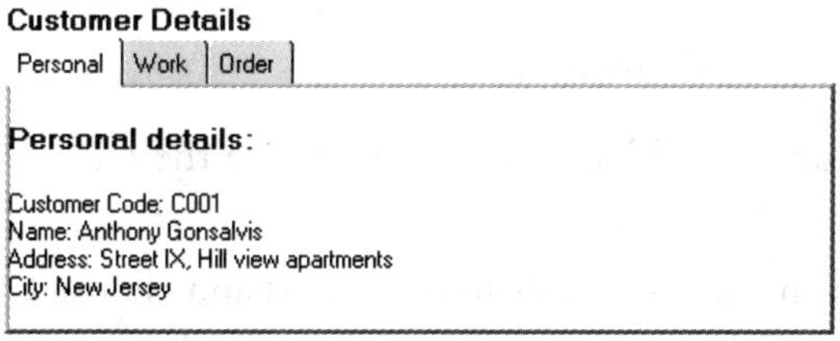

FIGURE 2.3 *A tabbed table*

- **Animated table.** This table displays one row at a time; each row is displayed after a specified interval. You can specify a transition style, such as rolling, wipe, explode, or dissolve, for each row to appear.
- **Caption table.** This type displays a caption for each row. Users can click the caption to view the content of the row. Figure 2.4 shows a sample caption table.

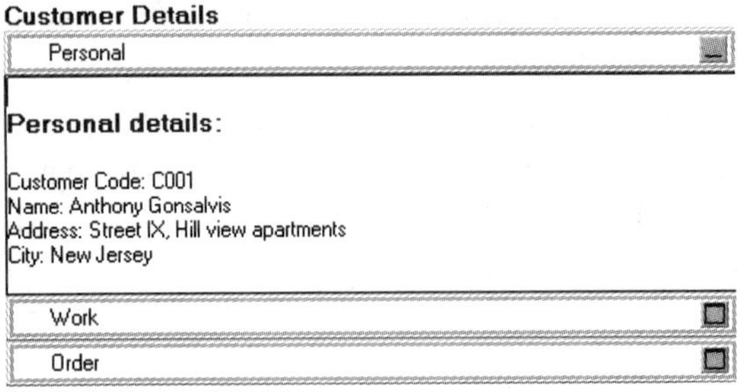

FIGURE 2.4 *A caption table*

- **Programmed table.** This table displays the rows based on a field formula or an action. This table also displays one row at a time. The procedure to create a programmed table has been explained in the section "Creating a Programmed Table."

Creating a Basic Table

To create a basic table, perform the following steps:

1. Open the page or the form in which you want to create the table in Domino Designer.
2. Place the cursor where you want the table to be located and choose Create/ Table. The Create Table dialog box appears, as shown in Figure 2.5.

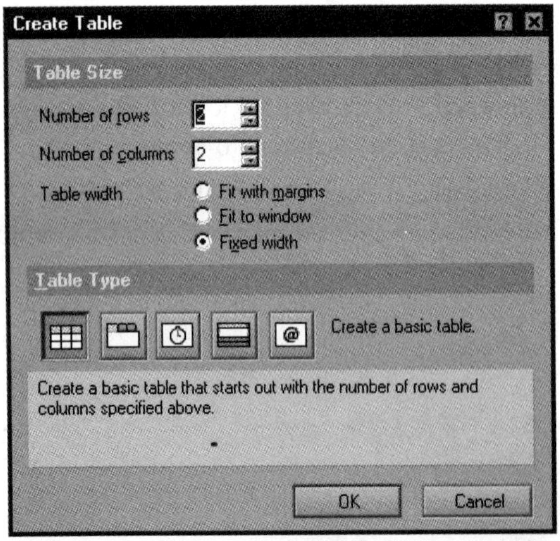

FIGURE 2.5 *The Create Table dialog box*

3. Under Table Size, select the number of rows and columns for the table and the table width.
4. Under Table Type, select the Basic table type to create a basic table.
5. Click OK to close the dialog box. A basic table is created.
6. Choose Table/Table Properties to open the Table dialog box and set the properties of the table, such as width, border, color, and margin.

Converting an Existing Table to Other Table Types

You can use the Create Table dialog box to create any of the five types of tables. If a table already exists and you want to convert it to another table type, you do not need to delete the existing table and create the new table from scratch. You can convert the existing table to another table type by modifying its properties. You can do so by using the Table Rows tab of the Table dialog box, as shown in Figure 2.6.

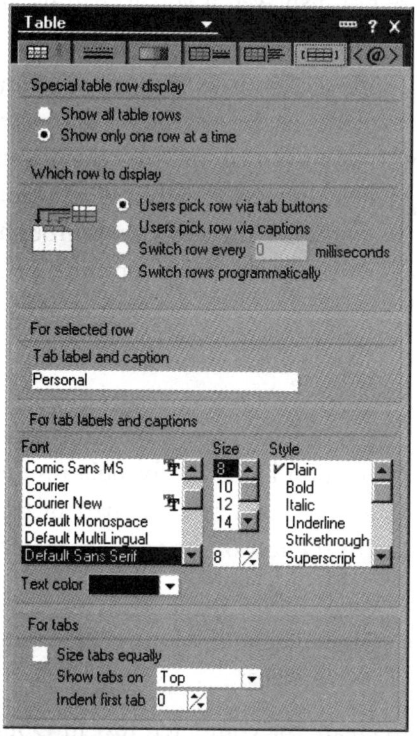

FIGURE 2.6 *The Table dialog box with the Table Rows tab active*

The Table Rows tab has the following sections:

- **Special table row display.** This section has two options, Show all table rows and Show only one row at a time. The Show all table rows option creates a basic table. To create any other type of table, select Show only one row at a time.
- **Which row to display.** This section contains four options. Select the Users pick rows via the tab buttons option to create a tabbed table. Select the Users pick rows via the captions option to create a caption table. Select the Switch rows every 2000 milliseconds to create an animated table. Using this option, you can change the time according to your requirements. To create a programmed table, select the Switch rows programmatically option.
- **Tab label and caption.** This section is used to specify the tab label and the caption for each row and is, therefore, applicable only to tabbed and caption tables. You can also use font formatting options for the specified label or caption. These options are not displayed if you're creating any other type of table.
- **Transition when switching rows.** This section is used to specify a transition effect, such as rolling, wipe, explode, or dissolve, for an animated table. This section is displayed only when you choose to create an animated table. You can also specify when the next row should be displayed. To specify this, select an appropriate option from the Cycle through rows list. The different options are Advance on click, Continually, Once when opened, and Once on click.

Creating Computed Text

Computed text displays dynamic content on a page. Since a page cannot contain fields, computed text helps to display information based on formula results on a page. Moreover, computed text displays the computed result as part of the text, and therefore, the result is better aligned with the rest of the text, compared with the alignment of the result with a field.

To create computed text that displays the system date in the format `Date: current date` at the top of a page, perform the following steps:

1. Open the page where you want to create the computed text in Domino Designer.

2. Place the cursor at the location where you want to add the computed text and choose Create/Computed Text. The Computed Text dialog box appears, as shown in Figure 2.7. You use this dialog box to set properties such as font, size, color, style, alignment, margin, and indentation for the text.

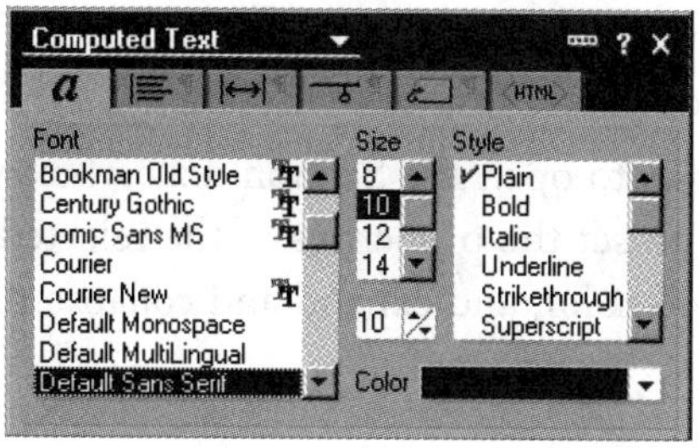

FIGURE 2.7 *The Computed Text dialog box*

3. To display the system date in the format `Date: current date`, write the following code in the Programmer's pane:

```
"Date: "+@text(@today)
```

The function `@today` returns the current system date, and the function `@text` is used to convert a date or number type value to text. This conversion is required to concatenate the date value with text. For more information on using functions and formulas, refer to Chapter 4, "Working with Formulas in Domino Designer."

4. Save the page and preview it in the Notes client to view the result of the computed text.

Creating Sections

Sections are used to group related information under a heading. Sections enable you to organize information in a compact manner because they can be collapsed or expanded. A special section called a *controlled access section* can also be created. Only authorized users can access this section. For more information on controlled access sections, refer to Chapter 8, " Securing Your Application."

Suppose you want to provide the contact details of the HR team for the users of the Employees database so that the users can contact the HR team if they have any queries regarding company policies. To create a section named Contact HR on the Company Policies page, perform the following steps:

1. Open the Company Policies page in Domino Designer.
2. Select the text on the page, starting from "For any queries contact the HR team at".
3. Choose Create/Section to convert the selected text into a section. The first line of the selected text becomes the title of the section.
4. Choose Section/Section Properties to open the Section dialog box as shown in Figure 2.8. Here you can set the properties of the selected section, such as title, border style and color, and expand and collapse rules.

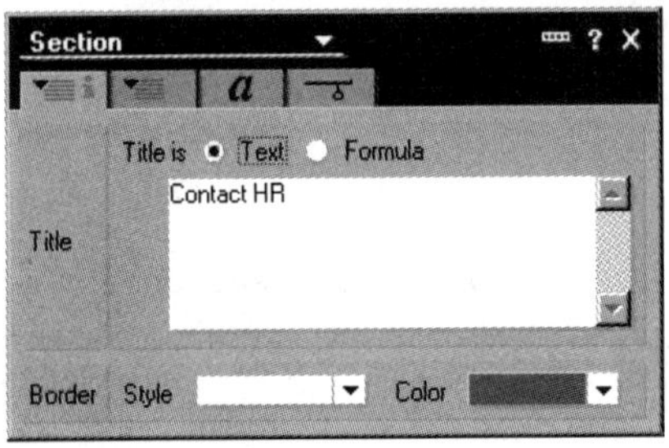

FIGURE 2.8 *The Section dialog box*

5. In the Section Title and Border tab, modify the Title field to read Contact HR. If you want a border around the title, select a border style and color.
6. Activate the Expand/Collapse tab to define whether or not the section should be collapsed or expanded when previewed, opened for reading, and opened for editing or printing. Select the Auto-Collapse section of the Opened for reading option to keep the section collapsed by default.
7. Activate the Font tab to set the font properties of the section title and then close the Section dialog box.

Figure 2.9 shows the Company Policies page after the section has been added.

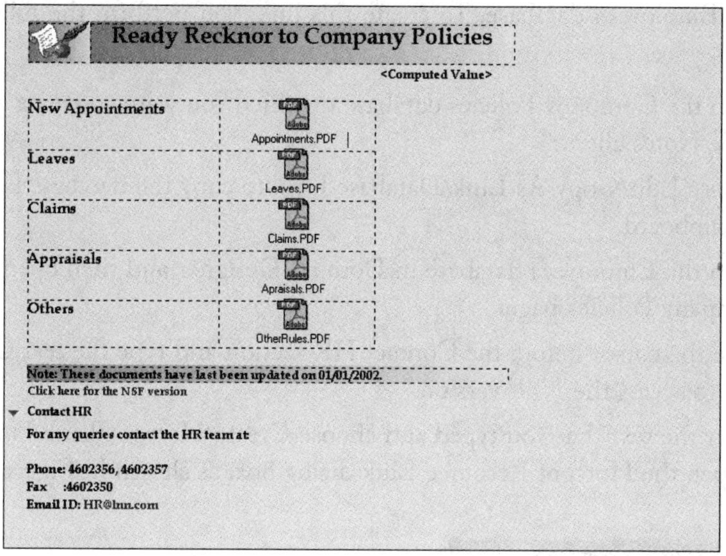

FIGURE 2.9 *The Company Policies page displaying the Contact HR section*

If you do not need the section at any point in time, you can delete it. To delete the section, select it and choose Section/Remove Section.

Creating Link Hotspots

A *link hotspot* is selected text on a page that links you to a particular design element, such as a view or a document, when clicked. You can create link hotspots to access other elements in the same database in which the link hotspot is created or a in different database. You can also create links to Web sites. The different types of link hotspots that you can create in Notes are as follows:

- **Link.** This links to a database, view, or document that has been copied to the clipboard.
- **Named element.** This links to named elements, such as pages, views, folders, navigators, framesets, and forms in the same or a different database.
- **URL.** This links to a Web site and is created by specifying the appropriate URL.

Suppose you have a database named Company Policies that stores all company policies. You want to create a link to this database from the Company Policies page in the Employees database. To create this link, you perform the following steps:

1. Open the Company Policies database to which you want to create a link in the Notes client.
2. Choose Edit/Copy As Link/Database Link to copy the database link to the clipboard.
3. Open the Employees database in Domino Designer and then open the Company Policies page.
4. Place the cursor before the Contact HR section and type the text Click here to access the NSF version.
5. Select the text that you typed and choose Create/Hotspot/Link Hotspot to open the Hotspot Resource Link dialog box, as shown in Figure 2.10.

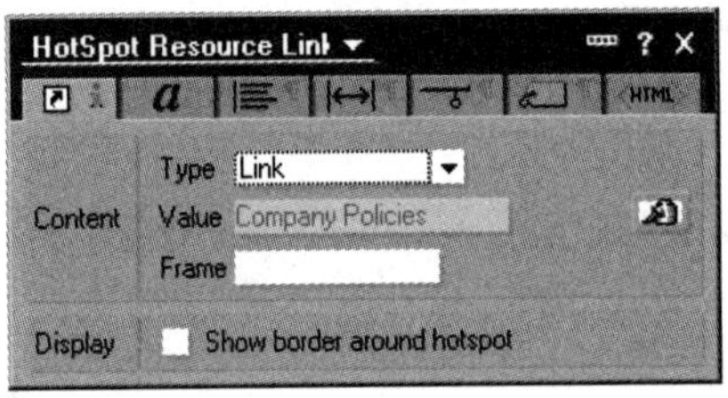

FIGURE 2.10 *The Hotspot Resource Link dialog box*

6. In the Hotspot Info tab, select the content type as Link. The database link is automatically pasted in the Value field. Format the hotspot, if required, by using the other tabs.
7. Preview the page in the Notes client and click on the link to test it.

To remove a link, select the link and choose Hotspot/Remove Hotspot.

Forms

Forms are used to collect information from users. In addition to the various objects that you can create on a page, a form contains fields. Users fill out the fields in a form and save it to create a document. Therefore, a form acts as a template to create multiple documents.

Creating a Form

When designing a database, you must plan the forms that you'll create in the database. A form is meant to collect related information from users, and, therefore you must decide the fields you'll be creating in advance. For information about the types of fields, refer to the section "Creating Fields" in this chapter.

In the Employees database, you need to have a form to collect employees' data. To create a layout for this form, perform the following steps:

1. Open the Employees database in Domino Designer.
2. In the Design pane, select Forms. The Forms work pane appears, displaying a list of all the forms in the database.
3. In the Forms work pane, click the New Form button. The work pane for a new form appears.
4. Choose Design/Form Properties to access the Form dialog box, as shown in Figure 2.11.

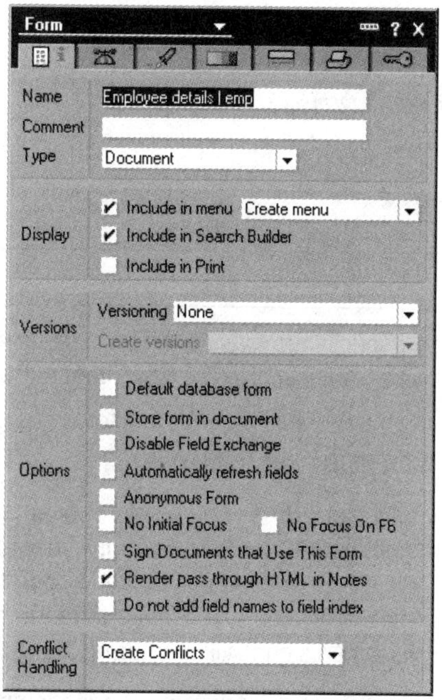

FIGURE 2.11 *The Form dialog box used to set the properties of a form*

5. In the Name field, enter **employee details** and click the check box to the field's right to save the name that you entered.
6. Activate the Background tab to select a background color or a graphic and then close the Form dialog box.
7. Type headings and labels for the fields that you want to include in the form to define the layout of the form, as shown in Figure 2.12.

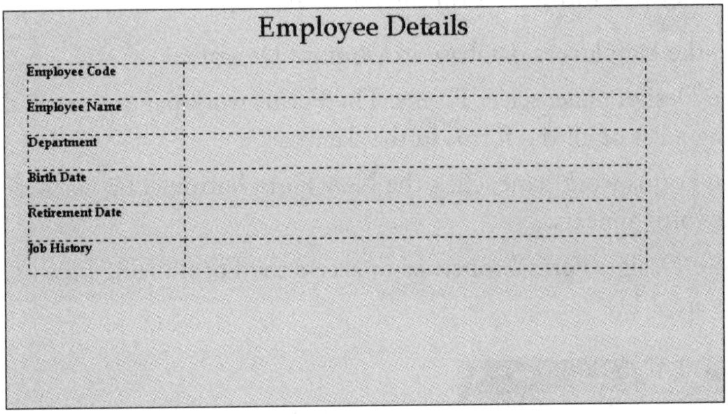

FIGURE 2.12 *A sample layout of the Employee details form*

8. Save and close the form.

NAMING A FORM

Form names are case-sensitive. You can specify an *alias* for the form by using the vertical bar (|), for example, Employee details | emp. The advantages of using an alias are:

- The alias is a simple name and is easy to use in a formula.
- It helps to change a form's display name later. When you create or open a document based on a form, the form name is used. If the form name is changed, the old documents based on the form will give an error when you try to open them. On the other hand, if you have used an alias, you can change the form name without changing the alias, and the documents can still open using the alias.

You can also create a *cascading name* by using the backslash (\), for example, Employee Forms\ Employee details. A cascading name is used to create a submenu under the Create menu.

The complete name of a form, including aliases and cascading options, can be up to 256 bytes long, though only the first 64 bytes appear on the Create menu.

Creating Fields

Fields are used to store information in a document. You can specify a field type to define the data that can be entered in the field. Table 2.1 lists the types of fields that you can create.

Table 2.1 Field Types

Type	Description
Text	Can contain letters, digits, and any special character, such as $, *, or ?
Date/Time	Can contain a date, time, or both
Number	Can contain digits and symbols, including + (plus), - (minus), % (percent), (decimal), E (scientific notation), and any currency symbol, such as $
Dialog list	Contains a predefined set of choices, which are displayed as a pop-up list
Checkbox	Contains a predefined set of choices, which are displayed as check boxes
Radio button	Contains a predefined set of choices, which are displayed as radio buttons
Listbox	Contains a predefined set of choices, which are displayed in a scrolling list
Combobox	Contains a predefined set of choices, which are displayed in a drop-down list
Rich Text	Can contain formatted text, embedded objects, and attachments
Authors	Contains the names of users with Author access to a database who can edit a document created by any user; refer to the section "The Authors Field" in Chapter 8
Names	Used to store Notes hierarchical names; displays names in abbreviated format, for example, Jessica/Inn; allows you to attach the address book or the access control list to the field for selecting names
Readers	Used to specify the names of users who are allowed to read a document; refer to the section "The Readers Field" in Chapter 8
Password	Displays each character entered by the user as an asterisk
Formula	Specifies the selection criteria for subscribing to the documents in a database; the result of the subscription is viewed in the headlines.nsf database
Time zone	Displays a list of available time zones in the world and a partial list of cities or locations where each time zone applies

(continues)

Table 2.1 Continued

Type	Description
Rich Text Lite	Similar to a Rich Text field but has an entry helper button next to it for quickly adding objects to the field; contains a down arrow button that is used to select the type of object you want to add to the field
Color	Displays a color picker on the form; the user can select a color that is stored in hexadecimal format

To create fields in the Employee details form, perform the following steps:

1. Open the Employee details form in Domino Designer.
2. Place the cursor in the cell next to the Employee Code label and choose Create/Field. The Field dialog box appears, as shown in Figure 2.13.

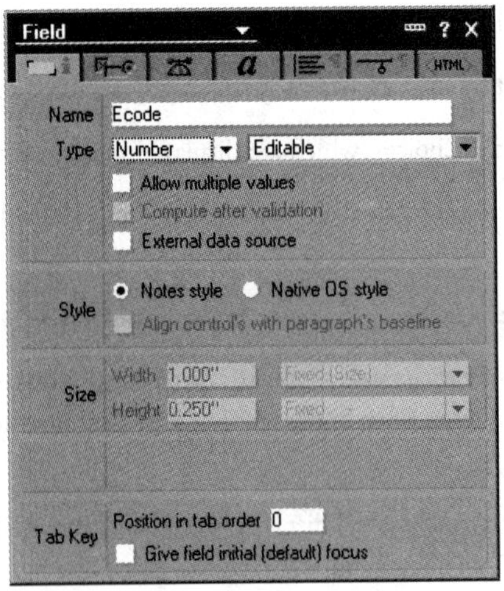

FIGURE 2.13 *The Field dialog box used to set the properties of a field*

3. In the Field Info tab, enter **ecode** in the Name field. From the Type list, select Number. To create a field with a fixed display size, select the style as Native OS Style.
4. Activate the Control tab and specify the number format, decimals, if required, for the ecode field. Specify other formatting options, such as currency symbol, parentheses, or punctuation. Notes picks up the format of the number from the user settings of the client computer. You can also choose a custom format by using this tab.

5. Activate the Advanced tab and specify the Help Description and Field Hint. Help Description is the message that appears at the bottom of the window. The Field Hint is the text that appears in the field when you move the cursor to the field. These options help the user to enter correct information in a field.
6. Activate the Font and Paragraph Alignment tabs to format the field content for the ecode field.
7. Place the cursor in the cell next to the Employee name label and create the field named **ename** of the type Names.
8. To provide the user with the Address dialog box to select the employee name from the address book, activate the Control tab, and from the Choices list, select Use Address dialog for choices.
9. Create a field named **Department** of the type Dialog list next to the Department label.
10. Activate the Control tab, and from the Choices list, select Enter choices (one per line).
11. Enter the department names **IT**, **ACCTS**, and **HR**. Click the Sort button to sort the choices. If you want to allow users to enter a value that is not present in the list, check Allow values not in list.
12. Next to the Birth Date label, create a field named **birthdate**. Select the Style as Calendar/Time control to display a datepicker with the field. A *datepicker* displays as a calendar and allows the user to select a date.
13. In the Control tab, check Display Date and clear Display Time to allow the user to enter only a date. The format of the date is picked from the User setting of the client computer. You can modify the format by selecting Custom from the Use preferences from list.
14. Create a field named **rdate** next to the Retirement Date label. Set the properties of this field similar to the properties of the birthdate field.

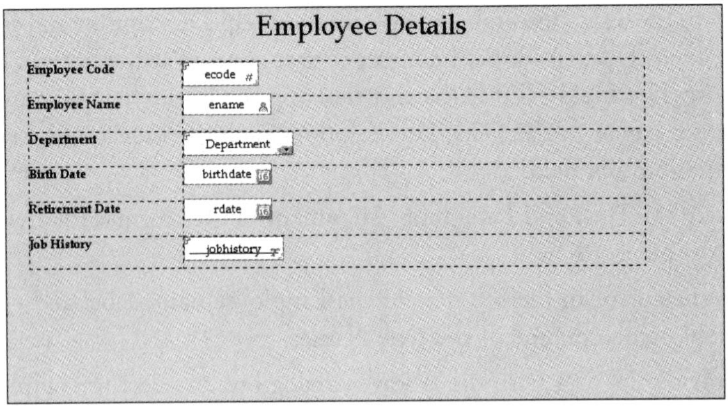

FIGURE 2.14 *A sample Employee details form*

15. Finally, create a field named **jobhistory** of the type Rich Text next to the label Job History. The form with all the fields is shown in Figure 2.14.
16. Save the form and preview it in the Notes client to create a document. You can create a document based on this form by choosing Create/Employee details.

Creating Form Actions

Actions provide shortcut methods to performing tasks in a design element. You can create actions for routine tasks, such as saving, closing, and editing a document. You can also create actions to perform complex tasks, such as approving a document, sending a notification, and changing the status of a field.

The different types of actions that you can create are as follows:

- **Button.** This action is used to display actions as buttons.
- **Check box.** This action is used to display actions as check boxes.
- **Menu separator.** This action is used to create a separator line on the Actions menu and does not have any associated action.

You can assign simple actions to an action or write formula, LotusScript, or JavaScript code. The actions that you create are available as options on the Action menu. You can also set action properties so that they are displayed as action buttons on the Action bar at the top of a form, a page, or a view.

To create an action called Save Document in the Employee details form, perform the following steps:

1. Open the Employee details form in Domino Designer.
2. Choose Create/Action/Action. The action is created in the Action pane, which is to the extreme right of the form. The Action dialog box also appears, as shown in Figure 2.15.

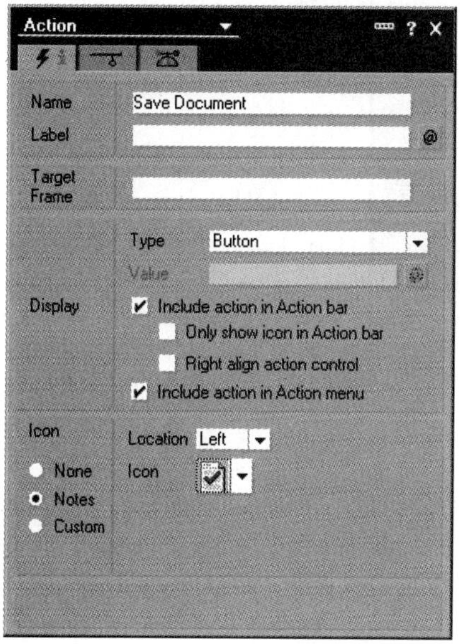

FIGURE 2.15 *The Action dialog box used to set the properties of an action*

3. In the Name field, enter the name of the action as **Save Document**.
4. From the Type list, select Button to create an action button.
5. In the Display section, check Include action in Action bar to display the action on the Action bar, and check Include action in Action menu to display it on the Actions menu.
6. To select an icon for the action, use the Icon section. Under Icon, select Notes and select the required icon from the Icon list. Alternately, you can choose Custom and select an image from image resources or write a formula.
7. Close the Action dialog box to return to the Programmer's pane for the action.

8. Select Simple action(s) from the Run list and click Add Action to display the Add Action dialog box, as shown in Figure 2.16.

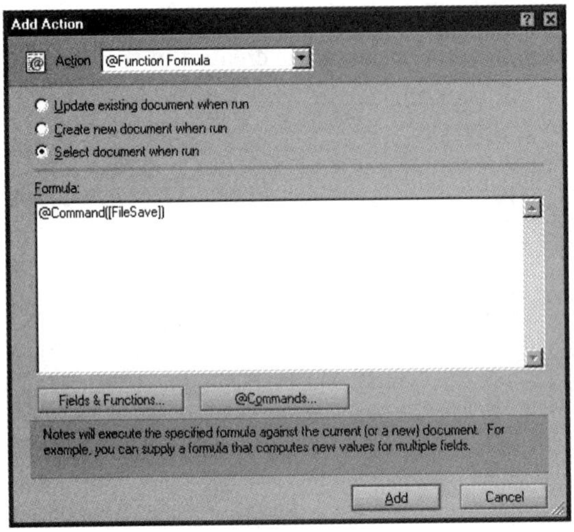

FIGURE 2.16 *The Add Action dialog box*

9. Display the Action list. This list displays various simple actions, such as Delete from Database, Copy to Database, and Send Message. In addition to these predefined actions, you can write your own formula. To do this, select @Function Formula from the Action list. For more information on formula language, refer to Chapter 4.
10. Under the Action list, select the Select document when run option.
11. Click the @Commands button at the bottom of the dialog box to view the list of all @Commands.
12. From the Available @Commands list, select `FileSave` and click Paste. The @Command is pasted in the Add Action Formula box. For information about @Commands, refer to the section "@Commands" in Chapter 4.
13. Click the Add button at the bottom of the Add Action dialog box to assign the selected simple action to the Save Document action.

The action is displayed in the Action pane to the extreme right of the form in Domino Designer. If this pane is not visible, choose View/Action Pane to view it. To test the action, save the form and preview it in the Notes client. Enter values in the field and click the Save Document button. The document is saved in the database.

Creating a Programmed Table

As already discussed, a programmed table displays rows based on a formula. A programmed table is associated with a field that is named after the table. For example, if you have assigned the name markstable to a programmed table, the field must be named $markstable. Each row in the table is also assigned a name. The formula in an action is used to assign the name of the row that you want to display to the $tablename field.

Suppose you want to create a quiz for the users of the Employees database. The questions and answers can be displayed in different rows of a single-column table. The user can view an answer by clicking the Show Answer button below a question. To create this programmed table, you perform the following steps:

1. Open the Employees database in Domino Designer.
2. Create a new form named Daily Quiz Question.
3. Place the cursor where you want the table to be located and choose Create/Table.
4. Under Table Size, select the number of rows as 2 and the number of columns as 1 for the table.
5. Under Table Type, select Programmed table and click OK to close the dialog box.
6. Choose Table/Table Properties to open the Table dialog box.
7. Activate the Table Programming tab. In the Name/Id field in the Table HTML Tags section, enter the name for the table as **quiztable**.
8. Click the first row in the Name field of the Row Tags section and enter **questionrow.**
9. Similarly, name the second row **answerrow.**
10. In the first row of the table, type a question, and in the second row, type its answer.
11. Under the table on the form, create a new field and name it **$quiztable.**
12. In the first row of the table, create a hotspot button by choosing Create/Hotspot/Button. Enter the label for the button as **Show Answer**. Figure 2.17 displays a sample form.

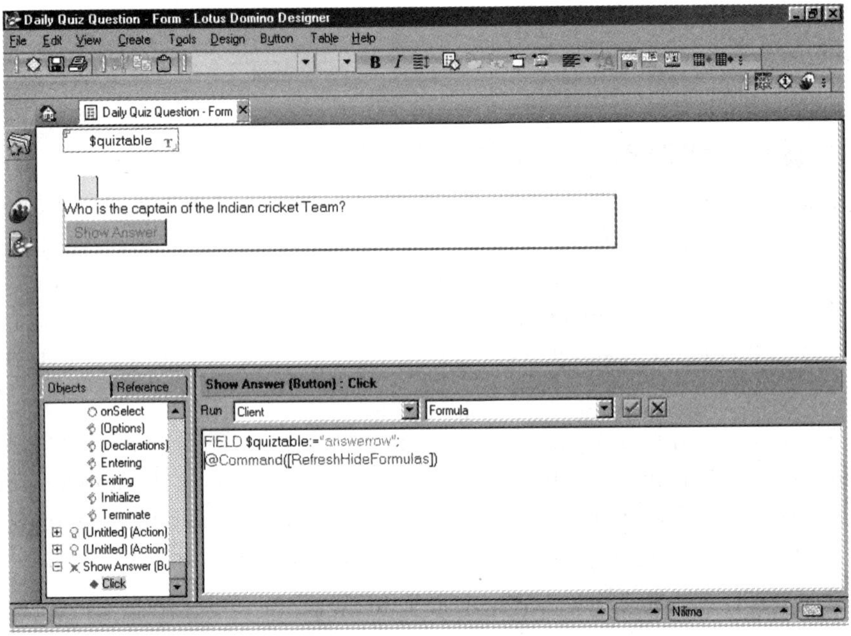

FIGURE 2.17 *A sample form containing a programmed table*

13. In the Programmer's pane for the Show Answer button, enter the following formula:

```
FIELD $quiztable:="answerrow";

@Command([RefreshHideFormulas])
```

    The first statement assigns the value answerrow to the field $quiztable. The next statement is used to refresh the hidden formulas in the form. This formula hides the row named questionrow and displays the row named answerrow. For more information on writing formulas, refer to Chapter 4.

14. Save the form and test the table by previewing it in the Notes client.

Using Hide When Options

Hide When options are used to display elements in a form or a page, such as text, fields, actions, hotspots, or actions, selectively to users. These options are available in the element's property box. You can hide selective elements from Notes users,

Web browsers, or mobile users. You can also hide selective elements on the basis of a document state. For example, you can specify the elements that should be visible when reading, editing, printing, or previewing a document. In addition, you can hide elements based on a formula.

The Save Document action button that you created earlier should be visible only when a document is in edit mode. This action button should be hidden when the document is opened for reading. To hide the Save Document action button when the document is in read mode, perform the following steps:

1. Open the Employee details form in Domino Designer.
2. Select the Save Document action in the Action pane.
3. Choose Design/Action Properties to open the Action dialog box and activate the Action Hide When tab.
4. Under Hide action when document is, check the Previewed for reading and Opened for reading options.
5. Close the dialog box and save the form.

To test the Hide When options, open an existing document in the Notes client. The Save Document action button should not be displayed. Double-click anywhere on the document to switch to edit mode. The Save Document action button should appear.

Views and Folders

Views and *folders* are used to list the documents in a database. They can be sorted or categorized to organize the documents. The basic difference between a view and a folder is that a view contains documents based on a selection condition, whereas a folder does not have a selection condition. A view contains all documents by default. However, you can specify a condition to see only certain documents in a view. A folder, in contrast, is empty by default. Documents are dragged manually to a folder. In the following sections, you'll learn how to create views and folders.

Designing Views

You can create one of the following types of views:

- **Shared.** This view can be accessed by all users who are allowed to read a database.
- **Shared, contains documents not in any folder.** This view displays documents that are not in any folder and can be accessed by all users with read access.
- **Shared, contains deleted documents.** This view displays documents that have been deleted for a specified time before purging them or until a user undeletes them. All users with at least read access can access this view.
- **Shared, private on first use.** This view can be accessed by all users with read access to a database. When the users access the view, a private copy of the view is created for them in the database.
- **Shared, desktop private on first use.** This view can be accessed by all users with read access. But when they access the view, a private copy of the view gets created for them. This private copy is stored in the desktop.dsk file on the user's workstation instead of in the database.
- **Private.** This view can be accessed only by the user who created the view.

The Employee details form in the Employees database is used to collect employees' data. To display all the employee records in the database, you need to create a view. To enable all users to access the employee records, create a shared view named All Employees. Perform the following steps:

1. Open the Employees database in Domino Designer.
2. In the Design pane, click Views. The Views work pane appears, displaying all the available views.
3. Click the New View button. The Create View dialog box appears, as shown in Figure 2.18.

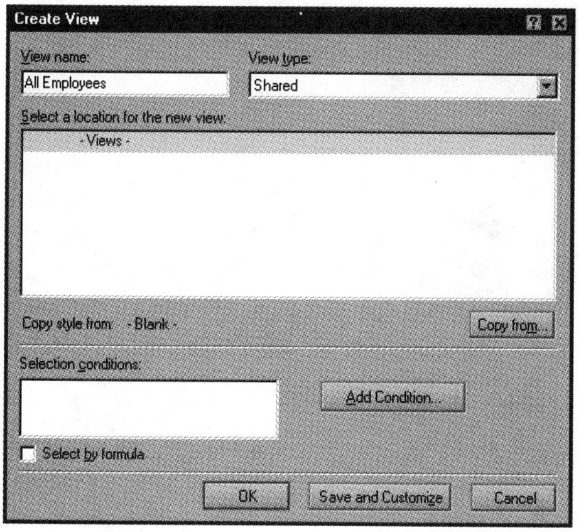

FIGURE 2.18 *The Create View dialog box*

4. In the View name field, enter the name of the view as **All Employees**.
5. From the View type list, select Shared to create a view that can be accessed by all users.
6. In the Select a location for the new view list, retain the default selection as Views. This option is used to specify the location where the view will be listed. Here you can select a view name to indent the new view under it.
7. Click the Copy from button to display a list of views in the database. You can inherit the design of the new view from one of these views. All Employees is the first view in the database; choose to create a blank view.
8. Click the Add Condition button to specify a document selection condition for the view. The Add Condition dialog box appears, as shown in Figure 2.19.

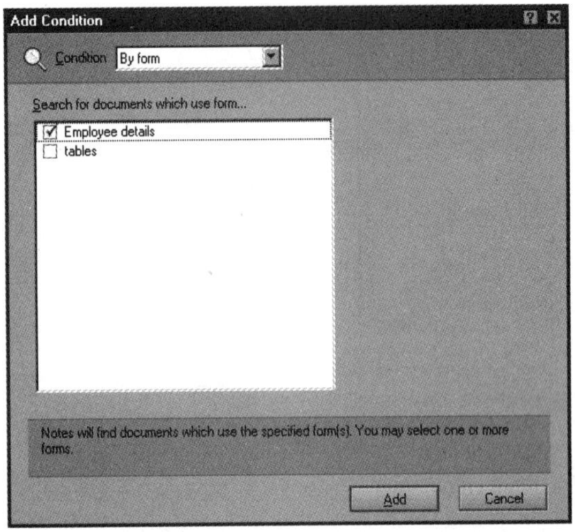

FIGURE 2.19 *The Add Condition dialog box, used to specify a document selection condition for a view*

The Condition list in this dialog box displays various options for specifying a condition, such as By author, to search on the basis of the creator of the document; By date, to search on the basis of the date of creation or date of modification of the document; By form, to search on the basis of the form used to create the document; and Multiple words, to search on the basis of certain words.

9. From the Condition list, select By form. In the Search for documents which use form list, check Employee details and click Add to specify the condition. This condition specifies that the view displays documents based on the Employee details form.

NOTE

Instead of using the Add Condition button, you can check Select by formula in the Create View dialog box to write the selection formula for the view. If you don't specify a selection condition at the time of creating a view, you can specify the condition later by using the View Selection event. To know more about this event, refer to the section "View Selection" in Chapter 4.

10. Click Save and Customize in the Create View dialog box to close the dialog box. The View work pane opens, and the View dialog box appears.
11. Activate the Style tab, as shown in Figure 2.20, to set the style for the view. You can set options such as background color, alternate row color, header style, and margins.

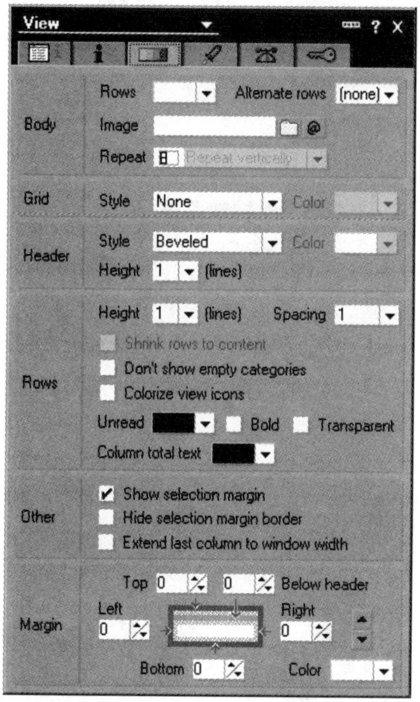

FIGURE 2.20 *The View dialog box with the Style tab active*

12. Close the View dialog box.
13. Click the first column and choose Design/Column Properties to open the Column dialog box.
14. In the Title field, enter the title as **Ecode**.
15. Activate the Sorting tab. Select the sort option as Ascending to sort the document in ascending order.
16. Close the Column dialog box.

17. In the Programmer's pane, from the Display list, select Field. This displays all the fields from all the forms in the Employees database. From the list of fields, select ecode to display all the employee codes in the first column.
18. Choose Create/Append New Column to add a new column to the view. Assign the title **Name** to the column and select the field ename for display.
19. Add one more column titled **Birthdate** to display the birthdate field.
20. Save the view and preview it in the Notes client.

Figure 2.21 shows the All Employees view.

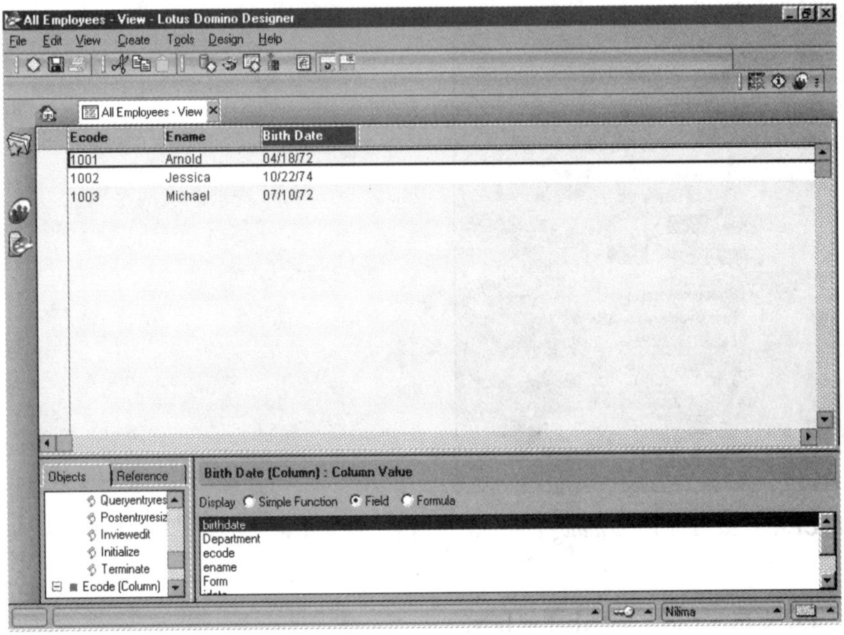

FIGURE 2.21 *A sample All Employees view*

Designing Folders

Folders are used as filing cabinets for documents. A user can manually move or copy documents into a folder. The different types of folders that you can create are:

- Shared
- Shared, private on first use

- Shared, desktop private on first use
- Private

Suppose you want supervisors at different levels to organize the details of their team members in separate folders in the Employees database. The folder in which they organize the details should only be accessible to them. Therefore, each supervisor needs to create a private folder. To create a private folder named My Teammates, you perform the following steps:

1. Open the Employees database in Domino Designer.
2. In the Design pane, click Folders to open the Folders work pane to the right of the Design pane.
3. Click the New Folder button. The Create Folder dialog box appears, as shown in Figure 2.22.

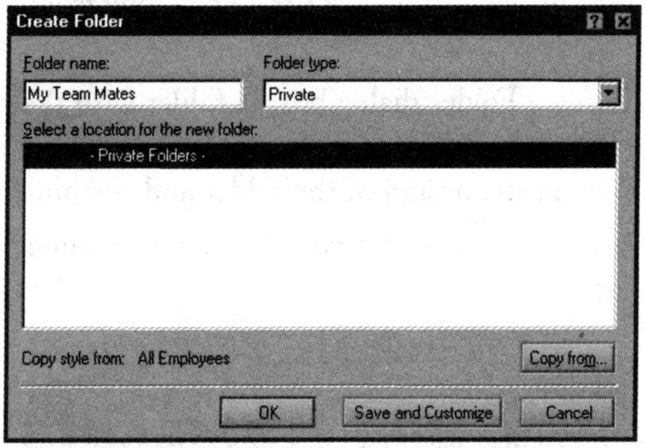

FIGURE 2.22 *The Create Folder dialog box*

4. In the Folder name field, enter the name of the folder as **My Teammates.**
5. From the Folder type list, select Shared, private on first use, to create a private folder for all users.
6. In the Select a location for the new folder list, retain the default selection as Folders.
7. Click the Copy from button to display a list of views and folders in the database, as shown in Figure 2.23. You can select a specific view or folder to create a folder based on an existing design. Since a view and a

folder have a similar design, you can also inherit the folder from the design of a view.

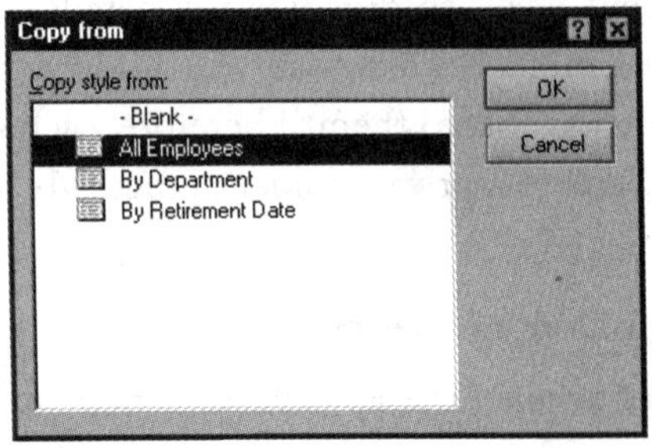

FIGURE 2.23 *The Copy from dialog box used to select a view or folder design for a new folder*

8. From the list of views and folders, select All Employees to inherit the design of the folder from this view and click OK. The Copy from dialog box closes.
9. Click OK to close the Create Folder dialog box. A folder with the same design as that of the All Employees view is created. You can also click Save and Customize to open the design of the folder and customize it.

To copy documents to the My Teammates folder, you can drag a document from a view and drop it on the folder.

Navigators, Outlines, and Framesets

Navigators, outlines, and framesets are used as navigation structures in a database.

Navigators provide a graphical interface for a user, allowing easy access to the various elements of a database.

Outlines provide a compact navigation structure to a database. An outline contains entries that are displayed hierarchically and can be expanded and collapsed. An *outline entry* is a link to a named element, such as a page, a frameset, a URL, a view, a database, or a document. An outline entry can also be assigned a formula that is executed when you click the entry.

A *frameset* is a collection of frames used to add a navigation structure to a database. A frame is one pane of a frameset, which can be used to display design elements such as page, view, folder, navigator, form, or another frameset.

When you open a database, you can set a navigator, an outline embedded in a page, or a frameset to open as the first element. This ensures that a user finds easy access to all the elements in the database.

In the following sections, you'll learn how to design a navigator, an outline, and a frameset. You'll also learn to set the launch properties of a database.

Designing Navigators

When you open a database in Notes client, a navigator can be displayed as a full screen navigator. It can also be displayed as a side navigator in the Navigation pane on the left of the application window, with a view in the right pane.

You can design a navigator by importing a graphic and creating links on it. You can also design a navigator by using the drawing tools available in the Navigator work pane.

To create a full screen navigator in the Employees database, perform the following steps:

1. Open the Employees database in Domino Designer.
2. In the Design pane, click Other and select Navigators.
3. In the right pane, click New Navigator to create a new navigator. The Navigator work pane appears.
4. Choose File/Import to import a graphic in the navigator. The Import dialog box appears, as shown in Figure 2.24.

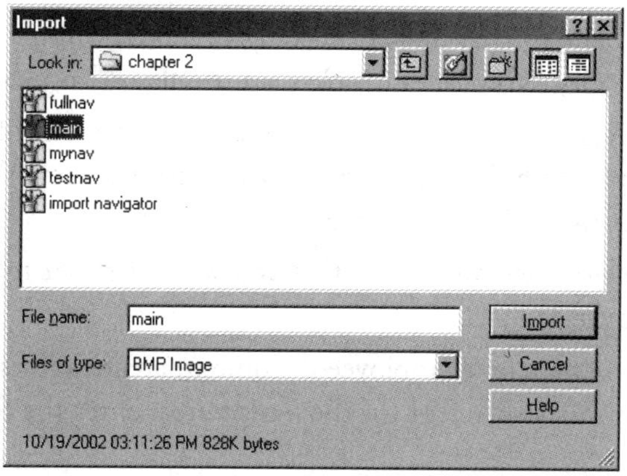

FIGURE 2.24 *The Import dialog box to import a file for a navigator*

5. Navigate to the directory that contains the image to be imported. You can import a file in BMP, GIF, JPEG, PCX, or TIFF 5.0 format. Select the Main.bmp file, the graphic for the navigator that you're designing, and click Import. Refer to Figure 2.25 for the graphic. The Import dialog box closes, and a message appears asking whether you want to import the image as a Graphic button or a Graphic background.
6. Select Graphic background to be able to create hotspots on the image. Hotspots are defined areas in a navigator that have an associated action, such as opening a view.
7. Click OK. The image is inserted as a background in the navigator.
8. Choose Create/Hotspot Rectangle to create hotspots on the image. You can create a hotspot circle or a hotspot polygon by using the options Create/Hotspot Circle and Create/Hotspot Polygon, respectively.
9. Mark the area of the image that you want to convert to a hotspot by clicking its top left corner and dragging the mouse pointer to the bottom right corner of the area. The Hotspot Rectangle dialog box appears.
10. In the Info tab, enter the name **Folderhotspot** for the hotspot and check Lock size and position to make sure the hotspot cannot be resized or repositioned.
11. In the HiLite tab, specify the highlight properties of the hotspot, such as the highlight border width and color. You also specify whether the hotspot should be highlighted when the mouse moves over the hotspot or only when the user clicks the hotspot. Choose the desired options and close the dialog box.
12. In the Programmer's pane for the hotspot rectangle, choose Simple action(s) from the Run list. You can also select a formula or LotusScript.
13. From the Action list, select Open a View or Folder. From the list of views and folders displayed next to the Action list, select the view that should open when the user clicks the hotspot.
14. Create hotspots for every view and folder that you want the user to access through the navigator.
15. To allow the user to create a new employee document, create a hotspot and select Formula from the Run list. In the Script area, enter the following formula:

```
@Command([compose];"Employee Details")
```

For more information on formulas, refer to Chapter 4.

16. Choose File/Save to save the navigator. Enter the name as MainNavigator when prompted. The navigator is shown in Figure 2.25.

FIGURE 2.25 *A sample full-screen navigator*

17. Select File/Close to close the navigator.

To launch the navigator when the database is opened, refer to the section "Setting Database Launch Properties" later in this chapter.

Designing Outlines

An outline is used to create links to views, pages, folders, and other design elements. An outline can also be used to execute actions or access URLs. Unlike a navigator, which can be displayed independently, an outline must be inserted in a page or a form.

To create entries for all the elements in the database, you can generate a default outline. You can then modify the default outline to suit your requirements. You can also design the outline from scratch by manually adding entries to the outline by using the Add Entry button.

To create an outline in the Employees database, perform the following steps:

1. Open the Employees database in Domino Designer.
2. In the Design pane, click Shared Code and then select Outlines to display the list of all the outlines in the database.
3. Click New Outline to create a new outline. The Outline work pane appears.
4. Click the Add Entry button to add a new outline entry. An entry is added to the outline, and the Outline Entry dialog box appears.
5. Enter a label for the outline entry and close the Outline Entry dialog box. To set other properties of the outline entry, refer to the section "Setting Outline Entry Properties."
6. Create other outline entries, as shown in Figure 2.26. You must add entries for each design element that you want to include in the outline.

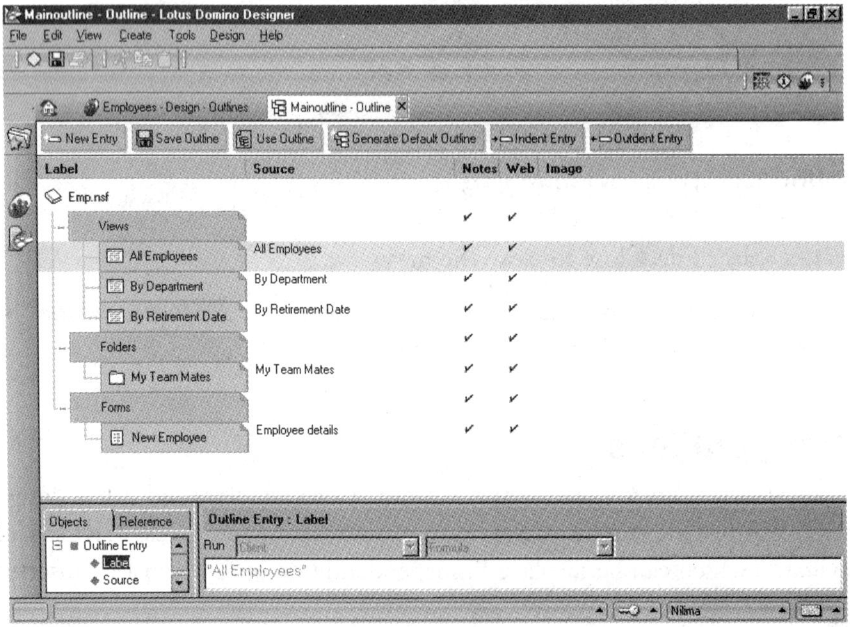

FIGURE 2.26 *A sample outline*

7. Use the Indent Entry and Outdent Entry buttons to move the entries horizontally and align them in a group.
8. Save the outline and enter its name as **Mainoutline** when prompted. Close the Outline work pane.

To test this outline, insert it in a page or a form. Refer to the section "Embedding an Outline in a Page."

Setting Outline Entry Properties

An outline can display one of the following items:

- **Named element.** This is used to display a database design element, such as a page, a form, a navigator, or a view.
- **URL.** This is used to specify the URL of a Web page to open a Web site.
- **Link.** This is used to create a link to a document, a database, an anchor, or a view. This option requires you to copy these objects as links and then paste them in the outline entry.
- **Action.** This is used to specify a formula, such as a formula to open a view.

An outline entry displays default images for each type of entry. You can choose to display a different image by using a formula or by selecting an image from the image resource. For information on image resources, refer to the section "Image Resources" in Chapter 3. You can also choose not to display any image with an outline entry.

To set outline entry properties, perform the following steps:

1. Open the outline Mainoutline, created in the previous section, in Domino Designer.
2. Double-click the outline entry All Employees to access its properties in the Outline Entry dialog box, as shown in Figure 2.27.

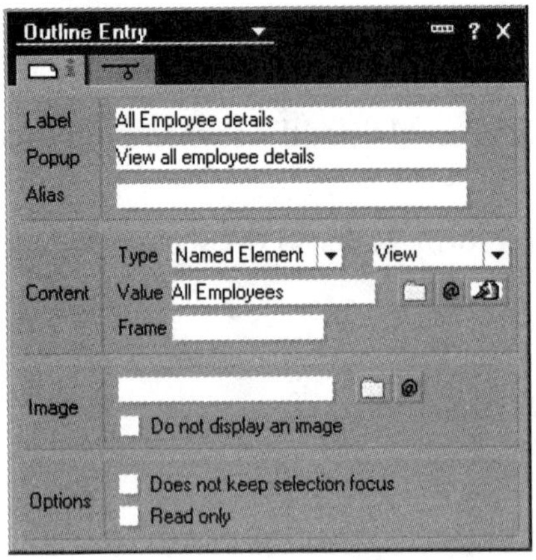

FIGURE 2.27 *The Outline Entry dialog box*

3. Edit the Label field to display the text All Employee details. If the label is long, it might get truncated when displayed to the user. You can enter the pop-up text in the Popup field. This text is displayed when the user moves the mouse over the truncated outline entry. Enter the pop-up text as View all employee details.
4. In the Content section, from the Type list, select Named Element. The Content section is used to specify the content that will be displayed when a user clicks the outline entry. The list of all the named elements in the database appears. From the list, select View. Next to the Value field, click the Browse button to select the view to be opened when a user clicks the entry. The Locate Object dialog box appears, as shown in Figure 2.28.

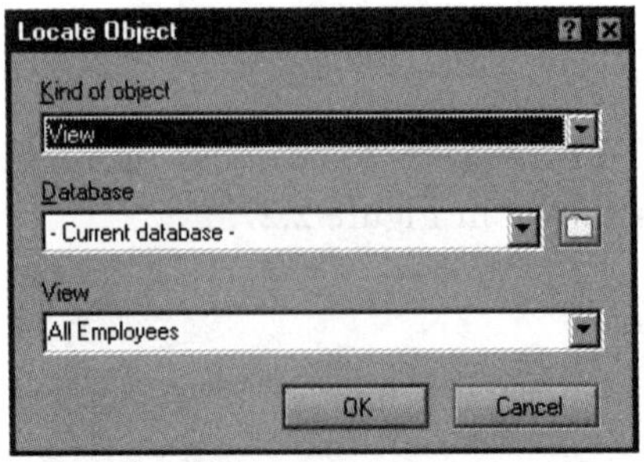

FIGURE 2.28 *The Locate Object dialog box to select the object to be linked to an outline entry*

5. In the Locate Object dialog box, from the View list, select All Employees and click OK to close the dialog box.
6. In the Image section, check Do not display an image to hide the default image that is displayed with the view.
7. Activate the Entry Hide When tab. Specify appropriate options to hide the outline entry in Notes 4.6 or later or Web browsers. You can also enter a formula to specify the hide condition for the outline entry.
8. Close the Outline Entry dialog box.
9. Similarly, set the properties of all other outline entries.

Embedding an Outline in a Page

To use an outline, you must embed it in a page or a form. You can click the Use Outline button in the Outline work pane to embed the outline in a new page. This creates the page and embeds the outline in the page. You can also embed the outline in an existing page or form.

Suppose you have created a page named oulinepage in which you want to embed the outline. To embed the outline Mainoutline in the outlinepage page in the Employees database, perform the following steps:

1. Open outlinepage in Domino Designer.
2. Choose Create/Embedded Element/Outline. The Insert Embedded Outline dialog box appears, as shown in Figure 2.29.

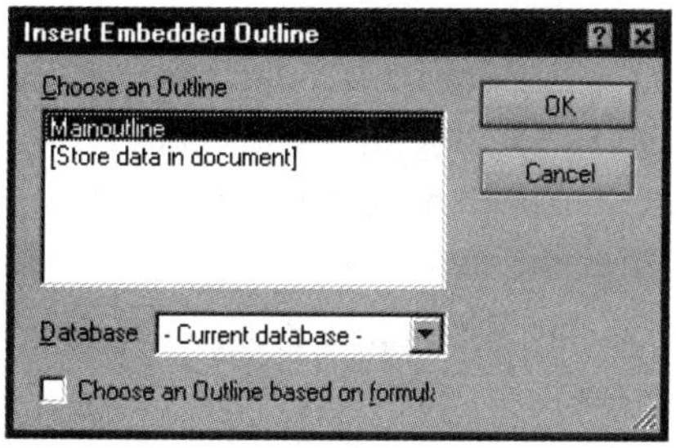

FIGURE 2.29 *The Insert Embedded Outline dialog box*

3. Select Mainoutline from the list and click OK. The outline is embedded in the page. You can choose an outline from another database by selecting the database from the Database list.

4. Format the outline by using the embedded outline properties, as shown in Figure 2.30.

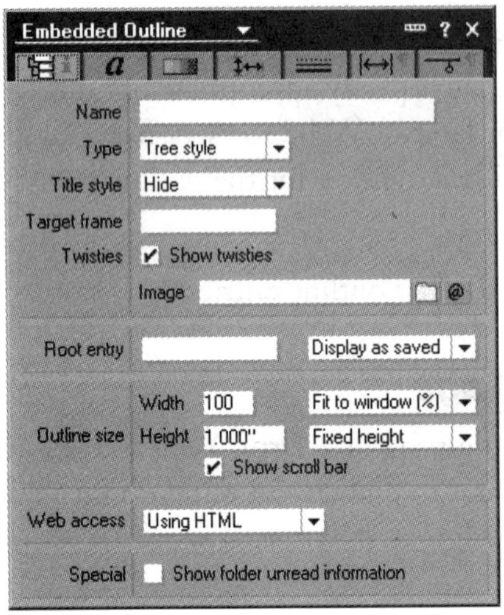

FIGURE 2.30 *The Embedded Outline dialog box*

5. Save the page and preview it in the Notes client.

Designing Framesets

A frameset consists of two or more frames. Each frame in a frameset displays content that can be of one of the following types:

- **Link.** This is used to create a link to a document, a database, an anchor, or a view. Creating a link requires you to copy these objects as links by using one of the options Database, Document or View Link from the Edit/Copy as Link menu and then paste them.
- **Named element.** This is used to display a database design element, such as a page, a form, a navigator, or a view.
- **URL.** This is used to specify the URL of a Web page to open a Web site.

Frame properties are set using the Frame dialog box. The Frame dialog box has the following five tabs:

- **Basics.** This tab is used to assign a name and content for a frame. A unique name must be assigned to each frame in a frameset. The content can be a URL; a named element, such as a page, a form, a frameset, a view, a folder, or a navigator; or a link, such as a document link, a view link, or an anchor. You can also specify a frame name in the field Default target for links in the frame. Specifying a value in this field ensures that a link from this frame always opens in the specified frame.
- **Frame Size.** This tab is used to specify the size-related properties of a frame. You can specify the width and height of a frame. You can prevent users from resizing a frame by setting the Allow Resizing option to No. A scrollbar can be displayed by selecting the Scrolling property. You can set the initial focus to one of the frames in the Notes client by using the Set Initial Focus property.
- **Frame Border.** This tab is used to set the style for a frame border. You can select a 3-D border. You can specify the border width, the border color, and the border caption. A border caption is used to display a caption at the top or bottom of a frame. You can also specify text properties such as color, font, font size, style, and background color for the caption.
- **Advanced.** This tab is used to specify the spacing between frames, margin height, and margin width. Margin width refers to the space between a frame border and the frame content. These properties are applicable only to browsers.
- **Additional HTML.** This is used for specifying HTML-related information. Refer to Chapter 6, "Working with HTML and JavaScript," for information on using HTML in Notes.

To create a frameset in the Employees database, perform the following steps:

1. Open the Employees database in Domino Designer.
2. In the Design pane, click Framesets.
3. In the right pane, click New Frameset to create a new frameset. The Create New Frameset dialog box appears, as shown in Figure 2.31.

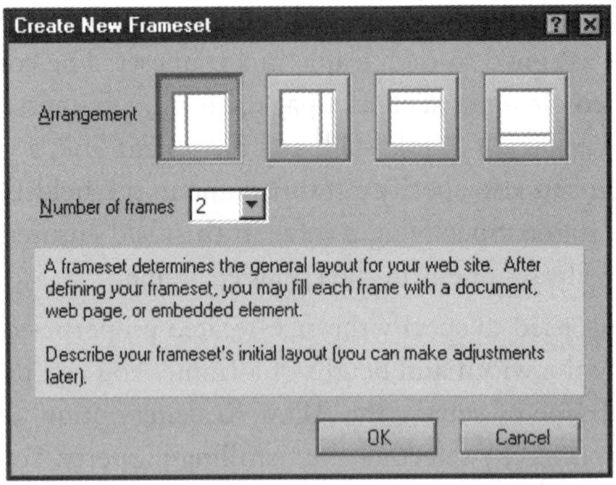

FIGURE 2.31 *The Create New Frameset dialog box*

4. Select 3 from the Number of frames list. If required, you can add more frames later.
5. Retain the default Arrangement option. The Arrangement option is used to define the layout of the frames in the frameset. Click OK to close the dialog box and open the Frameset work pane, as shown in Figure 2.32.

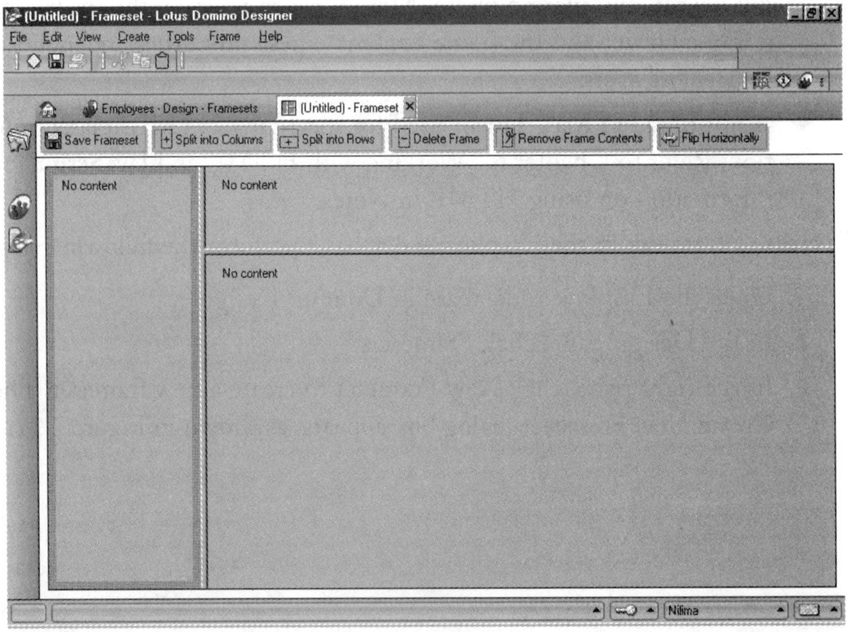

FIGURE 2.32 *The Frameset work pane*

NOTE

You can modify the frameset layout. To add more frames horizontally, select any frame and click Split into Rows. To add more frames vertically, select a frame and click Split into Columns. To remove a frame, select the frame and click Delete Frame.

6. Choose Frame/Frameset Properties to enter a title for the frameset. The Frameset dialog box appears, as shown in Figure 2.33.

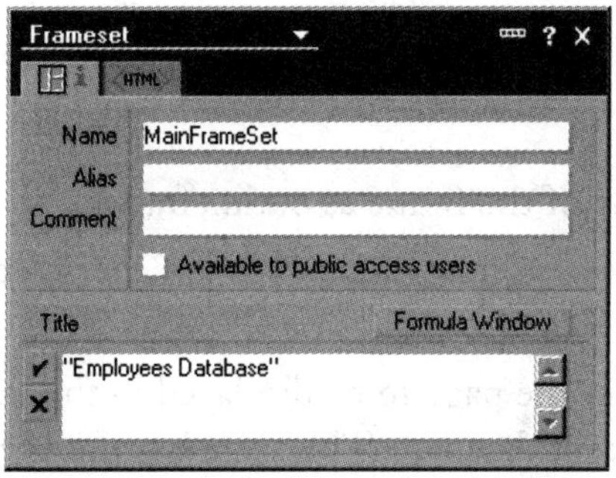

FIGURE 2.33 *The Frameset dialog box used to set the properties of the frameset*

7. In the Basics tab, specify Employees Database as the title of the frameset. You can also specify an alias and a comment for the frameset.
8. Right-click the left frame and select Frame properties from the shortcut menu to display the Frame dialog box, as shown in Figure 2.34.

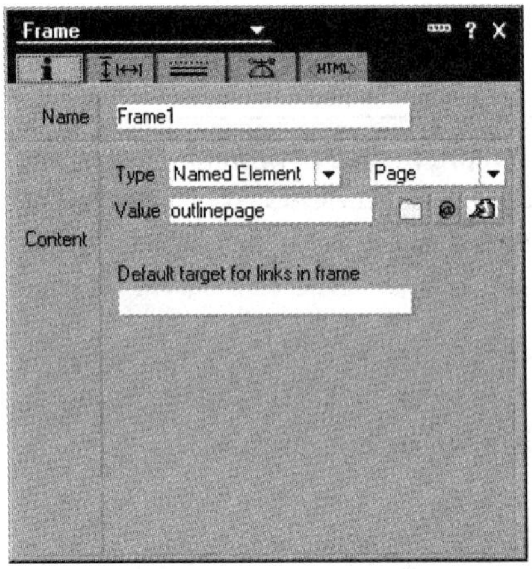

FIGURE 2.34 *The Frame dialog box used to set the properties of a frame*

9. In the Basics tab, enter the name of the frame as outlineframe.
10. Select the type as Named Element in the Content section and select the named element as Page.
11. Click the Browse button to select the page to be displayed in the frame. Select outlinepage from the current database. This page has the outline Mainoutline embedded in it.
12. Suppose you have also created a page named Header that contains the database heading. Select the content of the Header page and the Employee details form as the content for the top right frame and the bottom right frame, respectively.
13. Click Save Frameset to save the frameset. Specify the name as Main-FrameSet when prompted.
14. Close the frameset.

The next section will demonstrate how to launch the frameset from a database.

Setting Database Launch Properties

Database launch properties are used to specify the first design element to be displayed to the user when a database is opened. Creating a customized design element, such as a navigator or a frameset, to launch a database makes it easy for the user to navigate the database. You can set one of the following options for launching a database:

- Open "About database" document
- Open designated Frameset
- Open designated Navigator
- Open designated Navigator in its own window
- Launch first attachment in "About database"
- Launch first doclink in "About database"

To launch the navigator MainNavigator full screen, set the launch properties for the Employees database as follows:

1. Open the Employees database in Domino Designer.
2. Choose File/Database/Properties to open the Database dialog box.
3. Activate the Launch tab to set launch options. Figure 2.35 shows the Launch tab of the Database dialog box.

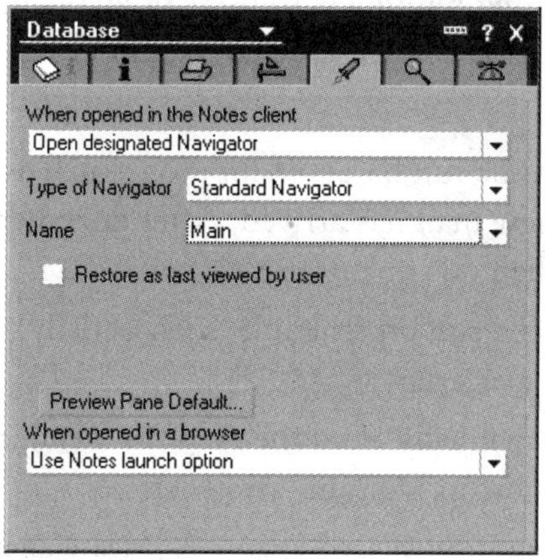

FIGURE 2.35 *The Database dialog box with the Launch tab active*

4. From the When opened in the Notes client list, select Open designated Navigator in its own window to launch the full screen navigator that you created.
5. From the Type of Navigator list, select Standard Navigator to choose a navigator. You can also select Page or Folders from this list to display a page or the default folder list, respectively. Select MainNavigator from the Name list.

> **NOTE**
>
> You can specify a different launch option for the Web browser or use the Notes launch option. To select a launch option for the browser, use the When opened in a browser list.

6. Close the Database dialog box.

Open the database in Notes client to test the launch option. This should open the full-screen navigator.

Agents

Agents are programs written using simple actions, formula language, LotusScript, or Java to automate actions such as sending reminders to users or archiving documents in a database. An agent is a database element that can be run in one of the following ways:

- **Based on an event.** An agent can be run based on an event, such as Before new mail arrives, After new mail has arrived, After documents are created or modified, and When documents are pasted.
- **On schedule.** An agent can also be run on schedule, such as daily, weekly, monthly, or more than once a day.
- **Manually.** An agent can be run manually from the Actions menu in the Notes client or from the Agents list in Domino Designer.

An agent can be created as a private agent or a shared agent. A private agent can be run only by its creator, whereas a shared agent can be run by other users as well.

An agent usually runs on documents. You can specify one of the following targets for an agent:

- All documents in database
- All new & modified documents
- All unread documents in view
- All documents in view
- All selected documents
- None

Select none if you want to specify an action that is not related to documents, such as sending a mail message.

Suppose you want to enable all users to delete documents from the Employee database by using the Actions menu. To create an agent, Delete Document, in the Employees database to delete documents from a view by using the Actions menu, perform the following steps:

1. Open the Employees database in Domino Designer.
2. In the Design pane, click Shared Code and then select Agents to display the Agents work pane to the right.
3. In the Agents work pane, click New Agent to create a new agent. The Agent dialog box appears, as shown in Figure 2.36.

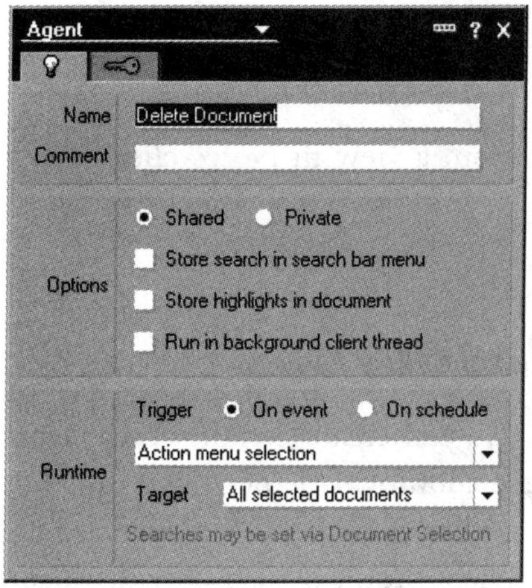

FIGURE 2.36 *The Agent dialog box used to set the properties of an agent*

4. Enter the name of the agent as Delete Document.
5. In the Options section, select Shared to create an agent that can be used by other users.
6. In the Runtime section, select a trigger option. The trigger defines when the agent will be executed. The trigger can be either an event or a schedule. To run the agent from the Actions menu, select On event as the trigger. From the Runtime list, select the Action menu selection option.

7. From the Target list, select All selected documents to delete selected documents in the view.
8. Close the Agent dialog box. This directs you to the Programmer's pane for the agent. You can use formulas, LotusScript, Java, or Imported Java to write the agent code. You'll learn about these programming options in later chapters. You can also use simple actions to select from a predefined set of actions.
9. From the Run list, select Simple actions(s). Click the Add Action button at the bottom of the pane to select an action. The Add Action dialog box appears.
10. Click Action to view a list of simple actions that can be assigned to the agent. Select Delete from Database and click Add to add the action to the agent. You can add multiple actions to the agent by using the same procedure.
11. Save and close the agent.

To run the agent, select any document from a view in Notes client and choose Actions/Delete Document.

Creating Database Resources

After the database design is complete, you can create certain other elements to enhance the database functionality. These additional elements are called *database resources*. For example, you can provide a suitable icon for the database to help a user identify the database in the Notes client. You can also provide documentation to facilitate the deployment and use of the database.

A *database icon* is a database resource that is displayed in the Bookmark pane and on the workspace. It helps identify a database quickly.

The "About Database" document is used to specify information about a database, such as its purpose, creator, and intended audience, and the "Using Database" document specifies detailed instructions for using a database.

Another database resource, *database script*, is used for writing formulas or LotusScript code at the database level. For information on database script, refer to the section "Database-Level Events" in Chapter 5, "Working with LotusScript."

The following sections explain the procedures for creating database resources.

Creating a Database Icon

A database icon is a graphical representation of a database. Therefore, you should select a database icon that clearly defines the purpose of a database. You can either draw a database icon in Domino Designer or use an existing graphic as an icon.

To create a database icon for the Employees database, perform the following steps:

1. Copy the image that you want to use as the database icon to the clipboard.
2. Open the Employees database in Domino Designer.
3. In the Design pane, click Other and then select Database Resources. The various database resources are Icon, "Using Database" Document, "About Database" Document, and Database Script.
4. Double-click Icon to open the Design Icon dialog box, as shown in Figure 2.37.

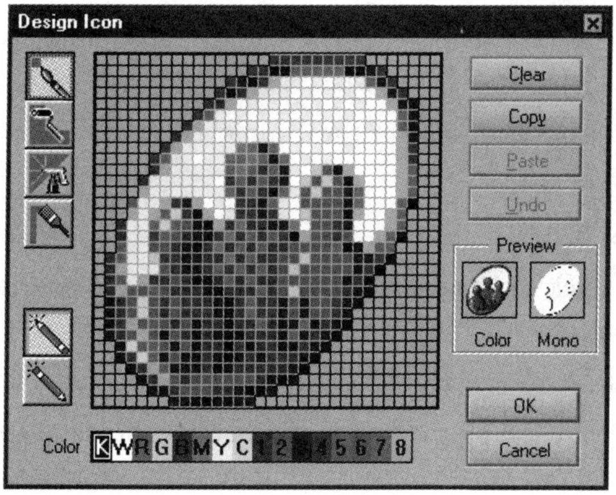

FIGURE 2.37 *The Design Icon dialog box*

5. Click Paste to paste the icon from the clipboard.
6. Click OK to save the icon.

Creating the "About Database" Document

You can view the "About Database" document in one of the following ways:

- By default, the "About Database" document opens automatically when the database is opened the first time in the Notes client.

> **NOTE**
>
> In the database launch properties, the Show "About database" document when database is opened for first time option is checked by default. You can also choose to display this document every time it is modified, by checking the Show "About database" document if modified option, in the database launch properties.

- You can display the "About Database" document every time a database is opened by selecting the Open "About database" document option as the database launch option.
- You can display the "About Database" document after a database is opened by choosing Help/About This Database.

To create the "About Database" document in the Employees database, perform the following steps:

1. Open the Employees database in Domino Designer.
2. In the Design pane, click Other and then select Database Resources to view the resource list.
3. Double-click "About Database" Document to open the document.
4. Design the document by typing the text that describes the database. You can also paste graphics and create hotspots. Figure 2.38 shows a sample "About Database" document.
5. Save the document and close it.

To view the "About Database" document that you created, select Help/About This Database.

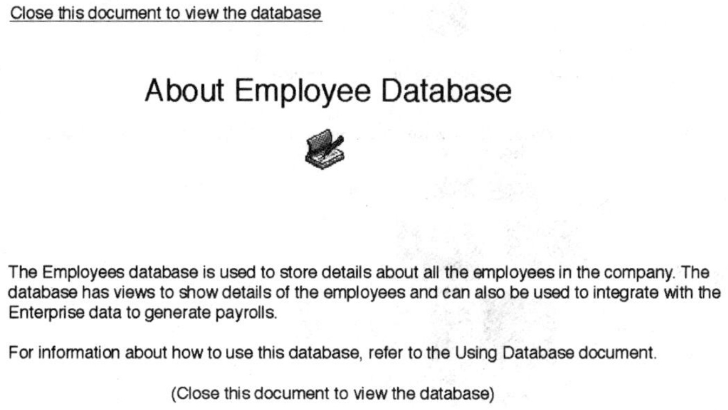

Close this document to view the database

About Employee Database

The Employees database is used to store details about all the employees in the company. The database has views to show details of the employees and can also be used to integrate with the Enterprise data to generate payrolls.

For information about how to use this database, refer to the Using Database document.

(Close this document to view the database)

FIGURE 2.38 *A sample "About Database" document*

Creating the "Using Database" Document

The "Using Database" document specifies detailed instructions for using a database. It explains the various options and design elements in the database and various deployment issues, such as the access control list to be set for the database.

To create the "Using Database" document, perform the following steps:

1. Open the Employees database in Domino Designer.
2. In the Design pane, click Other and then select Database Resources to view the resource list.
3. Double-click "Using Database" Document to open the document.
4. Design the document by typing text that describes the steps to use the database. Figure 2.39 shows a sample "Using Database" document.

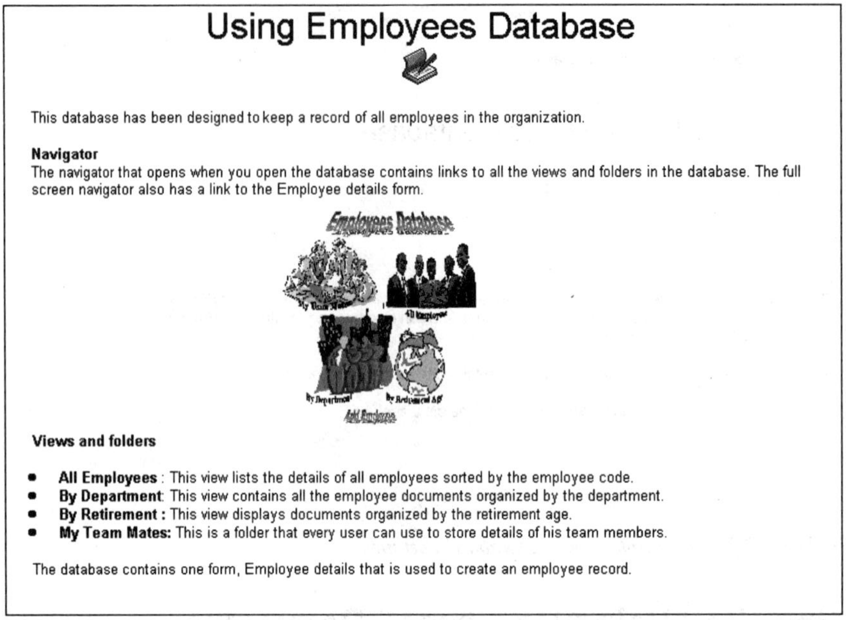

Using Employees Database

This database has been designed to keep a record of all employees in the organization.

Navigator
The navigator that opens when you open the database contains links to all the views and folders in the database. The full screen navigator also has a link to the Employee details form.

Views and folders

- **All Employees** : This view lists the details of all employees sorted by the employee code.
- **By Department**: This view contains all the employee documents organized by the department.
- **By Retirement :** This view displays documents organized by the retirement age.
- **My Team Mates:** This is a folder that every user can use to store details of his team members.

The database contains one form, Employee details that is used to create an employee record.

FIGURE 2.39 *A sample "Using Database" document*

5. Save the document and close it.

To view the "Using Database" document that you created, select Help/Using This Database.

Summary

In this chapter, you learned to design the various design elements in a database. You learned to create pages and insert different types of objects such as tables, computed text, sections, and links on a page. You learned to create form and add fields and labels on it. You also learned to create views, folders, framesets, outlines, navigators, and agents. Finally you learned to set the database launch properties and create various database resources such as the "About Database" document, the "Using Database" document and the database icon.

Chapter 3

Working with Shared Resources

Domino Designer R6 lays heavy emphasis on the sharing and reusability of design elements and code. In Domino Designer, you can create and store a shared resource, such as an applet, once in a database and use it in multiple places in a single database or across databases. Creating a shared resource provides many benefits. First, it reduces development time. Instead of creating each element from scratch, you can reuse the existing shared resources in your application, leading to faster development. Second, shared resources enable the easy maintenance of applications. Finally, shared resources save on disk space because a shared resource is stored only in one place. In contrast, a design element that is not shared needs to be stored in multiple places, wherever it is being used.

In this chapter, you'll learn how to create and use shared resources, such as image, file, applet, style sheet, and data connection resources. You'll also learn how to use some other resources, such as shared fields, subforms, and shared actions.

Image Resources

An *image resource* is used to store an image, which can be used in multiple places. For example, if you want to use non-Notes icons for action buttons, such as Save, Close, and Exit, you can store these graphics as image resources in your database. If you change any of these graphics, the change is reflected in all the places where these graphics are used when you refresh the image resource.

You can insert an image resource in a page or a form or use it as a background image. You can also use an image resource as an icon in an outline or action button.

Creating an Image Resource

An image resource is created from a graphic in GIF, JPEG, or BMP format. However, the image resource can store graphics only in GIF or JPEG format. Therefore, when you create an image resource using a graphic in BMP format, it is automatically converted to JPEG format.

To create an image resource, perform the following steps:

1. Open the database in which you want to create an image resource in Domino Designer.

2. Click Shared Resources in the Design pane. It expands to show all the types of shared resources that can be created.
3. Click Images. The Images work pane appears, as shown in Figure 3.1.

This pane displays all the image resources in the current database. The pane also contains options to create, open, refresh, and export an image resource.

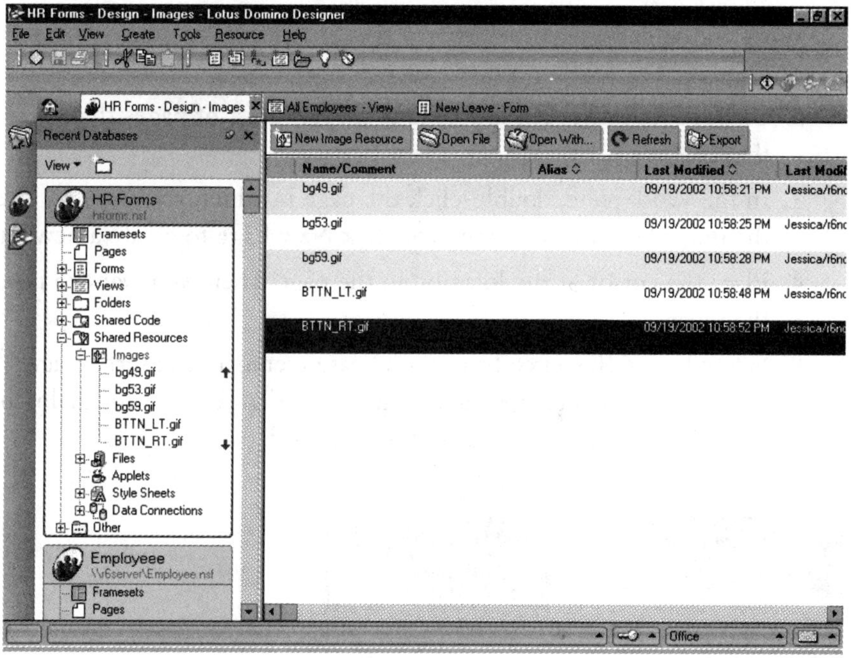

FIGURE 3.1 *The Images work pane*

4. Click New Image Resource to create a new image resource. The Open dialog box appears in which you can select the file to be added as an image resource. Notice that you can only select images in GIF, JPEG, or BMP format.
5. Navigate to the directory where the image is stored and select the file. You can select multiple files by pressing the Ctrl key (for a noncontiguous selection) and the Shift key (for a contiguous selection).
6. Click Open to add the image as a resource to the database.

Inserting an Image Resource in a Page

You can insert an image resource in different types of design elements in your databases. You can insert it as a graphic in a page, a form, a view, or a folder. You can insert it as a background in a page or a form. You can also insert it as an icon in action buttons or outlines.

To insert an image resource in a page, perform the following steps:

1. Open the database in which you want to insert the image resource in Domino Designer.
2. Click Pages in the Design pane to display a list of pages that exist in the database.
3. In the Work pane, double-click the page in which you want to insert the image resource to open it or click New Page to create a new page.
4. Place the cursor at the location in the page where you want to insert the image.
5. Select Image Resource from the Create menu. The Insert Image Resource dialog box appears, as shown in Figure 3.2. This dialog box lists all the image resources in the current database.

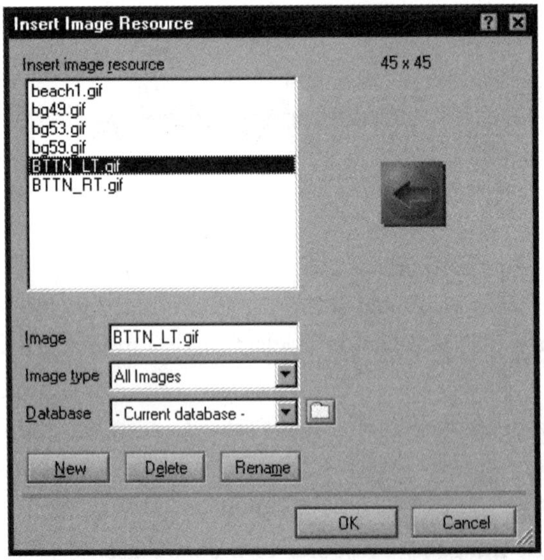

FIGURE 3.2 *The Insert Image Resource dialog box*

NOTE

To view the image resources in a different database, select the database from the Database list or click the Choose Database button. The Choose Database dialog box appears, and you can select a database either from the server or from your local disk.

6. In the Insert Image Resource dialog box, select the Image type as GIF Images or JPEG Images to view specific images. Otherwise, leave the All Images option selected to view both types of images.
7. From the Image resource list, select the desired image and click OK. The selected image stored as an image resource is inserted in the page.

File Resources

You can share files, such as HTML or GIF files, among databases by creating a *file resource*. For example, suppose you want to use a Company Information page, created in HTML, in all existing databases. To do so, you can create a file resource to share the file across databases.

Creating a File Resource

To create a file resource, perform the following steps:

1. Open the database in which you want to insert the file resource in Domino Designer.
2. In the Design pane, click Files under Shared Resources to open the Files work pane.
3. In the Work pane, click New File Resource. The Open dialog box appears, as shown in Figure 3.3. Here you can select the file that you want to add to the database as a resource.

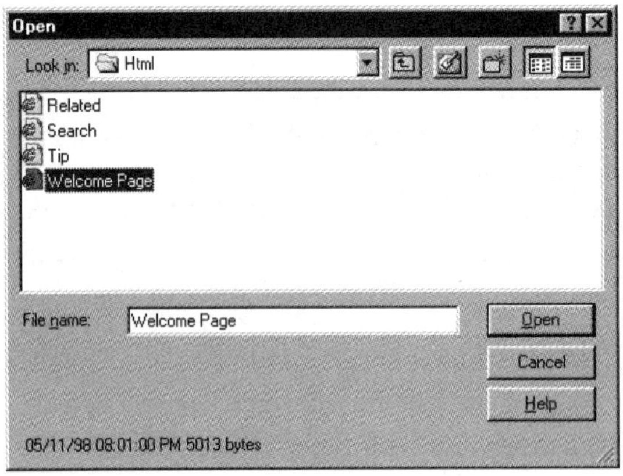

FIGURE 3.3 *The Open dialog box used to select the file to be stored as a file resource*

4. Navigate to the directory that contains the file to be stored as a resource and select the file.
5. Click Open. The file is added to your database as a resource. Also, the resource properties in the File Resource dialog box appear, as shown in Figure 3.4. You can use this dialog box to view and modify the properties of the file resource.

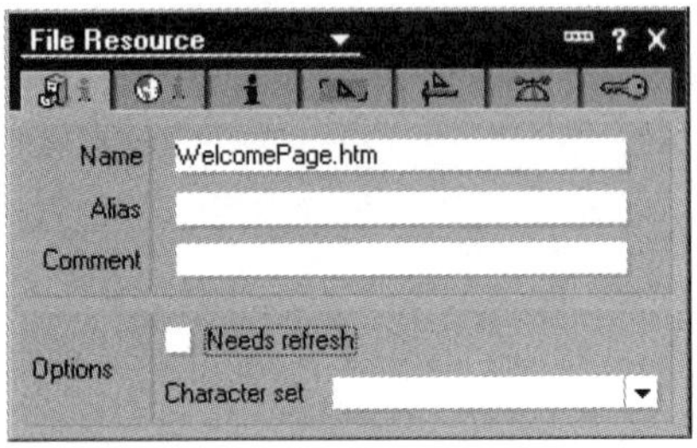

FIGURE 3.4 *The File Resource dialog box, displaying the file resource properties*

Inserting an HTML File Resource in a Page

The file resources created in a database can be used in different design elements for different purposes, according to the type of the file used to create a resource. For example, you can use a CSS file to apply a style sheet to a form or a page, a GIF file to insert an image, or an HTML file to insert the HTML code in a page or a form.

To insert an HTML file—Welcome.htm, stored as a file resource in a database—in a page, perform the following steps:

1. Open the database that contains the page in which you want to insert the HTML file in Domino Designer.
2. Click Pages in the Design pane to display the Pages work pane.
3. Double-click the page to open the page on which you want to insert the file resource or click New Page to create a new page.
4. Place the cursor where you want to insert the HTML file on the page.
5. Select Insert Resource from the Create menu. The Insert Resource dialog box appears, as shown in Figure 3.5.

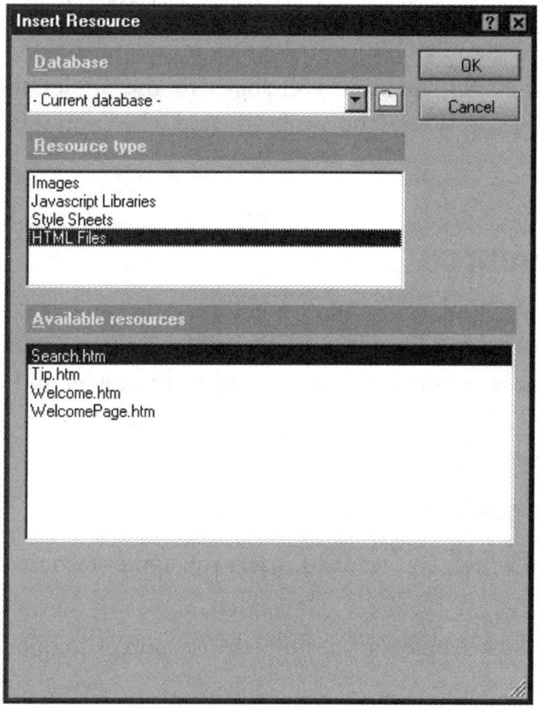

FIGURE 3.5 *The Insert Resource dialog box to insert a file resource*

6. Select the database that contains the file resource from the Database list or click the Choose Database button. The Choose Database dialog box appears. You can select a database from either the server or the local

disk. Select Current database to use a file resource stored in the current database.

7. Select the Resource type as HTML Files to view all the HTML file resources in the selected database.
8. From the Available resources list, select Welcome.htm and click OK. The HTML file is inserted on the selected page.
9. Preview the page to see the content of the inserted HTML file.

Applet Resources

You can insert a Java applet in a form, page, or document in a Notes application. A Java applet may consist of several files, such as Class and GIF files or other image files. You can store these applet files as resources in a database and reference them across databases. If you make any changes to the applet files, the change is reflected in all the places where the applet is used when you refresh the applet resource.

Creating an Applet Resource

To add the functionality of Java applets to a page or a form, you can insert applets in them. For example, a Java applet, caption, is used to add a caption at the top of a page or a form. You can pass a parameter, captiontext, to this applet and display the text in an attractive format. You can create an applet resource to store applets that are used in multiple design elements.

To create an applet resource, perform the following steps:

1. Open the database in which you want to insert the applet resource in Domino Designer.
2. In the Design pane, click Applets under Shared Resources to open the Applets work pane.
3. In the Work pane, click the New Applet Resource button. The Locate Java Applet Files dialog box appears, as shown in Figure 3.6. Here you can select the files that make up the applet that you want to import as an applet resource.

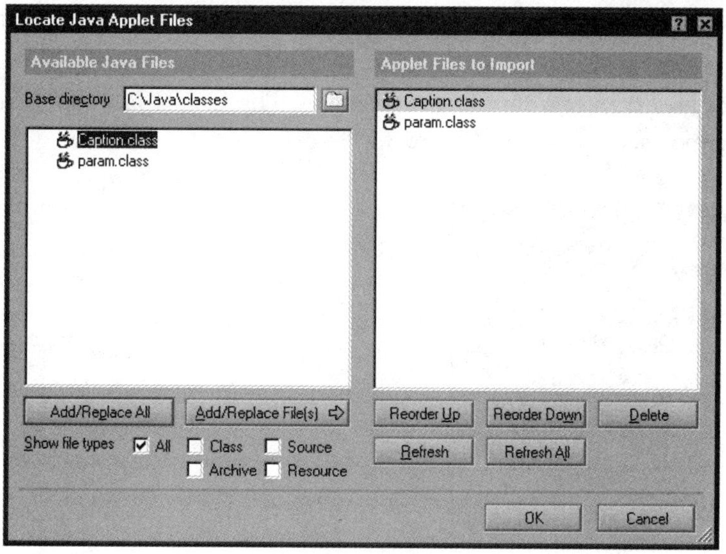

FIGURE 3.6 *The Locate Java Applet files dialog box to select the applet resource files*

4. In the Base directory field, enter the name of the directory where the class files for the applet are located. Or click the Locate file button to select the base directory.
5. From the displayed class files, select the files that you want to import and click the Add/Replace File(s) button.
6. Click OK. This creates an applet resource that you can use in any form or page within or across databases.

Inserting an Applet Resource in a Page

You can insert an applet in a form, a page, or a document to provide them with the applet's functionality. Perform the following steps to insert an applet stored as a resource in a page:

1. Open the database that contains the page in which you want to insert the applet resource in Domino Designer.
2. Click Pages in the Design pane to display the Pages work pane.
3. Double-click the page in which you want to insert the applet to open it or click New Page to create a new page.

4. Place the cursor at the location where you want to insert the applet on the page.
5. Select Java Applet from the Create menu. The Create Java Applet dialog box appears, as shown in Figure 3.7.

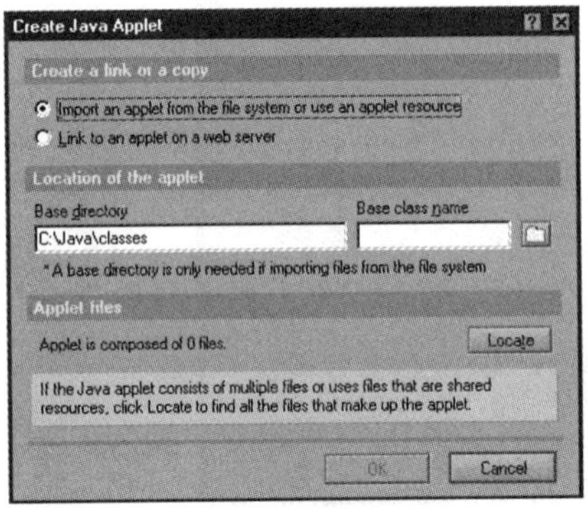

FIGURE 3.7 *The Create Java Applet dialog box to insert an applet resource in a page*

6. Under Create a link or a copy, the option Import an applet from the file system or use an applet resource is selected by default. Under Location of the applet, clear the Base directory field and click Locate to open the Locate Java Applet Files dialog box, as shown in Figure 3.8.

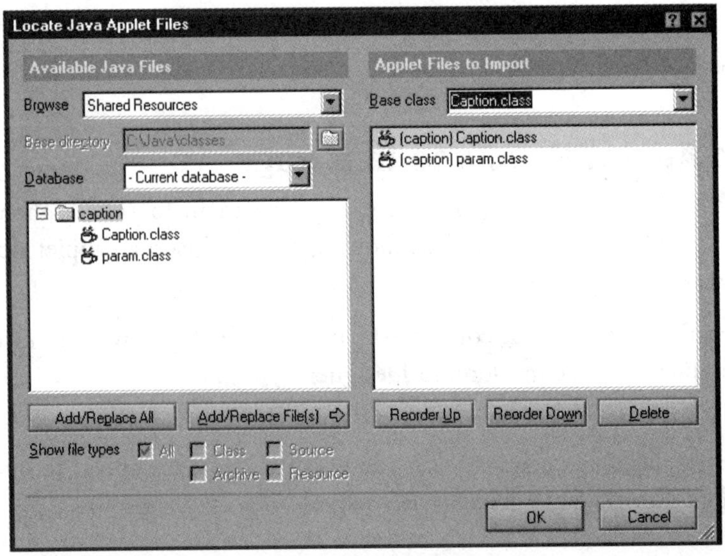

FIGURE 3.8 *The Locate Java Applet Files dialog box to select applet files from the applet resource*

7. From the Browse list, select Shared Resources. The Database list is activated.
8. From the Database list, select the database in which you created the applet resource. If you created it in the current database, select Current database. All the applet resources created in the selected database are displayed.
9. Select the applet resource that contains the applet to be inserted. Click Add/Replace All to add all the class files in the resource to the Applet Files to Import list on the right.
10. From the Base Class list, select the name of the base class. This class is used to run the applet.
11. Click OK to close the Locate Java Applet Files dialog box.
12. Click OK to close the Create Java Applet dialog box. The Java applet is inserted on the selected page.
13. Select Applet Parameters in the Object pane to add any parameters required to run the applet. Click Add in the Programmers pane to display the Add Parameter dialog box, as shown in Figure 3.9.

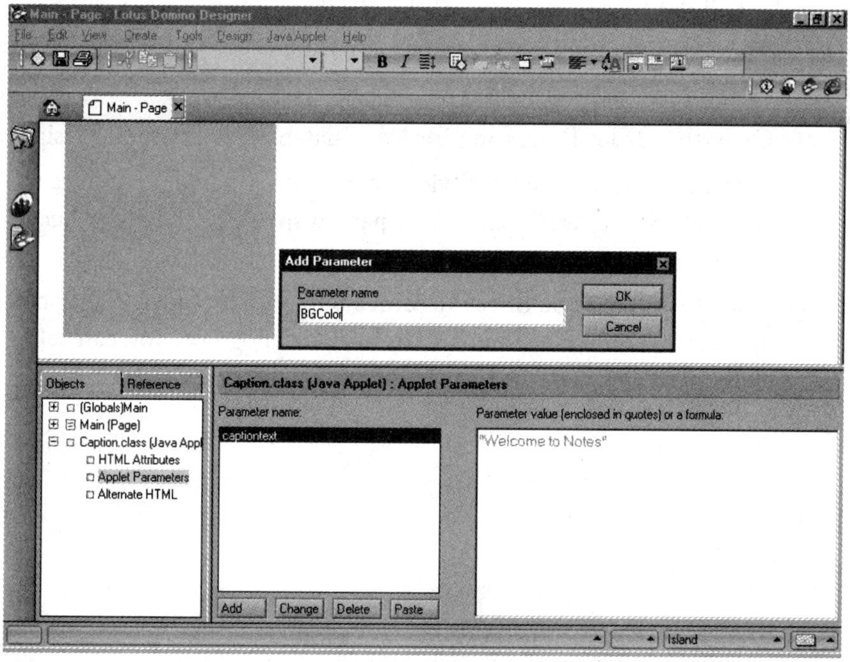

FIGURE 3.9 *The Add Parameter dialog box to add parameters to the Java applet*

14. Enter the name of the parameter. For example, enter BGColor to specify the background color of the applet and click OK.
15. Enter the value of the parameter enclosed in quotes, for example, "00ff00", in the Parameter Value box. Similarly, set all the required parameters.
16. Preview the page to load the applet.

Style Sheet Resources

A *style sheet* is used to apply standard formatting to multiple HTML documents. It contains formatting information about various parts, such as the Body, Paragraph, Header, and Links of a document. In Notes databases, you can store a style sheet as a style sheet resource and then apply it to all your pages and forms to give them a standard look.

Creating a Style Sheet Resource

Order Processing for Wow is an online order-processing database. To standardize the look of all the forms and pages of this database, suppose that you have developed a style sheet file, style1.css. To create a style sheet resource in the Order Processing for Wow database, perform the following steps:

1. Open the Order Processing for Wow database in Domino Designer.
2. In the Design pane, click Style Sheets under Shared Resources to view the Style Sheets work pane. This pane displays all the style sheet resources in the database.
3. Click the New Style Sheet Resource button. The Open dialog box appears, as shown in Figure 3.10. In this dialog box, you can select the style sheet file that you want to add as a style sheet resource.

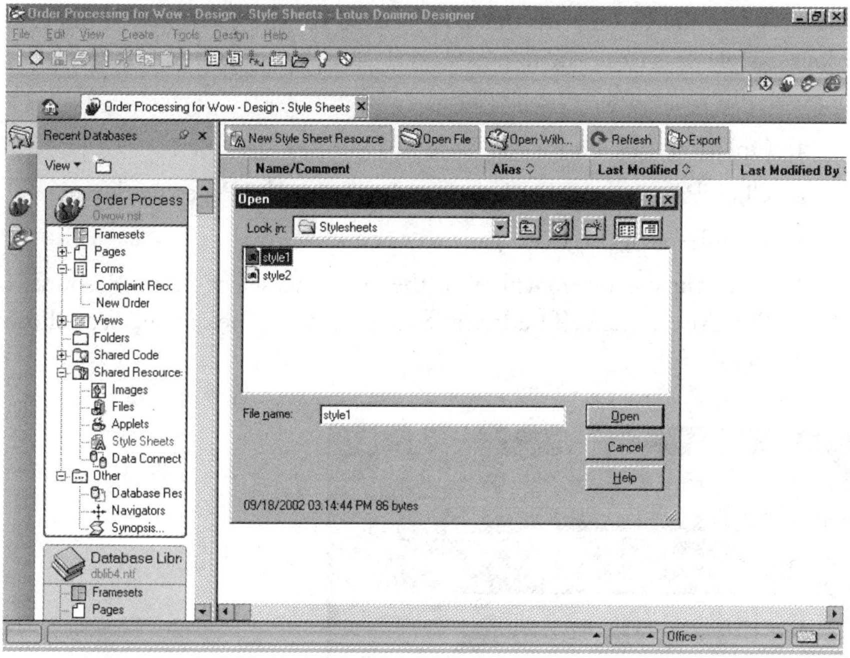

FIGURE 3.10 *The Open dialog box to select a style sheet for creating a style sheet resource*

4. Navigate to the directory where the style sheet file is stored, select the file style1.css, and click Open. This adds the style sheet style1.css as a resource to the database and opens the style sheet properties in the Style Sheet Resource dialog box.
5. Modify the name of the style sheet resource if required, and in the Comment fields, enter a comment about the style sheet resource.
6. Close the Style Sheet Resource dialog box.

Attaching a Style Sheet Resource to a Page

You can attach the style sheet resource to a page, a form, or a subform to apply the defined styles. You can attach a style sheet resource from the current database or from another database. Suppose you have developed a database named HR Forms as a repository of all HR related forms, such as Leave, Medical Reimbursement, and Conveyance Vouchers. You want to apply the same style as applied to the forms and pages in the Order Processing for Wow database to the

Intro page in the HR Forms database. To do so, you must attach the style sheet resource style1.css from the database to the Intro page of the HR Forms database by performing the following steps:

1. Open the HR Forms database in Domino Designer.
2. Click Pages in the Design pane to display the Pages work pane.
3. Double-click the Intro page to open it.
4. Place the cursor anywhere on the page and select Insert Resource from the Create menu. The Insert Resource dialog box appears, as shown in Figure 3.11.

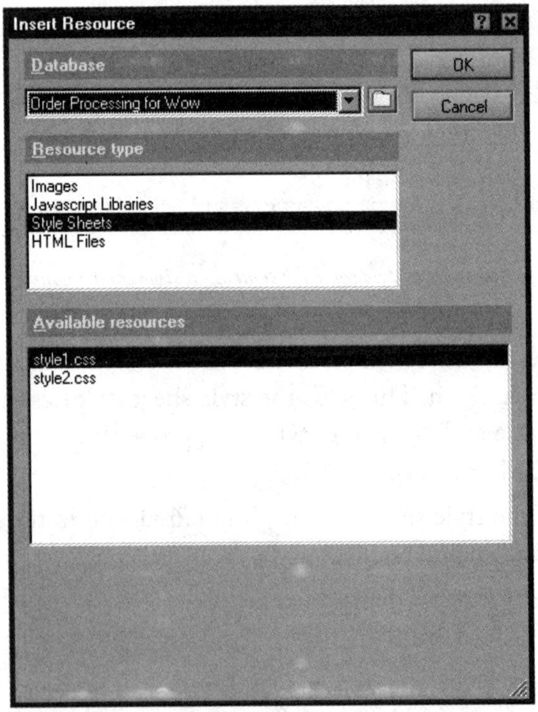

FIGURE 3.11 *The Insert Resource dialog box, displaying the options to select a style sheet resource*

5. From the Database list, select the Order Processing for Wow database.
6. To view the style sheet resources in the selected database, select Style Sheets as the Resource type. All the style sheets that you added to the Order Processing for Wow database are displayed.

7. Select style1.css from the Available resources list and click OK. The style sheet style1.css is attached to the Intro page.
8. Preview the page to view the modified format. The page is formatted according to the formatting options defined in the style1.css file.

CAUTION

If you change the style sheet file, you must refresh the style sheet resource to apply the changes made to the style sheet to all the design elements referencing it.

Data Connection Resources

Domino provides services for connecting a Domino database to enterprise systems, such as RDBMS (*Relational Database Management Systems*), TP (*Transaction Processing*) systems, and ERP (*Enterprise Resource Planning*) systems, or unstructured data. This feature lets you create powerful applications that use the data storage and processing capabilities of an enterprise system, for example, Oracle, as well as the power of Domino to share, replicate, manage, and secure data.

DECS (*Domino Enterprise Connection Services*) provides realtime form-based connectivity to enterprise data. DECS is loaded as a task on the Domino server. When you load DECS on the server, the DECS Administrator database used to configure DECS is automatically created. To configure DECS, you need to do two configurations in this database: one, create data connections to create a realtime connection to a back-end database, and two, define realtime activities. The detailed procedure to configure DECS is covered in Part V titled *Creating a Notes Application to Access Non-Notes Databases* of this book.

In Domino Designer, data connections can be created locally in a database to connect to enterprise data.

NOTE

On the Domino server that has the database configured for accessing an external database, you must create a data source reference for the external database. For example, to connect to a Microsoft Access database from a Windows NT server, you can use the Windows System Tools utility to specify the Access database as a data source and ODBC as the driver to use for data exchange.

A data connection resource is created in a database so that you can use it in the forms in the same database or other databases to set up realtime access to enterprise data. Using a form created for realtime access, you can add, update, or delete data directly in the back-end database, without storing it in Notes.

Suppose you have an Access database named Emp.dbf. This database contains a table named Employee, which you want to access directly in the form of a Notes database named Employees. You have a data source named EmpSource for the Emp.dbf database on the server. To create a data connection resource for the Employees database to access Emp.dbf, perform the following steps:

1. Open the Employees database in Domino Designer.
2. In the Design pane, click Data Connections under Shared Resources to view the Data Connections work pane. This pane displays the existing data connection resources and allows you to create new data connection resources.
3. Click New Data Connection Resource. The Data Connection dialog box appears, as shown in Figure 3.12.

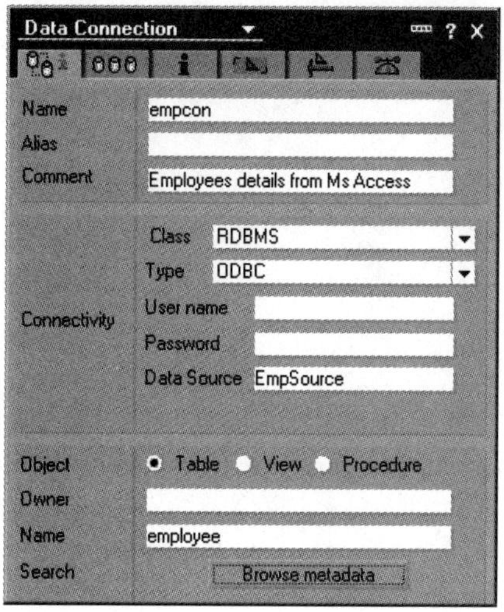

FIGURE 3.12 *The Data Connection dialog box, displaying data connection resource properties*

4. In the Name field, enter Empcon as the name for the data connection resource. You can also specify an alias and a comment. If you specify an alias and use that in the formulas and scripts used, you can change the name of the data connection resource without changing any formulas or scripts where you're using this resource.
5. From the Class list, select RDBMS.
6. From the Type list, select ODBC. This list contains various options, such as Oracle, Sybase, and DB2. It also has generic options, such as ODBC for back-end databases that do not have a native driver.
7. Enter your user name and password, if applicable. In this case, leave the User name and Password fields blank, because the Emp.dbf database does not have a user name and a password defined.
8. In the Data Source field, enter EmpSource.
9. Specify the object as Table.
10. Click Browse metadata to view the available objects in the selected data source. Because the selected object type is a table, a list of all the tables and their columns is displayed, as shown in Figure 3.13.

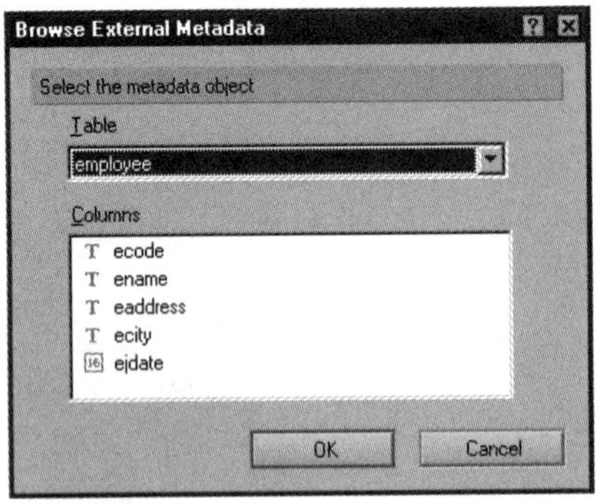

FIGURE 3.13 *The Browse External Metadata dialog box, displaying the tables and columns in the EmpSource data source*

11. Select employee as the table name and click OK.
12. Close the Data Connection dialog box. Optionally, you can specify additional properties using other tabs.

You'll learn to use a data connection resource in Part V titled "Creating a Notes Application to Access Non-Notes Databases" of this book.

Other Types of Shared Resources

Besides the five types of shared resources discussed, a Notes database contains certain other objects, such as fields, actions, and subforms, which can be shared within or across a database. You can also create script libraries in LotusScript, JavaScript, or Java to store the shared and reusable code in a database. In this section, you'll learn about shared fields, subforms, and shared actions.

Shared Fields

Fields that display the name of the person who created a document and the date of the creation of a document are used in almost all forms. The properties of these fields, such as field type or data type, remain the same in all the forms. Moreover, the formulas that you write on the fields' events are the same. You can save a lot of time by creating these fields as shared fields. Then, whenever required, you can insert the shared field in a form. If you need to make any change to a shared field, you can make the change in one place, and it will be reflected in all the places where the field has been used.

Creating a Shared Field

You can create a shared field in two ways. You can either create a new shared field or convert an existing single-use field (a field that is not shared) in a form into a shared field.

Creating a New Shared Field

To create a new shared field named CreateDate in the Employees database, perform the following steps:

1. Open the Employees database in Domino Designer.
2. In the Design pane, click Fields under Shared Code. The Work pane displays a list of shared fields in the current database.
3. Click the New Shared Field button. A new shared field is created, and the Shared Field dialog box appears, as shown in Figure 3.14.

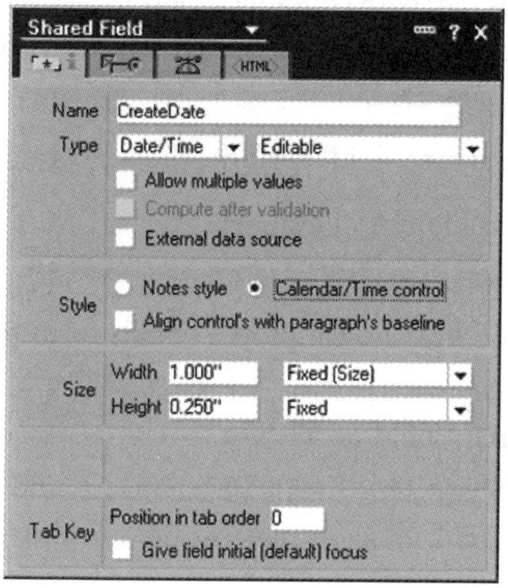

FIGURE 3.14 *The Shared Field dialog box, displaying the properties of a shared field*

4. In the Name field, enter CreateDate as the name of the shared field.
5. From the Type list, select Date/Time as the data type for the shared field.
6. Set other properties of the shared field as required and close the Shared Field dialog box. The Programmer's pane for the shared field is displayed.

7. In the Programmer's pane, you can write formulas or other types of code, such as LotusScript or JavaScript, for the field events. For example, to display the current system date in the CreateDate field by default, select the Default Value event in the Objects pane and write the following formula:

```
@Today
```

   This formula is also shared and will be executed whenever the field is inserted in a form.

8. Close the Programmer's pane for the shared field. An alert is displayed with the message, "Do you want to save this Shared Field?" Click Yes to save the shared field.

Converting an Existing Field in a Form to a Shared Field

You can convert an existing field in a form into a shared field. For example, the form Employee details in the Employees database contains a field named Department, which you want to use in other forms of the database. To save time, convert the existing Department field into a shared field.

To convert the Department field into a shared field, perform the following steps:

1. Open the Employees database in Domino Designer.
2. Click Forms in the Design pane.
3. In the Forms work pane, double-click the Employee details form to open it.
4. On the form, click the Department field to select it.
5. From the Design menu, select Share This Field. This converts the Department field into a shared field. You can use this field in the form of any database without recreating it.

Using a Shared Field in a Form

You can insert the Department shared field in any form in the Employees database or any other form in another database on the server. To insert this shared field in a form named New Leave in the HR Forms database, perform the following steps:

1. Open the HR Forms database in Domino Designer.

2. Click Forms in the Design pane to display the list of forms in the database.
3. In the Forms work pane, double-click the New Leave form to open it.
4. Place the cursor at the location where you want to insert the Department field on the form.
5. Type the label Employee department for the field.
6. From the Create menu, select Insert Shared Field. The Insert Shared Field dialog box with a list of all the shared fields in the current database appears, as shown in Figure 3.15. You can also select another database from the Database list to insert a shared field from that database.

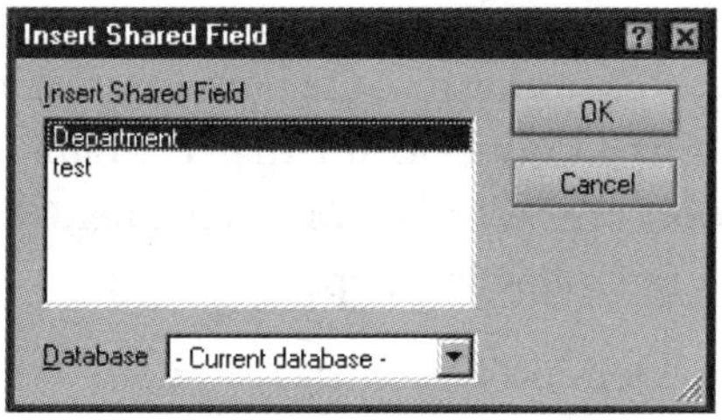

FIGURE 3.15 *The Insert Shared Field dialog box, displaying the list of shared fields in a database*

7. Select the Department field to insert it into your form and click OK. The Department field is inserted into your form. A shared field has a border darker than that of a single use field.

NOTE

You can also use the Insert Resource option on the Create menu to insert a shared field into your form. To view the shared fields in the selected database, you must select the Resource type as Shared Fields.

Subforms

A *subform* is a design element that can be shared among multiple forms. You can place a set of common form elements—such as fields, text, graphics, actions, or any other element or object that you can have in a form—on a subform and then use the subform with other forms. For example, you can use subforms to standardize the headers and footers of all the forms in a database.

Unlike a form, a subform does not have its own properties. Instead, a subform shares the properties of the form in which it is inserted. Therefore, a subform does not show up separately from the parent form when you create a document. Using subforms saves a lot of design and maintenance time. You need to make any changes required only once in a subform. These changes will be reflected automatically in all forms that use the subform.

Creating a Subform

Suppose you want to display the details about the author of a document at the bottom of each form in the HR Forms database. You can create a subform that contains all the required fields and insert this subform at the bottom of each form in the database. To create a subform named AuthorInfo that contains details about the name, department, and location of the author of a document and the date of creation of a document, perform the following steps:

1. Open the HR Forms database in Domino Designer.
2. In the Design pane, click Subforms under Shared Code. The Subforms work pane displays a list of all the subforms in the database.
3. Click New Subform to create a new subform.
4. Create the four required fields, along with the appropriate labels to design the subform, as shown in Figure 3.16.
5. From the Design menu, select Subform Properties to open the Subform dialog box. In the Name field, type AuthorInfo. You may also type a comment in the Comments field.
6. Set the other properties as required and close the subform. Notes displays a message prompting you to confirm whether you want to save the subform.
7. Click Yes to save the subform.

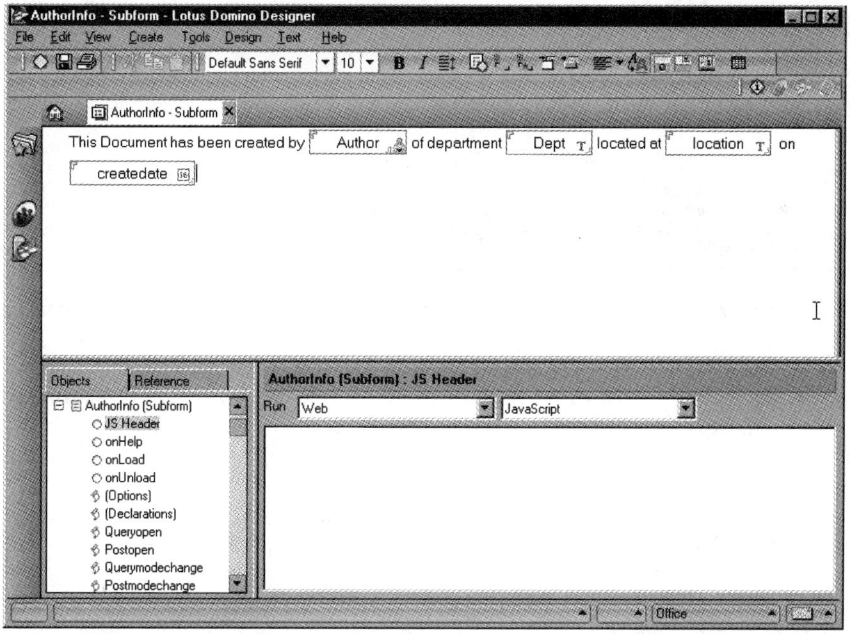

FIGURE 3.16 *The AuthorInfo subform*

Inserting the Subform in a Form

To insert the AuthorInfo subform in the New Leave form in the HR Forms database, perform the following steps:

1. Open the HR Forms database in Domino Designer.
2. Click Forms in the Design pane to display the list of forms in the database.
3. In the Work pane, double-click the New Leave form to open it.
4. Place the cursor at the bottom of the form to insert the subform as a footer.
5. From the Create menu, select Resource/Insert Subform. The Insert Subform dialog box with a list of all the subforms in the current database appears, as shown in Figure 3.17. You can also insert a subform from a different database.

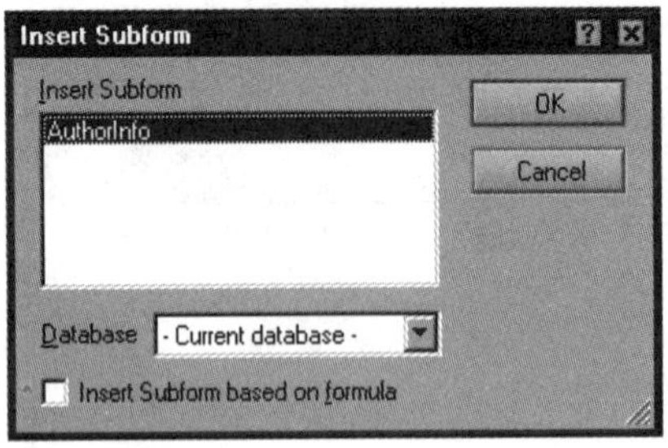

FIGURE 3.17 *The Insert Subform dialog box, displaying a list of subforms in the database*

6. Select the AuthorInfo subform and click OK to insert the subform in the New Leave form.

> **NOTE**
>
> A subform can also be inserted based on a formula. Such a subform is called a *computed* subform. To insert a computed subform in your form, select Insert Subform based on formula instead of selecting the subform name. A subform is added as an object in the Objects pane. Then write the formula that evaluates the name of the subform in the Default Value event. This subform will be inserted dynamically when a document is created from the form.

Shared Actions

Shared actions are reusable actions that can be created in a database and used in various forms, views, or pages. You can create all commonly used actions, such as Save Document, Close Document, Delete Document, and Edit Document, as shared actions and insert them wherever required to save designing and maintenance time.

Creating a Shared Action

To create a new shared action named Delete Document to mark a document for deletion, perform the following steps:

1. Open the database in which you want to create the shared action in Domino Designer.

2. In the Design pane, click Actions under Shared Code. The Actions work pane displays a list of all the shared actions in the current database.
3. Click New Shared Action. A new shared action is created, and the properties of the shared action are displayed in the Shared Action dialog box, as shown in Figure 3.18.

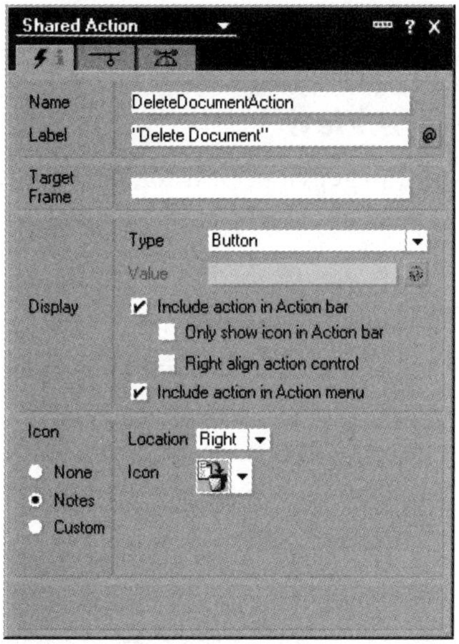

FIGURE 3.18 *The Shared Action dialog box, displaying the properties of a shared action*

4. In the Name field, enter Delete Document as the name of the shared action.
5. In Domino Designer, you can use formulas to assign labels to actions. In the Label field, enter the formula to assign a label to the shared action as "Delete Document".
6. Notice that the Type list shows Button, indicating that the action is displayed as a button. You can also choose Checkbox or Menu separator from the Type list.
7. Under Icon, select Notes, and from the Icon list, select an icon for the button.
8. Close the Shared Action dialog box. The Programmer's pane used to write the code for the action is displayed.

9. In the Click event, choose Simple action(s) and click the Add Action button to display the Add Action dialog box.
10. Select the action as Delete from Database and click Add. The action is assigned to the shared action.
11. Close the shared action. Notes displays a message prompting you to confirm if you want to save the changes.
12. Click Yes to save the shared action.

Inserting the Shared Action in a View

A shared action can be inserted in a form, page, view, or a folder. To insert the Delete Document shared action in the All Employees view of the Employees database, perform the following steps:

1. Open the Employees database in Domino Designer.
2. Click Views in the Design pane to display the list of views in the current database.
3. In the Views work pane, double-click the All Employees view to open it. This displays the view properties in a View dialog box.
4. Close the View dialog box.
5. From the Create menu, select Insert Shared Action. The Insert Shared Action dialog box with a list of shared actions in the current database is displayed, as shown in Figure 3.19.

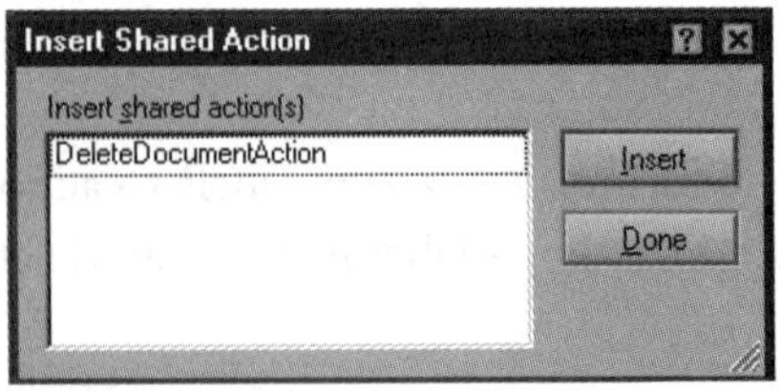

FIGURE 3.19 *The Insert Shared Action dialog box, displaying a list of shared actions in a database*

NOTE

You cannot insert a shared action that has been created in another different database.

6. Select the Delete Document action and click Insert. You can add multiple actions by selecting each action and then clicking Insert. Finally, click Done to close the Insert Shared Action dialog box. This inserts all the selected actions in the view.

Summary

In this chapter, you learned about the different types of shared resources in a database. A shared resource helps a developer save design and maintenance time. You learned how to create and insert different types of shared resources, such as an image resource, a file resource, an applet resource, and a style sheet resource. You also learned how to create a data connection resource. Finally, you learned to create and use shared fields, subforms, and shared actions.

Chapter 4

Working with Formulas in Domino Designer

Domino Designer provides an IDE (*Integrated Development Environment*) for programming. The IDE allows you to write code using formulas, LotusScript, JavaScript, or Java. The use of various languages gives you the flexibility to design robust applications for use in Notes, on the Web, or both.

In this chapter, you will learn the basics of formula language, some important @Functions, and @Commands. You will also learn how to use the events in various design elements to write formulas.

Basics of the Formula Language

Formula language has been an integral part of Notes since its first release. Formula language is different from programming languages. Unlike programming languages, formula language does not have constructs, such as iteration or condition checking. Although there are certain formula elements called *@Functions*, which can be used to achieve iteration or condition checking, they do not provide you with the complete flexibility of a programming language. Besides, the functionality of formula language is limited to built-in functions because you cannot create user-defined functions. In spite of all these limitations, formula language is easy to use. You can choose this language to perform most tasks, such as calculations, validations, and user interaction.

A *formula* consists of one or more statements that are executed in sequence. If you use multiple statements, they must be separated with a semicolon (;). A statement comprises of one or more of the following components:

- Variables
- Constants
- Operators
- Reserved words
- @Functions
- @Commands

Variables

Variables are used to store values. They are the named storage areas in the memory where the data being accessed is stored. There are two types of variables, *temporary* and *field*.

Temporary Variables

Temporary variables are created by assigning values to them in a formula. These variables do not have a specific datatype and automatically assume the datatype of the value assigned to them. For example, the following statement creates a variable named `A`. This variable automatically assumes a numeric datatype, because the value assigned to it is a number `10`.

```
A:=10
```

Next the variable named `B` is assigned a time-date value, and therefore, the datatype of the variable is time-date.

```
B:=[10/10/99]
```

Temporary variables have a local scope. They can be used only in the formula where they have been created. For example, if you create a temporary variable in one action button, you cannot refer to it in another action button or any other place. Defining a variable with the same name creates a new temporary variable.

It is also possible to reassign a variable in the same formula. For example, the following statements are valid:

```
A:=10;
A:=15
```

You can also reassign a value of a different datatype to the same variable. For example, in the following code, the variable named `A` is first assigned a numeric value `10` and then it is reassigned a textual value `Apple`.

```
A:=10;
A:="Apple"
```

Field Variables

Field variables or fields are created as part of the form design. You can also create and access these fields in the formula. To do so, the reserved word `FIELD` is used. For example, the following statement assigns a value `1001` to the field `ecode`. If the field `ecode` does not already exist, this statement creates the `ecode` field with the specified value in the current document.

```
FIELD ecode:=1001
```

When designing a form, you specify the datatype of a field in the Field dialog box. However, if you create a field using a formula, the field can have a datatype of text, number, or time-date, depending on the value assigned to the field.

> **NOTE**
>
> If you do not use the `FIELD` reserved word while assigning a value to a field from a formula, the field name is treated as a temporary variable and the value is not assigned to the field.

Constants

Constants are the values that are assigned to the variables. There are three types of constants in formula language: *text*, *number*, and *date and time*.

Text Constants

Any value, character or number, enclosed in quotation marks (" ") or curly braces ({}), is a text constant. The following is an example of a text constant defined using double quotation marks:

```
Name:="Jessica"
```

The following statement defines a constant using curly braces:

```
Country:={Canada}
```

If you want to use quotation marks in a text constant enclosed in quotation marks or braces in a text constant that is enclosed in braces, you must precede these characters with a backslash. A backslash serves as an escape character. If you want to use a backslash as part of the text constant, you must use two backslashes in each place. The following examples demonstrate how to use the backslash character in constants. The first example assigns a path to the variable `FilePath` and has backslashes as part of the path itself.

```
FilePath:="C:\\Lotus\\Notes\\Data"
```

The next example has curly braces as part of the constant. Note the use of backslash in this example.

```
Message:={Pls. write the amount in \{\}}
```

Number Constants

A number constant can contain a digit from 0 to 9, plus (+) or minus (-) signs, a decimal (.), and the character (E) for scientific notation. Unlike text constants, you do not enclose number constants in any delimiters. A few examples of number constants are as follows:

```
Age:=10;
Average:=75.5;
Temperature:=-4;
Salary:=12E3
```

You can perform arithmetic operations such as addition, subtraction, multiplication, and division on number constants.

Date and Time Constants

Date and time constants are used to assign values to variables of the type time-date. All date and time constants are enclosed in square brackets, as shown in the following statement:

```
Startdate:=[10/09/2000]
```

When assigning a date, the date format must match the default date format of the operating system. If you do not specify the year in the date, the current year is assigned by default. For example, the following statement automatically assumes the date to be 10/09/2002:

```
Startdate:=[10/09]
```

You can also specify time in a date and time constant. You can specify the time either in a 24-hour format, such as [22:00], or a 12-hour format, such as [10:00 pm].

You can also combine the date and time and assign as follows:

```
Meetingtime:=[10/10/2002 11:00 AM]
```

Operators

Formula language provides operators for various operations, such as addition, multiplication, concatenation, and comparison. Types of operators include *assignment*, *arithmetic*, *comparison*, *logical*, *list*, and *unary*.

The Assignment Operator

The assignment operator is used to assign a value to a variable. The assignment operator in the formula language is a colon and an equal sign (:=). For example, the following statement assigns a value `100` to the variable `Days`:

```
Days:=100
```

The assignment operator can also be used to assign values or results of expressions. You can use either constants or variables in the expressions. For example, consider the following statements that use the assignment operator.

The variable `Name` is assigned a constant value `Jessica`.

```
Name:="Jessica"
```

The variable `HRA` is assigned the result of the expression `Basic*0.4`.

```
HRA:=Basic* 0.4
```

The variable `PostalAddress` is assigned the result of the expression `Address+City`.

```
PostalAddress:= Address+city
```

Arithmetic Operators

Arithmetic operators are used to perform calculations on numbers. The various arithmetic operators are addition (+), subtraction (-), multiplication (*), and division (/).

You can use multiple operators in a single statement. The multiplication and division operators have an equal precedence with one another, but a higher precedence over addition and subtraction. For example, in the following statement, division takes place before addition. Therefore, the result assigned to the variable `A` is 14 instead of 9.

```
A:=10+8/2
```

You can change the order of evaluation by using parentheses. Parentheses have the highest precedence. Therefore, if you rewrite the previous statement using a parenthesis, the addition takes place first. The value assigned to the variable `A` is 9.

```
A:=(10+8)/2
```

If you are using two operators with the same precedence, the order of evaluation is from left to right. In the following example, multiplication and division have the same precedence, but multiplication is performed first because the multiplication operator is to the left of the division operator. The result 25 is assigned to the variable A.

```
A:=10*5/2
```

You can also use the subtraction operator to subtract a time-date value from another time-date value. For example, the following formula returns 777600, the difference in number of seconds:

```
[10/10/2002] - [10/01/2002]
```

To get the result in some other format, you must convert it appropriately. For example, to get the difference in number of days, you must divide the result by 86400, and therefore write the formula as follows:

```
Duration:=([10/10/2002] - [10/01/2002])/86400
```

Comparison Operators

Comparison operators are used to compare two values of the same datatype. All comparison operators return either True or False. If the values being compared are of different datatypes, an error is returned. Comparison operators, along with their examples, are listed in Table 4.1.

Table 4.1 Comparison Operators

Operator Name	Symbol	Example
Equal	=	`City="Phoenix"` returns True if the variable `City` contains the value `Phoenix`.
Not Equal	!=,<>,><	`City!="Arizona"` returns True if the variable `City` contains any value other than `Arizona`.
Greater than	>	`Rate>100` returns True if the variable `Rate` contains a value greater than `100`, otherwise, it returns False.
Greater than or equal	>=	`Rate>=100` returns True if `Rate` contains a value greater than or equal to `100`, otherwise, it returns False.
Less than	<	`Distance<20` returns True if the variable `Distance` contains a value less than `20`.
Less than or equal	<=	`Distance<=20` returns True if the variable `Distance` contains a value less than or equal to `20`.

Logical Operators

Logical operators evaluate multiple logical statements to return either True or False. There are three logical operators, which are described in Table 4.2.

Table 4.2 Logical Operators

Operator Name	Symbol	Description	Example
AND	&	Returns True if all the conditions are True. If any of the conditions is false, it returns False.	`Department="IT" & Location="Phoenix"` returns True if both the conditions are true.
OR	|	Returns True if any of the conditions is True. If both the conditions are false, it returns False.	`State="Phoenix" ¦ State="Arizona"` returns True if the variable `State` contains either `Phoenix` or `Arizona`, otherwise it returns False.
NOT	!	Evaluates the reverse of an expression.	`Status!="Rejected"` returns True if the field `Status` contains any value other than `Rejected`.

List Operators

A field or temporary variable containing multiple values is called a *list*. For a field to be a list, you must enable its *allow multiple values* property.

List operators operate on lists. There are two list operators:

- **Colon (:).** The list concatenation operator. It is used to concatenate a value to a list. For example, in the following statement, three values are concatenated to create a list named `list1`:

  ```
  List1:="Apples":"Mangoes":Grapes"
  ```

  The following example concatenates the value `Banana` to `list1`:

  ```
  List2:=List1:"Banana"
  ```

- **Square brackets ([]).** Represents a list subscript. This operator returns a specific member of a list. For example, `List1` returns the second element from `List1`, where `List1` contains `"Apple":"Mangoes":"Grapes"`. Therefore, `List1` returns `Mangoes`.

CAUTION

The list concatenation operator must be used with elements of similar datatypes.

The list subscript starts from 1. Using a subscript less than 1 or greater than the number of elements in the list results in an error.

You can use the arithmetic and comparison operations with lists. These operations can be performed using either of the two operators, *pair-wise* and *permutation*.

Pair-Wise Operators

These operators act on two lists in such a way that each individual element in one list pairs with the corresponding element in the second list. Therefore, the first element of the first list pairs with the first element of the second list, the second element of the first list pairs with the second element of the second list, and so on. For example, in the following statements, `List1` and `List2` have been added to obtain a new list, `List3`, which stores `8:10:12`.

```
List1:=1:2:3;
List2:=7:8:9;
List3:=List1+List2
```

Similarly, subtracting `List1` from `List2` results in `6:6:6`. `List1*List2` results in `7:16:27` and `List2/List1` results in `7:4:3`.

Pair-wise comparison operators, such as (=), (>), and (<), compare corresponding elements of a pair of lists. These operators return True if even one of the pair satisfies the condition. For example, `List1>List2` returns False because none of the elements in `List1` is greater than the corresponding elements in `List2`.

Permutation Operators

Permutation operators act on the lists by pairing each element of the first list with every individual element of the second list. For example, the following statements result in `8; 9; 10; 9; 10; 11; 10; 11; 12` by adding each element of `List1` with every possible element of `List2`.

```
List1:=1:2:3;
List2:=7:8:9;
List3:=List1 *+ List2
```

The various permutation operators are:

- *+ (Permuted addition or permuted concatenation)
- *- (Permuted subtraction)
- ** (Permuted multiplication)
- */ (Permuted division)
- *= (Permuted equal)
- *< (Permuted less than)
- *> (Permuted greater than)
- *<= (Permuted less than or equal)
- *>= (Permuted greater than or equal)
- *<> (Permuted not equal)

Unary Operators

Unary operators act on a single value. In formula language, there are two unary operators, Positive (+) and Negative (-). These operators are used to specify the sign of a number.

Following are the examples of unary operators:

`+2` represents a positive number 2

`-5` represents a negative number 5

An unsigned number represents a positive number. For example, `5` represents the positive number 5.

Reserved Words

Formula language has some special keywords, such as `FIELD`, that perform specific functions. These keywords are called *reserved words*. By convention, all reserved words are written in uppercase, though they are not case-sensitive. A reserved word is always the first word in a statement. There are five reserved words in formula language: `DEFAULT`, `ENVIRONMENT`, `FIELD`, `REM`, and `SELECT`.

DEFAULT

The `DEFAULT` keyword is used to assign a value to a field that does not exist in a document. When you use `DEFAULT` with the field that already exists, the current value of the field is used. But if the field does not exist, the value specified with the `DEFAULT` keyword is used. For example, in the following statements, if the document already contains the `sendto` field, the `@mailsend` @Function sends a message to the name specified in the field. But if the `sendto` field does not exist in the document, the message is sent to `Admin/LNN`.

```
DEFAULT sendto:="Admin/LNN";
@mailsend(sendto)
```

ENVIRONMENT

The `ENVIRONMENT` keyword is used to create entries in the user's notes.ini file. These entries can then be used as global variables and can be accessed from any document in any database. For example, the following statement creates an entry named `preference` in the notes.ini file. The value `Oriental` assigned to the entry can be accessed to display the appropriate food menu to a user when the user orders lunch online.

```
ENVIRONMENT preference:="Oriental"
```

NOTE

The entries remain in the notes.ini file even when Notes is shut down. Therefore, these entries can also be used to store static values that can be accessed across sessions.

FIELD

You are already familiar with the FIELD keyword. It is used to assign a value to a field in a document. If you assign a value to a field without using the FIELD reserved word, it creates a temporary variable with that name.

For example, the following statement assigns a value Y to the field named Mailed. If the field Mailed already exists in the document, FIELD replaces its value with Y, otherwise it adds a new field named Mailed to the current document and assigns the value Y to it.

```
FIELD Mailed:="Y"
```

REM

The REM keyword marks a comment entry. The comment following REM must be enclosed in quotation marks or curly braces. For example, the following statement is a comment entry:

```
REM "This is a Comment Entry"
```

Following is another way to write a comment:

```
REM {This is also a Comment}
```

If the comment entry contains quotation marks, you can use the escape character, backslash (\), before each quotation mark to negate the special meaning of these quotation marks. For example, the following statement illustrates the use of backslash:

```
REM " @Prompt([Ok];\"Error Message\";\"Pls. enter correct value in the field \") "
```

SELECT

The SELECT keyword is used for selecting documents in a view, a replication formula, or an agent. The SELECT keyword must be followed by an appropriate condition. For example, the following statement selects all the documents whose State field contains the value Phoenix:

```
SELECT State = "Phoenix"
```

You can combine multiple conditions by using logical operators. For example, the following statement selects all the documents whose `State` field contains either `Phoenix` or `Arizona`:

```
SELECT State="Phoenix" ¦ State="Arizona"
```

The default condition with `SELECT` is `@All`, which is an @Function that selects all the documents. Therefore, if no selection condition is specified, all the documents are selected for replication, agent execution, or display in a view.

@Functions

@Functions are built-in Notes formulas that are used to perform specific actions, such as converting a string to uppercase or sending a mail to a user. @Functions always return a value. The syntax of an @Function is:

```
@Functionname(argument1;argument2;…;argumentn)
```

Note that an @Function begins with the symbol `@`. The arguments are enclosed in parentheses. For example, the `@UpperCase()` @Function, which converts a string to uppercase, takes one argument:

```
@UpperCase(name)
```

If multiple arguments are required, separate them with semicolons. For example, the `@MailSend()` @Function, which sends mail to specific recipients, takes multiple arguments:

```
@MailSend(to;copyto;blindcopyto;subject;remarks;bodyfields;[flags])
```

However, if the @Function does not require any argument, do not use empty parentheses. For example, the following @Function, which returns the username, does not require any argument:

```
@UserName
```

NOTE

Although the @Function names are not case-sensitive, it is a convention to write them in proper case. For example, the `@UserName` @Function is written in proper case.

Some @Functions require keywords as arguments. Enclose these keywords in square brackets and, by convention, write them in uppercase, as shown:

```
@Prompt([OK];title;message)
```

In this example, `OK` is the style of the message box to be displayed to the user and therefore used as a keyword.

Domino Designer provides you with a rich collection of @Functions. These @Functions can be categorized in several groups, such as conversion @Functions, iterative @Functions, and string @Functions. The following subsections discuss the different categories of @Functions.

Data Conversion @Functions

Data conversion @Functions are used to convert a value of one datatype into another. The following are examples of data conversion @Functions.

- **`@TextToNumber`.** Converts a text string passed as a parameter to a number. For example, the following expression returns a value **`3000`** as a number that can be used for arithmetic calculations:

  ```
  @TextToNumber("3000")
  ```

  If the text string cannot be converted to a number, an error is returned. For example, the first expression returns `1200`, whereas the second returns an error.

  ```
  @TextToNumber("1200Rs.");
  @TextToNumber("Rs. 1200")
  ```

- **`@TextToTime`.** Converts a valid string into a time-date value. For example, the following expression generates the date **`08/10/2002 4:00 PM`**.

  ```
  @TextToTime("08/10/2002 4:00 PM")
  ```

  You can also use `today`, `yesterday`, and `tomorrow` as arguments to this @Function to retrieve the respective dates.

- **`@Text`.** Convert a numeric, time-date, or rich-text value to a string. For example, the following expression returns the text string **`1000`**.

  ```
  @Text(1000)
  ```

  The next example returns the `startdate` as a text string.

```
@Text(startdate)
```

`@Text` with a rich text field may be used to extract plain text from a rich text field.

Besides the data conversion @Functions, @Functions such as `@IsText`, `@IsNumber`, and `@IsTime` check the datatype of the argument that is passed to them. For example, `@IsText` returns True if the argument passed to this @Function is of the type text, otherwise it returns False.

Iterative @Functions

Iterative @Functions are used for executing statements in a loop. These @Functions allow you to execute statements repetitively based on a condition and are comparable to the iterative blocks in a programming language. There are three iterative @Functions in formula language.

- **`@DoWhile`.** Used to execute one or more (up to a maximum of 254) statements iteratively until a condition is true. The condition is checked after executing the loop once. Therefore, the loop gets executed at least once. For example, the following statements display the first five members of a list named `ItemList` and each time increments `n` by `1`.

```
n:=0;
@DoWhile(@Prompt([OK];"List Values";ItemList[n]);n:=n+1;n<=5)
```

- **`@For`.** Used to perform an iteration. This @Function contains initialization, condition checking, increment, and the statement to be executed. The condition is checked before executing the loop. For example, the following statement displays the first five members of a list named `ItemList`.

```
@For(n:=1;n<=5;n:=n+1;
@Prompt([OK];"List Values";ItemList[n])
```

- **`@While`.** Used to execute one or more statements iteratively until a condition is true. The condition is checked before executing the loop. For example, the following statements display the first five members of a list named `ItemList` and each time increments `n` by `1`.

```
n:=1;
@While(n<=5;@Prompt([OK];"List Values";ItemList[n]);n:=n+1)
```

String @Functions

String @Functions are used to work with strings or variables of text datatype. Some commonly used string @Functions are described in Table 4.3.

Table 4.3 String @Functions

@Function	Description	Example
`@UpperCase(string)`	Converts the value passed as an argument to uppercase.	`UpperCase("it")` converts `@it` to uppercase and returns `IT`.
`@LowerCase(string)`	Converts the string to lowercase.	`@LowerCase("ROGER")` returns `roger`.
`@ProperCase(string)`	Converts the string to proper case	`@ProperCase("new york")` returns `New York`.
`@NewLine`	Adds a new line between strings.	`"B-4355"+@NewLine+"Marine Drive"` returns `B-4355 Marine Drive`.
`@Length(string)`	Returns the number of characters in the string.	`@length("New York")` returns `8`.
`@Left(string;N)`	Extracts N characters from the left of a string.	`@Left("New York";3)` returns the string `New`.

Mathematical @Functions

Mathematical @Functions work on numeric data. Some commonly used @Functions are listed in Table 4.4.

Table 4.4 Mathematical @Functions

@Function	Description	Example
`@Max(n1;n2)`	Returns the maximum of two numbers.	`@Max(10;20)` returns `20`. This @Function may also be used with number lists to extract the larger values from a pair of lists.
`@Min(n1;n2)`	Returns the minimum of two numbers.	`@Min (10;20)` returns `10`. This @Function may also be used with number lists to extract the smaller values from a pair of lists.
`@Round(n1)`	Rounds off a number to the nearest whole number.	`@Round(24.57)` will return `25`. `@Round(24.57;10)` will return `20`, where `10` is the rounding factor.
`@sqrt(n1)`	Returns the square root of a number.	`@sqrt(4)` returns `2`.
`@Modulo(n1;n2)`	Returns the remainder when n1 is divided by n2.	`@Modulo(9;2)` returns `1`.

User Interaction @Functions

User interaction @Functions are used to take input from users. Some commonly used user interaction @Functions are:

- **`@Prompt([Style];Title;prompt)`**. Displays a dialog box to a user and returns a value based on user's interaction. `@Prompt` has several styles and can be used to display various types of dialog boxes to a user. The following example displays an alert with an `OK` button and a prompt.

  ```
  @Prompt([OK];"Hello";"How Are You")
  ```

  The following example displays the prompt with three buttons, `Yes`, `No`, and `Cancel`:

  ```
  @Prompt([YesNoCancel];"Save Document";"Do You want to save the document")
  ```

- **`@DialogBox(form)`**. Displays the form specified in a dialog box. The form shares fields with the currently open document. Therefore, this @Function can be used to accept values of the current document using a dialog box. For example, the following expression displays the `Date_fields` form in a dialog box titled `Enter Dates`. The `AutoVertfit` and `AutoHorzfit` options ensure that the size of the window is automatically adjusted to the size of the form.

```
@DialogBox("Date_fields";[AutoHorzfit]:[AutoVertFit];"Enter Dates")
```

User Environment @Functions

User environment @Functions are used to access user information, such as username, mail file name, access level, roles and privileges to a database, and the platform on which Notes is installed, from a user's desktop. Some commonly used user environment @Functions are described in Table 4.5.

Table 4.5 User Environment @Functions

@Function	Description	Example
`@UserName`	Returns the current username based on a user's ID.	`@UserName` returns `CN=Jessica/O=r6notes` if the user is using this ID.
`@Name([Keyword];name)`	Returns the component specified as the keyword from the name.	`@Name([CN];"Jessica/r6notes")` returns `Jessica`. `@Name([Abbreviate];@username)` returns `Jessica/r6notes`, the abbreviated format of user name.
`@PlatForm`	Returns the currently running platform version of Notes/Domino.	Returns values such as `Windows/16, Windows/32, UNIX`.
`@MailDbName`	Returns the name of the server and the mail file name of the current user.	The return value is of the format server; `mail directory\mailfilename`.

@Commands

@Commands are used to perform Notes commands. All the standard menu commands available in Notes, Domino Designer, and the Domino Administrator clients can be performed using @Commands. Some of these menu commands include opening a database, view, or document; saving a document; closing a window; creating a form, view, action, or subform; and opening the remote console for an administrator. Many other special actions, such as editing a profile document or running spell check, can also be performed using @Commands. Unlike @Functions, @Commands do not return a value.

There are two types of @Commands, *@Command* and *@PostedCommand*. @PostedCommand is always executed at the end after all @Commands have been executed.

All @Commands take a keyword enclosed in square brackets as the first argument. This keyword is the action that the @Command performs. Depending on the first argument, that is, the action, more arguments may or may not be required. For example, `@Command([FileSave])` is used to save a document, which is the same action performed when you select Save from the File menu. Notice that the keyword `FileSave` is enclosed in square brackets. This action requires no further parameters.

To open a particular view, you need to specify its name. The keyword to open a view is `OpenView`. Therefore, the @Command used to open a view named `All documents` is `@Command([OpenView];"All documents")`. Note that this action requires one more argument, which is the name of the view.

@Commands may be used in actions, button hotspots, action hotspots, and events. Some commonly used @Commands are listed in Table 4.6.

Table 4.6 Commonly Used @Commands

@Command	Description
`@Command([FileSave])`	Saves the current document that is open in edit mode.
`@Command([FileCloseWindow])`	Closes the current document or view window. If the document is in edit mode, Notes prompts the user to save the document before closing it. This command is always executed after all the @Functions.

(continues)

Table 4.6 Continued

@Command	Description
`@Command([CloseWindow])`	Closes the current document or view window. Unlike FileCloseWindow, it does not execute after all other @Functions.
`@Command([FilePrint])`	Displays the Print Document or the Print View dialog box, depending on where the command has been executed, and can be used to print a document or a view.
`@Command([EditDocument])`	Used to change the mode of the document. If the document is in read mode, it changes to edit mode, and if the document is in edit mode, it changes to read mode. You can use `@Command([EditDocument];"1")` to change the document to edit mode regardless of the current mode.
`@Command([OpenView];View)`	Opens the specified view. If you omit the second argument, the view name, the default view of the database is opened.
`@Command([OpenNavigator];Navigator)`	Opens the specified navigator.
`@Command([ToolsRunMacro];Agent)`	Runs the specified agent. This command is used to run agents from events or action buttons.
`@Command([Compose;Server:database;form)`	Creates a new blank document in the specified database with the specified form. To create a document in the current database, use null for server and database.
`@Command([ViewRefreshFields])`	Recalculates the fields in the current document if it is open in edit mode. If used in a view, it refreshes the view.

Writing Formulas in Domino Designer

So far, you learned the basic components of formulas. You write formulas in the events of various design elements, such as forms, views, action buttons, and agents of a database. The formulas are evaluated when the events are triggered. To write formulas in the events of various design elements, you use the Programmer's pane.

In this section, you will learn how to use the Programmer's pane. You will also learn to write formulas in some of the commonly used events of forms and views in a Notes database.

Using the Programmer's Pane

To display the Programmer's pane for a design element such as a form, you must open the design element in the Domino Designer. Figure 4.1 displays the Programmer's pane for a form titled emp.

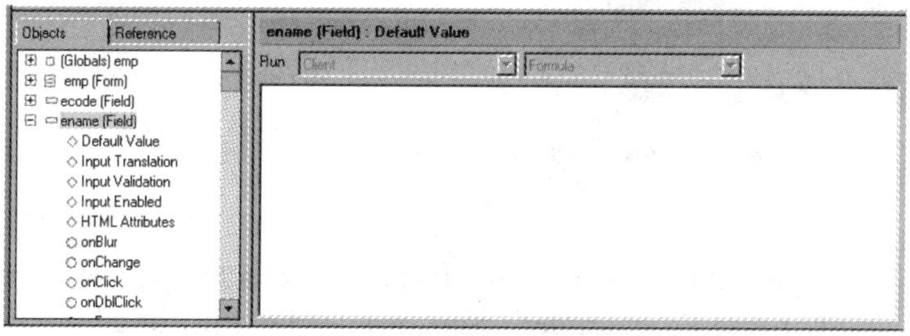

FIGURE 4.1 *Programmer's pane for the emp form*

The Programmer's pane is divided into two vertical panes, *InfoList* to the left and the *Script area* to the right. Further, InfoList has two tabs, *Objects* and *Reference.* The Objects tab opens the Object pane that lists all the objects and the associated events in the currently open design element. For example, if you are working on a form, the Objects tab displays all the objects in the form, such as fields and hotspots, and the associated events are listed under these objects. The Reference tab contains context-sensitive language reference.

When you select an event in the Objects pane, the Script area displays two lists at the top. The first list has two options, *Web* and *Client.* This list is activated only if it is allowed to write different code for the Web and the Notes client in that event. The second list displays all possible languages that you can use for coding in the selected event. If you can use only one of the possible languages, that language is selected and the list is disabled. The Reference tab displays the complete language reference for the language selected for an object.

The code that you write in the Script area is color coded; that is, it shows different code elements, such as reserved words, constants, remarks, or errors, in different colors. You can modify the color and font of the code in the Script area. To do so, right-click anywhere in the Script area and select Programmer's Pane Properties from the context menu. The Programmer's Pane dialog box appears, as shown in Figure 4.2.

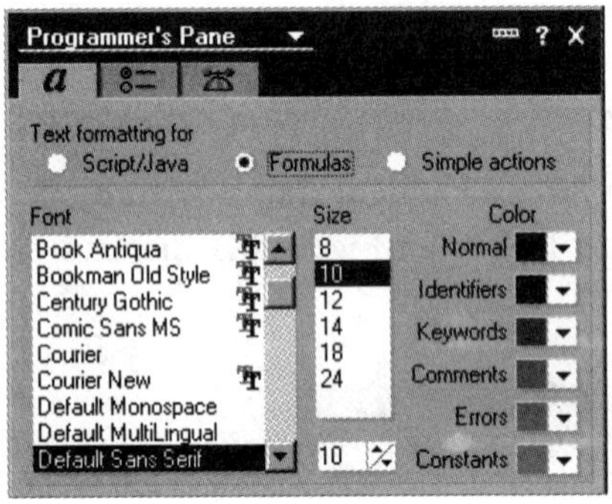

FIGURE 4.2 *The Programmer's Pane dialog box*

The Programmer's pane has the *type-ahead* feature. In this feature, whenever you type the @ symbol in the Programmer's pane, it pops up a list of all @Functions for you to choose from. When you select an @Function, it is inserted and pop-up text describing the attributes of the @Function is displayed for your help.

Writing Formulas in a Form

As already mentioned, the formula language is event-based. Therefore, all programming code is written in specific events of specific objects in a design element. In this section, you will learn to write formulas in some important events of a form.

Window Title

Window Title is a form-level event and is used for assigning a window title to the form. You can select the Window Title event from the Objects tab of a form and write the formula in the Script area. If you want to assign a static title to the window, type the title as a text constant. For example, to assign a title to the emp form in the Employees database, write the following text:

```
"New Employee Form"
```

You can also assign a dynamic title to the window by using a formula. For example, the following code assigns the title `New Employee Form` if the document is new. When you save the document, the title changes to `Employee Details for Roger Binny` if the `ename` field on the form contains the value `Roger Binny`.

```
@if(@IsNewDoc;"New Employee Form";"Employee Details for "+ename)
```

Value

The *Value* event is associated with all types of computed fields, *Computed*, *Computed for Display*, and *Computed when composed*, in a form. In this event, you can write the formula to evaluate the value of the computed field. For example, in the emp form, the `retirement date` is a computed field and is calculated as 60 years of age. To calculate this, enter the following formula in the Value event of the `retirement date` field:

```
@Adjust(birthdate;0;0;60;0;0;0)
```

The preceding formula adds `60` years to the `birthdate` field and calculates the retirement date of the employee.

Default Value

The *Default Value* event is associated with an editable field in a form and is used to assign a default value to the field. This is evaluated only at the time of creation of the document and if the user changes it, the changed value is stored in the field.

For example, to assign a default value as the current date in the field `DateOfJoining`, write the `@Today` formula in the Default Value event. Similarly, to assign the current username to the `Ename` field, enter `@UserName` in the Default Value event.

Input Translation

The data entered by the user is not always in the format that you want to store it in. The *Input Translation* event is used to convert the data entered by a user in a field in your desired format. This event is executed when a form is saved or refreshed. For example, to store the content of the `Ename` field in proper case, type the following formula in the Input Translation event of the `Ename` field:

```
@ProperCase(Ename)
```

Input Validation

The *Input Validation* event is used to validate or check the value entered by a user in a field in a form, such as a blank field, a numeric value in a given range, or a unique value in a field. This event is raised when you save or refresh a form. The input validation formula has a standard format. All input validation formulas must be written using @Functions named `@Failure` and `@Success`. The `@Failure` @Function is used to specify that the value entered is not valid, and the `@Success` @Function is used to specify a valid value.

For example, to ensure that a user does not leave the `Department` field blank, enter the following formula in the Input Validation event of the `Department` field:

```
@If(department=NULL;@Failure("Enter a value for the Department");@Success)
```

Writing Formulas in a View

Like forms, you can write formulas in many events, such as form formula, column formula, or view selection formula in a view. The two most commonly used events are described in the following subsections.

Column Formulas

Column formulas are used to define the content of a column in a view. To enter a formula for a view column, perform the following steps:

1. Open the view in which you want to write the formula in Domino Designer.
2. Click the column in which you want to enter the formula to select it. Note that the Column Value event for the selected column gets highlighted in the Objects tab.
3. Choose Formula from the Display options, and in the Script area, enter the formula. For example, to display the content of the `Ename` field in the column, write:

   ```
   Ename
   ```

   Besides a field name, the column formulas can contain fields and/or text concatenation, as follows:

   ```
   Firstname+" "+ Lastname
   ```

The column formula can also contain @Functions, as follows:

```
@left(Firstname;1)+" "+@Lastname
```

4. Click the green check mark to save the formula that you have entered.

View Selection

Another important view event where you can write formulas is *View Selection.* This event is used to define the selection criterion for the documents to be displayed in the view. All view selection formulas are written using the `SELECT` reserved word.

For example, to select all the documents created using the emp form in the Employees database, perform the following steps:

1. Open the view in which you want to write the view selection criteria in Domino Designer.
2. Select the View Selection event in the Objects tab of the view.
3. Select Formula from the Run list, and write the following formula:

```
SELECT form="emp"
```

4. Click the green check mark to save the formula that you have entered.

Consider another example. To select all the documents where the `Department` field contains the value `IT` or `System`, enter the following formula:

```
SELECT Department="IT" ¦ Department="Systems"
```

Summary

In this chapter, you learned the basics of formula language. You learned about the various elements of the formula language, such as variables, constants, keywords, operators, @Functions, and @Commands. You also learned how to work in the Programmer's pane. Finally, you learned to write formulas in some commonly used events of a form and a view.

Chapter 5

Working with LotusScript

LotusScript is an object-oriented scripting language. It is a cross-product language used in multiple Lotus products, such as Lotus Notes, Lotus 123, WordPro, and Approach. LotusScript provides you with a wide range of programming constructs, such as iteration, branching, and error handling. LotusScript allows you to perform complex functions that are not possible by using the formula language.

In this chapter, you will learn the basics of LotusScript. You will learn the various components of the language, such as operators, constants, variables, and identifiers, and also the programming constructs, such as block statements, compiler directives, comments, and iterations. You will also learn about the Domino object model and the various Notes classes.

Basics of LotusScript

LotusScript is an object-oriented, BASIC-compatible language. It has all the features of traditional programming languages, such as blocks, iterations, and condition checking.

As an object-oriented language, LotusScript uses predefined classes to access the Notes database elements. Using these classes, you can also perform complex functions, such as accessing back-end enterprise data or using OLE (*Object Linking and Embedding*) objects.

Components of LotusScript

Like any programming language, LotusScript has its own set of elements and constructs. This section discusses the components of LotusScript.

Identifiers

An *identifier* is a user-defined name given to a variable, a constant, a subroutine, a function, or a class. An identifier must start with an alphabet letter, can contain alphabet letters, numbers, and underscores, and can be up to 40 characters long. The identifiers are not case-sensitive; `Ecode` is same as `ecode`. The identifiers can be suffixed with a type suffix such as % for integer, $ for string, or & for long.

Labels

A *label* can be used to transfer the control of a program to a specific line of code using statements, such as `GoTo`, `GoSub`, `Resume`, or `On Error`. For more information about these statements, refer to the section "Branching Statements." A label is similar to an identifier. Like an identifier, a label can be up to 40 characters long and must begin with an alphabet letter. Unlike an identifier, a label is used to name a statement or a group of statements. A label must be written at the beginning of a line and must end with a colon (:). You cannot use any type suffix with a label. The following example illustrates the use of a label named `handleerror` to transfer control in a program:

```
On Error 11 GoTo handleerror
.
.
handleerror:
MsgBox " Error, Can't execute"
```

Keywords

Keywords are predefined words with a special meaning in LotusScript,such as Rem These keywords can refer to LotusScript statements, built-in functions, built-in constants, and datatypes. For example, `Len()` is a built-in function that returns the number of characters in a string. `Like` is a LotusScript operator to determine whether or not a given pattern matches a string. `MsgBox()` is a built-in function that displays a message to the user and waits for acknowledgement.

Variables and Constants

Variables and *constants* are identifiers for memory locations where data of a specific type is stored. A variable refers to a value that can be manipulated during run time, whereas a constant value is fixed and cannot be changed during run time.

A variable can be of any of the datatypes listed in Table 5.1.

Table 5.1 LotusScript Datatypes

Datatype	Value Range	Description
Integer	-32,768 to +32,767	Signed short integer with a size of 2 bytes. The type suffix is %.
Long	-2,147,483,648 to +2,147,483,647	Signed long integer with a size of 4 bytes. The type suffix is &.
Single	-3.402823E+38 to +3.408823E+38	Single precision floating point number with a size of 4 bytes.
Double	-1.7976931348623158+308 to +1.7976931348623158+308	Double precision floating point number with a size of 8 bytes. The type suffix is #.
Currency	-922,337,203,685,477.5807 to +922,337,203,685,477.5807	Fixed point integer scaled to four decimal places. The type suffix is @ and it takes 8 bytes for storage.
String	Limited by available memory	String with a size of 2 bytes per character. The type suffix is $.

Besides the datatypes described in the preceding table, LotusScript supports user-defined and variant datatypes. A *user-defined* datatype is used to group related data of different datatypes in a single variable. For example, you can create a user-defined datatype named `emp_record` to group the name, age, and joining date of an employee.

Variants are variables that are defined without a datatype. A variant can hold any of the LotusScript datatypes except user-defined types. Variants can also change their datatype, depending on the value assigned to them.

A variable can be explicitly declared by using the `Dim` statement, as follows:

```
Dim str as string
```

`str` is a variable with string datatype. For more information on declaring variables, refer to the section "Declarations." You can also declare a variable by using the type suffix, as follows:

```
Dim str$
```

You can declare a variable implicitly by directly assigning a value to it. For example, the following expression declares an integer type variable `c` by using the type suffix `%` and assigns it a value `100`:

```
C%=100
```

A constant can be a built-in LotusScript constant, such as `NOTHING`, `TRUE`, or `FALSE`, a user-defined constant, or a constant defined in one of the LSS files, such as LSCONST.LSS.

NOTE

The LSCONST.LSS file contains a set of constants that can be used in place of numeric arguments in some LotusScript statements to improve the readability of these statements. For example, to display a message to a user, you can use the `MsgBox()` function. The return value of this function is a number in the range 1 to 7 based on the button the user clicks. Instead of using the numbers, you can refer to the return values by a name, such as `IDOK`, `IDCANCEL`, or `IDABORT`, if you use the LSCONST.LSS file.

LSS files are available only after you include the file by the `Use` statement, as follows:

```
Use LSCONST.LSS
```

You can create a user-defined constant by using the `const` statement. For more information on declaring constants, refer to the section "Declarations." For example, the following statement defines a constant named `Normal` with value `37`:

```
Const Normal=37
```

Literals

A *literal* is a constant value assigned to a variable. A string literal is enclosed in a pair of double quotation marks (" "), a pair of vertical bars (||), or open and close braces ({}). For example, in the following statement, a literal `Arnold` is assigned to the variable `Name`:

```
Name="Arnold"
```

To include a quotation or a vertical bar in a literal string, you must use the character twice to delimit the string. For example, the following string contains `Julie` in double quotes. To preserve the double quotes in the string, each of the double quotes around `Julie` is preceded with an extra double quote:

```
" The girl named ""Julie"""
```

However, a number literal is not delimited by any character. For example, no delimiter is used in the following statement:

```
Ctr=100
```

Operators

LotusScript has a wide range of operators that can be used to manipulate various datatypes. The assignment operator in LotusScript is an equal sign (=). The other types of LotusScript operators are described in the following sections.

Arithmetic Operators

Arithmetic operators operate on numeric values. In addition to the arithmetic operators in the formula language, that is, addition (+), subtraction (-), multiplication (*), and floating point division (/), LotusScript has the following operators:

- **Integer Division (\).** Used to divide one number by another. The numbers are rounded to the nearest integer before the division and any fractional part of the result is dropped. For example, `3\2` returns `1`.
- **Exponentiation (^).** Used to raise a number to a power. For example, `2^3` raises `2` to the power of `3` and returns `8`.
- **Module (Mod).** Used to find the remainder when a number is divided by another. For example, `5 mod 2` returns `1`.
- **Negation (-).** This is a unary operator and is used to return the negative value of a number. For example, `-50` changes the sign of the number 50 to negative.

Comparison Operators

Comparison operators are used to compare two expressions or values. All comparison operators return a logical value, True or False. The comparison operators can be used for comparing both numeric and string datatypes, but the two expressions being compared must be of similar datatypes. The comparison operators available in LotusScript are equal (=), not equal (<>, ><), greater than (>), greater than or equal (>=, =>), less than (<), and less than or equal (<=, =<).

Logical Operators

Logical operators are used to combine multiple logical statements. The logical operators return a logical value, True or False, after evaluating all the logical statements. The logical operators in LotusScript are:

- **AND (AND).** Returns True if both the expressions being evaluated are true. Even if one of the expressions evaluates to false, the AND operator returns False.
- **OR (OR).** Returns True if any of the expressions being evaluated are true. Even if one of the expressions evaluates to true, the OR operator returns True.
- **Negation (NOT).** Used to logically negate an expression.
- **Exclusive OR (XOR).** Returns True if only one of the expressions is true. If none or both of the expressions are true, XOR returns False.
- **Equivalence (EQV).** Returns True if either both expressions are true or both the expressions are false.
- **Implication (IMP).** Performs a logical implication on two expressions.

String Operators

The string operators are used with string datatypes. The operators used with string datatypes in LotusScript are:

- **Concatenation (+ or &).** Used to concatenate two strings. For example, `"New" & "York"` returns `NewYork`. You can use the & operator to ensure concatenation even if used with numbers. For example, `10 & 3` returns `103`. If you use the + operator with strings, it performs concatenation, whereas with numbers, the + operator performs addition.
- **Contains (Like).** Used to check whether or not a string matches a pattern string. The pattern string can contain special characters, such as ? for any one character, * for any number of characters, # for a digit from 0 to 9, [characters] to specify any one of the characters specified in the brackets, and [!characters] to specify any character except the ones specified in the brackets. For example, `city Like "N*"` will return True for any city that begins with *N*.

Programming Constructs in LotusScript

A script in LotusScript consists of one or more statements. LotusScript statements can be comments, compiler directives, declarations, definitions, block or iterative block statements, or flow control statements.

Declarations

Declaration statements, or *declarations*, are used to declare variables and constants and instantiate classes. You also use these statements for forward declaration of procedures.

Variables are declared using the keyword `Dim`. For example, the following statement declares a variable `I` of the type integer:

```
Dim I as integer
```

`Dim` can also be used to create an instance of a class. For example, the following statement creates an instance of the `NotesDatabase` class:

```
Dim db as new NotesDatabase
```

`NotesDatabase` is a Domino back-end class that represents a Domino database. To read more about this class, refer to the section "Overview of Domino Classes."

> **NOTE**
>
> By default, the variables are nonstatic and private. *Nonstatic* indicates that the variables are not saved between subsequent calls to a procedure or function in which they are declared. *Private* indicates that the variables are only visible in that procedure or function. You can use `Public`, `Static`, or `Private` keywords with the `Dim` keyword to define the scope of the variable being declared.

A constant is declared using the keyword `Const`. For example, the following statement declares a constant named `temp` with value `98.6`:

```
Const temp=98.6
```

The value of `temp` cannot be modified in the script.

You can use the `Declare` statement for forward declaration of any procedure that has not been defined. The forward declaration of a procedure makes it possible to refer to the procedure in the script. For example, the following statement is a forward declaration for a function `isvalid()`:

```
Declare function isvalid(param1 as single) as single
```

Comments

Comments are nonexecutable statements used for inline documentation for your code. You can specify a comment using any of the following methods:

- **Begin a line with an apostrophe (').** For example, the following statement is a comment using an apostrophe in the beginning:

  ```
  'This is a comment
  ```

  An apostrophe can also be used for inline comments. In the following example, `declares a variable` is a comment because it is written after an apostrophe:

  ```
  Dim ctr as integer  'declares a variable
  ```

- **Begin a line with the `Rem` keyword.** In the following statement, `Rem` is used to mark the line `this is also a comment` as a comment:

  ```
  Rem this is also a comment
  ```

- **Enclose statements within `%Rem` and `%End Rem` compiler directives for multiple line comments.** When you use `%Rem` and `%End Rem` directives, the compiler ignores all text between them. The following example illustrates a multiple line comment:

  ```
  %Rem
  This is a comment
  that spans multiple lines
  %End Rem
  ```

COMPILER DIRECTIVES

A *compiler directive* is a special instruction to the compiler and is carried out at compile time. The character % specifies a compiler directive. For example, `%Rem` directs the compiler to discard the statements till `%End Rem` is encountered. Another compiler directive is `%Include`. The `%Include` directive directs the compiler to insert the text of a file such as an LSS file in place of the directive. `%Include` is written in the Options or Declarations section of an object. For example, the following statement inserts the LotusScript constants file in the script:

```
%Include "LSCONST.LSS"
```

Flow Control Statements

Flow control statements are used to control or alter the flow of execution of a script. Flow control statements include block statements, iterative statements, branching statements, and termination statements. The following subsections explain these flow control statements.

Block Statements

Block statements are used to execute a set of statements, or a block, based on certain conditions. There are two block statements in LotusScript, which are described in the following subsections.

The IF Statement

The `IF` statement is used to check for a condition and execute a set of statements if the condition is true. If the condition is false, another set of statements is executed. There are two types of `IF` statements, described below:

- **`If... Then... Else.`** Used to execute one of the two given sets of statements based on a specified condition. For example, in the following statements, the user is asked for input that is assigned to a variable named `iname`. If the user does not enter a value, a message `name has not been entered` is displayed; otherwise, the name is displayed to the user in a message box.

```
Dim iname as string  'declare a string type variable iname
'accept the value of iname from the user
iname=Inputbox("Enter Name", "Name")
If iname="" Then
    MsgBox "Name has not been entered"  'Display a message
Else
    MsgBox "Name is "&name
End If
```

- **`If... Then... ElseIf`.** Used to specify multiple conditions and execute a block when any one of the conditions is true. For example, in the following statements, the user is asked to enter a department code. Based on the entered code, an appropriate message is displayed.

```
Dim dept As Integer
dept=Inputbox("Enter Department Code","Department")
If dept=10 Then
    Msgbox "IT"
Elseif dept=20 Then
    Msgbox "SALES"
Elseif dept=30 Then
    Msgbox "HR"
Else
    Msgbox "Invalid Dept Code"
End If
```

The Select Case Statement

The `Select Case` statement is used to execute a block based on the value of an expression specified with `Select`. For example, in the following code, the user is asked to input the value of the Department code, which is assigned to a variable named `dept`. Based on the value in `dept`, one of the `Case` statements is executed and the `Select` statement ends. If none of the conditions is evaluated as true, `Case Else` is executed.

```
Dim dept As Integer
dept=Inputbox("Enter Department Code","Department")
Select Case dept
Case 10:
    Msgbox "IT"
Case 20:
    Msgbox "SALES"
Case 30:
    Msgbox "HR"
Case Else
    Msgbox "Invalid Dept Code"
End Select
```

Iterative Statements

Iterative statements are used to execute a block of statements more than once, based on a condition. LotusScript has four types of iterative statements, `Do`, `While`, `For`, and `Forall`. These iterative statements are described in the following subsections.

The Do statement

The `Do` statement is used to execute a block while a condition is true or until the condition becomes true. The conditions are specified with `While` or `Until` statements. If no condition is specified, the `Do` loop becomes an endless loop. The following are the types of `Do` loops in LotusScript:

- **`Do...Loop`.** This is an endless loop because it has no condition. This loop must be terminated with an `Exit Do` or a `Goto` statement. For example, the following `Do` loop displays the message `Hello` endlessly:

```
Do
   Msgbox "Hello"
Loop
```

- **`Do While...Loop`.** A condition can be added to a `Do` loop using `While` or `Until` statements. A `While` loop executes as long as the condition is true. For example, the following code displays the message `Hello` as long as `I` is less than `5`. The loop terminates when `I` becomes equal to `5`.

```
Dim I as integer
I=0
Do While I<5
    MsgBox "Hello"
    I=I+1
Loop
```

  A variation of this loop is `Do ... Loop While`. In the case of this loop, the body of the loop is executed before checking the condition. For example, in the following code, although the value of `I` is `6` and the condition `I<5` is not true, the loop will still be executed once.

```
Dim I as integer
I=6
Do
```

```
    MsgBox "Hello"
    I=I+1
Loop while I<5
```

- **`Do Until ... Loop`.** This loop executes as long as the condition specified is false and terminates as soon as the condition becomes true. For example, the following code displays the message `Hello` until `I` is not equal to `5`. When `I` becomes equal to `5`, the loop terminates.

  ```
  Dim I as integer
  I=0
  Until I=5
    MsgBox "Hello"
    I=I+1
  Loop
  ```

  `Do ... Loop Until` is used to execute the loop at least once without checking the condition.

The For ... Next Statement

The `For ... Next` statement is used to execute a block a specified number of times. This loop does not require a separate counter to be incremented as it is part of the loop. For example, the following loop prints `Hello` five times:

```
Dim I as Integer
For I = 1 to 5
    MsgBox "Hello"
Next
```

The While... Wend Statement

This loop executes a set of statements repeatedly while a condition is true. For example, the following loop prints `Hello` five times:

```
Dim I as Integer
While I < 5
    MsgBox "Hello"
    I=I+1
Wend
```

Branching Statements

Branching statements are used to transfer control from one place in a script to another. The commonly used branching statements are listed below:

- `GoTo Label`. Transfers control to the specified label unconditionally. For example, in the following code, if Location is not blank, then control is transferred to the statements following the label `StartPrint`.

```
If Location is <> "" then
Goto StartPrint
.
.
StartPrint:
Print name
Print location
```

- `On ... GoTo`. Transfers control to a label if a condition specified with `On` is met. When the called subroutine is completed, program execution is resumed at the statement next to the `GoTo` statement. For example, in the following statement, control is transferred to `grade_one` if grade has value `1` and `grade_two` if grade has a value `2`.

```
Dim grade as integer
Grade=Inputbox("Enter Grade","Grade")
On grade% GoTo grade_one,grade_two
```

- `GoSub`. Resumes the program execution at the statement following `GoSub` after the called subroutine is completed. For example, in the following statements, control is transferred to `mysub` from `mainsub`. After `mysub` is executed, control is returned to the line after `GoSub`.

```
Sub mainsub
.
.
GoSub  mysub
.
.
mysub:
    Messagebox "Well Done"
   return
End Sub
```

Termination Statements

Termination statements are used to terminate a subroutine, that is, a named procedure or a loop. There are two termination statements, `End` and `Exit`.

- **End.** The `End` statement is used to terminate the currently running script and also any procedures that called the script. The following code displays the use of `End` for termination of a `Do... Loop`. The loop prints the value of `I` starting from `1` and increments `I` each time. When `I` becomes equal to `5`, the loop terminates. The `Print` statement after `Loop` is not executed.

```
Dim I As Integer
I=1
Do
    Msgbox I
    I=I+1
    If I=5 Then
     End
   End If
Loop
Print "I is 5"
```

  The `End` statement is also used to mark the end of a function or subroutine of a loop, as follows:

```
Sub printname (name as string)
    print name
End Sub
```

- **Exit.** The `Exit` statement is used to terminate a procedure or a loop before it reaches its logical end. `Exit` is followed by the procedure that you want to terminate. For example, to exit a function, write `Exit Function`, and to exit a `For` loop, write `Exit For`. When you use exit a loop, execution resumes at the first statement after the end of the block. In the following example, the value is printed until `I` is less than `5`. When `I` becomes equal to `5`, the loop ends. The `Print` statement after `Loop` is executed in this case.

```
Dim I As Integer
I=1
Do
```

```
    Msgbox I
    I=I+1
    If I=5 Then
      Exit Do
    End If
Loop
Print "I is 5"
```

Procedures

Procedures are sections of a script that can be invoked by a name. A procedure makes the script more readable and allows you to organize reusable code.

Procedures in LotusScript are either functions or subroutines. Each of these is explained below:

- **Function.** A *function* is a named procedure that optionally takes parameters and returns a single value. LotusScript has a number of predefined functions for performing a variety of operations with numbers, date, and string datatypes. For example, the `Today()` function returns the system date, `Now()` returns the system date and time, `Len()` returns the number of characters in a string, and `IsEmpty()` checks whether an expression is empty.

  Besides the built-in functions, you can create your own functions using the `Function….End Function` statement. For example, the following code creates a user-defined function named `AddNumbers()`. This function takes two integers and returns their sum. The value to be returned from the function is assigned to a variable having the same name as the function.

  ```
  Function AddNumbers (n1 as integer, n2 as integer) as integer
     Addnumbers=n1+n2
  End Function
  ```

- **Subroutine.** A *subroutine*, or a *sub*, is also a named procedure like a function, but a subroutine cannot return a value. It is used to perform a series of operations without returning a value. For example, the following statements define a sub named `Printstr` that displays the value of the string passed as an argument:

  ```
  Sub Printstr (xstring as string)
      MsgBox " The value in the string is  "& xstring
  End sub
  ```

Overview of Domino Classes

LotusScript uses predefined Domino classes to access data in Notes. These Domino classes can access various elements of a database, such as database, form, view, ACL, and field. For example, the `NotesDatabase` class represents a database and contains properties and methods that allow you to manipulate a Notes database.

Domino classes are classified into two categories, front-end and back-end classes. A front-end class, also known as a UI (User Interface) class, represents an object visible to the user on the screen, such as workspace, database, or navigator. Domino Designer has eight front-end classes. For example, `NotesUIWorkspace` represents the current Notes workspace, `NotesUIDocument` represents the document a user is currently working on, and `NoteUIView` represents the current view if the user is working on a view.

A back-end class is used to manipulate an object in the back-end. For example, `NotesDatabase` class represents a Notes database that may or may not be one of those with which the user is currently working. Figure 5.1 displays the Domino front-end and back-end classes and their hierarchy.

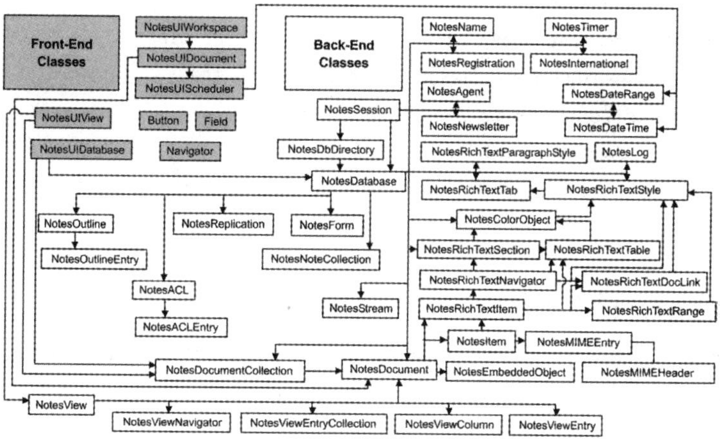

FIGURE 5.1 *The Domino objects for LotusScript*

A detailed description of all these classes is given in Appendix A "Domino LotusScript Classes" of this book.

To perform any action using LotusScript, such as opening a document, saving a document, or sending a mail message, the Notes objects, like document or field, are accessed using the Domino classes. The following subsections describe some of the commonly used classes to illustrate how to use Domino classes in LotusScript.

The NotesUIWorkspace Class

`NotesUIWorkspace` is a front-end class and represents the object with which the user is interacting, such as the current document or the desktop. This class contains three other front-end classes: `NotesUIDatabase`, `NotesUIDocument`, and `NotesUIView`. The `NotesUIDatabase` class refers to the current database that the user is working with, `NotesUIDocument` refers to the currently open document, and `NotesUIView` refers to the currently open view, if the user is working in a view.

One of the most common uses of the `NotesUIWorkspace` class is to manipulate the document that the user is currently working with. For example, the following statements are used to assign a value `Arnold` to the field `ename` in the currently open document:

```
'declare and instantiateNotesUIworkspace object using the method new
Dim ws as new NotesUIWorkspace
Dim uidoc as NotesUIDocument ' declares the NotesUIDocument class
'instantiates the NotesUIDocument class by setting it to the
'document open in the workspace.
Set uidoc=ws.CurrentDocument
' assigns a value "Arnold " to the field ename in the current document
Call uidoc.FieldSetText("ename","Arnold")
```

The NotesSession Class

`NotesSession` is a back-end class. This is a very important class because it represents the complete Notes environment at the time when the script is being executed. Some of its properties include:

- **`CommonUserName`.** Contains the common name component of a username.
- **`NotesVersion`.** Contains the version of Notes that the user is running.
- **`UserName`.** Contains the complete hierarchical name of the user.
- **`Platform`.** Contains the OS platform on which Notes is running.
- **`CurrentDatabase`.** Contains the name of the database that the user is currently working on.

The class also contains methods such as `New` to create a new instance of the class and `getdatabase()` to create a `NotesDatabase` object.

There can be only one instance of the `NotesSession` class for a user. Therefore, if you create multiple instances of this class, all of them refer to the same instance. The following example displays some properties of the `NotesSession` class:

```
'Declare and instantiate the NotesSession objectDim s as New NotesSession
'display the current user's name
Msgbox s.UserName
'display the release of Notes on which the script is running
MsgBox s.NotesVersion
```

This class is the starting point for most of the back-end scripts that access the objects that the user is working with, such as the current database.

The NotesDatabase Class

The `NotesDatabase` class is used to access Notes database objects. The properties of this class include database properties, such as:

- **`File name`.** Contains the full file name of the database including the extension.
- **`Filepath`.** Contains the path and the file name of the database. On a server, the path returned is relative to the data directory.
- **`Size`.** Contains the size of the database in bytes.
- **`Created`.** Contains the date and time of creation of the database.
- **`ACL`.** Contains the access control list for a database.

The methods include methods to create a new database, to create a database from a template, to search a database, to replicate a database, and so on. The following example shows the script to create a mail message from the current database and send it to a user:

```
'declare and instantiate the NotesSession object
Dim s As new NotesSession
'declare the NotesDatabase object
Dim db as NotesDatabase
'set db to the current database
Set db=s.CurrentDatabase
```

```
'declare a Notesdocument object
Dim doc as notesDocument
'set doc to a new document in the database db
Set doc=new NotesDocument(db)
'set the value of field form of the document doc to "Memo"
doc.form="Memo"
'set the values of subject and body fields
doc. subject=" Message from LotusScript" doc.body="This is a test message from
script" '
'sends the document to user Jessica/notesr6
doc.send(false, "Jessica/notesr6")
```

LotusScript Events

LotusScript is an event-based language. When you perform certain actions, such as opening a database, deleting a document, opening a document, or closing a database, you can write the script to perform your desired tasks. For example, to record the number of times a database is opened by anyone, you can increment a counter whenever a user opens the database. This can be implemented in the PostOpen event of the database.

The events in a database are identified at several levels, such as database level, view level, form level, and field level. Most of the event names usually start with Query or else Post. *Query events* are used to execute codes before an event takes place. For example, QuerySave is executed before saving a document. *Post events* are used to execute codes after the event has taken place. For example, PostSave is executed after the document has been saved.

Common Object Events

All the objects for which you can write scripts have two events that are common to them, Initialize and Terminate. Besides these common events, every object also has two areas, (Options) and (Declarations), used for writing specific code.

Initialize

The *Initialize* event for an object is raised when the object loads in memory. For example, when you open a database, the Initialize event for the database is raised.

When you open a document, the Initialize event for the form is raised, followed by the Initialize event for every field, because each field is loaded in sequence from top to bottom and left to right. In the Initialize event, you can write scripts that you want to execute when the specific object loads.

Terminate

The *Terminate* event for an object is raised when the object unloads. For example, when you close a database, the Terminate event for the database is raised. When you close a document, the Terminate event for every field is raised, because each field unloads in the sequence from top to bottom and left to right, followed by the Terminate event for the form. In the Terminate event, you can write scripts that you want to execute when the specific object unloads.

(Options)

The (Options) area is used to specify compiler options, such as using .LSS constant definition files or loading a LotusScript extension file.

.LSS files are used to associate values with symbolic texts. Using these files in your script, you can write scripts that are more readable. For example, you can use the error constant file LSERR.LSS in the (Options) area by specifying the following statement:

```
Use "LSERR.LSS"
```

Now instead of referring to errors by the error numbers, you can refer to them by names, such as `ErrTypeMismatch` or `ErrDivisionByZero`, defined in the LSERR.LSS file.

To use the LotusScript predefined constants file LSCONST.LSS, specify the following code in the (Options) area:

```
Use "LSCONST.LSS"
```

This file contains a definition of constants, such as return values for message boxes or different styles of message boxes.

You can also load LotusScript extensions (LSX) or the .LSX files to extend the functionality of LotusScript. For example, to access ODBC data sources using scripts, you must include the LotusScript extension file LS:DO (LotusScript:DataObject).

This adds the ODBC classes to Domino objects. To load the LS:DO LSX, write the following statement in the (Options) area:

```
USELSX "*lsxodbc"
```

The asterisk symbol is used to include the ODBC extension files for all platforms.

(Declarations)

The (Declarations) area is used to declare variables at the object level. These variables are available to all the events associated with that object. For example, if you declare a variable named `counter` in the (Declarations) area of the form, all the form-level events can access this variable. However, the variable `counter` cannot be used in the field-level events of that form.

To declare variables in an object that can be accessed globally at all levels, you must declare them in the (Declarations) area of the (Globals) section in that object. (Globals) is located in the Objects tab of the Programmer's pane for every object.

Database-Level Events

Database-level events are raised in response to the activities performed at the database level, such as opening or closing a database. All the database-level events are listed in the Database Script object in a database. To open the Database Script object for a database, perform the following steps:

1. Open the database that you want to work on in Domino Designer.
2. In the Design pane, click Other and then click Database Resources. This displays four resources: Icon, "About Database" Document, "Using Database" Document, and Database Script.
3. Double-click Database Script. This opens the Database Script in the right pane and displays all the database-level events. Table 5.6 lists the database-level events.

Table 5.6 Database-Level Events

Event	Description
Postopen	Raised after a database is opened and after the initialize event has fired.
Querydocumentdelete	Raised when you select a document in a view and press the Delete key. The event is raised before the document gets marked for deletion.
Querydocumentundelete	Raised when you select a document marked for deletion and press the Delete key to undelete the document. The event is raised before removing the trash can symbol from the document.
Postdocumentdelete	Raised when you mark a document for deletion and then press F9 key to remove the document from the view. The event is raised after the document is deleted.
Querydragdrop	Raised when you drag a document in a database to a view or a folder. The event is raised before the drag-and-drop takes place.
Postdragdrop	Raised after the drag-and-drop operation has been executed.
Querydroptoarchive	Raised before a document is dropped in an archive database.
Postdroptoarchive	Raised after dropping the document in the archive.
Queryclose	Raised just before the database is closed.

Form-Level Events

Form-level events are raised in response to activities performed in a document, such as opening or closing a document, changing the document from read mode to edit mode or vice versa, and recalculating formulas in a document. The form-level events can be accessed in the form's object pane. The form-level events are listed in Table 5.7.

Table 5.7 Form-Level Events

Event	Description
QueryOpen	Raised when you open a document, before it is opened.
Postopen	Raised after a document is opened, and before the initialize event has fired.
QueryModeChange	Raised before changing the mode of a document from read to edit or vice versa.
PostModeChange	Raised after changing the mode of document from read to edit or vice versa.
QueryRecalc	Raised before refreshing the formulas in a document.
PostRecalc	Raised after all the formulas in the document are refreshed.
QuerySave	Raised before saving a document.
PostSave	Raised a document is saved.
QuerySend	Raised just before the current document is mailed.
PostSend	Raised after the current document has been mailed.
QueryClose	Raised before closing a document.

Field-Level Events

The field-level events are raised in response to the activities performed at the field level, such as moving focus to a field or removing focus from a field. These events are used to write scripts on fields. The field-level events are listed with every field in a form. Following are the field-level events in a form:

- Entering. Raised when the cursor enters a field, either by clicking the field or pressing the Tab key.
- Exiting. Raised when the cursor leaves a field.

Summary

In this chapter, you learned the basic components of LotusScript, such as variables, constants, literals, and operators. You also learned the programming constructs, such as iteration, block statements, termination statements, and comments. You learned about Domino LotusScript classes and events in a database where you can use LotusScript. Finally you learned to use these LotusScript language elements to write code using classes such as NotesUIWorkspace, NotesSession and NotesDatabase.

Chapter 6

Working with HTML and JavaScript

Domino applications that are accessed from the Notes client can also be accessed from the Web. But this requires the HTTP task or the Domino Web server task running on the Domino server. When you access Domino applications from a Web client, the Domino Web server automatically converts Domino design elements, such as forms, pages, views, and navigators, to HTML (*Hypertext Markup Language*) and JavaScript. This feature of the Domino Web server allows you to design a single application that works both for the Notes client and the Web client.

Although Domino allows you to design a single application that can be accessed from Notes as well as the Web, the same application might appear and behave differently in the two clients. The reason is that there are certain Notes features that are not supported on the Web and there are certain features of a Web application that are not supported in Notes. Therefore, when designing applications for both clients, you need to remember what works in which client. For example, the LotusScript UI (*User Interface*) classes are not supported on the Web. JavaScript has its own set of classes that may be used to achieve similar functionality. You can use JavaScript to implement features that LotusScript or formula language do not support. Similarly, HTML may be used to add formatting features, such as maximum field length, that are not available in Notes.

In this chapter, you will learn how to use HTML in various design elements in Domino applications. You will also learn about the JavaScript Object Model and some common implementations of JavaScript in Domino.

Using HTML in Domino Design Elements

HTML is used for creating and formatting Web pages. You might want to use HTML in Domino applications for two reasons:

- To make the application more attractive and user-friendly for Web users
- To reuse existing HTML pages

In this section, you will learn to write HTML in various design elements in a database.

Adding HTML to a Form or a Page

When you develop a Notes application that may be accessed from both clients, Notes and Web, you can choose to design the forms or pages in Notes and enhance them using HTML. Alternatively, you can completely design the forms or pages in HTML. If you design a form or a page in Notes, the Domino Web server automatically converts the form or page into HTML and presents it to the browser. However, if you design a form or a page using HTML, you must mark the HTML as Pass-Thru HTML. The HTML code marked as *Pass-Thru HTML* specifies to the Domino Web server that the form or the page does not require conversion and should be passed on directly to the browser. For more information on Pass-Thru HTML, refer to the section "Pasting HTML."

The following sections explain the various methods of adding HTML to a form or a page.

Importing HTML

If you already have an HTML file that you want to use in a form or a page in Notes, you can import it. As an example, an IT consultant, Groupway Inc., has designed a database, IT Services, to record all interactions with its customers. Until now, the company was using an HTML file named survey.htm to conduct surveys to get feedback about its services. Following is the HTML code for the survey.htm file:

```
<HTML>
<BODY TEXT="000000" BGCOLOR="FFFFD0">
<FORM>
<H1 ALIGN=center><B>Customer Record</B></H1>
<HR>
<BR>
<TABLE BORDER=0 CELLSPACING=0 CELLPADDING=0>
<TR VALIGN=top><TD WIDTH="142"><B>Full Name</B></TD><TD WIDTH="334">
<INPUT NAME="FullName" VALUE=""></TD></TR>
<TR VALIGN=top><TD WIDTH="142"><B>Company </B></TD><TD WIDTH="334">
<INPUT NAME="Company" VALUE=""></TD></TR>
<TR VALIGN=top><TD WIDTH="142"><B>Address</B></TD><TD WIDTH="334">
<INPUT NAME="Address" VALUE="" onBlur="CheckField(this)"></TD></TR>
<TR VALIGN=top><TD WIDTH="142"><B>City</B></TD><TD WIDTH="334">
<INPUT NAME="City" VALUE=""></TD></TR>
```

```
<TR VALIGN=top><TD WIDTH="142"><B>State</B></TD><TD WIDTH="334">
<INPUT NAME="State" VALUE=""></TD></TR>
<TR VALIGN=top><TD WIDTH="142"><B>Zip</B></TD><TD WIDTH="334">
<INPUT NAME="Zip" VALUE=""></TD></TR>
<TR VALIGN=top><TD WIDTH="142"><B>E-Mail</B></TD><TD WIDTH="334">
<INPUT NAME="EMail" VALUE=""></TD></TR>
</TABLE>
<BR>
</FORM>
<HR>
</BODY>
</HTML>
```

The company now wants to use the same form design to get the feedback in Notes. Instead of redesigning the form, you can import the survey.htm file into the Notes form by performing the following steps:

1. Open the IT Services database in Domino Designer.
2. Click Forms in the Design pane to display the list of forms available in the database.
3. Double-click the IT Survey form to open it.
4. Choose Import from the File menu. The Import dialog box appears, as shown in Figure 6.1.

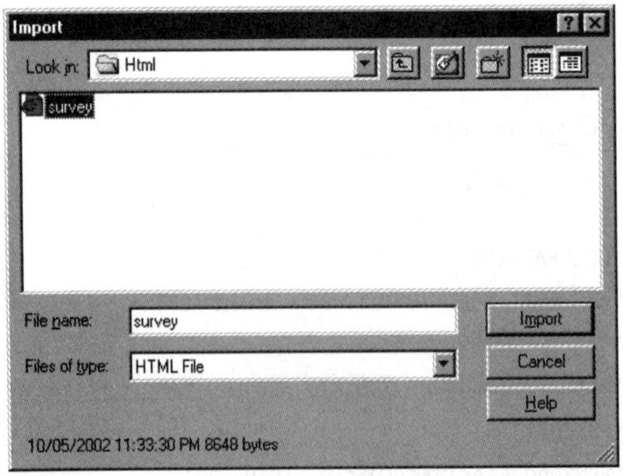

FIGURE 6.1 *The Import dialog box to import an HTML file to a form*

5. Navigate to the desired directory to select the file, survey.htm, to be imported. Select the file type as HTML from the Files of type list and click Import. This imports the file survey.htm on the form IT Survey, as shown in Figure 6.2.

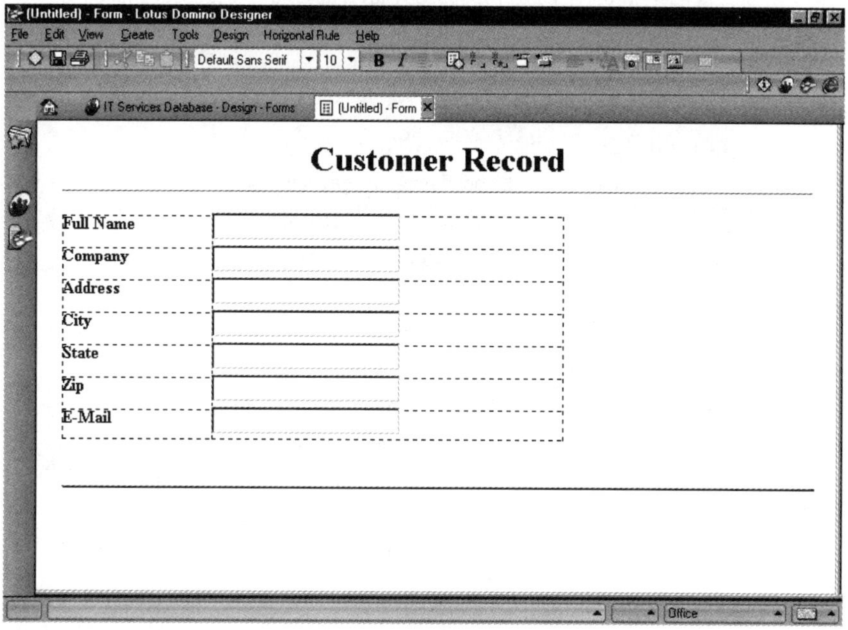

FIGURE 6.2 *The IT Survey form created by importing the survey.htm file*

Notice that Domino Designer automatically translates the HTML tags to form elements such as fields and text and creates a form readily usable both in Notes and on the Web.

Pasting HTML

At times, you may want only a part of an HTML document, such as the contact details at the end of an HTML page, instead of importing the complete file to your form. In such situations, you can copy just the necessary tags to the clipboard and then paste them in your form or page. For example, you have the HTML code in the HTML file welcome.htm for creating a contact data table as given:

```
<P align=justify><B><FONT color=#600000 face=Verdana size=3>
Contact us:</FONT></B></P>
      <TABLE border=1 borderColor=#cc3333 cellPadding=5 cellSpacing=0
      width="65%">
        <TBODY>
        <TR>
          <TD width="21%">
            <P align=center><IMG border=0 height=26
            src="c:\sp_files/telephone.gif" width=35></P></TD>
          <TD width="79%"><FONT face=Verdana size=2>480-515-5743<BR>
          480-515-0568<BR></FONT></TD></TR>
                  <TD width="21%">
            <P align=center><IMG border=0 height=43
            src="c:\sp_files/mail.gif" width=45></P></TD>
          <TD width="79%"><FONT face=Verdana size=2><A
            href="mailto:IThelpdesk@lnn.com">IT Help Desk</A> <A
            href="mailto:ITManager@lnn.com"><BR>IT Manager</A>
            </FONT></TD></TR></TBODY></TABLE>
</P>
```

To add this table at the end of the Intro page in the IT Services database, you can copy this HTML code and paste it on the Intro page. To do so:

1. Open the welcome.htm file in Notepad and copy the HTML code for the contact data table to the clipboard.
2. Open the IT Services database in Domino Designer.
3. Click Pages in the Design pane and double-click the Intro page to open it.
4. Place the cursor at end of the Intro page and choose paste from the Edit menu to paste the HTML code. The HTML code gets pasted as HTML and is not translated into form elements as in the case of import.
5. To ensure that Domino does not convert the HTML text and passes it on directly to the browser, highlight the HTML code and select Pass-Thru HTML from the Text menu.

The HTML written on a form or a page is displayed as plain text in the Notes client. To make the Notes client process the HTML, check Render pass through HTML in Notes. in the Form Info tab of the form properties.

Entering HTML Directly

You can enter HTML tags directly on a page or a form to enhance the functionality of the page or form. You can also use HTML tags to embed JavaScript code on a page or a form. The HTML entered must be marked as Pass-Thru HTML. If the form or page will be used in the Notes client as well, you must either hide the HTML from Notes users or render it in Notes for them so that they do not see the HTML tags as plain text.

The following steps show you how to enter the HTML code to create a Submit button at the end of the IT Survey form in the IT Services database:

1. Open the IT Services database in Domino Designer.
2. Click Forms in the Design pane and double-click the IT Survey form to open it.
3. Place the cursor at the location where you want to enter the HTML tags, in this case, at the end of the form.
4. Type the following code to create a button named Save Document that sits between two horizontal rules and submits the document:

```
<hr>
<INPUT TYPE="BUTTON" VALUE="Save Document" onClick="submit()">
<hr>
```

5. Highlight the HTML code and select Pass-Thru HTML from the Text menu.
6. Select Form Properties from the Design Menu to open the Form dialog box. In the Form Info tab, check Render pass through HTML in Notes.
7. Save the form and preview in either Notes or a browser to see the Save Document button at the bottom of the form.

Adding HTML in the HTML Head Content Event

The *HTML Head Content* event in a page or a form is used to pass information to the `<HEAD>` tag of the HTML document that is created when the form or page is viewed in a browser. The `<HEAD>` tag of an HTML document contains other tags like the <META> tag. The <META> tag is used to specify a description for your Web page when it is searched by a search engine such as Yahoo or Lycos. You can also use this tag to add keywords by which a user can search to retrieve your Web page.

For example, whenever Web users search for any of the words *software*, *hardware*, or *training*, you can display a link to the home page of the IT Services database. To do so, add the <META> tag "keywords" to the HTML Head Content event of the home page in the IT Services database as follows:

1. Open the IT Services database in Domino Designer.
2. Click Pages in the Design pane, and double-click HomePage to open it.
3. Select the HTML Head Content event in the Object pane.
4. In the Script area, enter the following code:

```
"<meta name=\"keywords\" content=\"Software Hardware Training\">"
```

This adds the <META> tag "keywords" to the <HEAD> tag in the document.

Adding HTML to Views and Folders

You can add HTML to a view or a folder column to apply formatting attributes for the Web access. To do so, open the View dialog box and check Treat view contents as HTML. This property overrides the default row and column settings for a view and uses the HTML formatting attributes stored in the view column.

CAUTION

When you check the view property Treat view contents as HTML, the view loses all its formatting when viewed in a browser. Therefore, you need to apply all formatting tags and links manually.

The IT Services database contains a view named By Performance. You want to add a column in this view to display the image good.gif if all the fields (s1qa, s1qb, s1qc) in the Survey form have a value "Agree" and the image poor.gif if all the values are "Disagree". To achieve this, perform the following steps:

1. Open the IT Services database in Domino Designer.
2. Click Views in the Design pane and double-click the By Performance view to open it. This opens the view properties in the View dialog box.
3. Click the Advanced tab and check the property Treat view contents as HTML.
4. Add a new column to the view and write the following HTML code in the Programmer's pane for the selected column:

```
@If(s1qa="Agree"&s1qb="Agree"&s1qc="Agree";
" [<img src=icons/good.gif border=0>]";
s1qa="Disagree"&s1qb="Disagree"&s1qc="Disagree";
"[<img src=icons/poor.gif border=0>]";null)
```

5. Save the view and preview it in a browser to see the images in the view.

Formatting Fields with HTML

You can format form fields for display on the Web using the HTML formatting tags. For example, you can set the field width and the maximum number of characters allowed in a field. You can also set the number of rows and columns for a rich text field.

You can add HTML to a field at the following two places in a form:

- Use the *HTML Attributes* event of the field. This HTML code must be enclosed in double quotes.
- Use the Field Extra HTML tab of the Field properties dialog box.

The Ccode field in the IT Survey form is used to store the customer codes and can only be four characters long. To specify the field width and maximum number of characters allowed in the field Ccode to 4 and format the rich text field suggestions, you can use the HTML Attributes event. Perform the following steps:

1. Open the IT Services database in Domino Designer.
2. Click Forms in the Design pane, and double-click the IT Survey form to open it.
3. Select the Ccode field on the form and then select the HTML Attributes event in the Object pane.

4. To set the number of characters allowed in the field to 4 and the maximum length of the field to 6, write the following code in the Script area:

```
"SIZE=4 MAXLENGTH=6"
```

5. Click the rich text field Suggestions and select the HTML Attributes event.
6. To set the number of rows to be displayed in the browser to 10 and the number of columns to 50 for the field, enter the following code:

```
"ROWS=10 COLS=50"
```

7. Save and preview the form in a browser to view the formatted fields.

Alternatively, you can write the HTML code in the Field Extra HTML tab of the field properties. For example, to set the size and maximum length of the Ccode field using the Field Extra HTML tab, perform the following steps:

1. Double-click the Ccode field to open the Field dialog box.
2. Activate the Field Extra HTML tab. This displays the option to use HTML on the field.
3. In the Other HTML tag field, enter the following code without quotes:

```
SIZE=4 MAXLENGTH=6
```

4. Save the form.

Using JavaScript in Domino Applications

JavaScript is an object-oriented scripting language used to add client-side processing to Web applications. Unlike formula language or LotusScript, which are executed by the Domino server, JavaScript is interpreted and executed by the browser. Therefore, JavaScript is used to perform actions such as field validation and field calculation that can be done by the browser, without submitting the form or performing a trip to the server.

In this section, you will learn about the basics of JavaScript and some implementations of JavaScript in Domino.

Basics of JavaScript

As an object-oriented scripting language, JavaScript has a predefined set of objects, such as window, document, or frame. You use these objects to access various parts of a Web page and perform actions such as changing the colors of a page, validating a field, or performing a calculation. JavaScript is case-sensitive. Therefore, all the object names, properties, and methods should be written in the same case as defined.

Like formula language and LotusScript, JavaScript is event-based. The elements such as a form or a page (which allow you to write JavaScript) have specific JavaScript events associated with them. For example, JS Header event is used to define all global variables and functions in a form or a page.

The following sections discuss the JavaScript Object Model, the different JavaScript events, and some common implementations of JavaScript in Domino. You can refer to Appendix C, "Working with JavaScript," for the complete coverage of JavaScript syntax.

Accessing Domino Design Elements Using JavaScript Objects

JavaScript has a well-defined object hierarchy. Objects in JavaScript are predefined; you cannot create custom classes. Most of the JavaScript objects are supported in Domino, and they map to the Domino design elements. Figure 6.3 displays the JavaScript Object Model.

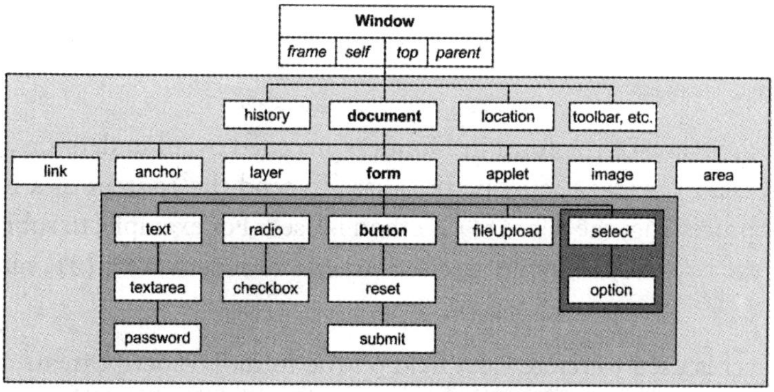

FIGURE 6.3 *The JavaScript Object Model*

You can access the object hierarchy in Domino Designer on the Designer Welcome page by selecting JavaScript Object Model from the Show me list. A detailed description of all these objects is given in Appendix C of this book.

The `window` object at the top of the hierarchy represents the currently opened object such as form, page, or view, and it contains all other Web page objects, such as the fields or the buttons. All the objects on a Web page are accessed through the `window` object.

As you are aware, every object has a set of properties and methods. You can access the properties of the `window` object by using the dot (.) operator as `window.property`. For example, `window.status` is used to display a message on the status bar. You can also invoke the methods in the `window` object. For example, `window.alert ("Welcome to Lotus Notes")` displays an alert to the user with the message passed as an argument.

The `document` object contained within the `window` object represents the content of the currently opened object. To access the properties of the `document` object, use the dot operator as `window.document.property`. For example, `window.document.fgColor` is used to set the foreground color of the document. `window.document.close()` is a method used to close the currently opened document.

The `form` object is contained in the `document` object. Because a Web document may be composed of multiple forms, the `form` object is always represented as an array. The first form is represented as `forms[0]`. You can access a form object in one of the following ways:

```
window.document.forms[0]
```

or

```
window.document._formname
```

`_formname` is the name of the form in Domino preceded by an underscore. If you have used an alias, `formname` must be the alias. To send the content of a form to the server for processing, the `submit()` method is used. For example, to submit the first form in the current document, use the `window.document.form[0].submit()` statement.

The `text` object is used to reference a field on the form. JavaScript treats all data as text and when this data is submitted to the server, Domino does the appropriate data conversion. Also, there are other types of input objects such as `checkbox`, radio, password, and textarea. For example, to reference a field fname in the form, write:

```
window.document.forms[0].fname
```

You can access the value of the field by using the value property of the text object as follows:

```
window.document.forms[0].fname.value
```

JavaScript Events in Domino Designer

As already mentioned, JavaScript is an event-driven language. You can trap the events to respond to user interactions such as submitting a form, clicking a button, or moving the mouse. Table 6.1 lists the JavaScript events.

Table 6.1 List of JavaScript Events in Domino Designer

Event	Associated Objects	Description
JS Header	Form, subform, or page	Used for code functions and to declare global variables
onBlur	Field, action, or hotspot	Raised when the focus moves out of the object
onChange	Field	Raised when the value in the field changes and the focus moves out of the field
onClick	Form, page, field, action, or hotspot	Raised when user clicks an object
onDblClick	Form, page, field, action, or hotspot	Raised when a user double-clicks an object
onFocus	Field, action, or hotspot	Raised when focus moves to an object or when the object is selected
onHelp	Form, subform, page, action, or hotspot	Raised when a user presses the F1 key or chooses help
onKeyDown	Form, page, field, action, or hotspot	Raised when a user presses a key over an object

(continues)

Table 6.1 Continued

Event	Associated Objects	Description
onKeyPress	Form, page, field, action, or hotspot	Raised when a user presses and releases a key over an object
onKeyUp	Form, page, field, action, or hotspot	Raised when a user releases a key over an object
onLoad	Form or page	Raised when a window completes loading
onMouseDown	Form, page, field, action, or hotspot	Raised when a user presses a mouse button over an object
onMouseMove	Form, page, field, action, or hotspot	Raised when a user moves a mouse over an object
onMouseOut	Form, page, field, action, or hotspot	Raised when the mouse moves out of an object
onMouseOver	Form, page, field, action, or hotspot	Raised when the mouse is moved into an object
onMouseUp	Form, page, field, action, or hotspot	Raised when a user releases a mouse button over an object
onReset	Form	Raised when a form is reset
onSelect	Field	Raised when a user selects text in a text object
onSubmit	Form	Raised before a form is submitted or saved
onUnLoad	Form, subform, or page	Raised before the user exits a document

Common Implementations of JavaScript in Domino

JavaScript is commonly used for client-side validations in Domino applications for Web clients. In the following sections, some common JavaScript implementations are discussed.

Displaying Field Help

For Domino applications that are accessed from Notes, you can provide instructions about the data to be entered in a field in the status bar. To do so, you enter the help description in the Advanced tab of the Field properties. To achieve the same for the applications that are accessed from the Web, you can use JavaScript. You can display and hide the message based on an event, such as the movement of the mouse over the field.

To display help when a user enters the mouse pointer in the field fname in the IT Survey form of the IT Services database, perform the following steps:

1. Open the IT Services database in Domino Designer.
2. Click Forms in the Design pane and double-click the IT Survey form in the Work pane to open it.
3. Click the fname field to select it.
4. Click the Objects tab to open the Object pane and select the onMouseOver event. Notice that Web and JavaScript are selected by default in the Script area.
5. Enter the following code to display field help on the status bar:

```
window.status="Please enter your name as registered in Notes"
```

6. To hide the display when mouse moves out of the field, select the onMouseOut event and write the following code:

```
window.status:=""
```

7. Preview the form in a browser to see the result.

Validating Fields

The formula written in the Input Validation event of a field is executed when a form is submitted from a browser, even if the form property Automatically refresh fields is set. This type of field validation has some disadvantages. For example, if a user has entered an incorrect value in a field, he comes to know about it only after submitting the form and not at the time of moving out of the field. The error message is displayed on a separate page, and therefore, the user has to use the back button of the browser to see the data. Also, if a user has entered incorrect values in multiple fields, he gets only the first message and not all messages for the incorrect values. Such problems can be avoided if the fields are validated at the same time that the values are entered. You can use JavaScript to achieve this.

The validation code for a field can be written in the events, onChange and onBlur. The onChange event is raised when the user changes the field value in the edit mode. The onBlur event is raised when the user exits the field in the edit mode.

CAUTION

The OnChange event fires only if you make any changes to the field. Therefore, if you want to validate an empty field, this event will not fire.

To validate that a user has not left the lname field of the IT Survey form blank, perform the following steps:

1. Open the IT Services database in Domino Designer.
2. Click Forms in the Design pane and double-click the IT Survey form in the Work pane to open it.
3. Click the lname field to select it.
4. Click the Objects tab to open the Object pane and select the OnBlur event. Notice that Web and JavaScript are selected by default in the Script area.
5. Enter the following code to validate the field:

```
var frm; // declare a variable frm
frm=window.document.forms[0]; // assign the current form to frm
if(frm.lname.value=="") // check if the lname field is blank
{
  alert("You must enter your last name");
  // display an error message.
  frm.lname.focus(); // return the focus to the lname field.
}
```

Computing Field Values

When you view a Notes form in a browser, all field value computations—such as concatenating two fields or performing arithmetic calculations using formulas or LotusScript—are executed on the Domino server after the form is submitted to the server. When the user submits the form, a new page with a Form processed message is displayed. Although the calculations take place in the document, the user can see them only when she opens the document. To view the result of calculations on the form itself, you can use JavaScript.

To compute field values, you can use two events, onChange and onFocus. The onChange event, as described earlier, is raised when the user makes any change to a field and OnFocus event is raised when the control moves to a field.

The formula for calculation for a field can be written in the OnChange event of the field on which the calculation is based so that the new value is calculated whenever the field changes. It can also be written on the OnFocus event of the field to be calculated. In this case, the calculation takes place when the control goes to the target field.

The e-mail field in the IT Survey form is to be calculated. The value of this field should include one character from the fname field, followed by a period (.), followed by the lname, and then the domain name @lnn.com. For example, if the fname field contains Arnold and the lname field contains `Grant`, the e-mail field must contain `A.Grant@lnn.com`. To compute the value for the email field, perform the following steps:

1. Open the IT Services database in Domino Designer.
2. Click Forms in the Design pane and double-click the IT Survey form in the Work pane to open it.
3. Click the e-mail field to select it.
4. Click the Objects tab to open the Object pane and select the OnFocus event.
5. In the Script area, enter the following code to automatically generate the field value when cursor moves to the field:

```
var frm; // declare  a variable frm
frm=window.document.forms[0]; // assign the current form to frm
frm.email.value=frm.fname.value.substr(0,1)+
"."+lname.value+"@lnn.com";
// extract 1 character from the value in fname, concatenate it with
//lname and the constant value "@lnn.com"
```

The `substr()` function is used to extract a substring from a string. The first argument is a number specifying the starting position, with 0 as the first position. The second argument is a number specifying the length of characters to be extracted.

Summary

In this chapter, you learned to use HTML and JavaScript in Domino design elements. You learned the various methods to use HTML in forms and pages. You learned to add HTML to Views and format fields using HTML. You also learned about the JavaScript Object Modeland the JavaScript events in Domino Designer. Finally, you learned some common implementations of JavaScript in a Domino database, such as displaying field help, validating fields, and computing field values.

Chapter 7

Working with Java

Java is a cross-platform, object-oriented programming language widely used for developing Web applications. It has a good collection of class libraries. It also has a strong network and TCP/IP supportthat enables you to create network-aware applications, such as the applications used for conducting e-business transactions.

Java also finds support in Domino. A Java program can access Domino objects through predefined classes. This allows you to use Java to manipulate databases and access the messaging, security, directory, data connectivity, and network services of the Domino server to automate business processes.

LotusScript is not fully supported on the Web. The only place where you can use LotusScript in a Web application is in agents, because agents are executed on the server. Therefore, when you create Domino Web applications, LotusScript provides you with restricted options. For a complete and efficient division of programming logic between the browser and the Domino server, Java comes into the picture.

For example, consider an online shopping mall application. This application presents a form to customers to place orders for any product. When a customer submits the form, an order document is added to the Order Processing database and a shipping order is placed in the Shipment database. When the order is shipped, the customer order history and the inventory record for the product is updated in Oracle in the customer and inventory tables. Simultaneously, the accounting system is notified to bill the customer's credit card. In this application, tasks such as the validation of the data in the form and dynamic modification of the content or look of the form are front-end tasks. These tasks can be accomplished using either Java applets or JavaScript. In contrast, creating shipment documents, updating customer order history and the inventory record for the product, and updating enterprise data are back-end tasks. These tasks can be handled by creating Java agents. Therefore, you can use Java to divide programming logic between the server and the browser, leading to easy and efficient maintenance of the application.

In this chapter, you'll learn about the basics of Java. You'll also learn about the various types of Java programs that can be executed on the Domino server and Java Domino classes. Finally, you'll learn how to create a Java agent.

Basics of Java

Java is a case-sensitive language. A Java program consists of *statements*. Each statement ends with a semicolon (;). Statements may be combined to form a block by enclosing them in curly braces ({}). A statement consists of one or more components, such as keywords, comments, literals, operators, variables, and programming constructs.

Keywords are reserved words that have special meaning in Java. Some keywords are `public`, `private`, `int`, `boolean`, and `char`. The keywords are used to perform actions such as declaring variables and classes, defining the scope of variables and classes, or writing programming constructs. However, keywords cannot be used to name user-defined variables, functions, and classes.

Comments are used for program documentation. Inline comments start with `//`, as shown below:

```
A=10; // shows an assignment
```

Comments that span multiple lines are enclosed between `/*` and `*/`, as shown below:

```
/* This complete line is a comment */
```

The following sections discuss the basic components of a Java program.

Datatypes, Variables, and Constants

Datatypes in Java can be categorized as primitive and derived datatypes. *Primitive datatypes* are built-in datatypes and are listed in Table 7.1.

Table 7.1 Primitive Datatypes

Datatype	Size	Description	Range
byte	8 bit	Byte-length integer	-128 to 127 if signed, 0 to 255 if unsigned
short	16 bit	Short integer	-32768 to +32767 (-215 to 215-1)
int	32 bit	Integer	-231 to 231-1
long	64 bit	Long integer	-263 to 263-1
float	32 bit	Single-precision floating point	+/- about 10^{39}
double	64 bit	Double-precision floating point	+/- about 10^{317}
char	16 bit	A single character	Any alphanumeric character
boolean	1 bit	A Boolean value	Either true or false

Derived datatypes are based on primitive datatypes. They consist of more than one primitive datatype and have methods to act on the datatypes. For example, String is a derived datatype that can store letters, digits, and other special characters. Also, the String datatype has methods for tasks such as concatenating two strings, searching for a substring, and extracting a part of a string. In addition to the existing derived datatypes, you can create your own derived datatypes. To do so, you need to create classes, which are discussed in the section "Objects and Classes."

Variables are named memory locations that hold data of a specific type. A variable name can start with a letter, an underscore (_), or a dollar sign ($). After the first character, a variable name can include any combination of letters and digits. A variable is declared using the following syntax:

```
<Data type> <Variable name>
```

For example, a variable, `age`, of the int type is declared as follows:

```
int age;
```

A variable, `firstname`, of the String type is declared as follows:

```
String firstname;
```

Variables are assigned values by using the assignment operator, =, as follows:

```
firstname = "Jessica";
```

Variables can also be assigned values at the time of declaration, as shown below:

```
int age = 20;
```

A special type of variable called a *constant* is a variable whose value never changes. You can use a constant to assign meaningful names to unchanging values. For example, 3.141592 is a constant value that represents pi, used in mathematical calculations. To declare a constant, you can use the keyword `final`. The following example shows the declaration of constants `pi` and `retirement_age`:

final float pi = 3.141592;

final retirement_age = 60;

Literals

Literals are the numeric, text, or Boolean values that are assigned to a variable. Based on the datatype in use for a variable, one of the following types of literals is assigned to the variable:

- **Number literal.** This is assigned to variables of one of the six numeric datatypes: byte, short, int, long, float, and double. For example, in the following statement, the variable `age` of the type int is assigned a value, `20`. The value `20` is a literal.

  ```
  int age=20;
  ```

  In the following example, the literal `2000.50` is assigned to a float type variable, `cost`.

  ```
  float cost=2000.50;
  ```

- **Character literal.** This is assigned to variables of the type char. A character literal is represented as a single character enclosed in single quotation marks. For example, the literal `a` is assigned to the variable `choice`, as follows:

  ```
  char choice='a';
  ```

  Character literals include some special escape characters, such as `\n` to represent a new line, `\t` to represent a tab, and `\b` to represent a backspace.

- **String literal.** This is assigned to variables of the derived datatype String. A string literal consists of a string of characters enclosed in double quotation marks. In the following example, the string literal `Steve` is assigned to the variable `uname`:

```
String uname="Steve";
```

- **Boolean literal.** This is assigned to variables of the type boolean. A Boolean literal can be either true or false. For example, to assign the value `false` to the variable `carryon`, you write the following statement:

```
boolean carryon=false;
```

Operators

Operators in Java may be classified as follows:

- **Arithmetic operators.** Addition (+), subtraction (-), multiplication (*), division (/), and modulus (%) are arithmetic operators. Modulus is similar to the Mod operator in LotusScript that finds the remainder of a division operation.
- **Assignment operator.** The assignment operator in Java is Equal (=). Java also has four shorthand assignment operators:

  +=: Used as `x+=y`. This statement is equivalent to `x=x+y`.

  -=: Used as `x-=y`. This statement is equivalent to `x=x-y`.

  *=: Used as `x*=y`. This statement is equivalent to `x=x*y`.

  /=: Used as `x/=y`. This statement is equivalent to `x=x/y`.
- **Unary operators.** Beside the unary operator (-), Java has two additional unary operators, increment (++) and decrement (—). These operators respectively increase and decrease the value of a variable by one. For example, `x++` increases the value of `x` by one and `x—` decreases the value of `x` by one.
- **Comparison operators.** Equal (= =), not equal (!=), less than (<), greater than (>), less than or equal (<=), and greater than or equal (>=) are comparison operators. Note that the comparison operator equal is represented as two = symbols.
- **Logical operators.** AND, OR, NOT, and XOR are logical operators.

The logical operator AND is represented as & or &&. If you use &, both the expressions combined by & are always evaluated. However, if you use &&, the expression to the right of && is never evaluated if the expression to the left of && is false.

The logical operator OR is represented as | or ||. The operator | evaluates both the conditions combined by | and returns true if any one of the conditions is true. However, the operator || returns true if the first expression is true, and it does not evaluate the second expression.

The logical operator NOT is represented as ! and the exclusive OR or XOR operator is represented as ^.

- **String operator.** The + operator is the string concatenation operator used to concatenate two strings. You can also use the shorthand operator += to add a string to the end of another string. For example, in the following statement, `India` is concatenated to the end of the string variable `address`:

```
address+="India";
```

Programming Constructs

Programming constructs are used to add logic to a program. Conditionals, loops, and error handling are some of the programming constructs available in any programming language. Some common programming constructs in Java are discussed in the following sections.

Conditionals

Conditionals are used to execute blocks (group of statements) based on a given condition. For condition checking, Java supports two constructs, `if…else` and `switch…case`.

The `if…else` construct is used to execute statements based on one condition. If the condition is true, statements following `if` are executed. If the condition is false, the statements following `else` are executed. The following example demonstrates the use of the `if…else` construct. The variable `grade` is assigned the value `A` if the variable `sal` has a value greater than `10000`, otherwise, the variable `grade` is assigned the value `B`.

```
float sal;
char grade;

.
.
if(sal>10000)
{
      grade="A";
}
else
{
      grade="B";
}
```

If you use the `if…else` construct, you need to use multiple `else` statements to compare a variable against a set of values. Using multiple `else` statements is too cumbersome. In such situations, the `switch…case` construct is useful. The following example demonstrates the use of the `switch…case` construct. The variable named `leaves` is assigned a value based on the value in the `grade` field.

```
char grade;
int leaves;
.
.
switch(grade)
{
case 'A':
      leaves=15;
      break;
case 'B':
      leaves=10;
      break;
case 'C':
      leaves=8;
      break;
default:
      leaves=0;
}
```

Loops

To execute a block multiple times (iterations or loops), Java has three constructs: `while`, `do…while`, and `for`.

In a `while` construct, the condition is checked first and then the block is executed. If the specified condition evaluates to false, the block is not executed even once. The following example demonstrates the use of the `while` construct:

```
while (I<10)
{
I=I+1;
}
```

In a `do…while` construct, the block is executed first and then the condition is checked. Therefore, the block is executed at least once even if the condition evaluates to false. The following example illustrates the use of the `do…while` construct:

```
do
{
I=I+1;
}while(I<10);
```

The `for` loop combines the counter initialization, condition checking, and increment in a single construct. First, the counter is initialized, and then the condition is checked. If the condition is satisfied, the block is executed and the counter is incremented. After the increment, the condition is checked again. The block is executed until the condition is satisfied. When the condition fails, the loop is terminated. The following example illustrates the syntax of the `for` construct:

```
for(I=0;I<10;1++)
{
//statements;
}
```

Exception Handling

Exceptions represent exceptional events, mostly errors, which may cause a program to fail. *Exception handling* is a built-in feature of Java that allows you to handle exceptional events and exit gracefully from a program.

You enclose the code that you suspect might raise exceptions, within a `try` block. A `catch` block follows a `try` block. If an exception occurs, it is passed to a `catch` clause as a parameter. For example, the following is the code for a function named `myfunction`. When zero divides a number, an exception, `ArithmeticException`, is raised, which is passed as an argument to the `catch` clause.

```
void  myfunction()
{
    try
    {
        100/0;
     }
   catch( ArithmeticException e)
   {
   System.out.println("Some error in calculation"+ e.getMessage());
   }
}
```

`getMessage()` is a method of the `Exception` class that returns the error message for the exception.

Objects and Classes

A *class* represents a collection of multiple objects of the same type. A class consists of attributes or properties and behaviors or methods. For example, if you are working with employee data, you can define a class called `Employee` that contains details about an employee, such as his name, age, and department. These details comprise the properties of the `Employee` class. The class can also contain methods, such as `add ()` or `delete ()`, to create the record for a new employee or delete the record of an employee, respectively.

A class is used to define a derived datatype. A class is declared using the keyword `class`, followed by the name of the class and the attributes and behaviors of the class enclosed in braces {}. The following code declares the `Employee` class that contains four fields: `ecode`, `ename`, `dept`, and `age`:

```
class Employee
{
     int ecode;
     String ename;
     String dept;
     int age;
}
```

The properties and methods of a class can be assigned a scope by using the access specifiers, `private` or `public`. If a method or a variable has been defined as `private`, it can be accessed only from within the class. A `public` variable or method is accessible to all other classes. You can use the keywords `public` and `private` to define variables and methods, as shown in the following code:

```
private int  age; //defines a private variable age
public int getAge(int ecode){
//…
//defines a public method
}
```

An *object* is an instance of a class. An object is declared using the `new` operator. For example, to create an object, `emprec`, of the `Employee` class, write the following statement:

```
Employee emprec = new Employee();
```

Methods

A *method* is a named block of executable statements like the procedures and functions in other programming languages, such as C. Methods are created within classes and are called the *members* of a class. A method has a name, a return type, and a sequence of statements enclosed in braces {}. For example, to check whether an employee is 60 years old and due for retirement, you can write the method `ToRetire ()` as shown below:

```
boolean ToRetire()
{
if age=60
return true;
else
return false;
}
```

The keyword `boolean` used prior to the function name indicates that the function returns a Boolean value. If the function does not return any value, the keyword `void` is used as follows:

```
void myfuction()
```

In addition to the specific member methods of a class, every Java program has a `main ()` method, which is always the first method to execute in a program. The complete structure of a Java program is discussed in the section "Structure of a Java Program."

Subclasses

You can reuse existing classes to create child classes, which inherit all the public methods and properties of the parent class. The parent class is called the *superclass,* and the child class is called the *subclass*. The concept of creating a subclass based on a superclass is called *inheritance*. The keyword `extends` is used to define a subclass. The following code defines a subclass named `SalariedEmp`, which is based on the `Employee` class:

```
class SalariedEmp extends Employee
{
float salary;
public float getsalary()
{
return salary;
}
}
```

In addition to the properties and methods of the `Employee` class, the `SalariedEmp` class has a property named `salary` and a method named `getsalary ()` to return details about the salary of an employee.

Interfaces

An *interface* defines a common set of attributes and behaviors that can be shared by multiple classes. A Java class can inherit from one superclass, but it can implement many interfaces.

Similar to a class, an interface is used to define a derived datatype. Unlike a class, an interface contains only the signature of a method. The body of the method is written in the class that implements the interface. An interface can also contain variables, but they must be constants.

An interface is declared using the keyword `interface`. An example of an interface named `fourwheeler` is shown below:

```
public interface fourwheeler
{
int WHEEL_COUNT=4;
int getPersonSeats();
int getLuggageSpace();
}
```

A class implements an interface by using the keyword `implements`. For example, to create a class named `car` that implements the `fourwheeler` interface, write the following code:

```
class car implements fourwheeler
{
int personseats=4;
int getPersonSeats()
{
return personseats;
}
}
```

Notice that the `getPersonSeats ()` method has been defined in the class `car` that implements the `fourwheeler` interface. The interface only contains the signature of the `getPersonSeats()` method.

Structure of a Java Program

A Java program consists of one or more classes. One of the classes contains a special method named `main ()`, which is the first method to be executed. The `main ()` method is declared as follows:

```
public static void main( String[] arguments)
    {}
```

The `public` keyword used with the `main ()` method indicates that the method can be called from any class. In contrast, a `private` method can be accessed only within the class in which the method is defined.

`static` indicates that the method belongs to the class in which it is defined and not to the individual objects of the class. `void` is used because the `main()` method does not return any value.

The following code illustrates a complete Java program. The `main ()` method creates an instance of the `Employee` class and initializes the class properties. The method `ToRetire ()` checks whether or not an employee is due to retire.

```
class Employee
{
     // attributes
     int ecode;
     String ename;
     String dept;
     int age;
     // Method to check if a person has retired
     boolean ToRetire()
    {
    if (age==60)
    return true;
    else
    return false;
    }
    // Main method
    public static void main( String[] arguments)
    {
     Employee emprec = new Employee();
     emprec.ecode=1001;
     emprec.ename= "Jessica";
     emprec.age=28;
     emprec.dept="IT";
     if (emprec.ToRetire())
     System.out.println("Due for retirement"); // Prints the output
     //to the system console
     else
     System.out.println("Not due for retirement");
    }
  }
```

Java in Domino

You can use Java for accessing Domino objects in multiple ways. You can use Java to create applications, agents, applets, and servlets.

Applications are stand-alone Java programs, which are invoked from the command line. If the Domino server is installed on the computer on which a Java application is hosted, the application can access Domino objects directly. Additionally, applications can access remote Domino objects by using IIOP (*Internet Inter-ORB Protocol*). For example, consider that you have a Domino server that hosts important databases. You have created a feedback database to collect feedback for the new magazine launched recently by your company. This magazine is accessible to users worldwide, and not all the users are using Lotus Notes. In addition, users are working on various platforms. You want to store the feedback of all users, regardless of whether or not they are using Lotus Notes. For this purpose, you can create a Java application that accesses the Domino database by using IIOP. Then you can distribute this application to all the users so that they work directly on the feedback database that you have created.

Agents

Agents are server-side programs that perform a variety of tasks, ranging from simple to advanced tasks. Some simple tasks include deleting a document from a database or sending a mail message in the background. Some advanced tasks include saving data posted from the Web to an Oracle database and creating automatic reports.

You can invoke agents from the Web as well as from a Notes client. From the Web, invoke an agent explicitly by using a URL as follows: **http://HostName/DatabaseName/AgentName?OpenAgent**. You can also invoke an agent from the Web implicitly by using server-side events.

In a Notes client, an agent is invoked explicitly either from the Action menu or from the agent list. You can also invoke an agent by creating a hotspot or an action and using the `RunAgent` or `ToolsRunMacro` @Command. For example, to invoke an agent named SaveData when a user clicks an action button, you can write the following code in an action button:

```
@Command([RunAgent];"SaveData")
```

Agents can be scheduled to trigger implicitly at specified intervals. You can have hourly, daily, weekly, or monthly agents. The agents may also be triggered implicitly by events, such as "Before new mail arrives", "After new mail has arrived", and "After documents are created or modified".

Java agents are highly secure. When invoked from a browser, the agents can be run using the identity of the user running the application. The agents allow access only to the databases and documents to which the user has access.

You'll learn to create a Java agent in the section "Creating a Java Agent."

Applets

Applets are Java programs used to enhance the user interface of a Notes or Web application by providing advanced graphical features, such as blinking or scrolling text and banners.

An applet consists of a collection of files, such as image and CLASS files. One of these files contains the main class, which is used to execute the applet. Unlike a Java application, an applet does not have a `main ()` method.

All applets are subclasses of the `Applet` class in the `java.applet` package. A *package* is a collection of related classes. For example, the `java.awt` package is used to provide classes for standard AWT (*Abstract Windowing Toolkit*) GUI (*graphical user interface*) controls and features, such as drawing and printing. You can use the `import` clause to import classes from a particular package. The code for a sample applet named `DisplayHeader`, which displays the message "Welcome to My Web Site!" on the page where it is inserted, is shown below:

```
//Import classes from the java.awt package
import java.awt.Graphics;
import java.awt.Font;
import java.awt.Color;
//define the class DisplayHeader as a subclass of java.applet.Applet
public class DisplayHeader extends java.applet.Applet
{
   Font f = new Font("Arial", Font.BOLD, 40);
   /*paint method is used to display something on the screen
and takes an instance of the class Graphics as a parameter*/
   public void paint(Graphics g)
{
```

```
        g.setFont(f);
        g.setColor(Color.blue);
        g.drawString("Welcome to My Web Site!",5,40);
    }
}
```

Applets are dynamically downloaded from the server and executed on the client computer. Since they are executed locally, they reduce the server load and enhance its performance.

A Domino server can host Java applets. Applets can be stored in a Domino database as a resource and then shared among different databases on the server. For more information on how to create and use an applet resource in a form or a page, refer to the section "Applet Resources" in Chapter 3.

In addition to accessing local Domino objects, applets can access remote Domino objects. To enable applets to access remote Domino objects, Domino has full integrated support for CORBA (*Common Object Request Broker Architecture*). However, to enable CORBA support, the DIIOP task must be loaded on the server and IIOP must be enabled. The DIIOP task enables the browser and the server to interact using the Domino Object Request Broker server program. To access Domino objects from remote clients, applets create proxy instances of the Domino objects and make calls to them as if they were stored locally. These calls to the Domino objects are passed over IIOP to the Domino Object Request Broker component of the Domino server. The Domino Object Request Broker server program then passes these calls to the real server objects and returns the response back to the applets.

Servlets

Servlets are Java programs that run on the server. Servlets are different from applets. Unlike applets, which are dynamically downloaded from the server and run on the Web page or document, servlets run on the server. Servlets are also different from Java agents. The Java agent loads following a request from a Web page, runs, and then unloads. In contrast, the servlet loads when the server starts or when it is requested and unloads when the server is shut down. Therefore, servlets help improve server-side processing and enable maintaining persistent connections to a database. For example, a servlet can be used to connect to enterprise data and retrieve it in response to a browser request. Since the servlet does not unload when the request is served, it provides quick access to the back-end data.

A servlet is created using a Java compiler and a Servlet API or any other Java development environment, such as IBM Visual Age for Java. To run a servlet on the Domino server, the Domino server should have a fully integrated Servlet Manager. Before you can use Servlet Manager to run a servlet, you must enable it in the server document. Additionally, you need to specify the directory where the servlet files are copied and the extension of the servlet files in the server document.

You can define the specific properties of servlets, such as URL mappings and initialization parameters, in a text file named servlet.properties located in the Domino directory. For example, to load a servlet as soon as Servlet Manager starts, you can specify the following statements:

```
servlets.startup=<servlet class> <servlet class> …
```

You can invoke a servlet from a browser by specifying URLs that contain either the servlet name or a name that the Domino administrator has mapped to the servlet by using the servlet.properties file. For example, to invoke the servlet dataconn in the servlet directory of the server's data directory, the URL used is **http://Servername/servlet/dataconn.**

All servlets are subclasses of the `HttpServlet` class. A servlet code sample is given below. This servlet, named ShowPageServlet, is used to display the message Form Successfully Processed as a formatted HTML page to a user. The servlet can be invoked in response to submitting a form from a browser.

```
import java.util.*;
import java.io.*;
import javax.servlet.*;
import javax.servlet.http.*;
Public class ShowPageServlet extends HttpServlet
{
 public void doGet (HttpServletRequest R, HttpServletResponse S)
        throws ServletException, IOException
    {
        S.setContentType("text/html");
        ServletOutputStream st = S.getOutputStream();
        st.println("<html>");
        st.println("<head><title>Message from Domino</title></head>");
        st.println("<body>");
```

```
            st.println("<h1>Form Successfully Processed</h1>");
            st.println("</body></html>");
        }
}
```

Java Domino Classes

Java has a set of built-in classes to access Domino objects. To access Java Domino classes, you must import the `lotus.domino` package in your program as follows:

Import lotus.domino.*

A class in this package is referenced as `lotus.domino.classname`. For example, the `Database` class can be referenced as `lotus.domino.Database`.

Java Domino classes are similar to the back-end LotusScript classes in functionality; only the syntax differs. For example, corresponding to the `NotesSession` class in LotusScript, there is the `lotus.domino.Session` class in Java, and corresponding to `NotesDatabase` in LotusScript, there is the `lotus.domino.Database` class in Java. Figure 7.1 displays Java classes for Domino.

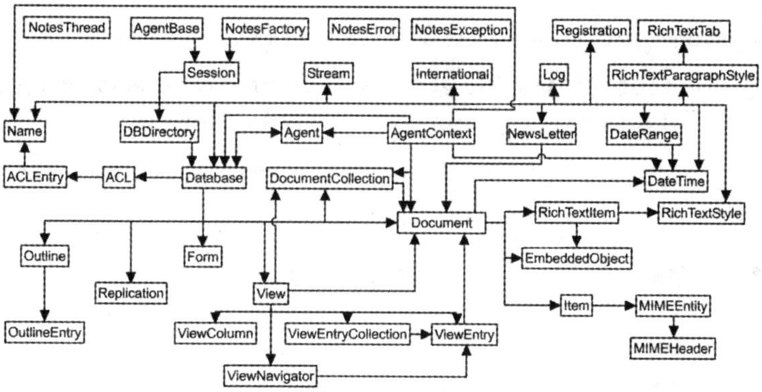

FIGURE 7.1 *Java classes for Domino*

The classes and interfaces in the `lotus.domino` package contain methods such as `getDatabase ()`. All method names follow a convention in which the first character of all words except the first word is an uppercase letter. For example, `getAllDocuments()` and `getDocumentByID()` are the method names used to select documents from a database.

The properties of the Domino objects in Java can be accessed using methods. To retrieve a property, a method name is of the form `getProperty`, and to set a property, the name is of the form `setProperty`. For example, to retrieve the title of a database, you use the `getTitle ()` method of the `Database` class. Similarly, to set the title, you use the `setTitle ()` method.

The properties that return Boolean values are prefixed with `is`. For example, the `isOpen()` method is used to check whether or not a database is open. The `isFTIndexed ()` method checks whether or not a database is full-text indexed.

Some commonly used classes are described in the following sections. For more information about Java Domino classes, refer to Appendix B, "Java Classes for Domino."

The AgentBase Class

The `AgentBase` class is used as a superclass for creating agents in Domino Designer. All agents must extend the `AgentBase` class and use the `NotesMain ()` method of this class for writing their code.

Some of the methods of the `AgentBase` class are:

- **`NotesMain ()`**. Equivalent to the `main ()` method of a Java program and begins the agent code
- **`getSession ()`**. Used to create a `Session` object
- **`getAgentOutput ()`**. Used to get a `java.io.PrintWriter` object, which is used to send print output to the browser or the Notes client

Consider the following example of an agent that displays the name of the current user:

```
// import java packages
import lotus.domino.*;
import java.io.PrintWriter;
// define the Java agent class as a subclass of AgentBase
public class JavaAgent extends AgentBase {
  public void NotesMain() {
  try {
        Session session = getSession();
        AgentContext agentcontext = session.getAgentContext();
        String p = session.getUserName(); //get the current username
        PrintWriter pw = getAgentOutput();// write the agent output
```

```
            // to the printWriter Object
            pw.println("username = " + p);// Print the username
        }catch(Exception e)
        {
            e.printStackTrace();
        }
    }
}
```

The Session Class

The `Session` class represents the current Domino environment and provides access to all other Domino objects in the environment. The `Session` class is similar to the `NotesSession` class in LotusScript and is used to access system properties, such as Notes version, platform, and the current username. It is also used to create independent objects, such as `DateTime`, `DateRange`, and `Name`.

A `Session` object is created from the `AgentBase` class, as follows:

```
Session s=AgentBase.getSession();
```

Some of the properties of the `Session` class are listed below:

- **`UserName`.** Contains the full name of the user or the server that created the session
- **`CommonUserName`.** Contains the common name of the user or server that created the session
- **`Platform`.** Contains the platform on which the session is running
- **`NotesVersion`.** Contains the release of the Domino server on which the session is running
- **`ServerName`.** Contains the full name of the server on which the session is running

To access these properties, you use the methods provided with the class. Some methods of the `Session` class are listed below:

- **`getDatabase()`.** Used to create a `Database` object
- **`getCommonUserName()`.** Used to obtain the common name of a user
- **`getPlatform()`.** Used to obtain the name of the platform on which the session is running

The Database Class

The `Database` class represents the back-end Domino database. A `Database` object can be created using the `Session`, `Dbdirectory`, or `AgentContext` classes.

Some commonly used properties of the `Database` class are:

- **`Created`.** Contains the date of creation of a database
- **`Filename`.** Contains the name of a database file
- **`ACL`.** Contains the ACL of a database

Some commonly used methods of the `Database` class are:

- **`isOpen()`.** Used to check whether or not a database is open
- **`getDatabaseTitle()`.** Used to obtain the title of a database
- **`grantAccess()`.** Used to modify the ACL of a database

The following agent displays the title of a database by using the `getTitle ()` method of the `Database` class. The `Database` object `db` is created using the `getCurrentDatabase()` method of the `AgentContext` class.

```
import lotus.domino.*;
import java.io.PrintWriter;
public class JavaAgent extends AgentBase {
                    public void NotesMain() {
                    try {
                    Session session = getSession();
                    AgentContext agentcontext = session.getAgentContext();
                    Database db = agentcontext.getCurrentDatabase();
                    String title = db.getTitle();
                    PrintWriter pw = getAgentOutput();
                    pw.println("Database Title = " + title);
                    } catch(Exception e)
                   {
                    e.printStackTrace();
                    }
                    }
}
```

The Document Class

The Document class is used to access a document in a database. A Document object can be created from Database, View, Newletter, or DocumentCollection classes.

The following statement declares an object named doc of the type Document by using the createDocument() method of the Database class.

Document doc=db.createDocument();

The following statement declares an object named doc of the type Document by using the AgentContext class. This object refers to the current document.

Document doc=agentcontext.getCurrentDocument();

Some of the properties of the Document class are:

- **IsProfile.** Used to check whether or not a document is a profile document
- **IsNewNote.** Used to check whether or not a document is new and has not been saved
- **Created.** Used to obtain the date of creation of a document

Some of the methods of the Document class are:

- **getItemValue().** Used to read field values from a document
- **replaceItemValue().** Used to write to the fields in a document
- **copyToDatabase().** Used to copy a document to a specified database

An example illustrating the use of the Document class is given in the next section.

Creating a Java Agent

To create a Java agent, you must create a subclass of the AgentBase class, as follows:

```
Public class JavaAgent extends AgentBase
```

When you extend a class from the AgentBase class, the agent initializes the Notes system and creates two objects, Session and AgentContext.

The AgentContext object represents the agent environment of the current program. It can be used to obtain information, such as the current database name using the `getCurrentDatabase()` method, the date and time of last execution of the agent using the `getLastRun()` method, or the list of documents the agent should act on using the `getUnprocessedDocuments()` method. To implement the agent functionality, you need to write the appropriate Java code in the `NotesMain()` method within the class inherited from the `AgentBase` class.

In this section, you'll create an agent in the online shopping mall application that was discussed earlier in the chapter. The online Order Processing database allows users to place orders on the Web. When a user places an order, an order document is created. You want a shipping request to be generated automatically in the database, whenever a user places an order. You can enable this by creating a Java agent and executing it from the WebQuerySave event of the Order form. This event is raised when a form is submitted on the Web. Perform the following steps to create the Java agent:

1. Open the Order Processing database in Domino Designer.
2. Click Shared Code in the Design pane and then select Agents. This displays the Agents work pane.
3. Click New Agent to create an agent. The Agent dialog box opens, as shown in Figure 7.2.

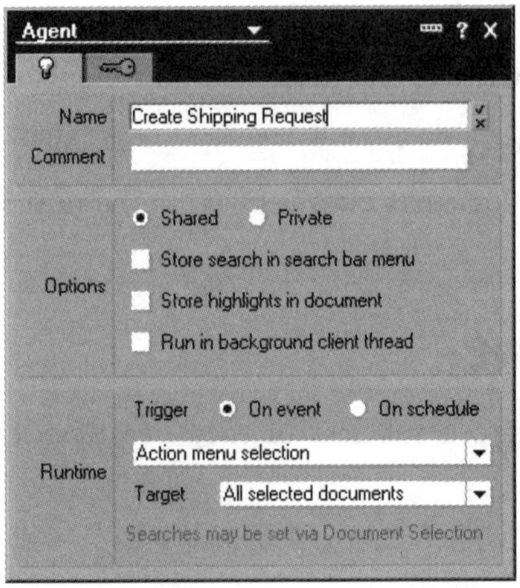

FIGURE 7.2 *The Agent dialog box to set agent properties*

4. In the Name field, enter the name of the agent as **Create Shipping Request**.

5. In the Options section, select the option Shared to create a shared agent.
6. In the Runtime section, select the Trigger option On event. Select the event as After documents are created or modified and close the Agent dialog box. This directs you to the programming pane for the agent.
7. Select Java from the Run list. Template code for the Java agent is automatically added to the Script area. The code is given below:

```
import lotus.domino.*; //import all classes from the lotus.domino package
//create a class JavaAgent as a subclass of the AgentBase class
public class JavaAgent extends AgentBase
{
public void NotesMain()
        {
        try
        {
        // declare an instance session of the class Session
        Session session = getSession();
       // declare an instance agentcontext of the class AgentContext
        AgentContext agentContext = session.getAgentContext();
       // (Your code goes here)
        }
        //handle exception
        catch(Exception e) {
                          e.printStackTrace();
                          }
      }
}
```

8. Place the cursor under the line `//(Your code goes here)` and type the agent code to create a shipping request document in the database. The complete agent code is shown below:

```
import lotus.domino.*;
public class JavaAgent extends AgentBase
{
public void NotesMain() {
    try
    {
    Session session = getSession();
```

```
        AgentContext agentContext = session.getAgentContext();
        Database db = agentContext.getCurrentDatabase();
        Document cdoc=agentContext.getDocumentContext();
        Document doc=db.createDocument();
        String ocust=cdoc.getItemValueString("cname");
        String oprod=cdoc.getItemValueString("pname");
        doc.appendItemValue("Form","shipment");
        doc.appendItemValue("customer",ocust);
        doc.appendItemValue("product",oprod);
        doc.save();
        } catch(Exception e)
        {
        e.printStackTrace();
        }
    }
    }
```

This agent uses the classes `Database` and `Document`. The current database obtained using the method `getCurrentDatabase()` of the `AgentContext` class is used to create an instance of the `Database` class. The `getDoumentContext()` method of the `AgentContext` class is used to create an instance, `cdoc`, of the `Document` class, which is pointing to the current document. Another instance, `doc`, of the `Document` class is created using the `createDocument()` method of the `Database` class. The `getItemValueString()` method of the `Document` class is used to read field values from the current document, and the `appendItemvalue()` method is used to write to the new document. The `save()` method of the `Document` class is used to save the document.

9. To enable the agent to run whenever an order document is saved, open the Order form and select the WebQuerySave event from the Object pane. This event already contains the following code:

   ```
   @Command([ToolsRunMacro]; "<Your agent goes here>")
   ```

10. Modify the command to add the agent name, as shown below:

   ```
   @Command([ToolsRunMacro]; "Create Shipping Request")
   ```

To test the agent, preview the Order form in a browser. Fill out the form and click the Save button. Open the Shipment Requests view to identify the shipment request that has been created.

Summary

In this chapter, you learned about the basics of Java. You learned the various language elements, such as datatypes, literals, variables and operators, the programming constructs such as conditionals, loops, and exception handling. You learned about objects, classes, methods, subclasses, and interfaces in Java. You also learned about the structure of a Java program. Then you learned about the various types of Java programs that can be executed on the Domino server and identified the various Java Domino classes. Finally, you learned how to create a Java agent.

Chapter 8

Securing Your Application

Domino enables you to implement security at multiple levels of an application. The different levels at which you can implement security are the server level, the database level, the design element level, and the document level. With Domino's comprehensive security model, you can create highly secured applications that may be shared by multiple users, without giving away any private information.

In this chapter, you'll learn about the Domino security architecture. You'll learn how to set up the ACLs (*Access Control Lists*) for a database. You'll also learn how to control access to views, forms, documents, sections, and fields.

Overview of Domino Security Architecture

An application in Domino is secured at multiple levels. The first level of security is *server-level security*. A user or a server trying to connect with the Domino server must be authenticated. The Domino server authenticates any user or server by checking its certificates and the public key. If a user is not authenticated, the user is not allowed access to any databases on the server. But if the user is authenticated, the Domino server checks the server access list to identify whether or not the user is allowed access to the server. If the user is denied access to the server, the user cannot access any database.

The administrator defines the following:

- The server access list in the server document stored in the Domino Directory.
- Security settings to specify who can access the server, cannot access the server, can create new databases, can create replica databases, and can create templates.
- Access to run various types of agents.
- A user as a Full Access Administrator in the server document. The Full Access Administrator gets Manager access to all the databases on the server, regardless of the ACL of the databases.

After a user is authenticated and is allowed access to the server, the user can access the server databases. *Database-level security* controls the access rights of the user to the database. Every database on the server has an ACL, which defines the access of a user to that database. The ACL also specifies roles and additional privileges used to further refine user access. You'll learn about the various access levels in the section "Setting Up an ACL."

In addition to the access rights defined in a database ACL, you can define *design-element-level security* to restrict access to individual design elements of a database such as forms, views, and agents instead of the entire database. For example, if a team is working to design an application, you can lock individual design elements. This ensures that no one else in your team can modify a design element while you're working on it.

The next security level is *document-level security*. Document-level security allows you to define access for individual documents in a database. You can use the Readers and Authors fields to control document-level access. You'll learn about these fields in the section "Controlling Access to Documents." You can also use a controlled access section to control the editing rights for a part of a document. Finally, you can encrypt a document to hide the content of certain fields from specific users.

Setting Up an ACL

The ACL of a database defines the access that a user has to the database. You can access the ACL of a selected database in Notes Client or Domino Designer by selecting File/Database/Access Control. The Access Control List dialog box has four tabs, as shown in Figure 8.1.

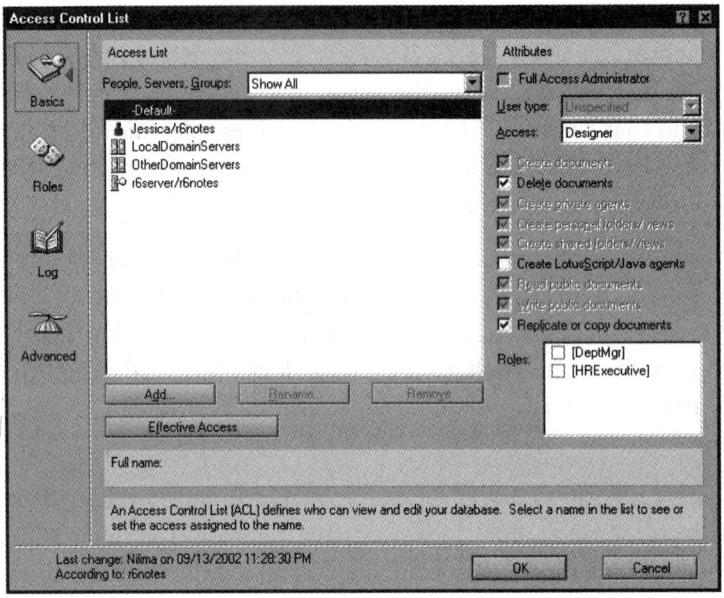

FIGURE 8.1 *The Access Control List dialog box*

Using the Basics tab, you can add, rename, or remove a user, server, or group. For each user, server, or group, you can set a user type, an access level, additional privileges, and roles. You'll learn about these terms in the subsequent sections.

Using the Roles tab, you can add, remove, or rename the roles that are displayed in the Basics tab. The Log tab shows the history of ACL change, such as the names of users who changed the ACL, the change made, and the date and time of the change.

Using the Advanced tab, you can define certain other access rights, such as the Maximum Internet name and password access for a database. You can also check the Enforce a consistent Access Control List across all replicas of the database option to maintain a standard ACL on all the replicas of the database.

NOTE

For databases stored in the local data directory of a user, setting up an ACL has no effect. Regardless of the access specified in the ACL, a user always gets the Manager access to a local database. Selecting the Enforce a consistent Access Control List across all replicas of the database option makes the ACL of a local database effective. The ACL of a database is also effective if the database has been created as a local replica of a server database.

Access Levels

Users can access a database with different access levels. For example, suppose you have a Company Policy database to store your company policy documents online. This database is accessible to all the users in your organization, but the users have different access rights. All executives can only read the documents. New policies are added by the HR group, but this group cannot edit the existing policies. A reviewer is responsible for updating any policy changes and is allowed to make changes to the existing policies. The users often need changes to the form and view designs. The group developer takes care of all design changes. The administrator assigns various types of access to different users.

There are eight access levels that you can assign to a user based on the user's requirements. These access levels are:

- **No Access.** Allows no permissions except for reading and writing public documents.

NOTE

To allow access to a specific form, like a feedback form or a registration form, to users assigned the No Access level in the database ACL, you can enable the Available to Public Access users property of the form. The documents created using these forms are called *public documents.* To read these public documents, you can create a view that has Available to Public Access users property enabled.

- **Depositor.** Allows a user to create documents, but not to read or edit the documents. This access is granted to users for applications where a user only needs to submit a document, such as a feedback form or a ballot box. The default access level for the server's outgoing mailbox database is Depositor, because in this database, mail messages only need to be delivered by the servers and then to be further routed by the router.
- **Reader.** Allows a user only to read the documents in a database. You can set Reader access as the default access for reference databases, such as a Company Policy database or a Technical Resource database.
- **Author.** Allows a user to read all documents and create new documents. With this access, a user can edit only those documents that he has created or to which he is an author—that is, included in the Authors field—but not all the documents in a database. You can set Author access as the default access for databases such as a Discussion database. A Discussion database would be used by multiple users to create new discussion topics and responses. Each user can edit the document that she has created, but can only read the documents created by other users.
- **Editor.** Allows a user to read documents, create new documents, and edit all the documents in a database, regardless of who created the documents. You can assign Editor access to users who need to make changes to documents created by others, such as the moderators of a Discussion database.
- **Designer.** Allows a user to modify the design of a database. Users with this access can also read documents, create new documents, and edit all the documents in a database, regardless of who created the documents. All the developers of a database must be given Designer access.
- **Manager.** Allows a user to modify the ACL of a database. Manager access also allows users to perform the actions that the user with Designer access can perform. This access is usually given to administrators. A user has Manager access to his mail database.

Additional Privileges

Each access level has a set of additional privileges, such as access to create private agents and create shared folders and views. These privileges further refine the access level for a user by allowing or disallowing certain actions within the purview of that access. For example, a person with Manager access has all privileges assigned to her by default. Of these, Delete Document and Replicate or Copy Documents is activated, which you may deactivate. You may clear the Delete Document option to prevent the accidental deletion of documents in an important database.

All additional privileges are listed under the Access list in the Access Control List dialog box. When setting the access level for a user, you can check or clear the privileges depending on the requirement. For example, a Reader by default is allowed to create personal folders and views. You can uncheck this privilege to remove it from a user with Reader access. However, for each access level, some of the additional privileges are automatically assigned and, therefore, cannot be checked or cleared. For example, a user with Designer access has the privilege to create personal folders and views that cannot be removed. The privileges that you can assign or revoke for each access level are as follows:

- Create documents
- Delete documents
- Create private agents
- Create personal folders and views
- Create shared folders and views
- Create LotusScript and Java agents
- Read public documents
- Write public documents
- Replicate or copy documents

User Types

You can set the ACL of a database to allow access to a user, a server, or a group. When you add any entry to the ACL, you must specify the user type, such as Person or Server. Specifying a user type is an extra security measure because it specifies the type of ID that needs to be used for a particular access type. For example, specifying a user type as Person ensures that a server or a group with the same name does not gain access to the database.

The various user types you can specify are as follows:

- **Person.** Refers to a user
- **Server.** Refers to a server

- **Person Group.** Refers to a group of users
- **Server Group.** Refers to a group of servers
- **Mixed Group.** Refers to a group of users and servers
- **Unspecified.** Used for the Default and the Anonymous entries

NOTE

When adding an entry in an ACL, you do not need to manually specify each user type. Instead, you can click Look Up User Types for Unspecified Users in the Advanced tab of the Access Control List dialog box.

Roles

Roles are used to define a group of users that may be assigned similar access. For example, the Resource Reservation (6.0) template stored on a server has a role, CreateResource. You can assign this role to all users to whom you want to grant access to create a resource in the reservation database.

Roles are an effective way to implement security in applications that need to be used by multiple users for different tasks. For example, in a Leave database, an employee fills out a Leave form and the manager approves it. The HR executive validates the leave application and updates the leave record. To allow multiple users (there can be many managers, for instance) to perform different tasks, you can use roles. Also, you can define access to certain sections of the form and hide different actions from different users.

Roles are different from groups created in the address book. Unlike groups, roles are applicable only to the database in which they are created. Role names appear in square brackets, for example, [Manager].

Creating Roles

You can create roles using the Roles tab of the Access Control List dialog box. To create a role, perform the following steps:

1. Open the database to which you want to add the roles in Notes Client or Domino Designer.

2. From the File menu, select Database and then select Access Control List. The Access Control List dialog box appears.
3. Activate the Roles tab. This displays the list of roles defined in the database.
4. Click the Add Role button to add a new role. The Add Role dialog box appears, as shown in Figure 8.2.

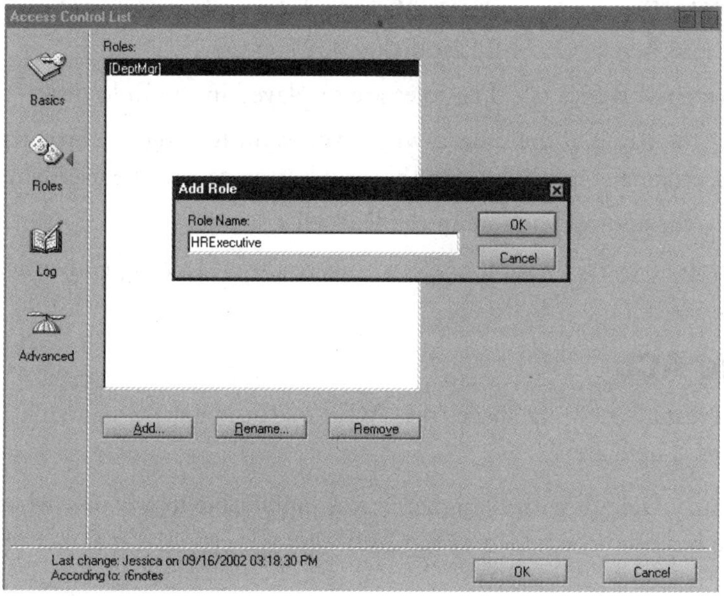

FIGURE 8.2 *The Roles tab, showing the Add Role dialog box*

5. Enter the name of the role and click OK. The role is added to the database.

Similarly, you can add more roles. The act of adding roles to the ACL and assigning them to users by itself has no significance. You must implement the roles in the design elements of the database. A role can be used to define access to a section of a form, a form access list, a view or folder access list, or the Readers and Authors fields.

You can use the Rename and Remove buttons to change and delete a role, respectively.

Assigning Roles

The Basics tab of the Access Control List dialog box displays all the available roles. You can use this tab to assign roles to different users.

Perform the following steps to assign a role to a user:

1. Open the database to which you want to add the role in Notes Client or Domino Designer.
2. From the File menu, select Database and then select Access Control List. The Access Control List dialog box appears.
3. Activate the Basics tab. The roles are displayed in the Roles list.
4. Select the name of the user to whom you want to assign a particular role. If a username is not listed, use the Add button to add the username.
5. Check the appropriate role in the Roles list.

Repeat the steps 4 and 5 for all users to whom you want to assign any role.

Changing the ACL

When you create a new database, the ACL of the database contains certain default entries. These are:

- An entry Default with Designer access (applicable to any user whose name has not been added to the ACL and who is not a member of any group added to the ACL)
- Local Domain Servers and Other Domain Servers groups with Manager access
- Name of the creator of the database with Manager access
- Server name with Manager access if a database is created on the server

When deploying an application, you may need to change these default entries as per your requirements. Perform the following steps to modify the ACL of a database:

1. Open the database whose ACL you need to modify in Notes Client or Domino Designer.
2. Choose File/Database and Access Control to open the Access Control List dialog box.

> **NOTE**
>
> You must have Manager access to a database to be able to change its ACL.

3. Activate the Basics tab and click the Add button to add a user, a server, or a group to the list. The Add User dialog box appears, as shown in Figure 8.3.

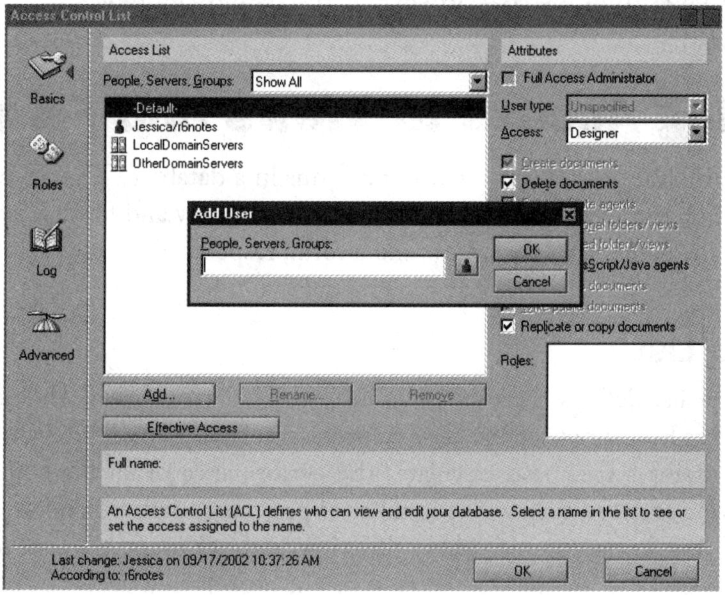

FIGURE 8.3 *The Add User dialog box*

4. In the Add User dialog box, you can either type a name or select it from Domino Directory or a local address book by clicking the button next to it.
5. Select an appropriate user type and appropriate access for the entry. To further refine the access level, you can optionally select or clear the additional privileges.
6. Assign a role for the entry if you've created roles.

NOTE

If you assign a particular access level to a user who belongs to a group that has a different access level, you can identify the effective access of the user by clicking the Effective Access button. This displays the effective access level, privileges, and effective roles of the user, taking into account all of the user's group memberships.

Repeat these steps for each entry that you add to the ACL. You can also change or delete any entry from the ACL by clicking the Remove button.

Controlling Access to Views and Forms

You can control access to specific views and forms in a database. This allows you to further refine the access given at the database level. View and form access lists help you set the access level for a view and a form, respectively.

View Access List

A view access list defines the users who can access a view. Users who are not included in this list cannot see the view. Suppose you have a Project Review database that contains a view that calculates the performance of all the employees based on various factors, such as the number of projects completed and customer feedback. If you do not want to share this view with all users, you can restrict access to the view by using the view access list. The default view access is All readers and above, which indicates that all users having Reader or higher access in the database ACL can access the view. You can modify this default setting to provide access to only selective users or roles. Users whose names are not included in the view access list cannot see the view at all.

CAUTION

Restricting a view to certain users does not ensure that access to documents has been restricted. Users can still create a private view displaying all documents to gain access to those documents. You must set up document-level security to restrict access to documents.

Perform the following steps to define a view access list:

1. Open the database that contains the view for which you want to define the view access list in Domino Designer.
2. Click Views in the Design pane. This opens the Views work pane that displays a list of views present in the database.
3. Double-click the view for which you want to restrict access. This displays the View dialog box.
4. In the View dialog box, activate the Security tab, as shown in Figure 8.4.

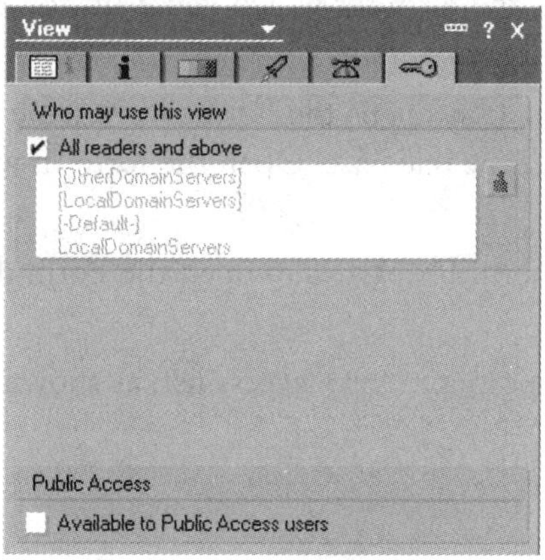

FIGURE 8.4 *The View dialog box with the Security tab active*

5. From the Who may use this view section, clear All readers and above and select specific users or roles to grant read access to them. Only these users will be able to see the view, and it will be hidden from all other users.

Form Access List

Users with Reader access can read all the documents in a database. If you want to restrict certain users from reading the documents created by using a particular form, you can define a form access list. For example, suppose a company has a Document Store database used to store all the important documents of the company. The database contains two types of documents, documents for all users and documents for a group of executives that cannot be seen by anyone else. Though the design of the two documents is the same, for the second type of documents, you can create a separate form and define the reader list for that form. When you define the reader list, a field by the name $Readers is added to all the documents and contains the names defined in the form reader list.

In addition to defining the reader list for a form, you can restrict users from creating documents using a particular form. For example, in a Technical Reference database, you do not want to allow users to create new topics. But you have a comments form that the users can use to send their comments and questions on any topic. This type of access can be defined in a form access list. Perform the following steps to define a form access list:

1. Open the database that contains the form for which you want to define a form access list in Domino Designer.
2. Click Forms in the Design pane. This opens the Forms work pane that displays a list of forms present in the database. Open the form to which you want to restrict access.
3. From the Design menu, select Form Properties to open the Form dialog box.
4. Activate the Security tab and modify the form access list, as shown in Figure 8.5.

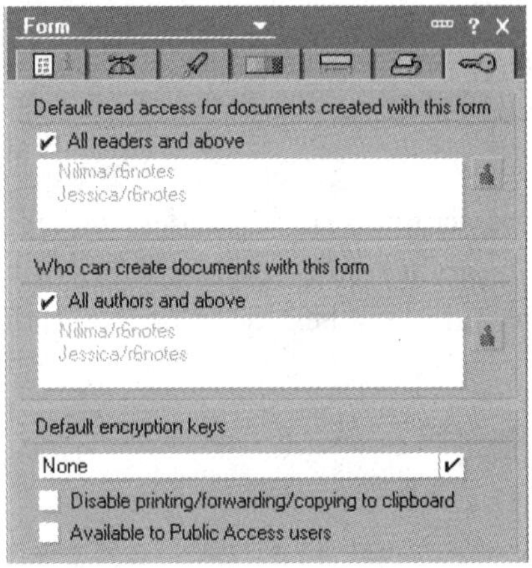

FIGURE 8.5 *The Form dialog box with the Security tab active*

5. In the Default read access for documents created with this form section, deselect All readers and above. From the list, select the names of users or roles to which you want to grant this access You can use the Add read

access button next to the list to add more users from the address book, but these users must have at least Reader access to the database.

6. In the Who can create documents with this form section, deselect All authors and above and select specific users or roles. You can also add usernames from the address book by using the Add create access button, but the users must have Author or higher access in the database ACL.

Controlling Access to Documents

You can define a form access list to restrict access to all the documents created by using a particular form. However, you may sometimes want to restrict access not to all documents of a specific type but only to selective documents. You can control access at the document level by using the Readers and Authors fields.

The Readers Field

The Readers field is used to define the readers for a document. Consider an Interoffice Memo database used to create memos to be shared among the employees in an office. Each memo is addressed to a group of people, and only these people must be able to read the memo. To implement, you use the Readers field to define the list of readers for the document. This field can be Computed or Editable. In the current scenario, you can make this field editable and allow the creator of the document to define the readers for the document. An empty Readers field allows all users who have Reader or higher access to the database to read the document.

NOTE

If a user's name is not included in the Readers field of a document, the user will not be able to read the document, even though the user may have Manager access to the database. For the same reason, servers will not be able to replicate documents with a Readers field in which their names are not included. Therefore, it is advisable to have an extra Readers field to ensure that LocalDomainServers and any other entries, such as the database administrator's name or the current user's name, are included by default to avoid any loss of documents.

Perform the following steps to add the Readers field to your form:

1. Open the database that has the form in which you want to create the Readers field in Domino Designer.
2. Click Forms in the Design pane. This opens the Forms work pane that displays the list of forms available in the database.
3. Double-click the form in which you want to add the Readers field to open it.
4. Place the cursor at the location on the form where you want to add the new field and type a label for the field.
5. Select Field from the Create menu to create a new field. This also displays the field properties in the Field dialog box.
6. Enter a name for the field and select Readers from the Type list.
7. Check the Allow multiple values option. This option allows you to enter more than one name in the field and hence specify multiple readers for the document. Refer to Figure 8.6.

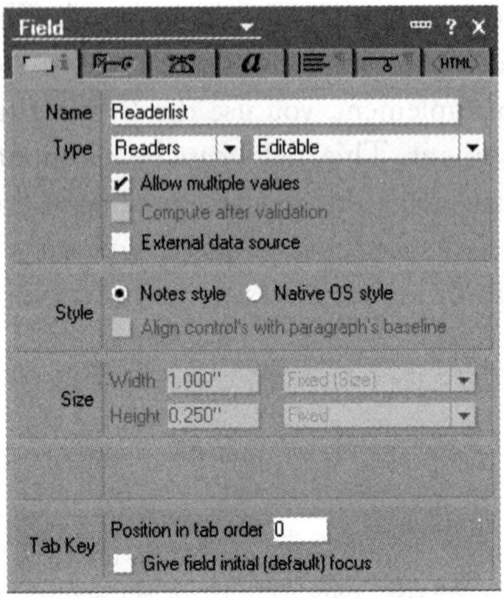

FIGURE 8.6 *The Field dialog box, displaying field properties for the Readers field*

8. Optionally, activate the Control tab and select Use Address dialog for choices from the Choice list so that the user can select names from the address book.

The Authors Field

The Authors field defines the authors of a document. Unlike the Readers field, which applies to users with all types of access, the Authors field is only applicable to users who have Author access to a database. If you have Editor or higher access, you will be able to edit a document even though your name is not included in the Authors field. If you have access less that Author, you will not be able to edit the document even if your name is included in the Authors field.

Consider a Leave database, where an employee creates a leave document by using the Leave form. The employee's manager then needs to edit the document. If you give a higher than Author access to the manager, he'll be able to edit all the documents in the database. To avoid this, give the default access as Author in the database ACL and create an Authors field in the Leave form. Assign the names of the employee and the manager to that field. The Authors field can be either Computed or Editable. In the current scenario, the field will be of the type Computed.

Perform the following steps to create the Authors field in your form:

1. Open the database that has the form in which you want to create the Authors field in Domino Designer.
2. Click Forms in the Design pane. This opens the Forms work pane that displays the list of forms available in the database.
3. Double-click the form to which you want to add the Authors field.
4. Place the cursor at the location on the form where you want to add the new field and type a label for the field.
5. Select Field from the Create menu to create a new field. This also displays the field properties in the Field dialog box.
6. Enter a name for the field and select Authors from the Type list.
7. Check Allow multiple values to allow a user to enter more than one name in the field and, hence, specify multiple authors for the document. Refer to Figure 8.7.

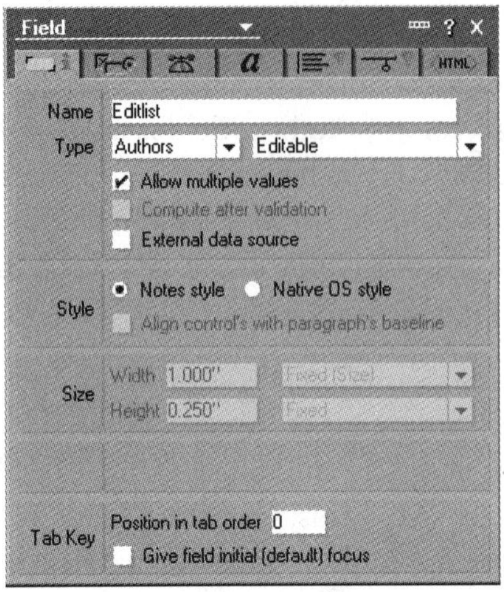

FIGURE 8.7 *The Field dialog box, displaying the field properties for the Authors field*

This creates an Authors field that allows users with Author access to edit documents that have been created by someone else.

Controlled Access Sections

Controlled access sections are used to control editing rights to a part of a document. Most applications, especially the workflow applications in Notes, require more than one person to write on the same document. For example, in a Leave database after the employee fills up her details, the manager needs to approve them and specify her comments. To ensure that only the manager can write in the Comments field and approve the document, you can place the fields in a controlled access section. When any user other than the manager tries to edit that section, a message appears indicating that only managers can edit the section.

Create a controlled access section by performing the following steps:

1. Open the database that has the form in which you want to create the controlled access section in Domino Designer.
2. Click Forms in the Design pane. This opens the Forms work pane that displays the list of forms available in the database.
3. Double-click the form to which you want to add the controlled access section.

4. Select the part of the form that you want to add to the controlled access section.
5. From the Create menu, select Section and then select Controlled Access Section. The selected part of the form is converted into a controlled access section, and the Form Section dialog box appears.
6. In the Section Title and Border tab, enter a title for the section in the Title field and select a border style and a color from the Style and Color lists, respectively.
7. On the Expand/Collapse tab, you can specify whether the section will be expanded or collapsed when an editor reads, edits, previews, or prints the document. You can specify the expand and collapse options for the section for users who do not have editing rights to the section separately.
8. On the Formula tab, specify the type of the section as Editable or Computed. Use Editable when you want the creator of the document to specify the editors of the section and use Computed when a formula defines the editors. In the formula, you can type the name of a person, a formula, or a role name. For example, to give editing rights only to the people with Manager roles, specify the section type as Computed and type "[Manager]" in the Access Formula field, as shown in Figure 8.8.

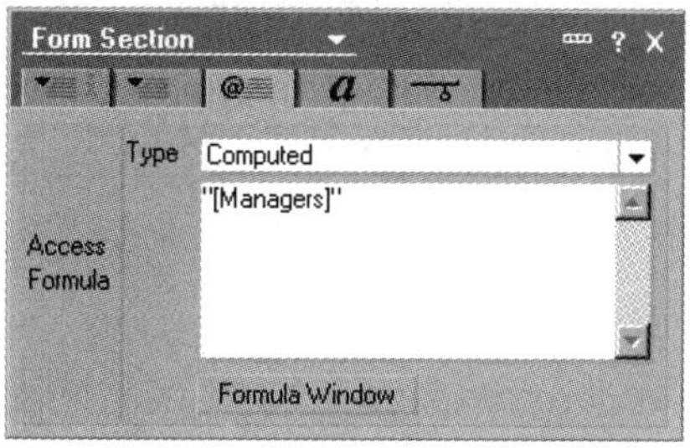

FIGURE 8.8 *The Form Section dialog box with the Formula tab active*

If your name is not included in the access formula of the section and you try to edit the document, fields other than those included in the section will become editable. If you click the section, a dialog box is displayed, as shown in Figure 8.9.

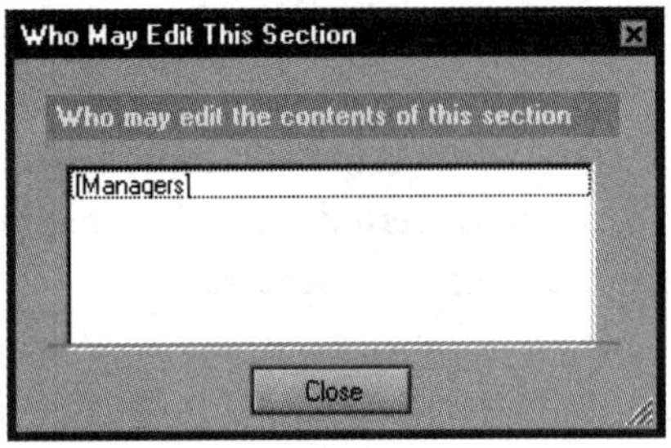

FIGURE 8.9 *A dialog box showing the editors of a controlled access section*

Document Encryption

Document encryption allows you to hide the data in one or more fields of a document from selected users. Encryption is implemented using keys. You can create encryption keys in your user ID and use them for encrypting documents. You may also use the public keys of users for whom you want to encrypt a document. If you create an encryption key and use it for encrypting a document, you must distribute this key to all the users with whom you want to share the data in the encrypted fields. If you encrypt a document using the public keys of the users, it is decrypted using the private keys stored in their user IDs. Therefore, only the users whose public keys have been used for encryption will be able to view the encrypted data.

Document encryption involves two actions: first, enabling encryption for certain fields, and second, attaching a key to the document.

Creating an Encryption Key

Perform the following steps to create an encryption key:

1. In the Notes client, select File/Security/User Security. You are prompted for your user ID password.
2. Enter the password and click OK. The User Security dialog box appears.
3. In the list displayed in the left pane of this dialog box, click Notes Data. This expands two categories, Database and Document.
4. Select Document. This displays Document Encryption details, as shown in Figure 8.10.

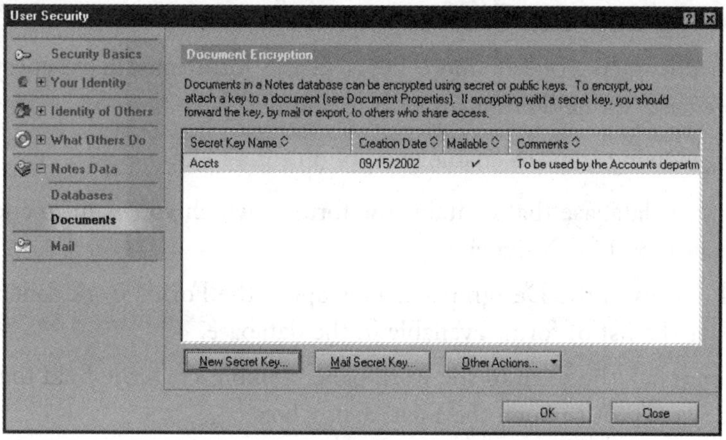

FIGURE 8.10 *The User Security dialog box, displaying Document Encryption details*

5. Click the New Secret Key button to create a new encryption key. The New Secret Encryption Key dialog box appears, as shown in Figure 8.11.

FIGURE 8.11 *The New Secret Encryption Key dialog box*

6. Enter a name for the new encryption key. For example, enter Projectleader in the Secret Key Name field.
7. Enter any comments for the key in the Comments field.
8. Click OK. An encryption key named Projectleader is created.

Enabling Encryption for Fields

To encrypt a document, one or more fields in the form must have encryption enabled. An encrypted field is shown with red borders.

Perform the following steps to enable encryption for a field:

1. Open the database that contains the form in which you want to encrypt fields in Domino Designer.
2. Click Forms in the Design pane. This opens the Forms work pane that displays the list of forms available in the database.
3. Double-click the form in the work pane. Double-click the field that you want to encrypt to open the Field dialog box.
4. In the Field dialog box, activate the Advanced tab.
5. In the Security Options list, check Enable encryption for this field, as shown in Figure 8.12.

FIGURE 8.12 *The Advanced tab of the Field dialog box to enable encryption for a field*

The border of this field becomes red, indicating that encryption has been enabled. When you apply an encryption key to the document, these fields are hidden from users who do not have the key.

Attaching an Encryption Key to a Document

To encrypt a document, you must attach a key to it. When you attach a key to a document, all the fields for which you have enabled encryption in that document are encrypted and are visible only to users who have the key in their user IDs. Perform the following steps to attach a key to a document:

1. Open the database that contains the documents that you want to encrypt in the Notes client.
2. Right-click the document to be encrypted and select Document Properties from the context menu. The Document dialog box appears.
3. Activate the Security tab and select a key from the Secret Encryption Keys list. This list shows all the keys that are present in your user ID. Refer Figure 8.13.

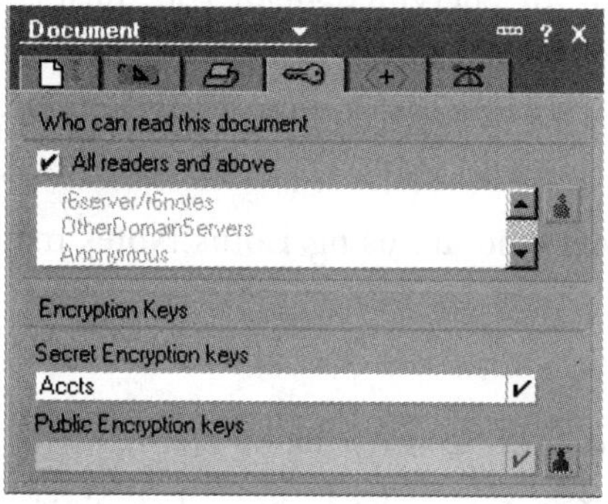

FIGURE 8.13 *The Document dialog box, displaying the option to attach an encryption key*

4. The document is encrypted with the key applied to the document. You can also encrypt the document by using the public keys of users. To do this, click the Add Public Key button next to the Public Encryption keys field. This button allows you to select the names of people for whom you want to encrypt the document.
5. To access the document encrypted with a public key, the user does not require any special encryption keys, because the documents can be decrypted using the user's private key present in the user's ID.

NOTE

You can attach a default encryption key to a form by selecting a key in the Security tab of the Form dialog box when you open the form in Domino Designer. This ensures that all documents are encrypted using this key by default, but a person having the editing rights to an encrypted document and possessing the key can apply a different key.

Mailing a Secret Encryption Key to Other Users

To enable users to view the content of an encrypted field, you must give the encryption key to them. You can either mail the key or export it to them on a floppy or shared disk, in which case, they will have to import this key into their user IDs.

You can mail the encryption key to users who are using Lotus Notes mail. Perform the following steps to do this:

1. Select File/Security/User Security.
2. Enter your password to view the User Security dialog box.
3. In the list displayed in the left pane of this dialog box, click Notes Data and then click Document.
4. In the Document Encryption details, shown in Figure 8.11, select the key that you want to mail.
5. Click the Mail Secret Key button. This displays the Mail Secret Encryption Key dialog box, as shown in Figure 8.14.

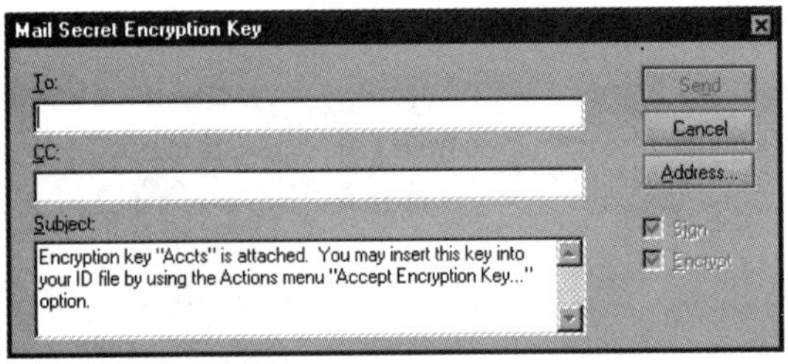

FIGURE 8.14 *The Mail Secret Encryption Key dialog box*

6. Enter the name of the person to whom you want to send the key in the To field. Enter a name in the CC field if you want to send a copy to someone else. You can also select the names by clicking the Address button.
7. Click Send. If you want to allow the recipients to send this key further to other users, check the Allow all recipients to forward the key by mail or export in the Secret Encryption Key Restrictions dialog box. This will send the key as a mail attachment to the users.

The users can accept this key by opening their mail messages and selecting Accept Encryption Key from the Actions menu. After accepting the encryption key, the users can access all the encrypted fields of a document that have been encrypted using the encryption key.

Encrypting a Database for Local Security

As mentioned earlier, the ACL of a database is not effective for a local database unless the database has been created as a replica of a server database or the Enforce a consistent ACL across all replica of the database option is selected in the Advanced tab of the ACL.

To prevent unauthorized access to a local database, you can encrypt the database locally. A database is encrypted using the public key of a user; therefore, only the person having the right user ID is able to open the database.

Perform the following steps if you want to encrypt a database:

1. Select the database from the Bookmark pane or the Workspace in the Notes client. If the database is not available in the Bookmark pane, choose File/Database/Open to bookmark it.
2. Choose File/Database/Properties to open the Database dialog box, as shown in Figure 8.15.

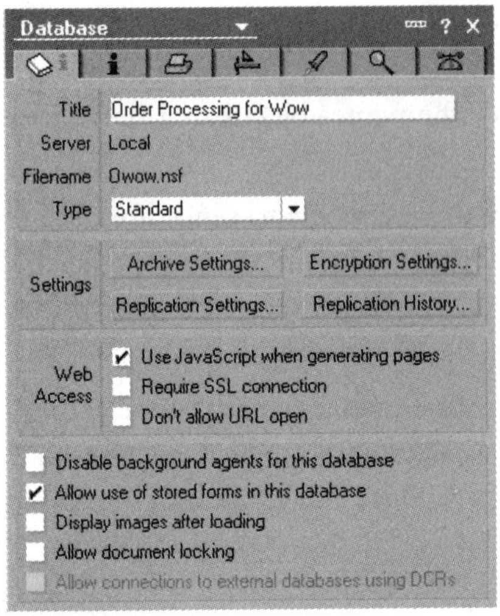

FIGURE 8.15 *The Database dialog box, displaying the Encryption Settings button*

3. Click the Encryption Settings button to access the Encryption dialog box, as shown in Figure 8.16.

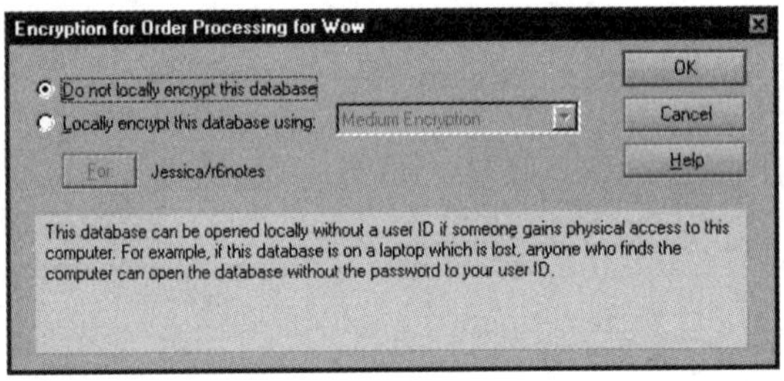

FIGURE 8.16 *The Encryption dialog box, displaying the option to locally encrypt a database*

4. Select Locally encrypt this database using and select an encryption level: Strong, Medium, or Simple. The stronger the encryption, the more secure it will be, and at the same time, the more time it'll take to decrypt. Therefore, Medium encryption is recommended.
5. Click OK. This encrypts the database for you, and nobody else will be able to open it.

CAUTION

You can click the For button to locally encrypt the database for another user, but when you do this, you will lose access to it yourself, because a database can be encrypted only for a single user.

Summary

In this chapter, you learned about the various security options available in Domino. The databases created in Notes are highly secure because of its multi-layered security model. You learned how to set the ACL of a database, how to define the security of the design elements, and how to secure a document or parts of a document. You also learned about document encryption. Finally, you learned how to encrypt a local database.

Chapter 9

Working with Templates

After you have designed a database, the next step is its deployment to make it available to users. Deployment of a database involves multiple tasks, such as copying the database to the Domino server so that the users can gain access to it and setting up the ACL (*Access Control List*) of the database for security. If the database is used in multiple locations, deployment also involves planning a replication strategy to synchronize the databases.

You can deploy a database either by copying it directly to the server or by copying a template, based on the database, to the server. The former method allows users to work directly on the database, while the latter allows users to create their own functional databases based on the template.

In this chapter, you'll learn what a template is, the purpose of using a template, how to create a template, and how to refresh the design of a database.

Defining a Template

A *template* is a basic Notes database design that users can use to create new databases. A template has an extension of .ntf, which stands for Notes Template Facility. A user has access to all the templates stored on the server or on his local hard disk when creating a new database. Therefore, the user is able to create a readily usable database without spending time on designing it.

Domino ships with a number of built-in templates, which the users can employ to create various types of databases. These templates help save the time and energy that goes into designing a database from scratch. All the system databases, such as the users' mail databases and personal and public address books, have a template associated with them. If a database has been deleted accidentally or has been corrupted, you could use the associated template to create or replace the database. Domino also ships with some other useful templates, such as the Personal Journal Template named Journal6.ntf. The Personal Journal database created using this template may be used to create documents for personal use. This database can be used as a notebook or a scribbling pad for creating a rough draft of your documents before they are distributed to others. Another useful built-in template is the Discussion database template named discsw6.ntf. This template can be used to create a discussion group for users to exchange their ideas and thoughts on any subject.

NOTE

After creating a database using a template, you can use the database as such or you can customize it to suit your requirements.

Besides using the templates available with Domino, you can also create a template from an existing database that you have designed and then deploy it on the server.

Creating a database template is useful if you want users to create their own database copies and work on them. A personal contact list, an expense database, or a personal picture book could be some of the databases that you could deploy as a template. The users can create the database by using the template you have deployed.

After you deploy a database, if you continue making changes to it, you can deploy the database as a template. Deploying a database as a template enables you to keep making changes without disturbing the functional, or live, database. You can make changes to the template and then affect the functional database by refreshing or replacing the design using the template.

Another use of templates is in a situation where you have hidden the design of the database from the users to prevent them from viewing or copying the design. Because this hides the design from you as well, to make any design changes to this database, you need to make changes to the template and refresh the design of the functional database with it.

Creating a database template is also useful in situations where you need to have a database on multiple servers. For example, imagine that there is a separate Action tracking database in every location of your company to track the activities of the people at a specific location. This database has been deployed on the server for each location. The design of the databases on all these servers must be standard. Any design changes required can be implemented in the template, and the databases across all the servers automatically get the updated design. For these updates, the Designer task needs to run on the servers. This task helps you make changes to the server templates, and then propagate them to all users. For example, you want to add a new letterhead containing the company logo to all the users mail files. To do so, make the change in the mail template named mail6.ntf, and the changes will be propagated to the user mail files when the Designer task runs.

NOTE

The databases across the servers get updated when the Designer task runs on the servers. This task by default runs at 1 A.M. However, the administrator may choose to run it at a different time.

CAUTION

Databases created on local hard disks must be updated manually.

Creating a Template

As already mentioned, besides the built-in Domino templates, you can create your own templates. Creating a template involves deploying an existing database as a template. To create a template from an existing database, you need to copy the database to the data directory of the server with the .ntf extension, if you want to make it a shared template. If, however, you want to create a template for personal use, you need to copy the database to the client with an extension of .ntf. After you copy the database as an .ntf file (on the server or on the client), you need to set the database design properties to specify it as a template.

Copying a Database

The steps to create a copy of a database with an .ntf extension are as follows:

1. In the Bookmark pane of Lotus Notes or Designer Client, select the database that you want to use to create a template from.

NOTE

If the database is not added to the Bookmark pane, select File/Database/Open to open or bookmark the database.

2. From the File menu, select Database, and then select New Copy to open the Copy Database dialog, as shown in Figure 9.1.

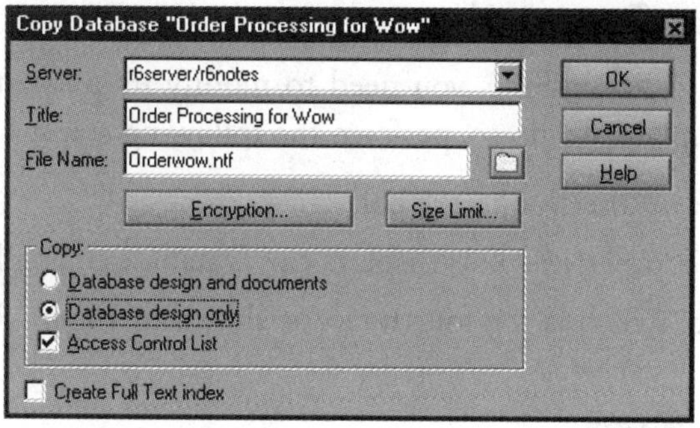

FIGURE 9.1 *The Copy Database dialog box to create a copy of the database with a .ntf extension*

3. From the Server list, select the server on which you want to create a template like r6server/r6notes. To create a template on your local hard disk, leave the default option as Local.
4. In the Title box, enter the title for the template. For example, Order Processing for Wow.
5. In the File Name box, change the extension to .ntf. This extension specifies that the new copy is a template.
6. In the Copy section, select the Database design only to copy just the design of the database and not any documents contained in it.
7. Check Access Control List to copy the ACL if you want to set up a standard ACL for the database. For example, you may have created certain roles in the ACL that have been implemented in your database.
8. Click OK.

NOTE

If you want to set up certain default ACL entries in the template so that they may be inherited by the databases that are created from this template, you must include these entries to the ACL of the template by enclosing them in square brackets. For example, the default access to a newly created database is Designer, and the creator of the database gets a Manager access. To give a Default access of Reader to the databases created from this template in the ACL of the template, add `[-default-]` with an access level as Reader. Similarly, any entry enclosed in square brackets gets propagated from the template to the database.

Modifying the Database Properties

After copying the database as an .ntf file, you need to modify its properties to specify the database as a template. To do so, perform the following steps:

1. Select the database from the Bookmark bar.
2. Select File/Database/Properties. This displays the Database dialog box.
3. Select the Design tab, which is the fourth tab, as shown in Figure 9.2.

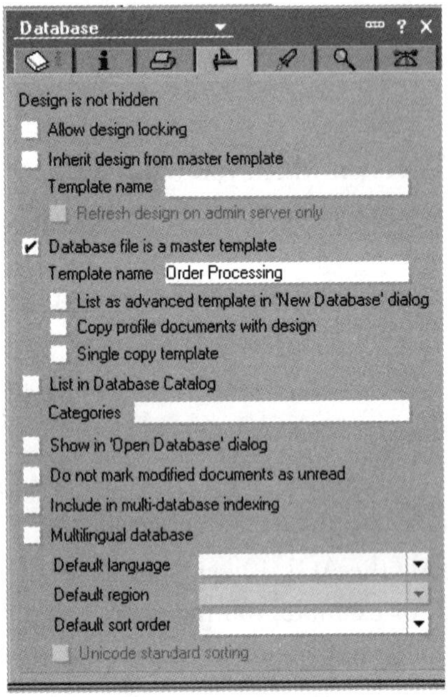

FIGURE 9.2 *The Database dialog box with the Design tab activated to set the template-related options*

4. Check Database file is a master template. In the Template name box, enter the name of the template.
5. Check List as advanced template in 'New Database' dialog if you want the template to be displayed in the advanced template list in the New Database dialog box.
6. Clear Show in 'Open Database' dialog if you do not want the template to be listed when a users accesses the Open Database dialog box to open a database.

7. Close the Database dialog box. Now this database is a template and can be used to create new databases.

NOTE

When you create a database using a template, the Inherit design from Master template option is checked for this database. In addition, the Template Name box has the name of the template from which the database has been created. If you want to associate the template with an existing database that is not based on a template, you can manually check this option and specify the name of the template that you want to associate with this database.

To test the template that you've just created, open the New Database dialog box. To do so, select File/Database/New. The template is listed in the dialog, as shown in Figure 9.3.

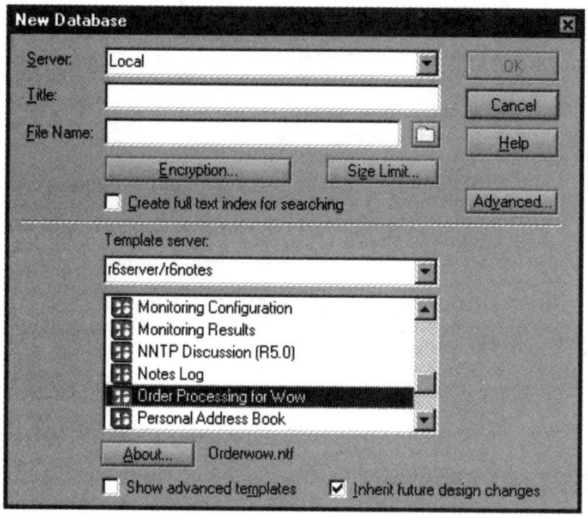

FIGURE 9.3 *The New Database dialog box showing the template you created*

Refreshing Design Changes

After you've deployed a database as a template on a server, users can use this template to create their own databases. If a user wants to inherit all changes made to the template in her database, the user needs to ensure that:

- The Inherit future design changes check box has been checked at the time of creation of the database
- The template and the database reside on the server

As explained earlier, the Designer task running on the server updates the designs of all such databases. For local databases, you need to update the design with the latest design changes in the template manually. Perform the following steps to manually refresh the design of a local database.

1. Select the database whose design you need to update.
2. From the File menu, select Database, and then select Refresh Design. You are prompted for the location of the template, as shown in Figure 9.4.

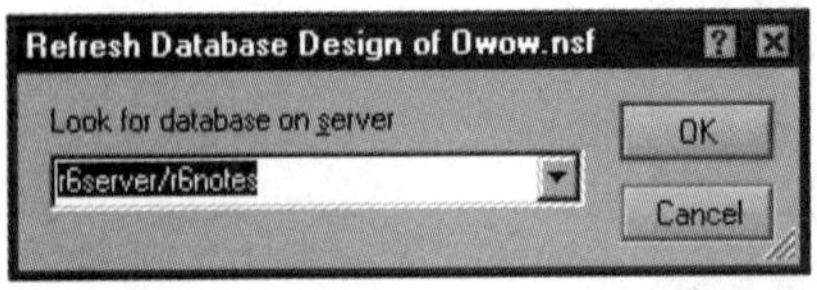

FIGURE 9.4 *The Refresh Database dialog box*

3. From the Server list, select the name of the server if the template is on a server. Otherwise, leave it as Local.
4. Click OK. A warning message is displayed, as shown in Figure 9.5.

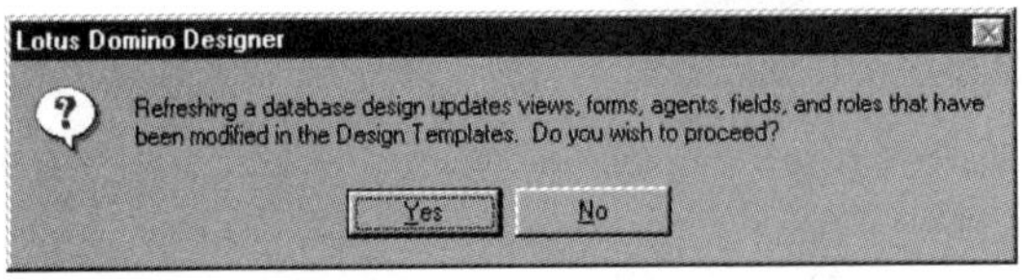

FIGURE 9.5 *A warning message while refreshing the design of the database*

5. Click Yes to continue refreshing the design. A message, "Design Refresh Completed," is displayed on the status bar, indicating that the design has been successfully refreshed.

Refreshing a design may overwrite the changes you made to the database you are using, which sometimes may not be desirable. It is possible to prohibit selective design notes of a database from getting updated during a design refresh. It is also possible to inherit different design elements from different templates.

Prohibiting a Design Note from Being Inherited

If you have made changes to the database that you want to keep—for example, you may have updated the Memo design of your mail database to add some personal details, such as your picture—you may not want these changes to be overwritten by a design refresh or replace. You can prohibit the design changes to update a specific design element by performing the following steps:

1. Open the database in Domino Designer.
2. In the Design Pane, select the design element whose design you want to prevent from being updated.
3. Right-click the design element in the work pane and select Design Properties. The Design Document dialog is displayed, as depicted in Figure 9.6.

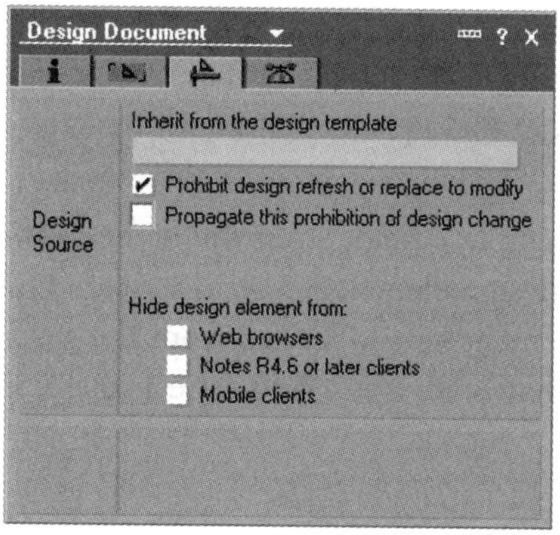

FIGURE 9.6 *The Design Document dialog box*

4. Click the Design tab, which is the third tab.
5. Check Prohibit design refresh or replace to modify. This will make sure that whenever the design of the database is refreshed or replaced, this element is not affected.

Inheriting the Design Element from a Different Template

After creating a database based on a template, you can ensure that the design of your database is regularly updated with any changes in the design of the template. You can also prohibit the update of certain design notes. You may also include certain design notes that are inherited from some template other than the master template for that database. For example, imagine that you want to use a standard welcome page or a navigator for all your databases. You have a created a template called StdForms, which contains all such standard design elements. To use that page in your database, you can copy it from that template and paste it into your database. Now you must ensure that this page or navigator design is updated whenever it is changed in the standard forms template, and also that refreshing design from the master template does not affect it.

Perform the following steps to inherit the design of the specific element from a different template:

1. Open the database in Domino Designer.
2. In the Design Pane, select the design element whose design you want to inherit from a different template.
3. Right-click the design element in the work pane and select Design Properties. The Design Document dialog is displayed, as depicted in Figure 9.7.
4. In the Inherit from the design template field, enter the name of the template from which you want the design element to be inherited. This will ensure that the design of this element gets inherited from the specified template only and not the one that is being used to refresh the design of the rest of the database.

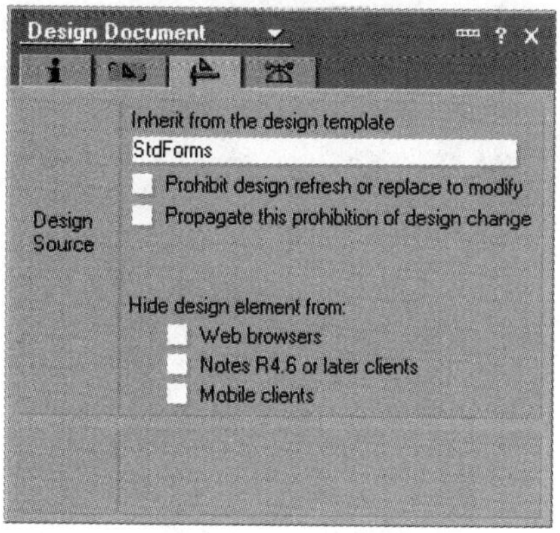

FIGURE 9.7 *The Design Document dialog box, depicting how to inherit changes from a different template*

Similarly, you can specify a template name for other design elements. Whenever you refresh the database design, the changes in the design element are received from the specified template.

Replacing Design Changes

Sometimes, you may want to change the template from which you are inheriting the changes to a database. For example, if you are upgrading from Domino R5 to Domino R6, you may want to update the mail database to make use of the latest features. To do so, you'll need to replace the design of the mail file with the new template. Other situations where you may need to replace the template for inheriting the design changes are when you've created a database using an incorrect template or some of the database design elements have got corrupted.

Perform the following steps to replace the design of a database:

1. Open the database either in the Notes Client or the Designer.

> **NOTE**
>
> In order to replace the design of a database, you must have at least a Designer access to the database.

2. From the File menu, select Database and then select Replace Design. The Replace Database Design dialog is displayed, as shown in Figure 9.8.

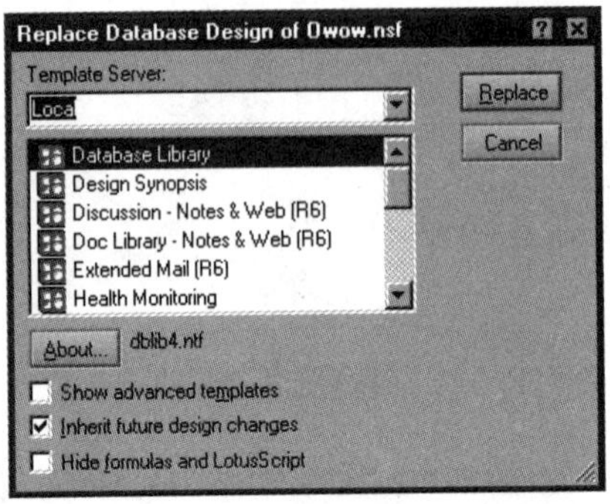

FIGURE 9.8 *Replacing the database design*

3. From the Template Server list, select the name of the server if the template is on a server. Otherwise, leave it as Local.
4. Select the template that you want to use to replace the design.
5. Select Show advanced templates if the template is listed as an advanced template.
6. Select Hide formulas and LotusScript if you want to hide the design of the database.
7. Click Replace. A warning message is displayed as shown in Figure 9.9.
8. Click Yes to proceed. A message on the status bar is displayed, stating that the design has been replaced.

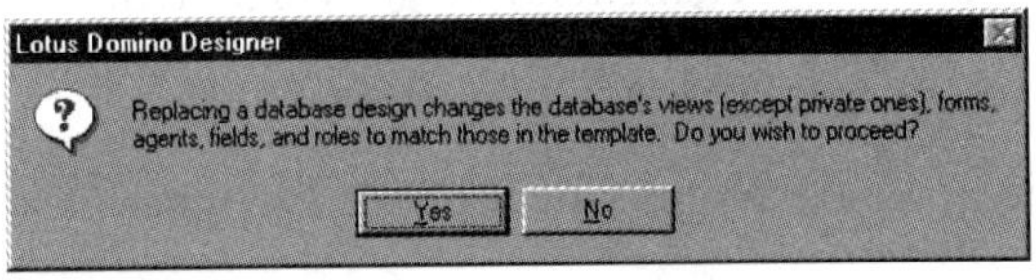

FIGURE 9.9 *A warning message before replacing the database design*

CAUTION

Replacing the design of a database deletes all the original design elements and adds the design elements from the new template to the database.

NOTE

As explained earlier, if you want to keep some original design elements even after replacing the design with a new template, you must check the Prohibit design refresh or replace to modify property of the specific design element.

Summary

In this chapter, you learned how to use templates in Lotus Notes. A template is a basic design of a database that can be used by users to create databases. Templates are created by copying the database design with an extension of .ntf and then setting the database properties. You learned how the changes could be propagated from a template to a functional database when the database and template are deployed locally or on the server. You can also selectively refresh the design of a database. Finally, you learned how to replace the design of a database to completely change the template being used.

PART II

Professional Project 1—Creating a Reference Application Using Notes

Project 1 Overview

In this project, you will create a Reference application named Employee Handbook. The application will be created using Domino Designer R6 and will be accessed by using Lotus Notes client.

The Employee Handbook application allows organizations to make an online version of their policies and procedures manual. The application can also store the different guidelines and forms used by the organization.

There will be two groups of users for the Employee Handbook application. The content authors will create the necessary content and the general users will use the application to access the available contents. The security aspects of the application will be implemented using database Access Control List (ACL) roles. Application features include content authoring, content presentation, search facility, and personalization features.

During the course of this project you will learn how to create forms, views, and navigational elements, and you will learn how to use full-text indexing and the search facility in a Notes application. In addition, you will learn how to implement security features for a Notes application.

The application deployment will be implemented using a distributed model. The replica copies residing in branch office servers and on local workstations of users will be updated by replicating with the central database that resides on the corporate office server.

Chapter 10

Structure of a Notes Application

In Part I of this book, you learned about creating the various design elements in a Notes application. This chapter further expands your knowledge base about creating a reference application. You will learn about the structural aspects of Notes applications, the various types of Notes applications, and the ways to create them.

Notes Applications and Databases

In general, an *application* is a collection of various data and design elements on any development platform. The design elements, which include data entry forms, programming code, and reports, are connected together based on a logic that is driven by the design objectives or the business logic. An application consists of a bunch of files that are loaded and run as per the application logic.

In Notes, a database is the basic container for all the design elements and the associated resources of an application. Therefore, the terms *application* and *database* are used synonymously in Notes.

Although a database contains all the design elements and application resources, you do not need to cram all the design elements of an application into a single database. Based on the size and complexity of the application, you can logically divide an application into one or more databases. In this manner, you are able to better organize your application and manage its complexities.

In addition to containing the design elements, Notes databases act as data repositories. The design elements and the data are clearly segregated in a database. This segregation helps you modify the design elements without disturbing the data and vice versa. Figure 10.1 depicts how the various elements are organized within a Notes database.

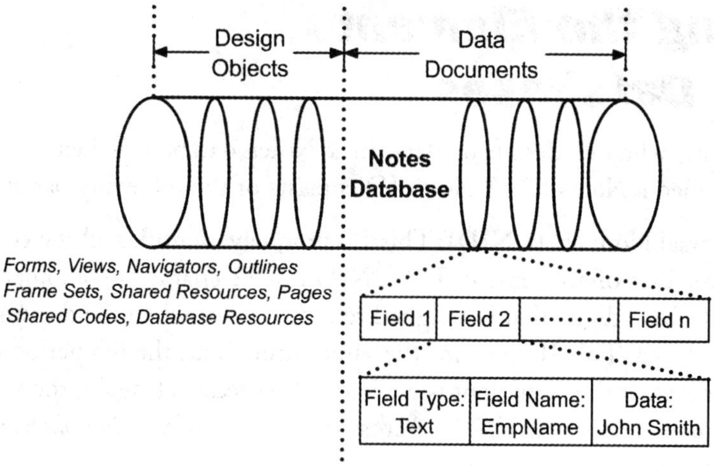

FIGURE 10.1 *Structure of a Notes database*

In a Notes database, a *document* is the basic entity for data organization. A document is similar to a record in a DBMS (*Database Management System*). A Notes database can contain none, one, or possibly thousands or millions of documents. All the documents contained in a Notes database need not be homogenous. For example, you can have documents related to employees' personal information and leave records in the same Notes database.

Fields constitute the basic data unit elements in a document. A field can store data of various types, such as text, number, date/time, and rich text. In addition, a document can contain objects, which can be OLE (*Object Linking and Embedding*) objects, file attachments, or almost anything you can think of, including another Notes database itself.

A Notes database acts as a data repository. In addition, a Notes application can use various data integration tools for connecting to relational databases, such as Oracle, SQL Server, and DB/2; ERP (*Enterprise Resource Planning*) systems, such as SAP, PeopleSoft, and J.D.Edwards; and transaction systems, such as CICS, IBM MQSeries, and IMS.

Identifying the Elements in Notes Databases

Every element, whether design or data, in a Notes database is identified by a unique ID, called a Notes ID. A Notes ID consists of the following parts:

- **Universal Note ID (UNID).** This ID uniquely identifies all the copies and versions of an element. The UNID is a 32-character combination of hexadecimal digits that is assigned to a document when the document is created first. This ID remains the same throughout the life period of the document. If the document is copied and pasted back again, the pasted document gets a new UNID. Across the replicas of the databases, a document has the same UNID.
- **Originator ID (OID).** This ID is used to identify a particular version of an element across all the copies of a database. This constitutes the UNID and a sequence number. Every replica of an element has the same OID. The OID changes when the element is modified.
- **Global Note ID (GNID).** This ID is used to identify the position of an element in any particular database. It consists of the database ID and the NID and is not changed even if the element is modified. Across the replicas of a database, an element has a different GNID. Unlike the OID, the GNID does not distinguish between different versions of the same element.
- **Note ID (NID).** This ID is used to identify a particular element in a specific database. It does not contain any information regarding the database in which the element is contained. This ID does not change when the element is modified.
- **Instance ID (IID).** This ID is used to identify a particular version of an element in a particular database. This ID does not contain any information regarding the database in which the Note is contained. This ID changes whenever a Note is changed.
- **Global Instance ID (GIID).** This ID is used to identify a particular version of an element in a particular database. Unlike the IID, this ID contains information regarding the database in which the element is contained.

The above-mentioned set of IDs is used to implement the mechanism of revision and replication in Notes.

Relation between a Form and a Document

A form is a template that contains various user interface elements and fields. A form is used for the following main purposes:

- To collect data from the users and store it in a document
- To present the existing data elements to the user in the form of a document
- To carry out data processing and implement the application logic

Each document contains a special field named Form to associate the document with a form. The Form field usually contains the name of the form with which you created the document, if it has not been changed programmatically after the document was created. However, you can modify the value of the Form field to associate the document with another form. Another way to override the form associated with a document while presenting the document is to use a Form Formula associated with various views. For example, you may use a form that captures the salary details and the personal details of an employee using a form. When others open this document using a specific view, you may use a form that contains only the personal details and not the salary details.

In addition to storing the name of the base form in the Form field of a document, you can select to store the form with the document. Although this method is useful to display documents even if they are moved to another database that doesn't have the same form, it may occupy more disk space and requires more system memory while the document is processed. Usually, this approach is used when documents need to be mailed to users who do not have access to the database in which the document and its form are stored.

Whatever the method, a document needs to be associated with a form in order to be displayed properly. Notes uses the following mechanisms in the specified sequence to decide which form should be used to display a document:

1. It checks whether or not a form is stored with the document. If yes, the stored form is used to display the document.
2. It checks whether or not a Form Formula is associated with the view from which the document is being opened. If a Form Formula is specified, Notes uses the specified form to display the document.
3. It checks the value contained in the Form field. If yes, it checks whether the specified form exists in the database in which the document is

contained. If it exists, Notes uses the specified form to display the document.

4. If all of the above fail, Notes displays an error indicating that the form (contained in the form field) cannot be located, but displays the document using the default form of the database.
5. If the database does not contain a default form, Notes reports an error indicating that the default form cannot be located and the document fails to open.

If none of the above works, Notes reports an error indicating that a form cannot be located to display the document.

Document Representations

When users are working with a document in a Notes client, a document can have one of the following representations:

- In-memory representation of a Notes UI document
- In-memory representation of a Notes back-end document
- On-disk representation, which is the document stored on the disk

Users interact with a document through the UI provided by the associated form. The in-memory representation of a Notes UI document is associated with the user interface. Therefore, when a user manipulates the document content through the associated form, he is manipulating the content of the Notes UI document. These changes are immediately reflected in the in-memory representation of the Notes back-end document. You will use the front-end classes in LotusScript and formula language to manipulate the UI representation.

On the other hand, if a user manipulates the in-memory representation of a Notes back-end document, the changes are not necessarily reflected in the Notes UI document, especially when the `AutoReload` property of the `NotesUIDocument` object is set to `false`. Therefore, it is required to explicitly reload the UI document so that the changes are reflected in the UI document. Otherwise the changes that you may have made to the back-end document will be overwritten by the front-end document when the front-end document is saved. This will result in a loss of all the changes you have made to the back-end document. One way to overcome this is to save the back-end document that was manipulated and discard the front-end document.

An on-disk representation is the document stored on the disk in the database. Any modifications that are made in a Notes UI document or a Notes back-end document are not reflected in the on-disk representation. These modifications need to be explicitly saved. Figure 10.2 depicts the different document representations in a Notes client. When a document is loaded in the memory, these representations are initialized from the left to the right, as shown in Figure 10.2. When the modifications are saved to the on-disk representation, the reverse direction is taken, as depicted in Figure 10.2.

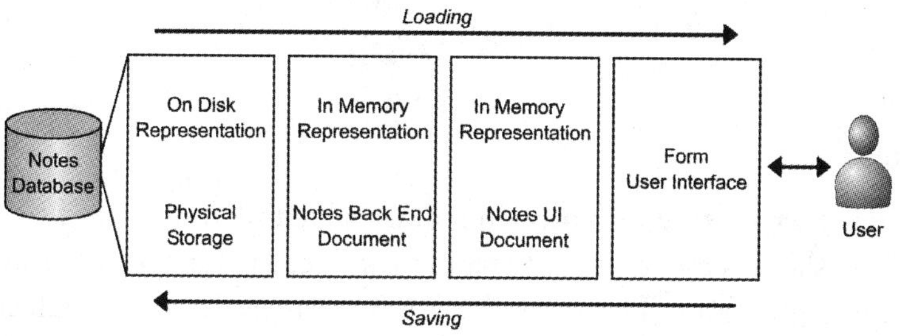

FIGURE 10.2 *Document representations in a Notes client*

When working with the formula language, you are dealing with the Notes UI document. In LotusScript, the various classes provide you with more flexibility to choose either a Notes UI document or a Notes back-end document. While programming in Java, you have only the back-end classes available.

When working on the Web, the document representations are different from the preceding representations. The document representations on the Web will be discussed in Part VI, "Creating a Web-Enabled Notes Application."

Multivalued Fields

Multivalued fields store more than one value separated by one of the following:

- Space
- Comma
- Semicolon
- New line

You can make the following field types into multivalued fields:

- Text
- Date/Time
- Number
- Dialog list
- Checkbox
- Listbox
- Authors
- Names
- Readers
- Formula

To access specific data elements stored in a multivalued field, you need to specify the index of the data element as `Fieldname[n]`. Here, `Fieldname` is the name of the field and `n` is the index. The index for a data element in a multivalued field can start from either 0 or 1, depending on the coding language used. The formula language uses n, starting from 1, while LotusScript or Java treats the content as an array with its lower bound at 0.

Authors and Readers Fields

The Authors and Readers fields are used to control document-level security. The Authors field controls the right to edit or update documents, while the Readers field controls the read access or the access rights to a document. Note that these fields can only be used to further fine-tune the database ACL (*Access Control List*) and cannot override the ACL. Therefore, if a user has an access right that is less than Author, you cannot provide edit access by listing her name in the Authors field. Refer to Chapter 8, "Securing Your Application," for further details.

Rich Text and Rich Text Lite Fields

Rich Text fields allow you to store any object in a Notes document. Usually a Rich Text field is used when you want to store a large volume of text or embed or attach objects to documents. Unlike the simple Text fields, Rich Text fields provide you with excellent formatting features. You can even use OLE objects stored in this field to open the objects from other non-Notes applications.

Rich Text Lite fields are Rich Text fields in which you can limit what the users can insert. During the design, you can select one or more of the following object types to specify the object type that can be inserted in a Rich Text Lite field:

- Pictures
- Shared images
- Attachments
- Views
- DatePicker
- Shared applets
- Text
- OLE objects
- Calendar
- Inbox

The most remarkable feature of this type of field is that it does not have any size limitations, as other field types have. Rich sets of programmable controls are associated with this field type in the formula language as well as in LotusScript and Java. This allows you to achieve remarkable manipulation and processing of the content in these fields.

Types of Notes Applications

Based on their behavioral characteristics, Notes applications are classified into the following categories:

- Reference applications
- Broadcast applications
- Collaborative applications
- Workflow applications

Reference applications are usually used to manage online reference material. Broadcast applications are used to deliver information simultaneously to a wide audience. Collaborative applications are used when teamwork is required and include discussion and tracking applications. Workflow applications are used to automate the manual flow of work with its online counterpart. These types of applications are covered in Chapter 1, "Overview of Domino Applications." The focus of this chapter is on reference applications, so their details are discussed in detail here.

As the name suggests, reference applications are mainly used to create, organize, and publish reference materials. In such applications, the emphasis is more on the ability for content publishing and organization than on complex design elements. Most of the time, the published content remains constant for a long period. A very good example of a reference application is an online handbook on company policies and procedures.

When designing a reference application, the following factors should be considered:

- It should be easy to create or author content.
- It should be easy to organize the content into different sections or chapters when authoring.
- It should be possible to segregate the content based on the target audience.
- A topics index should be provided so that users can easily understand the organization of the content.
- Searching for a word or a phrase should be easy.
- It should enable navigation to the related topics.
- The content should be valid for a time period.

User interaction with a reference application involves either authoring the content or reading the published content. The authoring is restricted to a few users who are responsible for creating content for the database. These applications tend to have very low to medium usage, and user access spreads evenly throughout a period of time. Usually users access the application periodically to see if any changes have been made to the existing content or new content has been published. Moreover, these applications, if replicated across servers, tend to use low-level priority for replication. This is because the content changes very infrequently.

Ways of Creating Notes Applications

There are different ways of developing Notes applications. The starting point you choose for your application depends on whether you are starting your application from scratch or from a base provided by an existing application. You can start the development in the following ways:

- By inheriting the design from a template
- By copying the design elements from an existing application
- By starting from a blank database

For the details of these methods, refer to Chapter 1.

Summary

In this chapter, you learned about the structural aspects of a Notes application database. You also learned about some of the design elements that require special consideration when creating an application. Finally, you identified the various types of Notes applications and the features of reference applications in particular.

Chapter 11

Project Case Study: Creating a Reference Application

In Chapter 10, "Structure of a Notes Application," you identified the design principles of a reference application. This chapter presents you with the case study of a typical reference application, the company policies and procedure manual for Munchausen Consulting Corporation.

Munchausen Consulting Corporation: The Present Scenario

Munchausen Consulting Corporation, headquartered in Boston, provides management and IT (*information technology*) consultancy services to medium to large corporations in the United States. The company is committed to providing zero-defect solutions to its clients. To ensure that the company meets its commitments, it focuses on its internal processes. Adherence to the processes by employees helps ensure quality and consistency across various consulting assignments that the company executes.

To stay competitive in the market and attract the best talents in the industry, Munchausen reviews its policies and guidelines twice a year. Until now, the company used to provide extensive training to its employees about the various policies and guidelines whenever there was a change. In addition, new hard copies of the employee handbook, incorporating the changes in procedures and policies, were distributed to the employees. This ensured a high degree of process adherence by the employees.

In the last two quarters, the company has seen exponential growth. To execute the growing number of assignments, the company has recruited more employees in the recent past. Despite the large work force inducted, there were serious problems associated with the quality of the last few consulting assignments that the company executed. The deterioration of quality was attributed to the lack of awareness among the employees about the various internal processes, policies, procedures, and guidelines of the company.

Taking note of the problem, the management constituted an internal task force to study the current situation and identify the root cause of why the employees are not adhering to the policies and procedures. The different reasons are as follows:

- The size of the employee handbook is very large. Therefore, if certain changes are made to the policies, a new employee handbook needs to be published. This involves time and cost. Sometimes the new employee handbook, incorporating the new policy changes, may not reach the employees in time because of the delay in printing.

- Whenever a new employee handbook needs to be published, the HR department undergoes a lot of pressure. This, in turn, affects the other HR activities.
- It is difficult to send the new employee handbook to the employees working at the customer site.
- The new handbook contains only the most updated policies and procedures. It is almost impossible to refer to the old policies and understand the actual changes that have occurred to an existing policy. This, in turn, leads to confusion whenever a policy change occurs.

Concluding the findings, the task force identified that the employees are not able to follow the processes because of the problems in the current manual employee handbook system. The task force, therefore, recommended replacing the existing manual system with a more efficient and cost-effective electronic publishing and distribution system.

Considering the recommendation by the task force, the company management has decided to automate the process of publishing the company policies and procedures. The company has its own IT department, which will implement the solution.

Munchausen Consulting Corporation: The Solution

The automated system of publishing the company policies and procedures will provide the following benefits:

- It will reduce the cost associated with publishing.
- It will speed up the creation and publication of the employee handbook.
- Employees can access the policies at any time from all the branches as well as customer sites.
- It will be possible to refer to old policies to identify the exact change in an existing policy.
- It will be possible to search for a particular policy based on a specified criterion.

The head of the IT department has assigned this project to a team, which consists of a project manager and two developers. The team studied the solution requirements and identified that the solution needs to be a reference application. The users of this application, the company employees, will use this application to refer to the company policies. The employees should be able to refer to these policies at any time from all the branches and customer sites. To implement this solution, the development team has decided to use Domino Designer R6. The reference application should provide the following features:

- Content Organization
- Content Publishing
- Personalization

The details of these features are discussed in the following sections.

Content Organization

The reference application is a repository of all company policies, procedures, guidelines, regulations, and formats to be used for various purposes, such as the leave application form. To enable the employees to use the application in an easy and efficient manner, the application needs to organize the content in the most appropriate manner. The content organization should map to the manual employee handbook so that the employees can relate to it when using the application. Therefore, the application organizes the content as follows in the next sections.

Parts

Parts, identified by a part number and a part title, are the first and highest level of organization. Parts are the logical organizational elements. The application is divided into the following five parts:

- **Policies.** This part contains all the company policies.
- **Procedures.** This part contains all the procedures and processes that are required to be followed by employees.
- **Guidelines.** This part contains the guidelines, which help the employees to avoid the usual pitfalls and mistakes they tend to make during consulting assignments.

- **Statutory regulations.** This part contains government regulations and laws that employees should be aware of during their tenure of employment with the company.
- **Forms to be used.** This part contains all the forms that the employees need to fill up. Examples of such forms are leave application forms, transfer request forms, loan application forms, employee benefits form, tax return filing forms, and so on.

Chapters

A part is further divided into chapters, which are logical organization elements and are used to group logically related content or documents. A chapter number and chapter title identify each chapter.

Sections

A section is the basic unit that holds the content. A section title identifies each section. Within a section, you can organize the content using various formatting features, such as headings, bullet lists, number lists, tables, and so on.

Table of Contents

The TOC (*Table of Contents*), as used in a manual employee handbook, helps identify the complete content organization in the application. It lists part elements at the top of the hierarchy, followed by chapters and sections.

Index

The index, as used in the manual employee handbook, is placed at the end of the book and contains an alphabetical listing of the subject along with the page numbers. An index helps users to quickly locate the page numbers through known words or phrases in the content.

The basic purpose of an index, to locate the required information, is solved by implementing search features in the application. Users can use this feature to locate all of the documents that contain a particular word or phrase. Therefore, the more powerful search feature can replace the index in the application.

Additional Features

To improve the user experience, it is a good idea to add certain features, which are over and above the basic application functioning. Following are the additional features of the application.

Personalization

The application will allow users to drag-and-drop the documents they refer to most to a particular area called MyReferences. In this manner, each user will have his own area where he can keep the most wanted documents and therefore quickly refer to them without following the complete navigational structure.

Highlighting New Documents

The application provides a mechanism by which the unread documents can be tracked. The documents, which are not yet identified by the user, are highlighted using a specific color. After the user reads a particular document, the document is highlighted with a different color. The application will maintain this feature on a per-user basis.

Tracking Changes

Whenever an existing policy or procedure is revised, it is required to track the old one. That will help users to understand the changes carried out to an existing document by comparing it with the older one. The application will allow the content authors to update the existing documents with version tracking.

Publishing

The content authors cannot be expected to complete the entire writing at one go. The application should provide a "Save as Draft" feature to address this problem. The documents that are saved using the Save as Draft feature will not be visible to the users, who include the readers, of the system. When the document is completely authored and the author uses the Publish option, the document will be made available to the readers.

Project Life Cycle

A project life cycle consists of phases, which allow better control and manageability of the project. The project begins with the project request, which can originate from end user groups, departments within an organization, or other organizations.

In this case, the project request is initiated at an organizational level by the top management of the company. After the project request, the project undergoes the following phases:

- Project initiation
- Project execution
- Project deployment

In the *project initiation* phase, the objectives, scope, risks, and costs associated with the project are identified. This phase also involves identifying milestones and deadlines and the team based on the required skills. In addition, a comprehensive plan is prepared for the activities to be performed during the various phases of the project life cycle. The complexity of this phase depends upon the size and complexity of the project.

The *project execution* phase involves coordination of the resources to execute the plan. This phase is further divided in to the following stages:

- Requirements analysis
- High-level design
- Low-level design
- Construction
- Integration and testing
- User acceptance testing

The final phase in a project life cycle, which is the *project deployment* phase needs explanation before discussing the other stages in detail. As the name suggests, during this phase, the application is deployed at the client location. In addition, support is provided to the client for a particular period that takes care of any bugs that might occur in the application after deployment.

The various stages in the project execution phase are discussed in the following sections.

Requirements Analysis

This phase involves identifying the various functional requirements of the application. The development team studied the current manual system of the employee handbook and interviewed the employees to identify their requirements.

The reference application has two types of users, authors and readers. The development team identified the following requirements for the content authors:

- Authoring content should be easy. It should be possible for the author to select the parts, chapters, and sections from a list wherever required.
- It should be easy to make changes to any existing policy.
- It should be possible for the authors to hide the documents that they are currently working on from the readers.
- After the content authoring, publishing should be easy.
- It should be possible to specify that certain policies and procedures apply to only specific employees.
- Only authorized users should be allowed to update the content.

For the readers, the following requirements were identified:

- The application interface should be simple so that readers can use the application without extensive training.
- The application organization should be simple to help readers navigate to different parts easily.
- Readers should be able to keep track of changed policies.
- Readers should be able to search documents based on specified criteria.
- Readers who are not connected to the network all the times should be able to access the policies and procedures locally. At the same time, they should be able to receive any updates made to the documents.

Based on the identified requirements, the development team decides to create a reference application, which is a database named Handbook, using Domino Designer R6.

High-Level Design

In the *high-level design* phase, the working of the application is identified. The various user interface screens are identified and presented to the client for approval. Based on the client feedback, the various user interface screens are finalized.

To identify the various user interface screens for the Handbook database, first identify how the authors and readers interact with the database.

Figure 11.1 shows the various user interactions with the system.

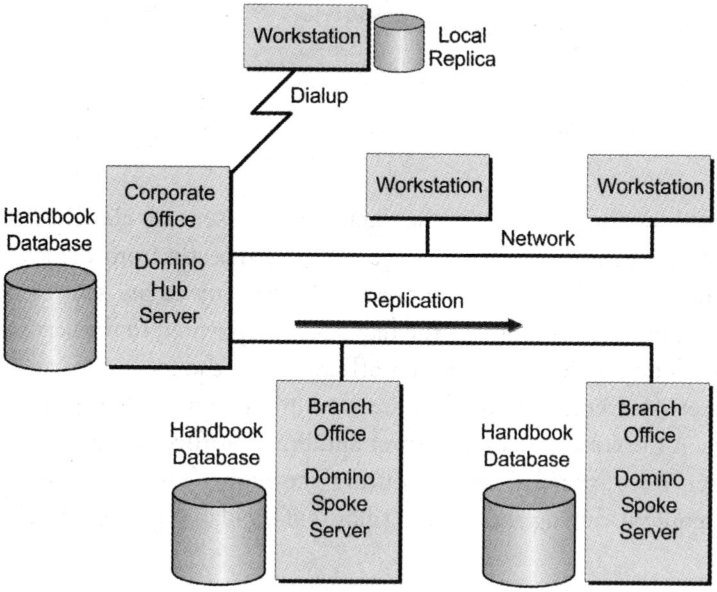

FIGURE 11.1 *User interactions with the Handbook database*

The user interactions can be classified as content authoring and content access. The content authoring allows the authorized authors to create, modify, and delete documents. The corporate office makes the policy decisions and a team from the HR department is responsible for keeping the documents up-to-date.

The content access, on the other hand, is limited to reading the existing policies and procedures. The employees access the content through a Topics index. They may also use the search facility to locate any content that matches specific criteria. The employees are scattered in branch offices and client sites in addition to the corporate office; all the employees should be able to access the Handbook database. The different employees can access the Handbook database in various ways or modes, as shown in Figure 11.2.

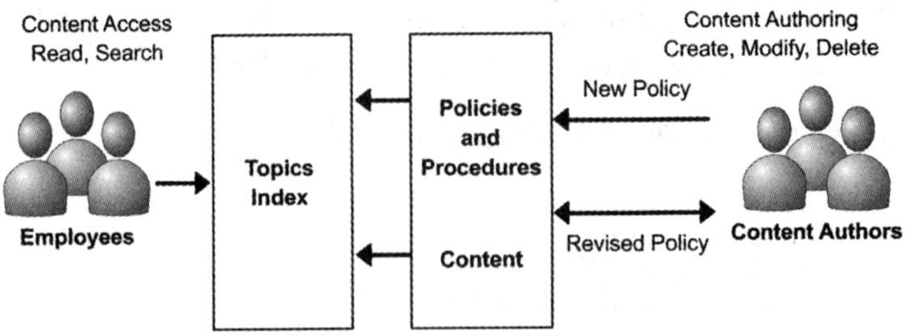

FIGURE 11.2 *User access modes*

Depending on how the users access the database, the users are classified into two categories. The first set of users access the database directly from the server over a local area network. As already mentioned, the employees are scattered across branch offices. For these employees, the database is replicated to the servers in the branch offices. The employees in branch offices access the local replicas available on their respective servers. The replicas are kept in synch using low-priority replications between the corporate office server and branch office servers. These replications happen once in a day, usually during the night. Therefore, any changes made to the content during the working hours is available to the branch offices the next day.

The second set of users are the employees located at the client sites and those who belong to the marketing department. They can connect to the branch office or corporate office using dial-up connectivity. Such users are called *mobile users*. It is not possible for these users to remain connected to the server for long periods. Therefore, a local replica copy is maintained on their workstations. Instructions will be given to them to replicate their Handbook database at least once day, preferably during the evening or night.

After identifying the user interaction with the database and the different modes in which different employees access the database, the development team identified the various user interface screens for the database.

For content authoring, a form needs to be created, as shown in Figure 11.3.

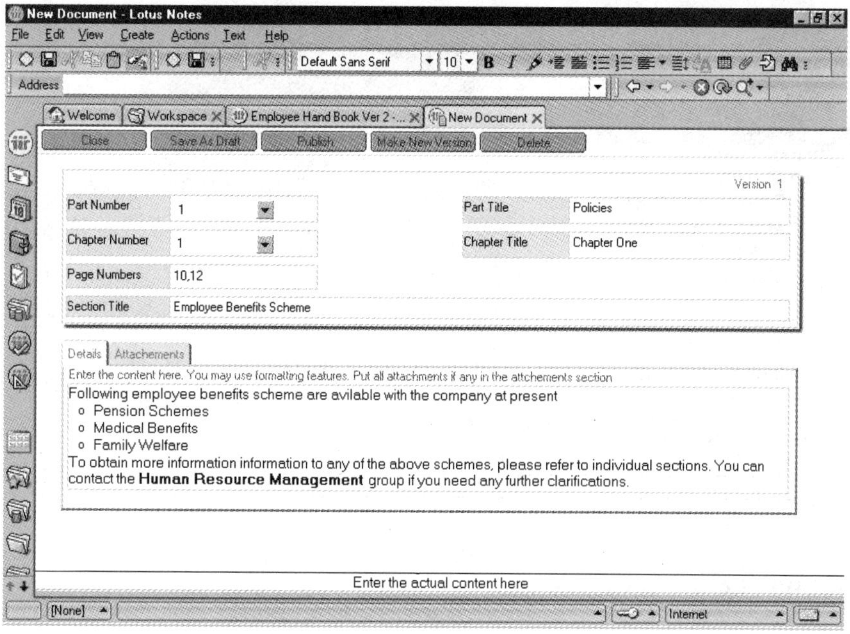

FIGURE 11.3 *Content authoring interface*

Readers can access individual documents using a view named Topics index, as shown in Figure 11.4.

Mixing the older versions with the latest versions of documents will unnecessarily confuse the readers. Therefore, the older versions of documents should be listed in a separate view whose design is similar to the Topics index view.

Similar to the Topics index view, which is available to all the users, readers, and content authors, the database should include a view that is available exclusively to the content authors. This view is similar to the Topics index view in design, but it lists the documents that are currently being authored.

Next, to provide the personalization feature that enables users to keep the documents they refer to most in a specific place for quick retrieval on demand, the database should allow users to create personal folders. If these folders are stored on the user's desktop, lot of space can also be saved on the server.

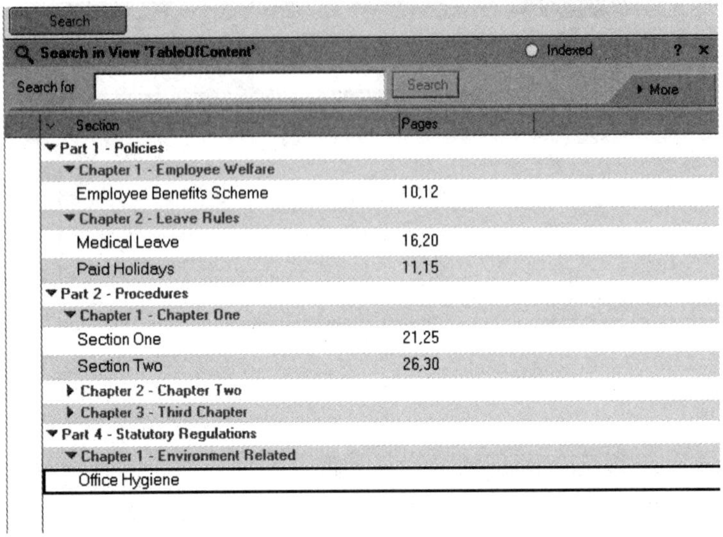

FIGURE 11.4 *The Topics index view*

After identifying the various forms and views, the database should provide an interface that connects these design elements for easy access. To connect the various database design elements, Notes provides navigators, outlines, and framesets. The first user interface screen that connects the various database design elements is shown in Figure 11.5.

To implement the search feature, you do not need to create a search engine exclusively. Instead, Notes provide this engine as a basic feature, called the Full Text Search feature, of the platform. To provide search capabilities to the application, you simply need to enable the full text search by creating a full text search index.

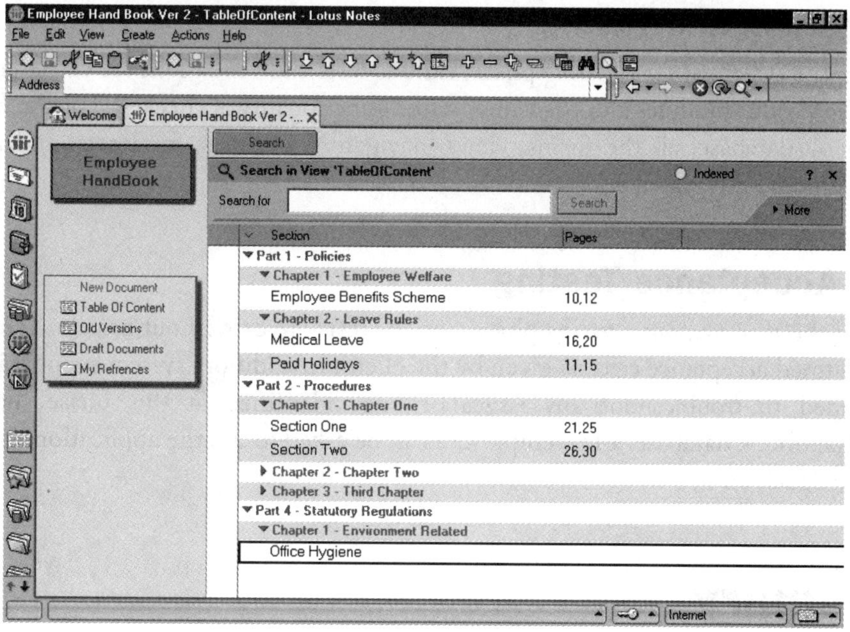

FIGURE 11.5 *The first screen*

Low-Level Design

During the *low-level design* phase, a detailed design of the various software modules is prepared using the high-level design. The team decides on the various standards, such as naming conventions for forms, views, and fields for a project. All these specifications are documented so that consistency can be maintained among the various modules for an application.

Construction

During the *construction* phase, various components of the application are coded. The various specifications identified during the low-level design are used to accomplish this. For the Handbook database, the forms, views, and other elements are constructed.

Integration and Testing

In the *integration and testing* phase, various tests and validations are carried out on the various modules and their integration functionality is checked. For the Handbook database, all the forms, views, navigators, outlines, framesets, and agents would be integrated and tested.

User Acceptance Testing

In the *user acceptance testing* phase, various tests are carried out based on the predefined acceptance criteria given by the client. In addition, system support is provided to troubleshoot any issues or bugs identified at this phase. For the Handbook database, a few employees can be asked to use the application and give feedback on it.

Summary

In this chapter, you learned how to analyze a problem and formulate a solution through a case study approach. You identified the different phases involved in a project life cycle and learned how to arrive at a high-level design for an application. The implementation of the solution, the Handbook database, will be covered in Chapter 12, "Creating a Reference Application."

Chapter 12

Creating a Reference Application

In the previous chapter, you looked at the case study and high-level design for the employee handbook application. In this chapter, you will learn to create the detailed design along with the application logic.

Design Elements

This section gives an overview of the Notes design elements, including forms, views, folders, the outline, the page, and the frameset, which will be used to implement the features of the employee handbook application.

ACL Roles

The database ACL (*Access Control List*) and roles control the security of the Notes application. For the handbook application, you will create a role called ContentAuthors defined at the ACL level. Only end users who are members of this role will have rights to create, modify, or delete documents in the handbook database. They need to have at least the Author access rights in the ACL along with the Create and Delete rights.

The readers, who are the employees at Munchausen other than the content authors, will require only Reader access. Servers will have the Manager access with the ContentAuthors role enabled. This ensures that documents will get replicated across servers properly.

Forms

The handbook application contains a single form. This section discusses the form properties and fields used in the form.

Form properties that are important from the design perspective are:

- **Form name.** Used to specify the name of the form. It is better to use a short name because the form will be used in various locations while programming for the application. Here the name of the form will be HandBook.
- **Form type.** Used to specify the type of form, such as Document. This form will be used to create documents and this property is specified to the Document type.

- **Display.** Used to specify how the form is displayed in the Notes client. The HandBook form will be included in the Create menu, the Search builder, and for printing.
- **Versioning.** Used to specify whether or not versioning will be enabled. For the HandBook form, this property is not enabled because this feature will be implemented using programming.
- **Options.** Used to specify various settings, such as whether or not the form needs to be stored in the document, whether the form should be refreshed automatically, and whether the documents created with this form need to be signed. For the handbook application, set this property as a default database form. By default, the form is not stored in the document, automatic refreshing is enabled, and document signing is disabled.
- **Conflict handling.** Used to specify how to handle any conflicts. In this application, set this property to Do not Create Conflicts to prevent the existence of two documents with different contents for the same policy or procedure.
- **Header.** Used to display all the fields belonging to the structural details, such as part and chapter of the document.
- **Form access rights.** Used to specify the rights for the application. The content available in the handbook application should be available for everyone. Therefore, set the Read access to all readers and above. However, the right to create documents using this form is restricted to the ACL role ContentAuthors.

Take a look at the fields used in this form along with their data types as listed in Table 12.1.

Table 12.1 Fields Used in the HandBook Form

Field Name	Data Type	Explanation
PartNumber	Combobox, Editable	This field is used to select the part number for choices. This is a mandatory field.
PartTitle	Text, Computed	This field is programmatically set when the part number is selected.

(continues)

Table 12.1 Continued

Field Name	Data Type	Explanation
ChapterNumber	Combobox, Editable	This field can either be selected from the existing list or a new chapter number can be entered. This is also a mandatory field.
ChapterTitle	Text, Editable	This field, a mandatory field, is programmatically set when the chapter number is selected.
SectionTitle	Text, Editable	This is a mandatory field used to enter the section title.
Body	RichText, Editable	This is an optional field used to capture the content of the document.
Attachments	RichTextLite, Editable	This is used to store attachments, if any.
VersionNumber	Text, ComputedWhenComposed	This is used to track the version number of the document. When a new document is created, this will have 1 as its default value. Afterwards, whenever Create new option is selected, this number will be incremented by one.
DraftMode	Text, ComputedWhenComposed	This field is set to Draft Mode when the document is saved as a draft. When published, the value is set to null.
DocumentReaders	Readers, ComputedWhenComposed	This field controls who can read the document at present and is used to implement the publishing feature.
Revised	Text,ComputedWhenComposed	This is used to implement the revision mechanism.
PageNumbers	Number,Editable	This is a multivalued field used to map the page numbers of the hard copy format.

The HandBook form contains the following actions:

- **Close.** Closes the document while in read mode.
- **Update.** Changes the mode of the document to edit and should be available only for content authors.
- **Save As Draft.** Saves the document in the draft mode. If clicked, this action sets the value of the DraftMode field on the form to Draft. In addition, the Readers field is set to ContentAuthors. Therefore, this action makes the document accessible only to content authors. This action is available only if the document is in edit mode.
- **Publish.** Makes the document available in the TableOfContents view for all users. If clicked, this action sets the DraftMode and Readers field to null. This action is available only for content authors.
- **Make New Version.** Creates a new version of the existing document. This action is available only for content authors.
- **Delete.** Marks the document for deletion. This action is available only to content authors.

Views

You can segregate views used in the application as follows:

- Views visible to the end user as part of the UI
- Internal views used for programming

There are three views used as part of the UI:

- **TableOfContents.** This view is used to list all the documents. This is the default view for the database and opens in the collapsed form. When opened, the focus is set to the last opened document, which allows the user to quickly locate the last read document. All the documents, except the revised or draft documents, are listed in the TableOfContents view. This view contains the following columns:
  - **Part.** This is a categorized column used to display the part number and part title.
  - **Chapter.** This is also a categorized column used to display the chapter number followed by the chapter title.
  - **Section.** This column is used to display the section title.

- **DraftDocuments.** This view is similar to the TableOfContents view, except for its selection formula. This view lists only those documents that are in draft mode. Only content authors can access this view.
- **VersionTracking.** This view lists all the revised documents. The documents that are revised are knocked out from the TableOfContents view. The VersionTracking view is very similar to the TableOfContents view, but version numbers are also listed.

Folder

The handbook application uses only one folder named MyReferences. Users can keep the documents they refer to frequently in this folder. The layout of this folder is the same as that of the TableOfContents view. To help users remove documents from this folder, an action `Remove Documents` is also provided.

Outline

The handbook application contains an outline named MainMenu for navigation. This outline provides the following links:

- **New Document.** Opens the HandBook form for creating new content documents
- **Table Of Content.** Opens the TableOfContents view
- **Old Versions.** Opens the VersionTracking view
- **Draft Documents.** Opens the DraftDocuments view
- **My References.** Opens the MyReferences folder

Page

The MainMenu outline must be embedded in a page to be used. For this purpose, the application uses only one page, named Outline page.

Frameset

The application uses a frameset named MainFrameset. When the application is started, this frameset will be launched first. The frameset contains the following two frames:

- **Left.** This frame appears to the left of the frameset and displays the page named OutlinePage, which contains the main navigation outline. The default target of this frame is set to the right frame.
- **Right.** This frame appears to the right of the frameset and displays the elements that are opened using the links in outline. It displays the TableOfContents view as the default content.

Developing the Application

In this section, you will perform the steps to create the employee handbook application. In the first phase, the general framework of the application will be created, followed by phase two, which will cover the steps to refine the UI of the application.

It is a good idea to create your first application on your local computer. After testing the application, you can deploy it on the server.

Phase I: Developing the Basic Framework

This section describes how to create the database and its various design elements.

Creating a Blank Database

Create a blank database on your local disk drive. Ensure that you select Blank in the Specify Template for New Database section. Specify the title as Employee Handbook and the file name as EmployeeHandbook.nsf.

Setting the ACL and the Role

The current ACL settings are sufficient for the application. However, you need to add a role, ContentAuthors, to the ACL. To do so, perform the following the steps:

1. Open the database ACL window.
2. Click the Roles tab.
3. Click the Add button. Enter ContentAuthors in the pop-up window, and click OK.
4. Enable the role for yourself by selecting your name and then the role.

Next, to make some of the formulas work on the local copy of the database, you need to enforce consistent ACL. To do this, perform the following steps:

1. In the database ACL window, click the Advanced tab.
2. Check the Enforce a consistent Access Control List across all replicas option.
3. Click OK to close the window.

Creating the Form

Open the database in the Domino Designer client. If the work pane for forms does not appear, click the Forms button in the Design pane. In the Form work pane, click the New Form button to create a new form. The Form designer opens in the work pane. Next, set the form properties. To do so, choose Design/Form Properties. Set the form properties as specified in Table 12.2.

Table 12.2 Form Properties

Property	Value
Name	HandBook
Type	Document
Include in menu	Checked, select Create menu in the drop-down down list
Include in Search Builder	Checked
Include in Print	Checked
Versions	None
Default Database Form	Checked
Conflict Handling	Do Not Create Conflicts

Clear the rest of the properties in this section of the form properties. Now the form properties box should like Figure 12.1.

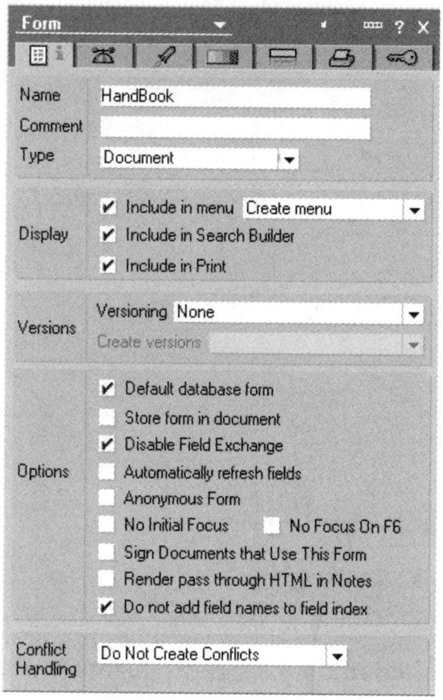

FIGURE 12.1 *Basic form properties*

To add a header to the HandBook form, perform the following steps:

1. Click the Header tab and check the Add Header to Form option. A line that looks like a horizontal ruler appears on the top of the form.
2. Specify the size as Fit to Content.
3. Specify scrolling as Yes.
4. Specify the border width as 1.

To specify the Form Access List, perform the following steps:

1. Select the Security tab in the form properties box (the one with the golden key).
2. In the section Default read access for documents created with this form, ensure that All readers and above is checked. Now clear All authors and above in the section Who can create documents with this form. This enables the list window.
3. Scroll down and select only the ACL role [ContentAuthors]. The form properties box appears, as shown in Figure 12.2.

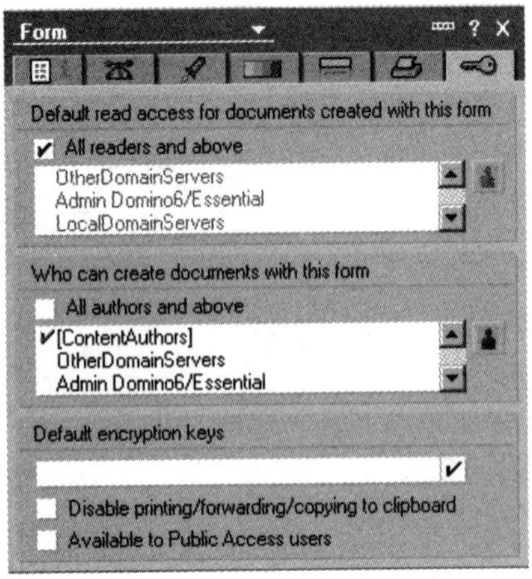

FIGURE 12.2 *Form access list properties*

Laying Out Fields

In this section, you'll lay out the fields listed in the Design Elements section. It is a good idea to create the field labels along with the fields so that users can identify the fields. To lay out the fields, perform the following steps:

1. Create a blank space by pressing the spacebar, and then press the Enter key to bring the cursor to the next line. It is a good practice to create text as the first element, even if it's a blank space.
2. Position your cursor in the work pane and type **Part Number**, the label for the field.
3. Leave a space to the right of the label, and keeping the cursor there, choose Create/Field. A field is inserted at the current cursor position and the field property box appears.
4. On the Basic tab, which is the first tab of the property box, enter the name of the field as PartNumber. Select Type as Combobox from the drop-down list. Select Editable from the other drop-down list. The field property box should look like Figure 12.3.

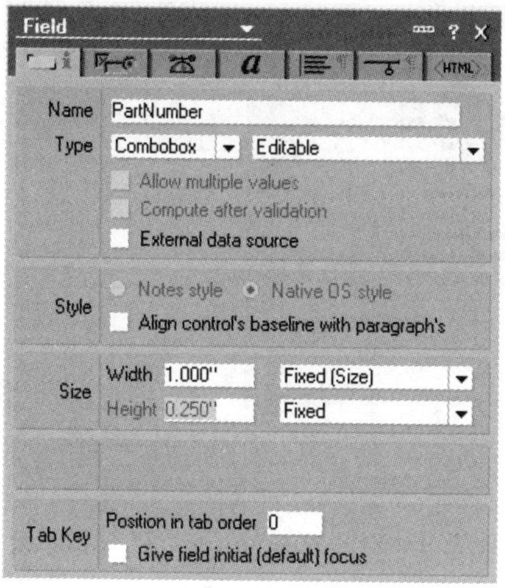

FIGURE 12.3 *Properties for PartNumber*

Close the field property box and perform the following steps to create the Part-Title field:

1. Position the cursor to next line.
2. Type the field label **Part Title** for the next field.
3. Leaving a space after the label, choose Create/Field. The field property box appears again.
4. Enter the details for the second field, specify the name as PartTitle, and select Text and Computed for field type from the drop-down list.
5. Enter the value for the field as PartTitle. The property box appears, as shown in Figure 12.4.

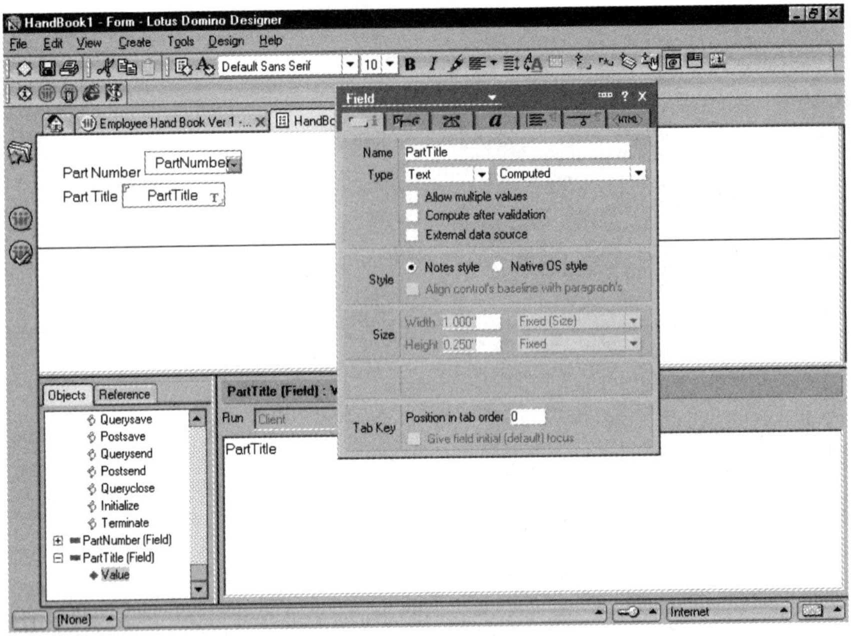

FIGURE 12.4 *Field properties for Part Title*

Repeat the steps for entering the values for the rest of the fields except the Body and Attachments fields. Ensure that you lay out all the fields and labels in the header area of the form.

Enter 1 as the value for the field VersionNumber. For the field ChapterNumber, in the Options sections in the second tab of the property box, check the Allow values not in list option and clear the rest of the check boxes. For the field PageNumbers, make sure that you check the Allow multiple values option. Now the HandBook form should look like Figure 12.5.

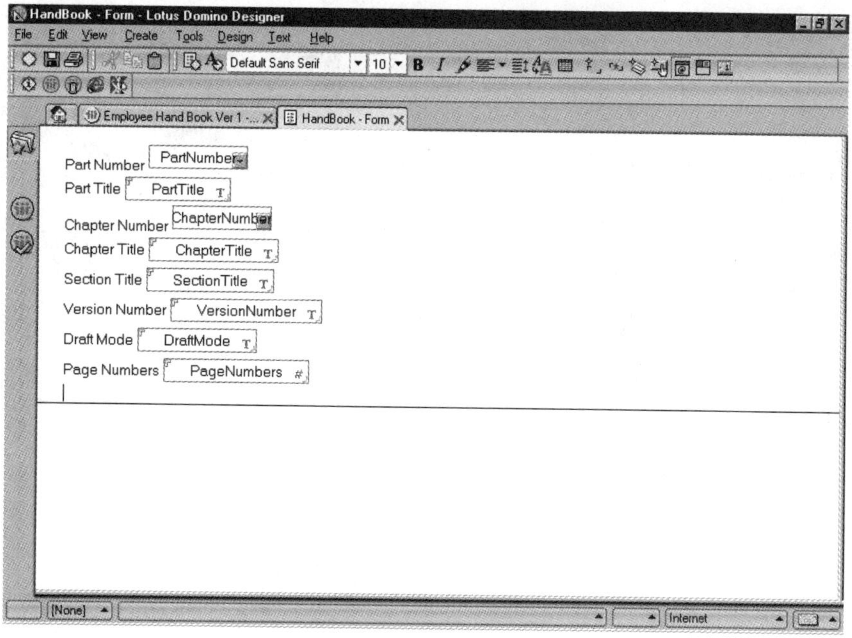

FIGURE 12.5 *Form with header fields*

Save the form, and place the cursor below the header section of the form to continue with the layout of rest of the fields.

1. Lay out the field Body, selecting the type as RichText, Editable.
2. Lay out the field Attachments below the Body field, selecting the type as RichTextLite, Editable.
3. Lay out the field Revised below the Attachments field and select type as Text, Computed when Composed. Enter "No" (note that No is in quotes) as the value. You need not enter a label for this field, because it is a field used for programming.
4. Lay out the field DocumentReaders next to the Revised field, and select type as Readers, Computed when Composed. Specify its value as DocumentReaders.

The complete form with all the fields is shown in Figure 12.6.

To preview the form, choose Design/Preview In Notes. When previewing, the form opens to compose a new document in the Notes client, as shown in Figure 12.7.

Perform the following steps to improve the look of the form:

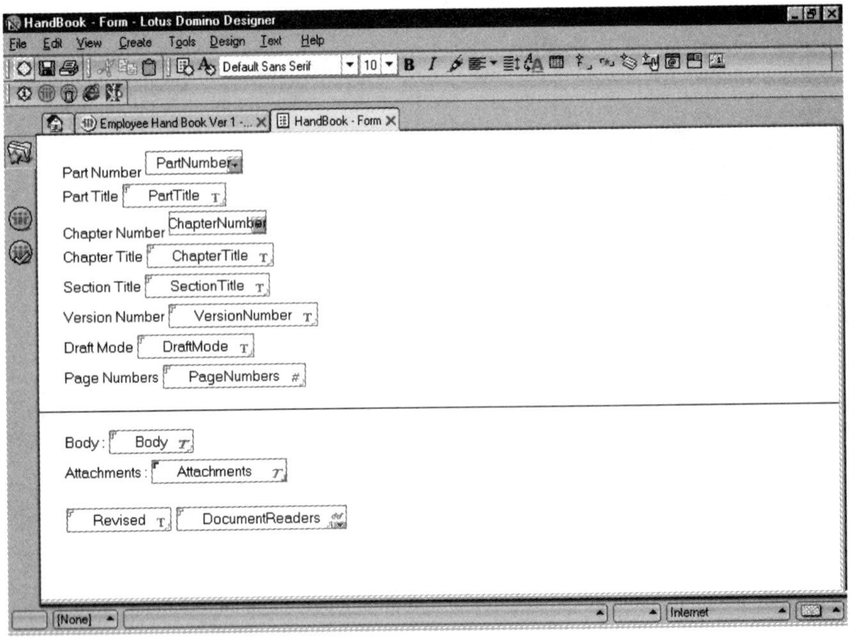

FIGURE 12.6 *The HandBook form with all the fields*

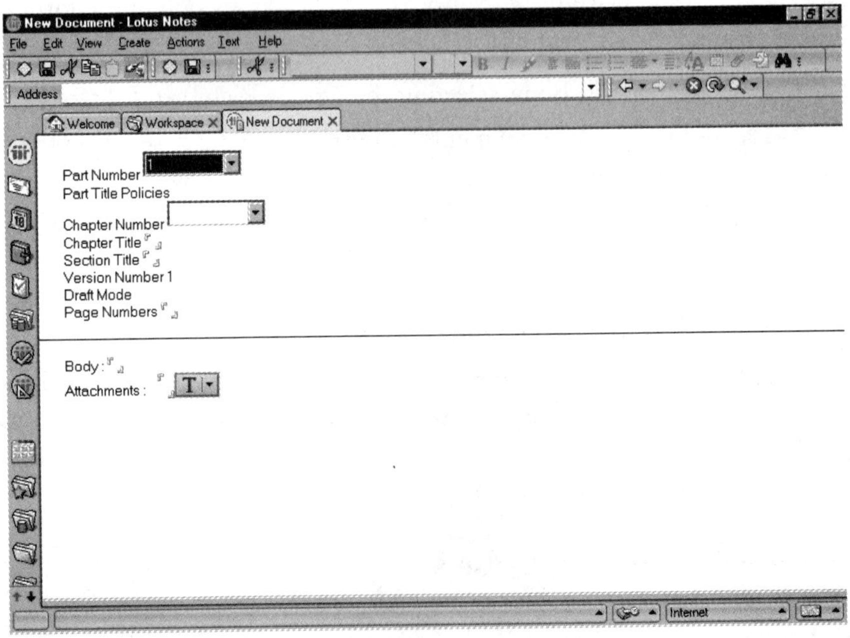

FIGURE 12.7 *Preview of the HandBook form in Notes client*

1. In Domino Designer, place the cursor to the left of the label Part Number and press Enter. Now position the cursor at the start of the empty space you created.
2. Choose Create/Table to open the Create Table dialog box. Enter the number of rows as 8 and number of columns as 2. Specify the table width as Fit with margins and table type as Create basic table (this is the default selection). Click OK to create the table. Your form should now look like Figure 12.8.

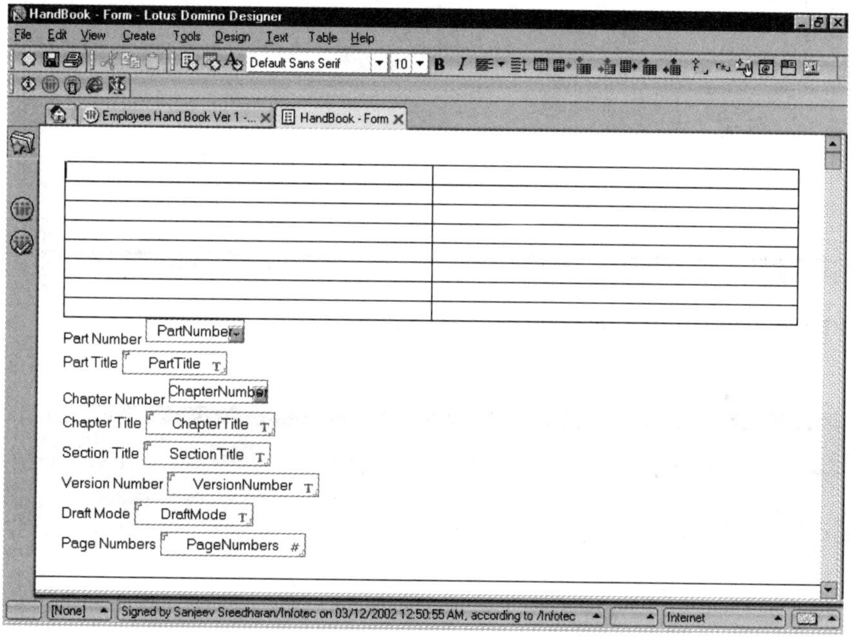

FIGURE 12.8 *The HandBook form with the table*

3. Cut and paste the field labels in the first column and its corresponding fields in the second column of the table. Complete this for all the fields in the form header region. At the end of this step, your form should look like Figure 12.9.

To reduce the space between field labels and fields, adjust the table column width of labels using the ruler. If the ruler is not available, choose View/View Ruler to turn on the ruler. Your form should now look like Figure 12.10.

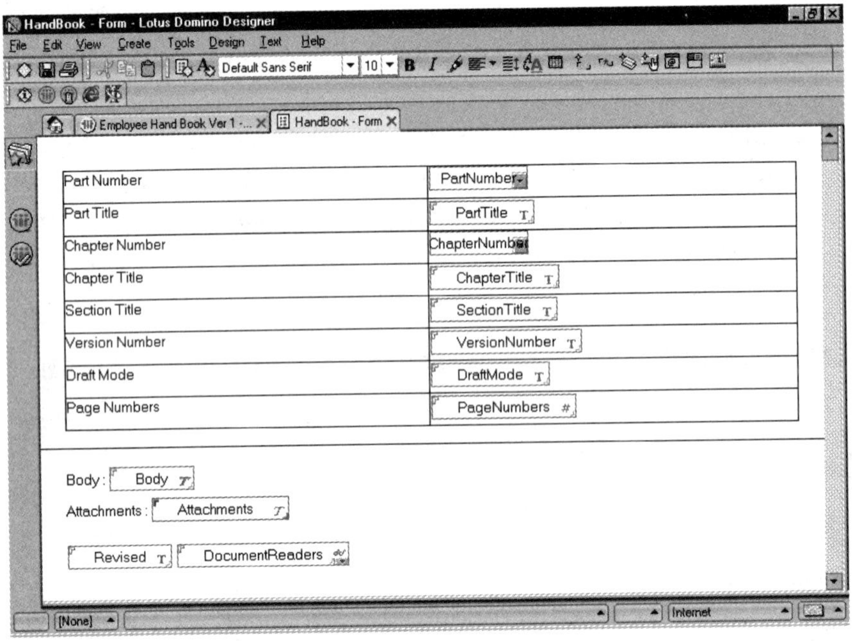

FIGURE 12.9 *The HandBook form with the fields in the table*

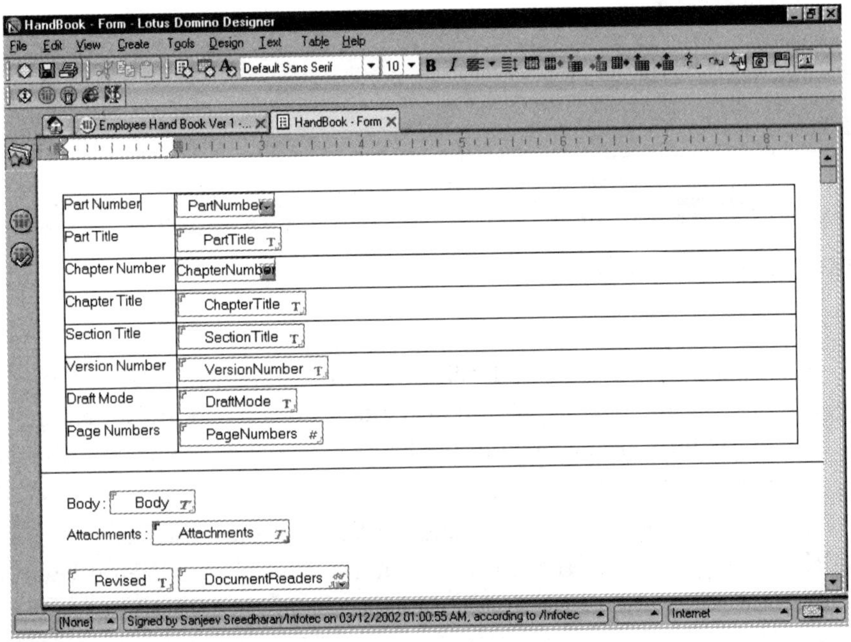

FIGURE 12.10 *The HandBook form with table width adjusted*

Set the scrolling property of the form header. Choose Design/Form Properties. Click the header property tab and set the Scrolling option as Auto.

Save your form now and preview it in Notes client.

Setting Formulas for Fields

To further refine the functioning of the form, you need to associate formulas with form fields. In Domino Designer, perform the following steps:

1. Enter the select list value for PartNumber field. Double-click the PartNumber field to open the property box. Select the second tab. In the Choices drop-down list, select Enter choice one per line. Enter select options for the field as 1 to 5 in different lines. In the options, check Refresh field on keyword change and clear the rest of the check boxes. The property box should look like Figure 12.11.

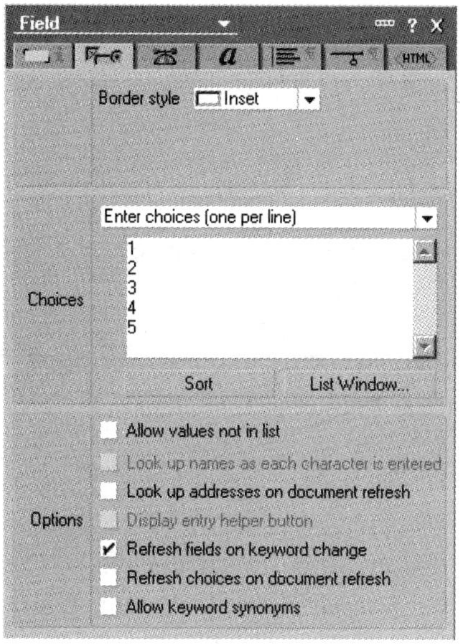

FIGURE 12.11 *PartNumber field properties*

2. Now enter the default value for the PartNumber field as 1. Note the value is listed inside quotes because it is a text value.
3. Set the formula for the PartTitle field. Enter the following formula:

```
PartTitleList := "Policies" : "Procedures" : "Guidelines" :
 "Statutory Regulations" : "Forms To Be Used";
PartTitleList[@TextToNumber(PartNumber)]
```

The first line of the preceding formula creates a text list, which contains the various permissible values for the part title, and assign that list to the temporary variable `PartTitleList`. The second line returns the nth value of this list as the value for the field. The index is formed by the current value of the PartNumber field being selected. The value of the PartNumber field is converted to the type number from text type, because the value expected for the index is number type.

PartTitle is a computed field; therefore, its value is computed according to the formula specified whenever the form is refreshed. As a result, when the user selects a part number, the field PartTitleList is evaluated as specified by the formula. When the part number changes, the part title corresponding to that part number is automatically updated.

Setting the Windows Title Formula

To set the Windows Title formula, perform the following steps:

1. Click anywhere on the form.
2. In the Objects pane, select HandBook(Form), and click Window Title.
3. In the Programmer's pane, enter the following formula:

```
@If(@IsNewDoc ; "New Document"; "Part " + PartNumber +
" - Chapter " + ChapterNumber
```

The `@if` statement checks whether the document currently opened is a new document. If it's a new document, it returns the value New Document. If an existing document is opened, the formula returns the value, which is formed by concatenating the values of the PartNumber and Chapter fields along with their corresponding labels. The value returned by the formula is displayed as the title for the window in which the document is open.

Creating Actions

To make the Action pane visible, choose View/Action Pane. To create your first action, perform the following steps:

1. Choose Create/Action/Action to open the action property box.
2. Enter the name of the action as Close.
3. Select type as Button from the drop-down list. Select Include in Action bar and Include in Action menu. Deselect the options Only show icon in Action bar and Right align action control. The action property box should look like Figure 12.12.

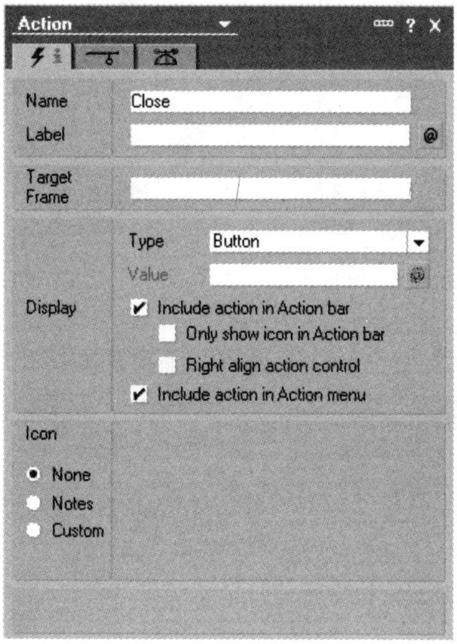

FIGURE 12.12 *The Close action properties*

4. Repeat steps 1 to 3 for creating the following actions: Update, Save As Draft, Publish, Make New Version, and Delete. After adding all the actions, your Action pane will look like Figure 12.13.

Next, preview the form to check how it appears in Notes client. The form should look like Figure 12.14.

However, if you click any of these buttons, nothing happens. You need to assign formulas to these actions.

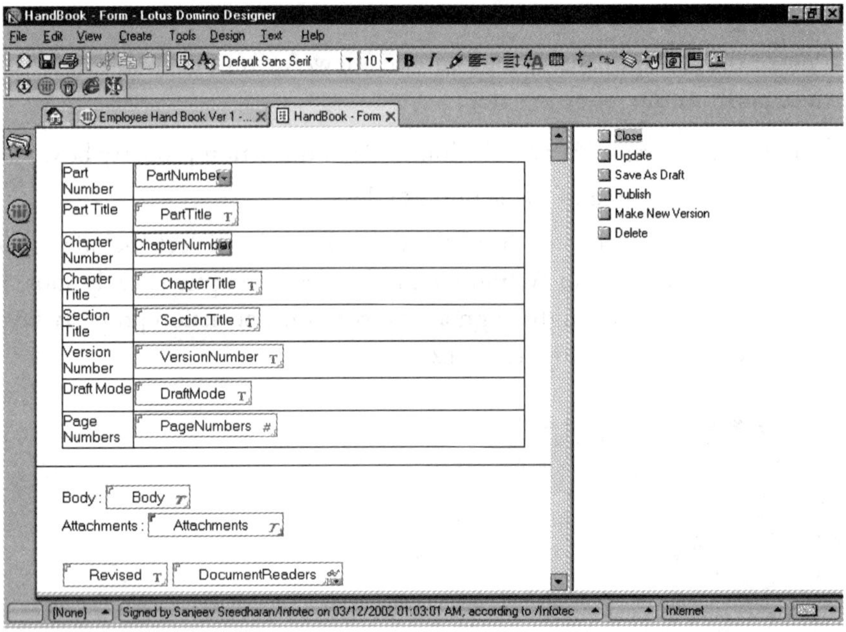

FIGURE 12.13 *Action pane listing all the actions*

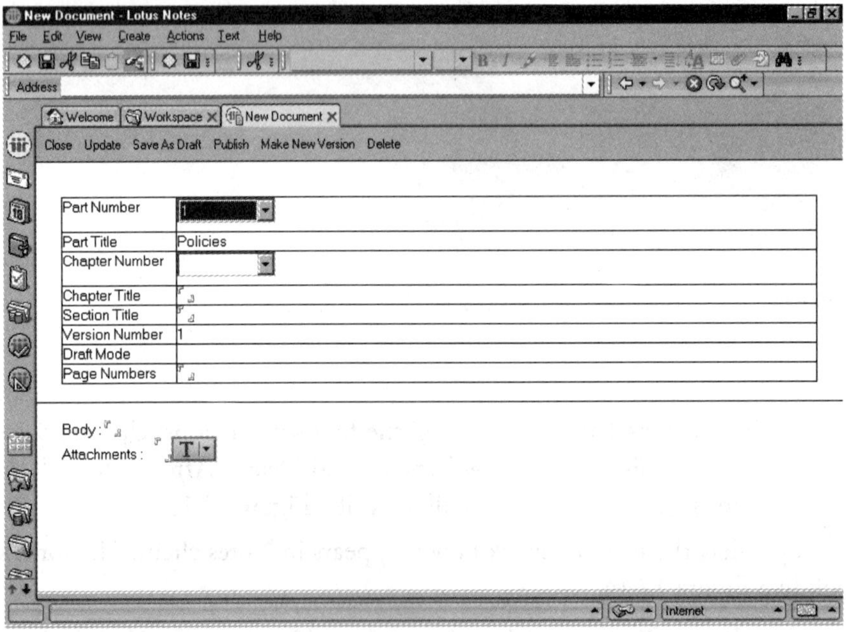

FIGURE 12.14 *Preview of the HandBook form with actions*

Assigning Formulas to Actions

In this section, you'll add the required formula to each action button to provide the required functionality.

Formula for the Close Action

To assign a formula to the Close action, perform the following steps:

1. Select the Close action in the Action pane.
2. In the Programmer's pane, from the two drop-down lists for the Run option, select Client in the first drop-down list and Formula in the second drop-down list.
3. Type the following formula in the formula window:

```
@Command([FileCloseWindow])
```

4. Click the Accept button to accept your formula. If you make a typographical error here, Notes will display an error.

Formula for the Update Action

To assign a formula to the Update action, perform the following steps:

1. In the Action pane, select the Update action.
2. In the Programmer's pane, from the two drop-down lists for the Run option, select Client in the first drop-down list and Formula in the second drop-down list.
3. Type the following formula in the formula window:

```
@Command([EditDocument])
```

4. To set the Hide When formula, double-click the action in the Action pane. In the action property box, click the second tab. Under the section Hide action when document is, check the options Previewed for editing and Opened for editing. Also check Hide action if formula is true, and clear the rest of the check boxes. Type the following formula in the formula window:

```
@UserRoles != "[ContentAuthors]"
```

   The preceding formula checks whether the current user is enabled for the ACL role to hide this action. If you are creating more than one role in any application use the `@IsMember` function instead of logical operators. The property box now looks like Figure 12.15.

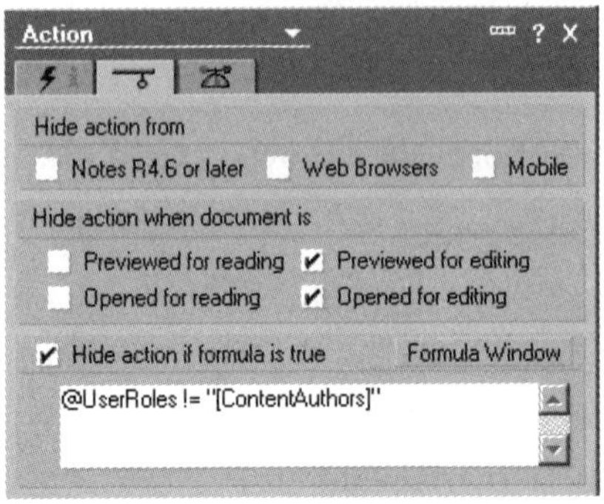

FIGURE 12.15 *Update action properties*

CAUTION

You need to be very careful when specifying the Hide When conditions. If you enable any other check boxes, you will not see the action button when it is required to show up.

Formula for the Save As Draft Action

To assign a formula to the Save As Draft action, perform the following steps:

1. For the Save As Draft action, specify the following formula in the formula window:

```
@SetField("DraftMode";"Draft");
@SetField("DocumentReaders";"[ContentAuthors]");
@PostedCommand([FileSave]);
@Command([FileCloseWindow])
```

2. To set the Hide When formula, under the section Hide action when document is, check Previewed for reading and Opened for reading, and clear the rest of the check boxes. The property box will appear, as shown in Figure 12.16.

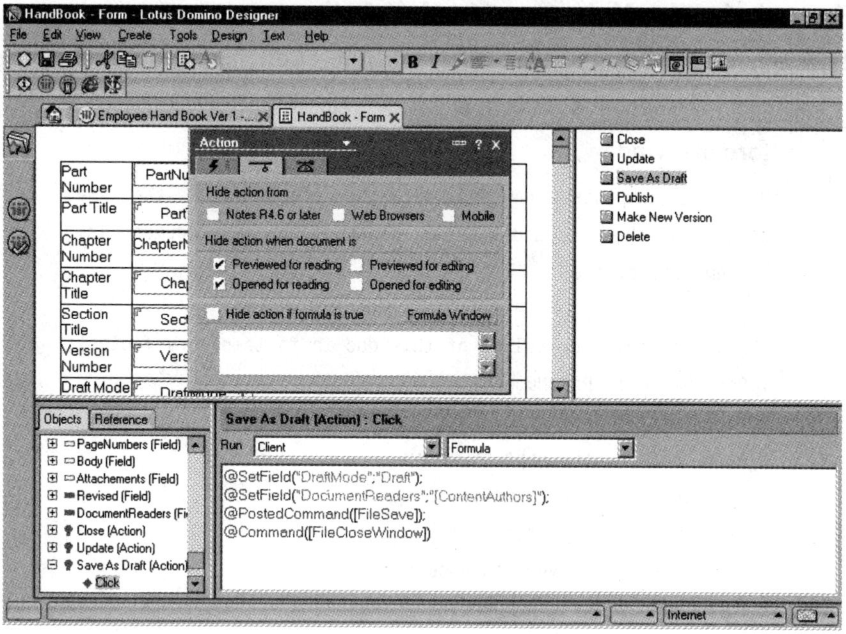

FIGURE 12.16 *Save As Draft action properties*

Formula for the Publish Action

To assign a formula to the Publish action, perform the following steps:

1. For the Publish action, enter the following formula in the formula window:

```
@SetField("DraftMode";"");
@SetField("DocumentReaders";"");
@PostedCommand([FileSave]);
@Command([FileCloseWindow])
```

2. To set the Hide When formula, under the section Hide action when document is, check the Previewed for reading and Opened for reading check boxes, and clear the rest of the check boxes.

Formula for the Make New Version Action

To assign a formula to the Make New Version action, perform the following steps:

1. For the Make New Version action, specify the following formula in the formula window:

```
REM {This composes a new doc, sets the default values the same
as that of this doc and Version number of the new document is
incremented by one};

REM {First hold the values of this doc in to temporary fields};
t_PartNumber := PartNumber;
t_PartTitle := PartTitle;
t_ChapterNumber := ChapterNumber;
t_ChapterTitle := ChapterTitle;
t_SectionTitle := SectionTitle;
t_VersionNumber := VersionNumber;
t_PageNumbers := PageNumbers;

REM {Set the Revision status to revised
for this document and save this doc};
@SetField("Revised";"Yes");
@PostedCommand([FileSave]);
REM {Create the new Document Now
and put a link to old document};
@Command([ComposeWithReference]; "" ; "HandBook" ; 1);
REM {Switch the formula context to the new document};
@UpdateFormulaContext;

REM {Set the default values
from the temporary holding fields};
@SetField("PartNumber";t_PartNumber);
@SetField("PartTitle";t_PartTitle);
@SetField("ChapterNumber";t_ChapterNumber);
@SetField("ChapterTitle";t_ChapterTitle);
@SetField("SectionTitle";t_SectionTitle);
@SetField("PageNumbers";t_PageNumbers);
```

```
REM {Increment the version number for the new document};
NewVersionNumber := @TextToNumber(t_VersionNumber) + 1;
@SetField("VersionNumber";@Text(NewVersionNumber));
REM {Write help text for the link};
@Command([EditGotoField];"Body");
@Command([EditInsertText];
"Click this link to access old version of this document -->")
```

2. To set the Hide When formula, under the section Hide action when document is, check Previewed for reading and Opened for reading check boxes, and clear the rest of the check boxes.

Formula for the Delete Action

To assign a formula to the Delete action, perform the following steps:

1. For the Delete action, specify the following formula in the formula window:

   ```
   @Command([EditClear])
   ```

2. To set the Hide When formula, under the section Hide action when document is, check Hide action if formula is true, and clear the rest of the check boxes. Type the following formula in the formula window:

   ```
   @UserRoles != "[ContentAuthors]"
   ```

Now preview the form in Notes client. Fill up the fields and test the action buttons. Change your user ID to another and see how the Hide When formulas are working based on users. Note that the users who are not in the ACL role ContentAuthors can see neither the form listed in the Create menu nor the action buttons Update and Delete. As a result, a normal user can only read a document. In addition, observe the behavior when the document is saved as a draft. When in draft mode, only those users who are in the ContentAuthors role can see the document.

Writing Field Translation and Validations

In the current form, content authors may save the document without entering the proper structural information for the document. To avoid this, you need to specify translation and validation formulas for fields.

Open the HandBook form in Domino Designer and perform the following steps:

1. Select the ChapterTitle field in the Objects pane.
2. Click Input Translation in the Objects pane for the ChapterTitle field.
3. Enter the following formula in the formula pane.

```
@Trim(@ThisValue)
```

4. Click Input validation in the Objects pane for the ChapterTitle field.
5. Type the following validation formula in the formula pane:

```
message := "You should enter value for  " + @ThisName;
@If(@ThisValue = "" ; @Failure(message);@Success)
```

Repeat steps 1 through 5 for the fields SectionTitle and PageNumbers. You may copy and paste the magic formula from the ChapterTitle field to save typing. `@ThisName` returns the name of the current field and `@ThisValue` returns the value of the current field. Using these two functions, you can program more generically rather than using the field names in formulas.

Preview the form again, and test the validations.

Creating Views

Open your database in Domino Designer and click Views in the Design pane. This opens the View designer in the work pane to the right.

Creating the TableOfContents View

Creating the TableOfContents view consists of the following steps:

- Creating the view
- Setting view properties
- Creating columns for the view

Creating the View

To create the TableOfContents view, perform the following steps:

1. Click the New View button in the work pane to open the Create View dialog box.
2. Enter TableOfContents in the View Name field.

3. From the View type drop-down list, select Shared.
4. In the Select the location for the new view list box, select View.
5. Check Select by formula.
6. In the Selection Conditions box, enter the following formula:

```
SELECT Form = "HandBook" & DraftMode !="Draft" & Revised != "Yes"
```

7. Click the Accept button to accept changes. The Create View dialog box should look like Figure 12.17.

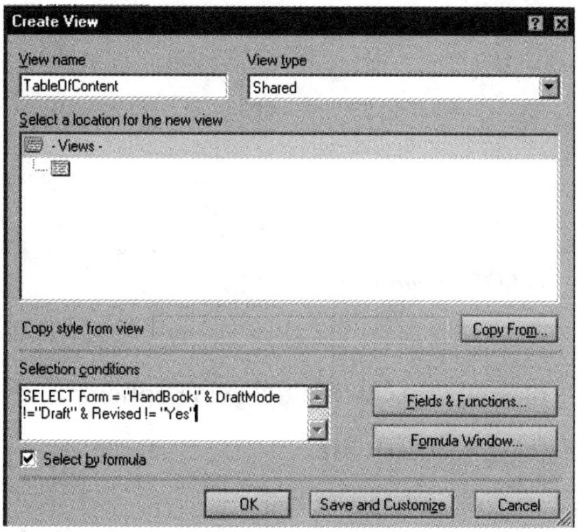

FIGURE 12.17 *The Create View dialog box for the TableOfContents view*

8. Click the Save and Customize button. This will open the view in the work pane.

Setting View Properties

If the view property property box is not displayed, choose Design/View Properties. To set the view properties, verify that Standard Outline is selected in the Basics tab of the view properties property box. Next click the Information tab and check the following options:

- Default when database is first opened
- Default design for new folders and views

- Collapse all when database is first opened
- Disable rest of the check boxes
- Select Go to last opened document, from the On Open pull-down list
- Select Refresh display from top row, from the On Refresh pull-down list

The view property box should look like the Figure 12.18.

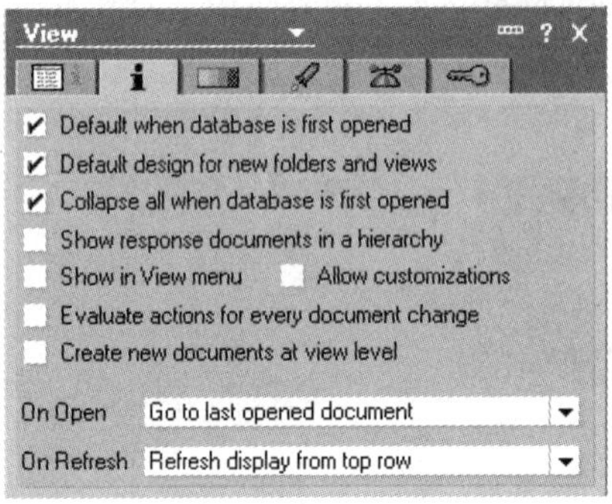

FIGURE 12.18 *Properties for the TableOfContents view*

In the Row section of the Display tab, specify the following options:

- Select 9 from the Height drop-down list.
- Select 11/4 from the Spacing drop-down list.
- Check Shrink rows to content.
- Against the Unread, pick up your favorite color from the color palette.

The view property property box should now look like Figure 12.19.

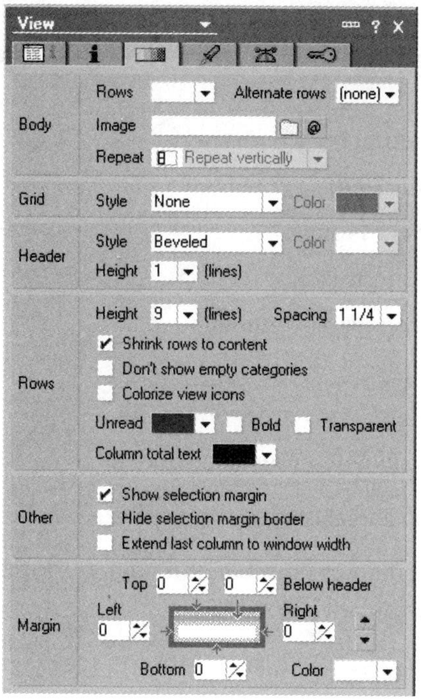

FIGURE 12.19 *Style properties for the TableOfContents view*

Now, click the Advanced tab and select Unread Documents Only from the Unread marks drop-down list.

Creating Columns for the View

To create the first column, which lists the Part Number and Part Title, perform the following steps:

1. Choose Create/Insert New Column.
2. Select the column by clicking the header.
3. In the column value window, select Formula against Display.
4. Enter the formula given below in the formula window:

```
"Part " + PartNumber + " - " + PartTitle
```

5. To set the column properties, double-click on the column header to open the column properties property box. Click the Sorting tab, and set the following options:

   In the Sort option, select Ascending.

   In the Type option, select Categorized.

   In the Totals drop-down list, select None.

   Clear the rest of the check boxes in this tab.

6. Click the Basic tab and set the following options:

   Enter `1` in the Width text box.

   Select None in the Multi-value separator drop-down list.

   Check the check box Show twistie when row is expandable.

Clear the rest of the check boxes in this tab and close the property box. Save the view.

Similarly, create the second column for Chapter Number and Chapter Title fields. Specify the following formula in the formula window:

```
"Chapter " + ChapterNumber + " - " + ChapterTitle
```

Next, create the third column for the Section Title field. Specify the following formula in the formula window:

```
SectionTitle
```

Set the column properties by using the Basic and Sorting tabs, as specified in Table 12.3.

Table 12.3 Column Properties for Section

Property	Value
Sort	None
Type	Standard
Totals	None
Title	Section
Width	25
Multi-value separator	None
Resizable	Checked

Create the fourth column for Page Number. Specify the following formula in the formula window:

PageNumber

Set the column properties by using the Basic and Sorting tabs as specified in Table 12.4.

Table 12.4 Column Properties for Page Number

Property	Value
Sort	None
Type	Standard
Totals	None
Title	Pages
Width	10
Multi-value separator	Comma
Resizable	Checked

The preview of the TableOfContents view in Notes client, in its fully expanded form, is shown in Figure 12.20.

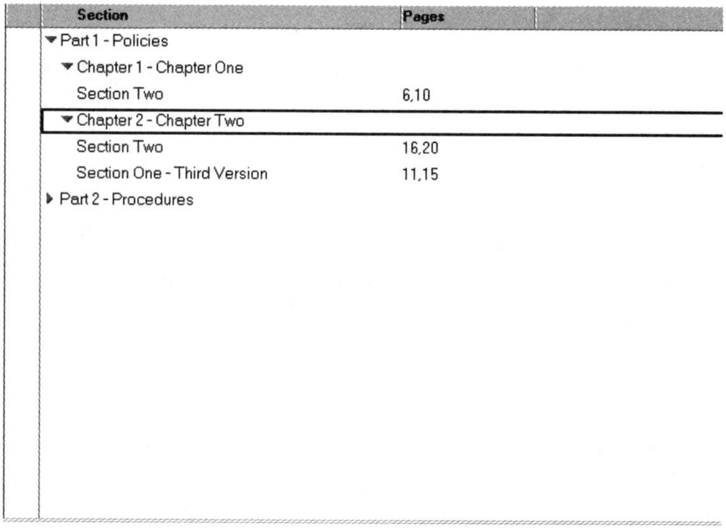

FIGURE 12.20 *Preview of the TableOfContents view*

Creating the DraftDocuments View

This view is similar to the TableOfContents view. Therefore, instead of going through the laborious steps of creating a new view again, use the shortcut method. Perform the following steps:

1. Click the New View button to open the Create View dialog box.
2. Specify the view name as DraftDocuments.
3. Specify the view type as Shared.
4. Specify the view location as View.
5. Click the Copy From button.
6. Select TableOfContents from the list box and click OK.
7. Check Select by formula.
8. In the Selection Conditions box replace the formula with the following:

   ```
   SELECT Form = "HandBook" & DraftMode ="Draft"
   ```

9. Click the Accept button.
10. Click the Save and Customize button.

Preview the view. If you have any documents that were saved as a draft, the documents will appear in this view. Notice that the documents that appear in this view will not appear in the TableOfContents view and vice versa.

Creating the VersionTracking View

Perform the steps listed in the following sections to create the VersionTracking view.

Create the View

Create the VersionTracking view by copying the existing TableOfContents or DraftDocuments view. Then modify the formula in the Selection Condition box to the following:

```
SELECT Form = "HandBook" & Revised = "Yes"
```

Customize the View

This view contains a column, which lists the version number.

Create a column named Version as the last column and set its properties as specified in Table 12.5.

Table 12.5 Properties for the Version Column

Property	Value
Title	Enter Version
Width	5
Multi-value separator	None
Resizable	Checked

Clear the rest of the check boxes on this tab and close the property box. Save the view. Preview the view. If you have created new versions for any documents by clicking the Make New Version action button, the old version documents should appear here.

Creating Folders

Open the Employee Handbook database in Domino Designer, and click Folders in the Design pane. The work pane switches to Folder designer.

Creating the MyReferences Folder

To create the MyReferences folder, perform the following steps:

1. Click the New Folder button in the work pane to open the Create Folder dialog box.
2. Enter MyReferences in the Folder Name field.
3. Select Shared, Desktop private on first use from the Folder Type drop-down list.
4. Click the Copy From button. Select TableOfContents from the list box.
5. Click the Save and Customize button.

To test the working of this folder, open the Employee Handbook database in Notes client. Click the MyReferences folder in the left pane. This will create a private folder for you on your desktop locally. Now drag-and-drop documents into this folder from any view.

After the documents are dropped or moved into the folder, it is not easy to remove them from there. Therefore, you need to add a mechanism to remove the selected documents from the folder. To implement this, create an action as follows:

1. Open the Folder in Domino Designer and turn on the Action pane.
2. Choose Create/Action/Action.
3. Set the properties for the action. Set the name of the action as **Remove Documents**. Select the type of the action as Button.
4. In the Programmer's pane, from the two drop-down lists for the Run option, select Client in the first drop-down list and Formula in the second drop-down list.
5. Enter the following formula for the action:

   ```
   @Command([RemoveFromFolder])
   ```

6. Save the folder.

Creating Navigational Structure

To implement navigation for the employee handbook application, you'll use an outline, a page, and a frameset.

Creating the Outline

Open the Employee Handbook database in Domino Designer. In the Design pane, click Shared Code and then click Outlines. This will switch the work pane to Outline designer.

Perform the following steps to create the outline:

1. Click the New Outline button.
2. Choose Design/Outline Properties to open the outline property box.
3. Set the outline properties. Specify the name of the outline as **MainMenu**. Next, clear both the check boxes under Options.

To create outline entry for composing a new document, perform the following steps:

1. Click the New Entry button. The outline property box appears.
2. Enter **New Document** in the Label field.

3. Select Named Element from the Type drop-down list in the Content section. Another drop-down list appears to the right. Select Form from this drop-down list.
4. Click the folder icon to the right of the Value box. The Locate Object dialog box appears. Select the following items from the drop-down list:

   Form for Kind of object

   Current database for Database

   HandBook for Form
5. Click OK to return to the property box.
6. Enter Right in the Frame text box.
7. Retain the rest of the values as default values. Click the Hide When tab of the property box.
8. Check Hide outline entry if formula is true. Enter the following formula in the formula window:

```
@UserRoles != "[ContentAuthors]"
```

9. Close the property box to return to the work pane.

To create an outline entry for opening the TableOfContents view, perform the following steps:

1. Click the New Entry button.
2. In the property box, enter **Table Of Contents** in the Label text box.
3. Select Named Element from the Type drop-down list in the Content section. Another drop-down list appears to the right. Select View from this drop-down list.
4. Click the folder icon to the right of the Value box. In the Locate Object dialog box, select the following items from the drop-down list:

   View for Kind of object

   Current database for Database

   TableOfContents for view
5. Click OK to return to the property box.
6. Enter Right in the Frame value text box.
7. Retain the rest of the values as default values and close the property box to return to the work pane.

To create an outline entry for opening the VersionTracking view, repeat the steps given for the TableOfContents view. For this outline entry, select VersionTracking view in place of TableOfContents. Also modify the label to Old Versions.

To create an outline entry for opening the DraftDocuments view, repeat the steps given for the TableOfContents view. Select the DraftDocuments view in place of TableOfContents. Also change the outline entry label to Draft Documents. In addition, enter the following Hide When formula for this outline entry:

```
@UserRoles != "[ContentAuthors]"
```

To create an outline entry for opening the MyReferences folder, repeat the steps given for the TableOfContents view. This time, select Folder as the object type. Select the folder MyReferences in place of TableOfContents. Change the label to My References.

Creating a Page

Open the Employee Handbook database in Domino Designer and click Pages in the Design pane. Perform the following steps to create the page:

1. Click the New Page button.
2. Choose Design/Page Properties to open the property box. Set the name of the page as **OutlinePage**. Clear all the check boxes under the Options section.
3. Close the property box to return to the work pane.

Now insert the outline you created earlier in this page as follows:

1. Press Enter and leave one line space.
2. Choose Create/Embedded Element/Outline. From the pop-up list, choose MainMenu and click OK.
3. Right-click the embedded outline and select Outline Properties to open the property box. Set the properties in the Basic tab listed in Table 12.6.
4. Close the property box and save the page.

Table 12.6 Properties of the Embedded Outline

Property	Value
Name	MainMenu
Type	Flat Style, Vertical
Title Style	Hide
Target Frame	Right
Width	Fit to content
Height	Fit to content

The property box should look like Figure 12.21.

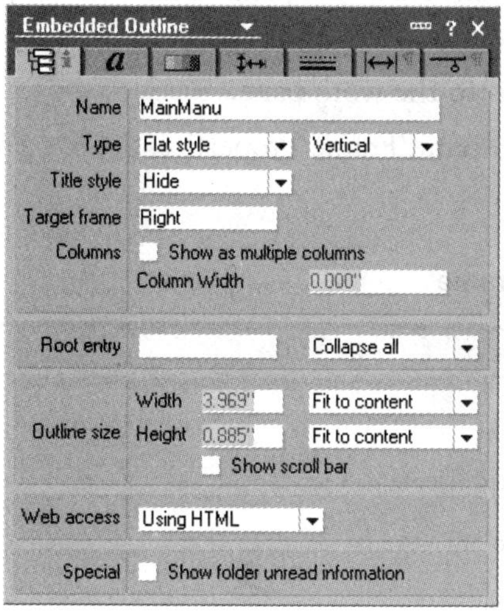

FIGURE 12.21 *Embedded Outline properties*

Creating the Frameset

Click Framesets in the Design pane. Perform the following steps to create the frameset:

1. Click the New Frameset button to open the Create New Frameset dialog box.
2. Select the first option under Arrangement and specify the number of frames as two. Click OK to create the frameset in the Frameset designer.

3. Choose Frame/Frameset Properties to open the property box.
4. Specify the name of the frameset as MainFrameset and close the property box to return to the work pane.
5. Select the left frame by clicking it. Choose Frame/Frame Properties. Set the following properties:

   Enter Left in the Name text box

   Select Named Element, Page from the Type drop-down list

   Select using folder icon or enter OutlinePage in the Value text box

   Enter Right in the Default target for links in this frame text box
6. Click the Frame Border tab of the property box and set the following properties:

   Clear the 3D Border check box.

   Clear Default against Border width check box, and enter 1 in the pixels value.
7. Close the property box to return to the work pane.
8. Select the right frame. Choose Frame/Frame Properties. Set the properties as specified in Table 12.7.

Table 12.7 Properties of the Right Frame

Property	Value
Name	Right
Type	Named Element, View
Value	TableOfContents
Show Action Bar	Enable
Show Header	Enable
Selection tracks mouse movement	Disable
Basic Simple appearance	Disable

Save the Frameset.

Applying the Navigational Structure

Perform the following steps to assign the navigational structure to the application.

1. Open the Employee Handbook database in Notes client.
2. Choose File/Database/Properties to open the database property box. Click the Launch tab.
3. In the When opened in Notes client drop-down list, select Open designated frameset.
4. In the Name drop-down list, select MainFrameset.
5. Close the property box. Close and reopen the database for the changes to take effect.

The application is now ready completely with all the functional features.

Phase II: Improving the User Interface

You probably would not like to roll out the application to users in its current form. This section will discuss how to improve the UI. Before you go ahead with the aesthetic aspects of the UI (*user interface*), create the mechanism for chapter number and title lookups.

Creating Chapter Title Selection Mechanism

A mechanism is required to provide the selection list for ChapterNumber field and to set the value of the ChapterTitle field based upon the selection of the Chapter Number. To implement this, you need to perform the following steps:

- Create lookup views
- Assign formulas to fields on the form

To create lookup views, perform the following steps:

1. Create a view named ChapterNumberLookUp with two columns. The first column is a sorted ascending and categorized column and displays the values from the PartNumber field. The second column is a sorted ascending column and displays the values from the ChapterNumber field.

2. Create another view named ChapterTitleLookUp. In the first column of this view, enter the following formula:

```
PartNumber +"#"+ChapterNumber
```

Make this column sorted ascending and categorized. In the second column, enter the value as ChapterTitle.

To assign formulas to the fields on the form, perform the following steps:

1. Double-click the field ChapterNumber to open the field property box.
2. Enter the following code in the choices formula window:

```
view := "ChapterNumberLookUp";
key := PartNumber;
@Unique(@Trim(@DbLookup( "" : "NoCache" ; ""; view ;
key ; 2 ; [FailSilent])))
```

3. Under Options in the second tab, check Refresh fields on keyword change and Refresh choices on document refresh. Close the property box.
4. Select the Input Translation event and enter the following formula:

```
view := "ChapterTitleLookUp";
key := PartNumber+"#"+ChapterNumber;
ChpTitle := @Unique(@Trim(@DbLookup( "" : "NoCache" ; ""; view ;
 key ; 2 ; [FailSilent])));
@If(ChapterTitle = ""; @SetField("ChapterTitle";ChpTitle);"");
REM {Keep the value of this field as the same};
ChapterNumber
```

5. Save the form.

Finishing Touches

For the search to work properly, make sure that you set up the Full Text Search for the database. Make sure to create the "Using Database" and "About Database" documents before you roll out the application.

Summary

In this chapter, you learned how to create a detailed design from the high-level design of a Notes application. You also learned to create the various design elements for the application based on the detailed specification.

PART III

Professional Project 2—Creating a Collaborative Application Using Notes

Project 2 Overview

In this project, you will create a Notes Discussion database, which is a collaborative application. A Discussion database allows people to share their thoughts and views using a common forum.

The Discussion database will allow people to start a discussion on any subject. Other users can contribute to the forum by posting responses to the main discussion topic. Users will also be able to create response to responses. Users will be able to create an interest profile which will keep the users informed using newsletters. All discussions will be presented in a tree structure for easy comprehension of the forum's structure.

While developing this application you will learn how to create document relationships in Notes applications. You will learn how to create a view in UI for presenting documents in a hierarchical manner that reflects the relationships between documents. You will also learn how to create an agent using LotusScript to generate and send newsletters in Notes applications. You will use the features of the `Newsletter` class available in LotusScript to implement the newsletter feature. You will learn how to perform search operations using LotusScript.

The application will be deployed in a distributed manner. The updating of distributed copies of the application will be achieved by using the Notes replication feature.

Chapter 13

Fundamentals of the Notes Collaborative Application

Domino provides a robust messaging facility, tightly integrated with tools to develop applications on a single platform. This enables you to develop and deploy secure, flexible, and scalable collaborative applications quickly and easily. Notes also provides a unified development framework to create applications for different target platforms. Deploying the same application for a range of clients, such as Notes clients, Mobile clients, and Web clients, enables you to maximize your target audience. You can use add-ons such as Lotus Sametime to provide real-time collaboration capability to your Notes applications.

This chapter covers the fundamentals of collaborative applications. It explains how a Discussion application fits into this framework. It also describes the development features of Notes that can be used to create a collaborative discussion application.

Basics of Collaborative Applications

Collaborative applications provide a framework for people to work together as a team. While transactional systems focus on data elements and associated processing, collaborative applications focus on connecting people and letting them sharing their thoughts and ideas. Because of this, these applications are considered complementary to each other.

While messaging achieves one-to-one communication, reference and broadcasting applications achieve one-to-many communication. Collaborative applications use the many-to-many model of communication.

Collaborative applications connect people separated by geography and time zones. Time convenience is a major advantage of these applications. Compared to other modes of communication—such as the telephone, where people have to respond immediately—collaborative applications provide a framework for people to respond at their own convenience. As a result, people tend to have better thought processes.

The application framework provides end users with services such as security, newsletter, archiving, and notification. Its also provides a UI for interacting with the application and acts as a repository. Figure 13.1 depicts the framework of a collaborative application.

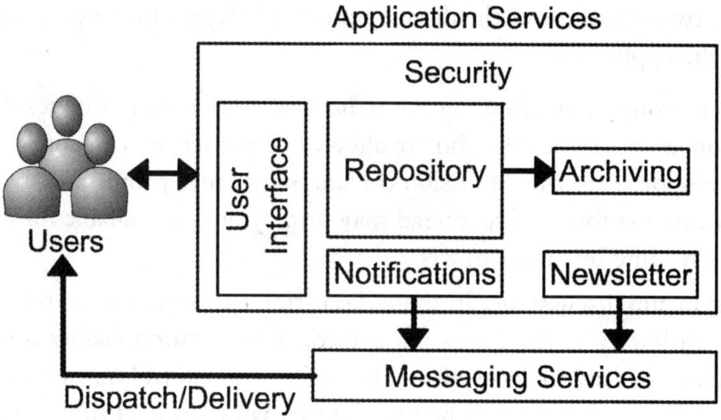

FIGURE 13.1 *Framework of a collaborative application*

Discussion forum and Team Room are examples of collaborative applications that are shipped along with Notes.

Uses of a Collaborative Application

These are some advantages of collaborative applications:

- They help people exchange thoughts and ideas and share mind space.
- These information sharing and collaboration tools are used for activities that require teamwork.
- They avoid day-to-day meetings by enabling discussions on issues and concerns among team members.
- They help to achieve better structuring for communication.
- They help in building a knowledge base.

Discussion Application as a Collaborative Application

A central repository is the heart of a discussion application. People can use it to store documents and contribute their ideas and thoughts. Other end users can access this central repository and post responses, which are also added to it. The main discussion document and its responses are called the *discussion thread.* For ease of use, they are grouped using categorization. Eventually, the entire discussion thread goes on to form a hierarchical tree.

There can be two variations of the discussion thread, depending upon the facility provided by the application.

- **Closed group discussions.** In these discussions, a person initiates the discussion, and only people who are allowed to participate can contribute their responses to the discussion thread. Sometimes people are invited to constitute the forum. The thread may or may not be available for viewing or reading by nonmembers.
- **Open forum discussions.** In these discussions, there are no restrictions on contributing to the discussion thread. A moderation facility is used to maintain the subject focus of the discussion and control unwanted language. The moderator may be the end user who initiated the discussion or another end user who will take on this responsibility. The moderator has the right to edit or remove any documents posted by other end users.

THE MESSAGING ENGINE

Invitations are often issued to inform people about the initiation of a discussion thread and invite them to participate in the discussion. For example, in closed group discussions, invitations are sent to people who constitute the forum.

The application uses a messaging engine to send these invitations. The messaging service also sends newsletters or notifications to end users when required.

Document Hierarchy in Notes

You can get the discussion thread to form a hierarchical tree by creating relationships among documents. In Notes, this is only a parent-child relationship between documents. Since it is not a data relationship as in relational databases, it is known as document hierarchy instead of data relationship. This hierarchical tree of documents is implemented using three different types of forms—document, response, and response-to-response—and a special type of view called *hierarchical view*.

Forms to Implement Document Hierarchy

The three form types mentioned above allow you to create documents that will have a parent-child relationship between them. Documents at a higher level in the tree are called *parent documents* and documents at lower levels are called *child* or *response documents*. To help build the tree structure, responses are divided into two levels, response documents and response-to-response documents. The relationship between response and response-to-response documents is also a parent-child one. Documents at the same level are called *siblings*.

Every child document, whether it is response or response-to-response, carries a reference or pointer to its parent. This reference is contained in a special field *$Ref*, which is added automatically to any response or response-to-response document. This field contains the UNID (*Universal ID*) of the parent document as its value. If you use this field as is, it forms a visual document link, which opens the parent document when clicked. The value of this special field $Ref can be used anywhere in formula language or LotusScript/Java where a UNID is expected.

View to Display Document Hierarchy

In the UI, visual representation for the document tree structure is achieved through the hierarchical view. This view shows the document hierarchy by using the view property Show response documents in a hierarchy in conjunction with the view column property Show responses only.

In hierarchical view, response documents are indented under the main document and response-to-response documents are indented under the response documents. Response documents are visible in a hierarchical view only if their parent document at the highest level of hierarchy is displayed. There can be a maximum of 32 levels of responses in a hierarchical view and 300,000 documents under each level.

To display the documents in a hierarchy, enable the Show response documents in a hierarchy property. If you do not enable this property, all the documents will be listed at the same level even if they have a tree structure internally. To create the document hierarchy, all the documents that form a part of the hierarchy should be in the same Notes database.

CAUTION

If you delete the parent document in the document hierarchy, all the child documents of the deleted document will become orphans and will disappear from the hierarchical view. You should remove the child documents before deleting the parent document.

INHERITING INFORMATION BETWEEN DOCUMENTS

You can inherit information from one document to a new document at the time of its creation. You may inherit selected fields or the entire document. For inheritance to work, you do not need a parent-child relationship between documents. To inherit fields from an opened or selected document, you need to enable the form property Formula inherit values from selected document for the inherited document. In addition, the value for the inherited fields should be the name of the fields in the document from which inheritance is made.

You may inherit the entire document as a link, collapsible rich text, or rich text by enabling the form property Inherit entire selected document into rich text field. For this to work, you should have at least one rich text field in the inherited document's form.

Adding Automations to Notes Applications

Automations help end users perform repeated tasks easily and speedily. You can achieve automations by adding or associating automation components, such as actions, hotspots, agents, or programs, to the Notes design elements.

The automation components, actions and hotspots automate user-activated tasks. Programs automate tasks that are triggered when events associated with Notes design elements take place.

Agents automate either user-activated tasks or perform operations in the background based on events or a schedule. While you need to associate all the automation components to other design elements to achieve automation, agents may be used as standalones.

You can implement task automation with any automation component by using simple actions, formulas, LotusScript, JavaScript, or Java. Simple actions achieve implementation without any programming. They are used to implement tasks of low levels of complexities. You can combine two or more simple actions, if required.

You have already used actions in forms and views to automate user-activated tasks in your earlier application, the employee handbook. In this part, you will use agents to achieve the automation of complex tasks in the background.

Newsletters

A *newsletter* is a special type of document, which contains information regarding other documents. You can include one or more documents in a newsletter. The newsletter documents contain only summary information about the documents that constitute the newsletter. This summary can be presented in two ways, as a snapshot of the document in picture format or as document links to the documents that form the newsletter itself. An example of a newsletter is notifying end users about new documents, which match their interest profiles, in a discussion database.

You can implement the newsletter feature using two approaches. One approach is by creating an agent using simple actions; the other is to use a program for this implementation. In the programming approach, you can use either LotusScript or Java. There are no features available in formula language for this.

While it is easy to set up an agent, which uses simple actions to implement the newsletter, it imposes certain limitations. It does not offer you the flexibility to handle complex tasks, such as creating newsletters based on interest profiles of end users.

You can use the `Newsletter` class for the implementation using LotusScript or Java. The methods and properties available for the class are the same in both LotusScript and Java, except for their naming conventions. In the current context, LotusScript is used. The methodology remains the same when you use Java. In Java, you will need to replace the names with their Java counterparts.

Newsletters are created from a collection of documents. The document collection is usually obtained by conducting a search in the database based on certain matching criteria. You can also create the document collection using other means as well.

There are three steps involved in implementing a newsletter feature programmatically:

1. Create the `Newsletter` object.
2. Format the content.
3. Send the newsletter to its target audience.

The complete implementation of newsletters in covered in Chapter 15, "Creating a Discussion Database."

Creating the Newsletter Object

You can create the Newsletter object in two ways. The first is by using the CreateNewsletter method of the NotesSession class. The second is by using the New method. In Java, you cannot use the New method because it is implemented as an interface. For both these ways, you first need to obtain a NotesDocument Collection object (a collection of NotesDocument objects), which has to be passed as an argument when creating the Newsletter object.

You can obtain the NotesDocumentCollection object by using the FTSearch or Search methods of NotesDatabase class. This approach is well suited while implementing the newsletter features by using agents that will run on the server based on a schedule. You can use the UnprocessedDocuments property of the NotesDatabase class to create a newsletter from user-selected documents in a view.

Formatting the Newsletter

After creating the Newsletter object, the next step is formatting the presentation of content in the newsletter. The Newsletter class has two methods and three properties:

- **FormatDocument.** This method renders the picture of the specified document in the newsletter's document collection. This is useful if you want to include very few documents in the newsletter. It is also helpful in cases where end users cannot access the database that contains the documents that are sent in the newsletter.
- **FormatMsgWithDocLinks.** This method creates links of all the documents in the NotesDocumentCollection object specified when creating the Newsletter object. These two properties control the formatting features. This method is ideal when you have large number documents to be included in the newsletter. It is imperative for end users to be able to access the database that contains the documents.
- **DoSubject.** This property controls the inclusion of a string describing the subject for each document. This property works in conjunction with the SubjectItemName property. It will not have any effect if you have not specified the SubjectItemName property.

- **SubjectItemName.** This property allows you to map any one field in the documents of the NotesDocumentCollection object as the subject. If the DoSubject property is not set, this property will not have any effect.
- **DoScore.** This property specifies whether to include the relevance score of each document in the newsletter. It works only if the NotesDocument Collection object used for creating the Newsletter object is sorted.

Set these three properties before calling the FormatMsgWithDocLinks method. These properties will not have any effect if the FormatDocument method is used to create the newsletter.

Sending the Newsletter

Both the methods FormatMsgWithDocLinks and FormatDocument return a NotesDocument object. You can use the Send method of the NotesDocument class to send the newsletter. You have to specify the form to be used when displaying the newsletter. If you use any special form to format the newsletter, make sure you attach it while using the Send method. Alternatively, you can set the form to memo, which is the default form for mail messages.

Using the Search Feature in Programs

Notes provides some very powerful search features. Although you have used the search feature for the last application, the employee handbook, it was limited to using search from the UI of the application. This section will focus on how to use this feature when you program.

In LotusScript and Java, the NotesDatabase class provides several methods to search for documents based on search criteria. Based on the type of search query used, these methods can be categorized under two groups, methods that use full-text search query and methods that use formula as the search query. All the methods listed below locate documents in a single database. To search for documents across multiple databases, you need to use the FTDomainSearch method. The complete implementation of the search feature is covered in Chapter 15.

Full-Text Search Methods

You can search for occurrences of words or phrases in documents by using full-text search methods. Search criteria, which are valid for a full-text search, can also be used as the search query for these search methods. In addition, you can use features such as treasures and stem words while using these methods.

These methods are available under this group:

- `FTSearch`
- `FTSearchRange`
- `UnprocessedFTSearch`
- `UnprocessedFTSearchRange`

`FTSearch` is similar to `FTSearchRange`, except that the former does not have a start parameter. The document collection returned by these search methods can be sorted either by relevance or by creation date of the document. When using the creation date, you can sort the collection in ascending or descending order.

`FTSearch` and `FTSearchRange` search all the documents present in the database. To exclude documents that have been searched once, use the `Unprocessed` methods. You can use `UnprocessedFTSearch` and `UnprocessedFTSearchRange` methods only in view actions and agents.

When they are used in agents, `Unprocessed` methods limit the search to documents that the agent considers unprocessed. In other words, you can use `Unprocessed` methods to search the documents that have been created or modified after the agent's last run. To mark the documents as processed and to exclude from any further searches, call the method `UpdateProcessedDoc` of the `NotesSession` class.

Although this search mechanism works in the absence of a full-text search index for the database, the search is much slower. If the sort options are specified, the document collection returned by the search is in sorted form. The main drawback of full-text search methods is that these methods do not return the correct result if the full-text search index of the database has not been updated. As a result, you have to be careful in using these methods for database that change dynamically. All the same, these are the most powerful and fastest search methods available today.

Formula Search Methods

You can use the @Function formula as the search query for these LotusScript or Java methods. Unlike the full-text search methods, these methods allow you to use complex search conditions that are more dynamic in nature.

There are two methods available under this group:

- `Search`
- `UnprocessedSearch`

Irrespective of whether the full-text index is updated or not, these methods always return the correct results. You can use a cut off date to limit the scope of the search. The document collection returned by these methods is not sorted.

If you use Java, follow the Java naming convention for all the search methods listed above.

Summary

In this chapter, you were introduced to the basic features of collaborative discussion applications. You familiarized yourself with the different ways of creating a newsletter and the programmable features available in Notes for newsletters including search mechanisms. You were also acquainted with the fundamentals of document hierarchy in Notes.

Chapter 14

Project Case Study: Creating a Collaborative Application

In this chapter, you will learn about creating a collaborative discussion application through a case study. You will learn how to create documents with relationship and inheritance and to use hierarchical views to display the document hierarchy. Also, you will update your knowledge base on how to add automation to a Notes application using agents.

Mars Retailers: The Present Scenario

Mars Retailers is one of the largest retailing companies in the United States, and it has diversified in different fields of the retailing business. The firm has its head office in New York and has outlets across various states in America and in the major cities of the United Kingdom.

Of late, because of the high level of competition from other such retailers and their aggressive marketing strategies, the market domination of Mars Retailers has decreased. The management reconsidered the current system to identify what was lacking. Currently, the company has its own set of policies and client relation programs in place to help maintain consistency in services and products the company offers from different outlets. If all the policies and programs are in place, the reason for the drop in sales is probably inefficient implementation in various outlets.

The management formed a separate team to identify the root cause of why the policies and programs are not being implemented properly. The team visited the different outlets at various locations and interviewed employees and customers of Mars Retailers.

The team identified that not all the outlets are following the standards maintained by the main outlet in New York. The team noticed that there is no proper means of communication between the main office and other outlets. At present, the company is using telephones as the main medium of communication between these outlets. This has resulted in a communication gap between the locations. Telephonic communication does not guarantee that discussions are documented. People tend to forget the quality control methods after some time. Different time zones between the United Kingdom and the United States has made communication a tedious process. This problem has affected the client relation process that is in place throughout the locations. It has been noted that the cost of communication is very high. The customer suggestion scheme that was implemented long ago is also not functioning properly. Suggestions assimilated in one location are not transferred to other locations in a timely manner to improve the quality of the support and service in other outlets. This is despite the fact that most of the outlets are interconnected through a wide area computer network, except those that are at remote locations.

The team, after studying all the processes involved, concluded that the existing modes of communication need to be replaced by a better mechanism. It suggested implementing a computerized collaborative application, which will help the people to work together. This will help the people in different locations to work as a team and save costs at the same time. In addition, the management can closely monitor the communications happening between different outlets and to frame effective marketing strategies quickly from time to time.

The management decided to implement the suggestion of a collaborative application to overcome the sales drop-off. To implement this solution, the management contacted an IT consulting firm. This firm suggested that a collaborative discussion application should be created using Domino Designer R6, which is a robust environment for developing and deploying collaborative applications. It also suggested that the customer suggestion scheme that is in place for the company could be implemented using the framework provided by this discussion application.

The management team asked the IT consulting firm to develop this application and implement it across all the outlets and the offices of the company in a very short period to check the drop-off the company was facing.

A Collaborative Discussion Application: The Solution

A collaborative discussion application will provide the following benefits:

- It will provide an excellent framework for achieving teamwork.
- It will capture all communications in a structured manner.
- It will reduce the cost of communication.
- It will provide convenience across time zones for participation in discussions.
- It will be possible to track all customer feedback in an organized manner.

The IT consulting firm has assigned this project a team, which consists of a project manager and two developers. Employees will use this application to contribute their ideas and discuss issues and problems within teams. In addition, the same application will be used for tracking the customer feedback.

The discussion application will contain mainly the following four types of documents:

- Main topic documents
- Response to main topic documents
- Response-to-response documents
- User interest profile

The functionality offered by each of these documents is described in the following sections.

Main Topic Documents

Main topic documents contain the main topic of discussion. In addition to the main discussion body, these documents contain the name of the person who initiated the discussion and the location of the initiator, the subject of the discussion, and the topic category. The topic category is used to specify whether the discussion is general or related to customer feedback. Main topic documents are used whenever a new discussion is initiated or customer feedback is entered.

Response to Main Topic Documents

These documents are created as responses to the main topic documents that already exist. Users can create the response to main topic documents either from the main topic documents or from the response-to-response documents.

Response to main topic documents contain the name of the person who created the document, the subject for the response, and the content of the response. These documents automatically inherit the subject, topic category, classification, and location of the main topic documents.

Response-to-Response Documents

These documents are the response documents to the response to main topic documents. These documents contain the name of the person who created the response-to-response document, the subject of the document, and the content of discussion. The subject, topic category, classification, and location of the response to main topic document are inherited from the parent document.

User Interest Profile

User interest profile is a document that lists the various attributes that constitute the user interest. This document contains details such as discussion contributors, topic category, classification, location, and subject of discussion. There can be only one interest profile allowed for each user. The application will dispatch a notification to those users who have created an interest profile if a matching document is found.

Project Life Cycle

The complete project life cycle has been discussed in detail in Chapter 11, "Project Case Study: Creating a Reference Application." Without indulging in the details of each of the phases, only the phases that are specific to the current discussion are detailed.

Requirements Analysis

The IT consultancy firm did a detailed study to gather the functionality requirements for the system and to understand the expectations for the system. The team consolidated the requirements as follows:

- All the users should be able to contribute their ideas.
- Users should be able to select topic category and location.
- Users should be able to view ideas contributed by others categorized by subject, topic category, location, or by username.
- Users should be able to respond with their own views to any ideas posted by others.
- Users should be able to respond to the responses posted by people other than the person who posted the main idea.

- Every discussion thread should be presented in a hierarchical tree to understand the sequences properly.
- Customer feedback should be segregated from general discussion topics.
- Users should be able to create their own interest profiles. The users will receive newsletters based on their interest profiles.

Based on the identified requirements, the development team decides to create a collaborative application, which is a database named Mars Retailers Discussion Forum, using Domino Designer R6.

High-Level Design

In the high-level design, the team first decided to identify the application model to be used. The development team needs to obtain an initial approval from the management before the actual development process starts.

The Notes discussion database can be implemented in the following two ways:

- Centralized implementation model
- Replication-enabled distributed model

In the centralized implementation model, there will be only one database, which can be accessed across the locations. This model has two main advantages:

- It is easy to maintain the application because there is only one database at one location.
- Users get the latest information because they use the same database to create as well as read documents.

However, there are a couple of disadvantages of the centralized implementation model:

- The access speed of the central database depends on the speed of the connection. When the server that hosts the database goes down, users cannot access the documents, leading to a complete hampering of work.
- It is difficult to predict the access patterns of the application. Therefore, it is difficult to plan the bandwidth usage for the communication links.

Figure 14.1 shows how a centralized implementation model works.

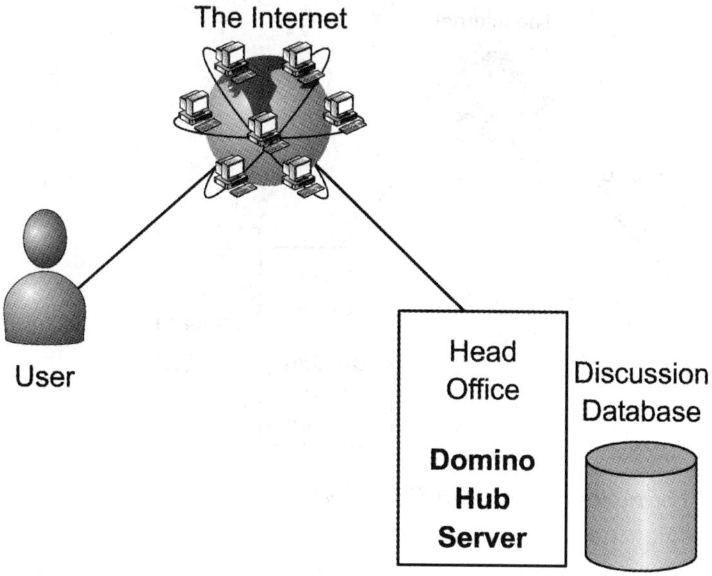

FIGURE 14.1 *The centralized implementation model*

In the replication-enabled distributed model, there are different replicas of the database at the different outlets and offices of the company. People are able to access the application without connecting to the central server. The main advantage of this model is that the access of information is faster, because users are accessing the local replica of the database.

The disadvantage for this model is that the users do not get the latest information. The updates happen only when the database is replicated. In addition, this model requires more effort to manage the application because of the number of locations where application copies are residing. Another problem is the storage space for the local workstations.

Figure 14.2 shows how a replication-enabled distributed model works.

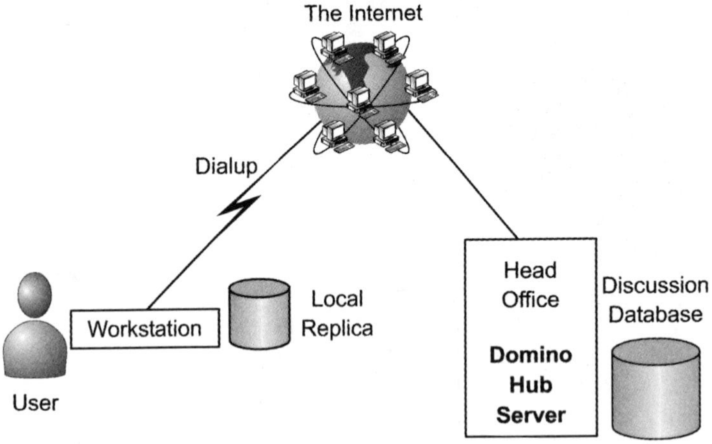

FIGURE 14.2 *The replication-enabled distributed model*

As you can see, the database stored locally at the workstations is replicated via the Internet with the database at the main server at the head office. In this manner, all the replicas are synchronized with the database at the server.

After a thoughtful consideration of the communications infrastructure and recurring cost of connectivity for Mars Retailers, the IT consultancy firm decided that the replication-enabled distributed model is best suited. It also noted that the application response time for users would be very fast.

Next, the team identified the user screens for the discussion application. A form needs to be created for initiating a discussion topic. Any document created with this form will be the top-level document in the hierarchy of the discussion thread. The Main Topic form is shown in Figure 14.3.

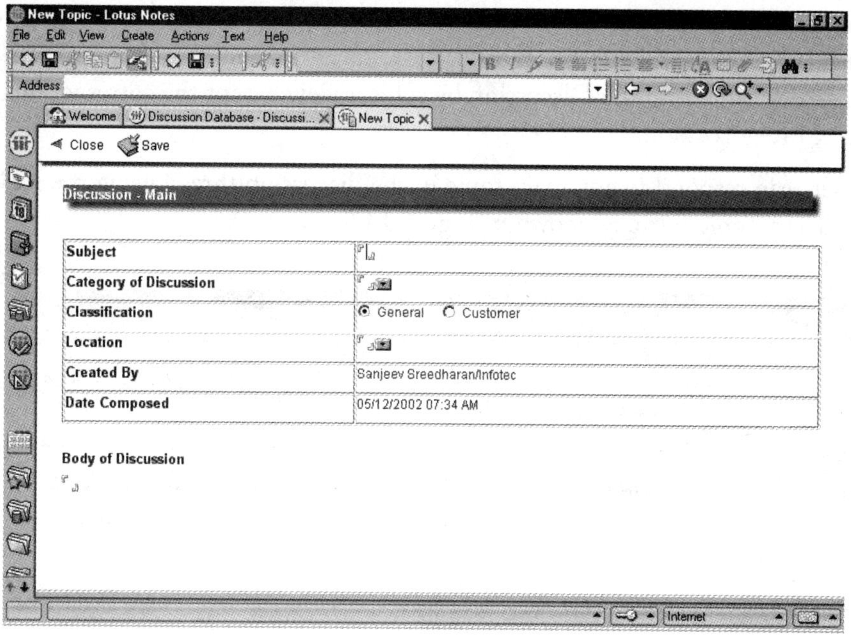

FIGURE 14.3 *The Main Topic form*

Readers access the available discussion topics through the view named Discussion by subject, as shown in Figure 14.4.

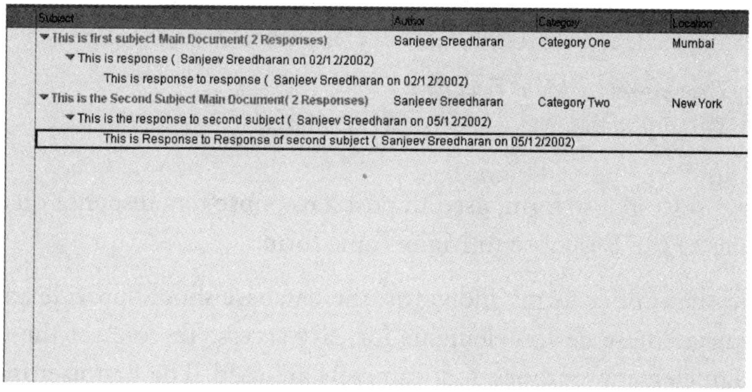

FIGURE 14.4 *The Discussion by subject view*

In addition to this view, the database contains other views, which display documents categorized by location, user, date, category, and classifications. All these views are similar to the Discussion by subject view except the corresponding top-level categorization.

Users can respond to any main topic in the discussion thread using the Response to Main Topic form, as shown in Figure 14.5.

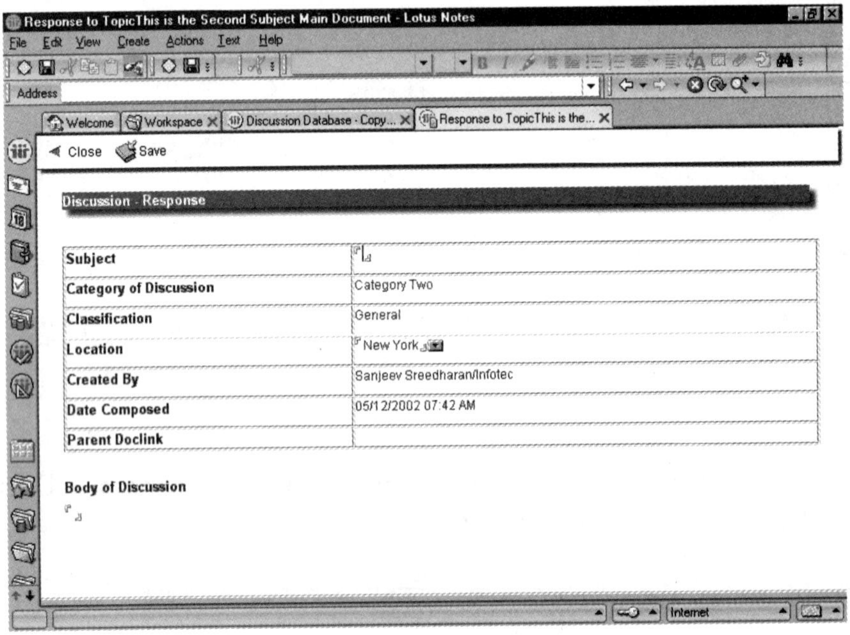

FIGURE 14.5 *The Response to Main Topic form*

The Response to Response form, used to post a response to a response on a main topic, is similar to the Response to Main Topic form.

In addition to the various forms and views, the database should provide an interface that connects these design elements for easy access. To connect the various database design element, outlines and framesets are used. The first user interface screen that connects the various database design elements is shown in Figure 14.6.

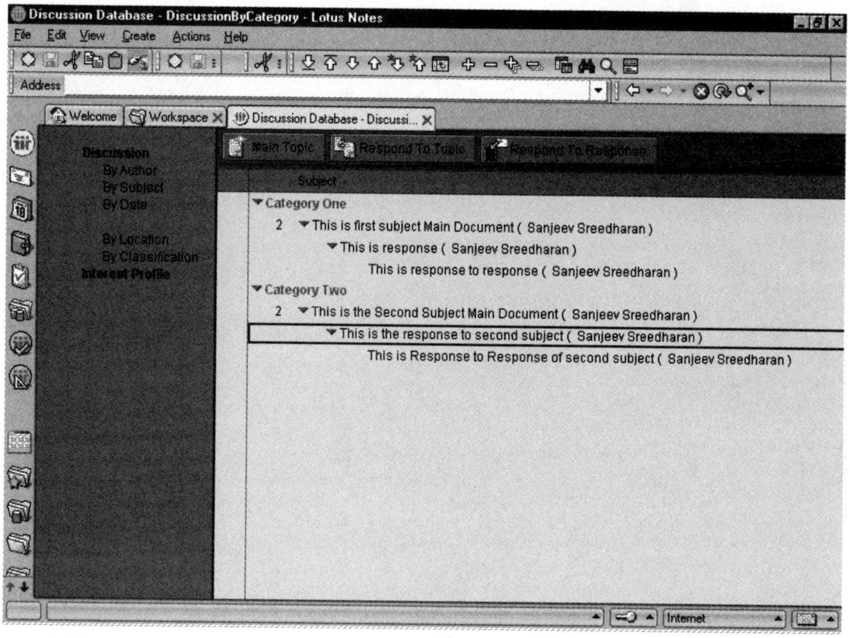

FIGURE 14.6 *The first user interface screen*

Summary

In this chapter, you learned how to formulate a solution for a collaborative application. You learned about the aspects of distributed and centralized implementation of Notes applications. Finally, you identified the design of the collaborative discussion application. In the next chapter, you'll learn the actual development of this application.

Chapter 15

Creating a Discussion Database

In the previous chapter, you saw the Mars Retailers case study. This company needs a collaborative discussion application for an efficient communication system among its employees. The application development team, hired by the company management, needs to develop a collaborative discussion application using Domino Designer R6. In this chapter, you will learn to create a discussion database in a systematic manner.

Planning for the Application

Before starting with the application development, you need to plan for the various activities involved in the development. Planning, of course, helps in a smooth execution of the development activities. The various planned activities are as follows:

1. Create the discussion database.
2. Create the following forms that are used in the discussion database:
   - Main Topic form
   - Response form
   - Response-to-Response form
   - Interest Profile form
3. Create the views to display the documents created using the preceding forms.
4. Create the outline for navigation to different elements in the database.
5. Embed the outline in a page.
6. Create a frameset to provide a user-friendly interface for the database.
7. Set up the database ACL.

The discussion application is targeted for the Notes users who will access the application using the Notes client. Therefore, you'll use the formula language and LotusScript for automation.

Creating the Discussion Database

As you already know, a database can be created as a blank database or it can be created by copying from another database or an existing template. The best way to create a discussion database is to create it from a template, because Lotus Notes is shipped with a Discussion template, DISCSW6.NTF. This template provides all the forms to track a discussion hierarchy and the views to display these documents in the hierarchical manner. Here, you will be creating the discussion database from scratch to get familiarized with the creation of the discussion database from the beginning. Perform the following steps to create the Discussion database:

1. In Domino Designer R6, choose File/Database/New to open the New Database dialog box.
2. In the Server list, select Local to create the database on the local computer. If you want to create the database on a Domino server, select the name of the server. The discussion database needs to be deployed on a Domino server because different users will be using the same database. Here, you can design the database on your local computer and then copy the database to the server for deployment.
3. In the Title box, specify the title for the database. It can have a maximum of 96 characters. Enter **Discussion Database** in the Title box.
4. Specify the file name as **Discussion.nsf**. Specify the location of the database as the Discussion folder on the local computer. Since you are going to create the database from scratch, you need not select any template name. Keep the template option as Blank, which is the default option. The New Database dialog box appears, as shown in Figure 15.1.

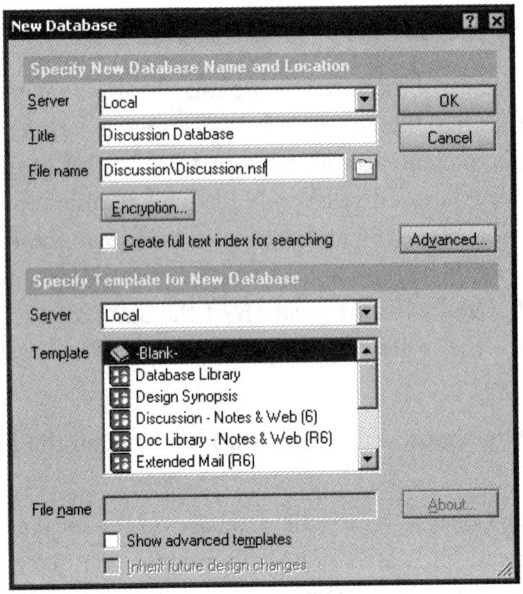

FIGURE 15.1 *The New Database dialog box*

5. Click OK to create the Discussion database.

Creating the Forms

To create a form in a database, open the database in Domino Designer. In this section, you'll create various forms in the Discussion database.

Creating the Main Topic Form

Perform the following steps to create the Main Topic form in the Discussion database:

1. Open the Discussion database in Domino Designer.
2. Click the New Form button to open a blank form in the work pane.
3. In the Form property box, specify the name of the form as **MainTopic**.
4. Specify the type as Document.

5. In the Display section, check Include in menu, and select Create menu from the drop-down list. Check Include in Search Builder and Include in Print.
6. Select None for the versioning.
4. Check Default database form and clear all other options in the Options section.
5. Select the Create Conflicts option in the In the Conflict Handling section.
7. Close the Form property box, and save the form.

Next, add a heading to the form to represent its purpose. To do so, leave a blank line and type the text **Discussion - Main** on the form. Center-align this text and press Enter to bring the cursor to the next line.

Then create the fields on the form. Refer to Table 15.1 to set the field properties.

Table 15.1 Properties of the Fields on the Main Topic Form

Label	Field Name	Type	Other Properties
Subject	Subject	Editable, Text	None
Category of Discussion	Category	Editable, Dialog list	The Allow values not in list property enabled
Classification	Classification	Editable, Radio button	Border style is None, Number of columns is 2, and Choices as General and Customer
Location	Location	Editable, Dialog list	The Allow values not in list property enabled
Created By	CreatedBy	Editable, Authors	None
Date Composed	DateComposed	Editable, Date/Time	The options, Display Date and Display Time, are enabled
Body of Discussion	Body	RichText	None

To make the form visually attractive, use a table to place the fields. Use the font styles for the labels and fields to suit your aesthetic requirements. Save the form and preview it in the Notes client. The complete Main Topic form is shown in Figure 15.2.

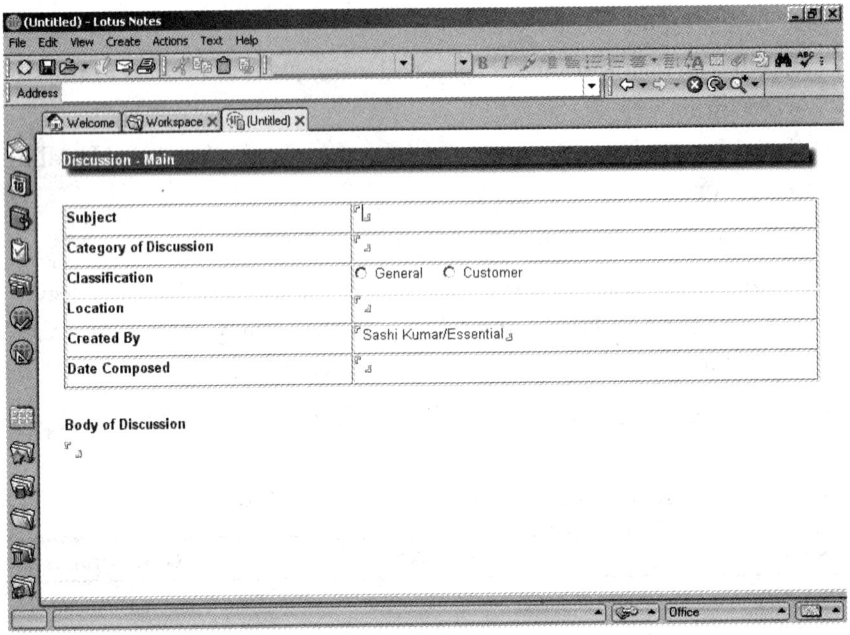

FIGURE 15.2 *The Main Topic form*

Adding Automation to the Main Topic Form

You will use action buttons to add automation to the Main Topic form. The action buttons are described in Table 15.2.

Table 15.2 Action Buttons on the Main Topic Form

Button	Description
Close	Used to close an opened document
Save	Used to save a document
Update	Used to update a created document
Respond To Topic	Used to create a response document to an existing Main Topic document

To create these action buttons, perform the following steps:

1. Create a new action button, specify the names of the action buttons as specified in Table 15.2, and click the Accept button.
2. In the Display row, clear the Include action in Action menu option.
3. Select Notes in the Icon row, select the location as Left, and select an appropriate icon to be displayed with the text.

After adding the action buttons, set the Action bar properties. In the Action bar property box, make the following changes:

1. In the Action bar Background tab, select a suitable color, say white.
2. In the Action bar Border tab in the Border style row, select a suitable color, say dark blue. In the Border effects row, select the option Drop Shadow and the width as 5. In the Thickness row, modify the top value to 1, and retain other properties as is.
3. In the Button properties tab, select the button background as white.
4. In the Button Font tab, specify the font as Arial, size as 9, style as Plain, and the color as black.

After creating the action buttons and setting action properties, the Main Topic form looks as shown in Figure 15.3.

Notice that the action buttons you have created will not function. To make these action buttons work, you need to assign code to each action button.

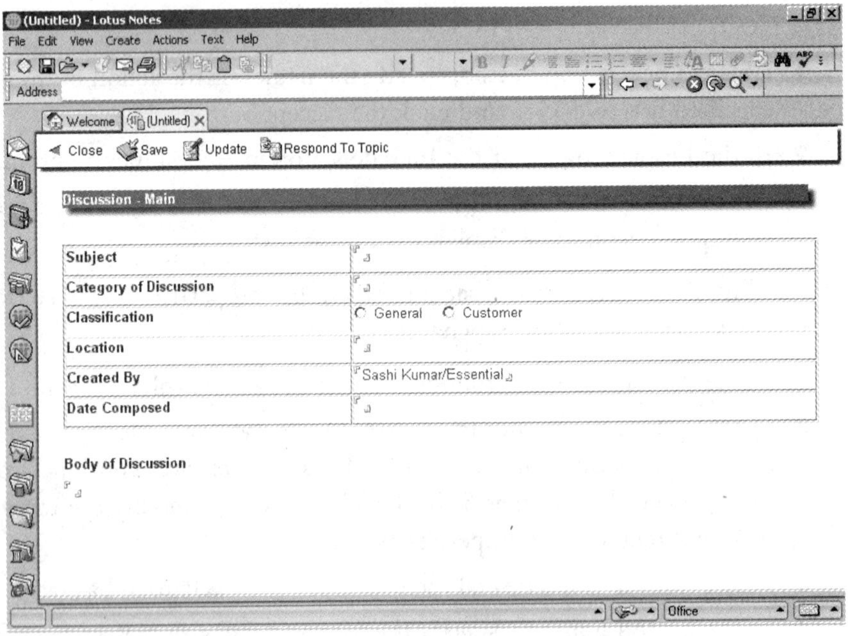

FIGURE 15.3 *The Main Topic form after adding action buttons*

Assigning Formulas to Main Topic Form

In this form, you will use formulas for coding because you need to build only a simple logic in the fields and action buttons already created. You will assign formulas to each field and action sequentially.

The Category Field

The Category field allows the users to select the category of discussion. The user can select an existing category, which is displayed in the DiscussionByCategory view. The user can also create a new category. To add code for the Category field, open the Field property box and activate the Control tab. In the Choices row, select the option Use formula for choices. In the formula window, add the following formula:

```
@Unique(@DbColumn("":"NoCache"; ""; "DiscussionByCategory"; 1))
```

In the previous formula:

- `@DbColumn` returns the values of the first column from the DiscussionBy-Category view in the Discussion database. Ensure that you create the view named DiscussionByCategory with the values from the Category field of the MainTopic form in the first column of the view. Otherwise, the preceding formula will return an error. For further information on @DbColumn function, refer to Chapter 18, "Creating a Customer Complaint Tracking Application."
- `@Unique` is used with the formula `@DbColumn` because there might be multiple documents with the same category listed in the view. `@Unique` returns you the unique text list from the first column of the Discussion-ByCategory view after removing the duplicate values from the list.

The Location Field

The Location field allows a user to select the location where the document is being created. This field lists the available locations. However, if the user's location is not the one among the listed locations, the user can create a new location.

To assign the choices for the Location field, activate the Control tab of the Field property box. In the Choices row, select the option Use formula for choices. In the formula window, enter the following formula:

```
@Unique(@DbColumn("":"NoCache"; ""; "DiscussionByLocation"; 1))
```

This formula fetches the unique values from the first column of the Discussion-ByLocation view. Again, ensure that you create the view named DiscussionBy-Location, which contains the values of the Location field in the first column of the view.

The CreatedBy Field

The CreatedBy field captures the name of the person who creates the document using the Main Topic form. Therefore, this field should display the username of the user who is currently logged into Notes. Moreover, the value of this field should not be changed by any user or when the document is refreshed. This field should be a Computed when Composed field.

In the Programmer's pane, enter the following formula for the value of the CreatedBy field:

```
@UserName
```

Here, `@UserName` returns the name of the user who is logged into the Notes client in canonical format. Because you have specified the field type as Authors, this formula will return only the name of the person in abbreviated format, the same way it is displayed in the Notes ID.

The DateComposed Field

The DateComposed field is used to capture the date on which the Main Topic document is composed. Because the date composed should not be allowed to be edited and should not be changed when refreshed, this field should be a Computed when Composed field.

In the Programmer's pane, add the following formula for the value of the DateComposed field:

```
@Created
```

`@Created` returns the time and date when the document was created.

The Close Action Button

The Close action button is used to close a window without saving the document. In the Programmer's pane for the Close action button, select the click event. In the right pane, specify the Run option as Client. In the formula window, enter the following formula:

```
FIELD SaveOptions := "0";
@Command( [FileCloseWindow] )
```

The `@Command([FileCloseWindow])` command closes the Main Topic form window without saving the document. `Field SaveOptions := "0"` suppresses the Notes prompt dialog box for saving the document when closing the window without saving.

The Save Action Button

This action button is used to save the document and close the window after saving the document. In the Programmer's pane for the Save action button, select the click event. In the right pane, specify the Run option as Client. In the formula window, enter the following formula:

```
@Command([FileSave]);
@Command([FileCloseWindow])
```

The `@Command([FileSave])` command saves the document and `@Command([FileCloseWindow])` command closes the window.

The Save action button should be visible only when the form is in edit mode. Therefore, in the Action property box, in the Action Hide When tab, check the options Previewed for reading and Opened for reading.

The Update Action Button

This action button enables a user to edit an existing Main Topic document. Therefore, this action button should be visible only when the document is opened in read mode. To hide this button in edit mode, select the options Previewed for editing and Opened for editing in the Hide When tab of the Action property box.

A Main Topic document should be editable only by the user who created it. The Update action button, therefore, should be hidden from all other users. To do so, in the Hide When tab of the Action property box, check Hide action if formula is true and write the following formula:

```
@UserName != @Name([Canonicalize];CreatedBy)
```

This formula checks whether the user who has logged into Notes is the same as the user who has created the document (value in the CreatedBy field). If the values are not equal, the formula hides the Update action button.

Next, in the Programmer's pane for the Update action button, select the click event. In the right pane, specify the Run option as Client. In the formula window, enter the following formula:

```
@Command([EditDocument])
```

This command is used to switch the document to edit mode.

The Respond To Topic Action Button

This action button creates a response document for a Main Topic document. Therefore, this button should not be visible when a user creates a new Main Topic document. To achieve this, specify the following formula in the Hide When tab of the Action property box:

```
@IsNewDoc
```

This formula hides the action button if the document is being created and not yet saved.

In the Programmer's pane for the Respond To Topic action button, select the click event. In the right pane, specify the Run option as Client. In the formula window, enter the following formula to create a document using the form `ResponseTo-Topic`:

```
@Command([Compose];"ResponseToTopic")
```

The Window Title

After assigning formulas for the action buttons, add a window title for the Main Topic form. To add a window title, in the Object tab info list, select the Window Title event and add the following formula:

```
@If(@IsNewDoc;"New Topic";Subject +" "+ @DocDescendants)
```

In this formula:

- `@IsNewDoc` returns a true value if the document is a new document and not yet saved.
- `@if` statement checks the return value of `@IsNewDoc`. If the value is true, the string "New Topic" is returned, which will be the window title. If the value is false, `@If` returns a string, which concatenates the subject and number of decedent documents.

After assigning formulas to the Main Topic form, the form is complete in design and function. When you preview the form in the Notes client, the form appears as shown in Figure 15.4.

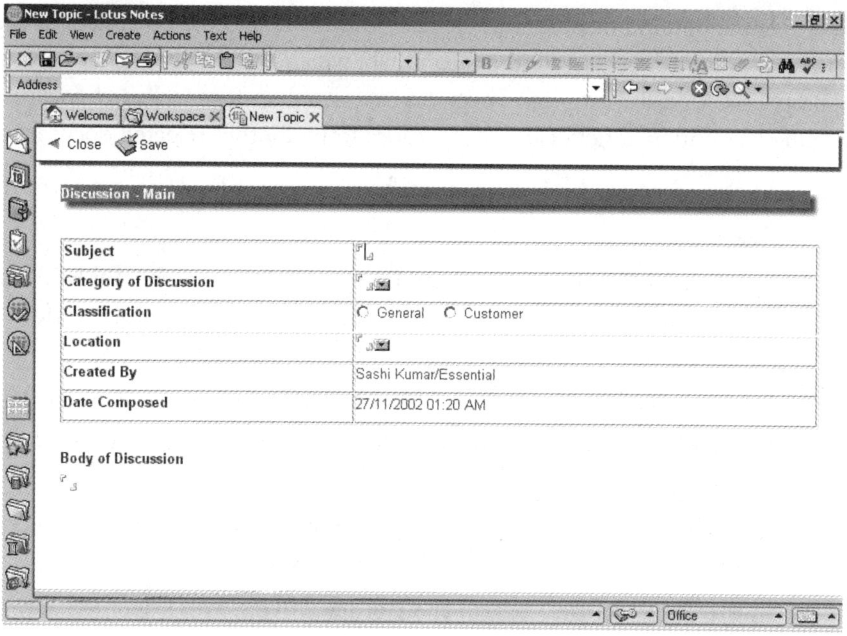

FIGURE 15.4 *The final Main Topic form*

Creating the Response to Topic Form

To create the Response to Topic form, create a new blank form, and set its properties as specified in Table 15.3.

Table 15.3 Properties of the Response to Topic Form

Property	Value
Form name	ResponseToTopic
Type	Response
Include in menu	Checked, Create menu
Include in Print	Checked
Options	Clear all options
Conflict Handling	Create Conflicts
Formulas inherit values from the selected document	Checked

To enable the option Formulas inherit values from the selected document as specified in the preceding table, activate the second tab, which is the Defaults tab in the Form property box. Check the option Formulas inherit values form selected document. By enabling this option, a field can inherit values from another selected document.

Next, add a heading to the form to specify its purpose. To do so, perform the following steps:

1. Create a table with one row and one column. Select the Table Width as Fit with margins. Select the table type as basic table, which is default, and click OK.
2. In the table, type the text **Discussion - Response** and left-align the text.
3. In the Cell Border Thickness section, click the Set All To 0 button to remove the border.
4. In the Table/Cell Background tab, in the Cell Color section, select a variation of sky blue as the background color.
5. In the Table Borders tab, in the Border Effects row, select the Drop Shadow option, and make the width 10.
6. Close the property window.
7. Set the property of the text Discussion - Response. In the Text property box, set the font to Arial, size to 10, style to Bold, and select color as white.

Then create the fields and their labels in another table. Refer to Table 15.4 for the field properties.

Table 15.4 Properties of the Fields in the Response to Topic Form

Label	Field Name	Type	Other Properties
Subject	Subject	Editable, Text	None
Category of Discussion	Category	Text	Computed when composed
Classification	Classification	Text	Computed when composed
Location	Location	Editable, Dialog list	The Allow values not in list property enabled
Created By	CreatedBy	Authors	Computed when composed
Creation Date	DateComposed	Date/Time	Computed when composed
Parent Doclink	ParentDocLink	Text	Computed for display

Outside the table, type the field label text as Body of Discussion. In the next line, create a field named Body, which is an editable Rich Text field.

Notes will not allow you to preview the form now because the form is of the type Response. Moreover, you haven't specified the values for the computed fields. In the Designer, the form appears as shown in Figure 15.5.

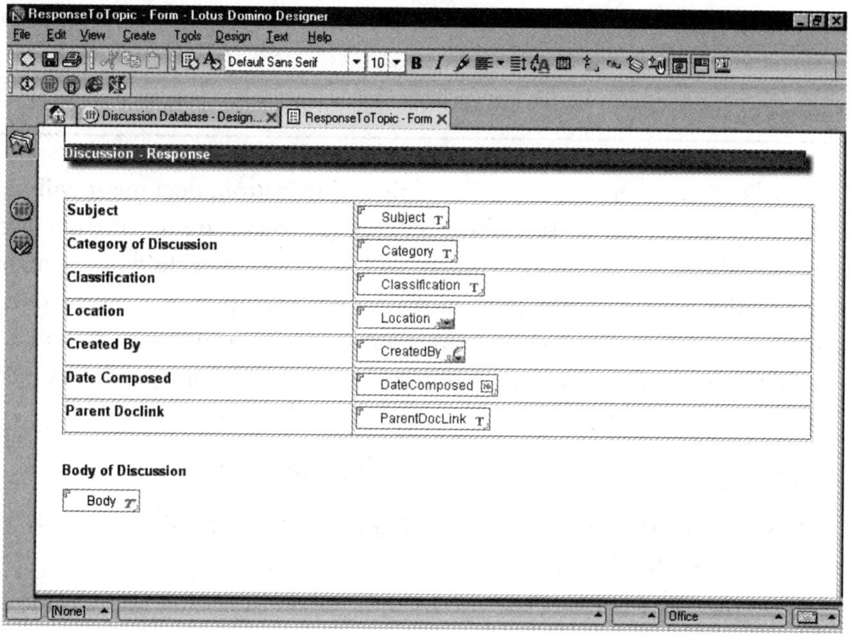

FIGURE 15.5 *The Response to Topic form*

Adding Automation to the Response to Topic Form

In this section, you will add the action buttons that will be used in the Response to Topic form. Table 15.5 lists the action buttons in the Response to Topic form.

Table 15.5 Action Buttons on the Response to Topic Form

Button	Description
Close	Used to close an opened document
Save	Used to save a document
Update	Used to update a document that already exists
Respond To Topic	Used to create a response document for the already created Main Topic document
Respond To Response	Used to create a Response-to-Response document

When you click on the Respond To Topic action button, document will be composed using the Response type form. Whenever you create documents using the Response type form, the new document will be created as a child to the main document in the hierarchy, irrespective of whether the open or selected document during composition of new document is a response or response to response document. If the form type is Response to response, the new, composed document will be created as the child of the selected or opened document.

To create the action buttons, perform the following steps:

1. Create a new action button, specify its name as specified in Table 15.5, and click the Accept button.
2. In the Display row, clear the Include action in Action menu option.
3. Select Notes in the Icon row, select the location as Left, and select an appropriate icon to be displayed with the text.

Next, set the Action bar properties. Follow the same steps as performed to set the Action bar properties of the Main Topic form. The same properties are set for the Action bar on both the forms to maintain a consistent look for the forms across the database. Now the Response to Topic form looks as shown in Figure 15.6.

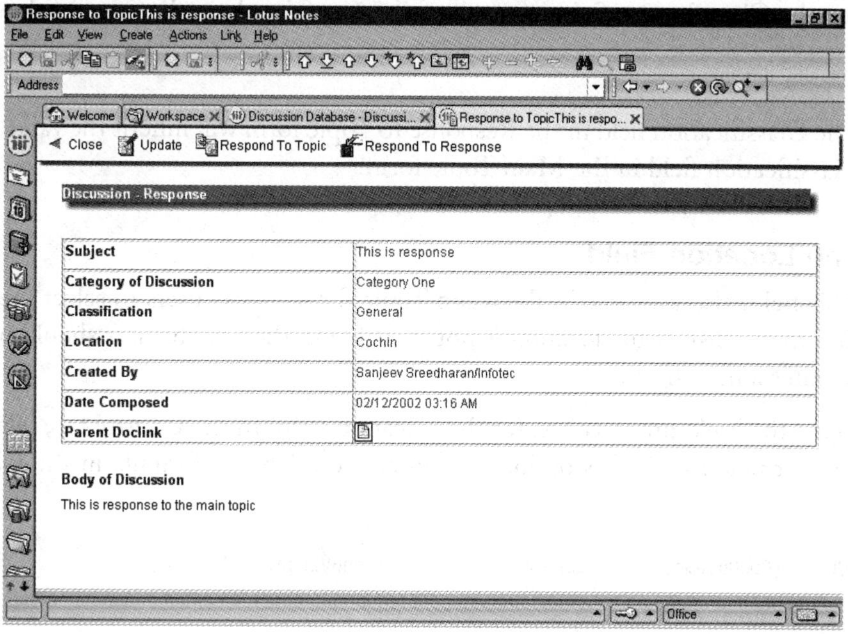

FIGURE 15.6 *The Response to Topic form after adding action buttons*

Assigning Formulas to the Response to Topic Form

In this section, you'll assign the formulas to the fields and action buttons in the Response to Topic form.

The Category and Classification fields

The Category and Classification fields are Computed when Composed fields and inherit the values from the parent document. For the Category field, assign the following formula in the value of the field:

```
Category
```

To inherit the field value from a selected document, you should specify the name of the field being inherited as the value for the field to which it is inherited. Therefore, the value of the Category field is specified as Category, which is the name of the field in the Main Topic form. The inheritance will happen because the Formulas inherit values from the parent document option is enabled in the Form property box.

For the Classification field, enter the following formula in the value of the field:

```
Classification
```

The Classification field in the Response to Topic form will inherit the value of the Classification field in the Main Topic form.

The Location Field

This field, also available in the Main Topic form, allows users to select the location from a list. If the location is not available in the list, the user should be able to enter a new location.

Open the Field property box for the Location field. In the Control tab, select the Use formula for choices option and enter the following formula in the Choices box:

```
@Unique(@DbColumn("":"NoCache"; ""; "DiscussionByLocation"; 1))
```

TIP

An alternative to specifying values in the Location field is to create a location profile document. Then try to fetch the values in the select list from that location profile document.

The CreatedBy, DateComposed, and ParentDocLink Fields

In the Programmer's pane, enter the following formula for the value of the CreatedBy field:

```
@UserName
```

For the DateComposed field, enter the following formula:

```
@Created
```

The ParentDocLink field displays a link to the parent document. Assign the following formula for the value of the ParentDocLink field:

```
$Ref
```

This formula will create a link of the parent document in the ParentDocLink field of the Response to Topic document. Clicking this link will open the parent document, which was selected when the document was created. $Ref is the name of the special field on a response document that stores the Universal ID of the parent document.

The Window Title of the Response to Topic Form

To set the window title of the form, enter the following formula in the Window Title event:

```
"Response to Topic" + Subject
```

This formula will display the subject along with the text "Response to Topic".

Formulas for the Action Buttons

Assign the following formula for the Close action button:

```
FIELD SaveOptions := "0";
@Command( [CloseWindow] )
```

For the Save action button, assign the following formula:

```
@Command([FileSave]);
@Command([FileCloseWindow])
```

Check the Hide When properties to make sure that the Save action button is visible when the document is in read mode.

For the Update action button, make sure the button is hidden in edit mode, check the Hide action if formula is true, and write the following formula:

```
@UserName != @Name([Canonicalize];CreatedBy):
```

Assign the following formula to the action button:

```
@Command([EditDocument])
```

For the Respond To Topic action button, assign the following formula:

```
@Command([Compose];"ResponseToTopic")
```

You do not need to show the Response To Topic action button when this document is new. Enter the following formula in the Hide action if the formula is true and click on the Accept button:

```
@IsNewDoc
```

For the Respond To Response action button, assign the following formula:

```
@Command([Compose];"ResponseToResponse")
```

This formula will open a new Response-to-Response form.

With this, the design of the Response to Topic form is complete. If you preview the form by selecting the form type as document, the form appears as shown in Figure 15.7.

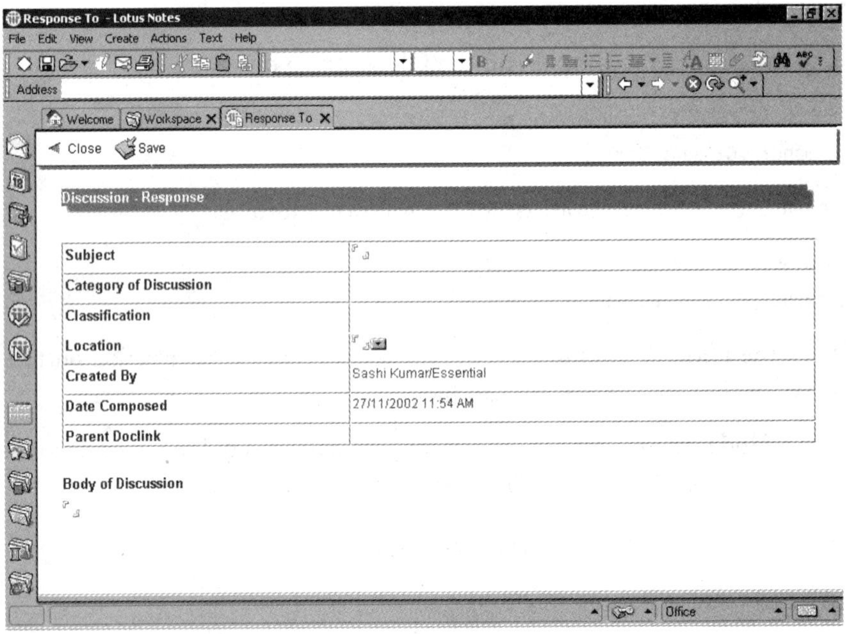

FIGURE 15.7 *The final Response to Topic form*

After previewing, modify the form type back to Response and save the form.

Creating the Response-to-Response Form

The Response-to-Response form is similar to the Response to Topic form. Therefore, instead of creating the Response-to-Response form from scratch, copy the Response to Topic form and make the necessary modifications. This section will only specify the changes you need to make on the copied Response to Topic form to make it the Response-to-Response form.

Perform the following steps:

1. In the Design pane, copy and paste the Response to Topic form. Note that the name of the pasted form is Copy Of ResponseToTopic form. Open the pasted form.
2. In the Form property box, in the Name box, modify the name Copy Of ResponseToTopic to **ResponseToResponse**.
3. Modify the form type to Response to Response and close the Form property box. Save the form.
4. Modify the heading of the form in the table to **Discussion - Response to Response**.
5. In the Window Title event, enter the following formula:

```
"Response to Response " + Subject
```

When previewed by changing the form type to document, the form should look as shown in Figure 15.8.

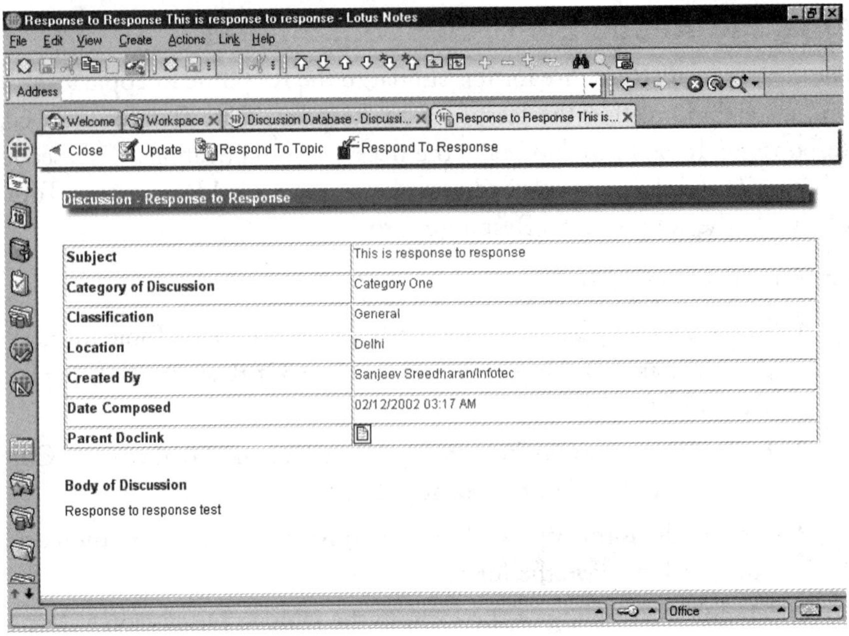

FIGURE 15.8 *The final Response-to-Response form*

Creating the Interest Profile Form

After creating the main forms Main Topic, Response to Topic, and Response-to-Response, you will now create the Interest Profile form. This form is used to capture the users' interests and to send them newsletters.

To create the Interest Profile form, create a new form and set its properties as specified in Table 15.6.

Table 15.6 Properties of Interest Profile Form

Property	Value
Form Name	InterestProfile
Form Type	Document
Include in menu	Clear
Include in Search Builder	Clear
Versioning	None
Options	Clear all options
Conflict Handling	Do not create conflict

Next, create a heading for the interest profile form, which will be dynamically customized for each user. Perform the following steps:

1. Create a table with one row and one column. Select the table width as Fit with margins. Select the table type as basic table, which is the default table type, and click OK.
2. In the table, type the text **Interest Profile For** and left-align the text.
3. Create a Field named UserName next to the text you typed. The field will be of the type Authors and Computed when Composed field.
4. Set the type of the UserName fields as Authors and Computed when Composed. Assign the following formula for this field:

   ```
   @UserName
   ```

5. Modify the table and text attributes in the same way as you did while creating the heading for the other three forms.

Next, under the form heading, type the text **Inform me of new documents created under these** and change the text properties to Arial, 10, Bold, and color to dark blue.

Create another table on the form and create the labels and fields inside this table. Refer to Table 15.7 for the properties of the fields on the Interest Profile form.

Table 15.7 Field Properties on the Interest Profile Form

Label	Field Name	Type	Other properties
Created By	CreatedBy	Editable, Names	The Allow multiple values and Use Address dialog for choices properties enabled
Subject	Subject	Editable, Text	The Allow multiple values property enabled
Category	Category	Editable, Dialog list	The Allow multiple values property enabled
Classification	Classification	Editable, Dialog list	The Allow multiple values property enabled
Location	Location	Editable, Dialog list	The Allow multiple values property enabled

Next, add automation to the fields on the form. Open the Field property box for the Category field, and in the Choices section, select Use formula for choices and enter the following formula:

```
@Unique(@DbColumn("":"NoCache"; ""; "DiscussionByCategory"; 1))
```

In the Field property box for the Classification field, in the Choices section, specify the choices as **General** and **Customer** in the Choice box. Also, check the options Show Field delimiters and Display entry helper button.

In the Field property box for the Location field, in the Choices section, select Use formula for choices and enter the following formula:

```
@Unique(@DbColumn("":"NoCache"; ""; "DiscussionByLocation"; 1))
```

After assigning the formulas for the fields, assign formulas for the action buttons. Assign the following formula for the Close action button:

```
FIELD SaveOptions := "0";
@Command( [CloseWindow] )
```

For the Save action button, assign the following formula:

```
@Command([FileSave]);
@Command([FileCloseWindow])
```

Modify the Action bar properties the same way you did for the other three forms.

To set the window title for the Interest Profile form, enter the following formula in the Window Title event of the form:

```
"Interest Profile for "+@Name([CN];@UserName)
```

This formula will display the text "Interest Profile for" concatenated with the name of the user who opened the Interest profile form.

Save the form and preview it in the Notes client. The Interest Profile form is shown in Figure 15.9.

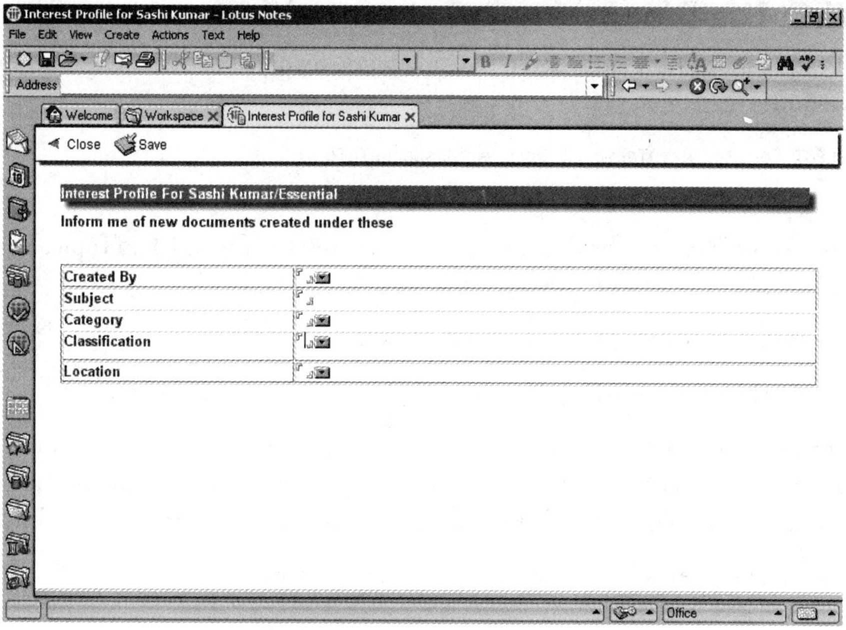

FIGURE 15.9 *The Interest Profile form*

Creating the Views

The Discussion database contains the following views:

- **DiscussionBySubject.** Lists documents categorized by discussion subjects.
- **DiscussionByAuthor.** Lists documents categorized by usernames.
- **DiscussionByDate.** Lists documents categorized by creation dates.
- **DiscussionByCategory.** Lists documents categorized by topic categories.
- **DiscussionByLocation.** Lists documents categorized by locations.
- **DiscussionByClassification.** Lists documents categorized by classifications.
- **InterestProfile.** Lists all Interest Profile documents categorized by user names. This is a hidden view.

Creating the DiscussionByCategory View

Create a new view and enter the following formula in the Select by formula window:

```
SELECT Form = "MainTopic" ¦ Form = "ResponseToTopic" ¦
        Form = "ResponseToResponse"
```

This formula selects the documents created using the forms MainTopic, Response ToTopic, and ResponseToResponse.

Alternatively, another formula can be used here:

```
SELECT Form = "MainTopic" ¦ @AllDescendants
```

Here, the first method is used to improve performance and reduce database size. One of the database properties, "Don't support specialized response hierarchy," will, when enabled, make the `@AllChildren` and `@AllDescendants` non functional.

The Create View dialog box should appear, as shown in Figure 15.10.

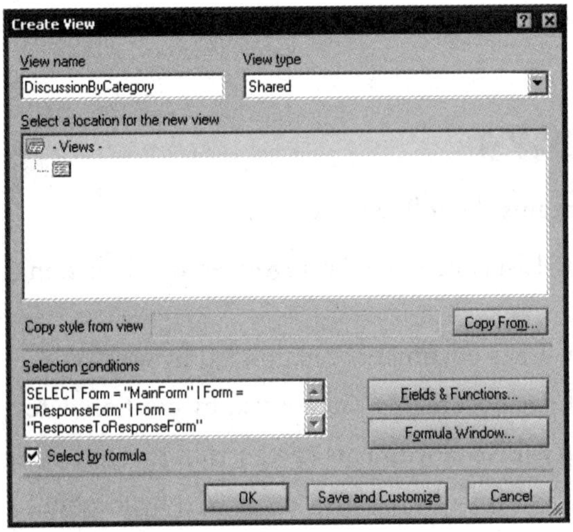

FIGURE 15.10 *The Create View dialog box*

Click the Save and Customize button to save the view and make changes in the view. You can start with customizing the DiscussionByCategory view. Set the view properties as listed in Table 15.8.

Table 15.8 Properties of the DiscussionByCategory View

Property	Value
Show response documents in hierarchy	Checked
Row color	Light blue
Alternate rows color	Light gray
Header style	Simple
Header color	Light blue
Row Height	5
Row Spacing	11/4
Shrink rows to content	Checked
Don't show empty categories	Checked
Unread	Dark red
Bold	Checked
Extend last column to window width	Checked
Unread marks	Standard (Compute in hierarchy)

Now the Style tab of the View property box appears as shown in Figure 15.11.

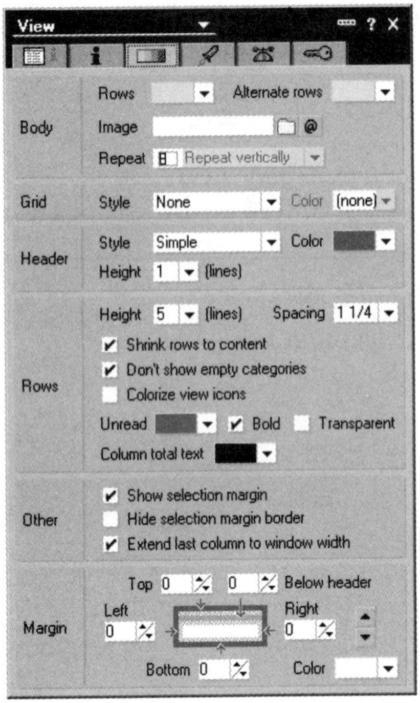

FIGURE 15.11 *The View property box with the Style tab active*

After setting the view properties, create the columns in the DiscussionByCategory view. Except one column, all of the column values in this view will be mapped to the fields on the Main Topic form.

Perform the following steps to create the view columns after deleting the default column, which was created when you created the view. Create a new column and set the Category field of the Main Topic form as the column value. Set other column properties as listed in Table 15.9.

Table 15.9 Properties for Column 1

Property	Value
Title	Make the title blank
Width	2
Resizable	Clear
Show twistie when row is expandable	Checked
Sort	Ascending
Type	Categorized
Font	Arial
Style	Bold
Text color	Dark green
Font size	Arial, 9
Title font	Arial, 9
Title style	Plain
Title text color	Black

Create a new column to the right of the first column. In the column properties, specify font as Arial, size as 9, style as Plain, and color as black. Assign the following formula for the column value:

```
@If( !@IsResponseDoc; @DocDescendants;"")
```

This formula will display the number of Response documents and Response-to-Response documents created for a particular main category form. The `if` condition checks whether or not a particular entry is a main document by using the `!@IsResponseDoc` formula. `@DocDescendants` returns the descendant count only on the row of the main document.

Create the third column, which will be used for sorting the documents based on the date of creation. Make the title blank and set the width to 2. Select Sorting option as Ascending. Check Hide column. For the value for the column, select the field DateComposed from the list of the fields.

Create the fourth column, which will display the Response and Response-to-Response documents in a hierarchical manner. Check the property Show responses only. Set the column width to 2 and clear the option Resizable. Check the option Show twistie when row is expandable option. Set the Font properties as Arial, size as 9, style as Plain, and color as black. Assign the following formula to the column value:

```
Subject + " (  "+@Name([CN];CreatedBy)+" )"
```

This formula will display the value of the Subject field in the Response and Response-to-Response documents with the common name of the person who has created the documents inside a square bracket.

Create the next column to show the Main Topic documents. Clear the property Show responses only. Assign Subject to the column title and set width to 20. Check the option Show twistie when the row is expandable. Set the Font properties as Arial, size as 9, style as Plain, and color as black. Check the option Resizable. Enter the following formula for the column value:

```
Subject + " (  "+@Name([CN];CreatedBy)+" )"
```

In this column, unlike the previous column, which will display the subject of the response documents, this formula will display the value of the Subject field in the Main Topic document with the common name of the person who has created the documents inside a bracket.

After creating the view columns, add the action buttons for creating the Main Topic, Response, and Response-to-Response documents from the view. Assign the following formulas to the actions:

- Main Topic action creates a new Main Topic document to initiate a discussion. Assign the following formula to the action:

  ```
  @Command([Compose];"MainTopic")
  ```

- Respond to Topic action creates a Response document for a Main Topic document. Assign the following formula to the action:

  ```
  @Command([Compose];"ResponseToTopic")
  ```

- Respond to Response action creates a Response-to-Response document. Assign the following formula to the action:

  ```
  @Command([Compose];"ResponseToResponse")
  ```

Next, modify the Action bar properties. To do so, perform the same steps that you performed to format the Action bar of the Main Topic form.

Save the view and preview it in the Notes client. The view is shown in Figure 15.12.

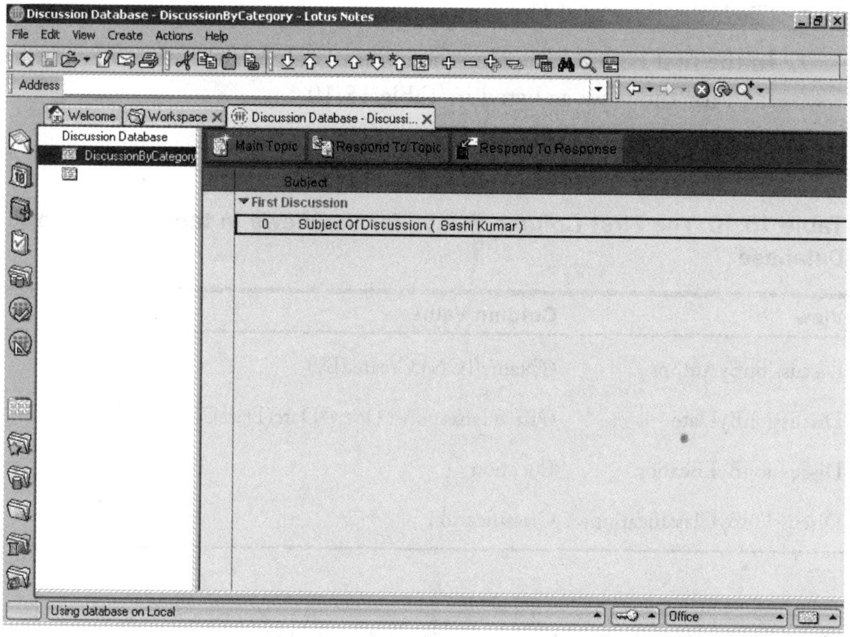

FIGURE 15.12 *The DiscussionByCategory view*

Creating the Other Views

The remaining views of the Discussion database are similar to the DiscussionBy-Category view except for the first column value. The first column of all the views is used for the highest-level categorization for each of the views. Therefore, to create these views, you can simply copy the DiscussionByCategory view and make the necessary changes.

To create the other views, except InterestProfile and DiscussionBySubject views, perform the following steps:

1. Create a new view and specify the name for the view.
2. Select view type as Shared.

3. In Copy style from view, click the Copy From button.
4. From the list, select DiscussionByCategory as the view from which the style has to be copied.
5. Retain the view selection formula as is.
6. Click the Save and Customize button.
7. In the first column, replace the column value with the corresponding field for the view as listed in Table 15.10.
8. Save the view and close the view window.

Table 15.10 The First Column Values for the Views in the Discussion Database

View	Column Value
DiscussionByAuthor	@Name([CN];CreatedBy)
DiscussionByDate	@If(!@IsResponseDoc;@Date(DateComposed);"")
DiscussionByLocation	Location
DiscussionByClassification	Classification

Creating the Discussion by Subject View

This view will be created the same way you have created the previous views by copying the DiscussionByCategory view. For this view, retain the view selection formula, as it exists.

Perform the following steps to make the variation in this view:

1. In the Column info tab of the first column property box, check the option Show responses only and Show twistie when row is expandable. In the second tab, specify Sort as None and Type as Standard. Check the option Ascent sensitive sorting and clear the other options in this tab. In the Font tab, select the Font as Arial, Size as 9, Style as Plain, and color as Black. Keep the other options as it is.

   Assign the following formula to the column value:

```
Subject + " (  "+@Name([CN];CreatedBy) + " on " +
    @Text(DateComposed;"S0")+ " from "+Location+")"
```

This formula will display the subject of the response documents with the name of the person who created it, date and location in the brackets.

2. Delete the next three columns of the view. Now you will be in the last column titled Subject.
3. In the first tab of the column property box, check the option Show twistie when row is expandable. In the second tab, select the Sort as Ascending and Type as Standard. In the third tab, select the Style as Bold and Text Color as a variation of green and let the other option be as it is.

   Assign the following formula to the column value:

   ```
   Subject + "( " +(@If(!@IsResponseDoc;@DocDescendants;""))
       +" Responses)"
   ```

   This formula will display the Subject of discussion with the number of response documents created under it.
4. Make a new column named Author. In the first tab of the column property box, only the Resizable option should be checked. In the Font tab, select the Font as Arial, Size as 9, Style as Bold, and Text Color as Black. In the Title tab, set the same font as you set for the text.

   Assign the following formula to the column value:

   ```
   @Name([CN];CreatedBy)
   ```
5. Create three more columns named 'Date', 'Category', and 'Location'. Change the column properties as you did for the previous columns. Select the respective field names as the Column value as listed in Table 15.11 for each of the columns created.

Table 15.11 The Column Values for Each of the Columns

View	Column Value
Date	DateComposed
Category	Category
Location	Location

Now, save and close the view. Notice the differences for this particular view when you preview the view in Notes client.

Creating the InterestProfile View

The InterestProfile view is a hidden view that lists only the Interest Profile documents categorized by username. Being a hidden view, this view will not be a part of the user interface. Instead, an agent will use this view for walk thru when generating newsletters. The agent will use this view to check if an interest profile exists for the user.

Perform the following steps to create the view:

1. Create a new view and assign the view name as (InterestProfile). Note the name is enclosed in parentheses to make the view hidden.
2. Select the view type as Shared.
3. Enable the Select by formula option. Enter the following formula in the Selection condition box:

   ```
   SELECT Form = "InterestProfile"
   ```

4. Click the Save and Customize button.

The InterestProfile view requires only one column, which will be used as the key column for lookups and to sort the Interest Profile documents.

Create only one column with the column title as User Name and the Sort option set to Ascending. For the value of the column, select the field named UserName from the available list of fields and save the view.

Adding Automation to the Application

In this section, you will learn how a newsletter is created and mailed to a user according to his interest profile. You will be using an agent to automate this process. In Domino, agents are used for processes such as handling repetitive tasks, automating workflow, and monitoring tasks.

Creating the Agent to Send a Newsletter

Since the newsletter has to be sent to the user, the agent needs to run daily. Every time the agent runs, it checks whether any documents have been created that match the conditions specified in the Interest Profile documents. This task doesn't involve any user interaction. The agent will be scheduled to run in the background and perform the task of sending newsletters periodically. Therefore, the agent needs to be a scheduled agent, which will run every night. The run time is selected as night because the agent will be able to get all the documents created during the day.

To create the agent, perform the following steps.

1. In the Design pane, expand Shared Code and click Agent.
2. Click the New Agent button to create a new agent. This will create a new agent and opens the Agent property box.
3. Enter InformUser in the Name box to assign a name to the agent.
4. Select the Shared radio button option to enable other users to use the agent. If you select Private, only the person who created the agent will be able to run the agent.
5. In the Runtime section, set the Trigger as On Schedule.
6. Select Daily from the Schedule drop-down list and click the Schedule button on the left side. The Agent Schedule dialog box appears.
7. In the Agent Schedule box, modify Start running agent at to 02:00AM. You can also modify the time after creating the agent. If you want to test the agent, modify the time to any other time convenient for you.
8. Select where the agent has to be run. If you want the agent to run on a server, select the name of the server from the drop-down list. In this case, select Local and click the OK button.
9. Select All new & modified documents from the Target drop-down list in the Runtime section.
10. In the Programmer's pane, from the Run list, choose LotusScript as the agent's Run option.

Before coding for the agent, identify the tasks that the agent performs. The following steps explain the logic of the agent code:

1. The agent gets the handle to the Interest Profile documents of all the users from the (InterestProfile) view and iterates (called *view walk thru*) through the documents individually until it reaches the last document in the view.
2. It checks whether or not the database is full-text indexed. If the database is full-text indexed, the agent uses the `FTSearch` method. Otherwise, the `Search` method is used.

3. The agent then tracks the user preferences and forms a search query, which will be used for searching. If there are no values in the profile document, control moves to the next document in the view.
4. If the search yields a result, the agent gets the collection of the documents, creates a newsletter, and sends it to the user who created the Interest Profile document.

Enter the following code in the Initialize event of the agent. Any line starting with an apostrophe is a comment. To make the comments stand out they are marked with rem, which is not required when you program.

```
Sub Initialize
    'Rem Declaration of variables
    Dim ns As New NotesSession 'declares and Initiates a new agent session
    Dim db As NotesDatabase
    Dim ProfileView As NotesView
    Dim ProfileDoc As NotesDocument
    Dim NotesDoc As NotesDocument
    Dim NewsLet As NotesNewsletter
    Dim DocCollection As NotesDocumentCollection

    Dim ByAuthor As Variant
    Dim ByCategory As Variant
    Dim BySubject As Variant
    Dim ByClassification As Variant
    Dim ByLocation As Variant

    'Rem Declaration of variable, to form a formatted string
    'for search query
    Dim strAuthor As String
    Dim strCategories As String
    Dim strSubject As String
    Dim strClassification As String
    Dim strLocation As String
    Dim IsCriteriaNull As Variant
    Dim SearchQry As String

    'Rem Initialization of objects
    Set db = ns.CurrentDatabase
```

```
Set ProfileView = db.GetView("(InterestProfile)")
Set ProfileDoc = ProfileView.GetFirstDocument

If ProfileDoc Is Nothing Then Exit Sub
'Rem Start walking thu the Interest profile view
Do While Not (ProfileDoc Is Nothing)
  If db.IsFTIndexed = True Then
    If Trim(ProfileDoc.CreatedBy(0)) <> "" Then
      ByAuthor = ProfileDoc.CreatedBy
      strAuthor = ""
      Forall value In ByAuthor
        If Trim(strAuthor) = "" Then
          strAuthor =  value
        Else
          strAuthor = strAuthor & "," & value
        End If
      End Forall
      SearchQry = "field CreatedBy contains " & strAuthor
    End If

    If Trim(ProfileDoc.Category(0)) <> "" Then
      ByCategory = ProfileDoc.Category
      strCategories = ""
      Forall value In ByCategory
        If Trim(strCategories) = "" Then
          strCategories =  value
        Else
          strCategories = strCategories & "," & value
        End If
      End Forall
      qry = "field Category contains (" & strCategories & ")"
      If Trim(SearchQry) = "" Then
        SearchQry = qry
      Else
        SearchQry = SearchQry & " Or " & qry
      End If
    End If
```

```
If Trim(ProfileDoc.Subject(0)) <> "" Then
  BySubject = ProfileDoc.Subject
  strSubject = ""
  Forall value In BySubject
    If Trim(strSubject) = "" Then
      strSubject =  value
    Else
      strSubject = strSubject & "," & value
    End If
  End Forall
  qry  = "field Subject contains (" & strSubject & ")"
  If Trim(SearchQry) = "" Then
    SearchQry = qry
  Else
    SearchQry = SearchQry & " Or " & qry
  End If
End If

If Trim(ProfileDoc.Classification(0)) <> "" Then
  ByClassification = ProfileDoc.Classification
  strClassification = ""
  Forall value In ByClassification
    If Trim(strClassification) = "" Then
      strClassification =  value
    Else
      strClassification = strClassification & "," & value
    End If
  End Forall
  qry = "field Classification contains
          (" & strClassification & ")"
  If Trim(SearchQry) = "" Then
    SearchQry = qry
  Else
    SearchQry = SearchQry & " Or " & qry
  End If
End If
```

```
If Trim(ProfileDoc.Location(0)) <> "" Then
  ByLocation = ProfileDoc.Location
  strLocation = ""
  Forall value In ByLocation
    If Trim(strLocation) = "" Then
      strLocation =  value
    Else
      strLocation = strLocation & "," & value
    End If
  End Forall
  qry = "field Location contains (" & strLocation & ")"
  If Trim(SearchQry) = "" Then
    SearchQry = qry
  Else
    SearchQry = SearchQry & " Or " & qry
  End If
End If

If Trim(SearchQry) <> "" Then
  SearchQry = SearchQry & " and (not(field
            Form contains InterestProfile))"
  Print SearchQry
  Set DocCollection = db.UnprocessedFTSearch(SearchQry, 0)
End If
Else

IsCriteriaNull = True
If Trim(ProfileDoc.CreatedBy(0)) <> "" Then
  IsCriteriaNull = False
  ByAuthor = ProfileDoc.CreatedBy
  strAuthor = ""     're-intializing
  Forall value In ByAuthor
    st = """" & value & """"
    If Trim(strAuthor) = "" Then
      strAuthor =  st
    Else
      strAuthor = strAuthor & ":" & st
    End If
```

```
  End Forall
End If

If Trim(ProfileDoc.Category(0)) <> "" Then
  IsCriteriaNull = False
    ByCategory = ProfileDoc.Category
    strCategories = ""
    Forall value In ByCategory
      st = """" & value & """"
      If Trim(strCategories) = "" Then
        strCategories =  st
      Else
        strCategories = strCategories & ":" & st
      End If
    End Forall
End If

If Trim(ProfileDoc.Subject(0)) <> "" Then
  IsCriteriaNull = False
  BySubject = ProfileDoc.Subject
  strSubject = ""
  Forall value In BySubject
    st = """" & value & """"
    If Trim(strSubject) = "" Then
      strSubject =  st
    Else
      strSubject = strSubject & ":" & st
    End If
  End Forall
End If

If Trim(ProfileDoc.Classification(0)) <> "" Then
  IsCriteriaNull = False
  ByClassification = ProfileDoc.Classification
  strClassification = ""
  Forall value In ByClassification
    st = """" & value & """"
    If Trim(strClassification) = "" Then
```

```
        strClassification =  st
      Else
        strClassification = strClassification & ":" & st
      End If
    End Forall
  End If

  If Trim(ProfileDoc.Location(0)) <> "" Then
    IsCriteriaNull = False
    ByLocation = ProfileDoc.Location
    strLocation = ""
    Forall value In ByLocation
      st = """" & value & """"
      If Trim(strLocation) = "" Then
        strLocation =  st
      Else
        strLocation = strLocation & ":" & st
      End If
    End Forall
  End If

  If IsCriteriaNull = False Then
    SearchQry = |Select Form != "InterestProfile" & ( |
      If Trim(strAuthor) <> "" Then
        SearchQry = SearchQry & |@Contains(@UpperCase(CreatedBy);
                    @UpperCase( | + strAuthor + | )) || |
      End If
      If Trim(strCategories) <> "" Then
        SearchQry = SearchQry & |@Contains(@UpperCase(Category);
                    @UpperCase( | + strCategories + | )) || |
      End If
      If Trim(strSubject) <> "" Then
        SearchQry = SearchQry & |@Contains(@UpperCase(Subject);
                  @UpperCase( | + strSubject + | )) || |
      End If
      If Trim(strClassification) <> "" Then
        SearchQry = SearchQry & |
                      @Contains(@UpperCase(Classification);
```

```
                    @UpperCase( | + strClassification + | )) || |
        End If
        If Trim(strLocation) <> "" Then
          SearchQry = SearchQry & |@Contains(@UpperCase(Location);
                       @UpperCase( | + strLocation + | )) || |
        End If
        SearchQry = SearchQry & |@AllDescendants)|

        Set DocCollection  = db.UnprocessedSearch
                                  (SearchQry, Nothing, 0)
      End If

      If DocCollection.Count > 0 Then
        Set NewsLet = New NotesNewsletter(DocCollection)
        NewsLet.DoSubject = True
        NewsLet.SubjectItemName = "Newsletter"
        Set NotesDoc = NewsLet.FormatMsgWithDoclinks(db)
        NotesDoc.Form = "Memo"
        NotesDoc.Subject = "Discussion Newsletter"
        Call NotesDoc.Send(True, ProfileDoc.UserName(0))
      End If
    End If
    Set ProfileDoc = ProfileView.GetNextDocument(ProfileDoc)
    Loop
      'Rem stamp all the documents as processed by this agent to
       'exclude them from next run
      Set DocCollection = db.UnprocessedDocuments
      For j = 1 To DocCollection.Count
        Set doc = DocCollection.GetNthDocument( j )
        Call ns.UpdateProcessedDoc( doc )
      Next
End Sub
```

Creating the Agent to Open the Interest Profile Form

This agent is required to show the user only her interest profile. You will create an agent that opens a new form if the user has not created an interest profile or opens the existing document if the user has created one.

Perform the following steps to create the agent:

1. Create a new agent named OpenInterestProfile.
2. Select agent as shared agent.
2. In the Run Time section, select the trigger as On event.
3. Select None as the Target in the Run Time Section. This is because the @Command will be used to run this agent.
4. In the Programmer's pane, from the Run list, choose LotusScript as the agent's Run option.

The agent first checks whether or not the user has an Interest Profile document listed in the Interest Profile view. If the user has already created an Interest Profile document, the agent opens the existing profile document for that user. Otherwise, the agent composes a new Interest Profile document.

Enter the following code in the Initialize event of the agent:

```
Sub Initialize
    Dim ns As New NotesSession
    Dim ws As New NotesUIWorkspace
    Dim uidoc As NotesUIDocument
    Dim db As NotesDatabase
    Dim profileVw As NotesView
    Dim profileDoc As NotesDocument
    Dim user As String

    user = ns.UserName
    Set db = ns.CurrentDatabase
    Set profileVw = db.GetView("(InterestProfile)")
    Set profileDoc = profilevw.GetDocumentByKey(user,True)

    If Not(profileDoc Is Nothing) Then
      Set  uidoc=ws.EditDocument(True,profileDoc, False)
    Else
      Call ws.ComposeDocument( "", "", "InterestProfile" )
    End If
End Sub
```

Adding Navigational Tools to the Application

You will use an outline, a page, and a frameset to provide the navigational capabilities for the application.

Creating the Outline

Create a new outline and assign the name MainOutline in the Outline property box. Next, create outline entries to create the links to the various design elements, such as view and agent. To create a new entry, you can use the New Entry button. Create the following entries:

- **Discussion.** This is a header entry. In the Outline Entry property box, check the Do not display an image option.
- **By Author.** This links to the DiscussionByAuthor view. In the Content section, select the type as Named Element, View. Specify the name of the view as DiscussionByAuthor. Check the Do not display an image option.
- **By Subject.** This links to the DiscussionBySubject view. Specify the name of the view as DiscussionBySubject. Check the Do not display an image option.
- **By Date.** This links to the DiscussionByDate view. Specify the name of the view as DiscussionByDate. Check the Do not display an image option.
- **By Category.** This links to the DiscussionByCategory view. Specify the name of the view as DiscussionByCategory. Check the Do not display an image option.
- **By Location.** This links to the DiscussionByLocation view. Specify the name of the view as DiscussionByLocation. Check the Do not display an image option.
- **By Classification.** This links to the DiscussionByClassification view. Specify the name of the view as DiscussionByClassification. Check the Do not display an image option.

◆ **Interest Profile.** This runs the OpenInterestProfile agent to open the Interest Profile document. In the Content section, select Action as the type and enter the following formula by clicking the @ button:

```
@Command([ToolsRunMacro]; "(OpenInterestProfile)")
```

Select all the outline entries starting form the By Author entry to the By Classification entry and click the Indent Entry button to indent the entries under the Discussion entry.

Save and close the outline. The outline is shown in Figure 15.13.

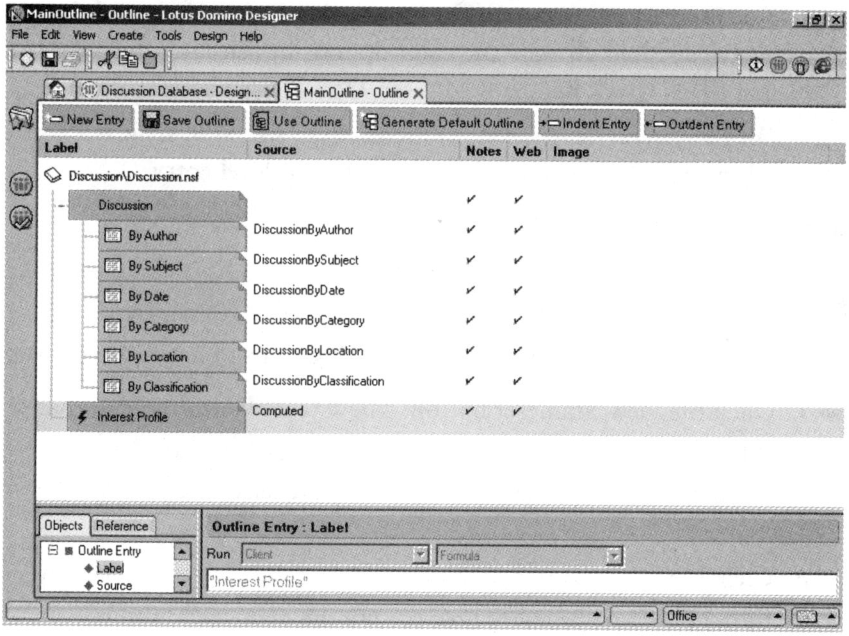

FIGURE 15.13 *Outline in Designer*

Creating the Page

After creating the outline, it needs to be used. To do so, you need to embed the outline in a page. To embed the outline in a page, create a new page and assign the name MainPage in the Page property box. In the Background tab, specify a variation of sky blue as the background color for the page.

Embed the outline in the page by performing the following steps:

1. Leave a blank line on the page and embed the MainOutline outline in the page. For the embedded outline, set the following properties in the Info tab:

   Assign the name MainOutline in the Name box.

   Clear the option Show twisties.

   Select the option Expand all in the Root entry section.

   Specify the height and width options as Fit to content.
2. In the Font tab of the Outline property box, set the following properties:

   Specify the font properties for the top-level entry: font as Arial, size as 9, style as Bold. Specify the color options by selecting the colors as Normal Black, Dark Red, and Moused Dark Brown.

   For the sublevel entry, select font as Arial, size as 9, style as Plain, and select the same color as selected for the top level entry.
3. Save and close the page.

Creating the Frameset

In the Frameset designer, perform the following steps to create a frameset:

1. Click the New Frameset button. The Create New Frameset dialog box appears.
2. Select the first frame in Arrangement and select 2 as the number of frames.
3. Click OK.
4. In the Frameset property box, specify the name as MainFrame.
5. Save the frameset.

Next, embed the page, MainPage, in the left frame.

1. Select the left frame by clicking it
2. In the Frame property box, specify the name of the frame as Left.
3. In the Content section, select the type as Named Element, Page. Select MainPage as the value for the page.
4. Enter Right in the Default target for links in frame box.

5. In the second tab, specify the width as 22. Set scrolling to Off and allow resizing to Off.
6. In the third tab, clear the 3D border check box. Clear Default as Border width and specify 2 pixels. Select the Border color as black.

In the right frame of the frameset, choose to display the DiscussionByCategory view:

1. Select the right frame by clicking it
2. In the Frame property box, specify the name of the frame as Right.
3. In the Content section, select the type as Named Element, View. Select DiscussionByCategory as the value for the view.
3. Specify Right in the Default target for links in frame box.

The frameset appears as shown in Figure 15.14.

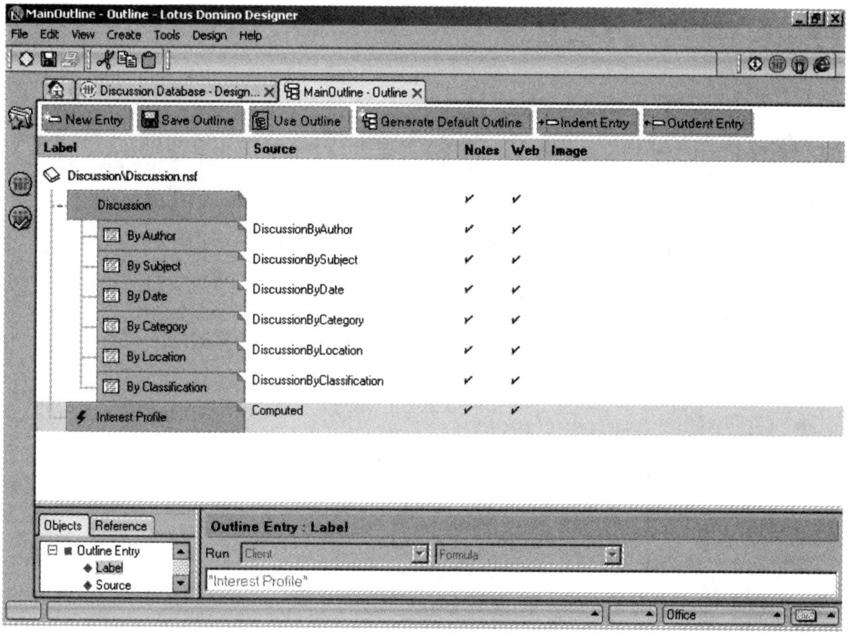

FIGURE 15.14 *The frameset*

Applying Navigational Structure

You will set the frameset that you created in the preceding section as the home page for the Discussion application. To set the frameset as the home page, perform the following steps.

1. Open the Database property box
2. In the Launch tab, in When opened in the Notes client section, select Open designated Frameset.
3. Select MainFrame as the name of the frameset.
4. Close the property box and double-click the database icon to see how the home page of the application looks.

With this, you have successfully finished the designing of the Discussion database. To finish the application, you need to set the ACL of the application.

Setting the ACL

After the development of the application is complete, the last step is to set the ACL for the application. The security of the application is controlled by the ACL. Set the access of the default user of the database as Author. This ensures that only the person who created the document will be able to edit the document. The Default access for normal users should be Author with following properties:

- Check Create Documents.
- Check Delete documents (the rights are controlled per document basis using the author field).
- Clear Create private agents.
- Check Create personal folders/views.
- Clear Create LotusScript/Java agents.
- Clear Write Public Documents.
- Check Replicate or copy documents.
- Add one or more privileged users with the Manager access with all properties.
- Add Servers with Manager access with all properties.

Summary

In this chapter, you learned how to create a Discussion database. You learned how to enforce document relationships and to create a hierarchical view to display the documents in a treelike structure. You also learned how to create a scheduled agent that will run in the background and an agent that will be invoked by the user. Using agents, you learned how to create a newsletter feature for a collaborative application.

PART IV

Professional Project 3—Creating a Workflow and Tracking Application in Domino

Project 3 Overview

In this project, you will learn to implement workflow and tracking in a Domino application. The project will walk you through the steps involved in creating a workflow and tracking application by using a Customer Complaint Tracking application.

The various participants who get involved in the sample Customer Complaint Tracking System can be listed as follows:

- The customer relations executive, who receives the complaint from the customer and logs it into the Customer Complaint Tracking System.
- The quality manager, who validates the complaint by visiting the customer and discussing the logged complaint with him. If the quality manager finds the complaint valid, he processes the complaint. If the complaint also involves a claim, he creates a claim record and informs the operations manager.
- The operations manager, who validates the complaint, as well as the claim associated with the complaint, and approves or rejects the claim amount.
- The accounts manager, who gives the final clearance for the claim amount and releases the payment for the claim.

In this chapter you'll create a Customer Complaint Tracking application to implement the following workflow and tracking functions:

- Send notifications to various people involved in the process.
- Send reminders to the people concerned if they do not take appropriate action in the stipulated time.
- Provide options for users to take action on the complaint.
- Create secured sections in the form so that only the person concerned can edit it.
- Track the status of the complaint by using a field.
- Create views to organize complaints.

The project uses an existing Domino database, customer.nsf, to look up the customer data.

The concepts that you'll learn through this project can be listed as follows:

- Components of workflow
- Routing documents and creating notification in a Domino application
- Creating controlled access sections
- Creating a field to record the workflow status
- Using `@DBColumns` and `@DbLookup` @Functions to access data from a Notes database
- Implementing roles

The project will be tested using Notes R6 client

Chapter 16

Introduction to Workflow and Tracking

Workflow enables people to communicate, collaborate, and coordinate business processes in the office. For example, consider the example presented in Chapter 1 "Overview of Domino Applications," about an employee applying for leave. He fills out a leave application form, which is then presented to his department manager for approval. Filling out the leave application form and presenting it to the department manager is communication. The department manager evaluates the application and decides whether or not to approve it. In the evaluation process, she is able to access the leave application and share her comments with the employee. This is collaboration. After the application is approved, the HR executive is informed about it, who in turn updates the employee's leave record. This is coordination. This automated communication, collaboration, and coordination constitutes a workflow application.

Tracking is an important feature of any workflow application, enabling users to identify the status or state of an activity at each stage of the workflow process. This helps save the time spent on manual tracking.

In this chapter, you'll learn about the basics of a workflow application. You'll learn the components of workflow and the tasks required to implement workflow. Finally, you'll learn how to implement tracking in a workflow application.

Components of Workflow

Workflow enables a group of people to achieve a goal in predefined ways by automating the repetitive part of work and presenting the right information to the right group of people at the right time. This definition of workflow indicates that a business process consists of the following elements:

- **Actions.** Predefined actions that are executed to achieve a goal
- **People.** The participants of the workflow process
- **Information.** The knowledge that is shared among people
- **Policies.** The business rules that control the process

Figure 16.1 illustrates the workflow involved in a leave approval process.

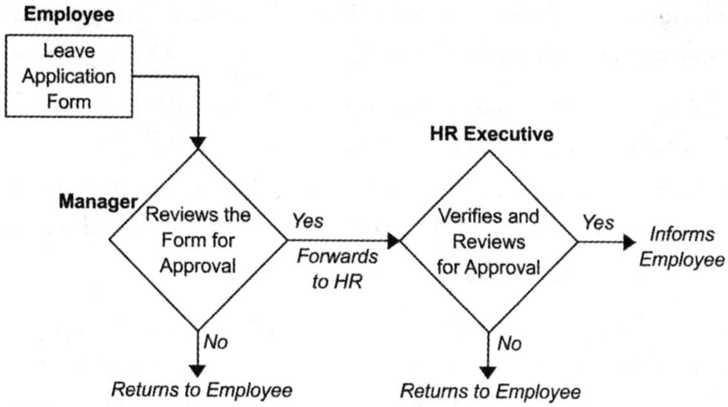

FIGURE 16.1 *The workflow involved in the leave approval process*

Based on the description of a workflow process, a workflow application consists of the following elements:

- Objects
- Roles
- Routes
- Rules

Objects

In all workflow processes, specific information is shared among a group of people. An *object* in a workflow process is the physical item used to share this information. A workflow object is usually a document. For example, in the leave approval process described earlier, the leave application is the object that is shared among the employees, the department manager, and the HR executive.

Each workflow object has a set life cycle with a start point and an end point. The start point for the leave document is the instant when the employee creates it. The end point is when the leave is approved at all levels or rejected at any level.

The people involved in workflow manipulate a workflow object. A document can be shared by keeping it in a centrally located shared database or by sending it to the concerned users through e-mail. However, sending the document to users has certain disadvantages, which are as follows:

- The document that is mailed is a copy of the original document. Therefore, multiple copies are created in the process of mailing it.
- It is difficult to track the status of the document at any stage because the changes occur in users' mail databases and not in the shared database.
- It is difficult to trace the document at any stage.

An alterative to sending documents through e-mail is sending notifications. A *notification* is a mail message sent to a person. It may contain a document link to the relevant document in a database. Creating a notification with a document link ensures that the document does not leave the database. A user can always come back to the database to check the status of the document. For example, in the situation discussed above, as soon as the employee fills out the leave application form, a notification is sent to the department manager; the notification provides a link to the leave document. The department manager can simply click the link to access the leave document and respond to it.

Notifications can also be created for sending automatic reminders. For example, consider the leave approval process under discussion. If the department manager fails to respond two days after an employee fills out the leave application form, an automatic reminder is sent to the department manager's mail database indicating that she needs to respond to the leave application.

A workflow process can have multiple workflow objects that are created either in parallel or serially. For example, imagine that a software-training institute has a New Training Orders database that is used to handle training orders received by the institute. Whenever the marketing manager fills out the form for a new training order, a training schedule, a faculty requisition, a courseware requisition, and a classroom requisition are generated automatically and sent to the respective departments. In this manner, multiple documents are generated in parallel with the order form.

Roles

Roles are the people involved in a workflow process. Being in a role, people may create content, make decisions, delegate work, and monitor the completion of work. In the leave approval process, the following roles can be identified:

- **Employee.** Fills out the leave application form
- **Department manager.** Approves or rejects the leave application submitted by the employee
- **HR executive.** Verifies and updates the leave record of the employee

The different roles in a workflow process can be mapped to the roles in the application database ACL. Defining roles in a workflow application helps in implementation of workflow logic independent of participants. It also helps in managing the security easily. You can also define what action each role is allowed to perform. For example, the action of approving or rejecting a leave application should be available only to department managers. Defining roles instead of achieving the same through usernames helps to achieve better flexibility and maintainability of the application by saving a lot of time and effort in rewriting code if participants change in a workflow Suppose the company discussed above has 1,000 employees, of whom 100 are department managers. All these employees will need to have access to the database and individual design elements. Department managers are transferred or promoted, and new department managers take their place. If you use usernames, you'll need to change your application every time a new employee joins as the department manager. Creating a role requires you to make the change only to the ACL.

Routes

A *route* defines the path that a workflow object follows during the process. It includes the start point, intermediary paths, and the end point of the object.

In the leave approval process, the following routes can be identified:

- From an employee to a department manager
- From a department manager to the HR executive
- From the HR executive back to the employee

In the case of exceptions, you can define alternate routes. For example, if the department manager rejects a leave application, a route from the department manager to the employee is followed.

The best way to implement routes in workflow is by using e-mail. At each step of the workflow process, the next person in the route is sent a notification about the action that he is required to perform. This ensures that all users concerned are informed in time and do not miss out when their action is due. Inserting a document link in the notification ensures that a user does not have to go around searching for the required documents. For example, in the leave approval process, when the employee fills out the leave application form and saves it, a notification is sent to the department manager informing her that she needs to take an action. A link in the notification enables the department manager to access the leave application by clicking it.

Rules

Rules are used to define business policies. These are the conditions that affect the workflow object. For example, an employee must fill out all the required fields in the leave application form and save it before it can be sent to the department manager. Another rule is that the department manager must approve the leave application before it is routed to the HR executive.

Rules are implemented using formulas and scripts . For example, a rule states that an employee must fill out the start date for leave and this start date must not be greater that the current date. This indicates that the start date field must have an input validation formula.

Rules are also used to define the security issues in the application. For example, if a rule states that only the department manager can take an action on a leave application and write comments, you must create a controlled access section, allowing access only to the department manager.

Implementing Workflow and Tracking

E-mail plays an important role in the implementation of workflow. A document can be mailed from an application database to another application database or to a user's mail database. It can also be mailed from a user's mail database to another user's mail database or an application database. The implementation of workflow involves basic functions, such as mail-enabling an application database, mail-enabling a form, and creating actions to send notifications.

Routing Documents

Routing is the process of mailing documents from one database to another. Whatever the route of a document is, the routing procedure can be described using Figure 16.2.

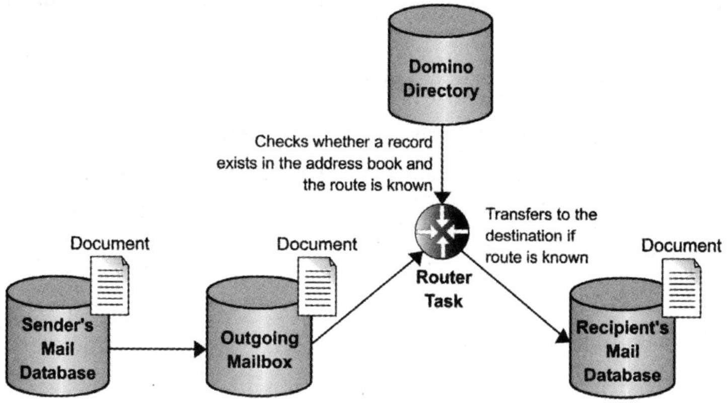

FIGURE 16.2 *The routing mechanism*

The routing mechanism consists of the following components:

- **Mail router.** This is a task that runs on the Domino server. It is responsible for routing e-mail to the databases on the same server or a different server.
- **Outgoing mailbox.** This is a database named mail.box on the Domino Mail server. This database temporarily stores all the mail that has to be delivered to users or databases.
- **Domino directory.** This is the public address book residing on the server. This database contains details about users, servers, and databases in the entire domain.
- **Mail-enabled databases.** These are databases on the server and are enabled for receiving e-mail. They include the user's mail databases and the databases that have a Mail-in database document in the Domino directory.

When a user sends an e-mail, it first goes to the outgoing mailbox. The router picks the e-mail from the outgoing mailbox and tries to find the destination address of the recipient from the Domino directory. Each user has a person document that contains the mail server and the mail file name for the user. For other types of databases, the Mail-in database document in the Domino directory contains information about the server on which a database is located and the file name of the database. The router delivers the mail to the specified mail file if the mail server is the current server. If not, it transfers the mail to the other server.

Creating a Mail-in Database Document

To mail-enable an application database, a Mail-in database document needs to be created in the Domino directory. A user with Author or higher access and a Net-Creator role can create a Mail-in database document. To create a Mail-in database document, perform the following steps:

1. Open the Domino directory on the Notes client.
2. Open the Mail-In Databases view and select Resources under the category Server.
3. Click Add Mail-in Database to open a new Mail-in Database document, as shown in Figure 16.3.

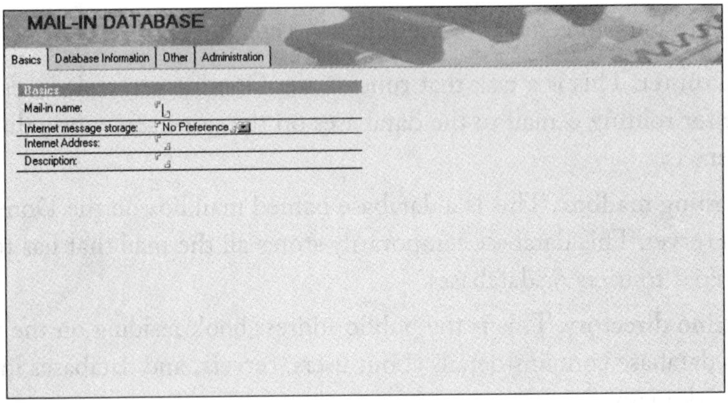

FIGURE 16.3 *Mail-in database document*

4. In the Basics tab, specify a Mail-in name for the database. This is the name used to address a database.
5. In the Database Information tab, specify the domain, server, and filename for the database.
6. Click Save and Close to save and close the document.

Now, when you create a mail message, you'll be able to send the mail to the application database by using its Mail-in name.

Mail-Enabling a Form

To enable users to e-mail documents based on a form, the form needs to be mail-enabled. A form that is mail-enabled must also have a method to address the document. The address of the recipient can be specified in a field named SendTo. This field is a reserved field and must contain the name of the user to whom the document needs to be mailed. You can also create the reserved fields CopyTo and BlindCopyTo to include the names of users in the CC or BCC list of the document that is mailed.

The various methods that can be used to mail-enable a form are listed below:

- Using the form property On Close: Present mail send dialog box
- Using the `MailOptions` reserved field
- Using the `@MailSend` @Function

Using a Form Property

You can enable the option On Close: Present mail send dialog box on the Defaults tab of the form properties box. When a user saves a document and closes it, Notes displays the Send Mail dialog box, as shown in Figure 16.4.

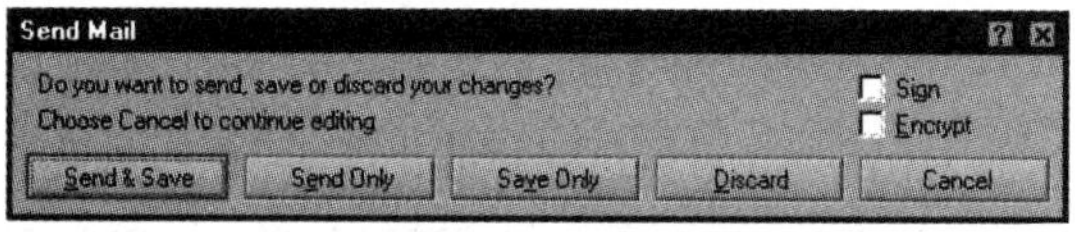

FIGURE 16.4 *The Send Mail dialog box*

In the dialog box, the user can select either the Send and Save option or the Send Only option and mail the document.

Using the MailOptions Reserved Field

`MailOptions` is a reserved field that can be assigned a value of either 1 or 0. The value 1 indicates that the document must be mailed, whereas the value 0 indicates that the document must not be mailed. This field can be created as a hidden computed field with a predefined value to automatically mail the document. It can also be made editable so that the user can decide whether or not she wants to mail the document.

Using the @MailSend @Function

The function `@MailSend` @Function is used without any parameters to mail a document to the user specified in the SendTo field. This function can be written on a form, a view action, a button, or an agent.

Sending Notifications

A notification is a mail message generated from a workflow application to send some information or reminder to a user. A notification can be generated using one of the following methods:

- **`@MailSend` @Function.** This function without parameters mails a document to a recipient. But if you specify one or more parameters with it, it sends a notification. For details about this @Function, please refer to Chapter 18, "Creating a Customer Complaint Tracking Application."
- **LotusScript.** You can also write LotusScript code to generate notifications. This method involves creating a new document; setting values for fields such as SendTo, CopyTo, Subject, and Body; and using the method named `send` of the `Document` class. For details about this method, please refer to Chapter 18.

Enabling Tracking

The main purpose of tracking is to ensure the availability of the status of the workflow process at any time. Tracking can be implemented in an application by using one or more of the following mechanisms:

- **Creating fields.** You can create fields that store the status of a document or the status of a workflow process. For example, in the leave approval process, you can create a field named `status` that displays the status of the leave application as New, Approved by DM, Rejected by DM, Approved by HR, or Rejected by HR. A user can identify the state of the leave application by looking at the `status` field.
- **Creating Views.** You can create views to display the status of the various documents. For example, a By Status view in the leave database displays all the documents organized by status of the leave application. Using this

view you can find the leave applications that have been approved or rejected or have been pending.

- **Creating consolidated reports.** You can generate scheduled reports that display a consolidated status of all the documents in the database. For example, in the New Training Orders database, you can create a report every weekend that provides information such as how many orders were generated, how many orders were implemented, and how many orders were completed. You can use scheduled agents to automate these reports.
- **Creating individual reports.** You can also generate scheduled reports that provide details about each phase in a workflow process. For example, in the New Training Orders database, you can create a report that displays the status of each activity for every training order, such as the status of the faculty, the courseware, or classroom requisitions. This report can be generated on a daily basis and can be used to monitor and plan the activities in the organization.
- **Creating a tracking table.** You can create a tracking table in a form that records the date and time and the person responsible for each action in the workflow process. For example, you can record the date and time and the person responsible for filling out the leave application, approving it, and finally verifying it.

Summary

In this chapter, you learned about the basic components of a workflow process. The chapter included the tasks required to implement a workflow process, such as creating a Mail-in database document, mail-enabling a form, and sending notifications. You also learned how to implement tracking in a workflow application.

Chapter 17

Project Case Study: Creating a Customer Complaint Tracking Application

In Chapter 16, "Introduction to Workflow and Tracking," you learned about the basics of workflow. In the next two chapters, you will learn how to implement workflow and tracking in a Notes application. To do this, you will create a customer complaint tracking application. This chapter discusses the case study for this project.

MMI Delivery Services: The Present Scenario

MMI Delivery Services started as Moving Meals Incorporated. This company started its operations in a small room with just five people. The company started taking orders for food from various restaurants in the town of Winslow and delivering them to the customer free of a delivery charge. The idea was an instant hit and the orders exceeded the expectations. Based on this success, the managing director Neil Edmond planned to diversify the operations and start delivering other items, such as movie tickets, cellular phone cash cards, and electronic items.

The operations manager was single-handedly responsible for controlling all operations, but the increasing volume of business started a whole lot of problems, such as orders not being delivered on time and delivery of damaged goods. To make sure that the customers did not lose faith in the company, MMI Delivery Services decided to follow up the problems with the customers. They even decided to pay back the customers for any damages. They assigned a quality manager, whose task would be to talk to the customers about the problems and solve them. Now they want an automated system that can help them log, process, track, and follow up with the customer complaints.

Customer Complaint Tracking System: The Solution

As mentioned in the preceding section, MMI Delivery Services intends to automate the CCTS (*Customer Complaint Tracking System*). The CCTS will allow them to log all customer complaints and to process these complaints by getting them verified and approved. It also has an option to create claim records to handle any damage charges. An extra level of approval would be required to approve these claims.

This system will help the company to record the actions taken on complaints and even do follow-ups. In addition, the CCTS has the facility whereby the customer can find out the status of a logged complaint. The following section describes a typical project cycle for developing this application.

Project Life Cycle

The development life cycle of a project involves three phases: project initiation, project execution, and project deployment.

The project initiation phase involves creating a comprehensive project plan. In addition, it also identifies team members and assigns responsibilities to them based on their skills..

The project execution phase involves the actual application development. This phase can be further divided into the following stages:

- Requirements analysis
- High-level design
- Low-level design
- Construction
- Integration and testing
- User acceptance testing

In Chapter 11, "Project Case Study: Creating a Reference Application," these stages were discussed in detail.

In the project deployment phase, the application is deployed at the client location. During deployment, support is provided to the client to handle any exceptions that may occur. Before proceeding further, take a look at each of the stages in the project execution phase.

Requirements Analysis

As the name suggests, during the requirements analysis stage, the team analyzes the various requirements that need to be fulfilled by the CCTS application. For this, the team working on the application studied various existing automated

CCTS applications, especially those involving claims. In addition, the team interviewed various customers who had benefited by these systems. As a result, the following requirements were identified for the customer complaint tracking application to be created. The application should:

- Be easy to use in terms of navigation
- Provide easy access to information through well-designed views
- Be secured such that only the responsible users can access the information and take actions
- Provide enough information at any stage about the status of the complaint to satisfy an inquiring customer

Based on the user requirements, the team decided on the design described in the next section.

High-Level Design

In the high-level design phase, the team decides on the working or functionality of the system. In addition, the various data input and output formats are finalized. The various operating requirements are also identified during this phase. Before the design is discussed, the various workflow elements required in the application are explained.

Workflow Analysis

The following elements were identified after analyzing the workflow of the application:

- **Workflow object.** The main workflow object in this application is the Complaint Request. Another workflow object identified is the Claim Record.
- **Start point.** The CRE (*customer relationship executive*) receives complaints from customers through phone calls, e-mails, or post and logs them into the system.
- **End point.** The quality manager closes the complaint after processing it.
- **Roles.** The different Roles identified are: CRE, QM (*quality manager*), OM (*operations manager*), AM (*accounts manager*), and MD (*managing director*).
- **Routes and rules.** Table 17.1 lists the routes, rules, and exceptions to rules in the workflow for the CCTS application.

Table 17.1 Routes and Rules in the CCTS Application

Route	Rule	Exception(s)
CRE to QM	Complaint is logged.	None.
QM to OM	Complaint is verified and claim record is created.	No claim record is created and complaint is closed.
OM to AM	Claim is approved by OM.	Claim is not approved by OM and returned to QM.
AM to QM	Claim is approved by AM.	Claim is not approved by OM and is returned to QM for review.

Figure 17.1 illustrates these elements through a workflow diagram.

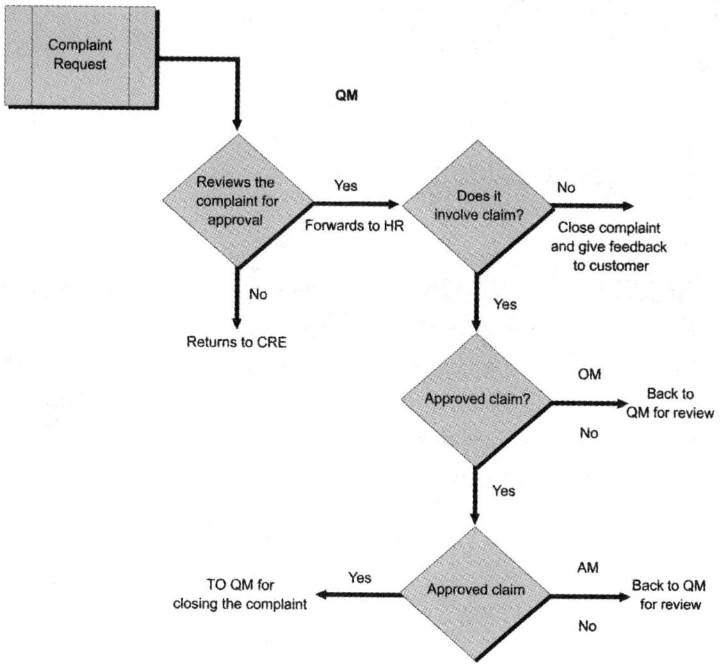

FIGURE 17.1 *The workflow analysis diagram for CCTS*

Design Analysis

Figure 17.2 displays the home page or navigator for the CCTS. This screen provides options to log new complaints as well as to view complaints in various formats. It also has an option for viewing the claim records and the acknowledgement letters sent to the customers and an option for database administration.

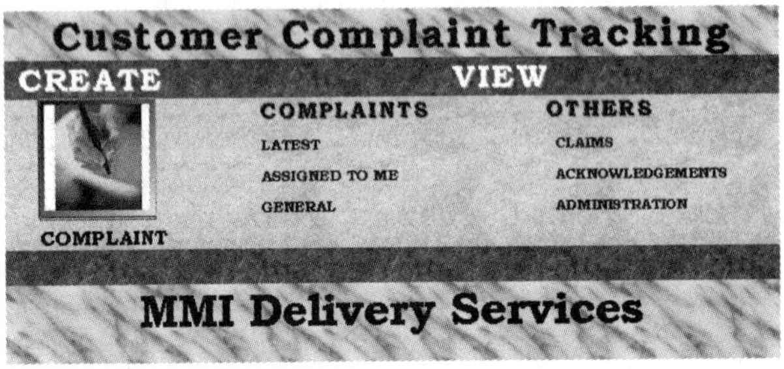

FIGURE 17.2 *The navigator for the CCTS*

Clicking the CREATE COMPLAINT link opens the Complaint Request form. This form is used to log a new complaint. A user fills in the details according to the complaints received from the customer. The customer details are fetched from the customer database on the basis of the Customer No. field. The complaints are classified as product-related complaints or service-related complaints. Figure 17.3 shows the Complaint Request form.

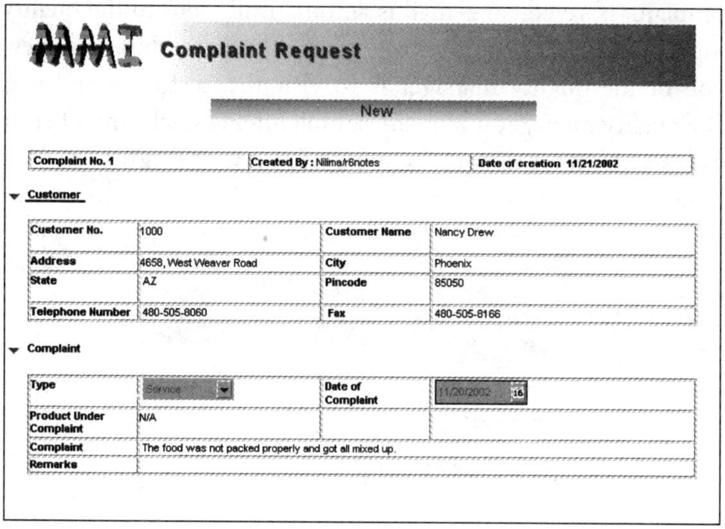

MMI Complaint Request

New

Complaint No. 1	Created By : Nilima/r6notes	Date of creation 11/21/2002

▾ Customer

Customer No.	1000	Customer Name	Nancy Drew
Address	4658, West Weaver Road	City	Phoenix
State	AZ	Pincode	85050
Telephone Number	480-505-8060	Fax	480-505-8166

▾ Complaint

Type	Service	Date of Complaint	11/20/2002
Product Under Complaint	N/A		
Complaint	The food was not packed properly and got all mixed up.		
Remarks			

FIGURE 17.3 *The Complaint Request form*

After the complaint has been saved, the user gets an option to print the acknowledgement letter to be sent to the customer. The acknowledgement letter can also be printed later. Figure 17.4 shows the format of the acknowledgement letter.

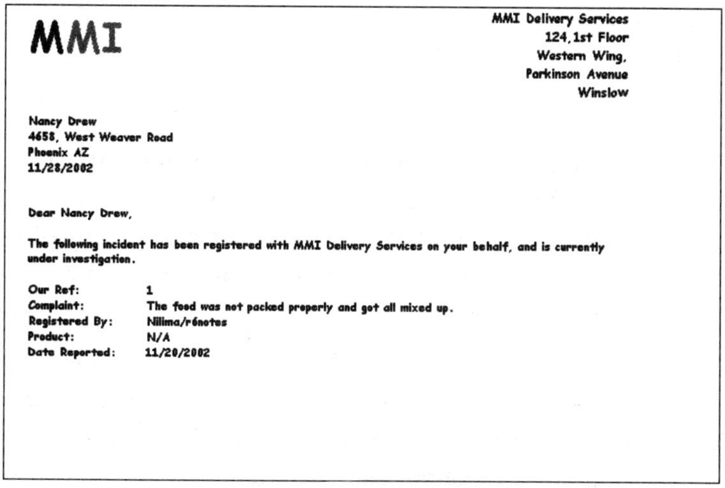

MMI

MMI Delivery Services
124, 1st Floor
Western Wing,
Parkinson Avenue
Winslow

Nancy Drew
4658, West Weaver Road
Phoenix AZ
11/28/2002

Dear Nancy Drew,

The following incident has been registered with MMI Delivery Services on your behalf, and is currently under investigation.

Our Ref:	1
Complaint:	The food was not packed properly and got all mixed up.
Registered By:	Nilima/r6notes
Product:	N/A
Date Reported:	11/20/2002

FIGURE 17.4 *Format of the acknowledgement letter sent to a customer*

When the complaint is saved, an e-mail is automatically sent to the quality manager and a copy to the managing director informing them about the new complaint. The job of the quality manager is to visit the customer and verify the complaint. The quality manager opens the complaint and clicks the QM's Report button to create a verification report. Figure 17.5 shows the format of the quality manager's report.

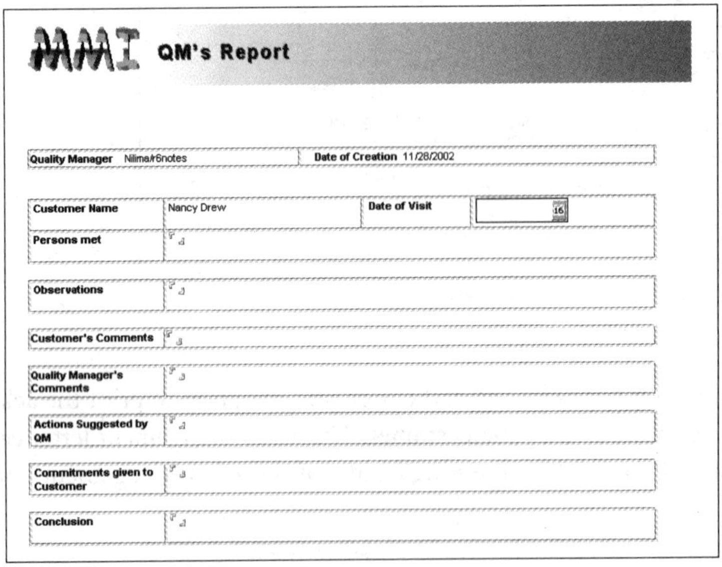

FIGURE 17.5 *The QM's Report*

Based on this report, the quality manager can reject a complaint, if there is no substance in it, by using the Reject Complaint button on the QM's Report. If the quality manager finds the complaint valid and the complaint also involves some claim, the quality manager creates a claim record by using the Claim Request button on the Complaint Request form.

The claim record needs to be approved at two levels. First the operations manager approves or rejects the claim. After an action is taken, the accounts manager is informed over e-mail and he can further approve or reject the claim. The approving authorities can approve an amount that is different from the actual claim amount. Figure 17.6 displays a sample Claim Request form.

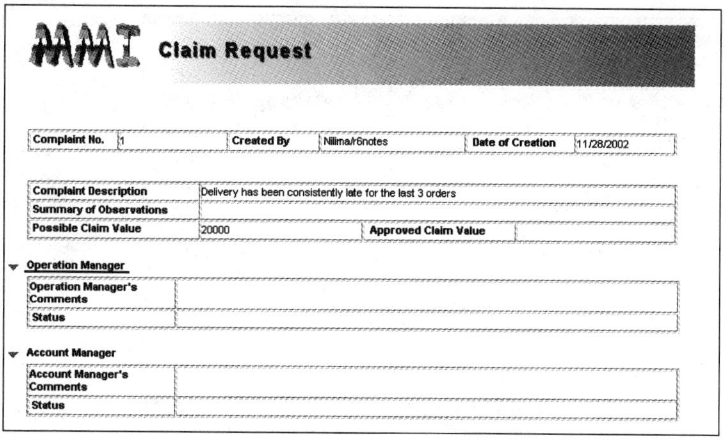

FIGURE 17.6 *The Claim Request form*

A complaint is closed in one of the following situations:

- The quality manager rejects the complaint after the customer visit.
- The quality manager finds that the complaint is valid but does not involve any claims. After processing the complaint, it can be closed.
- The complaint involves a claim amount and the approving authorities approve the amount. The quality manager, after processing the complaint, closes it.

In case any of the approving authorities do not approve the claim amount, the quality manager contacts the customer and updates the QM's Report and the claim record.

The option to close the complaint is available in the Complaint Request form. The complaint status is also visible on the Complaint Request form.

The complaints that have been recorded can be viewed in various ways. The VIEW—LATEST option on the navigator displays the complaints that have been logged in the last seven days. Figure 17.7 displays the Latest Complaints view.

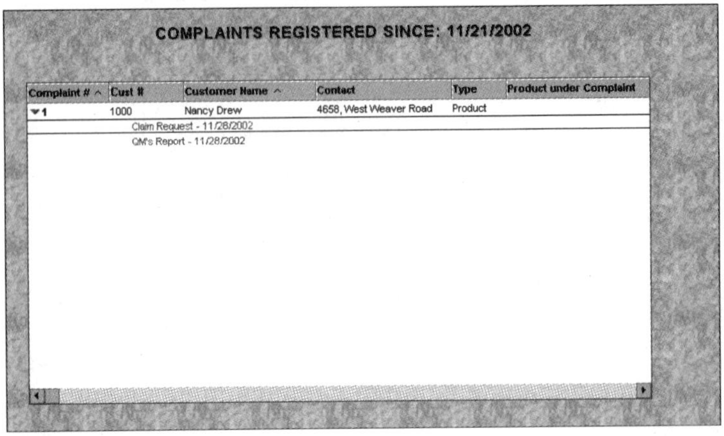

FIGURE 17.7 *The Latest Complaints view*

The VIEW—ASSIGNED TO ME option on the navigator displays the complaints that have been logged by the current user. Figure 17.8 displays the My Complaints view.

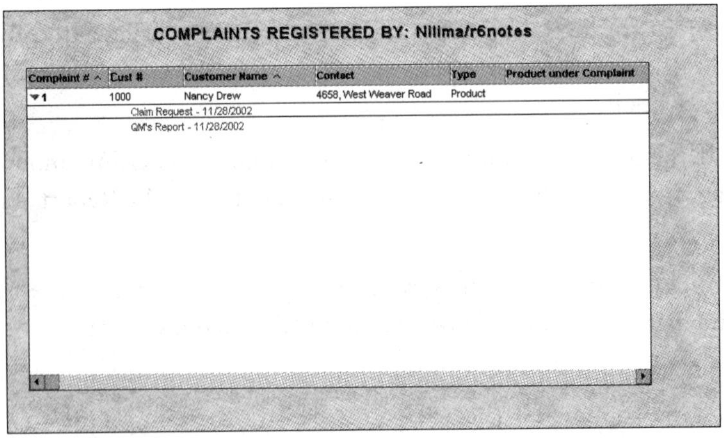

FIGURE 17.8 *The My Complaints view*

The VIEW—GENERAL option displays all the views in the database and the documents in the currently selected view, as shown in Figure 17.9.

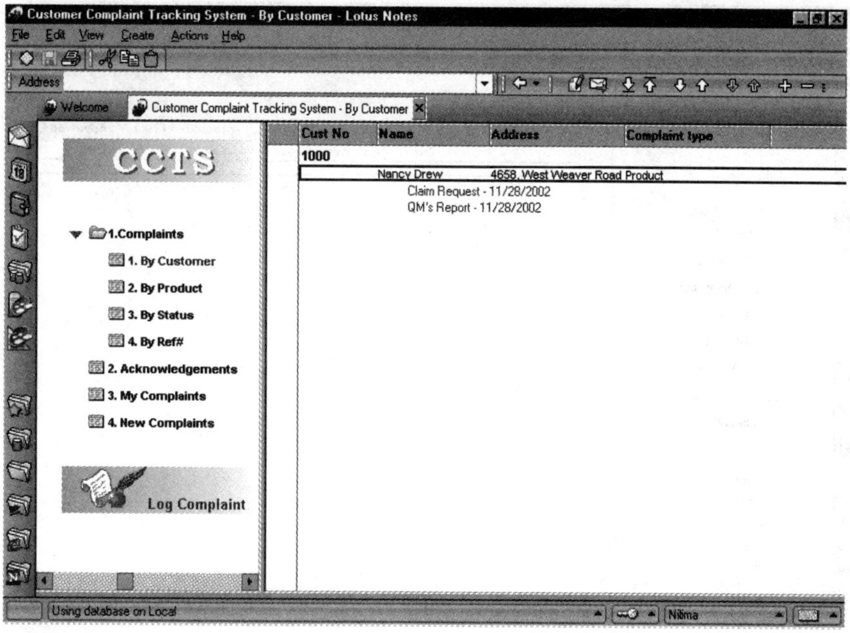

FIGURE 17.9 *The Database view*

There are four methods to view a complaint:

- By Customer
- By Product
- By Status
- By Reference Number

The option Acknowledgements in Figure 17.9 displays the acknowledgement letters created. The My Complaints and New Complaints options are for navigating to the My Complaints and Latest Complaints views from here. You can also create a new complaint request by clicking the Log Complaint link.

Clicking the VIEW—CLAIMS option on the navigator displays the Claims view. This view gives a total of the approved and the possible claim values, as shown in Figure 17.10.

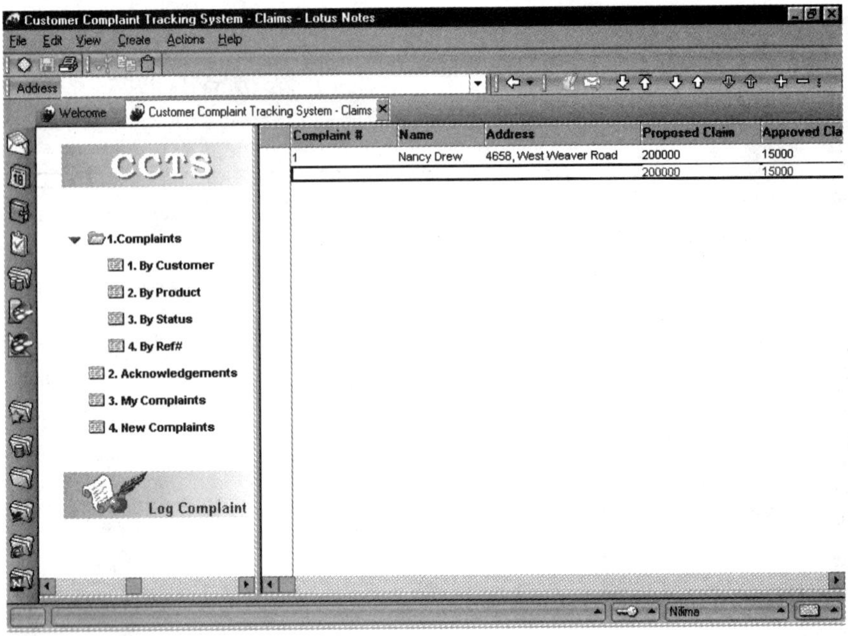

FIGURE 17.10 *The Claims view*

The VIEW—ACKNOWLEDGEMENTS option may be used to view the acknowledgement letters, as described earlier, directly from the navigator.

The VIEW—ADMINISTRATION option on the navigator is for the database administrator to update the database profile, which is used to store global values.

The CCTS contains a Send Reminder agent. If the quality manager does not submit a quality manager's report within seven days of creation of the complaint record, this agent sends a reminder to the QM. If she does not respond, then an e-mail is sent to the managing director.

Low-Level Design

In the low-level design phase, a detailed design of the various software modules is prepared using the high-level design. The team decides on the various standards, such as naming conventions for forms, views, and fields for a project. All these specifications are documented so that consistency can be maintained among the various modules for an application. The CCTS team also documents the various standards that they will follow while constructing this project.

Construction

In the construction phase, various components of the application are coded. The various specifications identified in the low-level design are used to accomplish this. In the CCTS case, the database forms and views and other elements are constructed.

Integration and Testing

In the integration and testing phase, various tests and validations are carried out on various modules and their integration functionality is checked. In the CCTS case, all the forms required, including the views, navigators, outlines, framesets, and agents, are integrated and tested.

User Acceptance Testing

In the user acceptance testing phase, various tests are carried out based on the predefined acceptance criteria given by the client. In addition, system support is provided to troubleshoot any issues or bugs identified at this phase. In the CCTS case, a few users can be asked to use the application and give feedback on it.

Summary

In this chapter, you learned about the MMI Delivery Services company that wants to maintain good customer relationships by giving a fast and effective response to customer complaints. You then looked at the proposed solution for this problem, the CCTS. Then you learned about the various requirements for this solution. Finally, the high-level and low-level designs of the CCTS of the application were discussed. In the next chapter, you will learn to create the various design elements required for the CCTS application.

Chapter 18

Creating a Customer Complaint Tracking Application

In Chapter 17, "Project Case Study: Creating a Customer Complaint Tracking Application," you learned about the CCTS (*Customer Complaint Tracking System*) application to be developed for MMI Delivery Services. You learned about the macro-level design of the application. The macro-level design described the types of features, such as forms, views, agents, and navigators, that need to be created for the application. In this chapter, you'll create the various elements in the CCTS application. To start with, let's create a database that'll be used to design the CCTS application.

Creating the Database

The CCTS application is a single database application. In addition, it will take input from the Customer database that is being used by MMI Delivery Services to store the customer details.

Because a workflow application involves multiple people, the CCTS database must be created on the server. However, while designing the application you can create it on local and later copy it to the server for testing. You'll be designing the database from scratch because there is no template available that suits the requirement. Create the new database with the following options:

- Server: Local
- Title: Customer Complaint Tracking System
- File Name: CCTS.nsf
- Template: Blank

Creating Forms

As identified in the high-level design, the CCTS application will contain the following five forms:

- Database Profile
- Complaint Request

- Acknowledgement Letter
- QM's Report
- Claim Request

Certain elements, such as some actions, will be common and therefore can be shared among these forms. Before you learn to design each individual form, you must design the shared elements in the database.

Creating Shared Elements

A database can contain various shared elements that reduce the development work of a database designer. You learned about shared resources in Chapter 3, "Working with Shared Resources." The shared resources identified for this database are shared actions and a Header subform. If you want to use images in your application, you can share them by creating image resources.

Shared Actions

Every form needs some basic actions that allow users to perform functions such as saving and closing a document, printing a document, editing a document, and closing a document without saving. Table 18.1 lists the shared actions to be created in the application. The table lists the name of the action, the language in which the code must be written, the code, and the Hide when options for the action, specifying under what conditions must each of these actions be hidden.

Table 18.1 List of Shared Actions

Action Name	Language	Code	Hide Action When Document Is:
Save & Close	Formula	`@Command([FileSave]);` `@Command([FileCloseWindow])`	Previewed for reading, Opened for reading
Close	Formula	`@Command([FileCloseWindow])`	None
Edit	Formula	`@Command([EditDocument])`	Previewed for editing, Opened for editing
Print	Formula	`@Command([FilePrint])`	None

Using the Table 18.1 as a reference, create the four shared actions described. Choose a suitable icon for these actions and leave the other action properties as default.

Subforms

Any group of design elements that are common in the forms must be created as a subform, which can be inserted in each form. In this database, the header area of each form contains the company logo and the title of the form. These elements are created as a subform called Header. Because the title of the form is different in each form, you can make it dynamic by creating a computed field on the subform with a value `Title`. This title can be defined individually in each form. Figure 18.1 displays the layout of the Header subform.

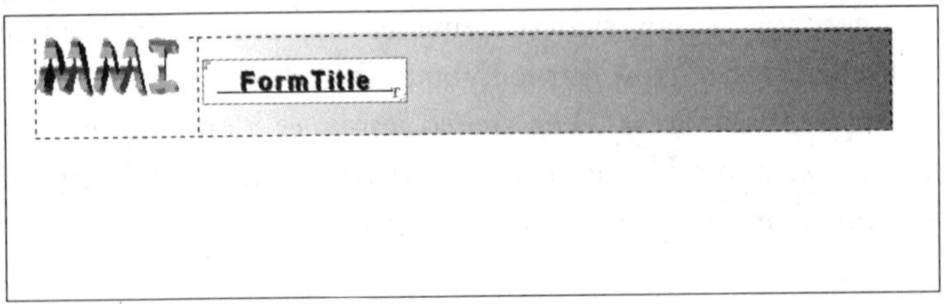

FIGURE 18.1 *The form layout for the Header subform*

Design the subform as shown in the layout. Create the FormTitle field of the type text and Computed when composed with a value as `Title`. Name the subform Header. Save and close the subform.

Creating the Database Profile Form

You can create a database profile to store field values that will be used across the database and also to define field values that are dynamic. A database profile is a good place to define the names of the users, such as the quality manager, the operations manager, and the accounts manager. The names of these users can be dynamically accessed from the database profile and need not be hard-coded in the form. This is useful if these users change, in which case, you can simply update the database profile instead of changing the form design.

The form contains four fields: MD, QM, OM, and AM. All these fields are of the type Names and have the property Use Address dialog for choices on the Control tab of the field properties enabled.

Follow the steps below to create the form for the database profile:

1. Create a new form in the CCTS database.
2. In the form properties, enter the name of the form as **DbProfile** and deselect the options Include in menu and Include in Search Builder from the Display section.
3. Design the form layout as shown in Figure 18.2.

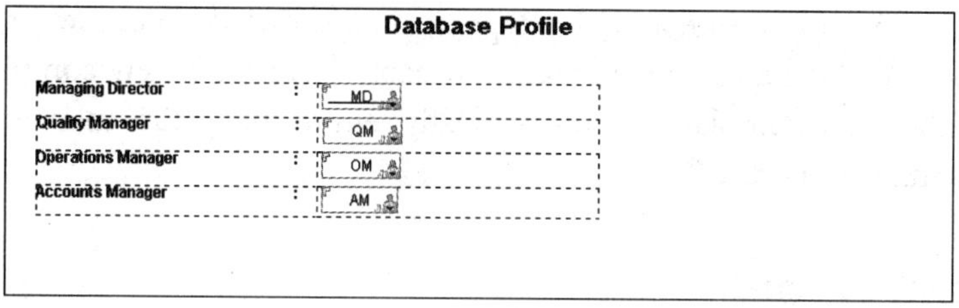

FIGURE 18.2 *The form layout for the DbProfile form*

4. Insert the Shared action Save & Close and save the form.

To create a profile document, you need to use certain special functions such as the EditProfile @Command. You can issue this command from an agent or a form or view action. To create an agentthatcreates the database profile based on the DbProfile form, perform the following steps:

1. Create a new agent in the database.
2. In the Agent dialog box, enter the name of the agent as **Update Profile**.
3. In the Runtime options, the Trigger is selected as Action menu selection by default. Select the target as **None**. This allows you to use @Commands.
4. Close the dialog box. Choose the option to run a formula, and in the Script area, enter the following code:

   ```
   @Command([EditProfile];"DbProfile")
   ```

5. Save and close the agent.
6. Run the agent from the Actions menu in the Notes client or the Agent/Run option in Domino Designer. This opens the database profile form. Add the appropriate names for the users and save and close the document.

These names can now be accessed in all other forms in the database to retrieve the required values.

Creating the Complaint Request Form

The main form that you'll design in this application is the Complaint Request form. This form is used to log new complaints. In addition to the shared actions, this form has actions to create a QM's Report, an acknowledgement letter, and a claim request. When the customer relation executive creates a new complaint, a notification about the complaint is automatically sent to the quality manager with a copy to the managing director.

Basic Form Layout

The Complaint Request form contains the labels and fields shown in Table 18.2.

Table 18.2 Description of Fields for the Complaint Request

Label	Field Name	Type
Complaint No.	ComplaintNo	Number, Editable
Created By	CreatedBy	Names, Computed when composed
Date of Creation	CreateDate	Date/Time, Computed when Composed
Customer No.	CustomerNo	Number, Editable
Customer Name	CustName	Text, Computed
Address	Address	Text, Computed
City	City	Text, Computed
State	State	Text, Computed
Pincode	Pincode	Text, Computed
Phone	Phone	Text, Computed
Fax	Fax	Text, Computed
Complaint Type	ComplaintType	ComboBox, Editable
Date of Complaint	DateOfComplaint	Date/Time, Editable

Label	Field Name	Type
Product under Complaint	ProductUnderComplaint	Text, Editable
Complaint	Complaint	Text, Editable
Remarks	Remarks	Rich Text, Editable

Perform the following steps to design the layout of the Complaint Request form:

1. Create a new form in the CCTS database.
2. To specify a window title for the form, select the Window Title event from the Objects tab and enter the following code in the Script area:

   ```
   @if(@IsNewDoc;"New Complaint Request";
   "Complaint No."+@Text(ComplaintNo))
   ```

   This formula displays the title New Complaint Request if the document has not been saved. After the document is saved, it displays Complaint No. and the value in the ComplaintNo field.
3. Place the cursor at the beginning of the form and create a field named Title with Type as Text and Computed when composed. In the Value event of this field, enter **"Complaint Request"**. Choose to hide this field from Notes users.
4. Place the cursor in the next line and insert the subform Header. The Header subform created earlier contains a field with the value as title. The Title field created on the form will act as the source for this field and the title of the form will get displayed in the header.
5. Next create labels and fields on the form. Figure 18.3 displays the organization of these fields on the form.

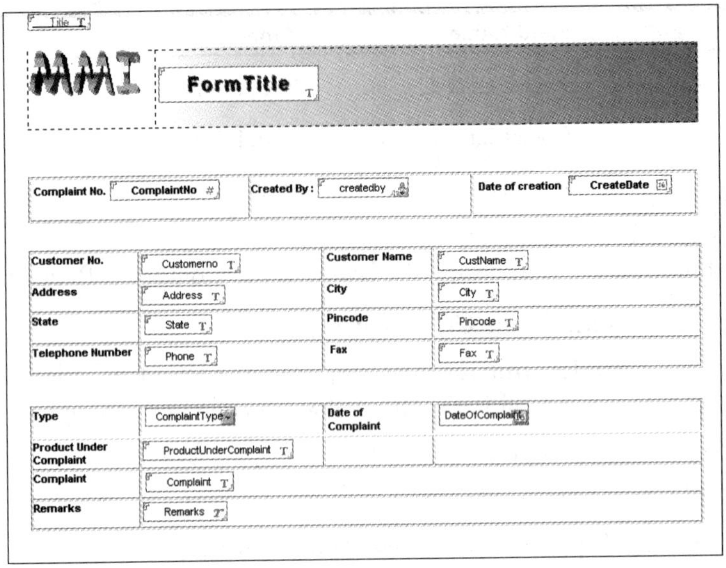

FIGURE 18.3 *The form layout for the Complaint Request form*

6. To specify the options for the ComplaintType field, double-click the field to access the field properties. Click the Control tab. Select Border style as None. From the Choices list, select the option Enter choices (one per line) and enter the choices as **Product** and **Service**, as shown in Figure 18.4.
7. To specify a Calendar control with the DateOfComplaint field for the user to select a date, select the option Calendar/Time control from the Field Info tab of the field properties.
8. Create a section named Customer Details that includes the customer related fields. Create another section named Complaint Details that includes the fields describing the Complaint.
9. Next open the form properties and set the form properties as described below:
   - In the Name field, enter **Complaint Request|CR** as the name of the form.
   - In the Options section, check Automatically refresh fields. This property is used to validate and recalculate the fields in the form as soon as you move out of a field. If this property is not selected, the fields

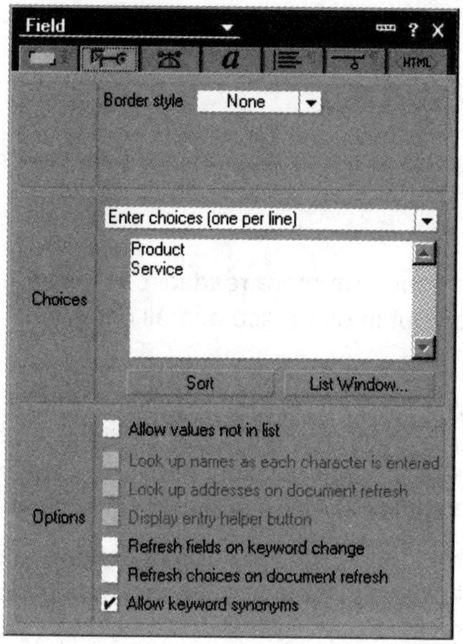

FIGURE 18.4 *The ComplaintType field properties for entering the choices*

in the form are recalculated only when the form is saved or the F9 (Refresh) key is pressed.

NOTE

Automatically refresh fields form property can slow down the display and the data entry time for your form.

10. Close the form properties and insert the shared actions Save & Close, Close, Edit, and Print created earlier using Create/Insert Shared Action.
11. Save the form layout.

TIPS FOR DESIGNING A FORM

Some of the tips to design a form include:

- Designing a form using tables helps you to better align the form elements and also to maintain the layout of the form even after the data has been entered in the fields.
- Grouping related information makes your form more readable. In this form, All customer-related fields have been put in one place and all complaint-related fields in another.
- Creating sections helps you make your form more compact and displays only relevant information to a user. If you want to create multiple sections in a form, you must create a separate table for each section, because a single table cannot be broken into multiple sections.
- The fields in a form are evaluated from left to right and top to bottom. A field whose value is used by another field in calculation should always be placed before the field using it for calculation.
- It is a good practice to group all hidden fields in a form at one location and apply a different font color and size to distinguish them. The fields whose values are predefined must be placed at the top and the fields whose values are determined during form calculation must be placed at the bottom of the form.

Adding Values for Computed Fields

After designing the basic layout of the form, you'll learn to write formulas for the Value event of the computed fields in the form.

The CreatedBy field records the name of the person who logs the complaint. To retrieve the username of the current user, you can use the @Username @Function. In a Text type field, this name displays in the canonical format. For example, a username Jessica/r6notes displays as CN=Jessica/O=r6notes. To display this name in the abbreviated format as Jessica/r6notes, enter the following formula in the value event of the CreatedBy field:

```
@Name([Abbreviate];@UserName)
```

TIP

The username in fields of the type Names, Readers and Authors is displayed in the abbreviated format without the use of the @Name @Function.

CreateDate field records the date on which the complaint is logged. To get the current system date, in the Value event of the CreateDate field, enter the following formula:

```
@Today
```

CustName, Address, City, State, Pincode, Phone, and Fax are the other computed fields in the form. The data in these fields is fetched from the Customer database that contains all customer details by matching the customer number entered by the user. The Customer database contains a view named CUSTLU created for this purpose. This view has the first column as customernumber, which is also the first sorted column of the view. The other columns are name, address, city, state, pin code, phone, and fax, in the same order.

In the value event of the customer name field, enter the following code:

```
@Dblookup("Notes":"NoCache";
"R6Server/R6Notes":"Customer.nsf";"CUSTLU";CustomerNo;2;[FAILSILENT])
```

This @Function searches the value in the customerno field in the customernumber column of the CUSTLU view and fetches the value of the customer name from the second column for the matching document. The keyword `[FAILSILENT]` ensures that if the matching value is not found in the view a null value is returned instead of an error message.

Similarly, add the formulas for the rest of the fields, as shown in the Table 18.3.

Table 18.3 Formulas for Customer-Related Computed Fields

Field Name	Formula
Address	`@Dblookup("Notes":"NoCache"; "R6Server/R6Notes":"Customer.nsf";"CUSTLU";CustomerNo;3; ;[FAILSILENT])`
City	`@Dblookup("Notes":"NoCache"; "R6Server/R6Notes":"Customer.nsf";"CUSTLU";CustomerNo;4; ;[FAILSILENT])`
State	`;@Dblookup("Notes":"NoCache"; "R6Server/R6Notes":"Customer.nsf";"CUSTLU";CustomerNo;5; ;[FAILSILENT])`
Pincode	`@Dblookup("Notes":"NoCache"; "R6Server/R6Notes":"Customer.nsf";"CUSTLU";CustomerNo;6; ;[FAILSILENT])`
Phone	`@Dblookup("Notes":"NoCache"; "R6Server/R6Notes":"Customer.nsf";"CUSTLU";CustomerNo;7; ;[FAILSILENT])`
Fax	`@Dblookup("Notes":"NoCache"; "R6Server/R6Notes":"Customer.nsf";"CUSTLU";CustomerNo;8; ;[FAILSILENT])`

ACCESSING DATA FROM A NOTES DATABASE

To access data from another Notes database, you can use the following two @Functions:

- `@DbColumn`. This is an @Function that is used to fetch a column from a Notes view or folder. For example, if you want to display the existing customer numbers to the user for selection, you can use @DbColumn to fetch the customer number column from a view in the Customer database. The syntax of @DbColumn @Function is as follows:

  ```
  @DbColumn(class:cache;server:database;view;columnnumber)
  ```

  In the above syntax, `class` denotes the type of database you are accessing. Use `Notes` or a null for a Notes database.

  `cache` is used to specify whether or not you want to store the data from the database in the cache. The options are `Cache`, `NoCache`, and `ReCache`.

ACCESSING DATA FROM A NOTES DATABASE (continued)

`server:database` specifies the location of the database. Server is the server on which the database is located; you can use null or empty quotations ("") for a local database. Database is the file name of the database. You can use null or empty quotations for the current database.

`view` is the name of the view that you are accessing to retrieve the data.

`columnnumber` is the sequence number of the column that you want to retrieve.

- `@DbLookup`. This is an @Function that is used to search for a key value in the first sorted column of a view and for all the documents where the key value is matched. It returns the content of a specified column or a field. For example, you can use this @Function to retrieve the customer name and address based on the value of the customer number from a view. In this view, the customer number is the first sorted column. The syntax of this @Function is as follows:

```
@DbLookup(class:cache;server:database;view;keyvalue;column-
number;keywords)
```

In this syntax, `keyvalue` represents the value that must be searched in the first sorted column of the view and `columnnumber` represents the column whose value must be returned for the documents that match the key value. Keywords can be used to specify one of the following options:

- `[FAILSILENT]` to return a null string if a matching value is not found in the view.
- `[PARTIALMATCH]` to return a value even if the key value matches just the beginning characters.
- `[RETURNDOCUMENTUNIQUEID]` to return the document UNID instead of the column value.

The rest of the arguments are the same as @DbColumn.

Sending a Notification

As mentioned earlier, when a complaint request is saved, a notification is sent to the quality manager, and a copy to the managing director, informing them that a new complaint has been logged.

Before writing the code for the notification, you must have the names of the quality manager and the managing director. The names of these users are stored in the database profile. To access these values in the form, create two new fields of the type text and computed, next to the Title field on the top. Name these fields MD and QM. Because these fields are placed on the same line as a hidden field, they will automatically be hidden. Enter the following code in the Value events of these fields:

```
In the field QM, enter @GetProfileField("DbProfile";"QM").
In the field MD, enter @GetProfileField("DbProfile";"MD").
```

Now select the QuerySave event of the form. Select to run a formula and enter the following code to send a notification:

```
@If(@IsNewDoc;@MailSend(QM;MD;Null;"New Complaint Request";
"A New Complaint Request has been created with a Complaint Number: "+
@text(Complaintno)+ " Pls. take required action";
Null;[IncludeDocLink]);Null)
```

Checking the state of the document using @IsNewDoc ensures that the notification is sent only once when the document is saved for the first time.

SENDING NOTIFICATION USING @MAILSEND

@MailSend is an @Function that is used to send notifications to users in a workflow application. The syntax of @MailSend is as follows:

```
@MailSend(SendTo;CopyTo;BlindCopyTo;Subject;Remark;BodyFields;[Flags])
```

Following is the description for each argument in the above syntax:

- `SendTo` evaluates to the names of the users to whom the notification is addressed.
- `CopyTo` is an optional argument that evaluates to the names of the users to whom a copy of the notification is sent.
- `BlindCopyTo` is an optional argument that evaluates to the names of the users whose names must be included in the blind copy list of the notification.
- `Subject` is an optional argument that contains the text you want to display in the subject field of the notification.
- `Remarks` is an optional argument that contains the text that you want to display in the body of the notification message.

SENDING NOTIFICATION USING @MAILSEND (continued)

- `BodyFields` is an optional argument that contains names of one or more fields from the form that you want to include in the message body of the notification. Fieldnames must be enclosed in quotation marks and multiple fields must be separated by a colon symbol.
- `Flags` is an optional argument that indicates one or more keywords specifying the priority or security of the memo. Some of the flags are:
  - `[INCLUDEDOCLINK]` to include a link to the originating document
  - `[SIGN]` to electronically sign the message
  - `[ENCRYPT]` to encrypt the message for the recipient
  - `[PRIORITYLOW]` to send the message as low priority

Creating an Acknowledgement Letter

The Acknowledgement Letter form has been designed with the purpose of allowing a user to print an acknowledgement for any complaint logged and send it to the customer. This form does not contain any editable fields and inherits most of the fields from the Complaint Request form.

The acknowledgement letter can be created after saving a complaint request using an action on the Complaint Request form. In the following subsections, you'll design the Acknowledgement Letter form and create the action on the Complaint Request form to create an acknowledgement letter.

Designing the Acknowledgement Letter Form

Table 18.4 specifies the field name, the type, and the formula for each of the fields that must be created in the Acknowledgement Letter form. The formula for inherited fields is the name of the field in the parent form whose value the field inherits.

Table 18.4 Details of Fields on the Acknowledgement Letter

Field Name	Type	Formula in the Value Event
CustName	Text, Computed when composed	CustName
CustAddress	Text, Computed when composed	Address
State	Text, Computed when composed	City+" "+State
Date	Date/Time, Computed when composed	@Today
CustomerNam	Text, Computed when composed	CustName
ComplaintNo	Number, Computed when composed	ComplaintNo
Complaint	Text, Computed when composed	Complaint
CreatedBy	Text, Computed when composed	CreatedBy
ProductUnderComplaint	Text, Computed when composed	ProductUnderComplaint
DateOfComplaint	Date/Time, Computed when composed	DateOfComplaint

NOTE

The fields that inherit from the parent document must be created as Computed when composed fields if you do not want the user to change their values later. This is because inheritance takes place only at the time of creation of a new document. If you want these fields to be editable, you can specify the inheritance formula in the Default Value event of the field.

To create the Acknowledgement Letter form perform the following steps:

1. Create a new form in the CCTS database.
2. Enter the Window Title as **"Acknowledgement Letter"**.
3. Create the layout of the form, as shown in Figure 18.5.

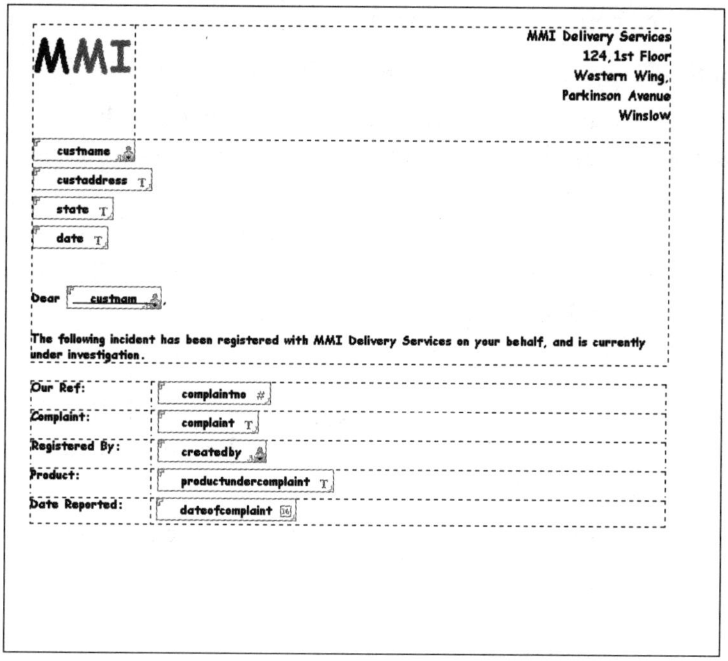

FIGURE 18.5 *The form layout for the Acknowledgement Letter form*

4. Open the form properties and set as described below:
   - On the Form Info tab, in the Name field, enter **Acknowledgement Letter|AL** as the name of the form.
   - From the Display section, deselect the option Include in menu to prevent a user from creating this letter directly using the menu.
   - To enable inheritance, click the Defaults tab and check the option On Create—Formulas inherit values from the selected document.
5. Close the form properties and insert the Save & Close and Print shared actions on the form.
6. Save and close the form.

Creating the Acknowledgement Letter Action

The Acknowledgement Letter action on the Complaint Request form gives the user the option to create an acknowledgement letter to be sent to the customer after logging the complaint. The acknowledgement letter can only be created once; therefore, the action is only available once.

To create the action, perform the following steps:

1. Open the Complaint Request form in Domino Designer.
2. Create a new action, and in the Action dialog box, enter the name as **Acknowledgement Letter.** From the Icon option, select Notes and select an appropriate icon for the action.
3. To hide the action, after the acknowledgement letter has been created once, in the Hide Action When tab of the action, check Hide action if formula is true and enter the following formula:

   ```
   ALCreated ="Yes"
   ```

4. Place the cursor next to the hidden fields at the top of the form and create a new field named **ALCreated** of the type Text and Editable. In the Default Value event of this field, enter **"No"**.
5. Close the action properties. In the Click event of the action, select Formula and enter the following code:

   ```
   @Command([EditDocument];"1");
   FIELD ALCreated:="Yes";
   @Command([Compose];"AL")
   ```

When a user clicks on this action, the document is changed to edit mode. The field ALCreated is updated to Yes. A new acknowledgement letter is created. The action hides because the value in the field ALCreated has become Yes.

NOTE

When you use the keyword FIELD to update a field using an action the document must be in the edit mode, otherwise the field is not updated. Add the formula `@Command([EditDocument];"1")` to all actions that are used to write to a field.

Creating the QM's Report Form

The QM's Report form is used by the quality manager to create the verification report for the complaint. This report is created based on the interaction of the quality manager with the customer. The QM's Report can only be created from an action on the Complaint Request form. This action is accessible only to the quality manager.

Designing the QM's Report Form

Table 18.5 lists the labels, field names, and the field types that you'll create in the QM's Report form.

Table 18.5 Details of Fields on the QM's Report

Label	Field Name	Type
Quality Manager	QMName	Names, Computed when composed
Date of Creation	CreateDate	Date/Time, Computed when composed
Customer Name	CustName	Text, Computed when composed
Date of Visit	DateofVisit	Date/Time, Editable
Persons Met	PersonsMet	Text, Editable
Observations	Observations	Text, Editable
Customer's Comments	CustomerComments	Text, Editable
Quality Manager's Comments	QMComments	Text, Editable
Actions Suggested by QM	Actions Suggested	Text, Editable
Commitments given to Customer	Commitments	Text, Editable
Conclusion	Conclusion	Text, Editable

To create the QM's Report form, perform the following steps:

1. Create a new form in the CCTS database.
2. Enter the Window Title as "**QM's Report**".
3. Place the cursor at the beginning of the form, and create a field named Title with Type as Text and Computed when composed. In the Value event of this field, enter "**QM's Report**". Choose to hide this field from Notes.
4. Place the cursor in the next line and insert the subform Header. The Header subform will display the title as QM's Report.
5. Create the layout of the form, as shown in Figure 18.6.

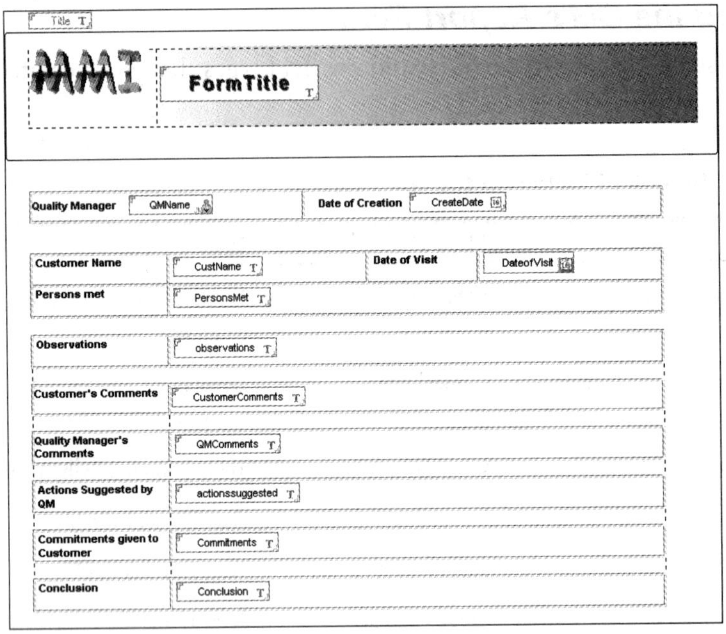

FIGURE 18.6 *The form layout for the QM's Report form*

6. Add the following formulas to the Value event of the computed fields:
   - ◆ QMName. @UserName
   - ◆ CreateDate. @Today
   - ◆ CustName. CustName
7. Open the form properties and set as described below:
   - ◆ On the Form Info tab, in the Name field, enter **QM'sReport|QMR** as the name of the form.
   - ◆ Select Type as Response.
   - ◆ From the Display section, deselect the option Include in menu to prevent a user from creating a QM's Report directly using the menu.
8. Insert the Save & Close, Close, Edit, and Print shared actions on the form.
9. Save and close the form. Because this is a response form, you will not be able to preview it. To test the form, use the QM's Report action on the Complaint Request form.

Creating the QM's Report Action

The QM's Report is created using the QM's Report form. It can be implemented exactly the same way as the Acknowledgement Letter action, but you will add a different functionality to this action. This action creates a QM's Report if it has not already been created. After the report is created, if a user clicks the action again, it displays the existing report. To add this action to the form, perform the following steps:

1. Open the Complaint Request form in Domino Designer.
2. Create a new action. In the Action dialog box, enter the name of the action as **QM's Report** and select an appropriate icon for the action.
3. To hide the action from all users other than a user with a QM role, in the Hide Action When tab of the action, check Hide action if formula is true and enter the following formula:

```
@IsNotMember("[QM]";@UserRoles)
```

> **NOTE**
>
> The @UserRoles @Function returns the list of roles that have been assigned to a user on a server database. On a local database, this @Function returns a null string.

> **TIP**
>
> If you want to test this @Function on a local database, you can enable the option Enforce a consistent Access Control List across all replicas in the database ACL.

4. Close the Action dialog box. In the Click event for the Action, select the Run option as LotusScript, and enter the following code:

```
Dim ws As New NotesUIWorkspace
Dim db As NotesUIDatabase
Set db=ws.currentdatabase
Dim doc1 As NotesDocument
Dim doc2 As NotesDocument
```

```
Dim col As NotesDocumentCollection
Set doc1=ws.currentdocument.document
Set col=doc1.responses
Dim found as variant
If col.count<>0 Then
    Set doc2=col.getfirstdocument
    Do Until doc2 Is Nothing
    If doc2.form(0)="QMR"Then
        found=True
        Call ws.editdocument(False,doc2)
        Exit Do
    Else
        Set doc2=col.getnextdocument(doc2)
    End If
    Loop
End If
If found=False  Or col.count=0 Then
    Set doc2=New notesdocument(db.database)
    doc2.form="QMR"
    doc2.custname=doc1.custname
    doc2.productundercomplaint=doc1.productundercomplaint
    call doc2.makeresponse(doc1)
    call ws.editdocument(True,doc2)
End If
```

The complaint request has two types of response documents—QM's Report and Claim Request. In the above code, a document collection of the response documents to the current document is created using the `responses` property of the `Document` class.

If the number of responses for the current document is 0, a new QM's Report is generated. If the number of responses is greater than 0, then the form field of each response document is checked for a value QMR. If a document with a form as QMR exists, it is opened and displayed to the user; otherwise, a new QM's Report is generated.

To create a new QM's Report, a new document is created. The fields that must be inherited from the current document, such as CustName and ProductUnder-Complaint, are assigned to the new document, and then the document is made as a response to the current document. Finally the document is opened in edit mode for the user.

Creating the Claim Request Form

The quality manager creates the claim request after finding that the complaint is valid and that it involves some amount of claim by the customer. The claim request is approved at two levels—the operations manager and the accounts manager. Both the managers can enter their comments and change the approved claim value.

Basic Form Layout

The Claim Request form is a response form to the complaint request. The complaint number in the Claim Request form is inherited from the parent complaint request. Table 18.6 lists the field labels, field names, and their types to be created on the Claim Request form.

Table 18.6 Details of Fields in the Claim Request Form

Label	Field Name	Type
Complaint No.	ComplaintNo	Number, Computed when composed
Date of Creation	CreateDate	Date/Time, Computed when composed
Complaint Description	Description	Text, Editable
Summary of Observations	Observations	Text, Editable
Possible Claim Value	PossibleClaim	Number, Editable
Approved Claim Value	Approved Claim	Number, Editable
Operations Manager's Comments	OMComments	Text, Editable
Status	OMStatus	Text, Computed
Accounts Manager's Comments	AMComments	Text, Editable
Status	AMStatus	Text, Computed

To create the Claim Request form, perform the following steps:

1. Create a new form in the CCTS database.
2. In the Window Title event of the form, enter **"Claim Request"**.
3. Place the cursor at the beginning of the form, and create a field named Title with Type as Text and Computed when composed. In the Value event of this field, enter **"Claim Request"**. Choose to hide this field from Notes users.
4. Next to the Title field, create three more hidden fields of the type Names, Computed. Name the fields **QM**, **OM**, and **AM**. Write the following codes in the Value event of the fields:
   - QM. `@GetProfileField("DbProfile";"QM")`
   - OM. `@GetProfileField("DbProfile";"OM")`
   - AM. `@GetProfileField("DbProfile";"AM")`
5. Place the cursor on the next line, and insert the subform Header. The Header subform will display the title as Claim Request.
6. Next create labels and fields as specified in Table 18.6. Figure 18.7 displays the organization of these fields on the form.

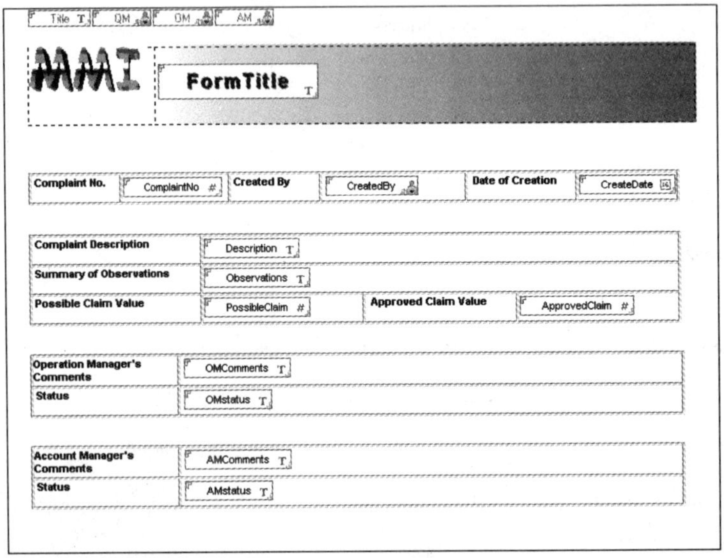

FIGURE 18.7 *The form layout for the Claim Request form*

7. Open the form properties and set as described below:
   - On the Form Info tab, in the Name field enter **Claim Request|CLR** as the name of the form.
   - Select Type as **Response**.
   - In the Options section, check Automatically refresh fields.
8. In the Value of events of the computed fields, enter formulas as specified in Table 18.7.
9. Insert the Save & Close, Close, Edit, and Print shared actions on the form.
10. Save and close the form. Because this is a response form, you will not be able to preview it. To test the form, open any complaint document and click the Claim Request action on it.

Table 18.7 Formulas for Computed Fields on the Claim Request

Field Name	Formula in the Value Event	Description
ComplaintNo	ComplaintNo	Value for this field will be assigned programmatically, so write the field name itself
CreatedBy	@UserName	To assign the current user's name
CreateDate	@Today	To assign the current system date
OMStatus	OMStatus	Value for this field will be assigned programmatically, so write the field name itself
AMStatus	AMStatus	Value for this field will be assigned programmatically, so write the field name itself

Creating Controlled Access Sections

Three users can work on the Claim Request form. They are as follows:

- **Quality manager.** The quality manager creates the claim request.
- **Operations manager.** The operations manager is the first-level approver.
- **Accounts manager.** The accounts manager is the second-level approver.

To ensure that only the concerned user can take the action and write the comments, you must create controlled access sections. You can create two controlled access sections in this form, one for the operations manager and the other for the accounts manager.

To create the controlled access sections, perform the following steps:

1. Highlight the operations manager's Comments and Status labels and the related fields.
2. Select Create/Section/Controlled Access. This creates a section of the highlighted fields and opens the Form Section dialog box.
3. In the Form Section dialog box, enter **Operations Manager** in the Title Text field.
4. Select the Expand/Collapse tab. For Editors, select Auto-expand section from the Opened for reading and Opened for editing lists. Click the down arrow next to the For Editors options and select For Non-Editors. Select Auto-expand section from the Opened for reading list and Auto-collapse section from the Opened for editing list.
5. Select the Formula tab. Select the Type as Computed and enter the Access Formula as "[OM]" to specify that only the users with role OM can edit the section.
6. Similarly, highlight the accounts manager's Comments and Status field and label and create a Controlled access section. Enter the section title as **Accounts Manager**. Click the Formula tab of the section properties, select the type as Computed and enter the Access Formula as "[AM]" to specify only users with role AM can edit the section.

Sending Notifications

The Claim Request form involves three users. Each user must be informed whenever he needs to take any action. The following notifications must be sent during the processing of the claim:

- When the quality manager creates a Claim Request, a notification must be sent to the operations manager informing her that a Claim Request has been created and she needs to take action on it.
- After the operations manager approves the claim, a notification must be sent to the accounts manager informing him that he must also verify the claim. If the operations manager rejects the claim, a notification must be sent to the quality manager.

- The quality manager must be informed about whatever action the accounts manager takes.

Quality Manager to Operations Manager

The operations manager is informed whenever a Claim Request is generated. This notification must be sent whenever the Claim Request is saved for the first time. You can write it on the QuerySave event of the Claim Request form. Select the QuerySave event in the form, choose to run a formula, and enter the following code:

```
@If(@IsNewDoc;@MailSend(OM;Null;Null;"Claim Request for Approval";
"A New Claim Request has been created.Pls. verify";Null;[IncludeDocLink]
);Null)
```

`@IsNewDoc` checks whether the document is being saved for the first time or subsequent times. The notification to the operations manager is sent only if the document is being saved for the first time.

Operations Manager to Accounts Manager

You can add two actions on the Claim Request form for the operations manager to approve or reject the claim. In the same actions, you can also write the code for sending the notifications to the appropriate users.

Create an action named Approve-OM. To make this action available only to the operations manager, write the following code in the Hide Action when tab of the action properties.

```
@Name([Abbreviate];@username)!=OM
```

In the Click event of the action, write the following code:

```
@Command([EditDocument];"1");
Field OMStatus:="Approved";
@MailSend(AM;Null;Null;"Claim for Approval";
"Pls. verify the claim request. It has been approved by the Operations
Manager";Null;[IncludeDocLink])
```

Similarly, create an action named Reject-OM. In the Hide Action When tab, enter the following code:

```
@Name([Abbreviate];@username)!=OM
```

In the Click event of the action, write the following code:

```
@Command([EditDocument];"1");
Field OMStatus:="Rejected";
@MailSend(QM;Null;Null;"Claim Rejected by Operations Manager";
"Pls. note that the claim for the complaint "+ @Text(ComplaintNo)+
" has been rejected by the Operations Manager";Null;[IncludeDocLink])
```

You can also make sure that the operations manager can only approve or reject once. To hide the action once the status field has been set, change the Hide Action When formula for both of these actions to the following:

```
OMStatus!=Null& @Name([Abbreviate];@username)!=OM
```

Accounts Manager to Quality Manager

The accounts manager to quality manager actions are created similar to the actions created for the operations manager.

Create an action named Approve-AM and write the Hide Action When formula as:

```
AMStatus!=Null& @Name([Abbreviate];@username)!=AM
```

In the Click event of the action, write the formula as:

```
@Command([EditDocument];"1");
Field AMStatus:="Approved";
@MailSend(QM;Null;Null;"Claim Approved by Accounts Manager";
"The Claim for the complaint "+ @Text(ComplaintNo)+
" has been approved by the Accounts Manager";Null;[IncludeDocLink])
```

Create another action named Reject-AM and write the Hide Action When formula as

```
AMStatus!=Null& @Name([Abbreviate];@username)!=AM
In the Click event of the action, write the formula as:
@Command([EditDocument];"1");
Field AMStatus:="Rejected";
```

```
@MailSend(QM;Null;Null;"Claim Rejected by Accounts Manager";
"The Claim for the complaint "+ @Text(ComplaintNo)+
" has been rejected by the Accounts Manager";Null;[IncludeDocLink])
```

Creating the Claim Request Action

Similar to the QM's Report, the Claim Request can also be created using an action on the Complaint Request form. This action creates a new Claim Request, if it does not already exist. If a Claim Request exists, then it should open the existing request.

To create a Claim Request action on the Complaint Request form, perform the following steps:

1. Open the Complaint Request form in Domino Designer.
2. Create a new action. In the Action dialog box, enter the name of the action as **Claim Request** and select an appropriate icon for the action.
3. To hide the action from all users other than a user with QM role, in the Hide Action When tab of the action, check Hide action if formula is true and enter the following formula:

   ```
   @IsNotMember("[QM]";@UserRoles)
   ```

4. Close the Action dialog box. In the Click event for the action, select the Run option as LotusScript and enter the following code:

   ```
   Dim ws As New NotesUIWorkspace
   Dim db As NotesUIDatabase
   Set db=ws.currentdatabase
   Dim doc1 As NotesDocument
   Dim doc2 As NotesDocument
   Dim col As NotesDocumentCollection
   Set doc1=ws.currentdocument.document
   Set col=doc1.responses
   Dim found as variant
   If col.count<>0 Then
       Set doc2=col.getfirstdocument
       Do Until doc2 Is Nothing
       If doc2.form(0)="CLR"Then
           found=True
           Call ws.editdocument(False,doc2)
   ```

```
                Exit Do
            Else
                Set doc2=col.getnextdocument(doc2)
            End If
            Loop
        End If
        If found=False  Or col.count=0 Then
            Set doc2=New notesdocument(db.database)
            doc2.form="CLR"
            doc2.complaintno=doc1.complaintno
            doc2.description=doc1.complaint
            doc2.observations=doc1.remarks
            call doc2.makeresponse(doc1)
            call ws.editdocument(True,doc2)
        End If
```

Setting the Status of the Complaint Request

The status of the complaint request is required to track the stage the complaint is in. This is useful for the users to be able to track any complaint and to tell customers the exact status of their complaints. Table 18.8 lists the different statuses that are identified for a complaint request.

Table 18.8 Status of the Complaint Request

Status	Description
New	When a new complaint is logged
Verified	When the QM's Report has been submitted
Rejected	If the complaint has been rejected
With Operations	If a claim record has been created and it is waiting for approval by the operations manager
With Accounts	If a claim record has been created and is waiting for approval by the accounts manager

Status	Description
With QM	If a claim has been rejected by the operations manager or the accounts manager, and when the accounts manager approves the claim
Closed	When the quality manager has closed the complaint after processing

The Status field is located on the Complaint Request form and is updated based on the actions taken. To set the status of the complaint request, perform the following steps:

1. Open the Complaint Request form in Domino Designer.
2. Place the cursor below the Header subform and create a new field.
3. Name the field status and set the type as Text and Computed when composed.
4. In the Value event of this field, enter **"New"**. This becomes the initial status of the complaint.
5. To update the status to Verified when the quality manager creates the QM's Report, open the QM's Report form. In the PostSave event of this form, enter the following formula:

   ```
   @If(@GetDocField($ref;"Status")="New";
   @SetDocField($ref;"status";"Verified");null)
   ```

   If the status of the complaint request is New, this formula updates it to Verified whenever the quality manager saves this report.
6. To set the status to Rejected when the quality manager clicks the Reject Complaint action on the QM's Report form, create a new action in the QM's Report form. Set the name as Reject Complaint and enter the following formula in the Click event:

   ```
   @SetDocField($ref;"Status";"Rejected")
   ```

   To make this action available only to the quality manager, in the Hide Action When tab of the action, check Hide action if formula is true and enter the following formula:

   ```
   @IsNotMember("[QM]";@UserRoles)
   ```

7. To set the status to With Operations when the quality manager creates a claim request and saves it, select the PostSave form event in the Claim Request form and enter the following formula:

```
@If(OMStatus=null;@SetDocField($ref;"Status";"With Operations"); null)
```

   The value of the status is updated only if the OMStatus field is null. This field gets a value when the operations manager takes an action.

8. To set the status to With Accounts when the operations manager approves the claim, select the Approve-OM action in the Claim Request form. Append the following formula to the existing code:

```
@SetDocField($ref;"Status";"With Accounts")
```

9. To set the status to With QM when the operations manager rejects the claim, select the Reject-OM action in the Claim Request form. Append the following formula to the existing code:

```
@SetDocField($ref;"Status";"With QM")
```

10. To set the status to With QM when the accounts manager takes any action on the claim, append the following formula to the existing code in the Approve-AM and the Reject-AM actions:

```
@SetDocField($ref;"Status";"With QM")
```

11. Finally, to set the status to Closed, open the Complaint Request form. Add a new action named Close Complaint. Hide the action from all users except the quality managers. In the Click event of this action, enter the following code:

```
@Command([EditDocument];"1");
FIELD Status:="Closed";
@Command([ViewRefreshFields])
```

UPDATING FIELDS IN A DOCUMENT

@SetDocField is an @Function that is used for updating a field in a document. The syntax of this @Function is:

```
@SetDocField(DocumentUNID;Fieldname;NewValue)
```

In the above syntax:

`DocumentUNID` is the unique document ID for the document to be updated. For the current document, you can use `@DocumentUniqueID`. For a parent document, you can use `$Ref`. `$Ref` is a reserved field in a response document that contains the document UNID of the parent document.

`Fieldname` is the name of the field that you want to update. It should be enclosed in quotation marks.

`NewValue` is the value that you want to assign to the specified field.

Another @Function, `@GetDocField`, is used to get the content of a field from a specified document. The syntax of this @Function is as follows:

```
@GetDocField(DocumentUNID;FieldName)
```

Creating Views

The CCTS database contains various views with the documents arranged by different categories to make them useful to users. The following are the views to be added to this database:

- By Customer
- By Status
- By Reference Number
- By Product
- My Complaints
- Latest Complaints
- Claims
- Acknowledgement Letters

By Customer View

The By Customer view displays the complaint documents categorized by the customer name. Table 18.9 lists the columns that this view must contain.

Table 18.9 Details of Columns in By Customer View

Column Title	Column Value Type	Column Value
Cust No.	Field	CustomerNo
Name	Field	CustName
Address	Formula	Address
Complaint Type	Field	ComplaintType
Product Under Complaint	Field	ProductUnderComplaint

To create this view, perform the following steps:

1. Create a shared view. Name it **By Customer**.
2. Add columns as specified in Table 18.9
3. Double-click the column Cust No to access column properties. On the Sorting tab, select Type as Categorized. On the Font tab, select the font as Arial, size as 9, and style as Bold. On the Column Info tab, check the option Show twisty when row is expandable.
4. For the rest of the columns, set the font as Arial, size as 8, and style as Plain.
5. Select the View Selection event and enter the following formula:

   ```
   Select form="CR"¦@AllDescendants
   ```

   The view will contain all the Complaint documents and their responses—the QM's Report and the claim request.

NOTE

The `@AllDescendants` @Function is used to include all the responses and the response to responses for a selected document.

6. To display the responses indented under the Complaint Request, check the view property Show response documents in hierarchy.
7. Add a new column after the Cust No. column. Select the Column Value type as Formula and enter the following code:

```
@If(form="QMR";"QM's Report - "+@Text(CreateDate);
form="CLR";"Claim Request - "+@Text(CreateDate);null)
```

8. Double-click the column and check the option Show responses only to make this column applicable only to the response documents. Set a different color for this column to distinguish the response documents.

   Figure 18.8 shows the layout of the By Customer view.

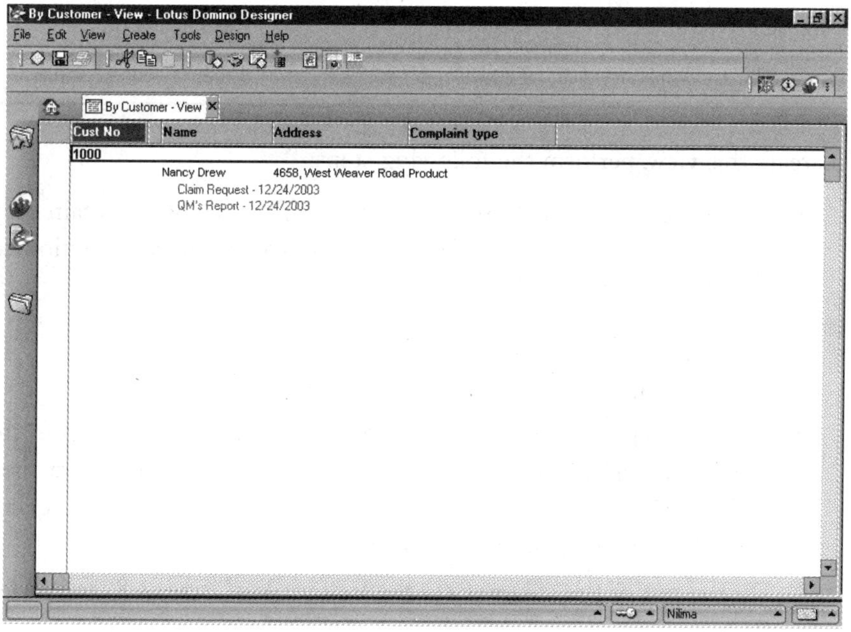

FIGURE 18.8 *By Customer view*

9. Save the view.

By Status View

The By Status view displays the complaint documents categorized by the status of the complaint request. Table 18.10 lists the columns that this view must contain.

Table 18.10 Details of Columns in By Status View

Column Title	Column Value Type	Column Value
Status	Field	Status
Cust No.	Field	CustomerNo
Name	Field	CustName
Address	Field	Address
Complaint Type	Field	ComplaintType
ProductUnderComplaint	Field	ProductUnderComplaint

To create this view, perform the following steps:

1. Create a shared view. Name it **By Status**. The view will contain only complaint requests. Check Select by formula and in the Selection conditions box, enter the following code:

   ```
   Select form="CR"
   ```

2. Add columns as specified in Table 18.10.
3. Double-click the column Status to access column properties. On the Sorting tab, select Type as Categorized. On the Font tab, select the font as Arial, size as 9, and style as Bold. On the Column Info tab, check the option Show twisty when row is expandable.
4. For the rest of the columns set the font as Arial, size as 8, and style as Plain.
5. Save the view.

By Reference Number View

The By Reference Number view displays the complaint documents organized by the Complaint Number. Table 18.11 lists the columns that this view must contain.

Table 18.11 Details of Columns in By Reference Number View

Column Title	Column Value Type	Column Value
Complaint No.	Field	ComplaintNo
Cust No.	Field	CustomerNo
Name	Field	CustName
Address	Formula	Address
Complaint Type	Field	ComplaintType
Product Under Complaint	Field	ProductUnderComplaint

To create this view, perform the following steps:

1. Create a shared view. Name it **By Reference Number.**
2. Add columns as specified in Table 18.11.
3. Double-click the column By Reference Number to access column properties. On the Column Info tab, check the option Show twisty when row is expandable. On the Sorting tab, select Sort as Ascending. On the Font tab, select the font as Arial, size as 9, and style as Bold.
4. For the rest of the columns, set the font as Arial, size as 8, and style as Plain.
5. To display the QM's Report, the Claim Request, and the Acknowledgement Letter indented under the complaint request, check the view property Show response documents in hierarchy.
6. Add a response only column after the Complaint No. column. Select the Column Value type as Formula, and enter the following code:

```
@If(form="QMR";"QM's Report - "+@Text(CreateDate);
form="CR";"Claim Request - "+@Text(CreateDate);null)
```

7. Save the view.

By Product View

The By Product view displays the complaint documents categorized by the product under complaint. This view includes only those documents where the complaint type is Product. Table 18.12 lists the columns that this view must contain.

Table 18.12 Details of Columns in By Product View

Column Title	Column Value Type	Column Value
Product	Field	ProductUnderComplaint
Cust No.	Field	CustomerNo
Name	Field	CustName
Address	Formula	Address
Complaint Type	Field	ComplaintType

To create this view, perform the following steps:

1. Create a shared view. Name it **By Product**. Copy the design of the view from the By Customer view.
2. Open the view in the Domino Designer, and in the View Selection event, enter the following code:

   ```
   Select form="CR" & ComplaintType="Product"
   ```

   The view will contain only those complaint documents where the complaint type is Product.
3. Click the last column in the view titled Product. Cut the column by selecting Edit/Cut. Click the first column in the view and select Edit/Paste. This pastes the Product column as the first column in the view.
4. Double-click the Product column. On the Sorting tab, select Type as Categorized. On the Font tab, select the font as Arial, size as 9, and style as Bold. On the Column Info tab, check the option Show twisty when row is expandable.
5. Double-click the Cust No. column. Deselect the option Show twisty when row is expandable. Click the Sorting tab and select Type as Standard.
6. For all the columns other than Product, set the font as Arial, size as 8, and style as Plain.
7. Save the view.

My Complaints View

The My Complaints view displays all those complaints that have been created by the current user. This view helps a CRE to quickly track the complaints that he has logged.

To create this view, perform the following steps:

1. Create a Shared, private on first use view named **My Complaints**. Copy the design of the view from the By Reference Number view.
2. Open the view in the Domino Designer and enter the following code in the View Selection event of the view:

```
SELECT(Form="CR"¦@AllDescendants)&
createdby=@Name([Abbreviate];@UserName)
```

3. Save and close the view.

Because this is a personalized view, you can embed this view on a page to make it more useful. Figure 18.9 shows the layout of the MyComplaints page.

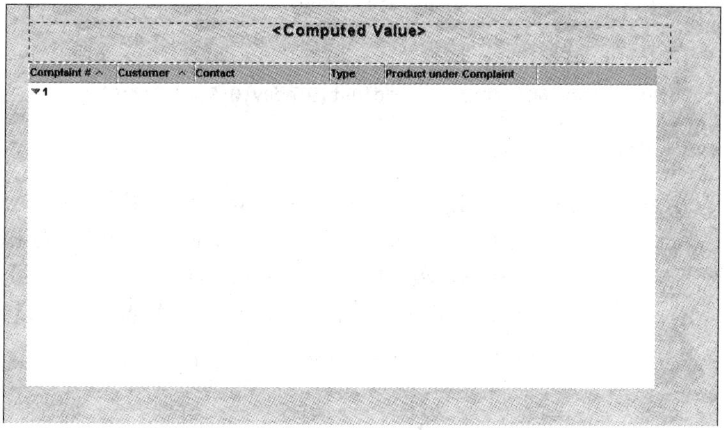

FIGURE 18.9 *The layout of MyComplaints page*

To create this page, perform the following steps:

1. Create a new page.
2. Name the page **MyComplaints** and apply a background to the page using page properties.

3. Create computed text at the top of the page. In the Value event, enter the following formula:

```
"COMPLAINTS REGISTERED BY: "+@Name([Abbreviate];@UserName)
```

4. On the next line, embed the view My Complaints using Create/Embedded Element/View
5. Save and close the page.

Latest Complaints View

The Latest Complaints view displays all those complaints that have been created during the last seven days. This view helps a user to quickly track the latest complaints logged.

To create this view, perform the following steps:

1. Create a Shared view named **Latest Complaints**. Copy the design of the view from the By Reference Number view.
2. Open the view in the Domino Designer, and enter the following code in the View Selection event of the view:

```
SELECT (Form="CR"¦@AllDescendants)
&CreateDate<=@Today &CreateDate>=@Adjust(@Today;0;0;-7;0;0;0)
```

3. Save and close the view.

Design a page for this view as well, because the document in this view will keep changing based on the current system date. When users access this view from the main navigator, they must be shown the date from when the complaints are being displayed in the view. The page is similar in layout to the MyComplaints page. Figure 18.10 shows the layout of the Latest Complaints page.

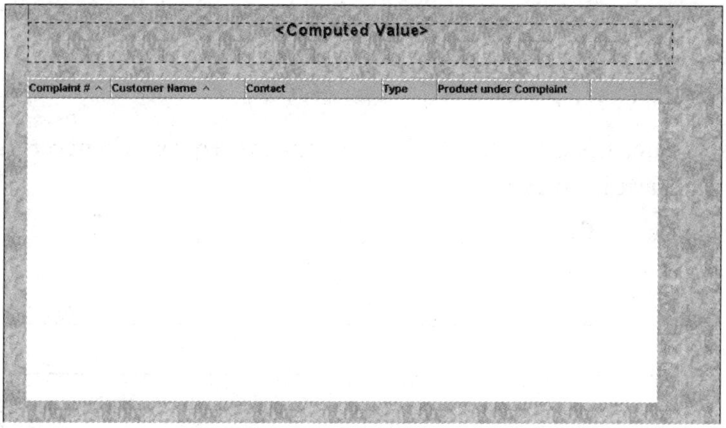

FIGURE 18.10 *The layout for Latest Complaints page*

To create this page perform the following steps:

1. Create a new page.
2. Name the page **Latest Complaints** and apply a background to the page using page properties.
3. Create computed text at the top of the page. In the Value event, enter the following formula:

   ```
   "COMPLAINTS REGISTERED SINCE: "+@text(@Adjust(@Today;0;0;-7;0;0;0))
   ```

4. On the next line, embed the view Latest Complaints.
5. Save and close the page.

Claims View

The Claims view displays the proposed and the approved claim values for complaints that have claims. The claim values are stored in the claim requests. Because the Claim Request form is a response form, the claim requests cannot be isolated in a view.

To create a view that that gives you the summary of the claim values, you can update these values in the complaint request. To achieve this, perform the following steps:

1. Open the Claim Request form in Domino designer.

2. Select the PostSave event of the form and enter the following code:

```
@SetDocField($ref;"ApprovedClaim";approvedclaim);
@SetDocField($ref;"possibleclaim";possibleclaim)
```

   This updates the claim fields in the complaint request whenever the claim request is saved.

3. Save and close the form.

NOTE

If you have already created documents for testing, to update the complaint request, you'll need to open the claim requests and save them once.

Now you can design the Claims view. Table 18.13 lists the columns that this view must contain.

Table 18.13 Details of Columns in Claims View

Column Title	Column Value Type	Column Value
Complaint No.	Field	ComplaintNo
Name	Field	CustName
Address	Field	Address
Proposed Claim	Field	PossibleClaim
Approved Claim	Field	ApprovedClaim

To create this view, perform the following steps:

1. Create a shared view. Name it **Claims.**
2. Add columns as specified in Table 18.13
3. For all the columns set the font as Arial, size as 8, and style as Plain.
4. In the View Selection event of the view, enter the following formula:

```
SELECT form="CR"&possibleclaim>0
```

5. Double-click the Proposed Claim column. Select the Sorting tab, and from the Totals list, select the option total to calculate the total of the Possible Claim value.
6. Repeat step 5 for the Approved Claim column.
7. Open view properties and select the Style tab. From the Rows section, select a different Column total text color. Figure 18.11 shows a sample Claims view.

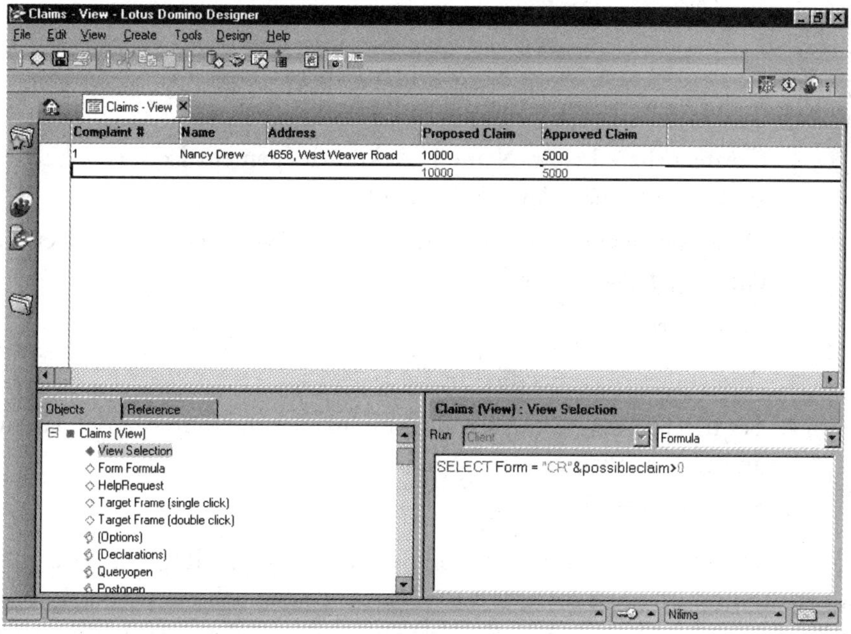

FIGURE 18.11 *The layout for Claims view*

8. Save and close the view.

Creating Acknowledgment Letters View

The Acknowledgement Letters view displays the acknowledgement letters. This view is the only place where these letters are displayed.

Table 18.14 lists the columns that this view must contain.

Table 18.14 Details of Columns in Acknowledgement Letters View

Column Title	Column Value Type	Column Value
Complaint No	Field	ComplaintNo
Name	Field	CustName
Address	Formula	Address
Complaint Type	Field	ComplaintType
Product Under Complaint	Field	ProductUnderComplaint

To create this view, perform the following steps:

1. Create a shared view. Name it **Acknowledgement Letters**. The view will contain only the acknowledgement letters.
2. Open the view in the Domino Designer and in the View Selection event enter the following code:

   ```
   Select form="AL"
   ```

3. Add columns as specified in Table 18.14.
4. Set the Text properties for all columns. Set the font as Arial, size as 8, and style as Plain.
5. Save the view.

The Acknowledgement Letter action on the Complaint Request form allows you to create the letter just once. If a user does not print the letter on the same day, it'll contain the date on which the letter was created whenever the letter is printed for sending.

You can create an agent that acts on all the selected documents in a view and sets the date of these letters to the current system date. You can also create an action in the view to run this agent. To create this action, perform the following steps:

1. Add a new action to the view.
2. Name the action **Set Date** and select an appropriate icon for the action.
3. Close the action dialog box and select Formula from the Run option in the Programmer's pane. Enter the following code for the action:

   ```
   @Command([ToolsRunMacro];"(SetDate)")
   ```

SetDate is the name of the agent to set the date of the documents.

To create the SetDate agent perform the following steps:

1. Create a New Agent and specify the following properties:
   - **Name.** SetDate
   - **Options.** Shared
   - **Trigger.** On event. Select event as Agent list selection
   - **Target.** All selected documents
2. In the Programmer's pane, select Formula and write the following code:

   ```
   FIELD date:=@Today;
   ```
3. Save and close the agent.

NOTE

Because the Trigger for SetDate agent is Agent list selection, it is saved as a hidden agent. To run this agent using the ToolsRunMacro @Command, you must use the name enclosed in parentheses as (SetDate).

Creating Workflow Agents

The database CCTS contains agents for a number of tasks. The agents in this database are listed below:

- Update Profile agent
- Set Date agent
- Send Reminder agent

You have already created the Update Profile and Set Date agents. In this section, you'll create the Send Reminder agent.

The Send Reminder agent is used to send a reminder to the quality manager if he does not submit a verification report within a period of seven days. If he still does not respond, the next day when the agent runs, it sends an e-mail to the managing director.

The Send Reminder agent will introduce you to the code required for creating a notification using LotusScript. In LotusScript, a notification is created by creating a new document; setting values for fields such as SendTo, Subject, and Body; and finally sending the document using the `Send` method of the `Document` class.

The properties of the Send Reminder agent have been listed in Table 18.15.

Table 18.15 Properties of Send Reminder Agent

Property	Value
Name	Send Reminder
Options	Shared
Trigger	On Schedule
Schedule	Daily
Target	All documents in the database

Create a new agent and set the properties as specified in Table 18.15.

In the Programmer's pane, select LotusScript, and write the code given below. In this example, the search method of the `NotesDatabase` class has been used to select documents of the type complaint request, with a status as New and that were created more than seven days earlier.

From the `NotesDocumentCollection` created, each document is checked for the number of reminders sent. If no reminder has been sent, a reminder is sent to the quality manager. If one reminder has been sent, then a notification is sent to the managing director. The number of reminders sent is recorded in a field named remsent in the Complaint Request form. This variable is initialized to 0. When the reminder is sent to the quality manager, the variable is set to 1, and when a notification is sent to the managing director, it becomes 2. After that, no notifications are sent. The class `NotesRichTextItem` has been used to format the body field of the message. The `AppendDocLink` method of this class is used to add a doclink to the message, the `AddNewLine` method is used to insert new lines in the message, and the `AppendText` method is used to add text to the message.

```
Dim s As New NotesSession
Dim db As NotesDatabase
Set db=s.Currentdatabase
Dim col As NotesDocumentCollection
Dim doc As notesdocument
Dim doc2 As Notesdocument
Dim rt As notesrichtextitem
Sstring="form=""CR"" & status=""New"" & (@Today-createdate)/86400>7"
Set col=db.search(Sstring,Nothing,0)
Set doc=col.GetFirstDocument
Do Until doc Is Nothing
       If doc.remsent(0)=0 Then
           Set doc2=New NotesDocument(db)
           Set rt = New NotesRichTextItem(doc2,"Body")
           doc2.sendto=doc.QM
           doc2.subject="Reminder for Complaint verification report"
           Call rt.AppendText("You have not submitted the Verification"_
           &"report for the following complaint request. Pls. do it")
           Call rt.AddNewline(2)
           Call rt.AppendDocLink(doc,"")
           doc2.Send False
           doc.remsent=1
       Elseif doc.remsent(0)=1 Then
           doc.remsent=2
           Set doc2=New NotesDocument(db)
           Set rt = New NotesRichTextItem(doc2,"Body")
           doc2.sendto=doc.MD
           doc2.subject="FYI: No response from QM for complaint no"_
           &doc.complaintno(0)
           Call rt.AppendText("The Quality Manager has not responded"_
           &"to the following complaint")
           Call rt.AddNewline(2)
           Call rt.AppendDocLink(doc,"")
           doc2.Send False
       End If
       doc.Save True,True
       Set doc=col.getnextdocument(doc)
Loop
```

SEARCH METHOD OF THE NOTESDATABASE CLASS

The `Search` method in the `NotesDatabase` class is used to search for documents specifying a condition. It returns the documents that match the condition as an object of the type `NotesDocumentCollection`. The syntax of this method is as follows:

```
Set NotesDocumentCollection=NotesDatabase.Search(search formula,
cutoff date,maximumdocs)
```

In the above syntax:

`search formula` is a Notes formula that specifies the search condition for the documents. The syntax of this condition must follow the rules for formula language. The formula must be enclosed in quotation marks (""). If the formula contains quotation marks, you can use double quotation marks. For example:

```
"form=""CR"""
```

The first and the last quotation marks are for the condition. Because CR is to be enclosed in quotation marks, two extra quotation marks have been used, one before each quotation mark around CR.

`cutoff` tells you that the documents that have been modified or created since the cutoff date are returned. If you do not want to give a cutoff date, you can use `Nothing`.

`maximumdocs` is the maximum number of documents that must be returned. If you want all documents, you can use a 0.

Creating a Navigation Structure

A database must have a user-friendly and attractive navigation structure to encourage users to use the application. Without an easy navigation structure, it is very likely that the users will avoid using the application or will not be able to utilize it to its full extent. The design elements in a database that help in designing a navigation structure are listed below:

- Framesets
- Outlines
- Navigator
- Page
- "About Database" document.

In this application, there are two navigation structures. The first is an "About Database" document, as shown in Figure 18.12

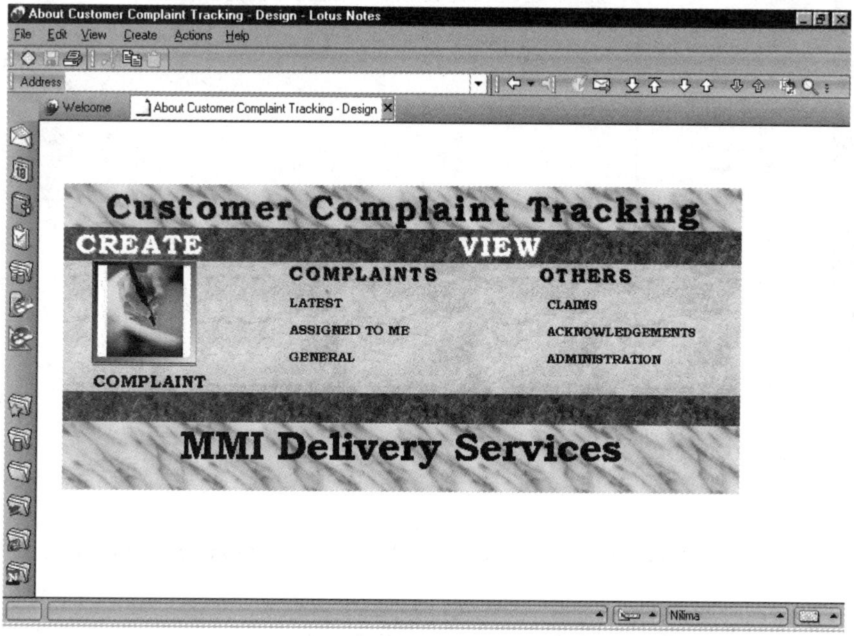

FIGURE 18.12 *The "About Database" document used as the main navigator*

The second navigation structure is a page titled NavPage launched as a side navigator, as shown in Figure 18.13

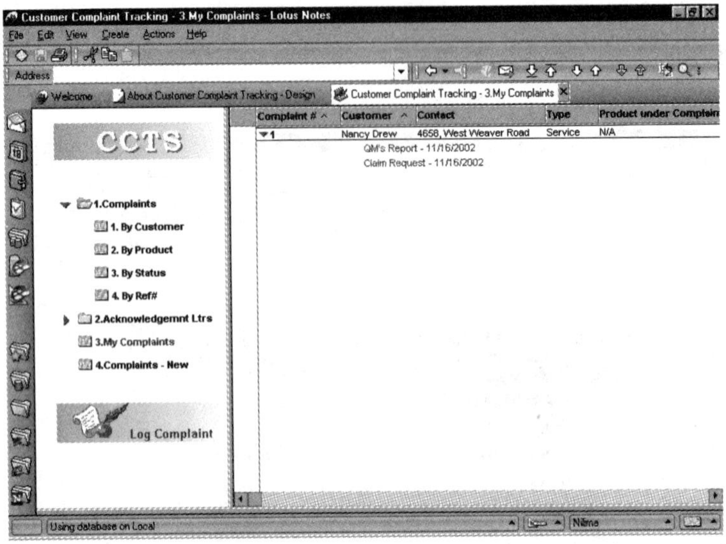

FIGURE 18.13 *A side navigator created using a page*

In the following sections, you'll design these two navigation structures.

Creating the "About Database" Document

The "About Database" document is being used as the main navigation structure in this database. Other than the labels, the "About Database" document contains two outlines—Complaints and Others—and a graphic hotspot.

Creating the Complaints Outline

You'll use the Complaints outline on the "About Database" document to provide links to the various views that display the complaint requests. This outline contains three entries. Table 18.16 lists the properties for these outline entries.

Table 18.16 Outline Entry Properties for the Complaints Outline

Label	Content Type	Content Value
LATEST	Named Element, Page	Latest
ASSSIGNED TO ME	Named Element, Page	MyComplaints
GENERAL	Named Element, View	By Customer

To create this outline, perform the following steps:

1. Create a new outline.
2. Add three entries to the outline with properties as specified in Table 18.16.
3. Name the outline **Complaints** and save and close it.

Creating the Others Outline

The Others outline is used on the "About Database" document to provide links to the Claims and Acknowledgement Letters views and to provide an option for database administration. This outline also contains three entries. Table 18.17 lists the properties for these outline entries.

Table 18.17 Outline Entry Properties for the Complaints Outline

Label	Content Type	Content Value
CLAIMS	Named Element, View	Claims
ACKNOWLEDGEMENTS	Named Element, View	Acknowledgement Letters
ADMINISTRATION	Action	@Command([EditProfile]; "DbProfile")

To create this outline, perform the following steps:

1. Create a new outline.
2. Add three entries to the outline with properties as specified in Table 18.17.
3. Name the outline **Others**. Save and close it.

Designing the "About Database" Document

Now that you've created the two outlines, open the "About Database" document in the CCTS database and design the navigation structure.

Figure 18.14 displays the layout of the "About Database" document.

FIGURE 18.14 *A layout of the "About Database" document*

Embed the two outlines on this document as shown in Figure 18.14. To create a new complaint request hotspot, insert an image and create an action hotspot by highlighting the image. Enter the following formula in the Click event of the action hotspot:

```
@Command([Compose];"CR")
```

Save and close the document.

Creating the NavPage Page

The NavPage is used as the side navigator when you access any of the views. This page contains an outline named AllViews and a text hotspot. Before you design the page, you must create the outline.

Creating the AllViews Outline

The AllViews outline is used on the NavPage and contains links to all the views in the database. Table 18.18 lists the properties for the outline entries in this outline.

Table 18.18 Outline Entry Properties for the Complaints Outline

Label	Content Type	Content Value
1. Complaints	None	None
1. By Customer	Named Element, View	By Customer
2. By Product	Named Element, View	By Product
3. By Reference #	Named Element, View	By Reference Number
4. By Status	Named Element, View	By Status
2. Acknowledgements	Named Element, View	Acknowledgement Letters
3. My Complaints	Named Element, View	My Complaints
4. New Complaints	Named Element, View	Latest Complaints

NOTE

The Complaints outline entry has been created in this outline as a category. No content has been assigned to it.

To create this outline, perform the following steps:

1. Create a new outline.
2. Add entries to the outline with properties as specified in Table 18.18.
3. Indent the entries 1. By Customer, 2. By Product, 3. By Reference# and 4. By Status, to categorize them under Complaints. Figure 18.15 displays the organization of the outline entries on the AllViews outline.

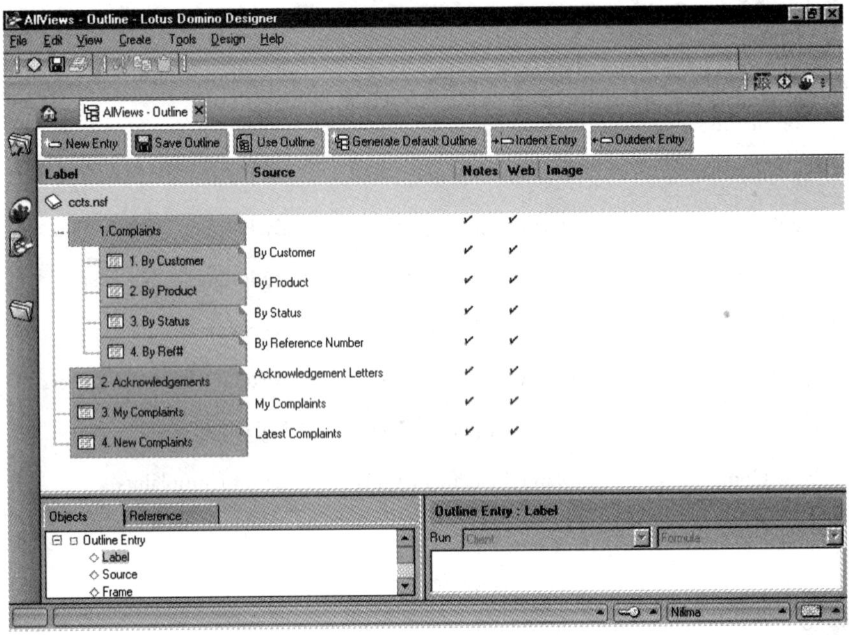

FIGURE 18.15 *The AllViews outline*

Name the outline AllViews. Save and close it.

Designing the NavPage Page

After you have designed the outline, you must embed it on a page to use it. The NavPage is the page you'll design for this purpose. To design this page, perform the following steps:

1. Create a new page named **NavPage**.
2. Insert a table with one column and three rows.
3. In the top row, enter the text **CCTS**.
4. In the second row, embed the outline AllViews using Create/Embedded Element/Outline.

5. In the third row, insert an image and enter the text **Log Complaint**. Highlight the text Log Complaint and create an action hotspot. Enter the following formula in the click event of the hotspot:

```
@Command([Compose];"CR")
```

6. Format the text and the embedded outline. To ensure that you can see the outline without any truncation, in the embedded outline properties, select the Width and Height as Fit to Content from the Outline size section on the Info tab. Figure 18.16 shows the layout for the NavPage page.

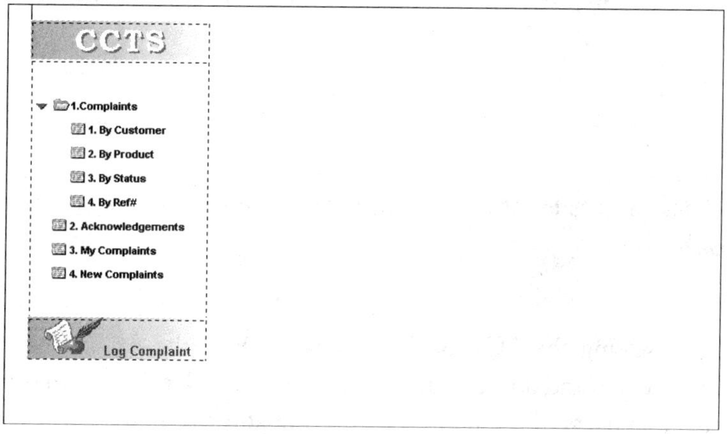

FIGURE 18.16 *The layout of NavPage page*

7. Save and close the page.

Setting the Database Launch Properties

The database launch properties are used to specify the element that must open whenever a database is opened. I have created two navigation structures. To launch the page NavPage, perform the following steps:

1. Open the database properties and select the Launch tab.
2. From When opened in Notes client, select the option Open designated Navigator.
3. Select the Type of navigator as Page and the Name as NavPage.

4. To open the "About Database" document each time the database is opened, select Open "About database" document from the When opened in Notes client option.

To test the navigation options, open the database from a Notes client.

Deploying the Application

After you have designed the CCTS application, you need to deploy it. As I mentioned earlier, this is a shared application; therefore, the database must reside on the server. As a first step in deploying the application, copy the CCTS database to the Domino server.

NOTE

If you do not have access to copy the database to the server, ask your system administrator for help.

The next step is setting the ACL of the database. Open the ACL of the CCTS database on the server and add the users with the access levels specified in Table 18.19. Select actual users of the database from the address book.

Table 18.19 Access Levels for Users

User	Access	Description
CRE	Author	The CRE will only create a complaint request and an acknowledgement letter.
Quality manager	Editor	The quality manager will make changes to the complaint request created by the CRE and create more documents.
Operations manager	Editor	The operations manager will work on the claim request created by the quality manager.
Accounts manager	Editor	The accounts manager will also work on the claim request created by the quality manager.
Managing director	Reader	The managing director will only monitor the database and will not be actively involved.

User	Access	Description
Database administrator	Manager	The database administrator will be responsible for changing the ACL of the database for assigning access and roles to required users. She will also be responsible for updating the database profile by using the ADMINISTRATION option on the main navigator.
Default	No access	To prevent nonusers of the database from opening it.

After setting the access levels, create the required roles. Following is the list of roles to be added to the database ACL.

- **QM.** For quality manager
- **OM.** For operations manager
- **AM.** For accounts manager
- **DA.** For database administrator

Add the roles to the database ACL and assign them to appropriate users. These roles have been implemented for hiding actions and for defining access for controlled access sections.

To restrict access to the ADMINISTRATION option on the Others outline embedded on the "About Database" document, open the Others outline in Domino Designer. Select the ADMINISTRATION entry and modify the formula to the following:

```
@If(@IsNotMember("[DA]";@UserRoles); @Prompt([Ok];"Authorization Error";
"You are not authorized to perform this action");
@Command([EditProfile];"DbProfile"))
```

This formula checks whether a user has the DA role assigned to him. If not, it displays an error message; if so, it opens the profile document. Update the profile document to add the names of the users and test the application.

Summary

In this chapter, you designed the customer complaint tracking application. By designing five forms for the CCTS, you learned to access data from another Notes database using the @DbLookup @Function. You also learned to implement workflow in the forms by sending notifications using the @MailSend @Function, by accessing fields from a database profile to get names of users involved in the workflow, and also by hiding elements based on roles and document state.

You learned to create and update a field for tracking the status of the complaint request. You learned to create a notification using LotusScript by creating a workflow agent to send reminders to a user. . You created the various views that are required for the CCTS database, as well as the navigation structures to help users to use the database with ease and to its full extent. Finally, you learned the various options that must be implemented for deploying the CCTS application before it can be used.

PART V

Professional Project 4—Creating a Notes Application to Access Non-Notes Databases

Project 4 Overview

In this project, you will learn to access enterprise data using LotusScript: Data Objects (LS:DO). You will access the enterprise data stored in an Oracle database by creating a Leave Processing application.

The various participants who get involved in a typical Leave Processing System can be listed as follows:

- The employee, who applies for leave by filling out the leave application.
- The department manager, who approves the leave applications of the employees who report to him.
- The HR executive, who verifies the leave record of the employee stored in the backend database to check whether or not the employee has leaves in his account.

In this chapter, you will create a Leave Processing application using Domino Designer R6. The Leave Processing application is a workflow application that takes data inputs from the back-end Oracle database. The Oracle database being used contains three tables:

- **Employee.** Stores the details about the employee
- **Dept.** Stores the department name and the manager name.
- **Leave.** Stores the leave details of the employee.

The Leave form will access these tables to read the data and display it in the form. The Leave Processing system contains two scheduled agents:

- A Credit Leaves agent runs on the first of every month to updates the leave record of the employee in the back-end database by assigning him leaves.
- The Update Leave Record agent runs every day. It updates the leave record of the employee whose leave starts on that day by reducing the leave balance by the number of leaves taken.

In this project, you will implement the three LS:DO classes:

- `ODBCConnection`
- `ODBCQuery`
- `ODBCResultSet`

The project introduction discusses the other methods of connecting to the back-end data sources, such as the @DB Commands and DECS.

Chapter 19

Accessing Non-Notes Databases from Domino

Domino Designer allows you to create applications that interact with enterprise data, such as relational databases. You can create applications that process data in Notes and then post it to a back-end database. You can also create applications that provide real-time access to enterprise data.

Notes application can use various data integration tools for connecting to relational databases (such as Oracle, MS SQL, and DB/2), Enterprise Resource Planning systems (ERPs such as SAP, PeopleSoft, and J.D.Edwards) and transaction systems (such as CICS, IBM MQSeries and IMS). You can use the following methods for connecting to non-Notes systems:

- DCR (Data Connection Resource) for form-based development using Domino Connectors and Open Database Connectivity (ODBC).
- @DB commands for programming with formula language using ODBC.
- LS:DO (LotusScript Data Objects) for programming with LotusScript using ODBC.
- DECS (Domino Enterprise Connection Services) for Domino server-based connectivity using Domino Connectors or ODBC.
- LC LSX (Lotus Domino Connector LotusScript Extension) for programming with LotusScript using Domino Connectors.
- UJDBC (Java Database Connectivity) for programming in Java.

In addition to the above native connectivity solutions, you can also use add-on connectivity solutions such as Lotus Enterprise Integrator (LEI) for high volume data transfers.

Native connectors are available for DB/2, Oracle, Oracle 8, Sybase, and OLEDB as standard connectors in Notes. For connecting to ERPs and other systems, Domino Connectors are available as add-ons.

This access to enterprise data enables you to create powerful applications that use the data storage and processing capabilities of an enterprise system, such as Oracle, as well as share, replicate, manage, and secure data.

In this chapter, you'll learn about the various methods to connect to enterprise data from Domino. You'll be introduced to the three @DB commands to access an ODBC (*Open Database Connectivity*) data source. You'll learn about LS:DO (*LotusScript:Data Objects*). You'll also learn to configure DECS and to use a Domino form for real-time access to back-end data. Finally, you'll learn to configure a Domino form to use a DCR configured in a Domino database.

Using @DB Commands

The formula language in Domino Designer provides certain @Functions that can be used to access back-end data. These @Functions are called @DB commands. @DB commands are used to access the relational databases through ODBC. Before you use these functions, you must check that the ODBC driver for the type of database to which you want to connect, such as Oracle, Sybase, or Microsoft Access, is installed. You must also register the data source for the database to which you want to connect with the ODBC driver manager on your computer.

@DB commands used for ODBC access are disabled if the Notes.ini file of a user contains the following entry:

```
NoExternalApps=1
```

The following are the three @DB commands in the formula language:

- @DbColumn
- @DbLookup
- @DbCommand

@DbColumn (ODBC Data Source)

The @DbColumn @Function is used to retrieve all the values in a specified column of a table from a specific data source. @DbColumn has certain limitations. This function can return a maximum of 64KB of data. Moreover, this function can only be used to retrieve data and cannot add, delete, or modify the back-end data.

The syntax for the @DbColumn function for an ODBC data source is as follows:

```
@DbColumn("ODBC":cache;data_source;user1:user2;
password1:password2;table;column:null_handling;"Distinct":sort)
```

In the preceding syntax:

- `ODBC` indicates that you are accessing an ODBC data source.

- `cache` specifies whether or not the data fetched should be cached for subsequent use. You can specify `cache` to cache the data, `NoCache` to fetch the data for each lookup and not to cache, or `ReCache` to refresh the cache with the latest data from the database.
- `data_source` is the name of the data source that you have created for the external database in the ODBC driver manager on your system.
- `user1:user2` are the user IDs or usernames that are required to access the external database. You can specify up to two user IDs.
- `password1:password2` are the passwords corresponding to the user IDs.

NOTE

The user ID and the password are used in combination. A password is required only if a user ID has been specified. You can use a single user ID as "user";"password" or two user IDs as "user1":"user2";"password1":"password2". If you do not specify any user ID or password, the user is prompted for it at run time if the data source requires a user ID and a password.

- `table` specifies the name of the table in the external database that you are trying to access.
- `column` specifies the column in the table that you want to retrieve.
- `null_handling` specifies how the null values in the column must be treated. By default, they are discarded. You can specify one of the following options: `fail` to generate an error message and not return any data, `discard` to discard null values and shorten the list, and `replacement string` to replace all null values with the replacement string. The replacement string must be enclosed within quotation marks.
- `"Distinct"` ensures that duplicate values are removed before the data is returned to Domino.
- `Sort` can be used with `"Distinct"` to sort the result. You can use the `ascending` or `descending` keyword as the option for sorting.

@DbLookup

The @DbLookup @Function retrieves the column values of those records in which a key column contains a specified key value. Similar to @DbColumn,

@DbLookup can return a maximum of 64KB of data and can only be used to retrieve data and not to add, delete, or modify the back-end data.

The syntax for the @DbLookup function for ODBC is as follows:

```
@DbColumn("ODBC":cache;data_source;user1:user2;
password1:password2;table;column:null_handling;keycolumn;keyvalue;"Distinct":sort)
```

In the preceding syntax, in addition to the parameters explained earlier, the parameters are:

- `keycolumn` specifies the name of the column used to search for a key value.
- `keyvalue` specifies the value for which you want to search in the key column.
- `"Distinct"` ensures that duplicate values are removed before the data is returned to Domino.
- `Sort` can be used with `"Distinct"` to sort the result. You can use the `ascending` or `descending` keyword as the option for sorting.

@DbCommand

The @DbCommand @Function is used to pass a command to an ODBC data source for processing and returns the data retrieved by that command. Like the other @DB commands, the @DbCommand function can also retrieve only 64KB of data.

The syntax for the @DbCommand function is as follows:

```
@DbCommand("ODBC":cache;data_source;user1:user2;
password1:password2;command_string:null_handling)
```

In the preceding syntax, `command_string` is used to specify the command to be executed. It can be an SQL statement, a command from a back-end DBMS, or the name of a procedure to be executed.

Using LS:DO

LS:DO is a LotusScript extension library used to provide classes for working with ODBC in LotusScript. You can use LS:DO to access the ODBC data source by using LotusScript programmatically.

You can use LS:DO to perform the following actions:

- Look up or retrieve the data stored in external databases
- Validate the data entered by a user against the data stored in external databases
- Update the data in external databases

LS:DO does not have the restriction of 64KB for data transfer as in case of @DB commands; therefore, it is especially useful for a large amount of data transfer. You can include LS:DO in your application by including the following statement in the (Options) event of the (Global) object or the agent:

```
UseLSX "*LSXODBC"
```

Domino runs on different platforms, and the LSX files for each of them has a different name. Using *LSXODBC indicates that the system should search its own Registry to find the exact name of the LSX file.

Including this library adds the following three classes to the LotusScript Domino object model:

- **ODBCConnection.** This class is used to create an ODBC connection.
- **ODBCQuery.** This class is used to specify the SQL statement to be executed.
- **ODBCResultSet.** This class is used to execute the SQL statement specified in ODBCQuery and to hold and manipulate the resulting values.

The following subsections explain the usage of these classes.

Creating a Connection to an External Data Source

You need to use the `ODBCConnection` class to create a connection to an external data source. To create a connection, perform the following steps:

1. Declare an object reference variable of the type `ODBCConection` as follows:

   ```
   Dim CON as ODBCConnection
   ```

2. Create a new `ODBCConnection` object as follows:

   ```
   Set CON= New ODBCConnection
   ```

3. Use the `ConnectTo` method of this class to create a connection. This method requires three parameters:
   - **Data source name.** This is the ODBC name of the external data source to which you want to connect.
   - **Username.** This is the name of the user ID that you need to specify only if the external data source requires one.
   - **Password.** This is the password associated with the user ID and is used only if the Username parameter has been used.

   The `ConnectTo` method returns True if the connection to the external data source is successfully established, otherwise it returns False.

   The following statement creates a connection to the data source named `EMP`, using a username as `scott` and the password as `tiger`.

   ```
   RetValue=CON.ConnectTo("EMP","scott","tiger")
   ```

> **TIP**
>
> The `ConnectTo` method displays the user ID and password dialog box during the execution of the code. If you have specified these arguments with the `ConnectTo` method and want to suppress the user ID and password dialog box , you can use the `SilentMode` property of the `ODBCConnection` class as follows:
>
> ```
> CON.SilentMode=True
> ```

4. Check for the value returned to see whether or not the connection was successful and display an appropriate message.

   ```
   If RetValue then
           MsgBox " Connected Successfully to EMP"
   Else
           MsgBox " Could not connect to EMP"
           MsgBox CON.GetExtendedErrorMessage
   End If
   ```

Some of the commonly used methods and properties of the `ODBCConnection` class are listed in Table 19.1

Table 19.1 Methods and Properties of the ODBCConnection Class

Name	Type	Description
`CommitOnDisconnect`	Property	Indicates whether the pending transactions are committed or rolledback on disconnect.
`DataSourceName`	Property	Is the ODBC name of the connected data source.
`SilentMode`	Property	Indicates whether or not the user ID password dialog box should be displayed during program execution.
`CommitTransactions`	Method	Commits all pending transactions if transaction mode is on.
`Disconnect`	Method	Disconnects from the data source.
`ListDataSources`	Method	Lists all registered data sources as an array.
`ListTables`	Method	Lists all available tables in a data source.
`ListFields`	Method	Lists all the column names in the table passed as an argument.
`ListProcedures`	Method	Lists all the executable procedures in the connected data source.
`RollbackTransactions`	Method	Rolls back all pending transactions if transaction mode is on.

Querying the Connection

After you have created a connection to the data source, you need to specify the information that is required from the data source. This is done using the `ODBCQuery` object. You first create an instance of the `ODBCQuery` object, set the `Connection` property of the `ODBCQuery` object to the connection created. This indicates that the information is required from the specified data source. The query is passed to the SQL property of the ODBCQuery object. The following code is used to perform these steps:

```
Dim CON as ODBCConnection
Set CON= New ODBCConnection
RetValue=CON.ConnectTo("EMP","scott","tiger")
            If RetValue then
                        MsgBox " Connected Successfully to EMP"
```

```
        Else
                MsgBox " Could not connect to EMP"
                MsgBox CON.GetExtendedErrorMessage
                Exit Sub
        End If
' Instantiate the ODBC Query object
Dim QR as ODBCQuery
Set QR = New ODBCQuery
'Set the Query object's connection property to Connection object
Set QR.Connection=CON
' Set the SQL property to specify the query to be executed
Set QR.SQL="select * from EMP"
```

The methods and properties of the `ODBCQuery` class are listed in Table 19.2.

Table 19.2 Methods and Properties of the ODBCQuery Class

Name	Type	Description
`Connection`	Property	Relates the query object to the connection.
`QueryExecuteTimeOut`	Property	Specifies a timeout value for the query execution.
`SQL`	Property	Indicates any SQL statement to be executed.
`UserRowID`	Property	Indicates whether or not the data in the back-end database is accessed based on the row ID.
`GetError`	Method	Returns the latest error code.
`GetErrorMessage`	Method	Returns the short error message text associated with an error code.
`GetExtendedErrorMessage`	Method	Returns the long descriptive error message text associated with an error code.

Retrieving the Data

After you have created a connection named `CON` using the `ODBCConnection` object and specified the data required by using the `ODBCQuery` object `QR`, you must execute the query to retrieve the data. The data retrieved is stored in an object called the *result set*. The result set is created using the `ODBCResultSet` class. The `Query` property of this class is set to the `ODBCQuery` object and then the `Execute` method executes the query and retrieves the data. The following code is required to perform these steps:

```
'Instantiate the ODBCResultSet object
Dim Result as ODBCResultSet
Set Result= New ODBCResultSet
'Set the Query property to the Query Object
Set Result.Query=QR
'Execute the query
Result.Execute
```

Some commonly used methods and properties of the ODBCQuery class are listed in Table 19.3

Table 19.3 Methods and Properties of the ODBCResultSet Class

Name	Type	Description
`CurrentRow`	Property	Returns the row number of the current row in the result set starting from 1.
`MaxRows`	Property	Returns the maximum number of rows to be fetched, 0 indicates all.
`ReadOnly`	Property	Indicates whether or not the data in the result set can be updated.
`AddRow`	Method	Adds the workspace for a new row in the result set.
`Close`	Method	Closes the result set.
`DeleteRow`	Method	Deletes the record represented by the current row in the result set from the specified table in the external database.
`FirstRow`	Method	Sets the current row to the first row in the result set.
`GetValue`	Method	Gets the value of a specified column from the current row in the result set.
`IsEndOfData`	Method	Indicates whether the cursor position is at the end of the result set.
`LocateRow`	Method	Locates a row that matches a specified field value.

Name	Type	Description
`LastRow`	Method	Sets the current row to the last row in the result set.
`NextRow`	Method	Sets the current row to the next row in the result set.
`SetValue`	Method	Sets a new value to a column.
`UpdateRow`	Method	Updates a changed row to the external database.

Using DECS

DECS provides real-time form-based connectivity to enterprise data. It provides live access to enterprise data or non-Notes data and applications, which include relational databases, transaction systems, and ERP systems. It is available in Notes release 4.6.3 and higher versions. DECS is loaded as a task on the Domino server. To run a DECS task on the Domino server successfully, you must add the following line to the Notes.ini file on the server:

```
EXTMGR_ADDINS=decsext
```

DECS Administrator Database

The DECS Administrator database is used to configure DECS. When you load DECS on the server, the DECS Administrator database is automatically created. Figure 19.1 shows the DECS Administrator database screen.

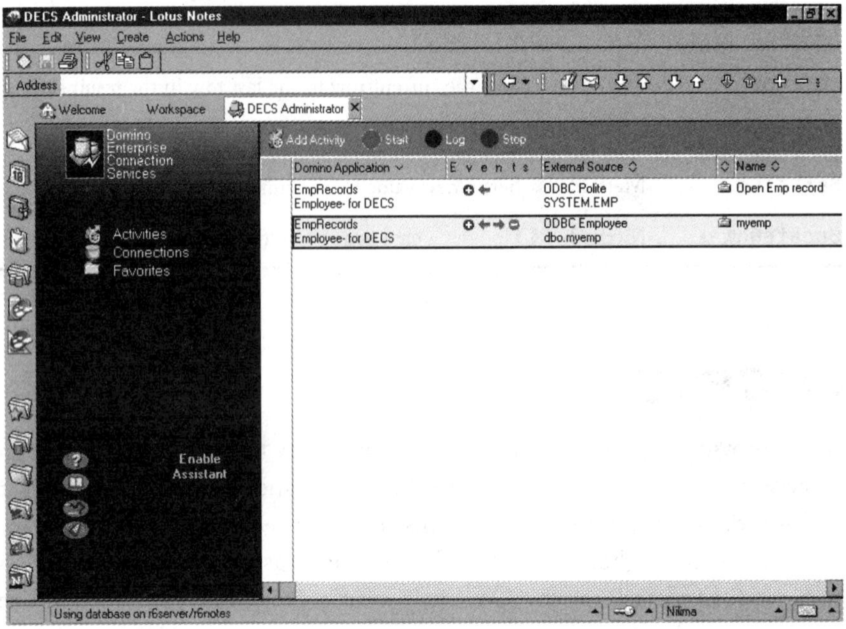

FIGURE 19.1 *The DECS Administrator database*

The DECS Administrator database contains two types of documents:

- **Connection.** A Connection document is used to define a connection to an external data source.
- **Virtual Fields Activity.** A Virtual Fields Activity document is created to monitor Notes forms. DECS connects these forms to the external data source through Lotus connectors. With the help of this document, a Notes user can open, create, update, and delete external system data directly from Notes.

As shown in Figure 19.1, the DECS Administrator database contains the following three views:

- **Activities.** The Activities view contains all the Virtual Fields activities that are configured in this database. This view contains actions to add a new activity, to start an activity, to stop an activity, and to view the log for a selected activity. Figure 19.2 displays the Activities view in the DECS Administrator database.

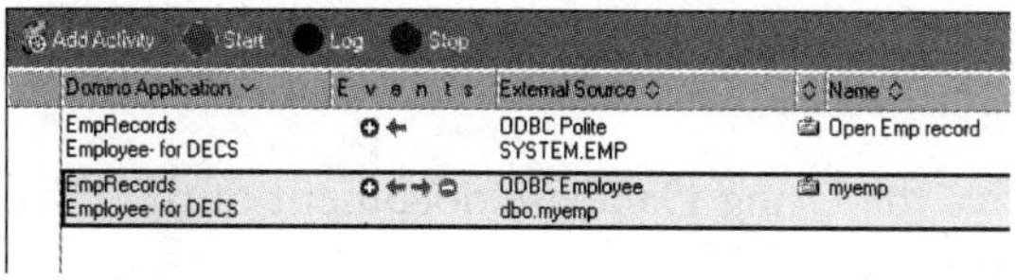

FIGURE 19.2 *The Activities view of the DECS Administrator database*

- **Connections.** The Connections view contains the Connection documents that are created in the DECS Administrator database. It contains one action named Add Connection, which is used to add a new connection. Figure 19.3 displays the Connections view in the DECS Administrator database.

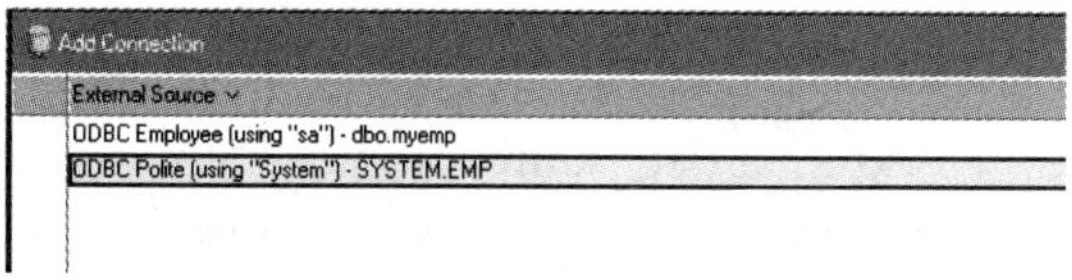

FIGURE 19.3 *The Connections view of the DECS Administrator database*

- **Favorites.** The Favorites view is a folder that you can use to store both connections and activities by dragging and dropping them into the Favorites folder. This folder contains options to add an activity, add a connection, start an activity, stop an activity, view the log of an activity, and remove a document from this folder. Figure 19.4 displays the Favorites folder in the DECS Administrator database.

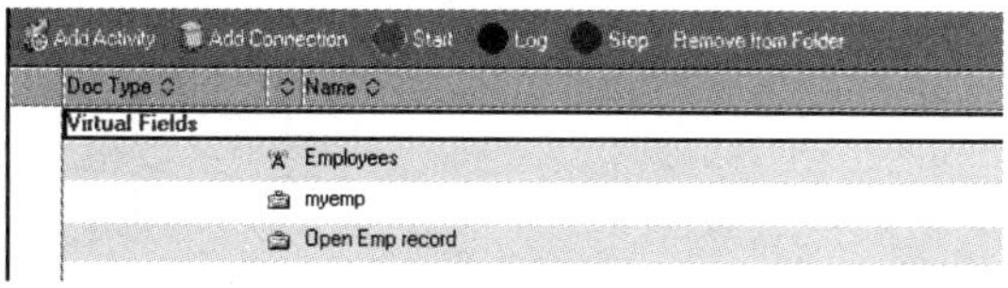

FIGURE 19.4 *The Favorites folder of the DECS Administrator database*

As shown in Figure 19.1, apart from the links to these views, the DECS navigator contains four icons, as described below:

- The Help icon displays the Using Database document of the DECS Administrator database.
- The Info icon opens the DECS User Guide Template database that is installed on the Domino database.
- The Running icon is a toggle that hides or displays a view containing the currently running activities.
- The Assistant icon is used to turn the User Assistant on or off. Turning the User Assistant on provides wizards for creating activities. You can also turn the User Assistant on by using the Enable Assistant link in the navigator.

Creating a Domino Application

You configure DECS to access an external data source from a Domino database. Before you configure the documents in the DECS Administrator database for accessing the external data source, you must design the Domino database that you'll use for this purpose. This database must contain a form that includes data fields that map to the data fields in the external data source. This form must have at least one field that maps to the key field in the external data source. Figure 19.5 displays a sample form that you can use to access the data from a data source.

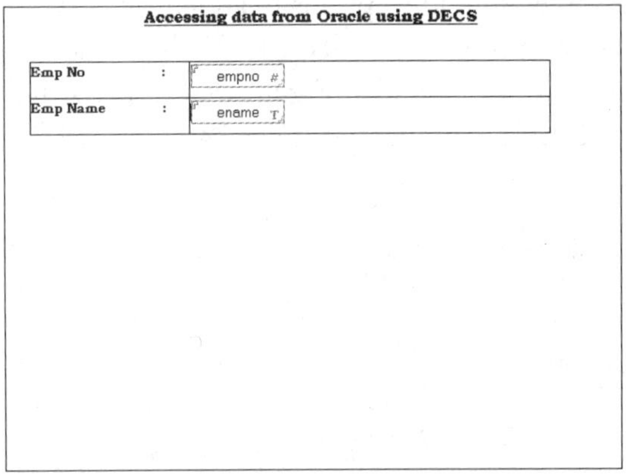

FIGURE 19.5 *A sample form used to access data from an external data source*

In addition, you must create a view that contains a column to display the key field. You will use this view to monitor the documents by using the Virtual Fields Activity.

Creating a Connection

A Connection document defines a connection to an external data source. Before creating a Connection document, you must ensure that the data source is configured and the connectivity software for the data source is installed on your server. To create a connection to an ODBC data source named Employee for the Microsoft SQL Server database, userdbs, perform the following steps:

1. Open the Connections view in the DECS Administrator database, and click the Add Connection action. This displays a list of supported data sources, as shown in Figure 19.6.

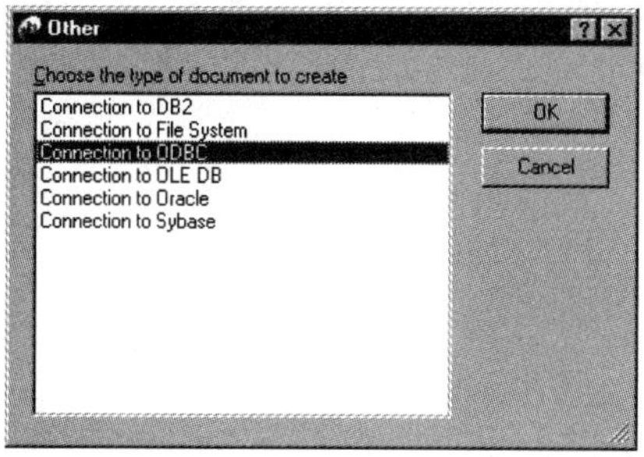

FIGURE 19.6 *The Other dialog box, displaying a list of supported data sources*

2. Select Connection to ODBC, and click OK to close the dialog box. This displays the Connection to ODBC document. Table 19.4 lists the fields in the Connection document.

Table 19.4 Fields in the Connection Document

Field	Description
Data Source	The name of the data source configured on the system.
Username	The username used to access the external database.
Password	The password for the specified username.
Selection Type	The type of metadata, such as tables, views, or procedures, that you want to choose from the data source.

(continues)

Table 19.4 Continued

Field	Description
Owner	The user from whose objects you want to select. Clicking the down arrow next to it displays a list of valid owners.
Name	The names of the selected type of objects. If you have selected Table, this displays the table names.
Fields	The fields from the selected table and their datatypes are listed here automatically.
Comment	To enter any comment for the connection.

Fill out the document as shown in Figure 19.7.

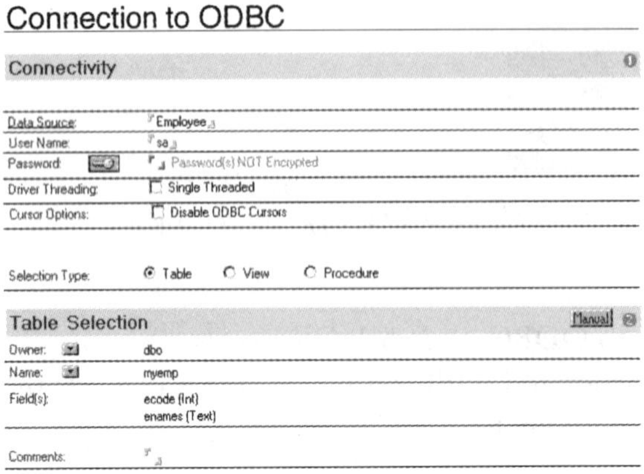

FIGURE 19.7 *The Connection to ODBC document*

Save and close the document. This adds a Connection document to the Connections view in the database.

Creating a Virtual Fields Activity

A Virtual Fields Activity is created to monitor a specific Notes form. In the activity, the fields in the Notes form are mapped to the corresponding fields in the external data source. By configuring this activity, a Notes user can open, create, update, or delete the external system data directly by using Notes.

NOTE

Before configuring a Virtual Fields Activity, you must design the Notes database and the form that you'll use to access the back-end data.

To create a Virtual Fields Activity in the DECS Administrator database by using User Assistant, perform the following steps:

1. Open the Activities view, and click the Add Activity option to create a new activity. This displays a message box displaying the steps involved in creating a Virtual Fields Activity, as shown in Figure 19.8.

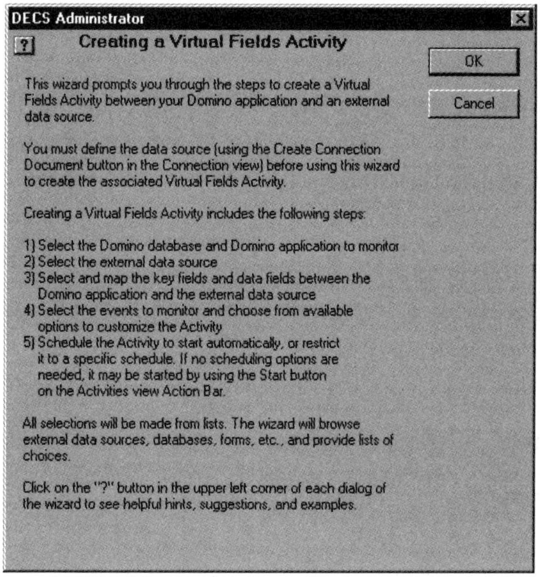

FIGURE 19.8 *Creating a Virtual Fields Activity by using User Assistant*

2. Click OK to close the message box. A list of the databases on the Domino server appears, as shown in Figure 19.9.

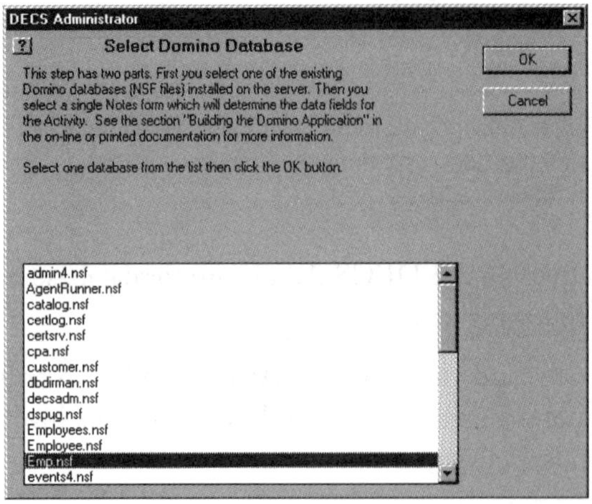

FIGURE 19.9 *Selecting a Domino database*

3. Select the database that contains the form you have designed for DECS, and click OK. The next screen containing a list of forms in the selected database is displayed, as shown in Figure 19.10.

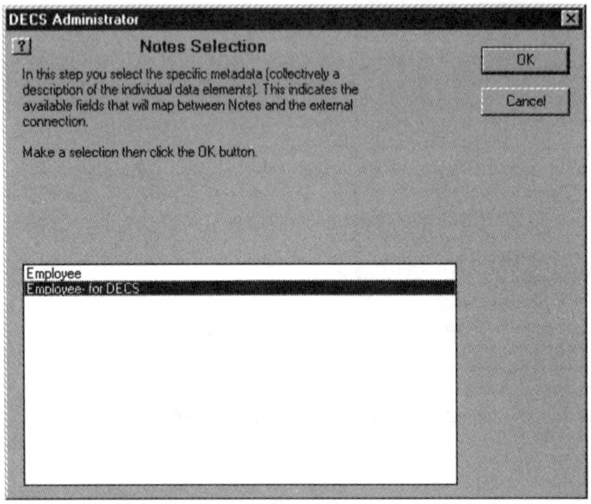

FIGURE 19.10 *Selecting a form to be used for mapping fields with external data*

4. Select the appropriate form that contains the metadata or the fields that can be mapped to the external data source, and click OK. The next screen appears, as shown in Figure 19.11.

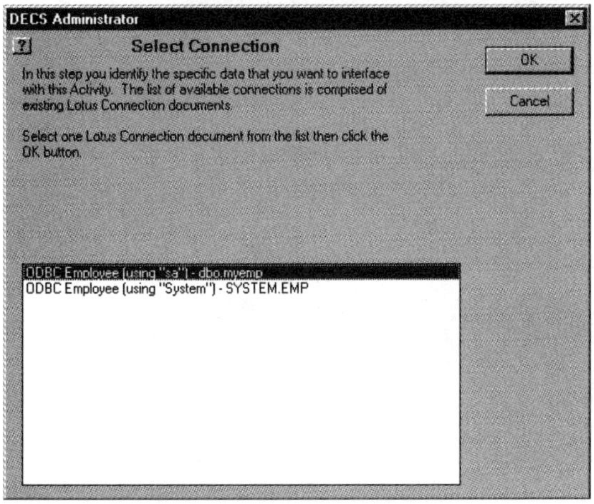

FIGURE 19.11 *Selecting a Connection document*

5. In this step, a list of connections in the DECS Administrator database are listed. Select the connection that you created for the required data source, and click OK.
6. A dialog box for mapping the fields of Domino and the external data source is displayed. In the Select Keys section, select the key field from both Domino and the external data source. In the Select Fields section map, the rest of the fields from the Domino form and the external data source appear, as shown in Figure 19.12. Click OK.

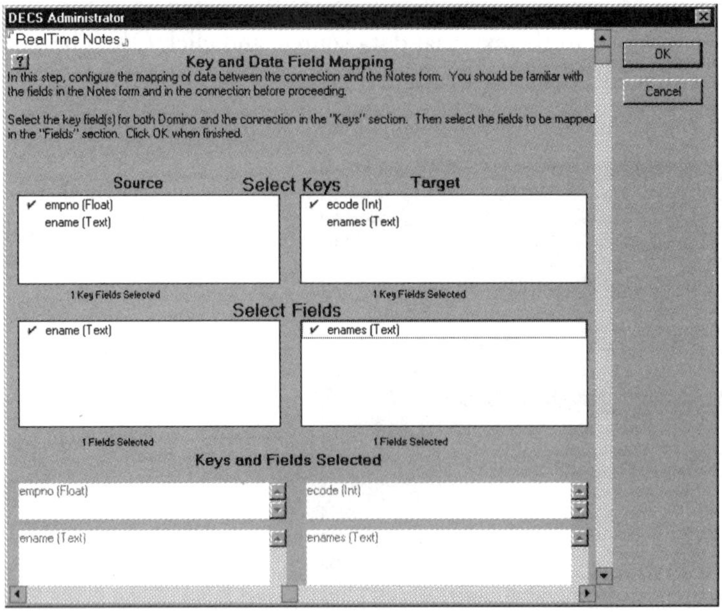

FIGURE 19.12 *Mapping the key fields and the data fields*

7. The next screen defines the document events that you want the activity to monitor. Select one or more events, as shown in Figure 19.13, and click OK.

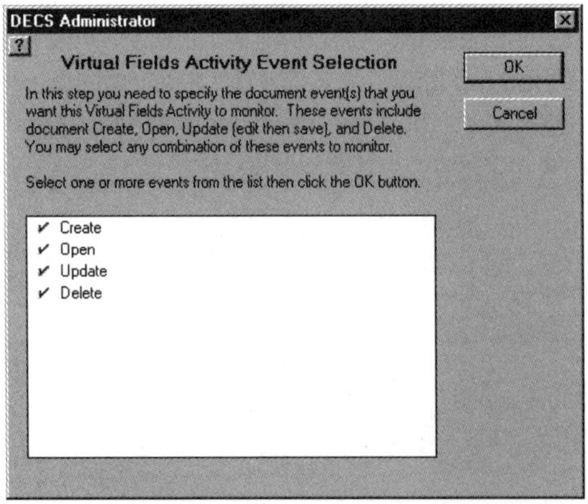

FIGURE 19.13 *Selecting Virtual Fields Activity events*

8. Finally, you are prompted for a name of the Virtual Fields Activity. Enter a unique name for the activity, and click OK. A message confirming that the activity has been created is displayed.
9. Close the message box. This takes you to the Virtual Fields Activity document, as shown in Figure 19.14.

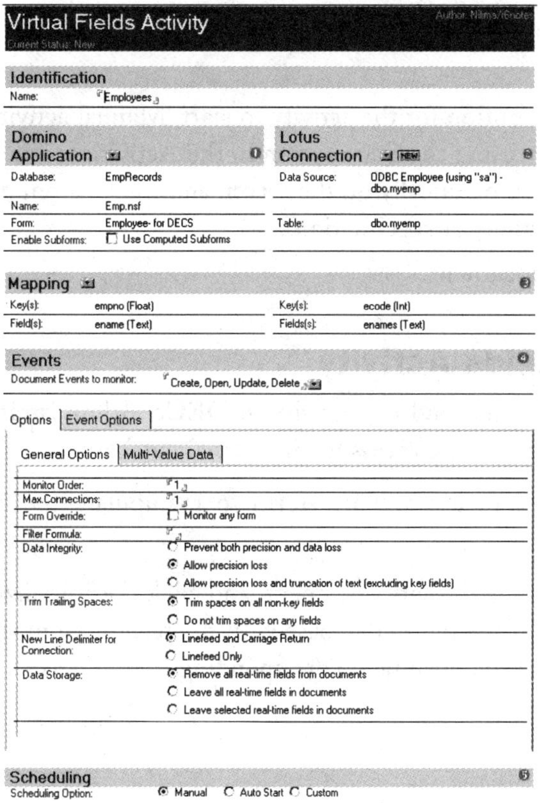

FIGURE 19.14 *The Virtual Fields Activity document*

10. The Options tab in the Events section of the activity document is used to specify options for the activity, such as data integrity, filter formula, and data storage. The Event options allow you to specify Notes formulas and the external data source procedures that you want to execute on each of the selected events. Figure 19.15 displays the event options for the Open event.

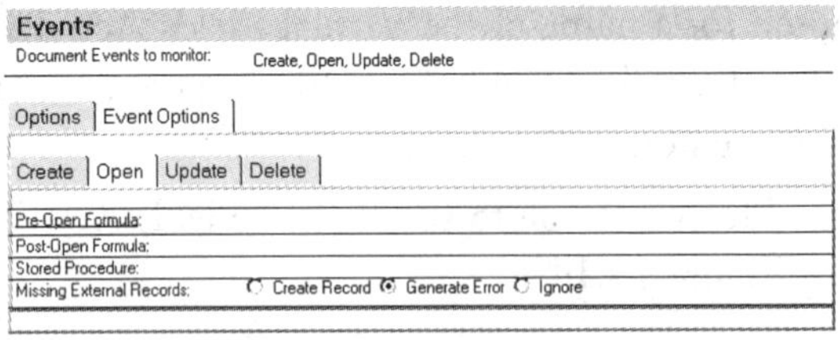

FIGURE 19.15 *The Event options for the Open event in the activity document*

11. Specify a scheduling option for the activity to start. Manual activities need to be started by using the Start option in the Activities view. Auto Start activities start automatically on the server, and the Custom option is used to start an activity at specific times.
12. Save and close the document.

Running the Virtual Fields Activity

After configuring the connection and the activity in DECS Administrator, you can use the Notes form for real-time access to an external database.

Perform the following steps to use a Notes form to manipulate the external database:

1. Open the Virtual Fields Activity document, and click the Initialize Keys action. This populates the Notes database with the records from the external data source. One document corresponding to each record is added to the database.

> **NOTE**
>
> The Initialize Keys action must be executed before starting the Virtual Fields Activity.

2. Select the Virtual Fields Activity, and click the Start action to start the activity.
3. Now open the Domino application that you designed for the purpose and navigate to the Notes view that you created to display the key for

the documents whose form you are monitoring. You can perform the following functions in the view:

- View a document by clicking on it. When the document opens, you will see the data that has been fetched from the external database.
- Update a document by clicking on the document you want to update and changing the values as needed. When you save the document, the changes will be reflected in the external database.
- Delete a document by pressing the Delete key. The changes will be reflected in the external database.
- Create a document by filling in the fields in the form. When you save the document, a new record is added to the external database.

Using a DCR

A DCR is a design element of a Domino database that is used to exchange data between a Domino database and an enterprise data source. A DCR is a shared resource that can be created once in a database and used in multiple forms across multiple databases.

To implement a DCR in a Domino database, you need to install and configure DECS on the Domino server. DCRs provide an alterative to the DECS Administrator database by allowing you to create connections in the database itself.

You must perform the following tasks to configure a DCR in a Domino database:

1. Install and configure DECS on the Domino server.
2. Create a data source reference to an external database that you want to access. For example, to access a Microsoft SQL Server database, you must specify the database as a data source and ODBC as the data driver to use for the data exchange.
3. Create a DCR to the external data source that you want to access from the Domino database. For information on creating a DCR, refer to the section "Data Connection Resources" in Chapter 3, "Working with Shared Resources."
4. For the database in which you want to use DCRs, on the Basics tab of the database properties, enable the property Allow connections to external databases using DCRs.

NOTE

The option Allow connections to external databases using DCRs, in the database properties, is enabled after a DCR has been created in the database.

5. The final task is to create a form to use the DCR. You define fields in the form that map to the external data.

Suppose you have created a DCR named EMPData in a database named Employees. This DCR is configured to access the EMP table in Oracle. Figure 19.16 displays the Data Connection dialog box for the EMPData DCR.

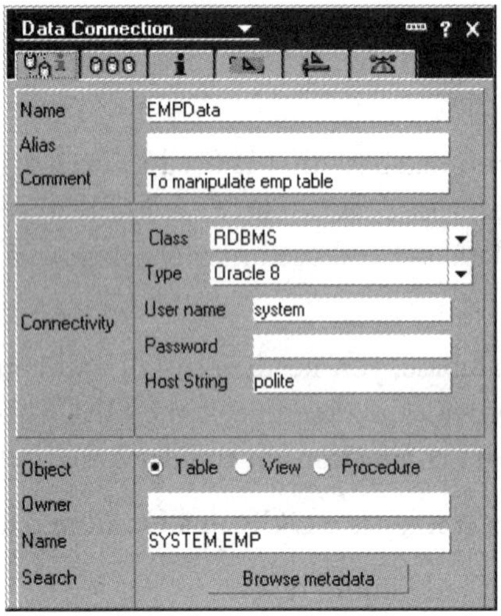

FIGURE 19.16 *The Data Connection dialog box for the EMPData DCR*

You have created a form, EmpForm, in the Employees database that contains fields corresponding to the fields in the EMP table. To configure this form to use the EMPData DCR, perform the following steps:

1. Open the form properties of EmpForm. Select the Defaults tab, and in the Data Source Options box, click the Browse button. This displays the Browse External Data Sources dialog box, as shown in Figure 19.17.

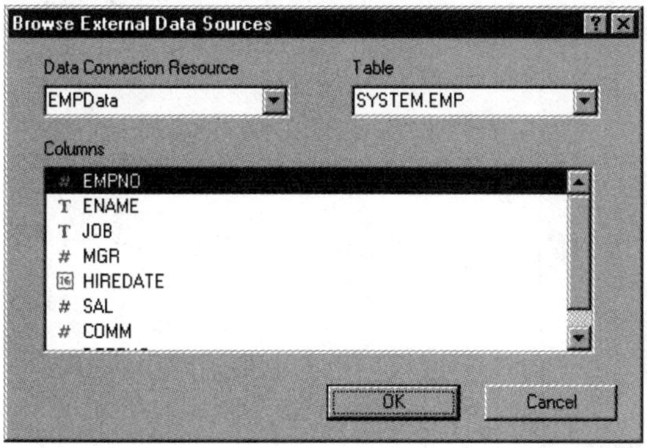

FIGURE 19.17 *The Browse External Data Sources dialog box*

2. From the Data Connection Resource list, select the DCR EMPData, and from the Table list, select System.EMP. Click OK to close the dialog box.
3. Double-click the empno field on the form to access its properties. In the Data Source Options dialog box, click the Browse button and select the DCR, Table, and the field corresponding to empno in the Emp table. Because empno is the key field, select the Key field option. Figure 19.18 displays the field properties after the specified options have been selected.

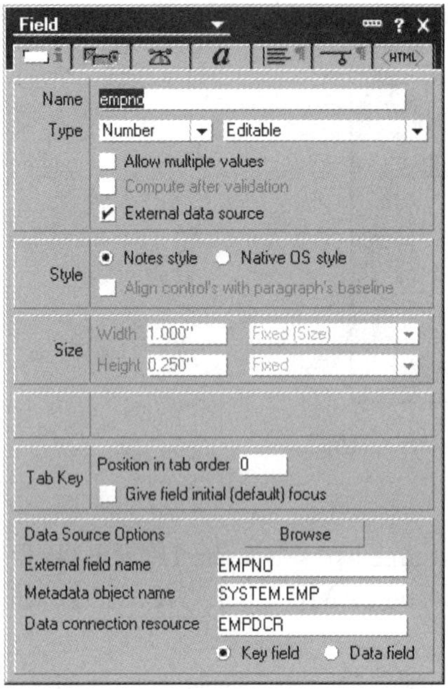

FIGURE 19.18 *The field properties displaying the data source options*

4. Repeat step 3 for all the fields that you want to map to the EMP table. Do not select the Key field option for these fields. Select the Data field option instead.
5. Save the form, and test it by using the Notes client. When you add any new data, it is added to the external data source. Similarly, if you open a document and update it, the corresponding record in the external data source table is updated.

Other Connection Solutions

Besides the tools mentioned in the previous sections to access the back-end non-Notes data, other tools are available. Some of these tools are as follows:

- LEI (*Lotus Enterprise Integrator*). LEI is used for high-volume data transfer and synchronization of data between Domino and a back-end database. It was previously called Lotus NotesPump and extends the DECS functionality beyond the real-time data sources. LEI provides visual tools to manage the integration of data sources without programming in order to initiate event-driven or scheduled high-volume data transfer between Domino applications and relational databases or other enterprise applications. LEI also supports programmatic data transfer by using LotusScript and Java classes.

- **LotusScript and Java classes.** LotusScript and Java include classes for enterprise data access. You can use these classes to customize applications to incorporate information from various back-end applications according to your business needs. The Domino server includes the LSX (*Lotus Domino Connector LotusScript eXtension*), which allows programmatic access to Domino connectors from LotusScript.
- **Domino connectors.** Domino connectors are used to provide native connectivity to external relational databases. You can access these connectors by using the forms-based development tool in DECS or the Domino object classes in the LotusScript or Java language.

Summary

In this chapter, you identified the need to access a non-Notes database from Domino and the various solutions available to access enterprise data. Domino Designer provides three @DB Commands to access an ODBC data source. LS:DOs provide classes for working with ODBC in LotusScript. You also configured DECS and used a Domino form for real-time access to back-end data. You learned about the Connection and Virtual Fields Activity documents in the DECS Administrator database and the steps to use an activity for accessing enterprise data source. Finally, you configured a Domino form to use a DCR configured in a Domino database.

Chapter 20

Project Case Study: Creating a Leave Processing Application

Chapter 19, "Accessing Non-Notes Databases from Domino," discussed the methods for connecting to enterprise data from Domino. In the next two chapters, you'll design a Leave Processing application that will access a non-Notes database using the LS:DO (*LotusScript:DataObjects*). This chapter discusses the case study and design specifications of the Leave Processing application that you will create in the following chapter.

KeepWell Pharmaceuticals: The Present Scenario

KeepWell Pharmaceuticals is a company with a global presence in the pharmaceutical market. It has offices in all major countries of the world and about 3,000 employees. It has an excellent IT infrastructure with most of its internal functions automated. It uses Oracle for data management and Lotus Notes for e-mail and calendars. The IT manager has decided to use Lotus Notes as a tool for internal workflow processes, such as leave processing, conveyance, medical, petty cash vouchers, and employee recruitment. Because the HR and financial data is on Oracle, the management wants to have an application that can operate with Oracle databases.

Leave Processing System: The Solution

As mentioned in the preceding section, the IT team intends to implement a Leave Processing System in Lotus Notes to take advantage of the workflow processing features in Lotus Notes. As per the existing process, the employees can take two leaves per month. These leaves are accredited to their leave account at the end of each month. For new employees, a leave record has to be generated in Oracle when they take their first leave.

The employees will use the Leave Processing System to apply for leave, which will then be approved by the department managers. If the department manager approves, then the request will be sent to the administration department for further approval. The administration department will verify the employee's leave record, stored in Oracle database, and based on availability, approve or reject the leave.

This system will send notifications at each step and record the approvals and rejections as in a workflow process. In addition, the leave data will be updated in the employee's leave record after the employee takes the leave. The following section describes the project cycle for developing an application.

Project Life Cycle

The development life cycle of a project involves three phases: project initiation, project execution, and project deployment. As discussed in earlier chapters, in the project initiation phase, a comprehensive project plan is prepared and the project team is identified. In the project execution phase, the team develops the required application. This phase is further divided into six phases: requirements analysis, high-level design, low-level design, construction, integration and testing, and user acceptance test. In the project deployment phase, the application is deployed at the client location. Deployment not only includes making the application available to the users, but also setting the security of the application and setting the administration options for easy management of the application.

Before proceeding further, take a look at each of the stages in the project execution phase.

Requirements Analysis

In this phase, the team studied the present system for leave processing. It interviewed various users to understand their requirements and expectations from the system. The team also studied a few existing automated Leave Processing Systems. Based on their understanding, they made presentations to the users. The following requirements were identified for the Leave Processing System to be created. The system should:

- Have a form that's simple to fill in
- Be easy to navigate
- Provide easy access to information through well-designed views
- Be secured such that only the authorized users can access the information and take actions
- Provide data integrity and consistency with the Oracle databases

Based on these requirements, the team decided on the design described in the next section.

High-Level Design

In this phase, the team decided on the working or functionality of the system and various data input and output formats. Various operating requirements were also identified during this phase. The following section discusses the workflow components for the system.

Workflow Analysis

The Leave Processing System is being implemented to combine the workflow functionality of Domino with the data processing capabilities of Oracle. To implement a workflow process, it is necessary to identify the various workflow elements in the application. The elements identified were:

- **Workflow object.** The main workflow object in this application is the leave request.
- **Start point employee.** This employee is responsible for filling up the leave requests.
- **End point.** This role is assigned to the HR executive, who verifies and gives a final approval for the leave.
- **Roles.** The different roles in the workflow are Employee, Department Manager, and HR Executive.
- **Routes and rules.** Table 20.1 lists the routes, rules, and exceptions to rules in the workflow for the Leave Processing System.

Table 20.1 Routes and Rules in the Leave Processing System

Route	Rule	Exceptions
Employee to Department Manager	Leave request is created.	None.
Department Manager to HR Executive	Leave is approved.	Leave is rejected.

Design Analysis

The Leave Processing System displays a side navigator, as shown in Figure 20.1, to the users when they open the database. This screen provides options to users to create a new leave request or view leaves organized in various ways.

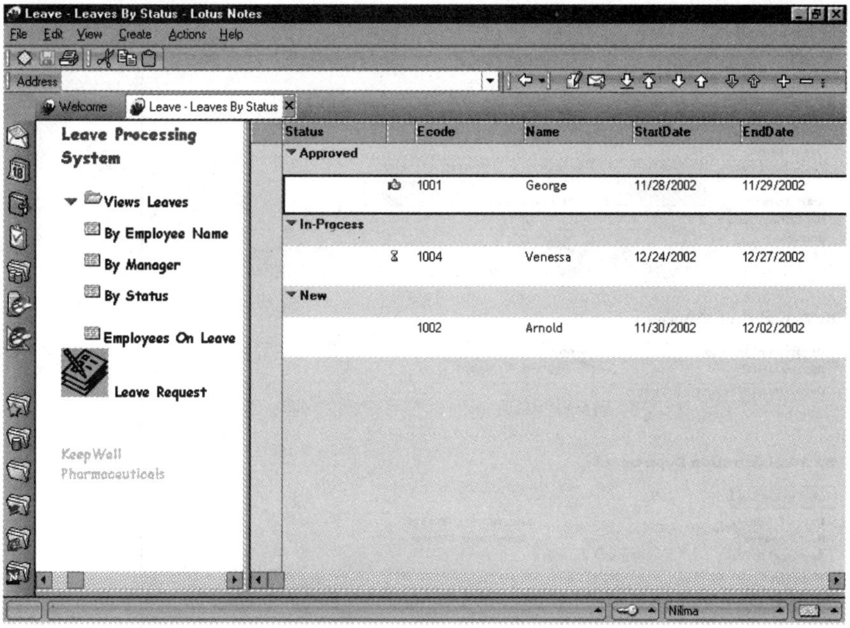

FIGURE 20.1 *The navigator for the Leave Processing System*

The Leave Request form, which appears after clicking the New Leave Request option and is shown in Figure 20.2, is used to apply for leave.

The employee enters the employee code, and the corresponding details, such as name, department name, and department manager's name, are automatically fetched from the back-end database and displayed. Then the employee fills in the leave details and saves and closes the leave request. A notification is sent to the department manager informing about the leave request. The department manager then processes the leave request and either approves or rejects the request. The form has fields that only the department manager can edit. If the leave is approved, a notification is sent to the HR executive informing him about the leave. If rejected, a notification is sent to the employee.

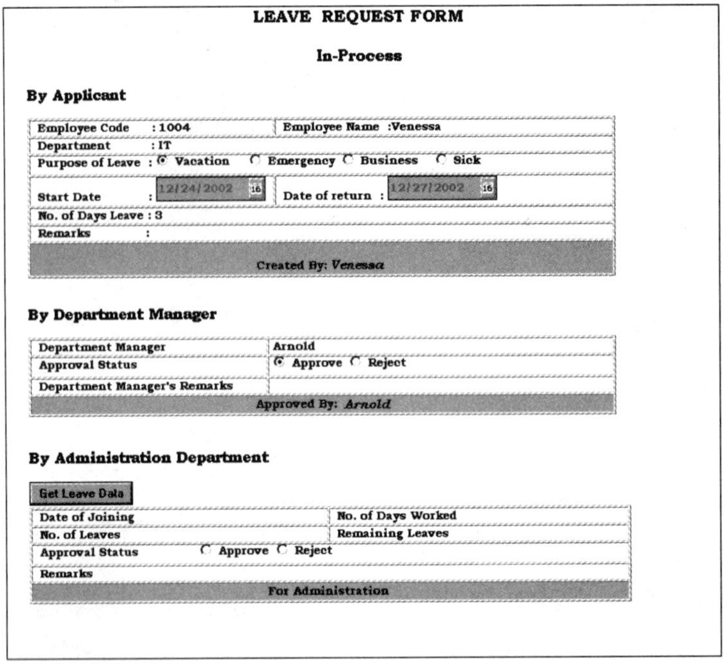
LEAVE REQUEST FORM

In-Process

By Applicant

Employee Code : 1004 | Employee Name :Venessa
Department : IT
Purpose of Leave : Vacation Emergency Business Sick
Start Date : 12/24/2002 | Date of return : 12/27/2002
No. of Days Leave : 3
Remarks :
Created By: Venessa

By Department Manager

Department Manager | Arnold
Approval Status | Approve Reject
Department Manager's Remarks |
Approved By: Arnold

By Administration Department

Get Leave Data
Date of Joining | No. of Days Worked
No. of Leaves | Remaining Leaves
Approval Status Approve Reject
Remarks
For Administration

FIGURE 20.2 *The Leave Request form*

The HR executive then verifies the employee's leave record by clicking the Get Leave Data button and accordingly approves or rejects the leave. A notification is sent to the employee informing her about the action taken.

The View Leaves option on the navigator organizes the existing leaves in four ways:

- Leaves by Status
- Leaves by Employee
- Leaves by Manager
- Employees on Leave

The Leaves by Status view is used to view the leaves organized by the status of the leave. This view uses icons to display the status of the view as Accepted, Rejected, or In-process. Figure 20.3 displays the Leaves by Status view.

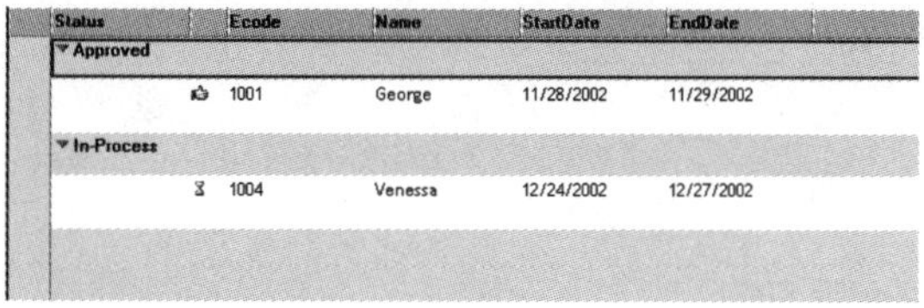

FIGURE 20.3 *The Leaves by Status view*

The Leaves by Employee view helps to see the leave records for a specific employee. Figure 20.4 displays the Leaves by Employee view.

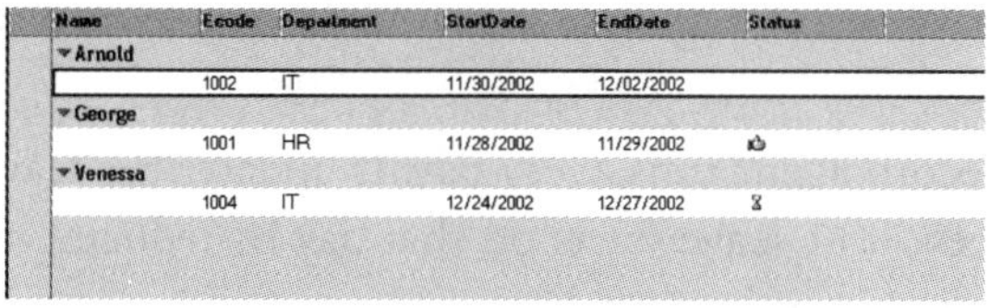

FIGURE 20.4 *The Leaves by Employee view*

The Leaves by Manager view displays the leaves organized by the department manager. This view helps the manager to view the leave records created by the employees of the department, based on which an action needs to be taken. Figure 20.5 displays the Leaves by Manager view.

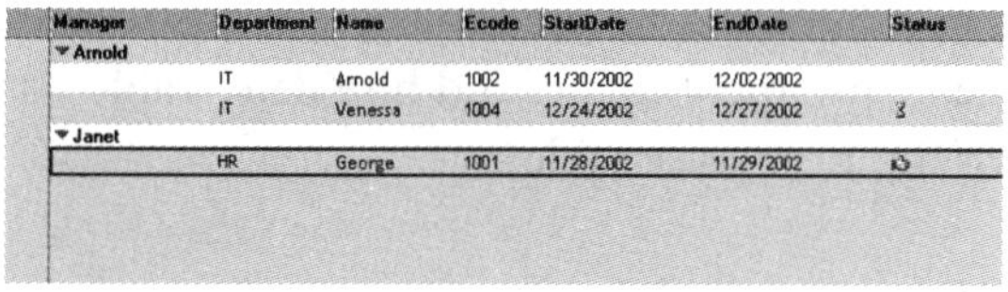

FIGURE 20.5 *The Leaves by Manager view*

The Employees on Leave view, as shown in Figure 20.6, displays leave records of the employees who are currently on leave.

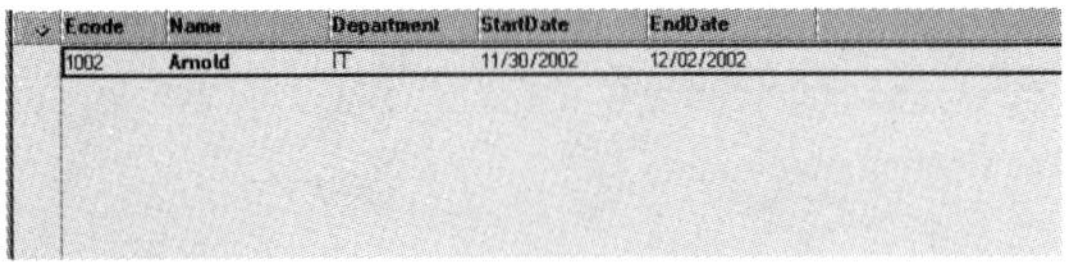

FIGURE 20.6 *The Employees on Leave view*

The Leave Processing System contains two scheduled agents:

- The Credit Leaves agent runs on the first of every month. It updates the leave record of the employee in the database by assigning him one leave if the employee's hire date is in within the last 15 to 30 days from the current date or two leaves if the hire date is before 30 days from the current date.
- The Update Leave Record agent runs every day. It updates the leave record of the employee whose leave starts on that day by reducing the leave balance by the number of leaves taken.

Low-Level Design

In this phase, a detailed design of the various design elements identified during the high-level design is prepared. The design includes specifications such as naming conventions for forms, views, and fields for the project. The development team for the Leave Processing System also documented these specifications. One such specification was the structure of the back-end tables.

- **The Employee table.** This table will be used to retrieve details about the employee such as name, department name, and hire date. Table 20.2 defines the structure of the Employee table.

Table 20.2 Structure of the Employee Table

Column Name	Data Type	Width
Ecode	Number	4
Ename	Varchar2	30
Dname	Varchar2	20
Salary	Long	10,2
Hiredate	Date	10

- **The Dept table.** This table will be used to retrieve the name of a department manager. The names in this table are consistent with the Notes usernames. Table 20.3 defines the structure of the Dept table.

Table 20.3 Structure of the Dept Table

Column Name	Data Type	Width
Dname	Varchar2	20
Manager	Varchar2	30

- **The Leave table.** This table will be used to obtain the leave details of all employees. Table 20.4 defines the structure of the Leave table.

Table 20.4 Structure of the Leave Table

Column Name	Data Type	Width
Ecode	Number	4
TotalLeave	Number	5
LeaveTaken	Number	5

Construction

In this phase, the application is developed according to the design specifications identified earlier. Chapter 21, "Creating a Leave Processing Application," discusses the development of the Leave Processing application.

Integration and Testing

In this phase, the application is deployed on the live server. The security is configured and the various roles identified are implemented. Several tests and validations are carried out on the different modules and their integration functionality is checked. The workflow process is also verified.

User Acceptance Test

In the *user acceptance* phase, the Leave Processing System will be made accessible to the users and various tests will be carried out based on the pre-defined acceptance criteria as given by the client. Any issues or bugs identified at this phase will be fixed. Users will be asked to give feedback on the same will be implemented in the system.

Summary

In this chapter, you learned about the KeepWell Pharmaceuticals company that wants to implement a Leave Processing System to incorporate workflow using Lotus Notes. The company wants to use the existing Oracle database for maintaining data. You looked at various requirements for this application and identified the design specifications for the applications. In the next chapter, you will learn to create the various design elements required for the Leave Processing System.

Chapter 21

Chapter 20, "Project Case Study: Creating a Leave Processing Application," discussed the design of the Leave Processing System to be developed for the Keep-Well Pharmaceuticals company. This chapter discusses how to create the various elements in the Leave Processing System. It covers how to access non-Notes databases through forms and agents using LS:DO (*LotusScript: Data Objects*). The first step is the creation of a database for the Leave Processing System.

Creating the Database

The database for the Leave Processing System needs to be created from scratch because this is a customized application. It is necessary to create the database on the server, but while designing it, you can create it on the local hard disk. To create the Leave Processing System, specify these options:

- Server: Local
- Title: Leave Processing System
- File Name: Leave.nsf
- Template: Blank

The Leave Request Form

The Leave Request form helps create a leave request. This form contains three sections:

- Applicant's section
- Department manager's section
- Administration section

These sections are explained in the following subsections.

Applicant's Section

The applicant's section displays details about the employee. The employee enters the employee code, while the name and department name are fetched from the

Employee table in the back-end Oracle database. The employee uses this section to fill in details about her leave, such as the purpose of leave or the start and end date of the leave. Figure 21.1 illustrates the layout of the applicant's section.

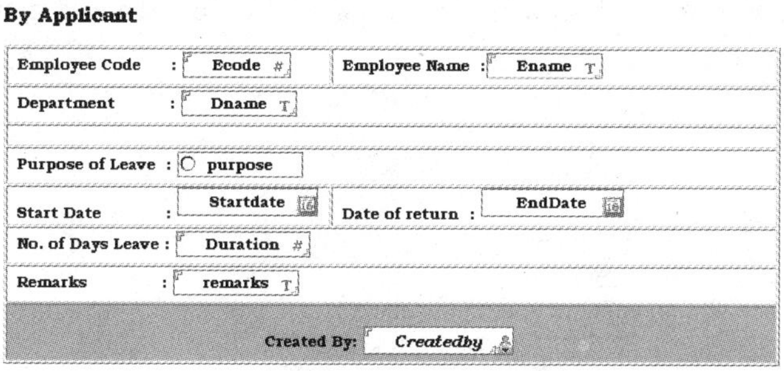

FIGURE 21.1 *The layout of the applicant's section*

The applicant's section in the Leave Request form contains labels and fields, as stated in Table 21.1.

Table 21.1 Description of the Fields in the Applicant's Section

Label	Field Name	Type
Employee Code	Ecode	Number, Editable
Employee Name	Ename	Text, Computed
Department	Dname	Text, Computed
Purpose of Leave	Purpose	Radio button, Editable
Start Date	StartDate	Date/Time, Editable
End Date	EndDate	Date/Time, Editable
No. of Days Leave	Duration	Number, Computed
Remarks	Remarks	Text, Editable
None	CreatedBy	Names, Computed when composed

This section contains four computed fields, and ename and dname are fetched from an Oracle table. In addition, the duration of leave is calculated based on the start and the end dates. The CreatedBy field contains the name of the user creating the leave request.

Department Manager's Section

The department manager uses the department manager's section to enter comments and take action on the leave request. This is a controlled access section and can only be edited by the person whose name has been specified in the DepartmentManager field. Figure 21.2 shows the layout of the department manager's section.

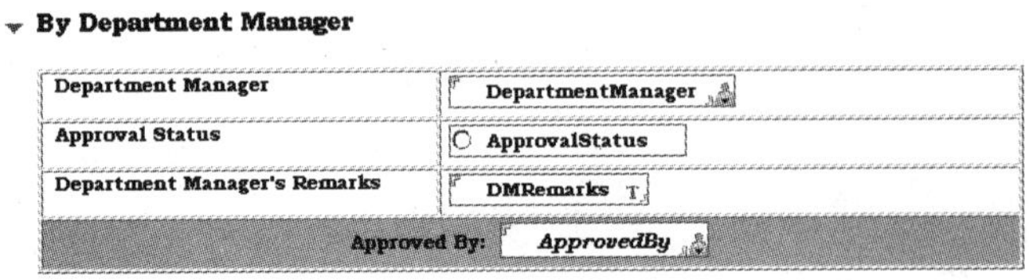

FIGURE 21.2 *The layout of the department manager's section*

The department manager's section in the Leave Request form contains labels and fields, as listed in Table 21.2.

Table 21.2 Description of Fields in the Department Manager's Section

Label	Field Name	Type
Department Manager	DepartmentManager	Text, Computed
Approval Status	ApprovalStatus	Radio button, Editable
Department Manager's Remarks	DMRemarks	Text, Editable
None	Approvedby	Names, Computed

The DepartmentManager field in this section is retrieved from Dept table in Oracle. The ApprovedBy field is automatically updated with the name of the person who updates the Approval Status.

Administration Section

The administration section is used by the HR executives in the administration department to process the leave. The HR executive uses the Get Leave Data button in the section to get details about the employee, such as the date of joining the company, the number of days of accrued leave, and the balance in the account, from the Leave table. Based on this data, the HR executive approves or rejects the leave. As a result, this section also contains fields for administration action and remarks. This is also a controlled access section and can be edited only by one who has been assigned the role HRE. Figure 21.3 shows the layout of the administration section.

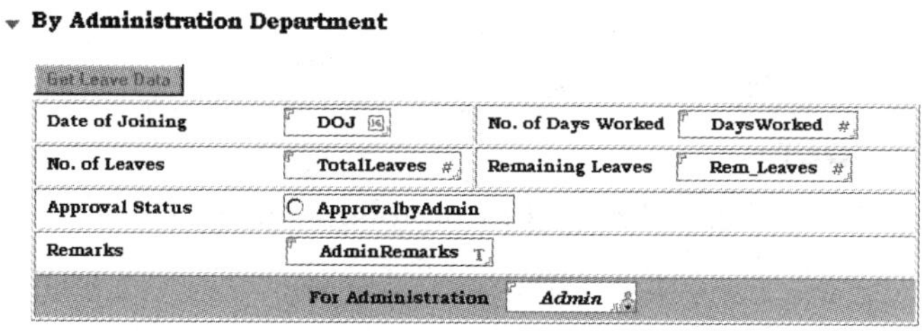

FIGURE 21.3 *The layout of the administration section*

The administration section on the Leave Request form contains labels and fields, as stated in Table 21.3.

Table 21.3 Description of Fields in the Administration Section

Label	Field Name	Type
Date of Joining	DOJ	Date/Time, Computed
No. of Days worked	DaysWorked	Number, Computed
No. of Days Leave Accrued	TotalLeaves	Number, Computed
Remaining Leave	Rem_Leaves	Number, Computed
Approval Status	ApprovalbyAdmin	Radio button, Editable
Remarks	AdminRemarks	Text, Editable
None	Admin	Names, Computed

In this section, the fields DOJ, DaysWorked, and TotalLeaves are retrieved from Oracle tables. The field Rem_Leaves is calculated based on the data retrieved from these tables. The Admin field is updated with the name of the person updating the ApprovalbyAdmin field.

Creating the Leave Request Form

In addition to fields and labels, the Leave Request form needs actions and programming code for various functions. This section covers how to design the Leave Request form.

Basic Form Layout

To design the layout of the Leave Request form, follow these steps:

1. Create a new form in the Leave Processing System database.
2. Select the Window Title event from the Objects tab of the new form and enter this code in the Script area:

   ```
   @if(@IsNewDoc;"New Leave Request";
   "Leave Requested By "+ Ename)
   ```

   This formula displays the title New Leave Request if the document has not been saved. After the document is saved, it displays Leave Requested By and the name of the employee who has applied for leave.
3. Enter the header for the form as **LEAVE REQUEST FORM**.
4. Place the cursor in the next line and create a field named Status. Specify the field type as Text and Computed. This field displays the status of the leave request.
5. In the next line, enter the section heading **By Applicant**. Below the section heading, create the fields and labels as described in Table 21.1.
6. To specify the options for the Purpose field, double-click the field to access the field properties. Click the Control tab. Select Border style as None. From the Choices list, select the option Enter choices and enter the choices as **Vacation, Business, Emergency,** and **Sick**.

7. In the Field Info tab of the field properties of the StartDate and the EndDate fields, select the option Calendar/Time control. This displays a Calendar control with these fields.
8. In a new line, enter the section title **By Department Manager**. Below this line, create the fields and label as specified in Table 21.2.
9. Specify Approve and Reject as the options for the ApprovalStatus field
10. Place the cursor in the next line and enter the section title **By Administration Department**. Below the section title, create the labels and fields as specified in Table 21.3.
11. For the ApprovalbyAdmin field, enter the options as Approve and Reject.
12. Next open the form properties and set the form properties as described below:
    - In the Name field, enter **Leave Request** as the name of the form.
    - In the Options section, check Automatically refresh fields.
13. Save the form layout. Figure 21.4 shows the complete form layout for the Leave Request form.

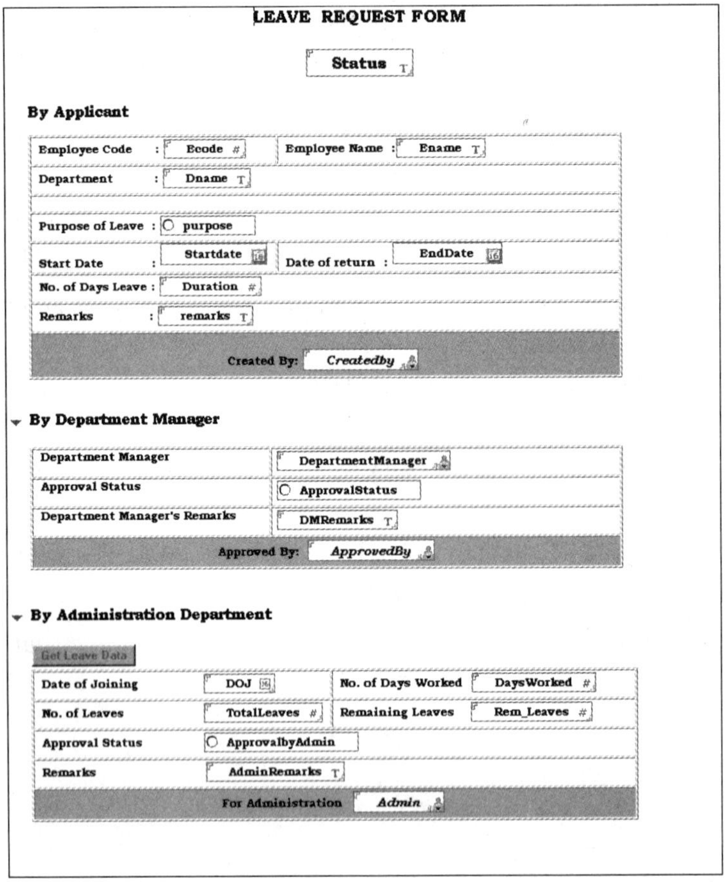

FIGURE 21.4 *The layout of the Leave Request form*

Adding Values for Computed Fields

After designing the basic layout of the form, write formulas to assign values to the computed fields in the form. The next sections explain the code required to assign values to these fields.

Status

The Status field displays the status of any leave request. This is updated at different stages during the processing of the leave request. Initially, the Status field displays the value as `New`. Therefore, select the Value event for this field in the Objects tab and enter this formula:

```
"New"
```

> **NOTE**
>
> The Status field must be of the type Computed when composed. If you create this field as type Computed and assign the formula `"New"`, all updates to this field from different places will finally be overwritten with New because computed fields values are calculated every time the document is recalculated.

CreatedBy

The CreatedBy field records the name of the person who fills in the Leave Request. To display the name of the current user, enter this code in the Value event of the CreatedBy field:

```
@UserName
```

The CreatedBy field is calculated only when the document is created and contains the name of the user who created the leave request.

ApprovedBy

The ApprovedBy field in the department manager's section contains the name of the person who approves or rejects the leave using the ApprovalStatus field. ApprovedBy is a computed field that will be assigned a value from the Approval-Status field. Therefore, in the Value event of the ApprovedBy field, enter **ApprovedBy**. To assign a value to this field, select the `OnChange` event of the ApprovalStatus field. The OnChange event shows Web and JavaScript as the default run options in the Programmer's pane. Select Client from the first list and select LotusScript from the second list, and enter this code:

```
Dim s As New NotesSession
Dim ws as New NotesUIWorkspace
Dim uidoc as NotesUIDocument
Set uidoc = ws.currentDocument
Call uidoc.fieldsettext("ApprovedBy",s.commonusername)
```

This code assigns the current username to the ApprovedBy field in the current document whenever the ApprovalStatus field is changed and the focus is moved out of the field.

Admin

The Admin field records and displays the name of the user who updates the ApprovalByAdmin field. In the Admin field, enter the formula `Admin`. To assign a value to the Admin field, select the `OnChange` event of the ApprovalByAdmin field, select to run LotusScript in the Client option, and enter this code:

```
Dim s As New NotesSession
Dim ws as New NotesUIWorkspace
Dim uidoc as NotesUIDocument
Set uidoc = ws.currentDocument
Call uidoc.fieldsettext("Admin",s.commonusername)
```

This code assigns the current username to the Admin field in the current document whenever the ApprovalByAdmin field is changed and the focus is moved out of the field.

Duration

The Duration field contains the duration of leave calculated by subtracting the leave start date from the leave end date. In the Value event of the Duration field, enter this formula:

```
@If(startdate=null¦enddate=null;null;(enddate-startdate)/86400)
```

If the startdate or the enddate fields are null, the calculation will result in an error message. As a result, before the calculation, the fields are checked for null values.

Ename, Dname, and Department Manager

The value in the Ecode field helps retrieve the values in the Ename, Dname, and the Department Manager fields from the back-end Oracle database. The code to retrieve these fields will be associated with the Ecode field, so in the Value event of these fields, enter the field names themselves. As explained in Chapter 19 "Accessing Non-Notes Databases from Domino" to use the LS:DO classes, you must include the LotusScript extension library for ODBC. Select the `(Options)` event of the (Globals)Leave Request object from the Objects tab and enter the following code:

```
UseLSX "*LSXODBC"
```

To assign values to these fields, select the OnChange event of the Ecode field. The code in the OnChange event of a field is evaluated whenever the field value is changed and the focus moves to another field.

In the Programmer's pane, select Client and LotusScript from the Run lists and enter this code:

```
Dim odbc As ODBCConnection
Dim qr As ODBCquery
Dim result As ODBCResultSet
Dim ws As NotesUIWorkspace
Dim uidoc As NotesUIDocument
Set odbc = New ODBCConnection
Set ws= New NotesUIWorkspace
Set uidoc=ws.CurrentDocument
Set qr=New ODBCQuery
Set result =New ODBCResultSet
Set qr.connection=odbc
Set result.query=qr
odbc.silentmode=True
var=odbc.connectto("empentry","notes","notesadmin")
If odbc.isconnected=False Then
        Msgbox "Could not connect. Contact administrator"
Else
      qr.SQL="select * from employee where ecode=" &_
      uidoc.FieldGetText("ecode")
      result.execute
      Call uidoc.fieldsettext("ename",Cstr(result.getvalue("ename")))
      Call uidoc.fieldsettext("dname",Cstr(result.getvalue("dname")))
      qr.SQL="select manager from dept where dname='"&_
      uidoc.FieldGetText("dname")&"'"
      result.Execute
      Call uidoc.fieldsettext("DepartmentManager",
      result.getvalue("manager"))
End If
```

This code executes a query in the back-end system to retrieve all the rows where the value in the ecode column matches the ecode in the current document. From the ResultSet, it reads the value of the Ename and the Dname columns and assigns them to the respective fields. Another query is executed to retrieve the value of the managername from the Dept table by matching the Dname field. This value is assigned to the DepartmentManager field in the document.

DOJ, TotalLeaves, Rem_Leaves

The DOJ, TotalLeaves, and Rem_Leaves fields are retrieved by the HR executive to verify the leave status of the employee who has applied for leave. The DOJ field is retrieved from the Hiredate column of the table Employee in the Oracle database. The table Leave contains the TotalLeaves and the LeavesTaken columns that populate the TotalLeaves and the Rem_Leaves fields. Rem_Leaves is the number of leaves remaining and is calculated by subtracting LeavesTaken from the TotalLeaves value. The HR executive should have an option by which the leave data can be retrieved from Oracle. To provide this option, follow these steps:

1. In the Leave Request form, under the section title By Administration Department, create a hotspot button by choosing Create/Hotspot/Button.
2. In the Button dialog box, enter the label as **Get Leave Data** and close the dialog box.
3. Select the Click event of the button and choose to run LotusScript in the Client.
4. In the Script area, enter this code:

```
Dim odbc As New ODBCConnection
Dim qr As New ODBCquery
Dim result As New ODBCResultSet
Dim ws As New NotesUIWorkspace
Dim uidoc As NotesUIDocument
Dim reml as Number
Set uidoc=ws.currentdocument
Set qr.connection=odbc
Set result.query=qr
odbc.silentmode=True
var=odbc.connectto("empentry","notes","notesadmin")
```

```
If odbc.isconnected=False Then
   Msgbox "Could not connect. Contact administrator"
Else
   qr.sql="select employee.ecode,hiredate,totalleave,leavetaken from _
           employee,leave where employee.ecode=leave.ecode
           and employee.ecode =" _
           & uidoc.FieldGetText("ecode")
   result.execute
End If
   reml=result.getvalue("totalleave")-result.getvalue("leavetaken")
   Call uidoc.fieldsettext("totalleaves", _
   Cstr(result.getvalue("totalleave")))
   Call uidoc.fieldsettext("rem_leaves",Cstr(reml))
   Call uidoc.fieldsettext("DOJ",Cstr(result.getvalue("hiredate")))
```

This code executes a query in the back-end system to retrieve the Ecode, Hiredate, TotalLeaves, and LeavesTaken columns from the Employee and Leave tables by joining them for those rows where the `ecode` matches the `ecode` in the current document. From the ResultSet, it reads the value of these fields and assigns them to the respective fields in the current document. The variable `reml` calculates the leaves remaining by subtracting LeavesTaken from TotalLeaves. The value is then assigned to the Rem_Leaves field.

DaysWorked

The DaysWorked field is a computed field that is calculated by subtracting the DOJ from the current system date. In the above code, DOJ field has been assigned a text value. As a result, before subtracting DOJ from @Today, convert it back to a DateTime value.

To calculate the DaysWorked, enter this formula in the Value event of the field:

```
@If(DOJ=null;null;(@Today-@TextToTime(DOJ))/86400)
```

Recall that in the preceding section, you assigned a text value to the DOJ field. Before using it for any calculations, you need to convert it to Date/Time type using the `@TextToTime` function.

Actions

The Leave Request form must contain the basic actions required for performing the basic functions, such as saving and closing a document, editing a document, and closing a document without saving. Table 21.4 lists the actions to be created in the form.

Table 21.4 List of Actions

Action Name	Language	Code	Hide Action When Document Is:
Save & Close	Formula	`@Command([FileSave]);` `@Command([FileCloseWindow])`	Previewed for reading, Opened for reading
Close	Formula	`@Command([FileCloseWindow])`	None
Edit	Formula	`@Command([EditDocument])`	Previewed for editing, Opened for editing
Print	Formula	`@Command([FilePrint])`	None

Using Table 21.4 as a reference, insert the four actions described on the Leave Request form. Choose a suitable icon for these actions.

Sending a Notification

As identified in the case study of the Leave Processing System, there are two routes for the leave request. When the employee fills out the leave request, a notification must be sent to the concerned department manager. When the department manager approves the leave request, a notification must be sent to the HR executive. If the department manager rejects the leave request, the employee must be notified. In addition, when the HR executive approves or rejects the leave request, the employee must be informed.

In this application, you have not created actions for approval and rejection of the leave request. This is done using radio buttons. Use the QuerySave form event to send notifications and to update the status of the leave request. The Status field contains a macro level status of the document. To store the status of every activity that takes place in the form, add a hidden field named WorkflowStatus in the form. Create the field of the type text and editable. In the Default value event of the field, enter "New".

When saving a document, the following actions occur:

- If the document is new, a notification is sent to the department manager informing her about the new leave request created. In addition to the notification, the Status field is assigned a value `In-Process` and the WorkflowStatus field is assigned a value `With DM`.
- If the WorkflowStatus field contains the value `With DM` and the ApprovalStatus field contains `Approve`, a notification is sent to the HR executive and the WorkflowStatus field is set to `With HRE`.
- If the WorkflowStatus field contains the value `With DM` and the ApprovalStatus field contains `Reject`, a notification is sent to the employee with the information that the leave has been rejected. The WorkflowStatus field is set to `Rejected By DM` and the Status field is set to `Rejected`.
- If the WorkflowStatus field contains the value `With HRE` and the ApprovalbyAdmin field contains `Approve`, a notification is sent to the employee with the information that the leave has been approved. The WorkflowStatus field is set to `Approved By HRE` and the Status field is set to `Approved`.
- If the WorkflowStatus field contains the value `With HRE` and the ApprovalbyAdmin field contains `Reject`, a notification is sent to the employee with the information that the leave has been rejected. The WorkflowStatus field is set to `Rejected By HRE` and the Status field is set to `Rejected`.

TIP

The following code assumes that you have a group name HRE in the Domino directory and an e-mail is sent to that group. You can create a database profile to store the name of the HRE and use it for sending the notification. For more information, refer to Chapter 18, "Creating a Customer Complaint Tracking Application."

Select the QuerySave event of the form. Select to run a formula and enter the following code for sending a notification:

```
@If(@IsNewDoc;@Do(
@MailSend(DepartmentManager;Null;Null;"New Leave Request";
"A New Leave Request has been created. Pls. take required action" ;
Null;[IncludeDocLink]);
@Setfield("WorkflowStatus";"With DM");
@SetField("Status";"In-Process"));
workflowstatus="With DM" & ApprovalStatus="Approve";@Do(
@MailSend("HRE";Null;Null;"New Leave Request";
" Leave Request has been created and approved by the Department Manager.
 Pls. take required action" ;Null;[IncludeDocLink]);
@Setfield("WorkflowStatus";"With HRE"));
workflowstatus="With DM" &approvalStatus="Reject";@Do(
@MailSend(Ename;Null;Null;"Leave Request Rejected";
" The Leave Request submitted by you has been rejected ";
Null;[IncludeDocLink]);
@Setfield("WorkflowStatus";"Rejected by DM");
@Setfield("Status";"Rejected"));
workflowstatus="With HRE" & ApprovalbyAdmin="Approve";@Do(
@MailSend(Ename;Null;Null;"Leave Request Approved";
" The Leave Request submitted by you has been Approved ";
Null;[IncludeDocLink]);
@Setfield("WorkflowStatus";"Approved by HRE");
@Setfield("Status";"Approved"));
workflowstatus="With HRE" & ApprovalbyAdmin="Reject";@Do(
@MailSend(Ename;Null;Null;"Leave Request Rejected";
" The Leave Request submitted by you has been Rejected ";
Null;[IncludeDocLink]);
@Setfield("WorkflowStatus";"Rejected by HRE");
@Setfield("Status";"Rejected"));Null)
```

NOTE

The `@Do` @Function performs multiple actions as part of another function. This @Function is useful when you want to execute multiple statements as part of an `@If` @Function.

The syntax of `@Do` is:

```
@Do(expressions)
```

You can give multiple expressions separated by semicolons.

Creating Sections

Three types of users use the Leave Request form. The employees use it to apply for leave, the department manager approves or rejects the leave and enters comments, and the HR executive from the administration department verifies the leave of the employee and gives a final decision regarding the leave. The actions taken by the department manager and the administration department must be restricted so that only the concerned people can perform them. To add this security to the form, create two controlled access sections, one for the department manager and the other for the administration department. To create these controlled access sections:

1. Highlight all the fields and text starting from By Department Manager and create a controlled access section.
2. In the Form Section dialog box that opens, select the Expand/Collapse tab. For Editors, select Auto-expand section from the Opened for reading and Opened for editing lists. Click the down arrow next to the For Editors options and select For Non-Editors. Select Auto-expand section from the Opened for reading list and Auto-collapse section from the Opened for editing list.
3. Select the Formula tab. Select the Type as Computed and enter the Access Formula as **DepartmentManager** to specify that only the user whose name is listed in the DepartmentManager field can edit the section.
4. Expand the section and delete the text By Department Manager to avoid duplication.

5. Next highlight all the fields and text starting from By Administration Department and create another controlled access section.
6. In the Form Section dialog box, select the Expand/Collapse tab. For Editors, select Auto-expand section from the Opened for reading and Opened for editing lists. Click the down arrow next to the For Editors options and select For Non-Editors. Select Auto-expand section from the Opened for reading list and Auto-collapse section from the Opened for editing list.
7. Select the Formula tab. Select the Type as Computed and enter the Access Formula as `"[HRE]"` to specify that only the users with the role HRE assigned to them can edit the section.
8. Expand the section and delete the text By Administration Department.

Creating Views

The Leave Request database contains four views. To make these views user-friendly, provide users with an action that create a new leave request. This action must be available in all four views and can be created as a shared action. Before designing the views, create a shared action named Create Leave Request. Choose to run a formula on the Click event of the action and enter the following formula:

```
@Command([Compose];"Leave Request")
```

The views that were decided upon for this database in the high-level design are:

- Leaves by Status
- Leaves by Employee
- Leaves by Manager
- Employees on Leave

Leaves by Status View

The Leaves by Status view displays the leave requests categorized by the status of the leave. The view shows three categories: Approved, Rejected, or In-Process. Table 21.5 lists the columns that this view should contain.

Table 21.5 Details of Columns in Leaves by Status View

Column Title	Column Value Type	Column Value
Status	Field	Status
None	Formula	`@If(Status="Approved";83; status="Rejected";84; status="In-Process";79;null)`
Ecode	Field	Ecode
Name	Field	Ename
Start Date	Field	StartDate
End Date	Field	EndDate

To create this view:

1. Create a shared view and name it **Leaves by Status**.
2. The view will contain all the leave requests, so leave the view selection formula to default as:

   ```
   SELECT @All
   ```

3. Add columns as specified in Table 21.5.
4. Double-click the column Status to access column properties. On the Sorting tab, select Sort as Ascending and Type as Categorized. On the Column Info tab, check the option Show twisty when row is expandable.
5. In the second column, which contains the formula to display the icons for the status of the leave, on the Column Info tab, select the option Display values as icons.
6. Format the view columns by specifying the font properties such as size, color, and style. Figure 21.5 shows the layout of the Leaves by Status view.

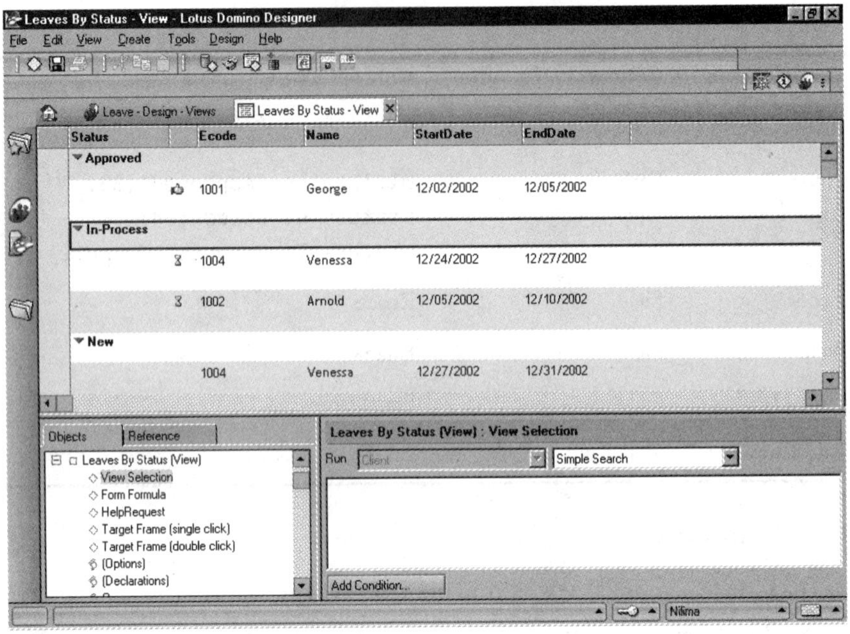

FIGURE 21.5 *Layout of Leaves by Status view*

7. Insert the shared action Create Leave Request.
8. Save and close the view.

Leaves by Employee View

The Leaves by Employee view displays the leave requests categorized by the name of the employee who has applied for leave. Table 21.6 lists the columns that this view should contain.

Table 21.6 Details of Columns in Leaves by Employee View

Column Title	Column Value Type	Column Value
Name	Field	Ename
Ecode	Field	Ecode
Department	Field	Dname
Start Date	Field	StartDate
End Date	Field	EndDate
Status	Formula	`@If(Status="Approved";83; status="Rejected"; 84;status="In-Process";79;null)`

To create this view:

1. Create a shared view and name it **Leaves by Employee.**
2. The view will contain all the leave requests; as a result, leave the view selection formula to default as:

   ```
   SELECT @All
   ```

3. Add columns as specified in Table 21.6.
4. Double-click the first column titled Name to access column properties. On the Sorting tab, select Sort as Ascending and Type as Categorized. On the Column Info tab, check the option Show twisty when row is expandable.
5. In the column titled Status, on the Column Info tab, select the option Display values as icons.
6. Format the view columns by specifying the font properties such as size, color, and style. Figure 21.6 shows the layout of the Leaves by Employee view.

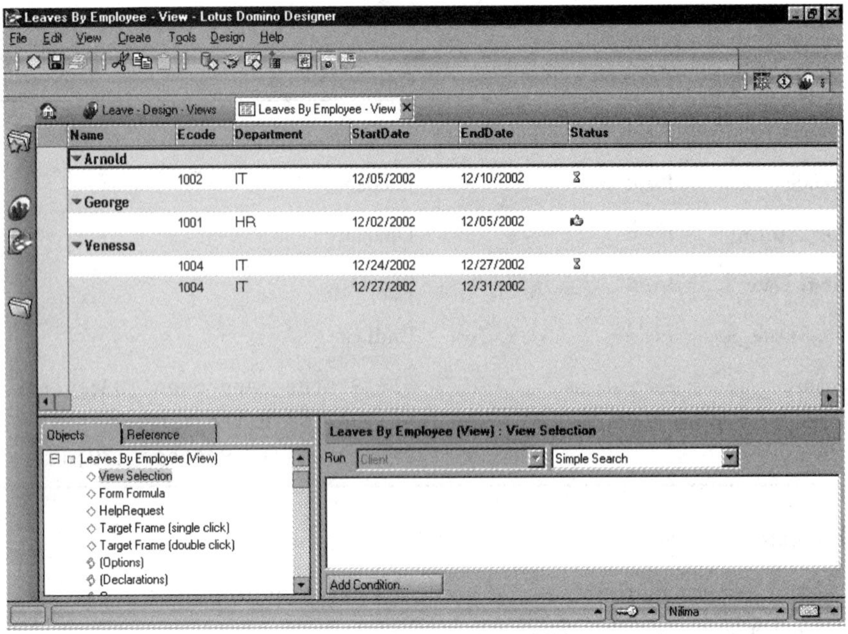

FIGURE 21.6 *Leaves by Employee view*

7. Insert the shared action Create Leave Request.
8. Save and close the view.

Leaves by Manager View

The Leaves by Manager view displays the leave requests categorized by the name of the department manager. This view helps a department manager monitor the leaves of the employees of the department. Table 21.7 lists the columns that this view should contain.

Table 21.7 Details of Columns in Leaves by Manager View

Column Title	Column Value Type	Column Value
Manager	Field	DepartmentManager
Department	Field	Dname
Ename	Field	Ename
Ecode	Field	Ecode

Column Title	Column Value Type	Column Value
Start Date	Field	StartDate
End Date	Field	EndDate
Status	Formula	`@If(Status="Approved";83; status="Rejected";84; status="In-Process";79;null)`

To create this view:

1. Create a shared view. Name it **Leaves by Manager**.
2. The view will also contain all the leave requests; as a result, leave the view selection formula to default as:

   ```
   SELECT @All
   ```

3. Add columns as specified in Table 21.7.
4. Double-click the first column titled Manager to access column properties. On the Sorting tab, select Sort as Ascending and Type as Categorized. On the Column Info tab, check the option Show twisty when row is expandable.
5. In the column titled Status, on the Column Info tab, select the option Display values as icons.
6. Format the view columns by specifying the font properties such as size, color, and style. Figure 21.7 shows the layout of the Leaves by Manager view.

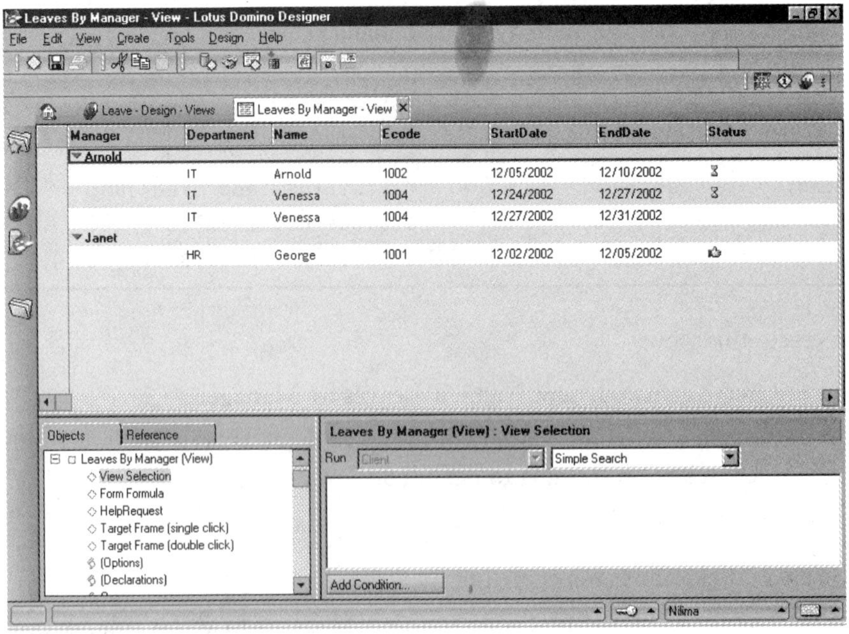

FIGURE 21.7 *Leaves by Manager view*

7. Insert the shared action Create Leave Request.
8. Save and close the view.

Employees on Leave View

The Employees on Leave view displays the details of employees currently on leave. Table 21.8 lists the columns that this view should contain.

Table 21.8 Details of Columns in Employees on Leave View

Column Title	Column Value Type	Column Value
Ecode	Field	Ecode
Name	Field	Ename
Department	Field	Dname
Start Date	Field	StartDate
End Date	Field	EndDate

To create this view:

1. Create a shared view. Name it **Employees on Leave**.
2. The view will contain only those leave requests that are currently running. As a result, in the view selection formula event, enter the following formula:

   ```
   SELECT status="Approved" & (startdate<=@Today & enddate>=@Today)
   ```

3. Add columns as specified in Table 21.8.
4. To organize the leaves in the ascending order of employee names, double-click the column titled Name to access column properties. On the Sorting tab, select Sort as Ascending.
5. To allow viewing the leaves in the ascending order of the leave end date, double-click the End Date column. On the Sorting tab of the column properties, check the option Click on column header to sort and select Ascending as the sort order. Checking this option displays a triangle next to the column title. Click the column title to sort the documents in the ascending order of the end date and click again to remove the sort order.
6. Format the view columns by specifying the font properties such as size, color, and style. Figure 21.8 shows the layout of the Employees on Leave view.

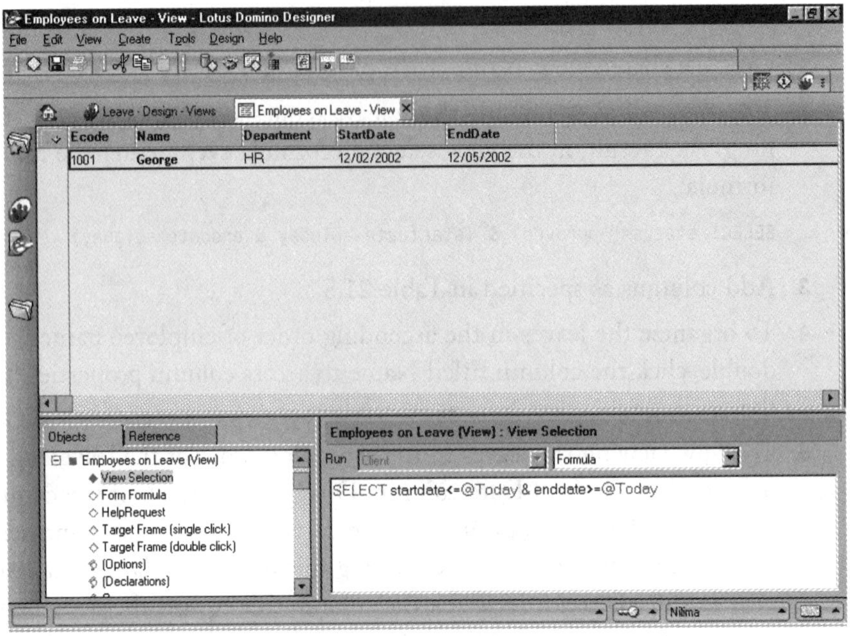

FIGURE 21.8 *The Employees on Leave view*

7. Save and close the view.

Creating Agents

The Leave Request database contains two agents to update the back-end data. The Update Leave agent runs every day. For all approved leaves starting on that day, it updates the LeavesTaken column in the Leave table by adding the value of the duration field.

The Credit Leaves agent runs on the first of every month. It updates the leave record of the employee in the Leave table by assigning one leave if the employee's hire date is in the last 15 to 30 days from the current date or two if the hire date is 30 days before the current date.

Update Leave Agent

To create the Update Leave Agent, create a new agent using the options specified in Table 21.9.

Table 21.9 Options for Update Leave Agent

Option	Value
Name	Update Leave
Options	Shared
Trigger	On Schedule
Schedule	Daily, at 1 AM
Target	All new and modified documents

In the Programmer's pane, select LotusScript. Select (Options) from the Object tab and enter this code in the Script area:

```
UseLSX "*LSXODBC"
```

Select the `Initialize` event and enter the following code:

```
Dim odbc As New ODBCConnection
Dim qr As New ODBCQuery
Dim result As New ODBCResultSet
Dim s As New notessession
Dim db As NotesDatabase
Set db=s.CurrentDatabase
Dim col As NotesDocumentCollection
Dim doc As NotesDocument
Set qr.connection=odbc
Set result.query=qr
odbc.silentmode=True
Call odbc.connectto("empentry","notes","notesadmin")
If odbc.isconnected Then
       Set col=db.Search("status=""Approved"" & startdate=@today"_
      ,Nothing,0)
       Set doc= col.GetFirstDocument
       Do Until doc Is Nothing
```

```
                qr.SQL="select ecode,leavetaken from leave where ecode= "_
                & doc.ecode(0)
                result.execute
                Call result.SetValue("leavetaken",_
                result.GetValue("leavetaken")+doc.duration(0))
                result.UpdateRow
                Set doc=col.GetNextDocument(doc)
                result.Close
        Loop
End If
odbc.Disconnect
```

This code first selects all documents where the status is `Approved` and the start date for the leave is the current system date. Next, for each document, it fetches the leave record for the employee from the Leave table in Oracle and updates the column LeavesTaken by adding the duration of the leave from the current document.

Credit Leave Agent

To create the Credit Leave Agent, create a new agent using the options specified in Table 21.10.

Table 21.10 Options for Credit Leave Agent

Option	Value
Name	Credit Leave
Options	Shared
Trigger	On Schedule
Schedule	Monthly, on day 1 at 2 AM
Target	All documents in database

In the Programmer's pane, select LotusScript. Select (Options) from the Object tab and enter the following code in the Script area:

```
UseLSX "*LSXODBC"
```

Select the Initialize event and enter the following code:

```
Dim odbc As New ODBCConnection
Dim qr  As New ODBCQuery
Dim result As New ODBCResultSet
Set qr.connection=odbc
Set result.query=qr
odbc.silentmode=True
Call odbc.connectto("empentry","notes","notesadmin")
If odbc.isconnected Then
	qr.sql="update leave set totalleave=totalleave+2 from employee,
	leave where employee.ecode=leave.ecode and
	employee.hiredate<getdate()-30"
	result.execute
	result.close
	qr.sql="update leave set totalleave=totalleave+1 from employee,
	leave where employee.ecode=leave.ecode and
	employee.hiredate<getdate()-15
	and employee.hiredate>getdate()-30"
	result.execute
	result.close
End If
```

This code executes the Update SQL statement to update the TotalLeaves column in the Leave table for the employee by the requisite number.

Creating a Navigation Structure

The Leave Request database contains a navigator for easy access to various options in the database. The navigator for this database will be designed on a page by embedding an outline. This page will be used as a side navigator. Figure 21.9 shows the navigator of the Leaves Request database.

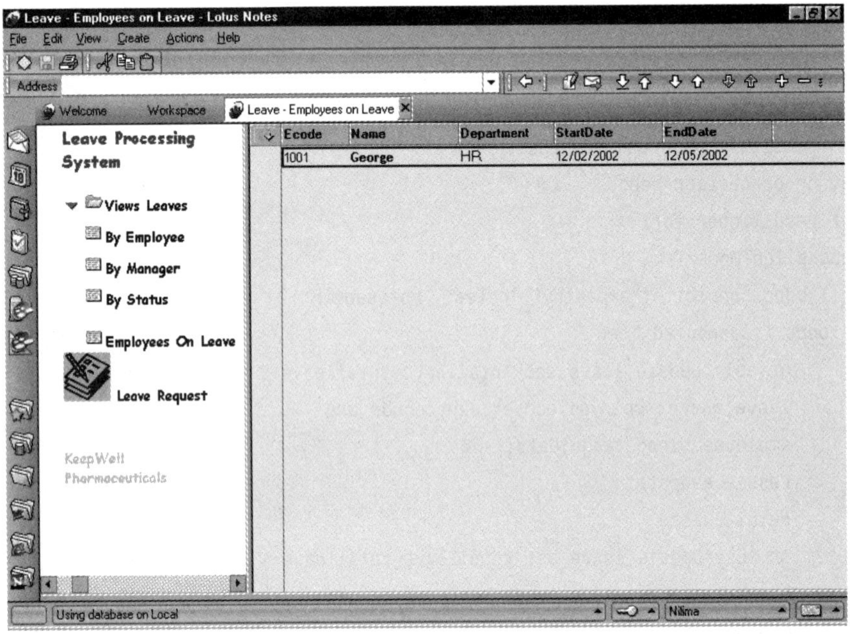

FIGURE 21.9 *The navigator in the Leave Request database*

To create this navigator:

- Create the outline
- Create the page
- Launch the page

Creating the Main Outline

Create a Main outline to design the navigation structure of the Leave Request database. Table 21.11 lists the properties for the outline entries for this outline.

Table 21.11 Outline Entry Properties for the Main Outline

Label	Content Type	Content Value
View Leaves	None	None
By Employee	Named Element, View	Leaves by Employee
By Manager	Named Element, View	Leaves by Manager
By Status	Named Element, View	Leaves by Status
Employees on Leave	Named Element, View	Employees on Leave

To create this outline:

1. Create a new outline named Main.
2. Add entries to the outline with properties as specified in Table 21.11.
3. Select the entries By Employee, By Manager and By Status by pressing Ctrl and clicking on the entries, and click Indent Entry action to group these three entries under the View Leaves entry. Figure 21.10 shows the layout of the Main outline.

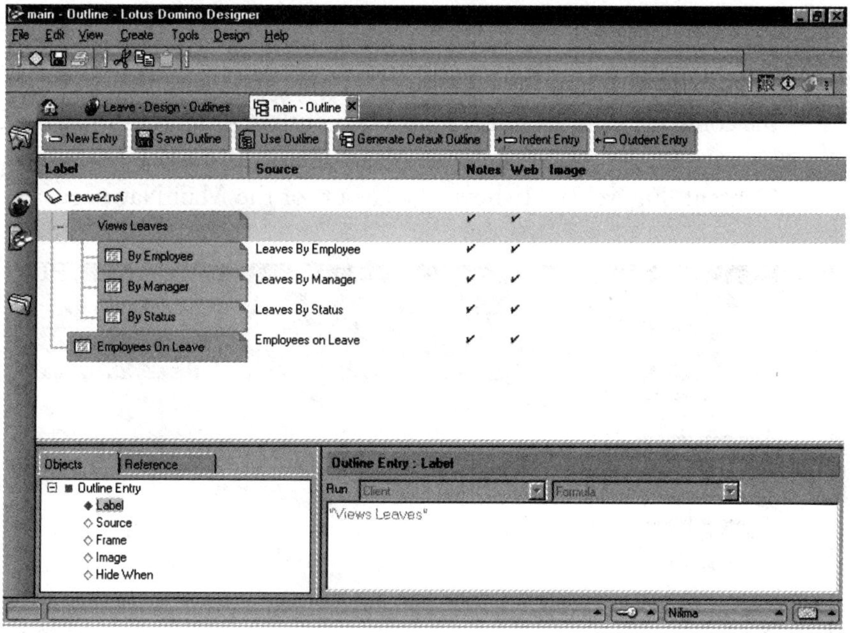

FIGURE 21.10 *The layout of the Main outline*

4. Save and close the outline.

Creating the MainNav Page

The MainNav is used as the side navigator in the Leave Request database. This page contains the designed outline and a hotspot to create a new Leave Request.

To design this page:

1. Create a new page named MainNav.
2. Enter the text **Leave Processing System** at the top of the page.
3. Take the cursor to the next line and embed the Main outline using the option Create/Embedded Element/Outline.
4. Paste an image and enter the text Leave Request on the next line. Highlight the image and create an action hotspot. Enter this formula in the Click event of the hotspot:

```
@Command([Compose];"Leave Request")
```

5. Format the text and the embedded outline. To ensure that you can see the complete outline, in the embedded outline properties from the Outline size section on the Info tab, select the width and height as Fit to Content. Figure 21.11 shows the layout for the MainNav page.

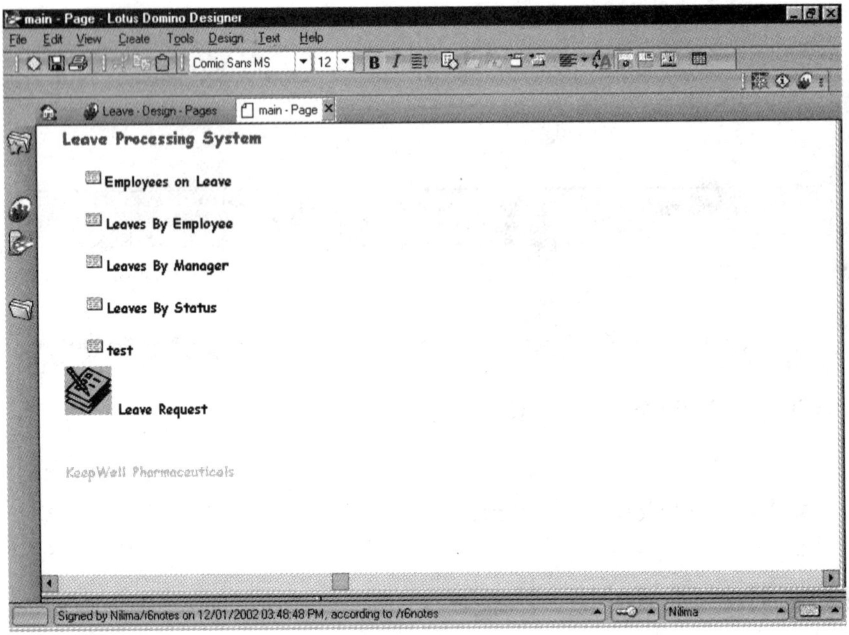

FIGURE 21.11 *The layout of the MainNav page*

6. Save and close the page.

Launching the MainNav Page

To view the MainNav page as the navigator, launch it by specifying the database launch properties. To specify the database launch properties of the Leave Request database:

1. Open the database properties and select the Launch tab.
2. From When opened in Notes client, select the option Open designated Navigator.
3. Select the Type of navigator as Page and from the list of pages displayed in the Name list, select MainNav.

To test the navigation options, open the database from a Notes client.

Deploying the Application

After designing the Leave Request database, deploy it in a live environment and test it. The Leave Request database must be copied to the server so that all users can use it. Copy the Leave Request database to the Domino server.

To set up security for the Leave Request database, open the ACL of the database on the server and add the users with access levels as specified in Table 21.12.

Table 21.12 Access Levels for Users

User	Access	Description
Department managers	Editor	The department managers update the leave request created by the employees.
HR executives	Editor	The HR executives also update the leave requests created by the employees.
Database administrator	Manager	The database administrator is responsible for changing the ACL of the database for assigning access and roles to required users.
Default	Author	This allows all employees of the organization to create a leave request.

Add a role HRE to the database ACL and assign it to the HR executives to allow them to edit the administration section in the Leave Request form.

Create a data source on the Domino server machine to access the Oracle database that contains the required tables. Name the data source **empentry**. Create a user named `notes` with a password as `notesadmin` to access this data source.

TIP

To make the application more flexible, create a database profile. In this profile, create fields for the username, user password, and the data source name. Access these fields in the Leave Request form and use them for connecting to the back-end data.

Summary

In this chapter, you designed the Leave Request Application. In Chapter 19, you were introduced to the three LotusScript classes ODBCConnection, ODBC-Query, and ODBCResultSet for accessing non-Notes databases: using LS:DO. In this chapter you implemented these classes to access non-Notes data. You also created agents to update the back-end data using these classes and used the QuerySave event to send notifications and update the status of the document.

PART VI

Professional Project 5—Creating a Web-Enabled Notes Application

Project 5 Overview

In this project, you will create an Online Order Processing System. Unlike the other applications you have developed thus far, this application will be accessed from a Web browser.

The Online Order Processing System is a business to business (B2B) application that allows customers to place orders and track their order's status online. The orders placed by customers are scrutinized by the order approval process. Once the order is approved, inventory transactions are executed. Customers are allowed to change their password, which will be synchronized with the Domino directory.

The functionality of the application is divided among three databases to achieve modularization. The three modules are products, clients, and orders. The Product database contains product information, warehouse details, and inventory transactions. The Client database contains the customer details and allows customers to change their passwords. The Order database contains customer orders, invoices, and features for order approval.

The application is developed in two phases. In the first phase, you will develop the basic framework for the application with all the functional features. In the second phase, you will enhance the application using HTML and JavaScript.

While developing this application you will learn how to program for server-side events and client-side events. Apart from learning the various techniques for developing a Web-enabled application, you will learn how to make use of CGI variables in a Domino Web application.

Chapter 22

Getting Started with a Domino Web Application

Up to this point, you learned to create various types of Domino applications to be accessed from the Notes client. For Domino applications, Notes client is just one among the many clients, such as Web browsers and mobile clients (PDA, mobile phone, and so on), which can be used to access applications.

In this chapter, you will learn the fundamental aspects for developing Domino applications for the Web. This chapter will focus on the various technology frameworks that you can use in Domino Web development. You will learn in detail how the Domino objects are dynamically translated to make your Web application accessible through browsers.

The Domino Architecture

Domino supports almost all the open standards available for the Internet. You can access or utilized the services of the DOM (*Domino Object Model*) using different technologies, such as CORBA (*Common Object Request Broker Architecture*), COM (*Component Object Model*), and SOAP (*Simple Object Access Protocol*). Because Domino supports so many Internet open standards, Domino application can be accessed from a wide rage of clients and platforms. Figure 22.1 depicts the various components of the Domino architecture.

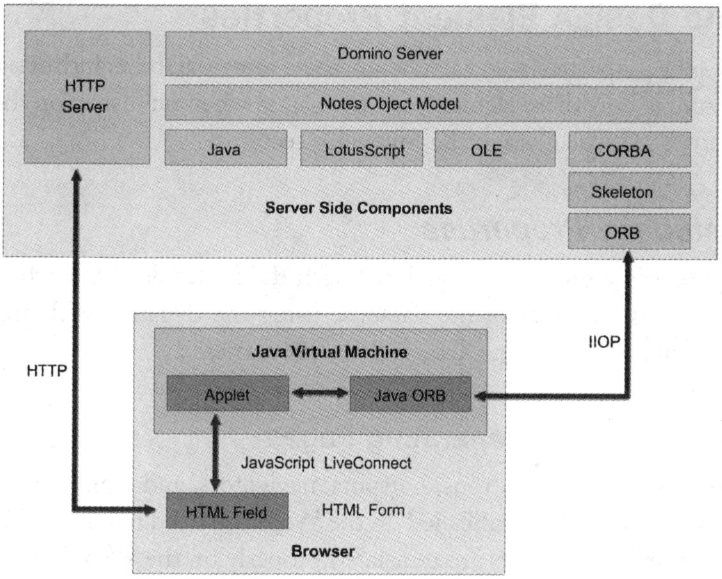

FIGURE 22.1 *Components of the Domino architecture*

> **NOTE**
>
> To make use of the technology framework provided by Domino and its various components, IBM Lotus ships additional development tools. Most of these tools can be downloaded from the Web sites **www.ibm.com** or **www.lotus.com**.

Fundamentals for Web Application Development

Before you get started with the development of a Web application, you need to understand the fundamentals of the various Domino design elements and their associated properties and behavior in a Web environment. In addition, you need to know the format in which the Domino objects will be translated when published on the Web.

Database and Design Element Properties

There are a few properties associated with the Notes database and design elements that control how these elements are translated when published on the Web. These properties are discussed in the following sections.

Notes Database Properties

There are quite a few properties associated with the Notes database, which controls the publishing behavior of the database using the dynamic Web engine of Domino. The following sections discuss these properties.

Use JavaScript While Generating Pages

This property controls how buttons, hotspots, navigators, and many other design elements are translated when published on the Web. You need to enable this property so that the design elements are translated properly on the Web. If you do not enable this property, you will be forced to work around with limited functionality, such as having only one button on the form that functions as a submit button. Enabling this option allows you to use most of the @Functions on the Web. However, few @Functions are not supported on the Web. In addition, the navigators and documents containing hotspots are displayed much faster because the hotspot formulas are not evaluated until clicked.

Don't Allow URL Open

When checked, this property will restrict the Domino URLs that users can use while accessing your application. This property, therefore, is very useful when you want to prevent users from accessing parts of your application using direct URLs. Accessing parts of your application, such as forms and views, using direct URLs may upset your application design and logic. However, this restriction may further restrict certain features, which you may wish to incorporate in your application by using direct URL invocation.

Require SSL Connection

This property is related to security rather than programmability of your application. If you check this property, only users who are using a SSL (*Secured Sockets Layer*) will be able to access your application. The SSL access may be of the following types:

- Anonymous access
- Authenticated access with username and password
- Authenticated access using an X.509 client certificate

To enable SSL for your application, the server on which your application is hosted should be enabled for SSL.

Multilingual Database

This property allows you to control the presentation language of some or all design elements of your application. If users access your application across linguistic regions, you should enable this property. This property, in conjunction with Domino Global Workbench, allows you to present your application in different languages.

Launch Property

The launch property, when opened in a browser, allows you to control the design elements that will be used as the first screen for your application when the application is accessed through a browser. You can set this property to be the same as that of the Notes launch property or you can set it to be different.

Design Element Properties

Table 22.1 summarizes some of the important properties of various design elements that need your attention when developing applications for the Web.

Table 22.1 Design Element Properties for the Web

Property	Design Element	Description
Generate HTML for all fields	Form	Controls whether the hidden fields on a form are published
Content Type	Form, Page	Controls how the content of a form, page, or document is translated
Character Set	Form, Page	Controls the character set for form or page content while using multilingual capabilities
Link Colors	Form, Page, Views	Controls the color characteristics of links used in a form, page, or view

(continues)

Table 22.1 Continued

Property	Design Element	Description
Auto Frame	Form, Page, Views	Controls whether the content is contained in a frameset or not
Available to public access users	Form, Page, Views	Controls the security aspect for public access of a form, page, or view
Background Graphics	Form, Page	Allows the use of graphics as the background element in a form or page
Treat View contents as HTML	View	Controls how the content of a view is translated while publishing
Use Applet in browser	View, Rich Text fields, Action, Outlines	Publishes views, Rich Text fields, actions, and outlines using Java applet rather than HTML

While some of the above properties are very specific to Web, few properties you can use seamlessly in Notes client and Web. Some of the above-mentioned properties require special attention. These properties are discussed in the following sections.

Generate HTML for All Fields

You are already familiar with hidden fields. You used these fields to implement programming logic when developing applications for the Notes client. You can modify the values for hidden fields using formula language @Functions and back-end and front-end classes.

When developing applications for the Web, the hidden fields are not available by default for programming. To make these fields available for programming access on the Web, you need to enable the Generate HTML for all fields property of the form. If you do not enable this property, Domino will not publish the hidden fields while translating the content for the Web.

After the Generate HTML for all fields property is enabled, all the hidden fields will be published using the HTML tag as follows:

```
<input name="FieldName" type="hidden" value="FieldValue">
```

Here, `FieldName` is the name of the field and `FieldValue` is the value of the field at the time of publishing.

When the form that has Generate HTML for all fields property enabled is accessed through a browser, you can even view the HTML code of the hidden fields on the translated form by choosing View/Source in the browser. All the hidden fields are listed toward the end of the HTML code. Even though the hidden fields are not visible to users, you can access these fields and manipulate their values using JavaScript.

CAUTION

Be careful when you use the Generate HTML for all fields for hidden fields that contain sensitive information and require security consideration. If users view the source of the published HTML in the browser, they will be able to see the values of the hidden fields.

Use Applet in Browser

Certain design elements, including views, actions, rich text fields, and outlines can be published using HTML or Java applets. When published using Java applets, these elements provide better user interfaces and functionality. Another advantage of using Java applets is their flexibility for better programmability. You can use JavaScript to access the properties and methods of these applets. For more information, refer to the section "Connecting Persistently to Domino Objects from a Browser" at the end of this chapter.

However, using applets has one disadvantage. When you use applets, the application performance decreases because applets need to be loaded in the browser. You need to be careful while enabling this property, especially if the users are going to access your application over slow dial-up connections.

Content Type

This property controls how the contents are translated when published for the Web access. You can chose from the options Notes, HTML, or Others. If you choose Others, you will have to specify the content type.

Every HTML page usually has a content tag, such as `Content-Type:text/html`, which defines the format for the content. If you choose the content type as HTML or Other, Domino passes the content to the browser as it is. For example, if you choose HTML or Other as the content type, the form is passed to the browser as it is and you will not be able to open the form in edit mode in the browser.

On the other hand, if you choose Notes as the content type, Domino adds the necessary HTML tags to the form or page header for the proper formation of an HTML page or form. Also, the Notes form will be translated to a proper Web form.

Domino Elements to HTML Translation

Domino provides a dynamic Web environment. In this environment, the Domino Web engine translates the Domino design elements and documents on the fly when an application is accessed through a browser. It is important to understand the HTML equivalent of Notes elements when they are translated to the Web elements.

Table 22.2 lists the Web equivalent of some of the important Notes elements when translated by the Domino Web engine.

Table 22.2 Domino Elements to HTML Translation

Domino Element	Translated HTML Equivalent
Text	`<INPUT TYPE="text" NAME=... ...>`
DateTime	`<INPUT TYPE="text" NAME=... ...>`
Number	`<INPUT TYPE="text" NAME=... ...>`
Rich Text	`<TEXTAREA NAME=... ...>` or `<APPLET NAME=... ...>`
Authors	`<INPUT TYPE="text" NAME=... ...>`
Readers	`<INPUT TYPE="text" NAME=... ...>`
Names	`<INPUT TYPE="text" NAME=... ...>`
Password	`<INPUT TYPE="password" NAME=... ...>`
Hidden Fields	`<INPUT TYPE="hidden" NAME=... ...>`
Formula	`<INPUT TYPE="text" NAME=... ...>`
Dialog List	`<SELECT><OPTION ...> ... </SELECT>`
Listbox	`<SELECT><OPTION ...> ... </SELECT>`
Combobox	`<SELECT><OPTION ...> ... </SELECT>`
Checkbox	`<INPUT TYPE="checkbox" NAME=... ...>`
Radiobutton	`<INPUT TYPE="radio" NAME=... ...>`

Domino Element	Translated HTML Equivalent
Action	`<A NAME=... onClick=... ...>`
Computed Text	`<SPAN ID=...> ... </SPAN>`
Link Hotspot	`<A HREF=... NAME=...>`
Text Pop-up Hotspot	inline text
Button Hotspot	`<INPUT TYPE="button" NAME=... ...>`
Formula Pop-up Hotspot	inline text
Action Hotspot	`<A HREF=... NAME=... onClick=...>`
Picture	`<IMG NAME=... ...>`
Image Resource	`<IMG NAME=... ...>`
Picture, Image Resource Hotspot	`<AREA NAME=... ...>`
Java Applet	`<APPLET NAME=... ...>`

If the content type for a form is selected as Notes, the HTML equivalent of the Notes form will be as follows:

```
<HTML>
<HEAD>
...
</HEAD>
<BODY onLoad=... onUnload=...>
<FORM NAME=... ... onSubmit=... onReset=...>
...
</FORM>
</BODY>
</HTML>
```

All the other elements that are contained in the form are enclosed within the starting and ending HTML tags.

Special Forms Used

Domino uses a set of special forms to achieve better formatting control for various Notes design elements when accessed through a Web browser. The names of these special forms start with $$ to distinguish them from the normal forms.

These forms contain certain special fields, which control how the elements are presented in a browser.

Some of these important forms and their purposes are as follows:

- **$$ViewTemplate.** This form is used to control the formatting features for views. You can associate a particular view template form with a specific view. To associate any view template to a Notes view, append the suffix `for viewname` to $$ViewTemplate, where `viewname` is the name of the view. For example, if the name of the view is `myview`, the view template form will have the name `$$ViewTemplate for myview`.
- **$$ViewTemplateDefault.** This is the default view template for all the views in a database. If there is no view template defined for a view, the view will be associated with this view template form. On the other hand, if a view template is defined for a view, it will override this default template.
- **$$NavigatorTemplate.** This form is used to control the formatting features of navigators. Similar to views, create these forms with the name `$$NavigatorTemplate for mynavigator` to associate a navigator named `mynavigator` with the template form.
- **$$NavigatorTemplateDefault.** This is the default navigator template form associated with all the navigators for which a template is not available.
- **$$SearchTemplate.** This form is used to customize the search results for a view search. To associate the template to the view named `myview`, create a form with the name `$$SearchTemplate for myview`.
- **$$SearchTemplateDefault.** This is the default search template form used to associate all the views for which a search template is not specified.
- **$$Search.** This form is used to customize the search inputs when a search URL is used.
- **$$SearchDomainTemplate.** This is the default search template for search domain URL used to customize the search results. This template is used if there are no template forms specified or the template specified in the search domain URL cannot be located.

In addition to the preceding template forms, Domino provides special forms to customize the default error messages:

- **$$ReturnDocumentDeleted.** This form is used to customize the message when a document gets deleted.
- **$$ReturnAuthenticationFailure.** This form is used to customize the authentication verification error returned by Domino. The authentication error can occur if the users enter a wrong username or password when challenged by Domino.
- **$$ReturnAuthorizationFailure.** This form is used to customize the access privilege error. This error occurs if the user does not have enough rights to the database to carry out the requested operation.
- **$$ReturnGeneralError.** This form is used to customize any other general error message that will be generated by Domino.

Domino URLs

To access Domino objects from a browser, HTTP or HTTPS protocol is used. This requires the use of URLs. A URL is the fundamental mechanism used to request for resources from any Web server. Domino has its own set of URL extensions to allow requests of various objects in the Domino database from a browser. A Domino URL has the following syntax:

```
http://Host/DominoObject?Action&Arguments
```

In this syntax,

- `Host` is the DNS name alias or IP address of the Domino server.
- `DominoObject` is a Domino extension construct for accessing Domino objects, such as database, view, document, form, navigator, agent, page, and frameset.
- `Action` is the operation required to be performed on the specified `DominoObject`, such as `?OpenDatabase`, `?OpenView`, `?OpenDocument`, `?OpenForm`, `?OpenPage`, and `?OpenNavigator`.
- `Argument` is the qualifier for the action requested to perform on the `DominoObject`.

Domino URLs can contain special identifiers, which include `$defaultView`, `$defaultForm`, `$searchForm`, `$file`, `$icon`, `$help`, `$about`, and `$first`.

For example, if you want to open the ByDate view in the sales.nsf database hosted on the salesserver and restrict the number of rows returned to 10, use the following Domino URL:

```
http://salesserver/sales.nsf/Bydate?OpenView&Count=10
```

Table 22.3 lists some of the important Domino URLs. For a complete reference of the Domino URLs, see Appendix D, "Domino URL Reference."

Table 22.3 Important Domino URLs

Domino Object	URL Action	Object Identifier
Database	?OpenDatabase	filename, __ReplicaID.nsf
View in HTML/Java Applet	?OpenView, or?OpenView	ViewName, ViewUniversalID, $defaultview
View in XML	?ReadViewEntries	ViewName, ViewUniversalID, $defaultview
About Document	/$about?OpenAbout	None
Help Document	/$help?OpenHelp	None
Icon	/$icon?OpenIcon	None
FrameSet	?OpenFrameset	FramesetName, FramesetUNID, FramesetNoteID
Agent	?OpenAgent	AgentName
Form in edit Mode	?OpenForm	FormNam, FormUniversalI, FormNoteID, $defaultform
Form in read mode	?ReadForm	FormNam, FormUniversalI, FormNoteID, $defaultform
Navigator	?OpenNavigator	NavigatorName, NavigatorUniversalID, NavigatorNoteID, $defaultNav
Create Document	?CreateDocument	Form, FormName
Delete Document	?DeleteDocument	View/Documentkey, view/DocumentUniversalID, View/DocumentNoteID, $first
Edit Document	?EditDocument	View/Documentkey, view/DocumentUniversalID, View/DocumentNoteID, $first

Domino Object	URL Action	Object Identifier
Open Document	?OpenDocument	View/Documentkey, view/DocumentUniversalID, View/DocumentNoteID, $first
Save Document	?SaveDocument	View/Documentkey, view/DocumentUniversalID, View/DocumentNoteID, $first
File Attachments	?OpenElement	Document/$File/FileName
Page	?OpenPage	PageName, PageUNID,PageNoteID
Domain Searching	templateform/?SearchDomain	
Site Search	?SearchSite	[$searchForm]
Search View	?SearchView	[$searchForm]
Authentication	&login	?OpenServer, ?OpenDatabase

NOTE

Notice that some of the objects can be accessed by using more than one object identifier. For some objects, such as documents and file attachments, object identifiers listed in square brackets are optional. You can use optional arguments with some of the URLs.

Programming in the Domino Web Environment

Notes client supports a rich set of events for event-oriented programming. You can use LotusScript, formula language, or JavaScript to write programs for these events and control the UI as well as the processing logic for your application. You use the front-end and back-end classes to access and manipulate Notes objects programmatically.

On the other hand, Web browsers offer extremely limited functionality compared to the Notes client. Domino provides a rich set of functionality for the various design elements on the Web, to match as closely as possible to what you get while using Notes client. However, a lot of the implementations are done using Java applets. Compared to the simple HTML files, these applets are heavy and will have an adverse impact on the loading time for your application in browsers.

Domino Object Model and Translation Mechanism

The Notes client provides you with a rich collection of Notes UI objects. These objects have been covered in detail in Appendix A, "Domino LotusScript Classes." However, in the Web programming environment, there are no front-end objects or Notes UI objects available. The question that arises is how you control the front end in a Domino Web programming environment. When users request for an object from the Domino server, the Domino server translates the native objects to its browser-compatible equivalent, which most of the time is HTML. These converted objects are then sent to the browser using HTTP. After the objects are sent to the browser, Domino loses control of the objects; the complete control is with the browser. When the user sends back another request, Domino again analyses the requested content and then translates it back to its native format to store inside the database.

It is interesting how Domino manages the translation of the Domino native objects to their browser equivalent and back. One of the Domino objects that undergoes the most complicated process is the Notes form. However, each of the other Domino objects, whether it is a document, view, or page, go through a similar process when translated back and forth. In addition, the caching mechanism is kept out of this discussion to make it simple for your understanding.

When the browser sends a request to the server using a Domino URL, Domino first checks for the security privileges for the user to access the requested object. If the user has the rights, Domino loads the form in the server memory from the database on the disk. On loading, the Web Query `Open` event is triggered and the associated agent is executed. Next, the form object undergoes different phases of parsing. Domino starts with the calculation of the default values for all the Editable and Computed when Composed fields on the form. If any formulas are used, they are computed. Then the values for the computed fields are generated. In the next step, it computes all the Hide When formulas. After all the calculations are over, the form is then translated to its HTML format and sent to the browser.

Domino server keeps the copy of the form in its memory. The duration for which the form is available in memory depends on the resources available, load factors, and certain other settings for the server. When the user submits the form using an HTTP POST operation, Domino first compares the posted content with the one available in the memory. If any discrepancies are found, Domino rejects the POST request. Only if the form matches the one that was served to the browser, except for the field value changes, does Domino accept the POST request. As the first step, Domino computes all the field translations followed by field validation formulas. If validation fails, an error is returned to the browser. Otherwise, Domino saves the document. The objects are then translated back to the Domino native format. Before the document is saved, the `WebQuerySave` event is triggered and the agent specified is executed. Finally, the document is saved in the database.

Web Programmable Events

As discussed in the preceding section, there are only two form events, `WebQueryOpen` and `WebQuerySave`, available for the server side programming on the Web. The following sections explain these two events. You may use the various JavaScript events for client side programming.

The WebQueryOpen Event

The `WebQueryOpen` event is triggered before Domino translates the Domino objects to their HTML equivalents and sends them back to the browser. You can use this event to invoke an agent to achieve complex processing. This event is equivalent to the `QueryOpen` event in the Notes client.

In Notes client, you had the freedom to use various UI features, such as dialog boxes, to capture data from the users and manipulate the document. However, on the Web, the limited functionality of HTML puts certain constraints on showing the information to the users. The only way to add some interactivity at the client side, which is the browser, is by using JavaScript. The creation of the HTML page can only be controlled when a document or form is loaded and using the `WebQueryOpen` event.

You can use LotusScript or Java for creating agents associated with the `WebQueryOpen` event. Simple actions are not available for this purpose. Using an @Function of formula language will restrict you from returning any information back to the browser. It is important to note that agents cannot be run in the browser as they are run in Notes client. However, they can be activated from the browser using the Domino URL, and when activated, they run on the Domino server that hosts the database that contains the agent.

The WebQuerySave Event

The `WebQuerySave` event is triggered before the document is actually saved to disk or mailed. The trigger occurs after all the field input validation formulas are executed. Like the `WebQueryOpen` event, you can associate an agent with this event to perform an operation on the document that is being saved or on any other documents. This event is equivalent to the `QuerySave` event in the Notes client.

When using LotusScript or Java, any agent outputs generated using the print statements are returned to the browser. You can even generate a complete HTML document by gathering data and content from other documents and sending it back to the browser. By setting the special field SaveOptions in the current document processed by the agent, you can restrict the document from being saved in the Domino database.

Sometimes the agent associated with the `WebQuerySave` event is used to redirect the URL in two ways, *explicit redirection* (also known as browser redirection) and *internal redirection.*

For explicit redirection, form a valid URL string to which you want to redirect the user. Then enclose the string in square brackets and print the string using a print statement. For example, if you want to redirect the user to `http://www.somhost.com/Mypage.html`, use the following statement in your agent:

```
redirectedurl$ = http://www.somhost.com/Mypage.html
'now print this In brackets
Print "["+ redirectedurl$ +"]"
'or to use directly
Print "[http://www.somhost.com/Mypage.html]"
```

The above program statements send the new URL to the browser, which will replace the existing URL.

If you want to send back some content that exists on the same Domino server, you can use internal redirection. For internal redirection, use double square brackets to enclose the URL, as shown below:

```
Internalurl$ = http://www.thisserver.com/Mypage.html
'now print this In double brackets
Print "[["+ redirectedurl$ +"]]"
'or to use directly
Print "[[http://www.somhost.com/Mypage.html]]"
```

The internal redirection saves the round trip and has better performance.

There is also a special field `$$Return`, which you can use in forms to send output to browser. You can use this field as a computed text field on the form and use HTML as the computed value for this field. Whenever the form is submitted, the value of this field is sent to the browser.

> **TIP**
>
> Avoid using explicit save of the document in the agent associated with the WebQuerySave event because this may result in incorrect results. Also, if the agent returns output to the browser, the $$Return field is ignored.

Using Agents with WebQueryOpen and WebQuerySave Events

When an agent associated with the `WebQueryOpen` or `WebQuerySave` events is invoked, the handle to the current document being processed is obtained through the `DocumentContext` property of the `NotesSession` object created in the agent. This property returns the `NotesDocument` object, which is involved in the current browser session. This object contains information about the Web session and enables you to access all the items in the document. This object also contains the values of all CGI (*Common Gateway Interface*) variables associated with the browser session and with the agent call. The CGI variables, even though added automatically by the Domino server, do not appear to the user if your form does not expose them explicitly. When the agent is invoked using the Domino URL, the Domino Web server uses the CGI variables to collect certain information about the user, such as username, browser type and version, and IP (*Internet Protocol*) address. After the document object handle is obtained, you can do whatever you want with the document.

You can use agents to control what is served to the browser by the Domino server.

Consider an example where a document contains two fields, FirstName and LastName, which store the name of an employee. However, you want to combine these two fields in a single field named FullName before the document is served to the browser. The form Employee is used to display the document. Perform the following steps:

1. Create an agent named EmpWebQryOpen with the following code:

```
Sub Initialize
Dim ns as New NotesSession
Dim contextdoc As NotesDocument

'obtain the context document
Set contextdoc = ns.DocumentContext

'next, use the contextdoc to do any processing on the document
 contextdoc.FullName = contextdoc.FirstName(0) +
                    " " +contextdoc.LastName
'you can do any complex processing here
'the output of following line is discarded
Print "This is my first web agent"
End Sub
```

2. Associate the agent with the `WebQueryOpen` event of the form, which is used to display the document. To do this, open the Employee form and in the `WebQueryOpen` event, enter the following formula:

```
@Command([ToolsRunMacro]; "EmpWebQryOpen")
```

3. Save the form.

Any output generated by an agent associated with the `WebQueryOpen` event, such as by using print statements, is discarded. This means that you cannot achieve URL redirection using the `WebQueryOpen` agent.

TIP

In a `WebQueryOpen` agent, you can customize the content, which will be served by Domino to match the display capabilities or functionality offered by the various browsers. To do so, you need to inspect the HTTP_USER_AGENT CGI variable for the browser.

Capturing CGI Variables

Domino supports most of the standard CGI variables. Table 22.4 lists some of the useful CGI variables available in Domino that you can use for programming.

Table 22.4 CGI Variables

CGI Variable	Description
Content_Type	Stores the content type of the data for HTTP POST and PUT
Content_Length	Stores the length of the content as provided by the browser
HTTP_Accept	Stores the MIME types specified by the HTTP headers, which the browser accepts
HTTP_Accept_language	Stores the languages as specified by HTTP headers, which the browser accepts
HTTP_Referer	Stores the referring URL from which the user accessed this URL
HTTP_User_Agent	Stores the type of the browser used by the user to send the request
Path_Info	Stores the extra path information from the server's root HMTL directory as provided by the user
Path_Info_Decoded	Stores the decoded Path_info, used to decode URLs containing space
Path_Translated	Stores the translated Path_info, which represents the actual path, not the virtual path
Query_String	Stores the query string parameter specified after the question mark (?) in the URL
Query_String_Decoded	Stores the decoded Query_String, which decodes the URL and query string which contain spaces
Remote_Addr	Stores the remote host's IP address
Remote_Host	Stores the remote host's name, which made the request
Remote_Ident	Stores the remote username retrieved from the server
Script_Name	Stores the virtual path to the script being executed; this can be used for self-referencing URLs
Server_Name	Stores the hostname of the server or IP address
Server_Protocol	Stores the request protocol's name and revision
Server_Port	Stores the TCP/IP port number of the server on which the request was received, such as 80,8080
Server_Software	Stores the version and name of the server

There are two ways to capture the CGI variables:

- **Create a field with the same name as that of the CGI variable you want to capture.** If you are using any fields other than editable fields, such as computed for display, specify the name of the CGI variable as the value for the field.
- **Use agents.** In the agents, you can access CGI variables using LotusScript or Java. For example, the following script captures the information regarding the browser using CGI variable in an agent:

  ```
  Dim ns as New NotesSession
  Dim contextdoc As NotesDocument
  Browsertype$ = contextdoc.HTTP_User_Agent(0)
  ```

  `contextdoc` will be the current document if the agent is run from the browser using `@Command([ToolsRunMacro])`. If you associate the agent with WebQueryOpen or WebQuerySave event, `contextdoc` will be the document, which is being currently processed.

Using HTML and JavaScript for Client-Side Programming

As already mentioned, Domino loses the control of the objects after it serves the content to the browser. You can control the UI or add features that make the application more interactive by using combination of HTML, DHTML, CSS, and JavaScript. While HTML is used to improve the look and feel of the UI, JavaScript is used to perform client-side processing.

There are various ways you can make Domino applications more dynamic. For example, consider an online order processing system. A user enters the quantity required for a product and the rate for the product is already available in the browser as part of the product information. Next, you need to calculate and display the amount, which is calculated using the formula `Quantity x Rate`. There are two ways to achieve this in Domino.

You can have a button provided on the UI, which the user needs to click to see the result of the computation. If the amount is displayed in the field Amount, you use the formula language to calculate the value for this field. When the user clicks the button, you simply need to refresh the form using the @function formula. To do so, you need to submit the form back to the Domino server. The Domino server performs the computation and generates a new HTML page, which contains the value of the Amount field. This new page is then sent back to the browser. In this method, a round trip to the server is required for even simple computations. This, in turn, impacts the performance of your application.

The second way of implementing the same logic is by using JavaScript. A simple JavaScript code can compute the amount using the values available in the Rate and Quantity fields and replace the value of the Amount field with the result of the computation. You may refer to Chapter 6, "Working with HTML and JavaScript" for the details on how to implement this functionality. Therefore, the complete computation happens in the browser without making a round trip to the server. In this way, the user can see the result immediately. In addition, you are making use of the computing power of the client computer rather than the Domino server. This, in turn, reduces the load on the server when thousands of users access your application.

Using JavaScript for Different Browsers

In the Notes client, JavaScript uses the Domino client DOM. However, when JavaScript runs in the browser, it uses the object model implemented by the browser. Therefore, you need to know the browser in which your JavaScript code will run and modify the program accordingly, but you cannot identify the browser unless you receive a request from the user. An alternate approach is to explicitly specify the browser compatibility for your application and limit accessibility to only those users who use the specified browser. In this case, you use the CGI variable HTTP_USER_AGENT. When you receive a request from the browser, you can check the browser type and accordingly serve the right set of JavaScript code to the browser. The leftmost 11 characters of this CGI variable specify which browser the user is using. You can use a simple @Functions to find this information, as shown below:

```
BrowserType := @Left(HTTP_USER_AGENT;11);
@If (BrowserType = "Mozilla 3.0";
    @Do(--this is a Netscape Navigator ----
        do what ever related to Netscape Navigator here ---);
    BrowserType = "MSIE 2.0" ;
    @Do(--this is a MS Internet Explorer -
        do what ever related to MSIE here-- );
    @Do(----the apps doesn't support ---do some thing here---))
```

Although the preceding code looks simple, it is a very powerful. In this way, you can dynamically assemble various JavaScript modules depending on the browser type. You can get an equivalent implementation of this in the `WebQueryOpen` agent that performs more complex tasks and generate the required JavaScript based on many CGI variables and Domino objects. This dynamic capability makes the Domino Web programming environment very powerful.

NOTE

What you can achieve using the JavaScript in the Web browser is limited to the amount of flexibility the browser provides. To complicate the matter further, various browsers behave in different ways even in basic implementations, such as how arrays are handled.

Connecting Persistently to Domino Objects from a Browser

In the Notes clients, it is possible for you to validate what the user entered by checking the entered value against the value of a field in a document in another database and inform the user about it right away. Domino provides you with a framework to achieve the same in a Web browser. You can do this by using JavaScript LiveConnect technology from Netscape in conjunction with Domino Java/CORBA framework.

The LiveConnect technology allows JavaScript in your Web page to communicate with Java applets within the browser. The Java applet can then initiate a communication channel with the Domino objects using CORBA over IIOP (*Inter-ORB-Protocol*). A CORBA-enabled Java applet in the browser can make CORBA-based remote (IIOP) calls to access run-time code from a remote Domino server. This allows the applet to access a remote Domino Session object, which is at the highest level in the DOM hierarchy. After you get access to a Domino Session, you can use it to access other objects in DOM and their properties and methods. Figure 22.2 depicts how DOM can be accessed using JavaScript LiveConnect.

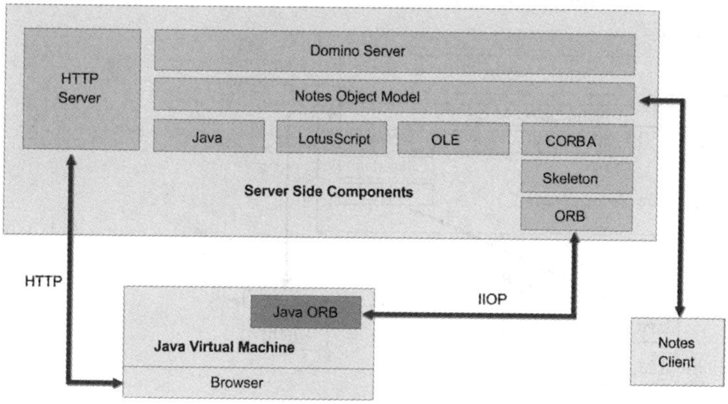

FIGURE 22.2 *Accessing DOM using JavaScript LiveConnect*

This framework allows an HTML page to have a persistent session with a Domino server. It also allows the use of the DOM through JavaScript using Live-Connect, which enables you to perform transactions without submitting the page every time to the server.

CORBA is the infrastructure specification for developing distributed, object-oriented applications. CORBA is based on the OMA (*Object Management Architecture*), which consists of five main components, ORB (*Object Request Broker*), Application Interfaces, Object Services, Common Facilities, and Domain Interfaces. Using CORBA, remote clients can invoke remote API residing on other computers. CORBA uses IIOP for communication over TCP/IP. Figure 22.3 depicts the CORBA implementation framework in Domino.

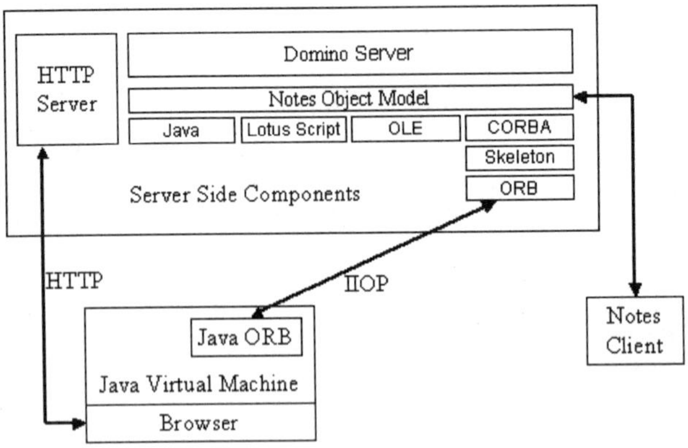

FIGURE 22.3 *Domino CORBA framework*

> **NOTE**
>
> To use CORBA, the DIIOP server task should be running on the server. In addition, you should enable the property Applet uses Notes CORBA classes for the applet.

Servlet Programming

Servlets are special Java programs that load and run when a request is made from the browser. You can also specify to load servlets at server startups. Unlike Domino agents, servlets remain in the server memory after they are loaded.

Domino ships with a built-in servlet manager, which loads and run the servlets. You can use the servlets to access Domino objects or other resources and create dynamic Web pages. Servlets are not limited to serve just HTTP requests but can provide services to any client. To use servlets in Domino, you should enable the Domino server for servlet support and specify any servlet properties in the server document stored in the Domino Directory. Once deployed, you can invoke the servlet from the browser using a URL. Refer to Chapter 7, "Working with Java" for more details.

Domino Designer does not provide any native support for creating servlets. You need to use third-party tools for the creation of servlets. One of the easily available tools is JSDK (*Java Servlet Development Kit*) from Sun Microsystems. Once compiled successfully, you can deploy the servlet on the Domino server. You can access the DOM in your servlet by importing the `lotus.domino.*` package.

Using XML in Domino Applications

Domino provides native API for working with XML in your Web applications. XML has become the de facto standard for data interchange between applications. Unlike HTML, which defines presentation standards for the content, XML is used for describing the structure for data elements. Describing the structure of the data makes documents more meaningful, especially if the documents need to be accessed using computer programs.

XML support is implemented in Domino using DXL (*Domino XML Language*). DXL contains the necessary tags and attributes for describing Notes documents, views, rich text, and other elements in the Domino database. In Domino, DXL is used to describe both the design and data elements in a database.

Domino Designer provides the following tools for handling XML:

- **Exporter.** To convert Domino design elements to XML format
- **Viewer.** To display XML document and elements
- **Transformer.** To transform XML into HTML using style sheets

In addition, Domino provides a list of APIs for programmatically processing DXL. These classes provide methods and properties for exporting, transforming, and processing DXL. Some of the main classes are:

- `NotesDXLExporter` for generating DXL
- `NotesDXLImporter` for processing DXL data
- `NotesXSLTransformer` for transforming DXL using XSLT classes
- `NotesDOMParser` for parsing the XML data into DOM tree structure

You can use XML tags in forms, views, and pages for presenting the content in XML format. You can also use agents, which are written using LotusScript or Java for generating and processing XML using the standard classes provided by Domino.

NOTE

To learn more about XML and how to work with XML in Domino, refer to Chapter 26, "XML in Domino."

Making Domino Applications Available for Web Services

Web Services provide the ability to make your application participate in process-to-process interaction without using a UI. This requires that the applications that participate in Web Service should have very high degree of standardization and interoperability.

The technology framework, which defines the Web Services, includes the following components:

- **XML.** For data interchange between applications.
- **SOAP.** The transport protocol. This provides the RPC (*remote procedure call*) facility by transporting the methods using HTTP POST request.
- **WDSL (*Web Service Description Language*).** Used to describe services, functions, parameters, and return values.
- **UDDI (*Universal Description, Discovery, and Integration*).** Provides directory services for publishing and finding Web Services.

You can use the tool SOAPConnect for LotusScript, which contains various LotusScript classes for implementing Web Services in your application. You can also use other tools, such as MS SOAP toolkit and .NET from Microsoft.

Summary

In this chapter, you learned about the different technology frameworks provided by Domino for creating Web applications. You also learned in detail about the dynamic translation mechanism for converting Domino objects into HTML and vice versa. You updated your knowledge base on the tools available for extending Domino applications using technology, such as LiveConnect, CORBA, XML, and Web Services.

Chapter 23

Project Case Study: Designing the Online Order Processing System

In the previous projects, you developed applications that were accessed using the Notes client. Most of these projects involved creating a single database. In this chapter, you will learn how to design a Notes application, which will be accessed through Web browsers. Perhaps for the first time, you will also learn how to design a Notes application, which consists of multiple Notes databases.

Online Order Processing System for MotoWare, Inc.

MotoWare, Inc. is an automobile spare parts sales and manufacturing company based in New York. It has been manufacturing and selling automobile spare parts for several years. MotoWare, Inc. has recently signed a contract with Shindler Motors, a leading car manufacturer.

One of the challenges faced by MotoWare is how to manage its growth. With the increase in business, the company needs efficient ways to manage the increase in staff and the inventory of automobile spare parts. The company aims at becoming a single point seller for all kinds of automobile spare parts.

Since the management lacks experience in adapting IT to its advantage, it has decided to appoint a consultant who can understand the challenge and suggest a suitable solution.

The consultant studied the current business procedures of the company for a month. These problems were identified in the current order management processes:

- Clients need to call up every now and then to check the status of their order.
- It is very difficult for the clients to find the specifications of various spare parts.
- There is no consolidation of data and many of the documents generated are lost.
- There is no specific procedure to prioritize orders. As a result, urgent orders tend to get sidelined while unimportant ones get processed.
- Since the process is manual, the lead times in item delivery are quite long.

- It is difficult for the higher management to keep track of the operational activities on any given day.
- There is no controlled inventory management system. This needs to be addressed very urgently.

The consultant suggested implementing a Web-centric online order processing system, which would help the company transform its core business process and improve the bottom line. The consultant recommended that the Domino Designer R6 platform was best suited for the system.

Keeping in view the seriousness of the situation, the management needed a solution as soon as possible. It appointed a team consisting of a project manager and five developers to develop and deploy the solution.

Project Life Cycle

The development team began with a detailed requirements analysis to gather the information required. For a detailed coverage of a typical project life cycle, refer to Chapter 11, "Project Case Study: Creating a Reference Application."

Requirements Analysis

The team carried out an in-depth study of the various processes in the current manual order processing and fulfillment cycle. After analyzing the problems with it, the team short-listed these tasks for improvement:

- The company needs to ensure that the orders are processed in a more transparent manner.
- The updated product catalog should be made available to the customers as fast as possible.
- The inventory needs to be maintained at an optimum level.
- The overall process needs to be faster and more efficient.

To improve on the current system, the development team identified certain functional modules that an online order processing application should provide:

- Client Management
- Product Catalog
- Inventory Management

- Order Management
- Invoice Management

Each of these modules is described in the following sections.

Client Management

This module will maintain the information pertaining to all clients. The Client Management module will manage the details of one contact person per client. This database will also provide the facility to locate client details sorted on name of the client, country, state, and name of the contact person.

Product Catalog

This module will provide a categorized listing of all spare parts, a listing sorted on product name, and the facility to add new categories. There will be a maximum of two levels of categories for the products. The product document will contain the details of the auto spare parts, such as product code, product name, specification, and price. A facility that allows clients to post their reviews about products will be provided.

Inventory Management

The company has a number of warehouses around the country. This module will maintain the quantity in stock for various products at these warehouses. Each warehouse would have a person in charge. Only the person in charge will be allowed to update the inventory of the items.

Order Management

This module will act as a repository for all the orders placed by clients. It will handle order entry and acceptance. Order acceptance and processing department will send dispatch notices to the warehouses against an order. The items to be dispatched will be collected from the warehouses and sent to the Dispatch department. The Dispatch department will generate the invoice and send the items mentioned in the order for delivery to the client.

Invoice Management

The Dispatch department generates invoices based on orders. This module will retain all invoices generated for the delivery of items against an order for future reference.

High-Level Design: Application Modules

Before discussing the high-level design of the online order processing application, you need to understand certain issues related to application deployment on the Web.

One of the most important issues when deploying any application on the Web is security. In Notes, the security framework uses PKI (*Public Key Infrastructure*), while on the Web, basic Web authentication uses usernames and passwords.

Another important issue is how to distribute the functionality of the application. You can use either a single database or multiple ones to distribute application functionality. Although using a single database is the simplest, it creates confusion in the design and number of documents. Another drawback of using a single database for all the modules of the application is security. A single database has its limitations if different security levels are to be assigned to different modules. The number of design elements in a database is another point to be considered. One of the key elements of design is the view. Every view has an associated index that is updated by the view indexer process. Performance is affected with the increase in number of views. Every time the view is opened, its index has to be updated. Documents increase the bulk of the database. Every time a new document is added, it has to be reflected in all the views. In light of this, you should keep a minimum number of views in a database.

When you deploy an application, think about whether the application needs to be spread across more than one server. Finally, decide on the design of the application in a rational step-by-step manner, keeping all these issues in mind.

The development team identified five modules to meet the company's requirements. All these modules are independent and can be implemented as separate databases. Each application needs a separate level of security. As a result, the team uses separate databases for each module.

The following sections discuss the high-level design of each module, which will be implemented as a separate database.

Client Management Module

This module maintains the list of clients. To capture the client details, create a form known as Client Profile. The client details to be captured are

- Name
- Address
- Phone
- Fax
- E-mail
- Contact person

The security model of the system allows access only to the end users registered in the Domino Address Book. The Notes administrator creates an end user and chooses a default password. The Client Profile form has a facility that allows the end user to change this password. The newly entered password is synchronized with the Person document in the Address Book. The design of the Client Profile form is shown in Figure 23.1.

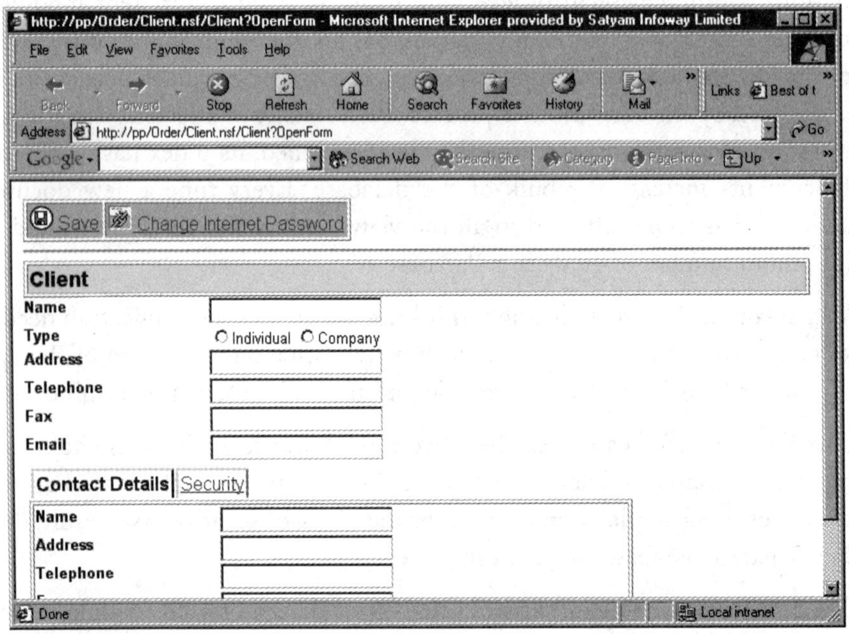

FIGURE 23.1 *The Client Profile form*

A single view known as Help Locate a Client Profile should be provided. This view should be sorted on client name, country, state, and the contact person. Since there will be only one document per client, there is no need for multiple views or categorization. The Client Management module interface is shown in Figure 23.2.

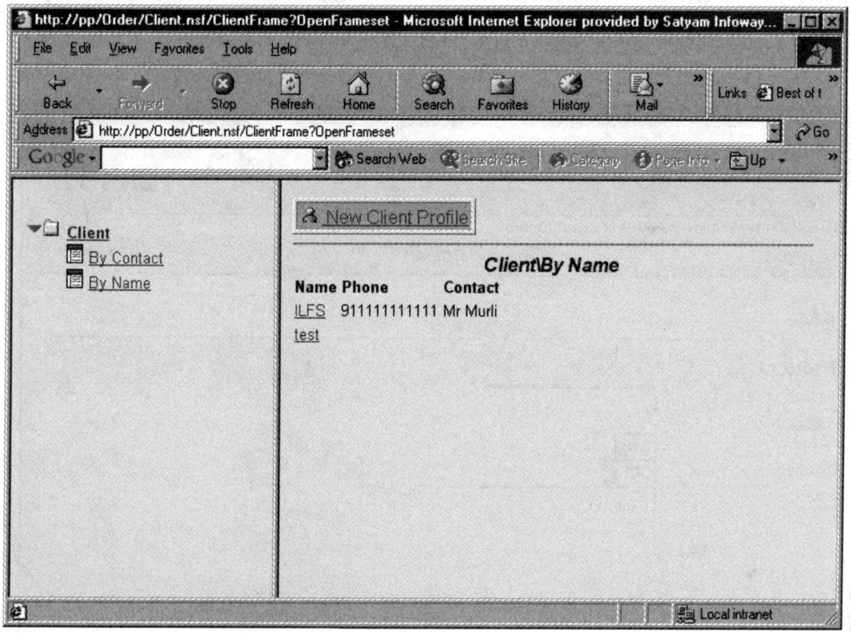

FIGURE 23.2 *The Client Management module*

Product Management Module

This module consists of two submodules:

- Product Catalog
- Inventory Management

Product Catalog

This module allows the end user to:

- Add a new product profile
- Edit an existing product profile

- Create a category and a subcategory of products
- Add the client's comments and reviews about a product

The Product Profile form captures product details such as name, price, and description. A file upload control should be provided to upload the specifications or images of the product. Each product is categorized using two levels, Category and Subcategory. The design of the Product Profile form is shown in Figure 23.3.

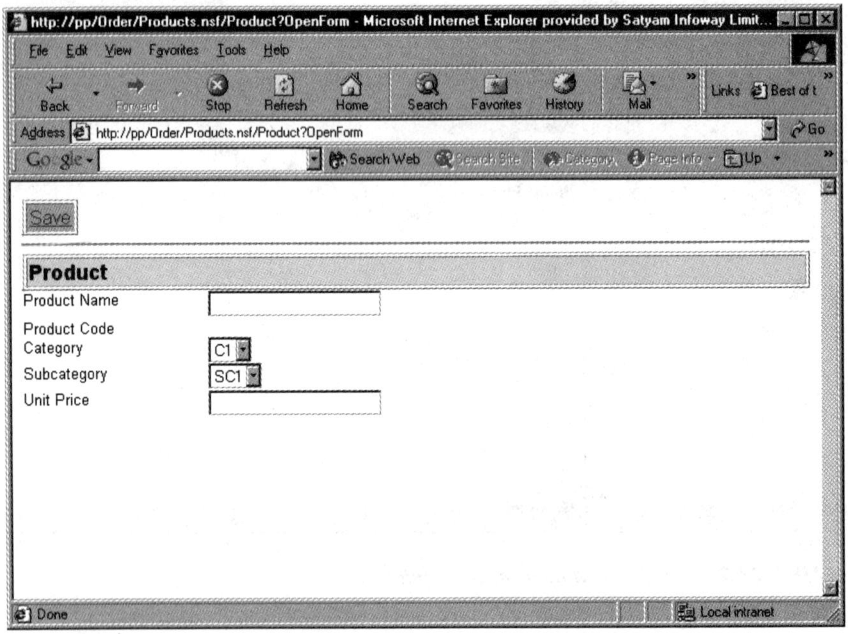

FIGURE 23.3 *The Product Profile form*

To categorize the products into two levels, define categories before using them. The two levels of categories are defined as two separate lists. To prevent the duplication of categories, before saving, check the corresponding view to see whether the name already exists. The subcategory and the category have not been linked and are used as two independent lists. The screen for entering the product category appears as shown in Figure 23.4.

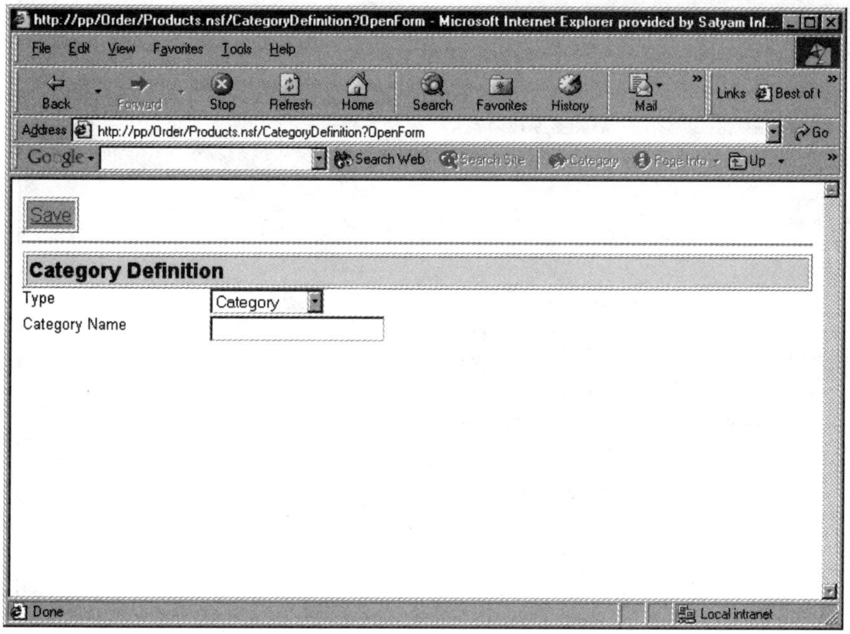

FIGURE 23.4 *Category definitions*

Clients should be allowed to provide their reviews and comments about the various products. Provide a Client Feedback form to capture client reviews and comments. This form should be response type. Clients use it to create Client Feedback documents in the form of responses to the Product Profile documents. The design of the Client Feedback form is shown in Figure 23.5.

Two views list the products categorized at the two levels, Category and Subcategory. A response type view is used to display the feedback from different clients. The interface of the Product Catalog module is shown in Figure 23.6.

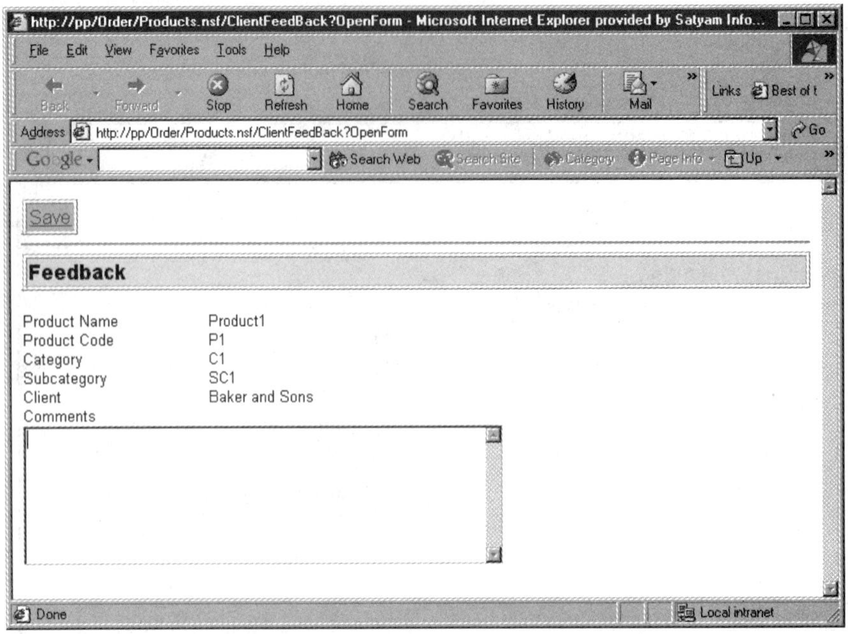

FIGURE 23.5 *The Client Feedback form*

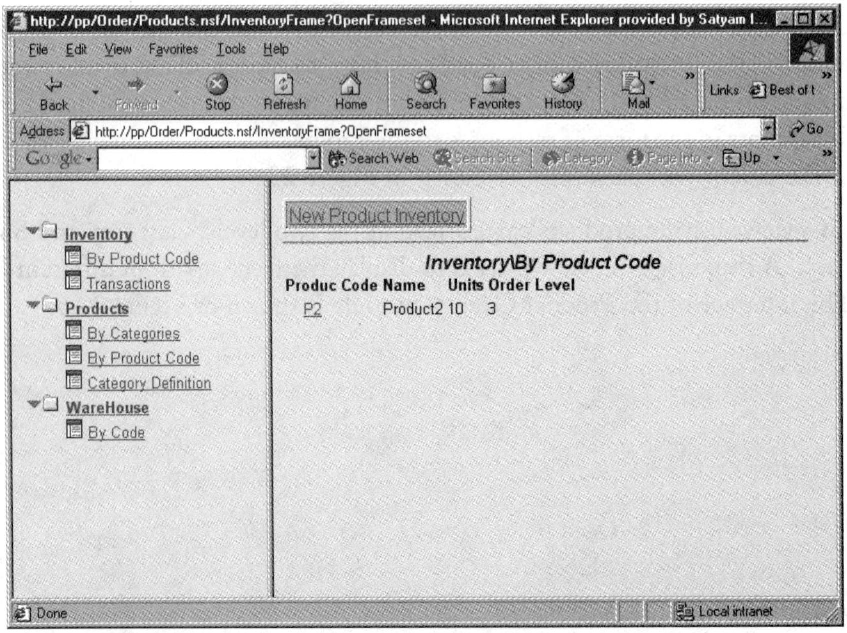

FIGURE 23.6 *The Product Catalog module*

Inventory Management

This module maintains the Warehouse and the Product Inventory masters. The Warehouse master defines the warehouses by stating the warehouse code, name, and the warehouse person in charge. The Warehouse master is shown in Figure 23.7.

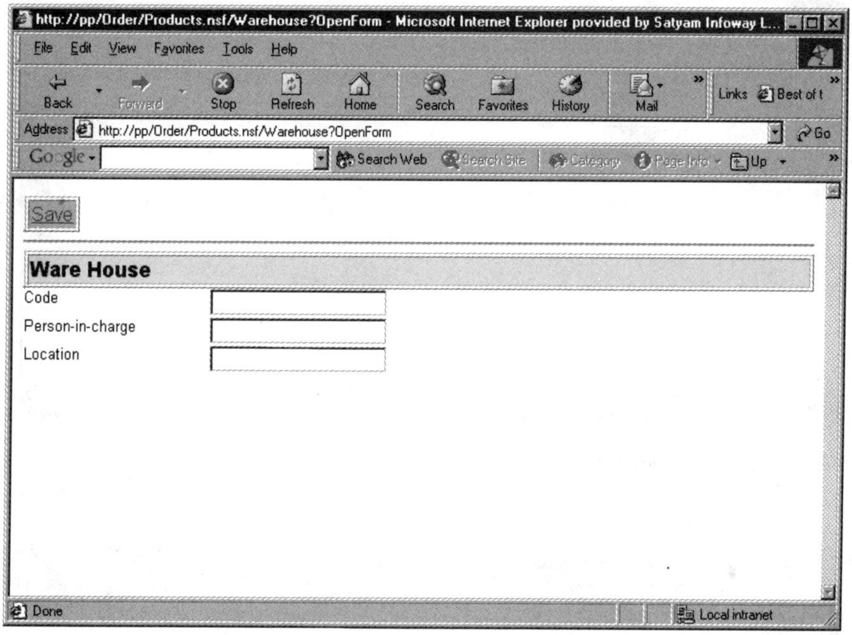

FIGURE 23.7 *Warehouse master*

The Product Stock master is the product master for a particular warehouse. It indicates the quantity of a product present in a warehouse. The warehouse person in charge is the only person authorized to update the Product Stock master, which is shown in Figure 23.8.

When an order is processed, an Inventory Transaction is generated. This transaction indicates the warehouses to which the product belongs and the quantity assigned to the order. Inventory Transactions act as dispatch requests for the warehouse. An Inventory Transaction is shown in Figure 23.9.

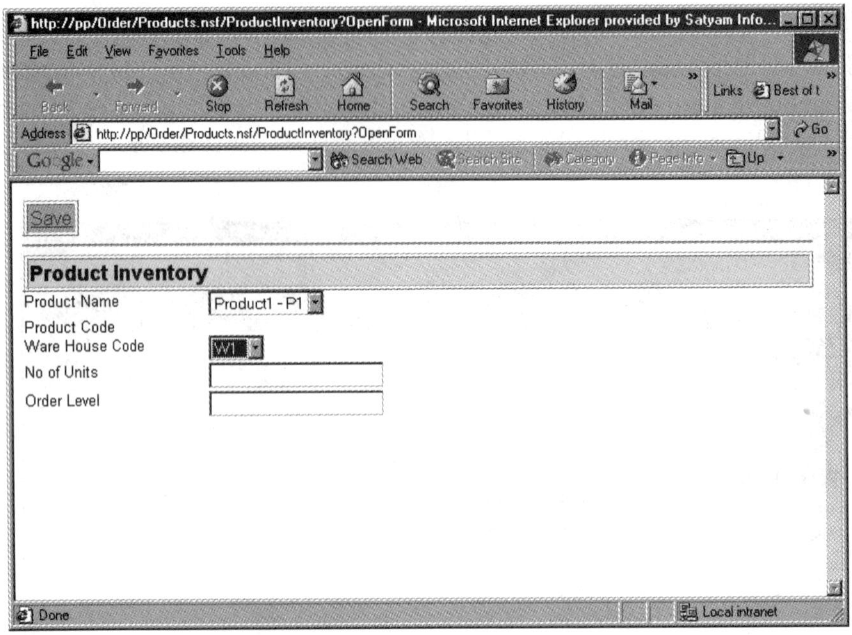

FIGURE 23.8 *Product Stock master*

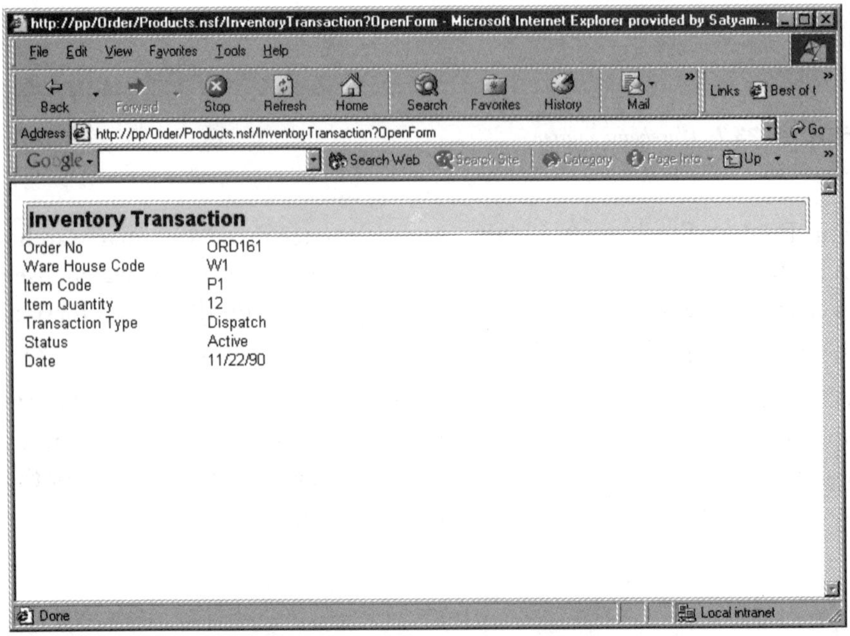

FIGURE 23.9 *Inventory Transaction*

The Inventory Management module provides these views:

- Warehouse listings of the products and their stock quantity. The products whose stock quantity is below the reorder level are indicated in red.
- The product listing across warehouses where the products are stored is also shown.
- A view lists all the products below their reorder levels.
- A listing of all the warehouses is provided.
- A separate listing of the warehouse transactions relevant to a particular warehouse is available to the warehouse person in charge.

The design of the Inventory Management module is shown in Figure 23.10.

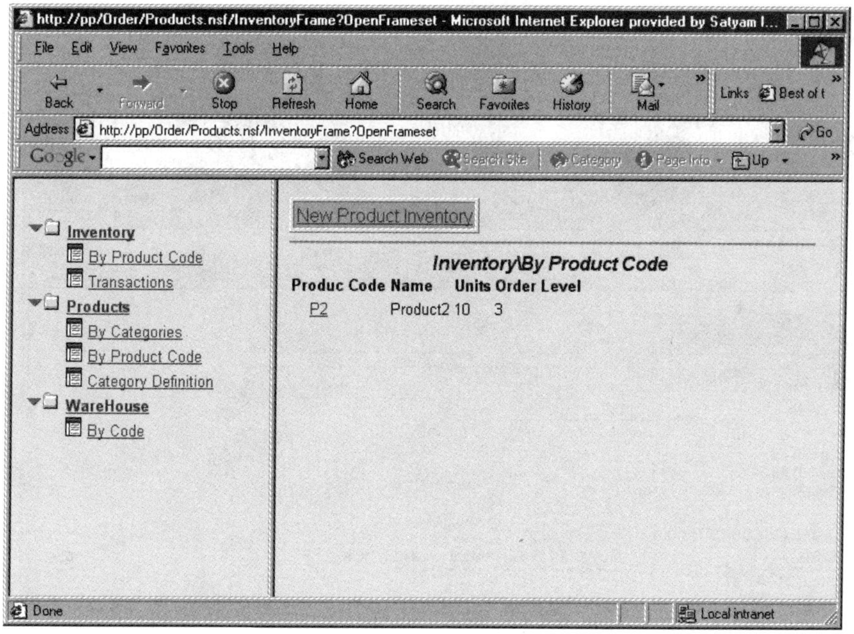

FIGURE 23.10 *The Inventory Management module*

Order Processing Module

This module consists of two submodules:

- Order Management
- Invoice Management

The main function of this module is to accept orders. It uses an Order form to accept an order from a client. After the client submits it, the order is placed for approval. The order processing authority fulfills the order by selecting the warehouses from which the order is to be fulfilled. An Inventory Transaction is created for each warehouse from which the product has been assigned.

An Order form automatically generates the order number, order status, client, and order type. The order number is a unique system-generated number. The order status changes from Open to Closed.

There are two sets of values for the products requested in an order. One contains the products that were requested, while the other lists the products that are actually provided. The list of products appears as a combobox. The second set of products is populated with values from the first set.

The design of the Order form appears as shown in Figure 23.11.

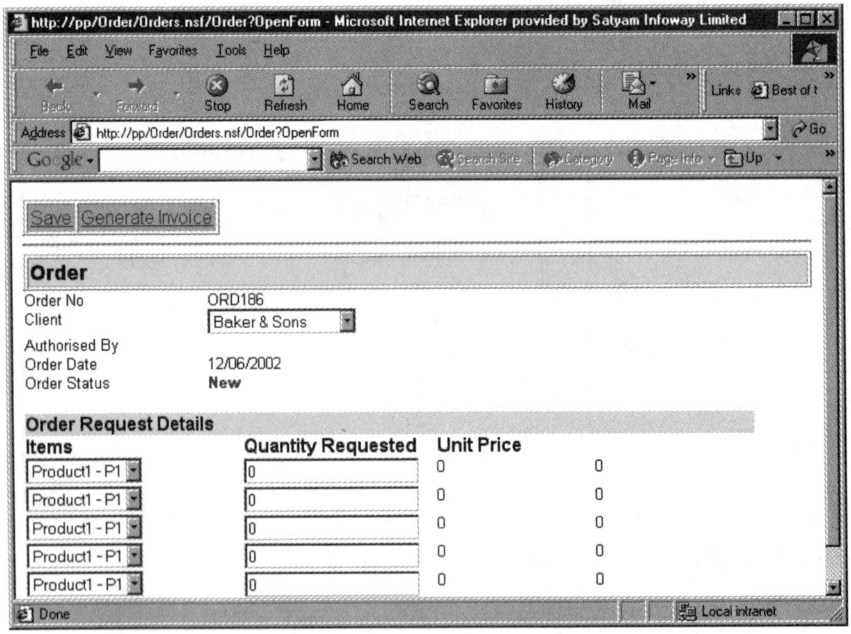

FIGURE 23.11 *The Order form*

When an order is dispatched, the invoice is sent along with it. The Invoice form generates invoices. This form provides details such as the date of invoice, name of the client, invoice number (auto-generated), order number, item pricing, and order total. Most of these details are captured from the corresponding Order document. The remaining fields, such as order total, need to be computed. The Invoice form appears as shown in Figure 23.12.

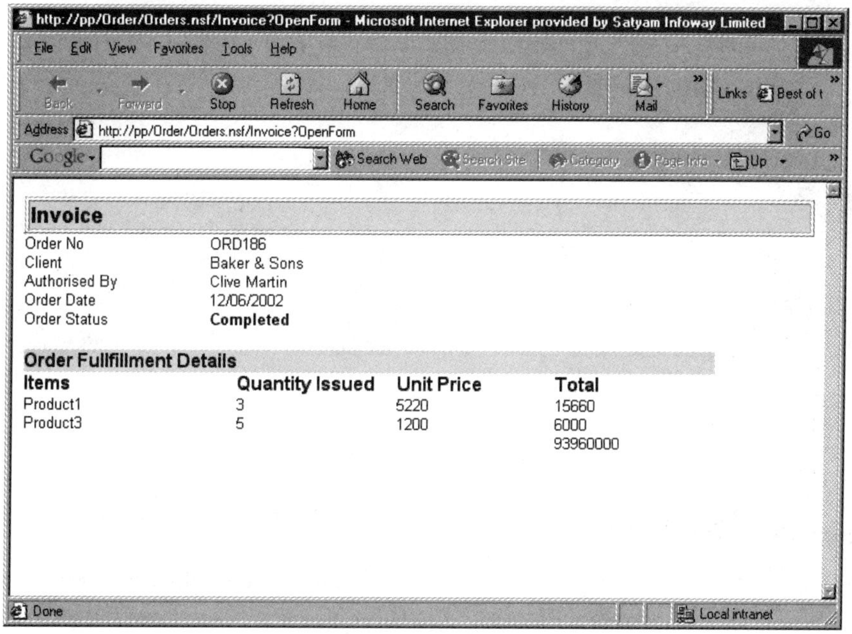

FIGURE 23.12 *The Invoice form*

The Invoice Management module provides two views, one for displaying invoices listed by the order number and the other for displaying invoices listed by the client code. The module also provides views for orders that are sorted by order date, order number, and client code. It also displays the status of the order as well as a list of pending orders. The Orders Processing module is shown in Figure 23.13.

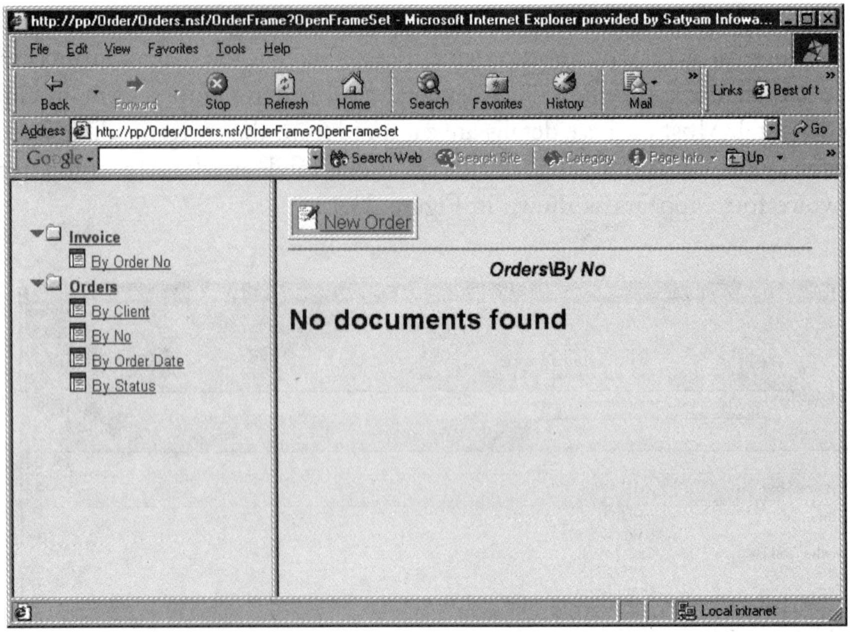

FIGURE 23.13 *The Order Processing module*

High-Level Design: Navigation

A two-frame layout helps you to navigate through the application. The left frame contains all the links and options for the end user. This layout uses framesets, pages, and outlines.

A frameset defines the two-frame layout. The navigator on the left frame is created using an outline embedded in a page. The outline offers you the flexibility of displaying options based on the end user. The end users recognized by the system are Client, Order Processing Agent, Warehouse In-Charge, and Finance. The screen that appears when end users access the application using a browser is shown in Figure 23.14.

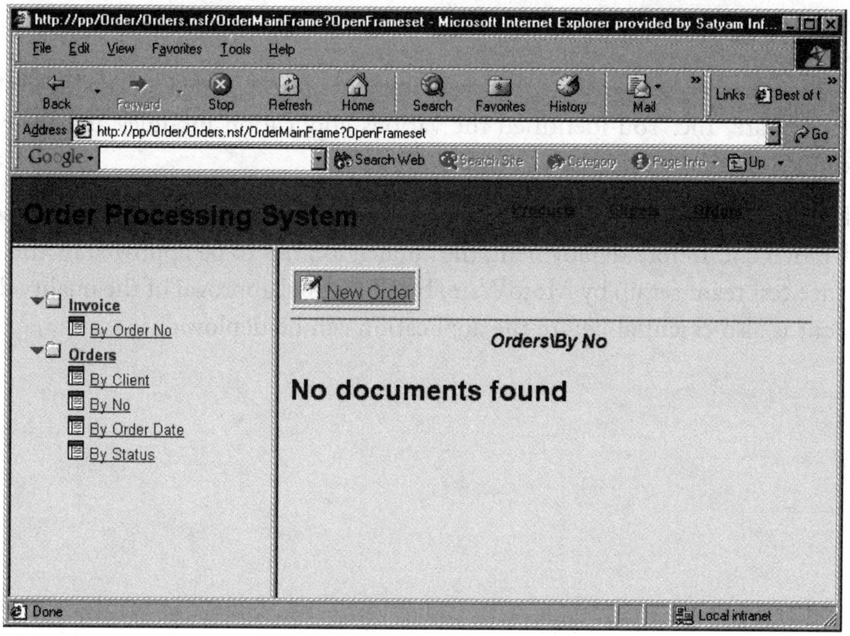

FIGURE 23.14 *The first user interface screen*

Figure 23.15 shows a flowchart that displays how various activities will be performed using the online order processing application.

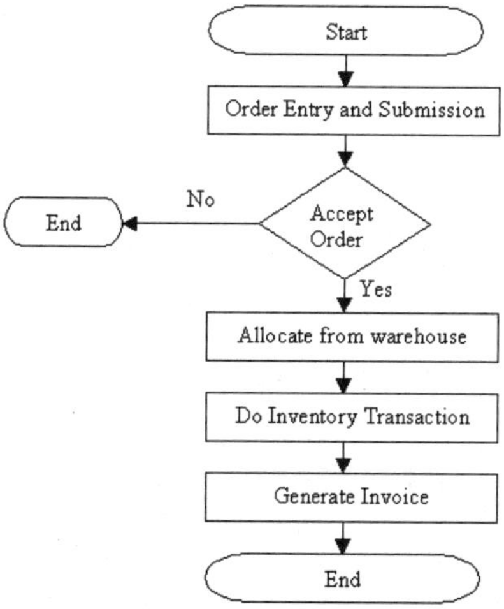

FIGURE 23.15 *Flowchart of the online order processing system*

Summary

In this chapter, you analyzed the requirements of the order processing system at MotoWare, Inc. You identified the various application modules and their high-level design.

The next chapter will cover the creation of the databases and also discuss their deployment. Before deployment, the application has to be approved by the acceptance test team set up by MotoWare, Inc. The final approval of the quality department is also essential before the application can be deployed.

Chapter 24

Developing an Order Processing System

You have seen the design outlined for the proposed order processing system in Chapter 23, "Project Case Study: Designing the Online Order Processing System," as part of the case study. In this chapter, you will create the application using a modular development approach. You will then integrate the different modules to provide the complete functionality of the application. You will learn how to create a multilevel navigational structure and how to program using the Web events in Domino applications.

The Order Processing System: An Overview

The online order processing system contains three modules or databases: Client, Products, and Orders. Let's quickly take a look at how this system works.

End users enter a URL to access this application in a browser. The first screen to appear is the Login screen, in which the end users enter their credentials. After the authentication, the home page of the application is displayed.

The home page has three sections: the top section is the banner, the left section is the module level navigation section, and the third section contains the content. The entire navigation for the application is achieved using Frameset. The banner section provides the top-level navigation for the order processing system. This allows users to switch between the three modules, namely Orders, Clients, and Products. The left section contains the navigational elements for the currently selected module. The content section displays the element corresponding to the selection made in the left section, which is the module level navigation.

To place an order, the user has to click on the New Order button. This button is available on one of the views, which will open in the content section of the Orders module. The user then has to select the items to be ordered and enter the quantity required. After the user submits the order, a new order with the status of "awaiting approval" is created.

To approve the order, the related personal has to select the warehouse in which the required item is available. When the order is approved, the quantity of the product is updated in the product master and an inventory transaction document is created in the Products module.

Now that you have reviewed the system functionality from its user perspective, you can start developing the system.

Creating the Order Processing System

The first step is to create the databases that will act as data repository for this application. As per the design of the application, you need to create three Notes databases, one for each of the three modules: Clients, Products, and Orders.

After creating the databases, you will create the design elements for each of the databases, including the shared actions, forms, views, outlines, pages, and navigational elements. Finally, you'll add the required functionality to the application through code.

Creating Databases

Open the Lotus Notes client and launch the workspace by clicking on the Workspace bookmark link available under the Databases bookmark folder. You may drag and drop the workspace bookmark to the Bookmark bar for accessing it later easily. To create a workspace page, right-click on it, and from the pop-up menu, select Create Workspace page.

NOTE

It is a good practice to keep database icons of a new application on a fresh workspace page. This will help you to organize all the databases involved in the application in a single place.

To launch the Workspace property box, as shown in Figure 24.1, right-click on the workspace page and select Workspace properties. Enter the page name as Order Processing.

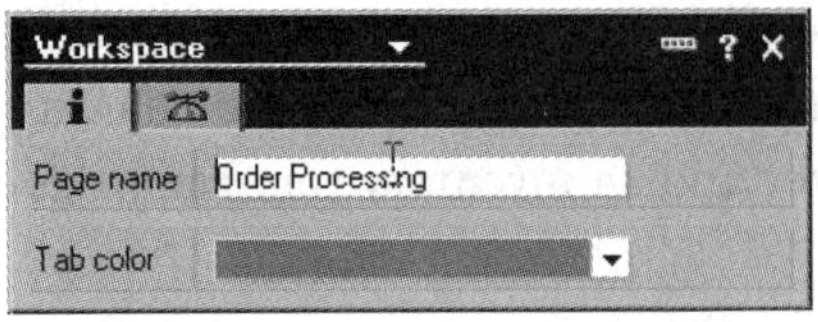

FIGURE 24.1 *The Workspace property box*

Creating the Orders Database

To create a new database, choose File/Database/New or press Ctrl+N. In the Create Database dialog box that appears, perform the following:

1. Select the server where you want to create the new database. In this application, the `PP/PRP` server has been selected. So far, you have been creating the entire application on your local workstation. While developing Web applications, you can preview design elements in browsers even if the databases are created locally. However, to effectively test the functionality as you progress with the development of a Web application, you should create the databases on a Domino server.
2. In the Title box, enter **Orders** to create the Orders database.
3. In the File name box, by default, the title you have specified followed with an .nsf extension appears. Note that this will create the file in the data directory, `root`, of the server. To create it within a subfolder named Order, change the file name to Order\Orders.nsf.

The database is being created from scratch; therefore, there is no need to specify the template. After performing the above-mentioned steps, the New Database dialog box should appear as shown in Figure 24.2.

4. Click OK to create the database.

The Orders database will be created under the Order folder in the Data directory of Domino. Notice that the database icon is added to your workspace.

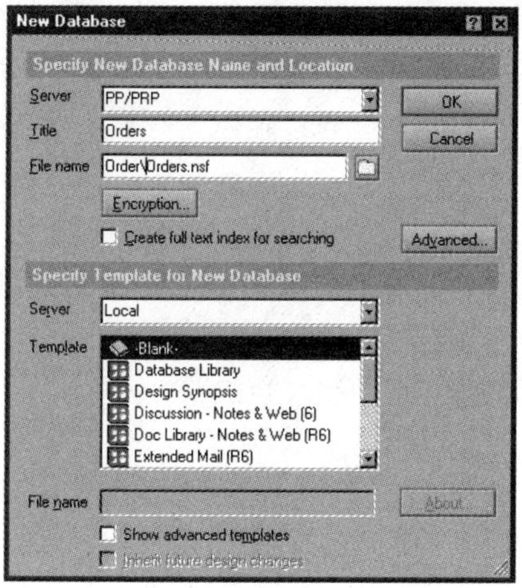

FIGURE 24.2 *The New Database dialog box for the Orders database*

Creating the Clients and Products Databases

Repeat the steps mentioned in the section "Creating the Orders Database," to create the Clients and Products databases. Create the databases under the Order folder as done earlier. To ensure this, verify that the file names are Order\Clients.nsf and Order\Products.nsf. Refer to Figures 24.3 and 24.4 for settings for these databases.

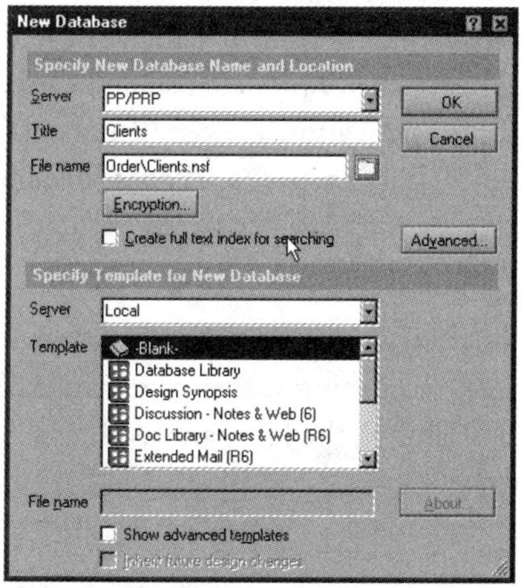

FIGURE 24.3 *The New Database dialog box for the Client database*

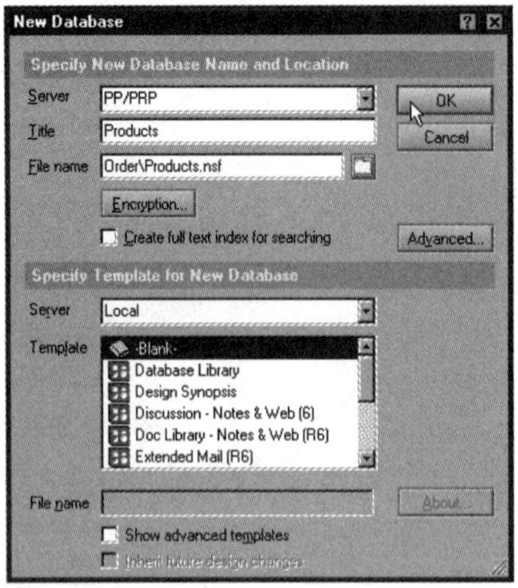

FIGURE 24.4 *The New Database dialog box for the Products database*

The next step is to create the home page of the application.

Creating the Home Page

Every Web application launches a default page when accessed, called the *home page*. Therefore, you will first design the home page for the order processing application. A typical Web-based application contains various types of pages, such as HTML, JSP/ASP, and PHP. These pages are typically stored under a single directory but as individual elements. In Domino, all the elements exist inside the database; therefore, the default directory has to point a particular database file. In this application, there are three database files, Clients.nsf, Products.nsf, and Orders.nsf. Because the Orders.nsf forms the heart of the application, choose Orders.nsf as the database to be launched. To do so, set the URL as `http://pp/Order/Orders.nsf`, where `pp` represents the host name of the server you have chosen to create the databases. This launches a page as shown in Figure 24.5.

This page is very primitive and needs to be designed according to the design specifications identified in the previous chapter. Accordingly, this page should have a three-frame layout, with the top acting as a banner, the left pane as the navigation bar, and the right pane as the content pane.

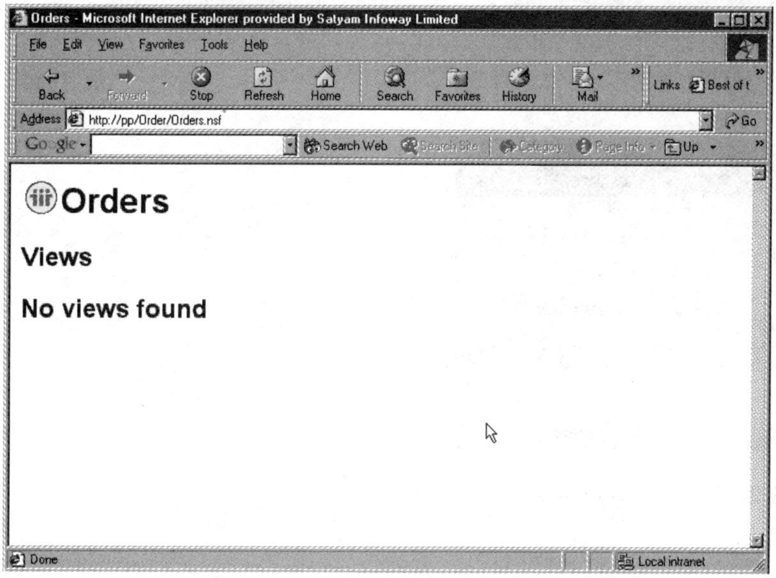

FIGURE 24.5 *The default home page*

To design this layout, you need to create a frameset. Perform the following steps to achieve this:

1. Right-click the Orders database icon in the workspace page Order Processing. From the menu, choose Open In Designer to open the database in the design mode. Next, create a new frameset and choose the layout as shown in Figure 24.6.

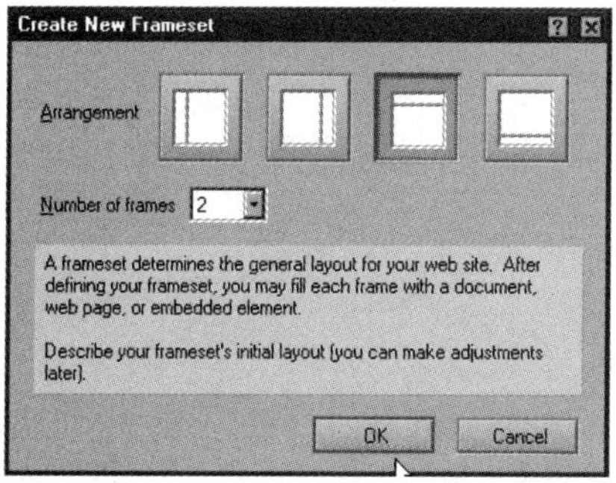

FIGURE 24.6 *The Create New Frameset dialog box*

2. In the Frameset properties, enter the name as **MainFrameset,** as shown in Figure 24.7.

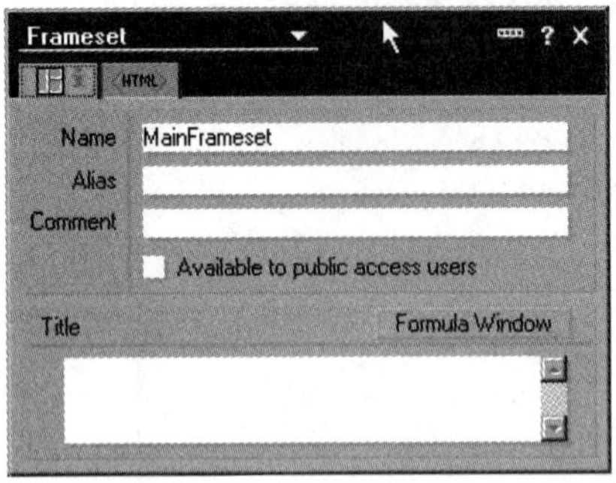

FIGURE 24.7 *The MainFrameset property box*

3. Click on the top frame and launch the Frame property box. Enter the name as **Banner** and the default target for the links in the frame as **Module.** The property box should look as shown in Figure 24.8.

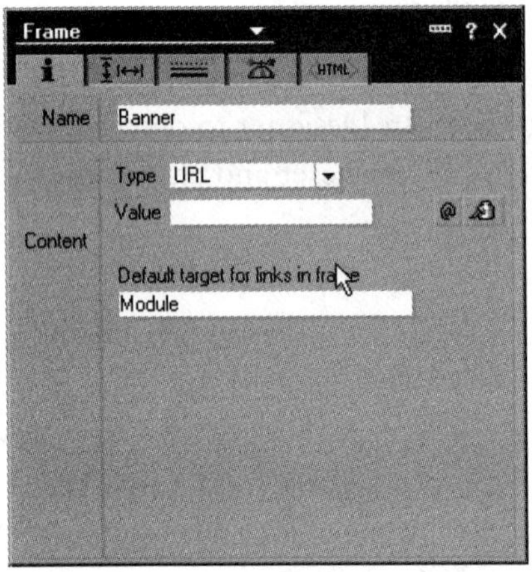

FIGURE 24.8 *The Banner Frame property box*

4. Click on the bottom frame to launch the frame's property box. Enter the name as **Module.** Notice that this frame has been set as the target for the top banner. Save the frameset.

Moving ahead, you need to create a banner page in the top frame and a frameset in the bottom frame. You will create this frameset for each of the three modules, because as the user navigates through different modules, the corresponding framesets are loaded. To do this:

1. Create a new page in the Orders module and name it **BannerPage.** Create a table with the dimensions 1 by 5 (1 row and 5 columns). Enter the title of the application and the names of the modules as shown in Figure 24.9.

FIGURE 24.9 *The BannerPage table*

2. Open the MainFrameset frameset and set the newly created banner page as the content for the top Banner frame, as shown in Figure 24.10.

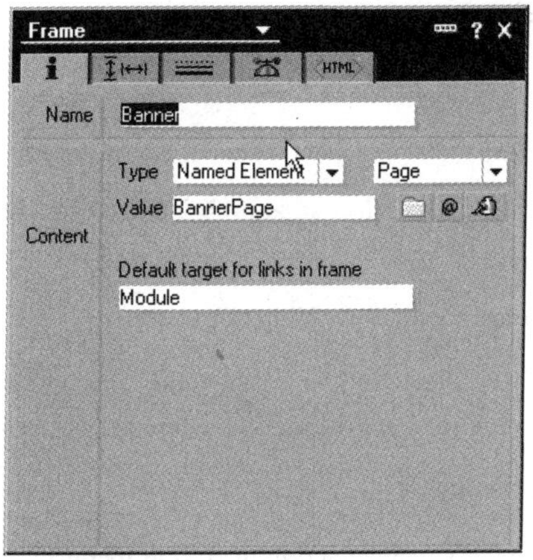

FIGURE 24.10 *The Banner page in the Banner frame*

3. Next, create individual framesets in each of the databases. Name the framesets **OrderFrame** in the Orders database, **ClientFrame** in the Clients database, and **ProductFrame** in the Products database. Select the default layout (the first option) for all these frames. In each of these framesets, name the left frame as **Nav** and the right frame as **Content**.

4. Open the Banner page and create hotspots on the text, Client, Products, and Order, to the respective framesets in the modules. On clicking these links, the corresponding framesets are loaded in the Module frame.

Adding Design Elements to the Clients Database

In this section, you will create the design elements for the Clients database, including shared actions, forms, views, outlines, pages, and navigation elements.

Creating the Shared Actions

Before proceeding, some common actions can be created. Some of the common actions are Edit, Save, and Cancel. Create the shared actions corresponding to these actions using the properties listed in Table 24.1.

Table 24.1 Properties for Actions

Action	Properties	Value
Edit	Name	Enter **Edit**
	Display	Deselect Include action in Action menu
	Icon	Select Notes
	Location	Select Left (Select an appropriate icon for the action)
	Action to be taken	Enter `@Command([EditDocument])`
	Hide when properties	Check Previewed for editing and Opened for editing (in the section Hide action when document is)
Save	Name	Enter **Save**
	Display	Deselect Include action in Action menu
	Icon	Select Notes
	Location	Select Left (Select an appropriate icon for the action)
	Action to be taken	Enter `@Command([FileSave]);` `@Command([FileCloseWindow])`
	Hide when properties	Check Previewed for reading and Opened for reading (in the section Hide action when document is)

Action	Properties	Value
Cancel	Name	Enter **Cancel**
	Display	Deselect Include action in Action menu
	Icon	Select Notes
	Location	Select Left (Select an appropriate icon for the action)
	Action to be taken	Enter `@Command([FileCloseWindow])`
	Hide when properties	Enter `@IsNewDoc` (in the section Hide action if formula is true)
New Client Profile	Name	Enter **New Client Profile**
	Display	Deselect Include action in Action menu
	Icon	Select Notes
	Location	Select Left (Select an appropriate icon for the action)
	Action to be taken	Enter `@Command([Compose];"";"Client")`
	Hide when properties	Enter `!(@IsMember("[Admin]";@UserRoles))` (in the section Hide action if formula is true)

Creating the Forms

The Clients database contains two forms, Client and ClientPasswordChange. The following section explains how to create these forms.

Creating the Client Form

Perform the following steps to create the Client form:

1. Click New Form to open a new blank form in the work pane for the Clients database.
2. Set the Form properties to the following.
   a. In the Name box, enter **Client**.
   b. In the Display section, clear all the options.

c. Select versioning to be None.

d. In the Options section, disable all the options in this section.

e. In the Conflict Handling section, select the option Create Conflicts.

f. Close the Form property box and save the form.

3. Add a heading to the form. To do so, perform the following steps:

   a. Create a 1-by-1 table. Select the Table Width as Fit with margins and click OK.

   b. Type Client Profile and left align the text. In the Text property box change font to Arial, size to 10, style to Bold, and select color as white.

   c. Open the Table property, in the Cell Border Thickness, click Set All To 0.

   d. In the Table\Cell Background tab, in the Cell color, select an appropriate background color.

   e. In the Table Borders tab, in the Border Effects row, select Drop Shadow and specify width as 10.

   f. Close the property window.

4. Create the Fields and the text associated with them inside the table. To do so, first create a 6 by 2 table under the previous table that you created. Select the Table Width as Fit with margins. In the first column of the table, enter Name, Type, Address, Telephone, Fax, and E-mail as the labels for the fields. Set the font as Arial, size as 8, and style as Bold for these labels. To create the fields for the labels follow the steps below:

   a. Create an editable field named ClientName of type Text.

   b. Create an editable field named ClientType of type Radio button. In the Control tab of the field, in the section Enter choices, enter the values **Individual** and **Company**. In the Display section, select the Number of columns as 2 so that the radio button choices appear in two columns.

   c. Create editable fields ClientAddress, ClientPhone, ClientFax, and ClientEmail and specify their type as Text.

   d. Specify the font as Arial, size as 8, and style as Plain for these text columns. The Client form appears as shown in Figure 24.11.

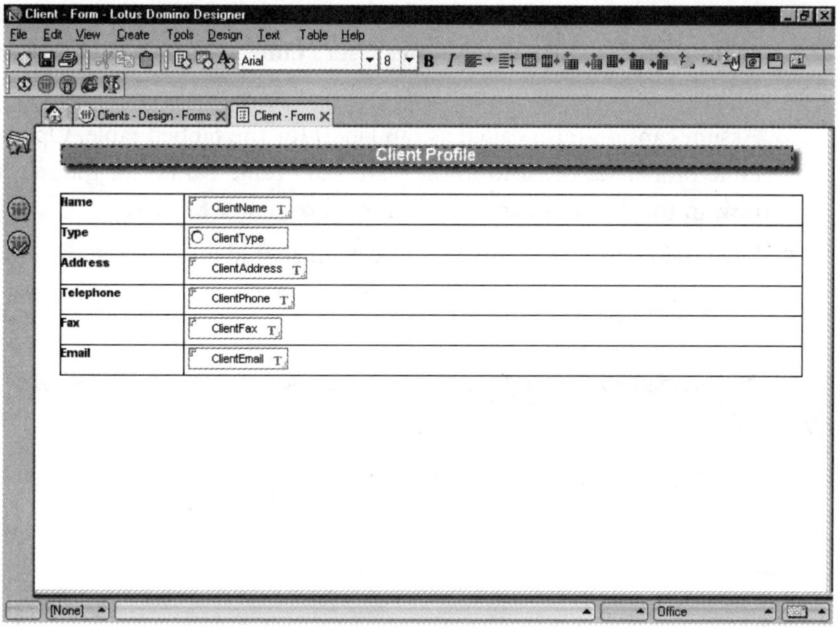

FIGURE 24.11 *Client form Design 1*

5. Create a 2-by-1 tabbed table under this table. Next, open the Table property box and in the sixth tab (Table Rows), in the section For selected row, enter the tab label and caption as **Contact Details** for the first tab and enter **Security** for the second tab. In the first tab of the table, create a 5x2 table. In the first column of this table, enter Name, Address, Telephone, Fax, and Email as the labels for the fields to be inserted in the second column. Create the fields for the labels with the properties as listed in Table 24.2.

Table 24.2 Fields for Contact Details

Field Name	Field Type
ContactName	Editable, Text
ContactAddress	Editable, Text
ContactPhone	Editable, Text
ContactFax	Editable, Text
ContactEmail	Editable, Text

In the second tab of the tabbed table, create a 1-by-2 table. In the first column of this table, enter **Notes User Name** as the label. Create an Editable field named ClientUserName of type Text.

Assign caption (also called as tab label) for the tabbed table. Open the table properties box and in the sixth tab (Table Rows) for the selected row, in the Tab label and caption text box, enter **Security**.

6. Save the form. The Client form design should appear as shown in Figure 24.12.

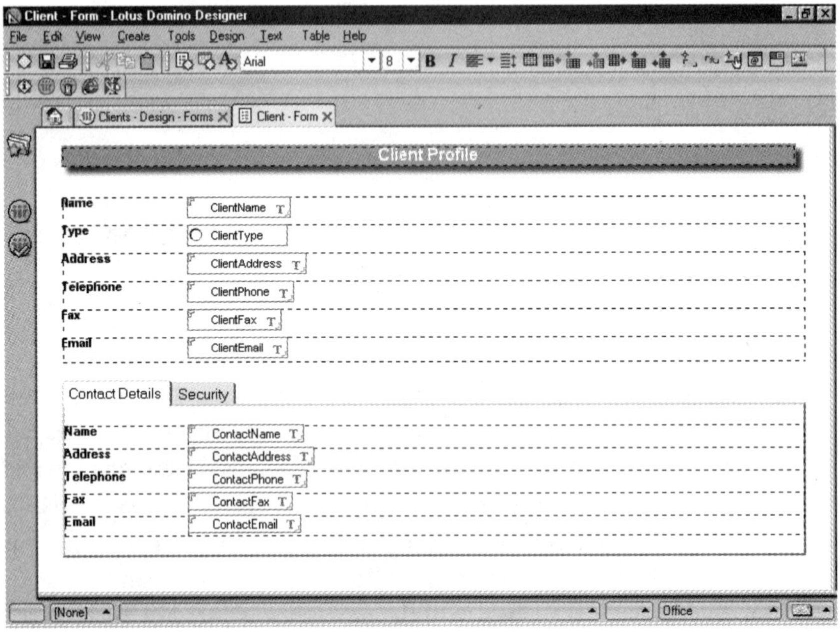

FIGURE 24.12 *Client form final design*

Click the Preview button to see the preview of the Client form, as shown in the Figure 24.13:

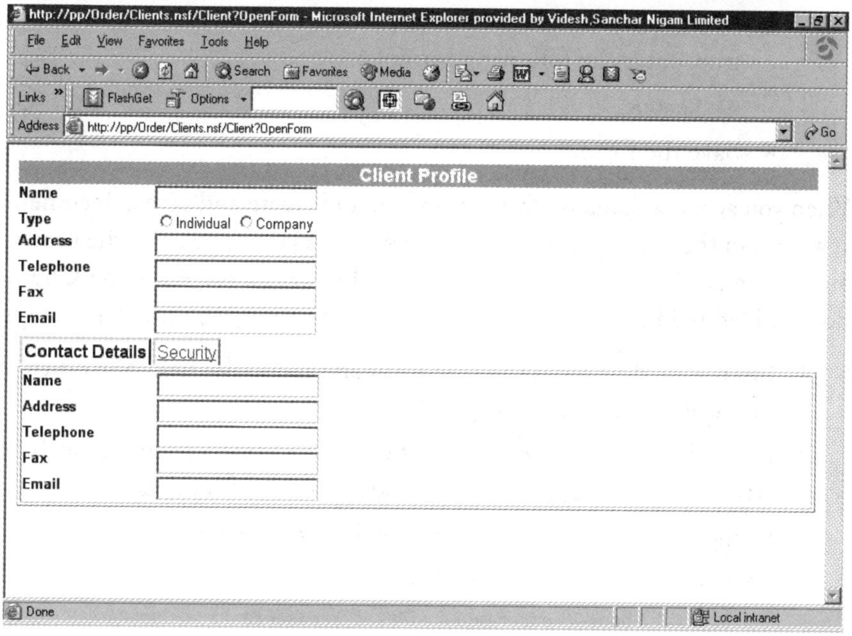

FIGURE 24.13 *Client form preview*

After creating the form, the next step is to add the shared actions to the form. To do so:

1. Open the Action pane and select the Create/Insert Shared Action menu. Select the actions Edit, Cancel, and Save.
2. Click Insert and Done to add these shared actions to the Action of the Client Profile form.
3. Adjust the sequence of the actions by dragging and dropping in the desired sequence. Keep Edit, Save, Cancel as the sequence.
4. Create a form action `Change Internet Password` to launch the Client-PasswordChange form. To create this action:
   - Create a new action and name it **Change Internet Password**. In the Display section, clear Include action in Action menu. In the Icon section, select Notes, and select the Location as Left. Finally, select an appropriate icon to be displayed with the text.
   - Enter the following formula for the action:

```
@Command([Compose];"";"ClientPasswordChange")
```

- In the Hide When properties, in the section Hide action if formula is true, enter the following formula:

  ```
  @IsNewDoc
  ```

- Save the form.

When you access a database from a browser and create and save a document based on a form in the database, a message `Form Processed` appears in the browser. You can customize this standard message. To edit this message for the Client form, add a hidden field `$$Return` in the form by performing the following steps:

1. Insert a field in the top of the form and name the field **$$Return**. Select the type as Text and Computed.
2. In the Hide Paragraph from section of the Hide When tab of the property box, check all the options to keep this field hidden.
3. In the value for the field, enter the following formula:

```
WebPage := "<style type='text/css'>
            body {font-family: 'Arial'} </style>";
WebPage := WebPage +
      "<h3>Your document has been successfully submitted</h3>";
WebPage := WebPage + "<hr><br><br>";
WebPage := WebPage +
    "Select a view from the outline pane on the left to continue";
       WebPage
```

Preview the form and save the form. A message as shown in Figure 24.14 appears.

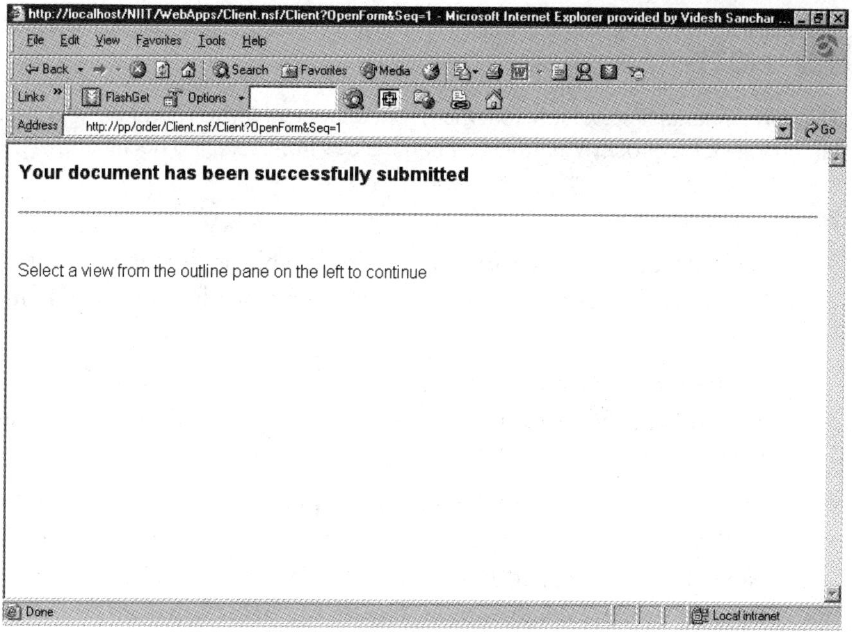

FIGURE 24.14 *Form Submit Message*

Creating the ClientPasswordChange Form

Perform the following steps to create the ClientPasswordChange form:

1. Click on the New Form button to open a new blank form in the work pane and set the form properties as listed in Table 24.3.

Table 24.3 Form Properties for the ClientPasswordChange Form

Field Name	Field Type
Form Name	ClientPasswordChange
Include in menu	Clear
Include in Search Builder	Clear
Include in Print	Clear
Conflict Handling	Create Conflicts
Formulas inherit values from selected document	Checked

NOTE

This form inherits field values from the Client document form. Therefore, it is important to check the property Formulas inherit values from selected document.

2. Add a heading to the form by creating a table as described in the section "Creating the Client Form." Enter the form heading text as **Change Password**.
3. Create the fields and the text associated with them inside the table as described in the section "Creating the Client Form." Set the font as Arial, size as 8, and style as Bold for these fields.
4. Create another 3-by-2 table under the previous table. Select the Table Width as Fit with margins. In the first column of the table, enter Name, Notes User Name, and Password as the labels for the fields to be inserted in the second column. Create the fields listed in Table 24.4. Set the font as Arial, size as 8, and style as Plain for these fields.

Table 24.4 Fields for ClientPasswordChange Form

Field Name	Field Type	Value
ClientName	Computed when composed, Text	ClientName
ClientUserName	Computed when composed, Text	ClientUserName
ClientPassword	Password, Editable	None
SaveOptions	Computed when composed field, Text	0

5. Save the form. The ClientPasswordChange form should appear as shown in Figure 24.15.

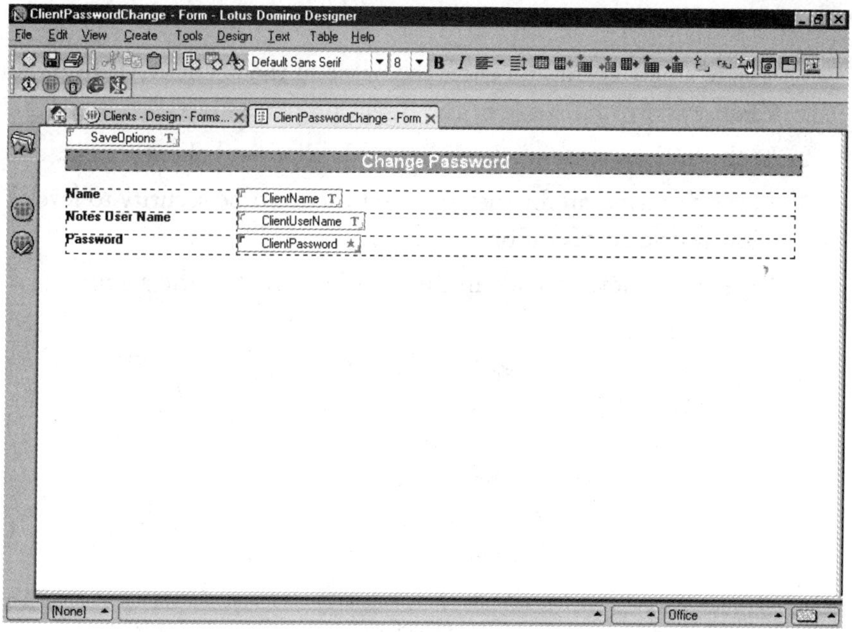

FIGURE 24.15 *ClientPasswordChange form design*

The next step is to add some of the shared actions. To do so:

1. Open the Action pane and select Create/Insert Shared Action to add the actions Cancel and Save. Click Insert and then Done to add these shared actions.
2. Adjust the sequence of the actions by dragging and dropping in the desired sequence. Keep the sequence as Save and Cancel.

To perform actions such as updating the document in the Address Book, one needs to use LotusScript. Therefore, you need to use a `WebQuerySave` agent. To use this, you should associate the agent you are going to create with the form event `WebQuerySave`. Associating the agent with the form will invoke the agent when an `HTTP POST` request is made to the server.

To associate the agent with the form event, enter the following formula in the form event `WebQuerySave` for the form ClientPasswordChange:

```
@Command([ToolsRunMacro]; "(WebQrySaveClientPasswordChange)")
```

Perform the following steps to create the agent:

1. Create a new agent and enter the name of the agent as **WebQrySave-ClientPasswordChange** in the Agent properties box.
2. In the options section, check Run in background client thread.
3. In the Security tab for the agent, set the runtime security to level 2 - allow restricted operations.
4. Enter the following code in the Initialize event of the agent:

```
Sub Initialize
        Dim session As New NotesSession
        Dim books As Variant
        Dim view As NotesView
        Dim persondoc As NotesDocument
        Dim doc As NotesDocument
        Dim done As Variant
        Dim person As String
        books = session.AddressBooks
        Set doc = session.DocumentContext
        done = False
        person = doc.ClientUserName(0)
        'check every Domino Directory,
        Forall b In books
                If ( b.IsPublicAddressBook ) And ( Not done ) Then
                        Call b.Open( "", "" )
                        ' look up person's  name
                        ' in the $Users view of address book
                        Set view = b.GetView( "($Users)" )
                        Set persondoc = view.GetDocumentByKey( person )
                        ' if person is found, update the password
                        ' in the Person document
                        If Not ( persondoc Is Nothing ) Then
                                persondoc.HTTPpassword = doc.ClientPasswordEnc
                                Call persondoc.Save(True,False)
                                done = True
                        End If
                End If
        End Forall
End Sub
```

The agent looks in each of the available Domino directories for the client whose password has to be changed. The Notes username is available in the field:

```
person = doc.ClientUserName(0)
```

This is the value inherited from the Client form. The name is looked up in the Domino directory in the `$Users` view, which is a hidden view. If the user is found, then the HTTPPassword field in the person document of the AddressBook is assigned the encrypted value of the new password, as shown here:

```
persondoc.HTTPpassword = doc.ClientPasswordEnc
```

In the code listing, notice that a field ClientPasswordEnc is being accessed. This field is used to provide the encrypted version of the password typed in by the user. You need to add this field to the form. Insert a new field at the bottom of the form and name it as ClientPasswordEnc. The field is a computed text field and has the following formula as its value:

```
@Password(ClientPassword)
```

In the Hide When tab, check all the options available under Hide paragraph from to make this a hidden field. Finally, in the `WebQuerySave` event of the form, add the following formula so that the agent created gets launched on the save of the form:

```
@Command([ToolsRunMacro]; "WebQrySaveClientPasswordChange")
```

Creating the Views

You need to create two views in the Clients module. They are:

- Client\By Contact
- Client\By Name

The following sections explain how to create these two views.

Creating the Client\By Contact View

To create this view, follow these steps: Create a new view and specify its name as **Client\By Contact.** This will create the view under the level Client. In the options tab of the View Property box, check the option Default when first opened and clear the option Show response.

In the selection formula for the view, enter the following formula:

```
SELECT ((Form = "Client"))
```

Close the property box and save the view. Add the columns to the view by setting the properties for the view as given in Table 24.5. Select Ascending as the Sort option for Name column.

Table 24.5 Columns and Properties

Column Name	Column Value
Name	ClientName
Phone	ClientPhone
Contact	ContactName

To provide an action to launch a new Client Profile, insert the shared action New Client Profile, as given below:

1. Open the Action pane of the view and select Create/Insert Shared Action to launch the Insert Shared Action dialog box.
2. Select the action New Client Profile and click on Insert button to add the shared action to the view.

Creating the Client\By Name View

To create the Client\By Name view, create a new view and enter the name as **Client\By Name**. Specify other details, such as type of view and copy from option.

> **NOTE**
>
> Notice that this time, the view style has been copied from the Client\By Contact view. To copy this view style, use copy style from view by selecting Client\By Contact This will reduce the creation effort since both are similar.

Click on the Save and Customize button to create the view. In the options tab of the View Property box, set the properties as listed in Table 24.6.

Table 24.6 View Properties for the Client\By Name View

Property	Value
Default when first opened	Clear
Show response documents in hierarchy	Clear

Now to list the correct documents in the view, enter the following formula for the view selection:

```
SELECT ((Form = "Client"))
```

Next, add the columns listed in Table 24.7 to the view.

Table 24.7 Columns for Client\By Name View

Column Title	Value
Contact	ContactName
Phone	ClientPhone
Name	ClientName

Open the Column property for the Contact column and select Ascending for the Sort option. To do so:

- Cut the Name column and paste it in place of the Contact column and change the sort from Ascending to None.
- Now cut the Contact column and paste it as the first column and add the sort as Ascending.

Observe that the New Client Profile action is added automatically because you have based the design of this view on the previously created view.

Creating the Outline

Now that the views have been created, you can create the outline very easily. To create the outline, perform the following steps:

1. Go to the Outline design view and click the New Outline button and give it the name **ClientOutline**.

2. Create two outline entries indented under the outline entry with label **Client**. Assign the labels for the outline entries as **By Contact** and **By Name**. Select content for the outline entries as Named Element and View. Assign values by selecting the views Client\ By Contact and Client\ By Name.

The outline will appear as shown in Figure 24.16:

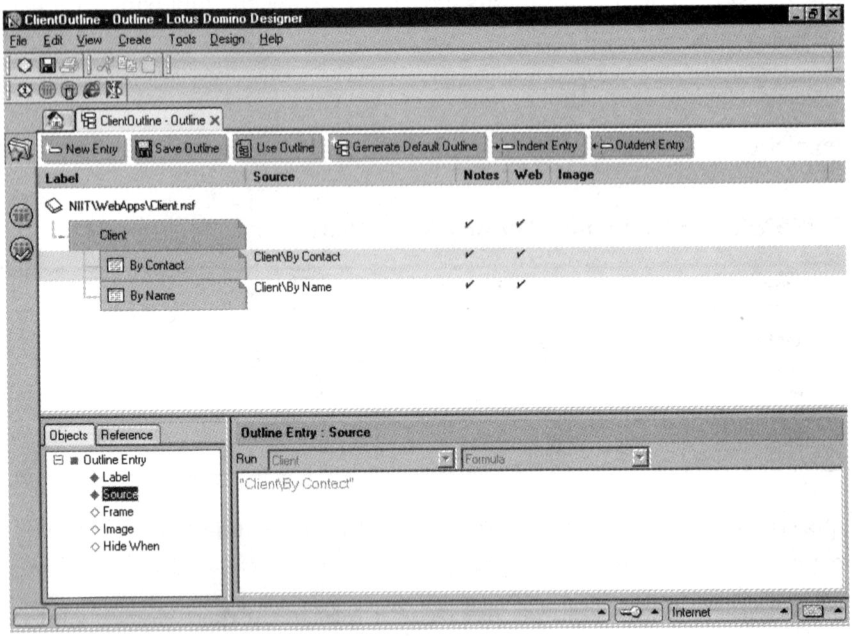

FIGURE 24.16 *The ClientOutline outline*

Creating the ClientNavPage Page

This page embeds the outline ClientOutline. To create the page and embed the outline, perform the following steps:

1. Create a new Page and open the Page Properties dialog box.
2. In the name field, enter **ClientNavPage**.
3. Click the Background tab and select the background color as 245,239,206 from the color palette.
4. Choose Create/Embedded Element/Outline, and select ClientOutline as the outline to be embedded.

5. Open the Embedded Outline properties box and set the outline properties as specified in Table 24.8.

Table 24.8 Properties of the ClientOutline View

Property	Value
Outline size – Height	Fit to window
Top level font	Size 8, Bold
Sub level font	Size 8, Plain

This page, when previewed in a Web browser, looks as shown in Figure 24.17.

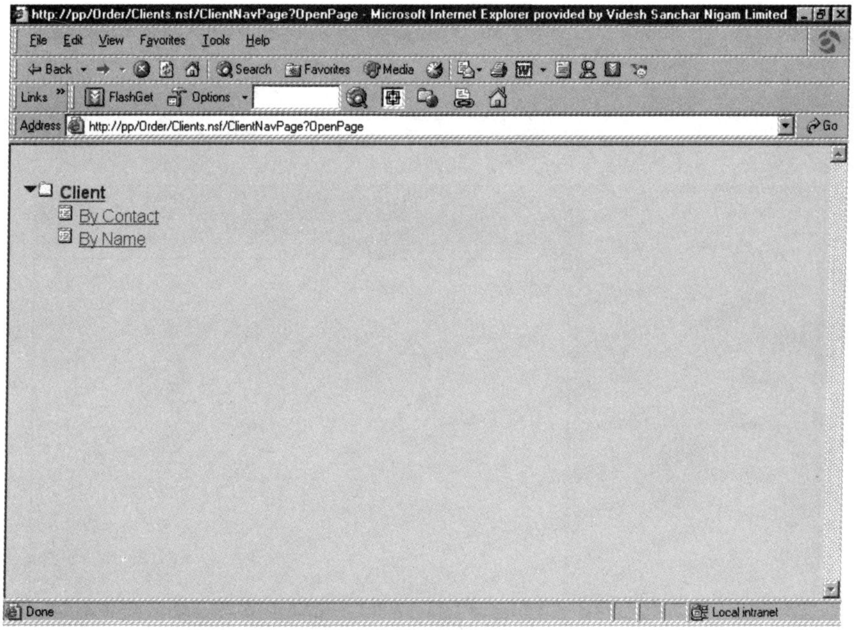

FIGURE 24.17 *The ClientNavPage page*

Creating the Navigational Elements

To complete the navigational framework of the Clients database, you need to add the appropriate pages to the ClientFrameset frameset. To do this, perform the following steps:

1. Open the ClientFrameset frameset.
2. In the property box for the frame Nav, set the page **ClientNavPage** as the content for the page. Adjust the width of the frame to contain the page properly.
3. In the property box of the Content frame, set the view **Client\By Name** as the content for the frame.

This frameset in the page designer appears as shown in Figure 24.18.

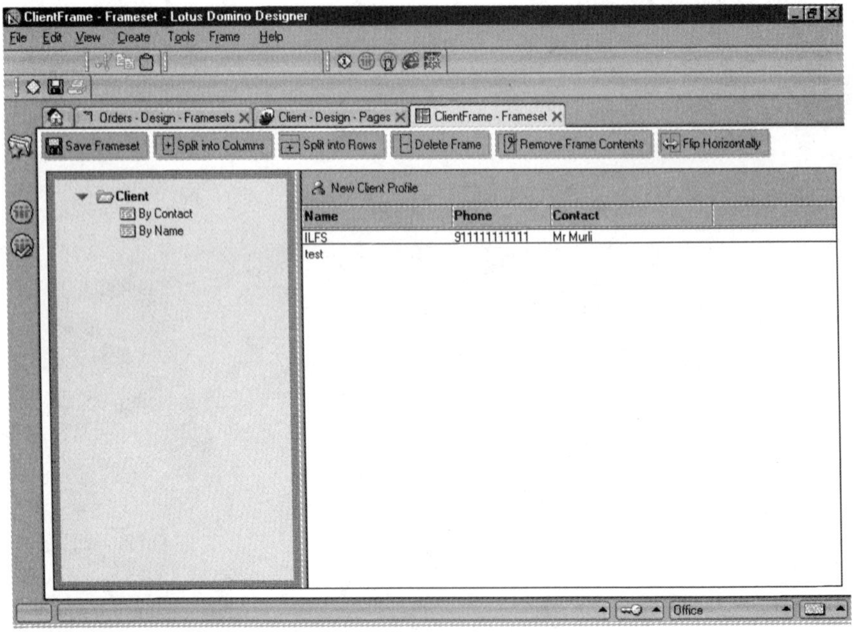

FIGURE 24.18 *The ClientFrame frameset*

Save the frameset and preview it in Internet Explorer. The frameset should look as shown in Figure 24.19.

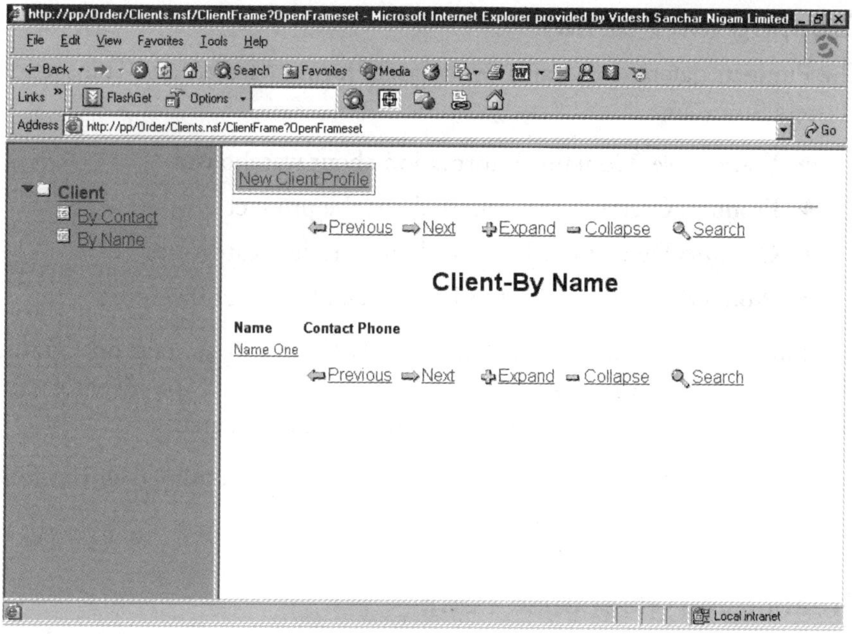

FIGURE 24.19 *The ClientFrame frameset preview*

Now that you have accomplished the task of designing the Clients database for your Online Order Processing system, proceed with the development of the other modules as discussed in the following sections.

Adding Design Elements to the Products Database

In this section, you will create the design elements for the Products database. You will create shared actions, forms, views, outlines, pages, and navigation elements.

Creating the Shared Actions

You have already created a set of shared actions, including Edit, Save, and Cancel, in the Clients database. Now, to save time and effort, copy the three actions from the Clients database and paste them into the Products database.

Creating the Forms

The Products database contains two types of forms: Masters and Transaction. The Masters forms are.

- **Warehouse.** Contains information about warehouses
- **Product.** Contains the details about the product
- **CategoryDefinition.** Used to define product categories
- **ProductInventory.** Used to keep track of product inventory

In addition to these forms, the Products database will contain one Transaction form, **InventoryTransaction**. This form is used to log all the inventory transactions that will happen when an order is placed and executed.

You will create all of the above forms using the steps outlined in the following sections.

Creating the Warehouse Form

This form is used to create the Warehouse masters. To create this form, perform the following steps:

Create a new form and open the property box. Set the properties of the form as shown in Table 24.9.

Table 24.9 Properties of the Warehouse Form

Property	Value
Name	Warehouse
Include in menu	Clear
Include in search	Clear

Now create the header for the form Warehouse using the steps specified for the Client form in the Clients database.

To lay out the fields, as in the previous forms, create a 3-by-2 table. In the first column, enter Code, Person-in-charge, and Location as labels. In the second column, create fields as listed in Table 24.10.

Table 24.10 Columns of the Warehouse Form

Field Name	Field Type
WarehouseCode	Editable, Text
WareHouseInCharge	Editable, Text
WareHouseLocation	Editable, Text

In Designer, the form will appear as shown in Figure 24.20.

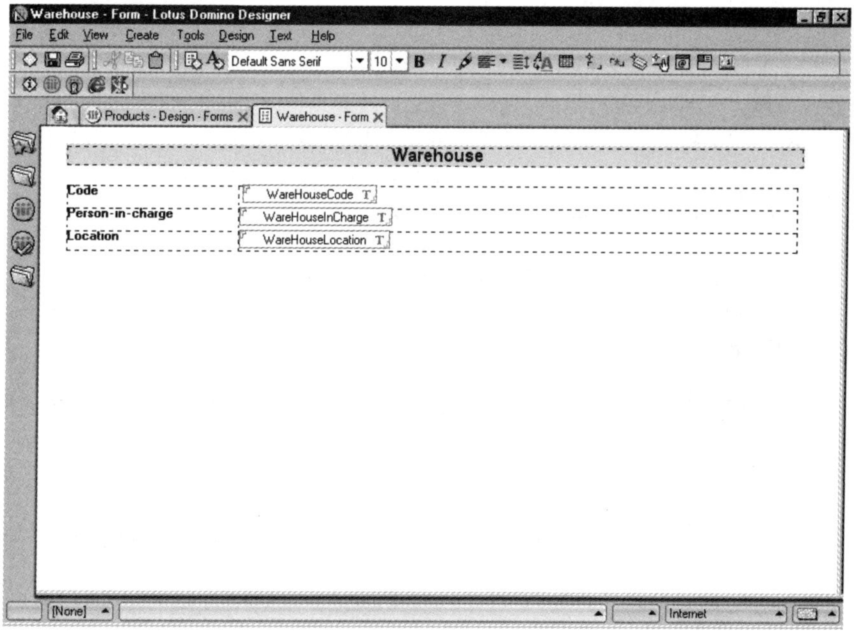

FIGURE 24.20 *The Warehouse form design*

The next step is to add the shared actions to the form. To do so:

1. Open the Action pane, select Create/Insert Shared Action, and select the actions Edit, Cancel, and Save.
2. Adjust the sequence of the actions by dragging and dropping in the desired sequence. Keep Edit, Save, and Cancel as the sequence.

In the Client form, `$$Return` was used to send an HTML message to the browser when the form gets submitted. In this form, `$$Return` is used to redirect to a default view. Perform the following steps to achieve the redirection:

1. Insert a field at the top of the form and name the field `$$Return`. Select the type as Text and Computed.
2. In the Hide Paragraph from section of the Hide When tab of the property box, check all the options to keep this field hidden.
3. In the value for the field, enter the following formula:

```
DB := @ReplaceSubstring(@ReplaceSubstring(@Subset(@DbName; -1);
" "; "+"); "\\"; "/");
View:="WareHouseByCode";
"[/"+DB+"/"+View+"]"
```

The above formula assembles redirection URL string and sends it to the browser. All the backward slashes are replaced with forward slashes and any spaces are converted to plus signs to achieve the proper format for the URL.

Next, to generate the warehouse code automatically, a LotusScript agent is necessary. Therefore, associate the agent that performs this task to the `WebQueryOpen` event of the form.

Now the form is ready to be previewed and appears as shown in Figure 24.21.

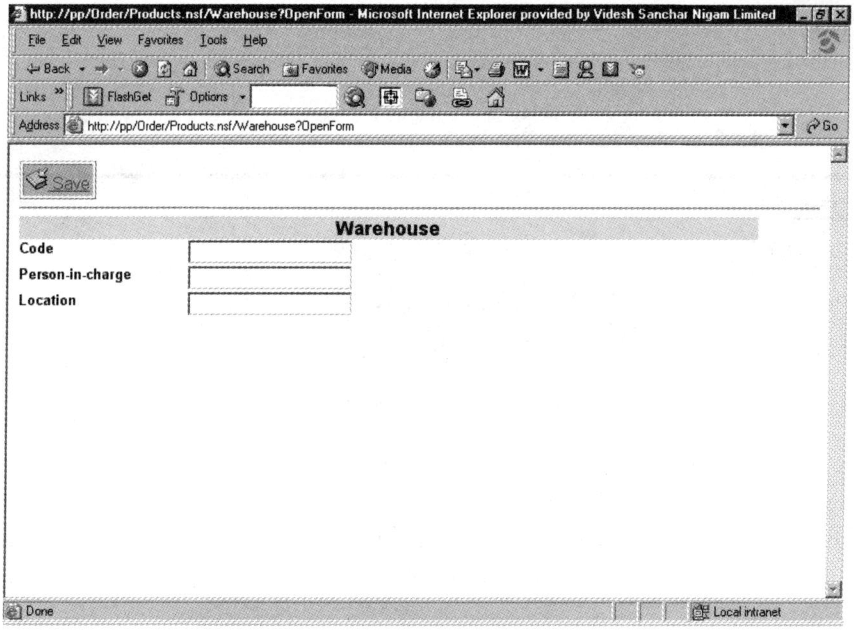

FIGURE 24.21 *The Warehouse form preview*

Creating the Product Form

This form is used to create the Product masters. Create this form using the steps discussed in the preceding sections on creating forms. Refer to Table 24.11 to set the properties of the form.

Table 24.11 Properties of the Product Form

Property	Value
Name	Product
Include in menu	Clear
Include in search	Clear

Create the header for the form by performing the same steps used for the Client form in the Clients database. Create a 5-by-2 table. In the first column, enter Product Name, Product Code, Product Category, Product Subcategory, and Unit

Price as labels. In the second column, create fields as per the properties listed in Table 24.12.

Table 24.12 Fields for the Product Form

Field Name	Type
ProductName	Editable, Text
ProductCode	Computed, Text
ProductCategory	Editable, Combobox
ProductSubcategory	Editable, Combobox
ProductUnitPrice	Editable, Number

The next step is to add some of the shared actions to the form. Repeat the steps used to add actions to the Product form.

You need to automate the ProductCategory and ProductSubcategory fields to display a list of the existing categories and subcategories of products. Perform the following to achieve this:

- **ProductCategory.** This field lists the existing product categories. In the second tab of this field, in the choices, select Use formula for choices and enter the following formula:

  ```
  view:="Products\\Category Definition";
  @DbLookup("";"";view;"Category";2)
  ```

- **ProductSubcategory.** This field lists the subcategories for the products. Select Use formula for choices and enter the formula given below:

  ```
  view:="Products\\Category Definition";
  @DbLookup("";"";view;"Subcategory";2)
  ```

You can also automate the generation of product codes. To do so, you need to create a LotusScript agent. Associate the agent that generates the product code with the WebQueryOpen event of the form.

In Designer, the form will appear as shown in Figure 24.22.

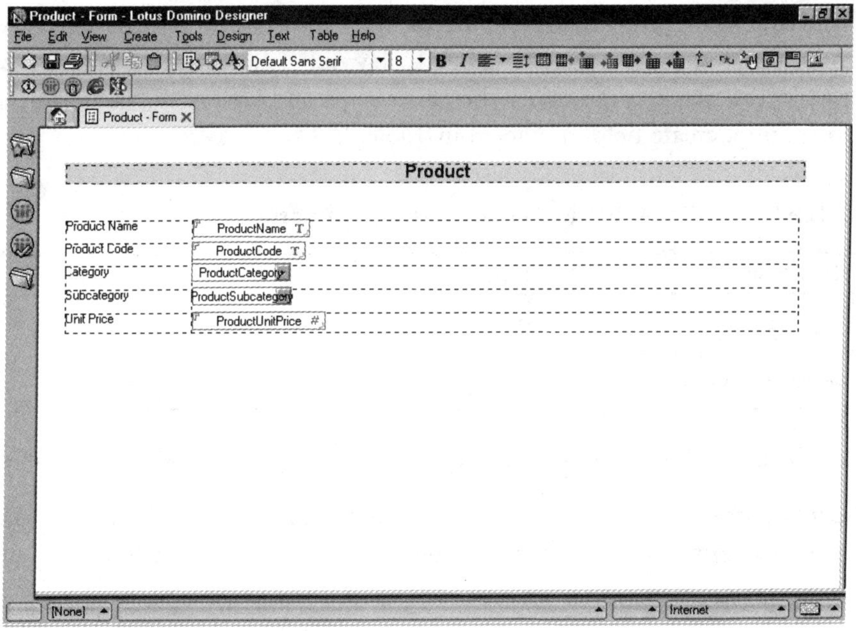

FIGURE 24.22 *The Product form design*

CAUTION

If you try to preview this form now, Domino will generate an error because the views used in the `@DbLookup` formula for the choices of the ProductCategory and Product-Subcategory field are not yet created.

Creating the CategoryDefinition Form

This form is used to define the various categories for the products. Create a new form and set its properties as given in Table 24.13.

Table 24.13 Properties of the CategoryDefinition Form

Property	Value
Name	CategoryDefinition
Include in menu	Clear
Include in search	Clear

Create the header for the form by performing the same steps used for the Client Profile form in the Clients database. To lay out fields properly, create a 2-by-2 table. In the first column, enter the labels Type and Category Name. In the second column, create fields as shown in Table 24.14.

Table 24.14 Fields of the CategoryDefinition Form

Field Name	Type
CategoryType	Editable, Combobox
CategoryName	Editable, Text

Enter values **Category** and **Subcategory** as the choices for the field `CategoryType`.

Next, add the shared actions Edit, Save, and Cancel as you did for the previous forms. To redirect the `$$Return` to a default view, perform the following steps:

1. Insert a field in the top of the form and name the field `$$Return`. Select the type as Text and Computed.
2. In the Hide Paragraph from section of the Hide When tab of the property box, check all the options to keep this field hidden. In the value for the field, enter the following formula:

```
DB := @ReplaceSubstring(@ReplaceSubstring(@Subset(@DbName; -1);
" "; "+"); "\\"; "/");
View:= "ProductsCategoryDefinition";
"[/"+DB+"/"+View+"]"
```

In Designer, the form will now look as shown in Figure 24.23.

Preview the form in browser. The form appears as shown in Figure 24.24.

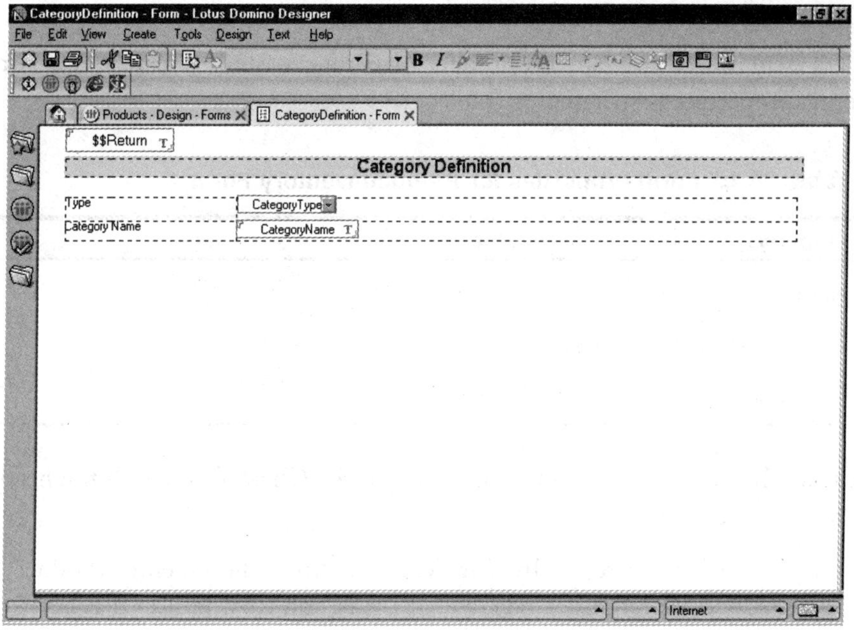

FIGURE 24.23 *The CategoryDefinition form design*

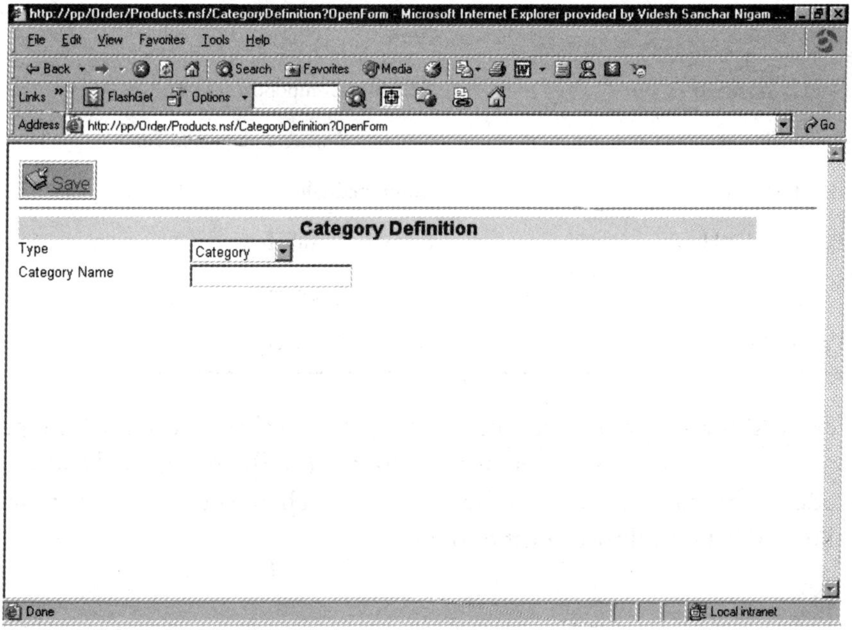

FIGURE 24.24 *The CategoryDefinition form preview*

Creating the ProductInventory Form

This form is used to maintain Product Inventory masters. Create a new form and set its properties as specified in Table 24.15.

Table 24.15 Form Properties for ProductInventory Form

Property	Value
Name	ProductInventory
Include in menu	Clear
Include in search	Clear

Create the header for the form, as shown in the Client form, with the heading as Product Inventory.

To lay out fields, create a 2-by-5 table. In the first column, enter Product Name, Product Code, Warehouse Code, No. of Units, and Reorder Level as labels. In the second column, create fields as listed in Table 24.16.

Table 24.16 Fields for ProductInventory Form

Field Name	Type
ProdInvName_d	Editable, Combobox
ProdInvName	Computed when composed, Text
ProdInvCode	Computed when composed, Text
ProdInvWareHouseCode	Editable, Combobox
ProdInvUnits	Editable, Number
ProdInvOrderLevel	Editable, Number

Next, add the shared actions Edit, Save, and Cancel as you did for the previous forms. Enter **ProdInvName** as the value for the ProdInvName field and **ProdInv-Code** as the value for the ProdInvCode field. Then, you need to automate the following fields to display a list of options:

- **ProdInvName_d.** This field provides the list of product codes and product names in the format "Product Name - Product Code". This list is based on a hidden view containing the products in the desired format. In the second tab of this field, from choices, select Use formula for choices and enter the following formula:

  ```
  view:= "Products\\ByProductCodeName";
  @DbColumn("";"";view;1)
  ```

  The preceding formula returns the value of the first column of the view Products\ByProductCodeName as a text list.

  The selection list available is a combination of product code and product name. However, since the product inventory is stored with code and name separated, you need to separate these two values from the select list and assign them to individual fields. To achieve this, first check the Refresh fields on keyword change in the Options section in the Control tab of the field property box of the ProdInvName_d field. Next, enter the following formula in the Input Translation event for this field:

  ```
  FIELD ProdInvName:= ProdInvName;
  FIELD ProdInvCode := ProdInvCode;
  @SetField("ProdInvCode";@Right(ProdInvName_d;" - "));
  @SetField("ProdInvName";@Left(ProdInvName_d;" - "));
  ProdInvName_d
  ```

- **ProdInvWareHouseCode.** This field provides the list of warehouses as a combo box. For this field, in the Choices section, select Use formula for choices and enter the following formula:

  ```
  view:= "WareHouse\\By Code";
  @DbColumn("";"";view;1)
  ```

  This formula returns a list of warehouses as a text list.

The design of the form will appear as shown in Figure 24.25.

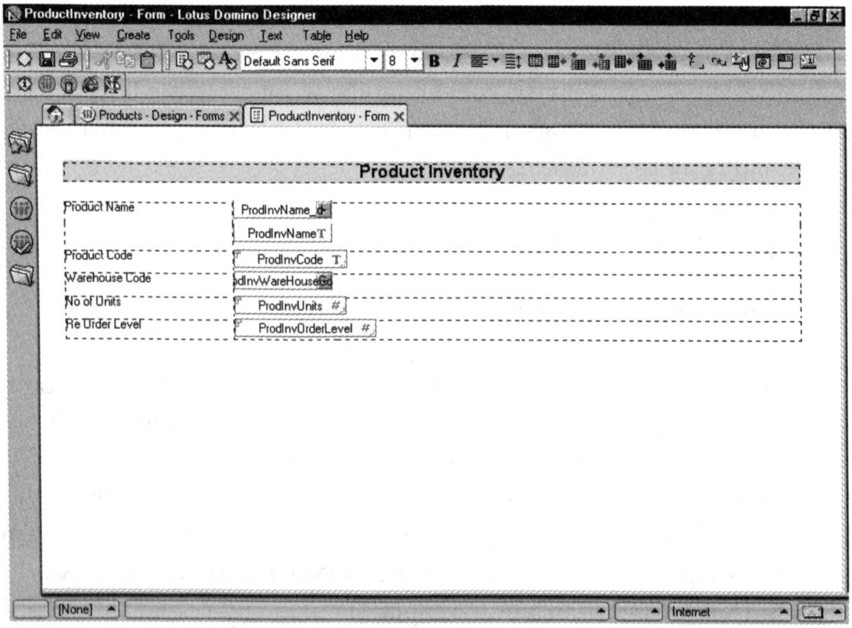

FIGURE 24.25 *The ProductInventory form design*

Creating the InventoryTransaction Form

This form is used to view the inventory transactions created as a result of the order processing. To create this form, perform the following steps:

1. Create a form named **InventoryTransaction**. The rest of the properties of the form remain the same as for the previous forms.
2. Create the header for the form Product Inventory.
3. As in the previous forms, create a 5-by-2 table. In the first column, enter OrderNo, Warehouse Code, Item Code, Item Quantity, Transaction Type, and Status as labels. In the second column, create fields as specified in Table 24.17.

Table 24.17 Fields for InventoryTransaction Form

Field Name	Type	Value
OrderNo	Computed when composed, Text	OrderNo
WareHouseCode	Computed when composed, Text	WareHouseCode
ProductCode	Computed when composed, Text	ProductCode
ProductQuantity	Computed when composed, Text	ProductQuantity
TransactionType	Computed when composed, Text	TransactionType
Status	Computed when composed, Text	Status

The design of the form will look as shown in Figure 24.26.

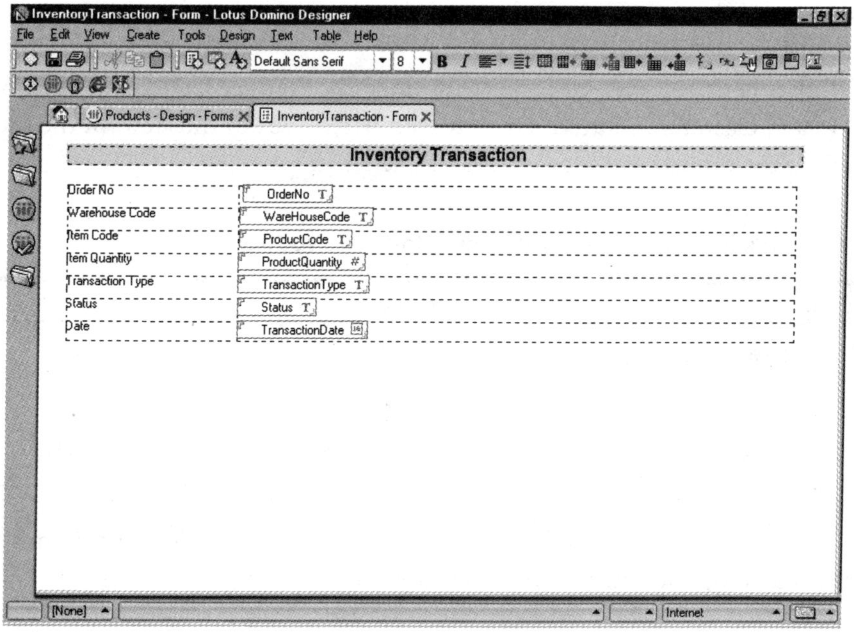

FIGURE 24.26 *The InventoryTransaction form design*

Because this form is used only for display purposes, there are no editable fields on this form. The agent will create the documents in the background when order confirmation happens.

Creating the Views

The Products module has the following views:

- Inventory\By Product Code View
- Inventory\Transactions View
- Products\By Categories View
- Products\By Product Code
- Products\Category Definition View
- WareHouse\By Code View
- (Inventory\ProductWarehouses) View
- (Products\By Product Code Name) View

The following sections detail the steps to create these views.

Creating the Inventory\By Product Code View

Create a new view by the name **Inventory\By Product Code,** and click on the Save and Customize button. Open the Properties box of the view. In the Options tab, set the properties as specified in Table 24.18.

Table 24.18 Properties for the Inventory\By Product View

Property	Value
Default when first opened	Checked
Show response documents in hierarchy	Cleared
Selection formula for the view	SELECT ((Form = "ProductInventory"))

Close the property box and save the view. You can now add the columns to the view based on the column properties listed in Table 24.19.

Table 24.19 Column Values for Inventory\By Product View

Column Title	Value
Product Code	ProdInvCode
Name	ProdInvName
Units	ProdInvUnits
Order Level	ProdInvOrderLevel

Set the property Sort to Ascending for the Product Code column.

Next, you need to add an action to this view to create a new inventory entry for a product. To do so, open the Action pane of the view and select Create/Insert Shared Action. Enter the name as **New Product Inventory** and clear the display options Include in action bar and Include in action menu.

Enter the following formula to the action button's Click event:

```
@Command([Compose];"";"ProductInventory")
```

Save the view.

Creating the Inventory\Transactions View

Create a view by the name **Inventory\Transactions**. Click on the Save and Customize button. In the view's properties box, in the Options tab, set the options as given in Table 24.20.

Table 24.20 Properties for the Inventory\By Product View

Property	Value
Default when first opened	Clear
Show response documents in hierarchy	Clear
Alias name	InventoryTransactions
Selection formula for the view	SELECT ((Form = "InventoryTransaction"))

Close the property box and save the view. Now add the columns listed in Table 24.21 to the view.

Table 24.21 Column Values for Inventory\By Product View

Column Title	Value
Order	OrderNo
WareHouse	WareHouseCode
ItemCode	ItemCode

Set the Sorting property for the column Order to Ascending.

Creating the Products\By Categories View

Create a view named **Products\By Categories**. Set its alias name as **ProductsByCategories** as done earlier. Remember to clear the response hierarchy to improve performance.

Specify the following formula as the selection formula for the view:

```
SELECT ((Form = "Product"))
```

Add the columns given in Table 24.22 to the view.

Table 24.22 Column Values for the Products\By Categories View

Column Number	Column Title	Value
1	None	ProductCategory
2	None	WareHouseCode
3	Product Code	ProductCode
4	Name	ProductName

Set the Sort property for first and second column as Ascending, and check the options Categorized and Show twistie when row is expandable.

Proceeding further, create an action named **New Product** and assign the following formula to the Click event:

```
@Command([Compose];"";"Product")
```

Save the view.

Creating the Products\By Product Code

Create a view named **Products\By Product Code.** Set its alias name as **Products-ByProduct** and clear the response hierarchy option.

Use the following as the selection formula for the view:

```
SELECT ((Form = "Product"))
```

Add the columns given in Table 24.23 to the view.

Table 24.23 Column Values for the Products\By Categories View

Column Number	Column Title	Value
1	Product Code	ProductCode
2	Name	ProductName
3	Quantity	ProductQuantity

Select the Sort property for column 1 as Ascending.

As done earlier, add an action named **New Product** with the following formula:

```
@Command([Compose];"";"Product")
```

Save the view.

Creating the Products\Category Definition View

Create a view with the name **Products\Category Definition** and alias name **Prod-uctsCategoryDefinition.** Use the following as the selection formula for the view:

```
SELECT ((Form = "CategoryDefinition"))
```

Refer to Table 24.24 to add the columns to the view.

Table 24.24 Column Values for the Products\Category Definition View

Column Number	Column Title	Value
1	None	CategoryType
2	Category	CategoryName

Select the Sort option as Ascending and check Categorized for column 1.

Next, create an action to create a new product category. Name the action as **New Category** and attach the following formula to the Click event of the action:

```
@Command([Compose];"";"CategoryDefinition")
```

Creating WareHouse\By Code View

Create a view with the name **WareHouse\By Code** and alias name **WareHouse-ByCode**. Use the following as the selection formula for the view:

```
SELECT ((Form = "Warehouse"))
```

Add the columns given in Table 24.25 to the view.

Table 24.25 Column Values for the WareHouse\By Code View

Column Number	Column Title	Value
1	WareHouse Code	WareHouseCode
2	Person In Charge	WareHouseInCharge
3	Location	WareHouseLocation

Select the Sort option for column 1 as Ascending.

Add an action **New Warehouse** to this view and assign the following formula to its Click event:

```
@Command([Compose];"";"Warehouse")
```

Save the view.

Creating the (Inventory\ProductWarehouses) View

This is a hidden view and will be used to handle programming requirements. Create a view with the name **(Inventory\ProductWarehouses)** and alias name **InventoryProductWarehouses**. Set the selection formula as:

```
SELECT ((Form = "ProductInventory"))
```

Add the columns to the view based on those given in Table 24.26.

Table 24.26 Column Values for the WareHouse\By Code View

Column Number	Column Title	Value
1	Product Code	ProdInvCode
2	Warehouse	ProdInvWareHouseCode

Select the Sort property as Ascending and check Categorized for column 1 and save the view.

Creating the (Products\By Product Code Name) View

This is a hidden view and, as mentioned earlier, will be used to handle any programming requirements. Create a view with the name **(Products\By Product Code Name)** and alias name **ProductsByProductCodeName**. Use the following as the selection formula for the view:

```
SELECT ((Form = "Product"))
```

This view will be used as a lookup view for the products with a combined key of product code and product name. Both values are combined together to retrieve the product name and code in a single lookup. This will improve the performance by reducing the number of lookups that are to be made from various forms and programs.

Create one column with a column title of **Product Code Name** and column value with the following formula:

```
ProductName +" - " + ProductCode
```

Select the Sort property for the column as Ascending.

NOTE

Although a title is not required for a hidden view, assign one to improve the readability and help with further maintenance of the application.

Creating the Outline

Create an outline named **ProductsOutline** as done earlier.

> **NOTE**
>
> Domino Designer generates the outline using the folders and views available in the current database.

The outline might look as shown in Figure 24.27.

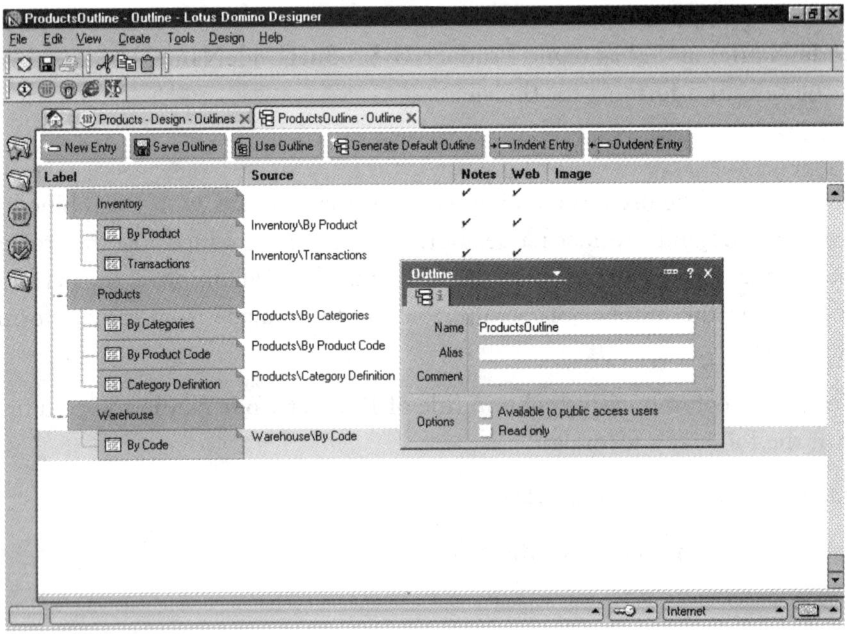

FIGURE 24.27 *The ProductsOutline outline*

Save the outline.

Creating the ProductsNavPage

The Products database will contain a page to embed the outline ProductsOutline. Perform the following steps to create this page:

1. Create a Page and open the Page Properties dialog box.
2. In the Name box, enter **ProductsNavPage.**
3. In the Background tab, select the background color 245,239,206.
4. Choose Create/ Embedded Element/Outline, and select ProductsOutline as the outline to be embedded.
5. Open the Embedded Outline properties box. Set the properties of the outline as specified in Table 24.27.

Table 24.27 Embedded Outline Properties

Property	Value
Property	Fit to window
Top level font	Size 8 Bold
Sublevel font	Size 8 Plain

Save the outline and preview in the Web browser. The page will appear as shown in Figure 24.28.

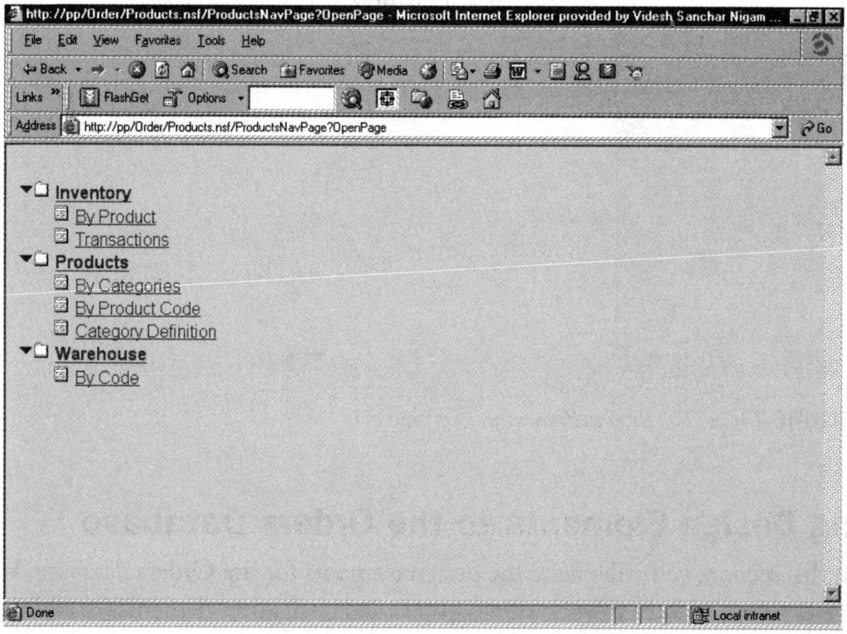

FIGURE 24.28 *The Products navigation page*

Creating the Navigational Elements

To complete the navigational framework of the Products database, you need to add the appropriate pages to the ProductsFrameset frameset. Perform the following steps to achieve this:

1. Open the ProductsFrameset frameset.
2. In the property box for the frame Nav, set the page **ProductsNavPage** as the content for the page.
3. In the property box of the Content frame, set the view **Inventory\By Product Code** as the content for the frame.

Preview the frameset in Internet Explorer. The frameset appears as shown in Figure 24.29.

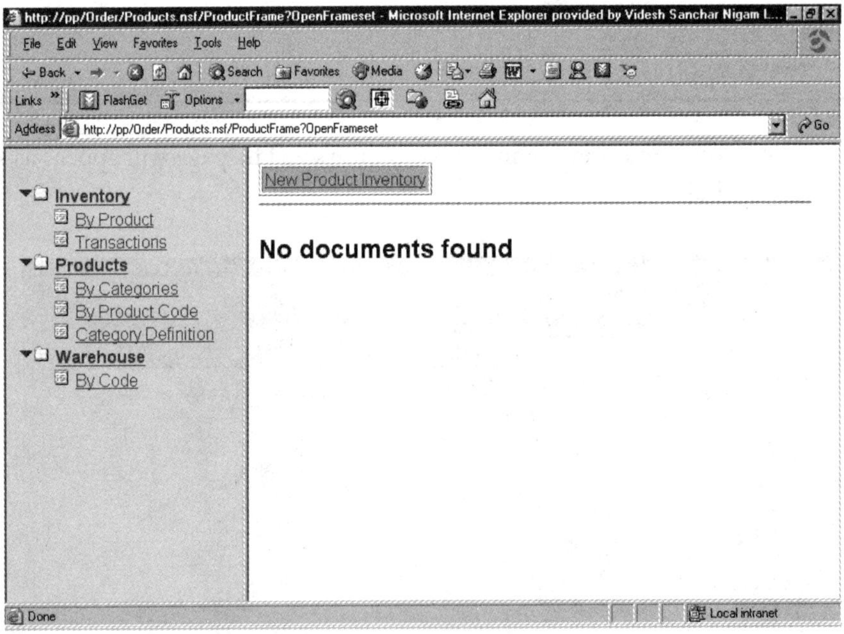

FIGURE 24.29 *The ProductFrame frameset preview*

Adding Design Elements to the Orders Database

In this section, you will create the design elements for the Orders database. You will create forms, actions, views, outlines, pages, and navigation elements. In addition, you will create various agents to implement certain functional features of the system.

Creating the Forms

The Orders database contains two forms, Order and Invoice. The Order form is used to capture the orders placed by users, and the Invoice form is used to display the invoice generated once the order is processed. In addition, the database contains two subforms, which are used in these forms. You will start with the creation of the subforms.

Creating the OrderRequestDisplay Subform

This subform is used to display the order details to the approver. An order can contain five items. To achieve this in a single form, five sets of similar fields are used.

TIP

An alternate is to create a single document per item details, but this will result in an increase of the number of documents. Another approach is to create fields, which contain the line item details as multi-valued fields. But, this will require more programming effort to manage the add, update, and delete functionality for line items.

Create a subform by name **OrderRequestDisplay** in the Orders database and lay out the fields listed in Table 24.28 in a tabular format.

Table 24.28 Fields for OrderRequestDisplay Form

Field Name	Type	Value
ItemRequest1	Computed when composed, Text	ItemRequest1
QtyRequest1	Computed when composed, Number	QtyRequest1
UnitPriceRequest1	Computed when composed, Number	UnitPriceRequest1
TotalPriceRequest1	Computed when composed, Number	TotalPriceRequest1
ItemRequest2	Computed when composed, Number	ItemRequest2
QtyRequest2	Computed when composed, Text	QtyRequest2
UnitPriceRequest2	Computed when composed, Number	UnitPriceRequest2

(continues)

Table 24.28 Continued

Field Name	Type	Value
TotalPriceRequest2	Computed when composed, Number	TotalPriceRequest2
ItemRequest3	Computed when composed, Number	ItemRequest3
QtyRequest3	Computed when composed, Text	QtyRequest3
UnitPriceRequest3	Computed when composed, Number	UnitPriceRequest3
TotalPriceRequest3	Computed when composed, Number	TotalPriceRequest3
ItemRequest4	Computed when composed, Number	ItemRequest4
QtyRequest4	Computed when composed, Text	QtyRequest4
UnitPriceRequest4	Computed when composed, Number	UnitPriceRequest4
TotalPriceRequest4	Computed when composed, Number	TotalPriceRequest4
ItemRequest5	Computed when composed, Number	ItemRequest5
QtyRequest5	Computed when composed, Text	QtyRequest5
UnitPriceRequest5	Computed when composed, Number	UnitPriceRequest5
TotalPriceRequest5	Computed when composed, Number	TotalPriceRequest5
TotalPrice	Computed, Number	nil

Enter the following formula as the value for the field TotalPrice:

```
TotalPriceRequest1+TotalPriceRequest+TotalPriceRequest3
+TotalPriceRequest4+TotalPriceRequest5
```

Save the subform.

In Designer, the subform will appear as shown in Figure 24.30.

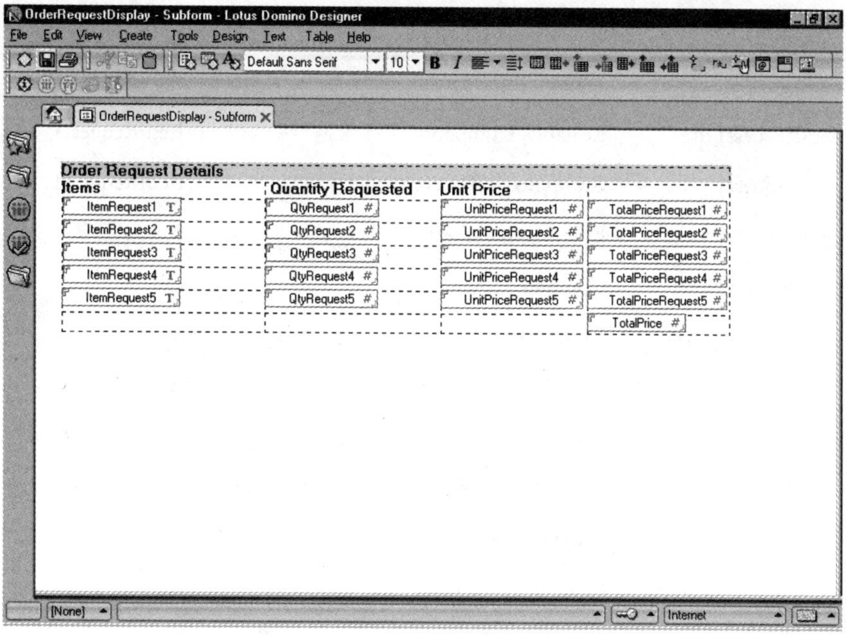

FIGURE 24.30 *OrderRequestDisplay subform design*

Creating the OrderRequestEditable Subform

This subform is used to display the order request section in an editable format. This subform is similar to the OrderRequestDisplay subform. Therefore, instead of creating a new form, copy the OrderRequestDisplay subform and paste it in the Orders database. Change its name to **OrderRequestEditable** and add the editable fields to the subform and change the properties of the existing fields to that listed in Table 24.29.

Create a hidden multi-valued text field by name **ItemRequestLookup**. Enter the following formula in the value event for the field:

```
view:= "ProductsByProductCodeName";
@Repeat("-";10):@DbColumn("";"":"order\\Products.nsf";view;1)
```

The above formula returns the list of product code and names, which will be a text list. Each element in the list will contain the product code and the product name separated by hyphen (-). The first element in the list is a string, hyphen (-), so that by default no product is selected.

Create the fields as listed in Table 24.29.

Table 24.29 Fields for OrderRequestEditable Form

Field Name	Type	Value
ItemRequest1_d	Editable, Combobox	ItemRequest1_d
ItemRequest1	Computed when composed, Combobox	ItemRequest1
QtyRequest1	Editable, Number	0
UnitPriceRequest1	Computed, Number	nil
TotalPriceRequest1	Computed, Number	nil
ItemNo1	Computed when composed, Text	ItemNo1
ItemRequest2_d	Editable, Combobox	ItemRequest2_d
ItemRequest2	Computed when composed, Combobox	ItemRequest2
QtyRequest2	Editable, Number	0
UnitPriceRequest2	Computed, Number	nil
TotalPriceRequest2	Computed, Number	nil
ItemNo2	Computed when composed, Text	ItemNo2
ItemRequest3_d	Editable, Combobox	ItemRequest3_d
ItemRequest3	Computed when composed, Combobox	ItemRequest3
QtyRequest3	Editable, Number	0
UnitPriceRequest3	Computed, Number	nil
TotalPriceRequest3	Computed, Number	nil
ItemNo3	Computed when composed, Text	ItemNo3
ItemRequest4_d	Editable, Combobox	ItemRequest4_d
ItemRequest4	Computed when composed, Combobox	ItemRequest4
QtyRequest4	Editable, Number	0
UnitPriceRequest4	Computed, Number	nil
TotalPriceRequest4	Computed, Number	nil
ItemNo4	Computed when composed, Text	ItemNo4
ItemRequest5_d	Editable, Combobox	ItemRequest5_d
ItemRequest5	Computed when composed, Combobox	ItemRequest5

Field Name	Type	Value
QtyRequest5	Editable, Number	0
UnitPriceRequest5	Computed, Number	nil
TotalPriceRequest5	Computed, Number	nil
ItemNo5	Computed when composed, Text	ItemNo5
TotalPrice	Computed, Number	nil

Now, enable the ItemRequest_d fields for product code and product name selection. To achieve this, perform the following steps:

1. In the control tab of the field property of the field ItemRequest1_d, check the option Refresh fields on keyword change. In the Choices section, select Use formula for choices and enter the following formula in the choice formula window:

   ```
   ItemRequestLookup
   ```

2. In the Input Translation event of field ItemRequest1_d, enter the following formula:

   ```
   FIELD ItemRequest1:=@Trim(@Left(@ThisValue;"-"));
   FIELD ItemNo1:= @Trim(@Right(@ThisValue;"-"));
   @ThisValue
   ```

   The above formula extracts the product code and product name from the selected value in the ItemRequest1_d field and assign them to individual fields. The value of the field is ItemRequest1_d is not altered.

3. Repeat the preceding steps 1 and 2 for the rest of the ItemRequest_d fields by changing the field suffix value to match the field suffix of the item line number.

   ```
   Enter the following formula as the value for UnitPriceRequest1 field:
   ProductsDb:="Order\\Products.nsf";
   view:="Products\\By Product Code";
   UnitPrice:=@DbLookup("";"":ProductsDb;view;ItemNo1;"ProductUnitPrice");
   @If(@IsError(UnitPrice);0;UnitPrice)
   ```

The above formula fetches the unit price for the selected product from the products database. Enter the above formula for rest of the UnitPriceRequest fields by changing the field suffix numbers to match the item line number.

For the TotalPriceRequest1 field, enter the following formula as their value:

```
UnitPriceRequest1*QtyRequest1
```

Enter the above formula for rest of the TotalPriceRequest fields by appropriately changing the field suffix number.

CAUTION

When entering the formulas shown above, make sure you change the suffix number to match the corresponding line item number.

Enter the following formula as the value for the field TotalPrice:

```
TotalPriceRequest1+TotalPriceRequest+TotalPriceRequest3
+TotalPriceRequest4+TotalPriceRequest5
```

Save the subform. The subform should look as shown in the Figure 24.31.

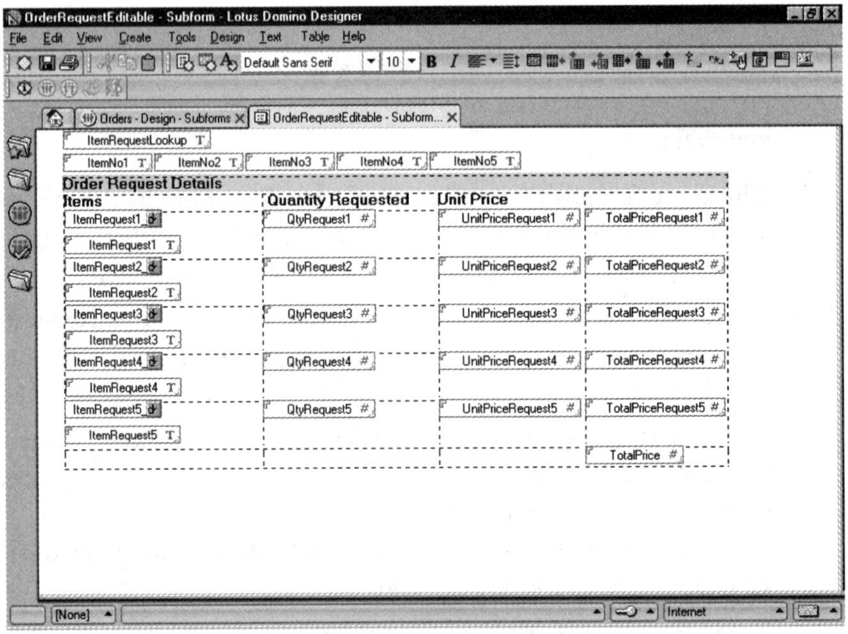

FIGURE 24.31 *The OrderRequestEditable subform design*

Creating the OrderFulfillment Subform

This is a subform to display the order fulfillment section during the order approval process. Create a new subform and assign the name **OrderFulfillment**. Create the fields on this subform as listed in Table 24.30.

At the top of the form, create a hidden multi-valued computed text field by name **WarehouseLookup**. Enter the following formula as the value for the field:

```
view:="Inventory\\ProductWarehouses";
db:="Order\\Products.nsf";
WareHouseList := @DbLookup(""; "":db; view; ItemNo1;2);
@If( @IsError(WareHouseList); "Not Available"; WareHouseList)
```

Now in each of the fields, Warehouse1 to Warehouse5, in the Choices section of the field property, select Use formula for choices and in the choices formula window, enter:

```
WarehouseLookup
```

Table 24.30 Fields for OrderFulfillment Form

Field Name	Type	Value
ItemIssued1	Computed, Text	ItemRequest1
Warehouse1	Editable, Combobox	Warehouse1
QtyIssued1	Editable, Number	0
UnitPriceRequest1_d	Computed for display, Number	UnitPriceRequest1
TotalPriceIssued1	Computed, Number	QtyIssued1 * UnitPriceRequest1
ItemIssued2	Computed , Text	ItemRequest2
Warehouse2	Editable, Combobox	Warehouse2
QtyIssued2	Editable, Number	0
UnitPriceRequest2_d	Computed for display, Number	UnitPriceRequest2
TotalPriceIssued2	Computed, Number	QtyIssued2 * UnitPriceRequest2
ItemIssued3	Computed, Text	ItemRequest3
Warehouse3	Editable, Combobox	Warehouse3

(continues)

Table 24.30 Continued

Field Name	Type	Value
QtyIssued3	Editable, Number	0
UnitPriceRequest3_d	Computed for display, Number	UnitPriceRequest3
TotalPriceIssued3	Computed, Number	QtyIssued3 * UnitPriceRequest3
ItemIssued4	Computed, Text	ItemRequest4
Warehouse4	Editable, Combobox	Warehouse4
QtyIssued4	Editable, Number	0
UnitPriceRequest4_d	Computed for display, Number	UnitPriceRequest4
TotalPriceIssued4	Computed, Number	QtyIssued4 * UnitPriceRequest4
ItemIssued5	Computed, Text	ItemRequest5
Warehouse5	Editable, Combobox	Warehouse5
QtyIssued5	Editable, Number	0
UnitPriceRequest5_d	Computed for display, Number	UnitPriceRequest5
TotalPriceIssued5	Computed, Number	QtyIssued5 * UnitPriceRequest5
TotalPriceIssue	Computed, Number	nil

For the TotalPriceIssue field, enter the following formula as the value:

```
TotalPriceIssued1+TotalPriceIssued2+TotalPriceIssued3+
TotalPriceIssued4+TotalPriceIssued5
```

Save the subform. In the Designer, the subform should appear as shown in Figure 24.32.

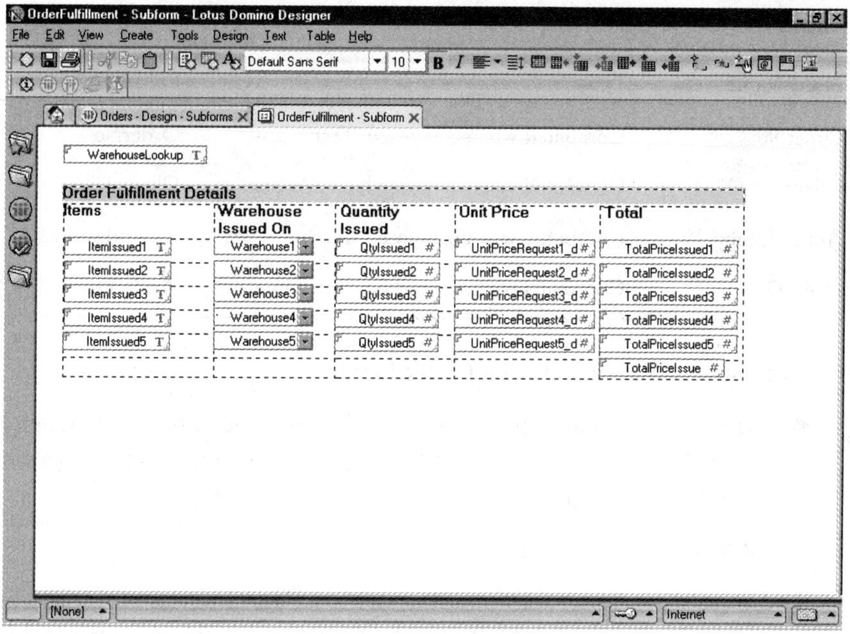

FIGURE 24.32 *The OrderFulfillment subform design*

Creating the Order Form

Users will access this form to place an order. In a single order form, a user can order five items. Create a form and set its properties as given in Table 24.31.

Table 24.31 Properties for Order Form

Property	Value
Name	Order
Include in menu	Clear
Include in search	Clear

Leave rest of the properties to their default values.

Create the header for the form as `Order`. As in the previous forms, create a 5-by-2 table. In the first column, enter Order No, Client, Authorized By, Order Date, and Order Status as labels. In the second column, create fields as listed in Table 24.32.

Table 24.32 Fields for the Order Form

Field Name	Type	Value
OrderNo	Computed when composed, Text	OrderNo
Client	Computed when composed, Combobox	Client
Authorizedby	Computed when composed, Text	Authorizedby
OrderDate	Computed when composed, DateTime	OrderDate

Add the following actions to the Order form:

- **Edit.** Create an action button named Edit. Check the Hide when properties Previewed and Opened for Editing. Enter the following formula in the Click event of the action:

  ```
  @Command([EditDocument])
  ```

- **Cancel.** Create an action button named Cancel. Clear all Hide when properties because this action will always be visible. Enter the following formula in the Click event of the action:

  ```
  @Command([FileCloseWindow])
  ```

- **Approve.** Create an action button named Approve and enter the following formula in the Click event of the action:

  ```
  @SetField("OrderStatus";"Approved");
  @Command([FileSave]);
  @Command([FileCloseWindow])
  ```

  In the Hide when properties, check Hide paragraph if formula is true. Enter the following formula in the Hide when formula window:

  ```
  OrderStatus !="Awaits Approval"
  ```

- **Reject.** Create an action button named Reject. Enter the following formula in the Click event of the action:

  ```
  @SetField("OrderStatus";"Rejected");
  @Command([FileSave]);
  @Command([FileCloseWindow])
  ```

In the Hide when properties, check Hide paragraph if formula is true. Enter the following formula in the Hide when formula window:

```
OrderStatus !=" Awaits Approval "
```

- **Submit.** Create an action button named Submit. Enter the following formula in the Click event of the action:

  ```
  @SetField("OrderStatus";"Awaits Approval");
  @Command([FileSave])
  ```

  In the Hide when properties, check Hide paragraph if formula is true. Enter the following formula in the Hide when formula window:

  ```
  OrderStatus !="New"
  ```

- **Generate Invoice.** Create an action button named Generate Invoice. Enter the following formula in the Click event of the action:

  ```
  @Command([Compose];"";"Invoice")
  ```

  In the Hide when properties, check Hide paragraph if formula is true. Enter the following formula in the Hide when formula window:

  ```
  OrderStatus !="Approved"
  ```

In the Client form, `$$Return` was used to send an HTML message to the browser when the form is submitted. In this form, the `$$Return` is used to redirect to a default view. To achieve this, perform the following steps:

1. Insert a field in the top of the form and name the field $$Return. Select the type as Text and Computed.
2. In the Hide Paragraph from section of the Hide When tab of the property box, check all the options to keep this field hidden.
3. In the value for the field, enter the following formula:

   ```
   DB := @ReplaceSubstring(@ReplaceSubstring(@Subset(@DbName; -1);
   " "; "+"); "\\"; "/");
   View:="WareHouseByCode";
   "[/"+DB+"/"+View+"]"
   ```

The above formula assembles the URL that will take the user to the view WareHouseByCode, which is in the current database.

Next, you need to add agents associated with the `WebQueryOpen` and `WebQuerySave` events. In addition, you need to create computed subforms to decide whether the order request section should be presented in the edit or read mode. Perform the steps specified in the following section to achieve all of this.

Creating Computed Subforms

Create two computed subforms to be loaded. The first one displays the order request section in the editable or display format as follows:

```
@If(OrderStatus="New";"OrderRequestEditable";"OrderRequestDisplay")
```

The second one hides the Approvers section:

```
@If(OrderStatus="New";"";"OrderFullfillment")
```

The above formulas will insert the appropriate subforms based on the order status. The order form in Designer should look as shown in Figure 24.33.

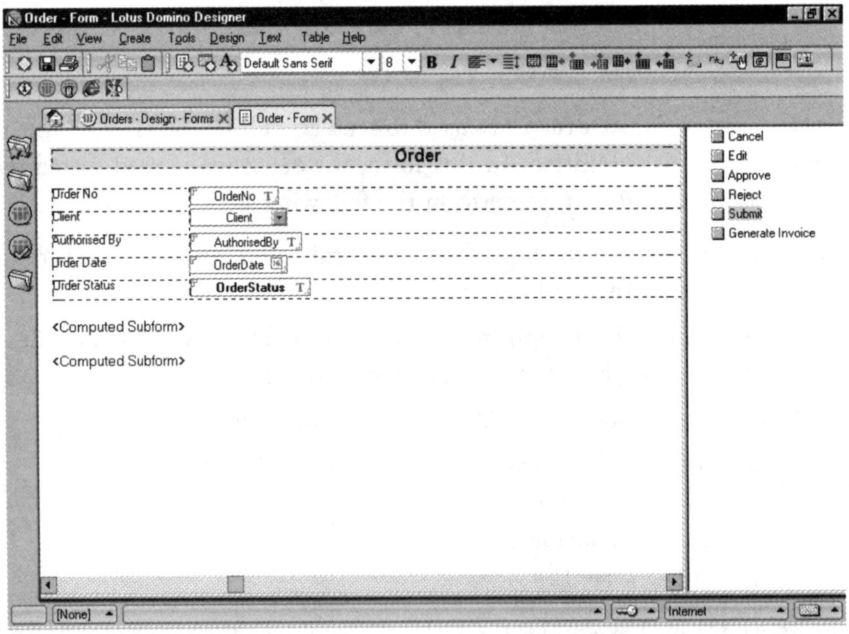

FIGURE 24.33 *Order form design*

Attaching Agents with the WebQueryOpen Event

To generate the order number automatically, an agent is necessary. Unlike the other agents, you will code this agent in Java. Associate this agent with the form by entering the following formula in the `WebQueryOpen` event of the Order form:

```
@Command([ToolsRunMacro]; "(WebQryOpenOrder)")
```

Now create an agent named **WebQryOpenOrder**. In the options select Shared, for Trigger, select On event and Agent list selection, and select Target as None.

In the Run option, select Java and enter the following code:

```
import lotus.domino.*;
public class JavaAgent extends AgentBase {

 public void NotesMain() {

    try {
          Session session = getSession();
          AgentContext agentContext = session.getAgentContext();
          //get the current database
          Database db = agentContext.getCurrentDatabase();
          //get the document context
          Document doc = agentContext.getDocumentContext();
          if (doc.isNewNote()){
             //get the order no view
             View view = db.getView("OrdersByOrderNo");
             //get the last order doc from the sorted view
             Document lastorderdoc = view.getLastDocument();
             String nextOrderno = "1";
             if (lastorderdoc != null) {
                //get the order number of the last order
                //increment it by one and assign it to the current order
                  Double lastOrderno =
Double.valueOf(lastorderdoc.getItemValueString("OrderNo"));
                nextOrderno = Double.toString(lastOrderno.doubleValue() + 1);
                doc.replaceItemValue("OrderNo",
 nextOrderno.substring(0,nextOrderno.lastIndexOf(".")));
             }
            else{
```

```
                    //this is the first order
                    doc.replaceItemValue("OrderNo", nextOrderno);
                } //lastorderdoc
            } //doc isNewNote
    } catch(Exception e) {
            e.printStackTrace();
        }
 }
}
```

Save the agent. The above code gets the last document from the Orders\By No view, the first column of which is sorted in the ascending order of the order number. Then, the order number from the last document is incremented by one and assigned to the new document.

Attaching an Agent with the WebQuerySave Event

When the order is approved, the inventory transaction is created. To do this, an agent needs to be associated with the `WebQuerySave` event of the Order form. Do so by entering the following formula in the `WebQuerySave` event:

```
@Command([ToolsRunMacro]; " WebQrySaveOrder")
```

Now create an agent named `WebQrySaveOrder`. Set the agent properties as explained for the WebQueryOpen event agent. From the Run option select Lotus Script and enter the following code in the Initialize event of the agent:

```
Sub Initialize
  Dim session As New NotesSession
  Dim productsDb As NotesDatabase
  Dim view As NotesView
  Dim invview As NotesView
  Dim doc As NotesDocument
  Dim transacdoc As NotesDocument
  Dim invdoc As NotesDocument

  Set doc = session.DocumentContext
  If doc.OrderStatus(0) = "Approved" Then
    'The order has been approved
    'connect to the Product database
```

```
Set productsDb = session.GetDatabase("","Order\Products.nsf")
If Not ( productsDb Is Nothing ) And productsDb.IsOpen Then
   'Print "Opened database"
   Print "<H3>Processing Details for the_
      Approved Order Number - " +doc.OrderNo(0) +"</H3>"
   Print "<BR>"
   Set invview = productsDb.GetView("InventoryByProductCode")
   For i = 1 To 5
      itemno = doc.GetItemValue("ItemNo"+Cstr(i))(0)
      If ( itemno <> "" ) Then
      'get the issued quantity for this line item
      QtyIssued = Cdbl(doc.GetItemValue("QtyIssued"+Cstr(i))(0))
      Print "Processing item " + Cstr(i) +_
          " Item Code " + itemno + " Issued qty " + Cstr(QtyIssued)
      Print "<BR>"
      'deduct from the inventory
      Set invdoc = invview.GetDocumentByKey(itemno)
      'check if stock entry present
      If Not (invdoc Is Nothing) Then
        'check if there is sufficient stock
        AvailableStock = Cdbl(invdoc.ProdInvUnits(0))
        If ( ( AvailableStock - QtyIssued )< 0 ) Then
           'issued more quantity than available in stock
           Print "Order Processing Failed for_
                 item " +Cstr(i) +
                 " - Insufficient stock_for the Item Code "
                 +itemno
           Print "<BR>"
        Else
           'reduce the inventory level by issued quantity
           invdoc.ProdInvUnits = AvailableStock - QtyIssued
           Call invdoc.save(True,False)
           'Succesful transaction
           'create the invetory transaction document
           Set transacdoc = productsDb.CreateDocument()
           transacdoc.OrderNo = doc.OrderNo
           transacdoc.WareHouseCode = doc.GetItemValue("Warehouse"+Cstr(i))
           transacdoc.ProductCode = itemno
```

```
                transacdoc.ProductQuantity =
                      doc.GetItemValue("QtyIssued"+Cstr(i))
                transacdoc.TransactionType =  "OrderDispatch"
                transacdoc.Status= "Active"
                transacdoc.TransactionDate= doc.GetItemValue("ItemNo"+Cstr(i))
                transacdoc.Form = "InventoryTransaction"
                Call transacdoc.Save(True,False)
                Print "Inventory Transaction created"
                Print "<BR>"
             End If 'end stock checking
             Else
             'could not locate the inventory entry doc for this product
                Print "Order Processing Failed_
                   - stock entry for the item _
                     code "+itemno + " not found"
                Print "<BR>"
             End If 'end invdoc isnothing
           End If' end itemno <> ""
        Next 'process next line item
        doc.OrderStatus = "Processed"
        Print "<BR>"
        Print "<B>Order Processing completed</B>"
     End If
   Else
     If doc.OrderStatus(0) = "Rejected" Then
        Print "<BR><BR><BR><BR>"
        Print "<H2> Order Rejected</H2>"
     Else
        'this is a new order
        Print "<H1> Order Saved </H1>"
        Print "<H2> Thank you for placing the order with us</H2>"
        Print "<Br> Your order is placed for approval._
              Your Order Number is -" + doc.OrderNo(0) +"</Br>"
     End If
   End If 'order = approved
End Sub
```

The above agent processes each line item in the order during the order approval process. For each line item processed, it checks if enough stock is available. If available, it adjusts the stock quantity and creates an inventory transaction document for that line item. The agent also shows how you can dynamically create formatted HTML and send it to browser.

Creating the Invoice Form

This form is used generate the invoice from the processed order. The actual layout would be more complicated and intrinsic for a real world invoice document. One chosen here is a simple layout to demonstrate the coding in generating such a document.

Create a form named Invoice and lay out the form as shown in Figure 24.34. To set the field properties, refer to Table 24.33.

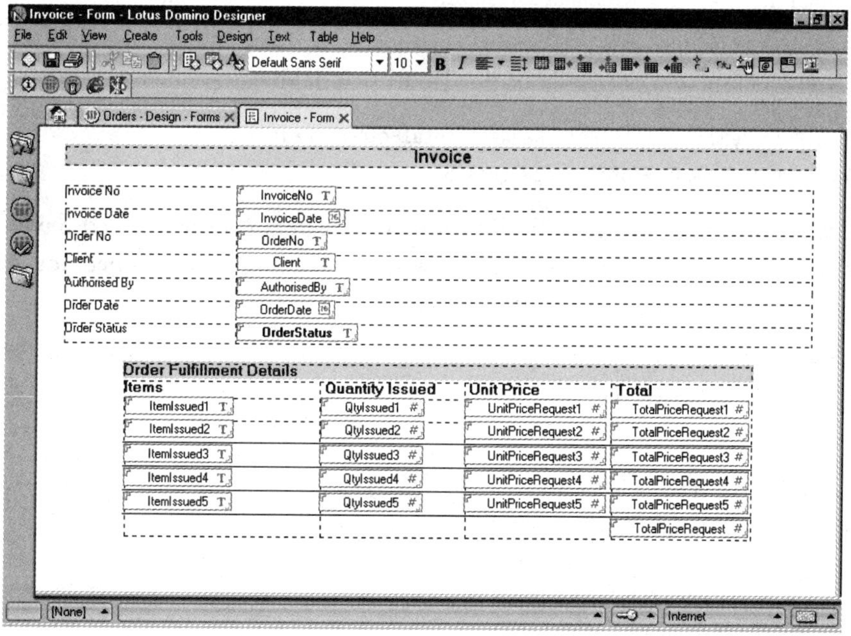

FIGURE 24.34 *The Invoice form design*

Table 24.33 Fields for the Invoice Form

Field Name	Type	Value
OrderNo	Computed when composed, Text	OrderNo
Client	Computed when composed, Combobox	Client
AuthorizedBy	Computed when composed, Text	AuthorizedBy
OrderDate	Computed when composed, Date	OrderDate
ItemRequest1	Computed when composed, Text	ItemRequest1
QtyIssued1	Computed when composed, Number	QtyIssued1
UnitPriceRequest1	Computed when composed, Number	UnitPriceRequest1
TotalPriceRequest1	Computed when composed, Number	UnitPriceRequest1* QtyIssued1
TotalPrice	Computed, Number	nil

Enter the following formula in the TotalPrice field value:

```
TotalPriceRequest1+TotalPriceRequest+TotalPriceRequest3+
Total PriceRequest4+TotalPriceRequest5
```

Create an action for saving the document. Create an action named **Save.** In the Hide when properties, check Previewed for reading and Opened for reading. Enter the following formula in the Click event of the action:

```
@Command([FileSave]);
@Command([FileCloseWindow])
```

Creating the Views

The Orders database contains the following views:

- Invoice\By Order No
- Orders\ By Client
- Orders\By No
- Orders\By Order Date
- Orders\By Status

To create the views, perform the steps outlined in the following sections.

Creating the Invoice\By Order No View

Create a view named **Invoice\By Order No** and specify its alias as **InvoiceBy-OrderNo.** In the selection formula for the view, enter the following formula:

```
SELECT ((Form = "Invoice"))
```

Save the view. Add the columns to the view as specified in Table 24.34.

Table 24.34 Columns for the Invoice\By Order No View

Column Number	Column Title	Column Value
1	By Order No	ProdInvCode
2	Client	Client
3	Order Date	OrderDate

Select the property Sort for column 1 as Ascending.

Creating the Orders\By Client View

Create a view named **Orders\By Client.** Set the alias name for this view to **OrdersByClient.**

In the selection formula for the view, enter the following formula:

```
SELECT ((Form = "Order"))
```

Save the view and add the columns as specified in Table 24.35.

Table 24.35 Columns for the Orders\By Client View

Column Number	Column Title	Column Value
1	Client	Client
2	Order No	Order No
3	Status	OrderStatus

Select the Sort property for column 1 as Ascending and check the Categorized option check Show twistie when row is expandable.

In this view, insert the shared action New Order, and in the click event of the action enter the following formula:

```
@Command([Compose];"Order")
```

Save the view.

Creating the Orders\By No View

Create a view named **Orders\By No** and enter the alias for the view as **Orders-ByOrderNo**. In the selection formula for the view, enter the following formula:

```
SELECT ((Form = "Order"))
```

Save the view and add the columns specified in Table 24.36.

Table 24.36 Columns for the Orders\By No View

Column Number	Column Title	Column Value
1	Order No	OrderNo
2	Status	OrderStatus
3	Client	Client

Set the property Sort to Ascending for column one.

> **TIP**
>
> Notice that this view is very similar to the previous one and can be created easily by swapping the columns. If you do so, remove the categorization on the Client Name.

In this view, insert the shared action New Order, as explained for the earlier view.

Creating the Orders\By Status View

Create a view named **Orders\By Status**. Enter the alias name for this view as **OrdersByStatus**. In the selection formula for the view, enter the following formula:

```
SELECT ((Form = "Order"))
```

Refer to Table 24.37 to add the columns to the view.

Table 24.37 Columns for the Orders\By Status No View

Column Number	Column Title	Column Value
1	None	OrderStatus
2	Client	Client
3	OrderNo	OrderNo

For Column 1, set the Sorting property as Ascending and type as Categorized.

TIP

This view can also be easily created by cutting, pasting, and swapping the columns.

Creating the Orders\By Order Date View

Create a view named **Orders\By Order Date** by copying and pasting the previous view. Remove the categorization for the first column and the alias name for the view. Arrange the columns to the view as specified in Table 24.38.

Table 24.38 Columns for the Orders\By Order Date View

Column Number	Column Title	Column Value
1	Order Date	OrderDate
2	Order No	OrderNo
3	Status	Status
4	Client	Client

For Column 1, set the Sorting property as Ascending.

Creating the Outline

To create the navigational features for the Orders database, you need to create an outline. You can create the outline easily by setting the Notes Designer to generate the outline entries automatically.

Go to the Outline design view and click the New Outline button. Then click the Generate Default Outline button. Designer generates the outline using the folders and the view pane. The outline might appear as shown in Figure 24.35. Save the outline by the name **OrdersOutline**.

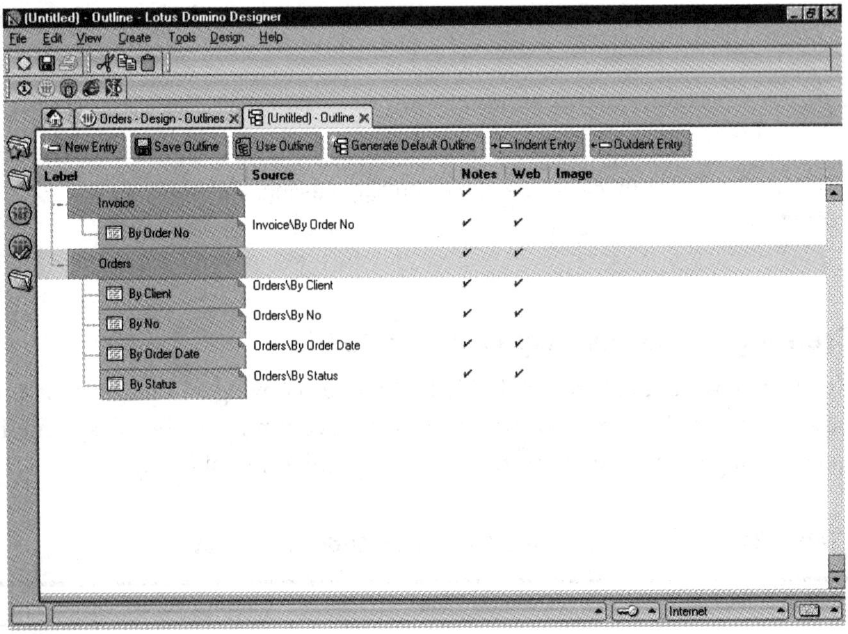

FIGURE 24.35 *The OrdersOutline outline*

Creating the OrderNavPage Page

The Orders database will contain one more page in addition to the already created BannerPage. The page OrderNavPage will embed the OrderOutline outline. Create a new page by name **OrderNavPage**. Perform the same steps explained for creating the ProductsNavPage to embed the outline, but by selecting the OrderOutline.

This page, when previewed in a Web browser, will appear as shown in Figure 24.36.

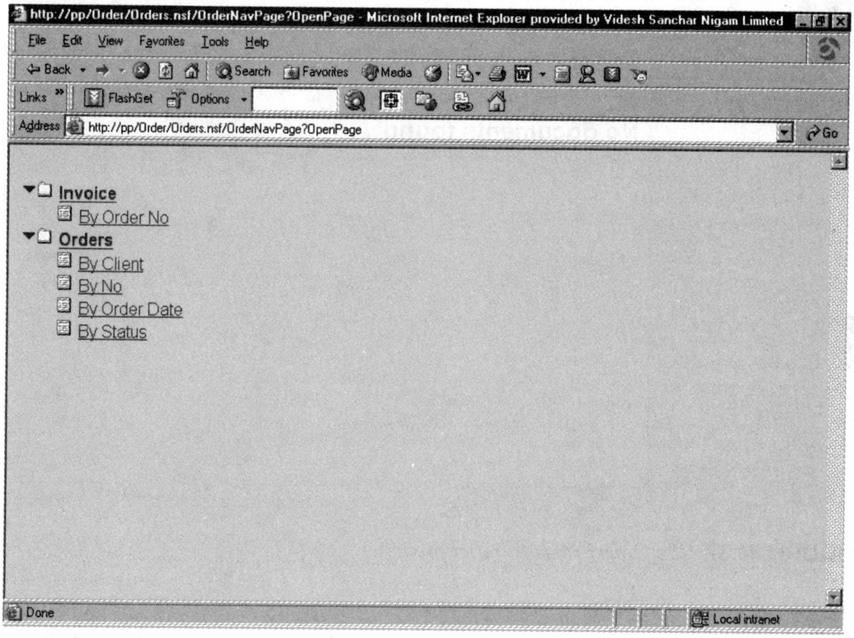

FIGURE 24.36 *The OrderNavPage page preview*

Creating the Navigational Elements

To complete the navigational framework of the Orders database, you need to add the appropriate pages to the OrderFrameset frameset. To do this, perform the following steps:

1. Open the OrderFrameset frameset.
2. In the property box for the frame Nav, set the page OrdersNavPage as the content for the page.
3. In the property box of the Content frame, set the view Orders\By No as the content for the frame.

This frameset, when previewed, will appear as shown in Figure 24.37.

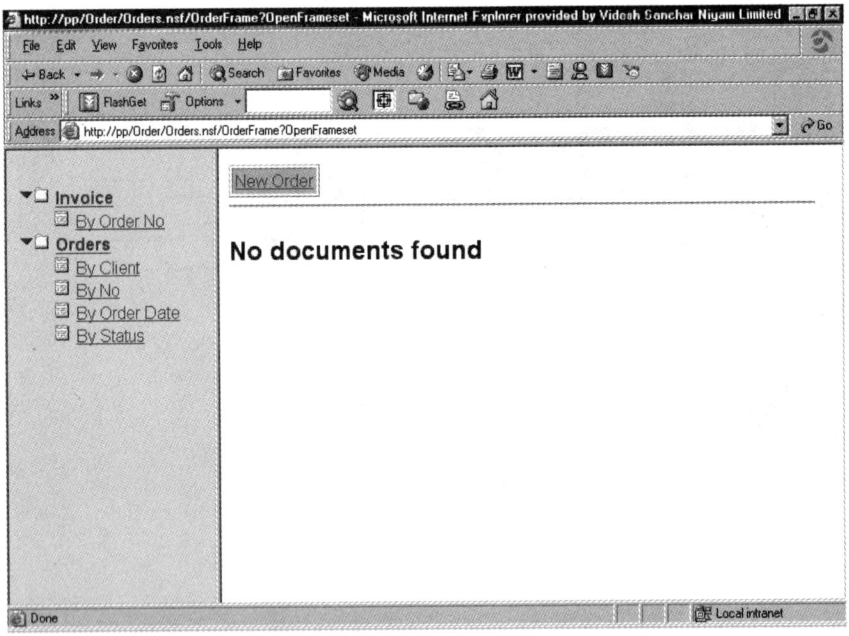

FIGURE 24.37 *The OrderFrame frameset preview*

Now open the MainFrameSet frameset. For the bottom frame, set the content as the OrderFrame frameset. Now, set MainFrameSet frameset as the home page for the database by setting the launch property when opened in browser option of the database property for the Orders database.

Now you have completed the basic framework of the application with the necessary navigational elements. If you open the application using the home URL of the application `http://pp/Order/Orders.nsf`, the MainFrameset frameset should automatically open as shown in Figure 24.38. In the URL, replace `pp` with the server host name.

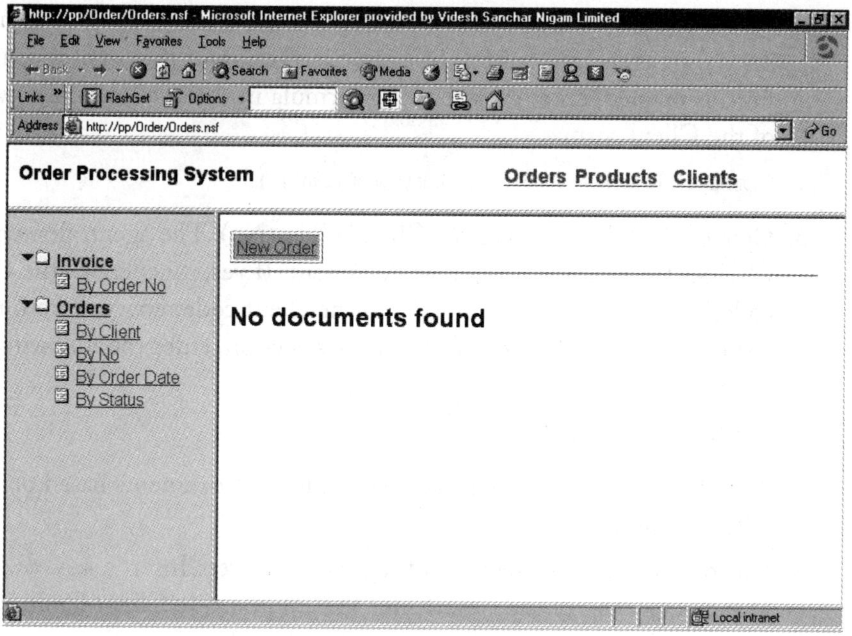

FIGURE 24.38 *The first screen of the application*

Enhancing the Order Processing System

In this section, you will learn to add more functionality to the online order processing application to enhance it further. Here, you will add code to identify clients and products. You'll add validations to check whether or not the client name and product category already exist.

Generating Client Code

In this section, you will add the code to generate unique client codes. Assuming that a single person creates the client documents, you can generate these codes when the form is opened for creation. If the documents have to be created by different persons at the same time, it would be safe to generate these codes when the document is saved. To generate the client code, perform the following steps:

1. Add a new field to the client form. Insert a new row on top of the first table, which contains the fields, and in the first column, type in the label **Client Code**. Create a new Editable, Text field with the name **ClientCode** and value as the field name.

2. To generate the unique client code during the creation of new documents, an agent is required. To enable triggering of the agent when the form is opened, enter the following formula in the `WebQueryOpen` event of the Client form:

```
@Command([ToolsRunMacro]; "(WebQryOpenClient)")
```

3. Create a hidden view named **(Client\ClientNo)**. The agent, first checks whether the document is a new document. If yes, it generates the client code. To do this, you add one (1) to the client code retrieved from the last document in the view. In the view selection, enter the following formula:

```
SELECT Form = "Client"
```

The above formula is used to display only the documents based on the Client form in the view.

4. Customize the view created in the preceding step. Insert a new column at the beginning of the view. Enter the column title **Client Code** and in the second tab of the column property, select the sort option as Ascending. In the column value window, select Field against Display. Select the field named **ClientCode** from the available list of fields. Save and close the view.

5. Create a new agent named **WebQryOpenClient**. Select On event, Agent list selection as the trigger type. Select None as the Target for the agent. From the Run option, select LotusScript. Enter the following Lotus Script code in Initialize event of the agent:

```
Sub Initialize
    Dim ns As New NotesSession
    Dim db As NotesDatabase
    Dim clientvw As NotesView
    Dim vwdoc As NotesDocument
    Dim curdoc As NotesDocument
    Dim lastclientno As Double
    Dim curclientno As Double

    Set curdoc = ns.DocumentContext
    Set db = curdoc.ParentDatabase
    Set clientvw = db.GetView("(Client\ClientNo)")
    Set vwdoc = clientvw.GetLastDocument
```

```
'Check whether the document is being newly opened or not
 If curdoc.Isnewnote Then
 'Check whether vwdoc is there or not.
 'If not there set the client code as 1
    If Not(vwdoc Is Nothing) Then
      'get the last document client code
      'and then  increment that by 1
       lastclientno = Cdbl(vwdoc.ClientCode(0))
       curclientno = lastclientno + 1
       Print Cstr(curclientno)
    Else
      'initialize the client code as 1
       curclientno = 1
       Print Cstr(curclientno)
    End If
 curdoc.ClientCode = curclientno
 End If
End Sub
```

Generating Unique Product Codes

In the Product form, you need to generate a unique product code for each product when the Product form is opened for creation of new documents. In addition, when saving the Product form, you need to check whether any other product with the same product name already exists.

First, you will automate the generation of the product code. In this case, you need not create a new field because the product code field exists. In addition, the ProductsByProduct view contains the first column as product code.

Now to generate the product code, in the `WebQueryOpen` event of the form, enter the following formula:

```
@Command([ToolsRunMacro]; "(WebQryOpenProduct)")
```

The above-specified code will trigger the agent `WebQryOpenProduct` when the form is opened. The logic to generate the product code is the same as that of client code.

Add the code given below in the `Initialize` event of the agent.

```
Sub Initialize
   Dim ns As New NotesSession
   Dim db As NotesDatabase
   Dim productvw As NotesView
   Dim doc As NotesDocument
   Dim curdoc As NotesDocument
   Dim lastproductno As Double
   Dim curproductno As Double

   Set curdoc = ns.DocumentContext
   Set db = curdoc.ParentDatabase
   Set productvw = db.GetView("ProductsByProduct Code")
   Set doc = productvw.GetLastDocument

   'Check whether the document is being newly opened or not
   If curdoc.Isnewnote Then
   'Check whether doc is there or not.
   'If not there set the product code as 1
      If Not(doc Is Nothing) Then
      'get the last document product code
      'and then  increment that by 1
         lastproductno = Cdbl(doc.ProductCode(0))
         curproductno = lastproductno + 1
         'Print Cstr(curproductno)
      Else
      '  initialize the product code as 1
         curproductno = 1
         'Print Cstr(curproductno)
      End If
      curdoc.ProductCode = curproductno
   End If
End Sub
```

The next step is to verify whether a product document already exists with the specified product name. If such a document exists, the newly created Product document should not be saved and an error message should be displayed. To do this, you need to check whether the product name is unique when the user saves the document.

First, create a view named **Products\ProductName** with Product Name as its first column and the column values sorted in the Ascending order. Enter the following formula as the view selection formula:

```
SELECT Form = "Product"
```

In the Product form, create a hidden computed when composed test field by name **SaveOptions**. Enter the value for this field as **1**. In the `WebQuerySave` event, enter the following formula, which will trigger an agent when saving the Product document:

```
@Command([ToolsRunMacro]; "(WebQrySaveProduct)")
```

Create a new agent named **WebQrySaveProduct**. This agent should first check whether the document is new. If the document is saved for the first time, you need to validate the document. Enter the following LotusScript code in the `Initialize` event of the agent:

```
Sub Initialize
   Dim ns As New NotesSession
   Dim db As NotesDatabase
   Dim productvw As NotesView
   Dim doc As NotesDocument
   Dim curdoc As NotesDocument
   Dim curproductname As String

   Set curdoc = ns.DocumentContext
   curproductname = curdoc.ProductName(0)
   Print curproductname
   'Check whether the document is being newly opened or not
   If curdoc.Isnewnote Then
     Set db = curdoc.ParentDatabase
     Set productvw = db.GetView("(Products\ProductName)")
     'Get the document using the current
     'documents product name as key
     Set doc = productvw.GetDocumentByKey(curproductname, True)

     'Check whether doc is there or not.
     'If there is not document with the same product name,
      'the name is unique
```

```
        If Not(doc Is Nothing) Then
       'The product name is not unique so exit with giving an error
            curdoc.SaveOptions = "0"
            Print "The document has not been_
            saved as the product name "+curprodcutname+" already exists"
            Exit Sub
        Else
       'The product name is unique save the form
            curdoc.SaveOptions = "1"
            Print "Document has been sucessfully saved"
        End If
    Else
       'If the document is not new save the edited changes
        curdoc.SaveOptions = "1"
        Print "Document has been sucessfully saved"
    End If
End Sub
```

Validating Category Name

In this section, you will add the code to validate the uniqueness of the category name belonging to a specific category type. To accomplish this task, you can use the existing view Products\Category Definition in the Products database. In the second column property, select the sort option as ascending for this view. You will create an array containing category types and category names from the first two column values of this view and use this array to check for uniqueness of the category name whenever a document is saved.

In the Category definition form in the Products database, create a hidden computed when composed test field by name **SaveOptions**. Enter the value for this field as **1**. Now, enter the following formula in the `WebQuerySave` event of the form:

```
@Command([ToolsRunMacro]; "(WebQrySaveCatDef)")
```

Save the form. This formula will trigger the agent when the document is saved.

Next, create a new shared agent named **WebQrySaveCatDef** in the Products database. Enter the following LotusScript code in the Initialize event of the agent:

```
Sub Initialize
        Dim ns As New NotesSession
        Dim db As NotesDatabase
        Dim categoryvw As NotesView
        Dim categorydoc As NotesDocument
        Dim curdoc As NotesDocument
        Dim keys( 1 To 2 ) As String

        Set curdoc = ns.DocumentContext
        'create the array with category type
        'and category name as the elements
        keys( 1 ) = curdoc.CategoryType(0)
        keys( 2 ) = curdoc.CategoryName(0)
        Print keys( 1 )
        Print keys( 2 )

        Set db = curdoc.ParentDatabase
        Set categoryvw = db.GetView("ProductsCategoryDefinition")
        'Get the document using the current documents type and name as key
        Set categorydoc = categoryvw.GetDocumentByKey(keys, True)

        'Check whether doc is there or not.
        'If there is not document with the same type and name
        'the name is unique
        If Not(categorydoc Is Nothing) Then
                'The category name is not unique
                'so exit with giving an error
                curdoc.SaveOptions = "0"
        Print "The document has not been saved as the Category name "_
         +keys( 2 )+ " already exists under the type "+keys(1)
                Exit Sub
        Else
                'The category name is unique save the form
                curdoc.SaveOptions = "1"
                Print "Document has been sucessfully saved"
        End If
End Sub
```

Setting up the ACL

To control the security aspects of the system, all three modules of the Online Order Processing application use database ACL roles. The application requires four roles to control the rights, as specified in Table 24.39.

Table 24.39 Database ACL Roles

Role	Rights
OrderApprover	Users assigned with this role can only edit the Order for approval. Create this ACL role in the Order database.
Sales	Users assigned with this role can only create and edit the Client data. Create this role in the Clients database.
WarehouseMgr	Users assigned with this role can only create Warehouse and edit Inventory documents. Create this role in the Products database.
ProductMgr	Users assigned with this role can only create Product documents. Create this role in the Products database.

Besides assigning the roles to the respective forms, you should modify the formula used for the Hide when properties of the Action buttons. Currently, the Edit action on the forms is a shared action. So to assign the roles independently, convert the shared action in each of the forms to individual ones. You can achieve this easily by creating a new action button in the corresponding forms and copying the formula for the Click event from the shared action. Then change the Hide when formula for the newly created action and delete the shared action from the form. To do so, perform the following:

- **Edit Action of the Order Form.** Change the Hide when formula to:

  ```
  !@IsMember(@UserRoles;"[OrderApprover])
  ```

- **Approve and Reject Action of the Order Form.** Change the Hide when formula to:

  ```
  OrderStatus !="Awaits Approval" ¦
  !@IsMember(@UserRoles;"[OrderApprover]")
  ```

- **Generate Invoice Action of the Order Form.** Change the hide when formula to:

  ```
  OrderStatus !="Processed"  ¦ !@IsMember(@UserRoles;"[OrderApprover]")
  ```

- **Edit Action of the Client Form.** Change the Hide when formula to:

  ```
  !@IsMember(@UserRoles;"[Sales])
  ```

- **Edit Action of the Warehouse Form.** Change the Hide when formula to:

  ```
  !@IsMember(@UserRoles;"[WarehouseMgr])
  ```

- **Edit Action of the Product Form.** Change the Hide when formula to:

  ```
  !@IsMember(@UserRoles;"[ProductMgr])
  ```

Now you need to assign the create rights to various forms based on the ACL role. To do this in the form properties security tab, clear the option all authors and above and then select the ACL role for each form as specified in Table 24.40.

Table 24.40 Create Rights for Forms

Form Name	ACL Role
Products	ProductMgr
ProductInventory	WarehouseMgr
Warehouse	WarehouseMgr
CategoryDefinition	ProductMgr
Invoice	OrderApprover
Client	Sales

Deploying the Application

To deploy the application, you will have to set up all three databases of the Online Order Processing system on a Domino server. The Domino server on which you deploy the application should be running the HTTP server task. If this task is not running, you can use the Domino server console command `Load HTTP` to load and run the HTTP.

In addition, sign all the databases using an appropriate user ID that has sufficient rights on the server and make the necessary changes to the server document in the Domino Directory. Refer to the Domino Administration Help database for more details about setting up a Web application in Domino.

Summary

In this chapter, you learned how to develop a Web-enabled application using Domino. You learned how to create agents for processing documents when opened or saved from a Web browser using the `WebQueryOpen` and `WebQuerySave` events of the form. In addition, you learned to control formatting and presentation of views for Web application by making use of view templates. You also learned how to create navigational features for Web-enabled Domino applications.

Chapter 25

Enhancing the Application Using JavaScript and HTML

In the previous chapter, you learned how to create the online order processing application using Domino Designer R6. In its current state, the application has certain shortcomings. The application does not provide any field validation. The databases in the application, therefore, are susceptible to incorrect data.

In this chapter, you will enhance the online order processing application that you created in Chapter 24, "Developing an Order Processing System." You'll enhance the UI and add field validations using HTML and JavaScript.

Enhancing the Client Database Design Elements

In the Client database, you'll perform the following tasks:

- Enhance the UI of the forms
- Add field validations to the forms
- Enhance the UI of the views
- Add an item selection mechanism for order entry

To start with, enhance the UI of the Client form.

Adding HTML to the Client Form

To enhance the look and feel of the Client form, you'll use HTML and perform certain modifications in the tables and text.

First, modify the properties of the heading table to provide a better look for the table. In the Table property box, set the cell border thickness to 0. Next, modify the properties of the heading text. Set the font as Arial, size as 10, and style as Bold.

Insert a single line break between the heading table and the content table. To achieve this, type the text `<Br>` between the heading table and the content table. Select the text and select Pass-Thru HTML from the Text menu. This inserts a blank line between the two tables when published on the Web. When any of the elements are selected as Pass-Thru HTML, it instructs the Domino translation engine not to translate the elements when published on the Web, but just pass them as they are.

Insert a horizontal rule prior to the heading Contact Details. To do this, enter the text <HR> prior to the heading. Select the text and then choose Pass-Thru HTML from the Text menu. You can also achieve the same result by choosing Create /Horizontal Rule. The idea of using <HR> was to show you how you can use HTML tags in forms or pages.

Another method for improving the layout of text, links, headers, margins, and so on in forms and pages is by using Cascading Style Sheet (CSS). This method will be used to enhance the forms of Products database. In this manner, you'll be familiarized to different techniques that can be used to improve the form layout.

You can set the margin size of the form by specifying the following code in the HTML Body Attribute event of the form:

```
"LEFTMARGIN=25 TOPMARGIN=3"
```

Now preview the form in a browser and observe the difference the two HTML tags have made to the look and feel of the form. Your form should look as shown in Figure 25.1.

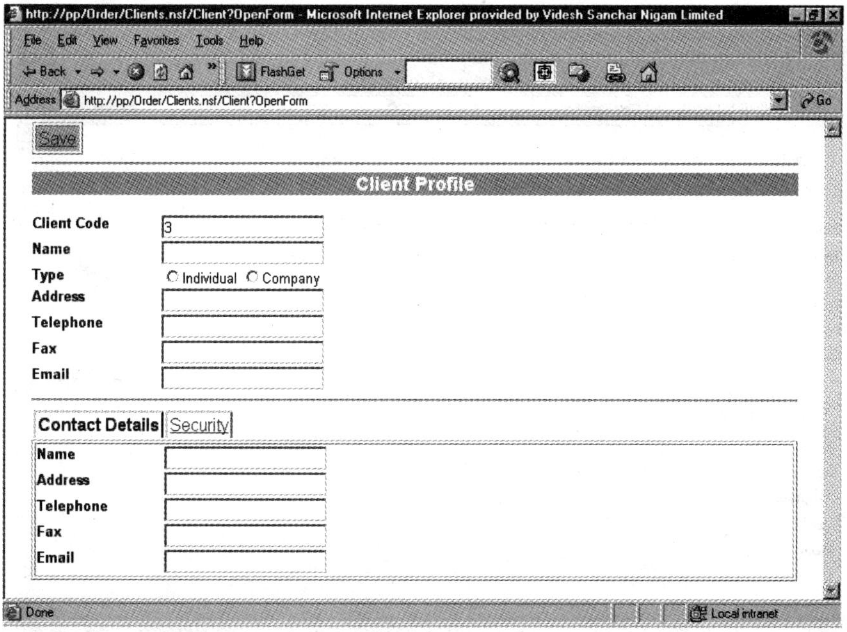

FIGURE 25.1 *The Client form after initial enhancement*

After the basic enhancement of the Client form, you will now use HTML to modify the field attributes of the form.

In the current form, the field for entering the Client Name is small. Therefore, to increase the width of the field, enter the following code in the HTML Attributes event of the field:

```
"Size=40"
```

This code will increase the width of the input text box to 40. Note that the default size of a text field is 20. The same may also be attained by specifying the above code without double quotes in the Field Extra HTML tab of the field property box.

Next, the Address field is too small to enter big addresses. In this case, you need to increase the height and width of the field. In the Field Info tab of the field property box, modify the type of the field to Rich Text. In the HTML Attributes event of the field, enter the following code:

```
"cols=30 rows=3"
```

In the Contact Details tab, increase the size of the ContactAddress field. Also, reduce the size of the ClientCode field. After the enhancements, the Client form will appear as shown in Figure 25.2.

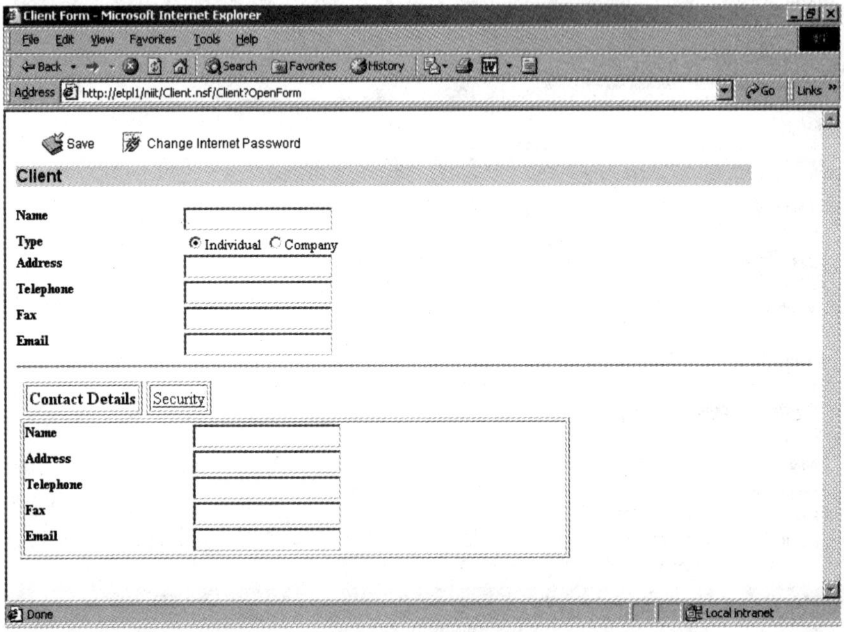

FIGURE 25.2 *The Client form after modifying the field attributes*

Adding Field Validations to the Client Form Using JavaScript

In this section, you will learn how to validate form fields using JavaScript in Domino. The Client form contains a shared action, Save, to save and close the form. However, the users could save the form without even specifying the name of the client. If the users are allowed to save incomplete documents or documents with incorrect data, the database will be full of incorrect documents.

You can validate form fields using formula language or LotusScript in the `WebQuerySave` event of the form. In this case, the form will take a round trip to the server for validation, resulting in an increased load on the server and slow performance. However, if you use JavaScript for validation, you can stop the HTTP POST to the server and perform the validations at the client side.

To validate the fields in the Client form, create a new action button that uses JavaScript to save the form. Before saving the form, you will validate the details that are entered in the Client form. You will be validating these fields: ClientName, ClientAddress, ClientPhone, and ClientEmail. To validate these fields, perform the following steps:

1. Create a new action button named Save.
2. In the Display section of the Action property box, clear Include action in Action menu.
3. In the Icon section, select Notes.
4. Select location of the action button as left and select an appropriate icon to be displayed with the text.
5. In the Hide When tab, check the options Previewed for reading and Opened for reading. This setting will hide the Save action button when the form is previewed or opened for reading.

Set the Action bar properties as follows:

1. In the Action Bar Info tab (first tab) of the Action bar property box, select the Web access display option as Using Java Applet.
2. In the Action Bar Background tab, select the background color as white.
3. In the Button properties tab, in the Button size section, select height as 10, width as background size, and select margin as Fixed size 2. Select the button background color as white.

4. In the Button font tab, select font as Arial, size as 9, style as Plain, and color as black.

Next, in the Programmer's pane, select the Run options for the action button as Web and JavaScript. Enter the following JavaScript code in the Click event of the Save button:

```
if (document.forms[0].ClientName.value == "")
{
    alert("You haven't entered a Name for the client. Please enter a Name
           and then continue.");
    document.forms[0].ClientName.focus();
    return false;
}
if (document.forms[0].ClientAddress.value == "")
{
    alert("You haven't entered an Address for the Client. Please enter
           the Address and then continue");
    document.forms[0].ClientAddress.focus();
    return false;
}
if (document.forms[0].ClientPhone.value == "")
{
    alert("You haven't entered a Phone No. for the client. Please enter
           the Phone No. and then continue.");
    document.forms[0].ClientPhone.focus();
    return false;
}
if (document.forms[0].ClientEmail.value == "")
{
    alert("You haven't entered an Email for the client. Please enter
           the Email and then continue.");
    document.forms[0].ClientEmail.focus();
    return false;
}

document.forms[0].submit();
```

The preceding JavaScript code checks whether or not the ClientName, ClientAddress, ClientPhone, and ClientEmail fields are empty. If a field value is null, an appropriate error message is displayed, the focus is set to the field, and the program execution stops. Otherwise, the form is submitted to the server.

You can also validate the field by placing the JavaScript code in the JavaScript field events, such as onBlur, onChange, or onClick. However, these validations will trigger only when the user enters that particular field or when the field loses the focus. Therefore, if the user does not set the focus to that field, the validation in that particular field will never trigger. For example, suppose you are validating whether or not the ClientPhone field in the Client form is null by using the onBlur event. If the user enters only the ClientName and submits the form, the form will get saved without performing the validation. Moreover, the maintenance of the code is difficult because the code is distributed across different fields. Therefore, it is better to use the full validation code in the click event of the Save action. Now preview the form in a browser. The form appears as shown in Figure 25.3.

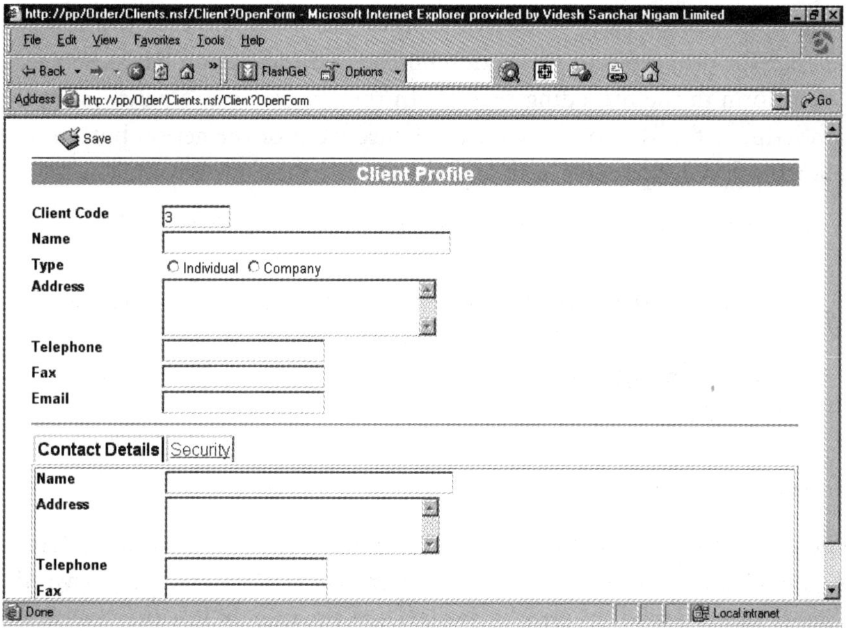

FIGURE 25.3 *The final Client form*

Enhancing the ClientPasswordChange Form

Enhance the look and feel of this form by using HTML in the same way you did for the Client form. In this form, you need to add only the <BR> text to insert a single line break between the heading table and the content table.

Now modify the field property of the ClientPassword field to reduce its width and restrict the users from entering not more than 10 characters as password. To achieve this, activate the Field Extra HTML tab (the last tab) of the field property box. In the Other HTML tag box, enter the following HTML code without quotes:

```
SIZE=10 MAXLENGTH=10
```

The preceding HTML code will not allow users to enter more than 10 characters as password.

Next, you need to validate the ClientPassword field in the form. You need to check whether the ClientPassword field is not null. If the user has not entered any value in this field, the user should not be allowed to save the document. To do this, remove the already existing Save button on the form and create a new Save button. Set the properties of this action button and the Action bar as you did for the Client form in the preceding section. In the Programmer's pane, select Web and JavaScript as the Run options for the Click event of the action button. Enter the following JavaScript code in the Click event of the Save button:

```
if (document.forms[0].ClientPassword.value == "")
{
    alert("You haven't entered a Password for changing the password.
            Please enter a Password and then continue.");
    document.forms[0].ClientPassword.focus();
    return false;
}
document.forms[0].submit();
```

The preceding JavaScript code checks whether or not the user has entered a value in the ClientPassword field. If the user has not entered a password in the ClientPassword field, an error is displayed to the user and further execution of the code is halted. Therefore, the form will not be saved until the user enters a password in the ClientPassword field.

Adding a View Template to the Clients Database

When a user tries to open a view, Domino uses a reserved form called *vie* *plate* to format the contents of the view. You can use a single view temp multiple templates, which associates with each view. You can assign a r name $$ViewTemplateDefault for a template form so that all the views in t application are formatted using the same template form. Refer to Chapter 23, "Project Case Study: Designing the Online Order Processing System," to see the listing of important template forms used by Domino. To create a view template in the Client database, perform the following steps:

1. Click the New Form button to open a new blank form in the work pane.
2. In the Form property box, specify the form name as **$$ViewTemplate Default**.
3. Disable all the Display properties.
4. Select none for versioning.
5. In the Options section, disable all the options.
6. Close the Form property box and save the form.

This creates a blank form. In this form, create a basic table with one row and four columns. In the first column, type the text **Previous**. Select the text and add an action hotspot to this text. In the Action Hotspot property box, set the following options.

1. In the first tab, specify frame as **_self**. This will open all the links that are opened from the hotspot in the same frame.
2. Clear the option, Show border around hotspot.
3. In the Font tab, specify font as Arial, size as 9, style as Plain, and color as blue.

In the remaining columns (left to right) of the table, type the following text: **Next**, **Collapse**, and **Expand**. Next, you need to add action hotspots to these text entries. To do this, follow the same steps as you performed for the **Previous** text.

After setting the action hotspot properties for all the text entries, you need to associate formulas for each of these. The following list provides the associated formulas with each of the action hotspots:

- **Previous.** This action should allow the user to move to the previous page if the view spans over multiple pages. To achieve this, enter the following formula in the Click event of the action:

  ```
  @DbCommand ("Domino";"ViewPreviousPage")
  ```

- **Next.** This action should allow the user to move to the next page if the view spans over multiple pages. To achieve this, enter the following formula in the Click event of the action:

  ```
  @DbCommand("Domino";"ViewNextPage")
  ```

- **Collapse.** This action should collapse the contents if the view contents are displayed in the expanded manner. The formula for this action is as follows:

  ```
  @Command([ViewCollapseAll])
  ```

- **Expand.** This action should expand the contents if the view contents are displayed in the collapsed manner. Enter the following formula in the Click event of the action:

  ```
  @Command([VieyouxpandAll])
  ```

You need to specify to the Domino to display a particular view using the template form. You can do this in one of the two ways:

- By embedding any view in the template form
- By creating a field named $$ViewBody in the template form. In this case, you can use the $$ViewBody field to display the view.

Create a one row by one column table. In this table, create an Editable text field named **$$ViewBody**. Save the form. In Designer, the form will look as shown in the Figure 25.4.

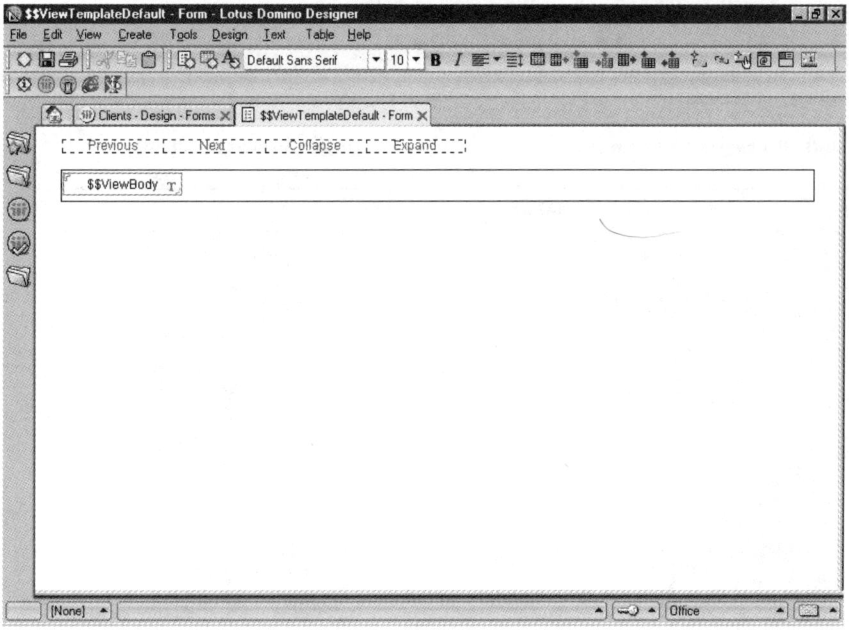

FIGURE 25.4 *The View Template form design*

Now if you open any of the views in the Clients database, the view will look as shown in Figure 25.5.

With the creation of the view template form, you have completed the enhancements for the Clients database. Copy the View Template form from the Clients database and paste it in the other two databases, Products and Orders.

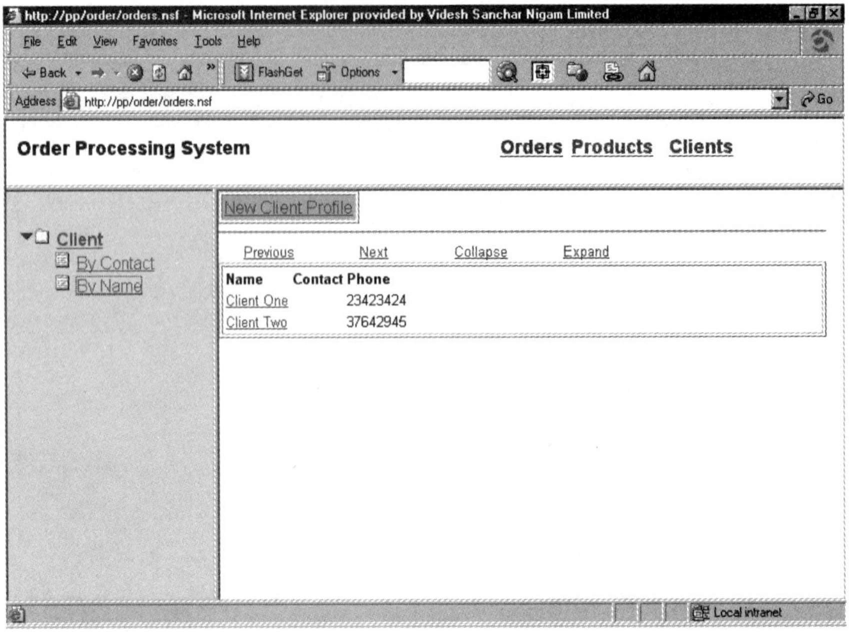

FIGURE 25.5 *A view with the View Template form applied*

Enhancing the Products Database Design Elements

In this section, you will enhance the design elements in the Products database. Begin with the first form, Category Definition.

Enhancing the Category Definition Form

As you already know, you use HTML to enhance the UI of forms. First, modify the heading attributes in the heading table of the Category Definition form. In the Table property box for the heading table, set the cell border thickness to 0. Also, modify the properties of the heading text. Set the font as Arial, size as 10, and style as Bold.

Next, insert a blank line between the heading table and the content table. In this case, you can try out a different method to convert the text to HTML without using the Pass-Thru HTML option. Enclose the `<Br>` tag in square brackets. Domino treats the tags enclosed in square brackets as HTML. Therefore, type the text [
] between the two tables. If you specify any text enclosed in square brackets, Domino treats it as Pass-Thru code and passes that to the browser without any translation.

Now you will create another line break after the first field on the form by inserting a row and then creating the line break. Type [
] in the blank row that you have inserted between the two rows. Enhance the action bar properties by performing the same steps you did for the Client form.

The Category Definition form appears as shown in Figure 25.6.

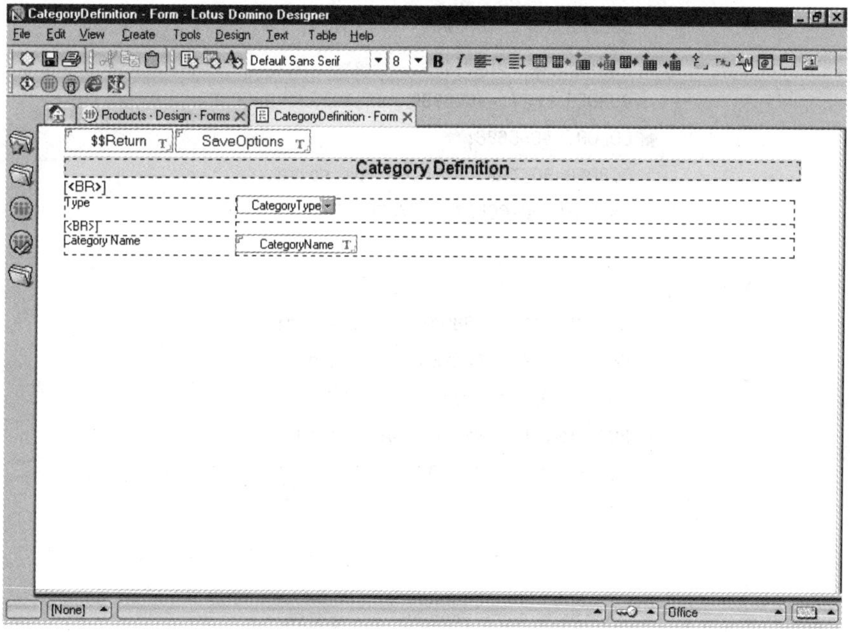

FIGURE 25.6 *The Category Definition form after initial enhancements*

Now you will enhance the layout of the form by using Cascading Style Sheets (CSS). You can do this in one of the following two ways:

- By creating style sheets as shared resources. For this, first create the style sheet with .css extension. Then, import the .css file by clicking the New Style Sheet Resource button in the Style Sheets option under Shared Resources.

- By creating the style sheet in a page. In this case, you can directly place your CSS code in the page and then save the page with the .css extension.

First, create a CSS page and then include it in the Category Definition form. Perform the following steps to create the CSS page:

1. Click the New Page button to open a new blank page in the work pane.
2. Enter the following style sheet code in the page:

```
INPUT {
            BORDER-RIGHT: #808080 1px solid;
            BORDER-TOP: #808080 1px solid;
            FONT: 13px arial;
            BORDER-LEFT: #808080 1px solid;
            COLOR: #666666;
            BORDER-BOTTOM: #808080 1px solid;
            BACKGROUND-COLOR: #F7F7F7
}
TEXTAREA {
            BORDER-RIGHT: #808080 1px solid;
            BORDER-TOP: #808080 1px solid;
            FONT: 13px arial;
            BORDER-LEFT: #808080 1px solid;
            COLOR: #666666; BORDER-BOTTOM: #808080 1px solid;
            BACKGROUND-COLOR:  #F7F7F7
}
SELECT {
            BORDER-RIGHT: #808080 1px solid;
            BORDER-TOP: #808080 1px solid;
            FONT: 13px arial;
            BORDER-LEFT: #808080 1px solid;
            COLOR: #666666;
            BORDER-BOTTOM: #808080 1px solid;
            BACKGROUND-COLOR:  #F7F7F7
}

A:link {
            text-decoration :none;
}
```

```
A:visited {
                text-decoration :none;
}

  .roll {
                font-family:Veranda;
                font-size:18pt;
                font-style:normal;
                font-weight:normal;
                letter-spacing:normal;
                text-decoration:underline;
}
  A.roll:hover {
                font-family:Veranda;
                font-size:16pt;
                font-weight:bolder;
                text-transform:capitalize;
                color:green;
}
```

3. In the Page property box, enter the page name as **Global_Ie.css**.
4. Save and close the page.

To create the style sheet as a shared resource, perform the following:

1. Open a text editor, such as Notepad, and paste the preceding code in it. Save the file as **Global_Ie.css**.
2. Switch to Designer and in the Design pane, expand Shared Resources. Then, select Style Sheets from the list of resources.
3. Click the 'New Style Sheet Resource' button on the top. This will open a dialog box. Specify the Global_Ie.css file that you have just created and then click the Open button to add the style sheet to the resources.

Now that you have created the CSS page and style sheet resource, go back to the Category Definition form to include the newly created CSS page in the form. To apply CSS to the form, enter the following code in the HTML Head Content event of the form:

```
db := @ReplaceSubstring( @Subset( @DbName; -1); "\\"; "/");
@If(@BrowserInfo("BrowserType")="Microsoft";
 "<link rel=\"stylesheet\" type=\"text/css\" href=\"/"+ db+
   "/global_ie.css\"><meta http-equiv=\"Pragma\" content=\"no-cache\">";
 "<meta http-equiv=\"Pragma\" content=\"no-cache\">"
   )
```

The preceding code applies the Global_Ie.css style sheet to the form. The style sheet is applied only if the browser is Internet Explorer. The code also provides a directive to the browser not to cache the form locally.

Alternatively, to associate style sheets with forms or pages, you can use the style sheet that was created as shared resource. To insert a shared resource style sheet, place the cursor where you want to insert the style sheet and choose Create/Resource/Insert Resource. Then, from the resource type, select style sheet and then select the style you want to apply from the Available resources list box.

Now preview the form in the browser. The form should appear as shown in Figure 25.7.

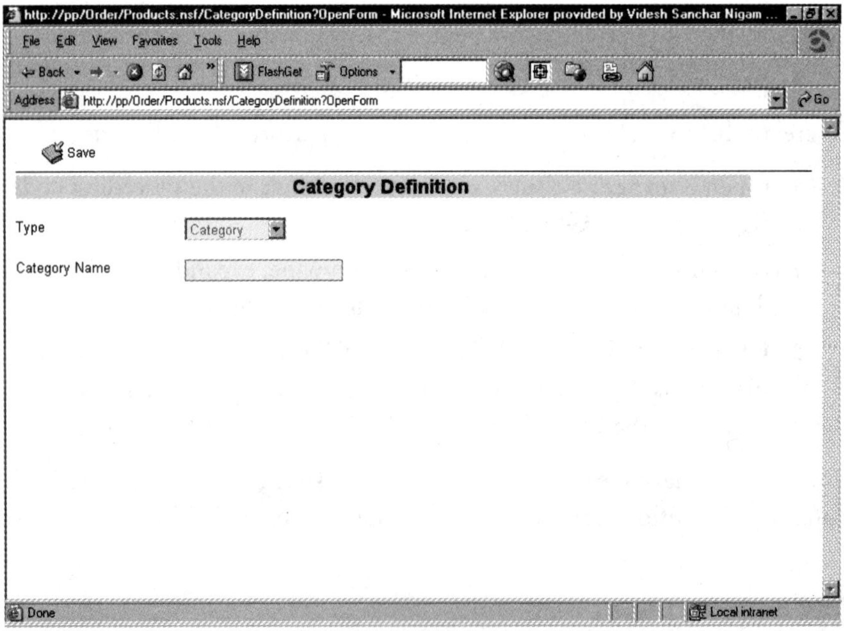

FIGURE 25.7 *The CategoryDefinition form after applying the style sheet*

Adding Field Validations to the Category Definition Form Using JavaScript

You will use JavaScript to validate fields in the Category Definition form the same way you did for the Client form. You'll validate the CategoryName field to check that the field is not left blank before saving the document in the Products database.

Remove the already existing Save action button and create a new action button named Save. In the Action property box, in the Display row, deselect the Include action in Action menu option. Select Notes in the Icon row, select the location as left, and select an appropriate icon to be displayed with the text.

In the Hide When tab, select the options Previewed for reading and Opened for reading. This will hide the action buttons when the form is being previewed or opened for reading. Modify the Action bar properties by performing the same steps as you did for the Client form.

In the Script area, select Web and JavaScript as the Run option. Enter the following JavaScript code in the action Click event:

```
if (document.forms[0].CategoryName.value == "")
{
    alert("You haven't entered a Name for the Category.
          Please enter a Category Name and then continue.");
    return false;
}
document.forms[0].submit();
```

The preceding JavaScript code checks whether or not the user has entered a value in the CategoryName field. If the field value is null, it will raise an appropriate error message and the further execution of the code will be halted. Otherwise, the form is submitted to the server.

Enhancing the Client Feedback Form

You will enhance the UI of the Client Feedback form the same way you did for the other forms. Set the table properties of the heading table the same way you did for the other forms. Next, add the text `[<Br>]` between the heading table and the content table. Also, modify the Action bar properties the same way you did for the other forms.

You don't need to validate any fields in this form, because the form is of type Response and so is loaded with all the field values. Users only need to enter their comments.

Before enhancing the ItemSelectionDlg form, you first need to modify the Item Selection view, which will be embedded in this form. The ItemSelectionDlg form will be opened from the Order form to enable the user to select the item that the user wants to order. The Order form exists in the Order database.

Creating Product Selection Dialog Box

You can implement the product selection mechanism while placing the order using a dialog box. To achieve this, you need to create a form and a view. The view, which will be HTML formatted, will be embedded in the form. Then, the form will be opened using JavaScript to open a dialog box for selection of products. The steps are explained in the following sections.

Creating the Products\Item Selection View

Create a new, shared view named **Products\Item Selection** in the Products database. Use the following selection formula for the view:

```
SELECT Form = "Product
```

Create the view columns as specified in Table 25.1.

Table 25.1 Columns in the Products\Item Selection View

Column No	Column Title	Column Value
1	None	ProductCategory
2	None	ProductSubcategory
3	None	See the formula below
4	Product Code	ProductCode
5	Product Name	ProductName

Set the first and second columns as Sorted Ascending and Categorized. For the third column, set the column width as 2 and enter the following formula in the value for column:

```
"[<INPUT TYPE=\"radio\" NAME=\"Product\" VALUE=\"" +ProductCode+
    " - "+ProductName+ "\"onClick>]"
```

The preceding HTML code creates a radio button with product code and product name separated with a hyphen (-). Notice that you can create radio buttons even in views using HTML. However, be careful to specify the code as a Pass-Thru HTML using the square brackets. Otherwise, Domino will display the HTML code rather than a radio button. You can use the same mechanism to convert a view column to a check box using the appropriate HTML code.

Save and close the view. When previewed in a browser, the view appears as shown in Figure 25.8.

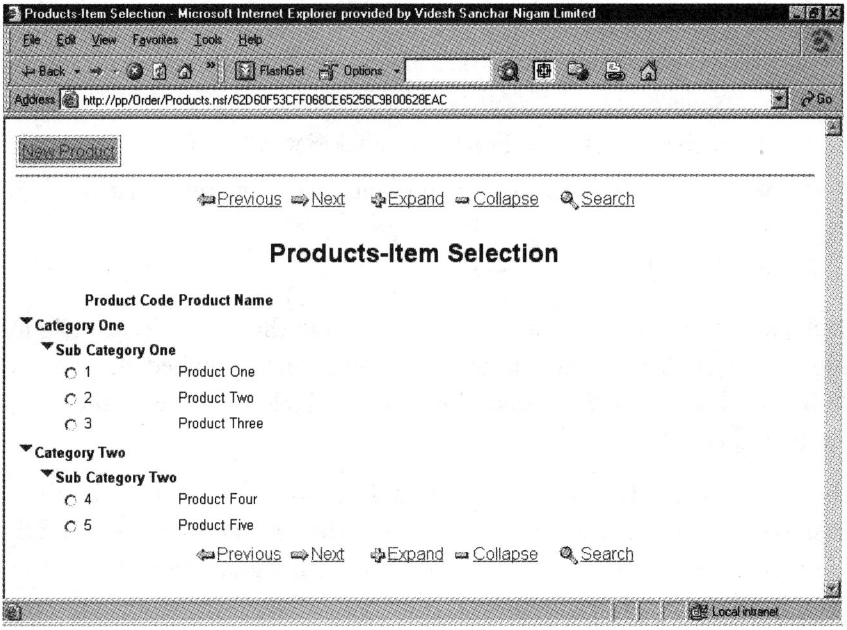

FIGURE 25.8 *The Item Selection view*

Creating the ItemSelectionDlg Form

The dialog box for allowing the selection of products when placing an order will be implemented using a form. You will create a new form in the Products database that will display the view you created earlier from which the user can select the product. Perform the following steps to create the form:

1. Click New Form to open a new blank form in the work pane.
2. Set the Form properties to the following:
   - In the Name box, enter ItemSelectionDlg.
   - In the Display section, clear Include in menu.
   - Select versioning as None.
   - In the Options section, disable all the options.
   - Close the Form property box and Save the form.
3. Add a heading to the form. Perform the following steps:
   - Create a 1x1 table. Select the table width as Fit with margins and click OK.
   - Type Product. Select the text and left-align it. In the Text property box, change Font to Arial, Size to 10, Style to Bold, and select color as black.
   - In the Cell Border Thickness, click Set All To 0.
   - In the Table\Cell Background tab, select an appropriate background color.
   - Close the property box.

Next, embed the view Products\Item Selection in the ItemSelectionDlg form. To embed the view, place the cursor where you want to embed the view. Choose Embedded Element \View. From the list of available views, select the view named 'Products\Item Selection'.

The ItemSelectionDlg form is opened from the Order form in the Orders database. A user can select the item to be ordered in the ItemSelectionDlg form. After the user selects the item, the selected item should be added to the Order form. In the Order form, five buttons corresponding to each line item exist, using which the ItemSelectionDlg form can be opened.

Create two hidden fields in the ItemSelectionDlg form. The first field named **Query_String** is a built-in CGI variable field. This field returns the URL, from which the window has been opened, after the '?' symbol. The second field named **SeqNo** is an editable field. This field captures the button number from which the window is opened. Enter the following formula as the Default Value for the SeqNo field:

```
@Right(Query_String;"&")
```

The preceding formula will return the string to the right of the '&' symbol in the Query_String field. Therefore, if the window is opened by clicking the first button in the Order form, the SeqNo field will have the value as **1**.

In addition to the two hidden fields, create two action buttons in the ItemSelectionDlg form. The first action button, OK, is used to add the selected item to the parent Order form. To achieve this, add the following JavaScript code in the click event of the action button:

```
thisform = window.document.forms[0];
parentform = window.opener.document.forms[0];
for (i=0; i< thisform.Product.length;i++)
{
    if (thisform.Product[i].checked == true)
    {
      var st = thisform.Product[i].value;
      j = st.indexOf('-');
      str1 = st.substr(0,(j));
      str2 = st.substr((j+1));

      if (thisform.SeqNo.value == "1") {
      parentform.ItemNo1.value = str1
      parentform.ItemRequest1.value = str2
    }
    if (thisform.SeqNo.value == "2")
    {
      parentform.ItemNo2.value = str1
      parentform.ItemRequest2.value = str2
    }
    if (thisform.SeqNo.value == "3")
    {
      parentform.ItemNo3.value = str1
      parentform.ItemRequest3.value = str2
    }
    if (thisform.SeqNo.value == "4")
    {
      parentform.ItemNo4.value = str1
      parentform.ItemRequest4.value = str2
    }
```

```
        if (thisform.SeqNo.value == "5")
        {
          parentform.ItemNo5.value = str1
          parentform.ItemRequest5.value = str2
          }
        }
}
self.close();
```

The preceding JavaScript code loops through all the radio button items in the form and looks for the one that is checked. It then extracts the product name and product code and sets the values for the same fields in the parent form, which is the Order form. The code checks for the button from which the window has been opened, and then inserts the respective values accordingly.

The second button, Cancel, is used to close the window without performing any operation. In the click event of this button, enter the following JavaScript code:

```
self.close();
```

Finally, center-align both the buttons and save the form. In Designer, the form will look as shown in the Figure 25.9.

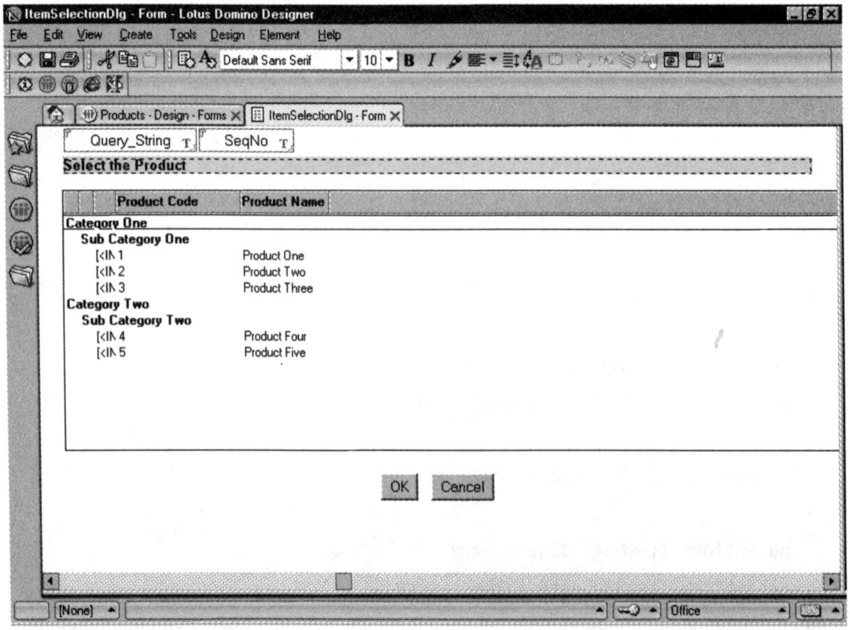

FIGURE 25.9 *The ItemSelectionDlg form design*

The rest of the steps for the completing the implementation of the dialog box mechanism is detailed in the section "Creating a Pop-up Dialog Box to Select Items."

Enhancing the Product Form

To enhance the UI of this form, follow the steps specified in the earlier forms. Next, use JavaScript to validate the form fields. You will validate two fields, ProductName and ProductUnitPrice. To do this, remove the already existing Save button, which has been inserted from the shared resources, and create a new action button named Save. Follow the same steps specified for the earlier forms to set the properties of the action button and the Action bar. In the Click event of Save action button, enter the following JavaScript code:

```
if (document.forms[0].ProductName.value == "")
{
    alert("You haven't entered a Product Name.
        Please enter a Product Name and then continue.");
    document.forms[0].ProductName.focus();
    return false;
}
if (document.forms[0].ProductUnitPrice.value == "")
{
    alert("You haven't entered an Unit Price for the Product.
          Please enter the Unit Price and then continue.");
    document.forms[0].ProductUnitPrice.focus();
    return false;
}
document.forms[0].submit();
```

The preceding JavaScript code checks whether or not the ProductName and ProductUnitPrice fields contain values. If the field value is null, it will raise an appropriate error message. Otherwise, it will submit the form using the HTTP POST operation.

Next, increase the size of the ProductName field and decrease the size of the ProductCode field using HTML attributes. Increase spacing between the fields by inserting new rows in the table and typing the **
** tag and marking it as Pass-Thru HTML.

Preview the form in Internet Explorer. The form should appear as shown in Figure 25.10.

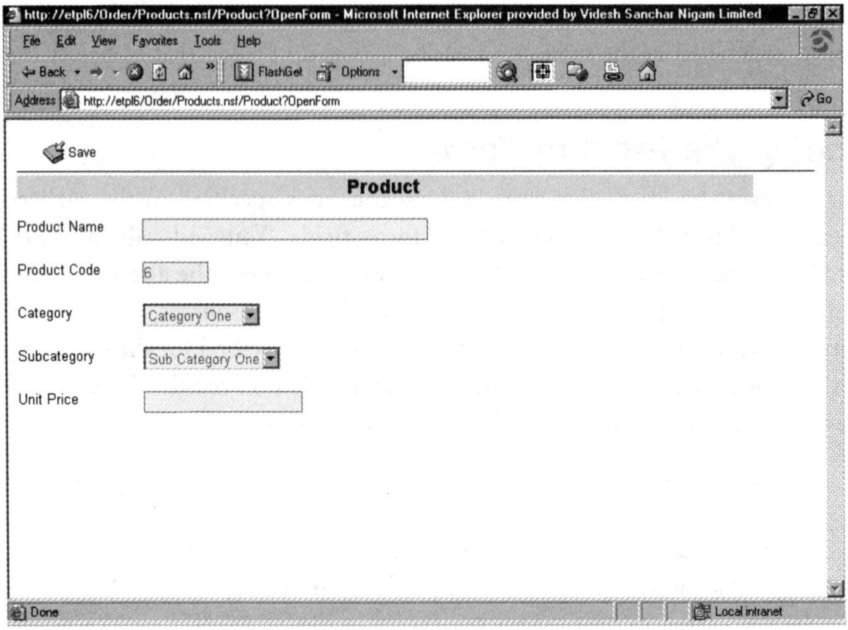

FIGURE 25.10 *The enhanced Product form*

Enhancing the Product Inventory Form

In the Product Inventory form, modify the heading table and text as you did for earlier forms and then add the HTML tags. Also, add the CSS page by entering the formula in the HTML Head Content event of the form. Set the action button and Action bar properties the same way as you did for earlier forms.

Next, create a new Save button as you did for the earlier forms. In the Click event of the action button, enter the following JavaScript code to validate the form fields:

```
if (document.forms[0].ProdInvUnits.value == "")
{
    alert("You haven't entered the No. of Units for the Product.
          Please enter the No. of Units and then continue.");
    document.forms[0].ProdInvUnits.focus();
    return false;
}
if (document.forms[0].ProdInvOrderLevel.value == "")
{
    alert("You haven't entered an Order Level for the Product.
```

```
            Please enter the Order Level and then continue.");
    document.forms[0].ProdInvOrderLevel.focus();
    return false;
}
document.forms[0].submit();
```

The preceding JavaScript code checks whether or not the user has entered the values for the ProdInvUnits and ProdInvOrderLevel fields.

Enhancing the Warehouse Form

Enhance the UI of this form in the same way you did for earlier forms.

Next, in the Click event of the Save action button, enter the following JavaScript code to validate the form fields:

```
if (document.forms[0].WareHouseCode.value == "")
{
    alert("You haven't entered the Code for Warehouse.
            Please enter the Code and then continue.");
    document.forms[0].WareHouseCode.focus();
    return false;
}
if (document.forms[0].WareHouseInCharge.value == "")
{
    alert("You haven't entered a Person In Charge for this Warehouse.
            Please enter the Person-in-charge and then continue.");
    document.forms[0].WareHouseInCharge.focus();
    return false;
}
if (document.forms[0].WareHouseLocation.value == "")
{
    alert("You haven't entered the Location for this Warehouse.
            Please enter the Location and then continue.");
    document.forms[0].WareHouseLocation.focus();
    return false;
}
document.forms[0].submit();
```

Enhancing the Orders Database Design Elements

The Orders database is the main module for user transactions. Therefore, this module should be highly user-friendly. In this section, you will enhance the design elements of the Orders database. Copy the page, which contains the style sheet from the Products database (Products.nsf) and paste it to the Orders database. Then, to associate the style sheet with any of the forms in the Orders database, copy the formula in the HTML Head Content event of any of the forms in the Products database and paste it in the HTML Head Content event of the form in the Orders database.

Enhancing the Invoice Form

There will be no user interactions in this form. Therefore, you do not need to perform any field validation in this form. You simply need to improve the UI. To do this, follow the same steps to enhance the UI of the other forms in the application. Insert a single line break between tables using the `<Br>` tag enclosed in square brackets. Additionally, you can include the style sheet in this form.

Enhancing the Order Form

Enhance the UI of this form in the same manner you did for the other forms.

Currently, there is no provision for the user to specify the date by when the order needs to be delivered. Therefore, add an editable field named LtDeliveryDate of type DateTime to the Order form. Because the form will be used by the Web clients, the date picker will not be published. On the Web, you need to use JavaScript to display date picker to users. To do this, add a button labeled Pick Date next to the LtDeliveryDate field. For this button, select Web and JavaScript as the Run options in the Programmer's pane. Then in the Click event of the button, enter the following JavaScript:

```
getMonth_and_Date(document.forms[0],'LtDeliveryDate');
                    putcal(this.form,'LtDeliveryDate')
```

In the preceding code, two functions named `getMonth_and_Date` and `putcal` are used. These functions open a new calendar window. When a user selects a date in the calendar, the selected date is set as the value of the specified field.

Next, you will add these JavaScript functions to achieve the required functionality. These functions are a set of reusable code that can be used in other parts of the application. In the JS Header event of the form, add the following JavaScript code:

NOTE

For the proper listing of code in the book, certain code lines are broken into two lines using underscores. When you enter the code, enter the code on a single line leaving out the underscore.

```
var month; var day; var year;
var delim = new Array(":","/","\\","-"," ",".");
var monthArray = new Array(0,31,29,31,30,31,30,31,31,30,31,30,31);
function vd(frm, fieldName,fieldLabel)
{
    //init
    dtString = eval("frm." + fieldName + ".value");
    // trim date string
    while ((dtString.charAt(0) == " ") && (dtString.length != 0))
      dtString = dtString.substring(1,dtString.length - 1)
    while ((dtString.charAt(dtString.length - 1) == " ")
                  && (dtString.length != 0))
      dtString = dtString.substring(0,dtString.length - 1)

    //get date components
    i = 0; startPos = 0; pos = 0;

    //get month
    do
    {
      pos = dtString.indexOf(delim[i], startPos);
      i++
    }

    while ((pos == -1) && (i < delim.length));
```

```
          if (pos == -1) return false;
        month  = parseInt(dtString.substring(startPos,pos),10);
        startPos = pos + 1;
        if ((month < 1) || (month > 12)) return false;
        //get day
        i = 0;
        do
        {
          pos = dtString.indexOf(delim[i], startPos);
          i++
        }
        while ((pos == -1) && (i < delim.length));
          if (pos == -1)return false;
        day  = parseInt(dtString.substring(startPos,pos),10);
        startPos = pos + 1;
        if ((day < 1) || (day > monthArray[month])) return false;

        //get year
        year = parseInt(dtString.substring(startPos,dtString.length),10);
        //check for leap year
        if ((month == 2) && (day == 29))
          if ((((year % 4) == 0) && ((year % 100) != 0)) == false)
          {
            return false;
          }

          //if you've gotten this far, return true
          return true;
        } // end function vd
    }
    function validateDate(form, dateFieldName,fieldLabel)
    {
        if (!vd(frm,fieldName,fieldLabel))
        alert(fieldLabel + " does not have a valid date")
    }//end function validateDate

    function getToday()
    {
```

```
        today = new Date();
        day = today.getDate();
        month = today.getMonth();
        month++;
        year = today.getYear();
        year = (year < 100) ? 1900 + year : year;
}

function getMonth_and_Date(form,fieldName)
{
        dtString = eval("form." + fieldName + ".value");
        // trim date string
        while ((dtString.charAt(0) == " ") && (dtString.length != 0))
          dtString = dtString.substring(1,dtString.length - 1)
        while ((dtString.charAt(dtString.length - 1) == " ")
                 && (dtString.length != 0))
          dtString = dtString.substring(0,dtString.length - 1)

        //get date components
        i = 0; startPos = 0; pos = 0;
        //get month
        do
        {
          pos = dtString.indexOf(delim[i], startPos);
          i++
        }
        while ((pos == -1) && (i < delim.length));
          if (pos == -1)
          {//there's no month
            getToday();
            return;
          }
        month  = parseInt(dtString.substring(startPos,pos),10) - 1;
        startPos = pos + 1;
        if ((month < 0) || (month > 12))
        { //no valid month
          getToday();
          return;
```

```
    }
    else
      month++;

    //get day
    i = 0;
    do {
      pos = dtString.indexOf(delim[i], startPos);
      i++
    }
    while ((pos == -1) && (i < delim.length));
      if (pos == -1){
        getToday();
        return;
      }
      day  = parseInt(dtString.substring(startPos,pos),10);
      startPos = pos + 1;
      if ((day < 1) || (day > monthArray[month])){
        getToday();
        return;
      }

    //get year
    year = parseInt(dtString.substring(startPos,dtString.length),10)
    year = (year < 100) ? 1900 + year : year;

}//getMonth_and_Date

function putDate(form,fieldName,value)
{
    eval("form." + fieldName + ".value=" + value)
}

function gm(num)
{
    var mydate = new Date();
    mydate.setDate(1);
    mydate.setMonth(num-1);
```

```
    var datestr = "" + mydate;
    return datestr.substring(4,7);
}

function gy(num)
{
    var mydate = new Date();
    return (1900 + eval(mydate.getYear()) - 4 + num);
}

function ud(mon)
{
    var i = mon.selectedIndex;
    if(mon.options[i].value == "2")
    {
      document.myform.day.options[30] = null;
      document.myform.day.options[29] = null;
      var j = document.myform.year.selectedIndex;
      var year = eval(document.myform.year.options[j].value);

      if ( ((year%400)==0) || (((year%100)!=0) && ((year%4)==0)) )
      {
        if (document.myform.day.options[28] == null)
        {
          document.myform.day.options[28] = new Option("29");
          document.myform.day.options[28].value = "29";
        }
      }
      else
      {
        document.myform.day.options[28] = null;
      }
    }

    if(mon.options[i].value == "1" ||
       mon.options[i].value == "3" ||
       mon.options[i].value == "5" ||
       mon.options[i].value == "7" ||
```

```
   mon.options[i].value == "8" ||
   mon.options[i].value == "10" ||
   mon.options[i].value == "12")
{

  if (document.myform.day.options[28] == null)
  {
    document.myform.day.options[28] = new Option("29");
    document.myform.day.options[28].value = "29";
  }

  if (document.myform.day.options[29] == null)
  {
    document.myform.day.options[29] = new Option("30");
    document.myform.day.options[29].value = "30";
  }

  if (document.myform.day.options[30] == null)
  {
    document.myform.day.options[30] = new Option("31");
    document.myform.day.options[30].value = "31";
  }
}

if(mon.options[i].value == "4" ||
   mon.options[i].value == "6" ||
   mon.options[i].value == "9" ||
   mon.options[i].value == "11")
{

  if (document.myform.day.options[28] == null)
  {
    document.myform.day.options[28] = new Option("29");
    document.myform.day.options[28].value = "29";
  }

  if (document.myform.day.options[29] == null)
  {
```

```
            document.myform.day.options[29] = new Option("30");
            document.myform.day.options[29].value = "30";
          }
          document.myform.day.options[30] = null;
        }

        if (document.myform.day.selectedIndex == -1)
          document.myform.day.selectedIndex = 0;
}

function showdate()
{
        var i = document.myform.month.selectedIndex;
        var j = document.myform.day.selectedIndex;
        var k = document.myform.year.selectedIndex;
        alert(document.myform.month.options[i].value + "/" +
        document.myform.day.options[j].value + "/" +
        document.myform.year.options[k].value)
}

function putcal(form, dateFieldName)
{
        var version = navigator.appVersion;
        if (navigator.appVersion.indexOf("Mac") != -1)
        {
//the following line is broken
          calwin =
            open("","calwin","width=300,height=300,_
                    resizable=yes,top=150,left=250");
        }
        else
        {
//the following line is broken
        calwin =
            open("","calwin","width=230,height=240,_
                    resizable=yes,top=150,left=250");
        }
        calccal(calwin,form,dateFieldName);
```

```
}

function calccal(targetwin,form,dateFieldName)
{

    var monthname = new Array(12);
    monthname[0] = "January";
          ] = "July";
    monthname[7] = "August";
    monthname[8] = "September";
    monthname[9] = "October";
    monthname[10] = "November";
    monthname[11] = "December";
    var endday = calclastday(eval(month),eval(year));
    mystr = month + "/01/" + year;
    mydate = new Date(mystr);
    firstday = mydate.getDay();
    var cnt = 0;
    var day = new Array(6);

    for (var i=0; i<6; i++)
      day[i] = new Array(7);
    for (var r=0; r<6; r++)
    {
      for (var c=0; c<7; c++)
      {
        if ((cnt==0) && (c!=firstday))
        continue;
        cnt++;
        day[r][c] = cnt;
        if (cnt==endday)
          break;
      }
      if (cnt==endday)
      break;
    }

     targetwin.document.open()
```

```
targetwin.document.writeln("<HEAD><STYLE>
      A:link{text-decoration:none};A:hover{color:red}</STYLE></HEAD>")
targetwin.document.writeln("<FORM><TABLE><TR VALIGN=TOP>");

var prevyear = eval(year) - 1;
targetwin.document.writeln("<TD><INPUT TYPE=BUTTON
           NAME=prevyearbutton VALUE='<<'"+
            " onclick='opener.month = " + month + ";
    //the following line is broken
            opener.year = " + prevyear +
            ";document.clear();opener.calccal_
              (opener.calwin,opener.document."
                + form.name + ",\"" + dateFieldName + "\")'></TD>");

var prevmonth = (month == 1) ? 12 : month - 1;
var prevmonthyear = (month == 1) ? year - 1 : year;

targetwin.document.writeln("<TD><INPUT TYPE=BUTTON
            NAME=prevmonthbutton VALUE=' < '"+
             //the following line is broken
           " onclick='opener.month = " + _
            prevmonth + "; opener.year = " +
            prevmonthyear +
            ";document.clear();opener.calccal_
            (opener.calwin,opener.document."
            + form.name + ",\"" + dateFieldName + "\")'></TD>");
targetwin.document.writeln("<TD COLSPAN=3 ALIGN=CENTER>");
var index = eval(month) - 1;
targetwin.document.writeln("<B>" + monthname[index] + " " + year +
            "</B></TD>");
var nextyear = eval(year) + 1;
var nextmonth = (month == 12) ? 1 : month + 1;
var nextmonthyear = (month == 12) ? year + 1 : year;
//the following line is broken
targetwin.document.writeln("<TD><INPUT TYPE=BUTTON
           NAME=nextmonthbutton VALUE=' > '"+
           " onclick='opener.month = " + nextmonth + ";_
            opener.year = " +
```

```
          nextmonthyear +
          ";document.clear();opener.calccal_
          (opener.calwin,opener.document."
          + form.name + ",\"" + dateFieldName + "\")'></TD>");
    //The following line is broken
  targetwin.document.writeln("<TD><INPUT TYPE=BUTTON
          NAME=nextyearbutton VALUE='>>'"+
          " onclick='opener.month = " + month + "; opener.year = " +
           nextyear +
           ";document.clear();opener.calccal_
              (opener.calwin,opener.document."
           + form.name + ",\"" + dateFieldName + "\")'></TD>");

  targetwin.document.writeln("</TR><TR>");
  targetwin.document.writeln("<TD>Su</TD>");
  targetwin.document.writeln("<TD>Mo</TD>");
  targetwin.document.writeln("<TD>Tu</TD>");
  targetwin.document.writeln("<TD>You</TD>");
  targetwin.document.writeln("<TD>Th</TD>");
  targetwin.document.writeln("<TD>Fr</TD>");
  targetwin.document.writeln("<TD>Sa</TD>");
  targetwin.document.writeln("</TR>");
//the following line is broken
  targetwin.document.writeln_
   ("<TR><TD COLSPAN=7><HR NOSHADE></TD></TR>");
  targetwin.document.writeln("<TR><TD COLSPAN=7><TABLE  WIDTH=\"100%\"
                BORDER=\"0\">");

  var selectedmonth = eval(month) - 1;
  var today = new Date();
  var thisyear = today.getYear() + 1900;
  var selectedyear = eval(year) - thisyear + 4;
  var conditionalpadder = "";

  for(r=0; r<6; r++)
  {
    targetwin.document.writeln("<TR>");
    for(c=0; c<7; c++)
```

```
        {
          targetwin.document.writeln("<TD>");
          if(day[r][c] != null)
          {
            if (day[r][c] < 10)
              conditionalpadder = " "
            else
              conditionalpadder = "";
//the following line is broken
            targetwin.document.writeln_
             ("<a href=\"javascript:window.close();" +_
                  "opener.document." + form.name + "." +_
                    dateFieldName + ".value =
                 '" + day[r][c] + "/" +  month + "/" + year + "'" +
                 "\">" + conditionalpadder + day[r][c] + conditionalpadder +
                 "</a>")
          }
          targetwin.document.writeln("</TD>");
        }
       targetwin.document.writeln("</TR>");
     }
     targetwin.document.writeln("</TABLE></TABLE></FORM>");
     targetwin.document.close()
}

function calclastday(month,year)
{
     if ((month==2) && ((year%4)==0))
       return 29;
     if ((month==2) && ((year%4)!=0))
       return 28;
     if ((month==1) || (month == 3) || (month == 5) || (month == 7) ||
          (month==8) || (month == 10) || (month ==12))
        return 31;
     return 30;
}

function calcnextmonth(month)
```

```
{
    if (month=="12")
      return "1";
    else
      return (eval(month)+1);
}

function calcnextyear(month,year)
{
    if (month=="12")
      return (eval(year)+1);
    else
      return (year);
}

function calcprevmonth(month)
{
    if (month=="1")
      return "12";
    else
      return (eval(month)-1);
}

function calcprevyear(month,year)
{
    if (month=="1")
      return (eval(year)-1);
    else
      return (year);
}
```

The preceding JavaScript code opens a new calendar window after checking the current date. Notice that in this code, HTML is used along with JavaScript to align the dates in the calendar window.

NOTE

You can create a JavaScript library to reuse the code across your applications. Whenever you want to use the functionality, simply copy the JavaScript library to the database in which you want to incorporate the date pickup functionality.

Creating a Pop-Up Dialog Box to Select Items

In the current Order form, whenever a user selects an item, the form is refreshed. When the user selects an item, a round trip to the server is made to fetch the details, such as item description and rate, from the database to the form. Therefore, each refresh involves a round trip to the server, which is time consuming and sometimes frustrating. In this section, you will modify the current item selection mechanism.

You will use a pop-up dialog box, implemented using JavaScript, to enable users to select items to be ordered. To achieve this, make the necessary changes in the Order form to capture certain CGI variables, which you will use in your JavaScript code. Add the fields to the Order form as listed in Table 25.2.

Table 25.2 Fields for the Order Form

Field Name	Type	Value
Server_Protocol	Computed for display, Text	Server_Protocol
Server_Name	Computed for display, Text	Server_Name
Server_Port	Computed for display, Text	Server_Port
Path_Info	Computed for display, Text	Path_Info
ConnectString	Computed for display, Text	See formula

For the ConnectString field, enter the following formula in the field value:

```
@Left(Server_Protocol;"/") +
"://"+Server_Name+":"+Server_Port+@LeftBack(Path_Info;"Orders")+"/Products.nsf"
```

The preceding formula uses the CGI variables to construct the URL, which will open the dialog box form from the Products database. The CGI variables are used to obtain the prefix part of the URL pointing to Products.nsf, such as hostname, database path, and server port.

Next, delete the existing ItemRequest1_d and ItemRequest2_d fields in the OrderRequestEditable subform. Make the ItemRequest1 and ItemRequest2 fields editable and clear the specified Hide When options. Create two buttons next to the fields ItemRequest1 and ItemRequest2 and enter the JavaScript code in the Click event of these buttons.

Enter the following JavaScript code in the Click event of the button next to the ItemRequest1 field:

```
a1=window.document.forms[0].ConnectString.value;
b1=a1+"/ItemSelectionDlg?OpenForm"+"&1";
win=open(b1,"win3" ,"height=300 width=600
          top=100 left=100 resizeable=no maximize=no
          systemMenu=no scrollbars=yes menubar=no toolbar=no
          statusbar=no locationbar=no personalbar=no")
Enter the following JavaScript code in the Click event of the button next to
IremRequest2 field:
a1=window.document.forms[0].ConnectString.value;
b1=a1+"/ItemSelectionDlg?OpenForm"+"&2";
win=open(b1,"win3" ,"height=300 width=600 top=100 left=100
            resizeable=no maximize=no systemMenu=no scrollbars=yes
//the following line is broken
            menubar=no toolbar=no statusbar=no_
              locationbar=no personalbar=no")
```

Notice that the only difference in the code for the two buttons is how the URL arguments are used while assigning the URL to the variable `b1`. The number after the `&` sign corresponds to the button number to which the code is associated.

Perform the steps mentioned earlier for implementing additional buttons associated with other item fields, if required.

Clicking on any of the button will pop up a dialog box as shown in Figure 25.11.

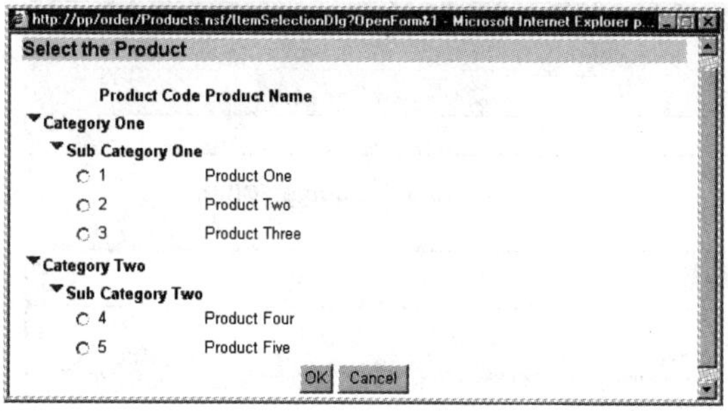

FIGURE 25.11 *The Product Selection dialog box*

The pop-up mechanism that you implemented can be used to perform tasks, which may involve even data transfer between databases and browser windows in the browser client.

Publishing Views using Applets

You can publish a view using Java applet when it is accessed from browsers. Publishing the view this way provides an interface which is very close to the interface you get in the Notes client. In this section, you will learn how to publish a view using an applet.

In Designer, open the view Products\By Categories of the Products database. Open the view properties box by choosing Design/View Properties. Click the Advanced tab. Check the option use applet in browser in the Web access section and save the view. Now open the view in the browser. The view will look as shown in Figure 25.12.

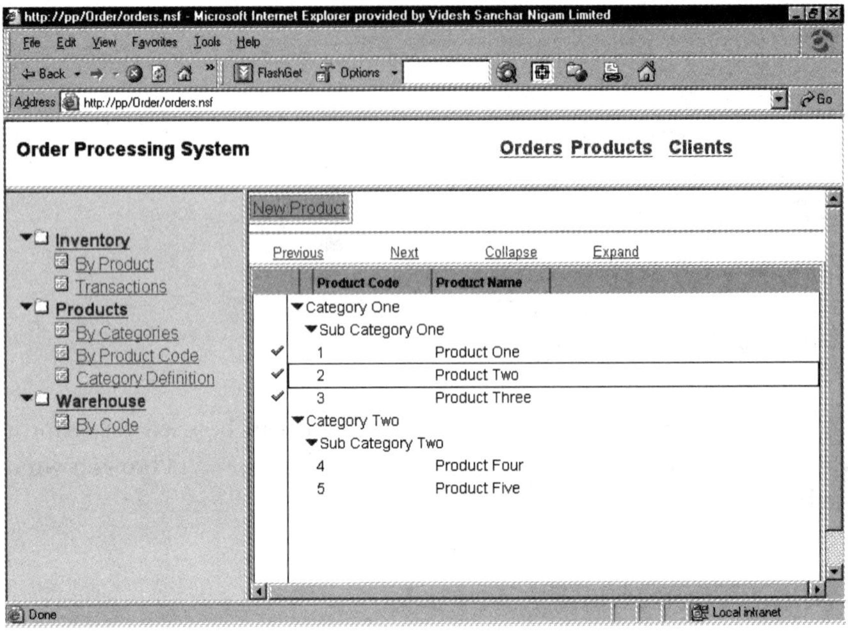

FIGURE 25.12 *The Product Selection dialog box*

Publishing a view using an applet will take more time for the view to load in the browser. Therefore, you need to be careful using this option when your application is accessed over low bandwidth connectivity to the Domino server.

Publishing Rich Text Fields using Applets

In the Notes client, Rich Text fields offer excellent formatting features such as the ability to select various text attributes, create bullet and numbered list, and add tables. But when you publish them on the Web using HTML, all these formatting features are lost. You can retain some of the formatting features of Rich Text fields in browsers by publishing these fields using applets.

Currently, the Product form of the Products database does not contain any field for entering a detailed description of the product. You will create a Rich Text field for this purpose and will then publish it using an applet. Perform the following steps:

1. Open the Product form in Designer
2. Append two rows to the existing table that contain field labels and fields.

3. In the first row of the newly appended rows, enter **
** and mark it as Pass-Thru HTML.
4. In the second row of the newly appended rows, enter **Description** as the field label and create an Editable Rich Text field by name **ProductDescription** in the fields column.
5. On the Field Info tab of the field property box, against the Web Access, select Using Java Applet in the Display option and save the form.

Preview the form in Internet Explorer. The form will look as shown in Figure 25.13.

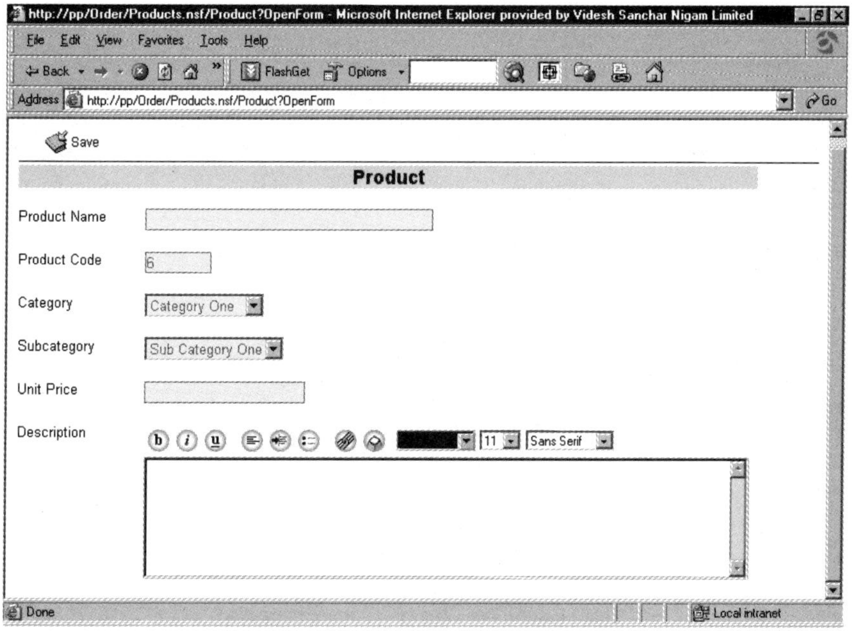

FIGURE 25.13 *The Description field published using an applet*

Like the view applets, using applets to publish Rich Text field will increase the load time for the form in browser.

Summary

In this chapter, you learned how to use HTML and JavaScript to enhance the UI and functionality of Domino applications. You also learned to use CGI variables, which can be accessed using JavaScript. Certain features of Domino, such as date picker, do not work for Web clients. In this chapter, you learned how to implement this feature for the Web using JavaScript. You also learned how to transfer data between databases through pop-up dialog boxes using JavaScript. You learned the tricks and methods for transforming a Notes view column to editable elements when published on the Web.

PART VII

Beyond the Lab

Chapter 26

XML in Domino

XML (*eXtensible Markup Language*) is a W3C (*World Wide Web Consortium*) defined standard that provides a format to present structured data. The data to be presented is stored in *XML documents*. These XML documents are similar to databases in the sense that they allow you to store data. XML documents, however, store data as plain text to enable multiple platforms to understand and interpret the data. XML thus provides a standard interface for interchanging data across Web applications, irrespective of platform.

Domino provides support for XML. The XML representation of Domino data is known as DXL. DXL provides a basis for importing and exporting XML representations of data to and from a Domino application.

In this chapter, you'll learn the basics of XML and about some of the specifications related to XML. In addition, you'll learn about the application of XML in Domino. You will create a simple form to create XML data, a view to group the XML documents, and a page to display the embedded view. You'll also create a LotusScript agent to help us access the page from a browser. Finally, you will learn about Domino DTDs (*Document Type Definitions*).

Introduction to XML

XML is a language used to create Web applications. It allows Web application designers to create their own customized tags, enabling the definition, transmission, validation, and interpretation of data between applications.

Some of the benefits of XML are:

- **Information sharing.** Any data can be stored in the XML format and be used by various tools that read data, write data, and transform data between XML and other formats. This is possible because of the separation of data and presentation.
- **Content delivery.** XML supports different users and channels, such as digital TV, Web, and multimedia. This helps in delivering e-business applications to customers through their chosen media.

- **Extensibility**. As the name suggests, XML supports extensibility by enabling users to create new tags.
- **Semantic information**. An HTML-based search engine cannot distinguish between a document authored by "John Brightly" or a document that describes a star that shines "brightly." On the other hand, XML builds semantic information into documents, making it possible to know the meaning of a document.

Besides these benefits, XML is an easily readable, tree-based, and easy-to-write language.

In order to view an XML document, it must be interpreted. An XML parser is used to interpret an XML file. The parser loads the XML file, validates the XML document, and creates a document tree structure or a data structure. Some browsers, such as Internet Explorer 5, have a built-in XML parser.

Some of the common specifications related to XML include:

- **DTD (*Document Type Definition*).** DTDs specify the rules for XML documents that make it easier for everyone to understand the structure and logic of your XML documents.
- **DOM (*Document Object Model*).** DOM enables navigation and modification in an XML document including adding, updating, or deleting content of elements. This also allows you to access XML data programmatically.
- **XML schemas.** XML schemas can be considered as a superset of DTDs and are also used to define the structure of XML documents.

DTD

DTD represents a set of rules that define the structure and logic of XML documents. The documents that store these rules are called DTD documents (referred to as DTDs from here on) and have the extension `.dtd`.

To better understand the concept of DTDs, compare them with the creation of tables in a database. When you create a table in a database system, you specify the columns, the data types for different columns, the validation rules for data within columns, and so on. Similarly, you can specify rules that can be used in XML documents, such as tags and attributes, by using a DTD. DTDs can be considered to be rule books for XML documents.

TIP

It's not essential for you to create a DTD for your XML documents. However, a DTD can be important to users who need to understand the structure of your XML documents or who need to create an XML document similar to the one you've already created. These users can refer to your DTD document to understand the structure and logic of your XML documents.

When you create a DTD document for an XML document, the XML document is checked against the rules specified in the DTD document. If the XML document adheres to all the DTD rules, the document is considered valid. Otherwise, the XML document fails to generate the desired output.

The components of a DTD are listed below:

- **DOCTYPE declarations.** The `<!DOCTYPE>` declaration contains the information about the location of the DTD.
- **Element declarations.** An element is a logical component of a document. Every element that is contained in an XML document must have a corresponding declaration in the DTD. The element declaration is used to validate the elements in the document.
- **Attributes declaration.** Attributes represent the characteristics of an element. An element can contain multiple attributes. For each element attribute that is used in an XML document, a corresponding attribute declaration must be specified in the DTD.
- **Content model.** The content model is used to describe the content of an element.
- **Entity declaration.** Entities are aliases associated with a group of data. These are used in a document to avoid typing long pieces of text repeatedly.

The general structure of a DTD is shown below:

```
<!DOCTYPE dtd-name
[
Element declaration(
Attribute declaration
]
>
```

Element Declaration

An element declaration specifies a single markup element. Every tag used in the XML document must be must be defined with an element declaration in the corresponding DTD.

The syntax to declare an element is:

```
<!ELEMENT element-name (element content-type)>
```

For example, consider a DTD, restaurant.dtd, that is used to define details about restaurants. The details include the following elements:

- RESTAURANT. Identifies the restaurant
- NAME. Identifies the name of the restaurant
- LOCATION. Identifies the location of the restaurant
- ADDRESS. Identifies the address of the restaurant
- PHONE. Provides the phone number of the restaurant
- REMARKS. Used to provide comments about the restaurant

The declarations for these elements are:

```
<!ELEMENT restaurant>
<!ELEMENT name>
<!ELEMENT location>
<!ELEMENT address>
<!ELEMENT phone>
<!ELEMENT remarks>
```

Attribute Declaration

Attribute declarations define the sets of attributes for an element. Every attribute used in the XML document must have a declaration in the corresponding DTD. All elements need not have attributes.

For example, in restaurant.dtd, attributes may be added to the RESTAURANT element.

An attribute TYPE with values as Continental, Chinese, Indian, Mexican, and Multicuisine can be added to the RESTAURANT element using the following declaration:

```
<!ATTLIST RESTAURANT TYPE (INDIAN | CONTINENTAL | CHINESE | MEXICAN | MULTICUISINE )
"CONTINENTAL" #REQUIRED>
```

The default value for an attribute is enclosed in quotation marks. `#REQUIRED` indicates that the attribute is mandatory and is required each time the element is used in a document.

Content Model

A content model is part of the element declaration and is used to describe the content of the element. There are three different types of content:

- **Data content.** This signifies text-based characters and is the most basic type of content. Data content can be specified either as `#CDATA` or `#PCDATA`. `#CDATA` is used to specify that the element contain data that is not to be parsed by the parser, whereas `#PCDATA` is used to specify that the element contains data that is to be parsed by the parser.
- **Element content.** This specifies the *child elements* that are contained in the element. In addition, element content specifies which of the child elements are required and the order in which these elements must appear in the document.
- **Mixed content.** Mixed content signifies both the data and element content.

An element with data is declared as shown:

```
<!ELEMENT element-name (data-type)>
```

An element with a child element is declared as shown:

```
<!ELEMENT element-name (child-element-name)>
```

Multiple child elements can be separated with a comma. In an XML document, the child elements must appear in the same sequence as they have been declared in the DTD. A question mark (?) after a child element indicates that the element is optional.

In the restaurant.dtd, the RESTAURANT element contains all the other elements. The restaurant.dtd, after adding the content model information, is as follows:

```
<!ELEMENT RESTAURANT (NAME, LOCATION, ADDRESS, PHONE, REMARKS?)>
<!ATTLIST RESTAURANT TYPE (INDIAN ¦ CONTINENTAL ¦ CHINESE ¦ MEXICAN
 ¦ MULTICUISINE ) "CONTINENTAL" #REQUIRED>
              <!ELEMENT NAME (#PCDATA)>
              <!ELEMENT LOCATION EMPTY>
              <!ATTLIST LOCATION TYPE (SOUTH¦NORTH¦EAST¦WEST) "SOUTH" )>
<!ELEMENT ADDRESS (#PCDATA)>
<!ELEMENT PHONE (#PCDATA)>
```

The keyword `EMPTY` can be used as the content-type to specify that the element has no child elements. The `ELEMENT LOCATION` is a singleton tag that does not require the start and the end tags.

Entity Declaration

Entities are used within a document to avoid typing long pieces of repetitive text. Such texts can be assigned an alias, which can further be used in the document. When the document is processed, the alias is replaced by the text specified.

Table 26.1 lists some of the predefined entities in XML.

Table 26.1 Predefined Entities in XML

Entity Name	Character
<	<
>	>
&	&
&quto	“
'	‘

Entities are of two types:

- **General entities.** A general entity is declared as follows:

```
<!ENTITY myaddress " 112 Vasant Enclave New Delhi -57">
```

This is an example of an internal entity, where the text phrase being mapped is in the entity declaration itself. An external entity maps the unique name to a block of text stored outside of the document. A general entity is referenced with & before the entity name.

- **Parameter entities.** Parameter entities are specified by %. These entities are similar to general entities but can be used only within the DTD.

Structure of an XML Document

An XML document consists of character data and the markup that describes the data. A sample XML document created based on restaurant.dtd is shown below:

```
<?xml version="1.0"?>
<RESTAURANT TYPE="CONTINENTAL">
        <NAME> Sensoi </NAME>
        <LOCATION TYPE="SOUTH" />
        <ADDRESS> West End, Wellingdon Street, New Delhi</ADDRESS>
        <PHONE>91-011-6854672</PHONE>
</RESTAURANT>
```

An XML document has the following components:

- XML declaration
- Elements
- Attributes
- Entities
- Comments

XML Declaration

An XML declaration is the first statement in an XML document. It is used to identify the document as an XML document. It is also used to specify processing instructions such as whether the application should process only the XML document or the DTD as well. The XML declaration may include attributes such as version and encoding. For example,

```
<?XML version= "1.0" encoding="UTF-8"?>
```

`<?` and `?>` signifies that XML is a processing instruction. The processing instructions are used to pass messages to the application processing the XML document. Such processing instructions can be placed anywhere in the document.

The attribute `version` specifies the version of the XML document. The `encoding` attribute is used to specify the character encoding used by the author. `UTF-8` corresponds to 8-bit ASCII characters.

Elements

Elements are the main components of a markup language and are defined in the DTD. Every XML document must have one *root* element. A root element describes the function of the document. In the restaurant.dtd example, `<RESTAURANT>` is the root element. The root element contains the other elements of the XML document.

Elements are specified using tags. A tag is specified with in angular brackets (< >). A tag can be a *paired tag* with a start tag (<element>) and an end tag (</element>). A tag can also be a *singleton tag* that does not have start and end tags and therefore cannot contain any elements or data. Singleton tags are signified with the `EMPTY` keyword in the DTD.

The text between the start and the end tags is defined as the *character data*. Character data may be any legal Unicode character except <.

Attributes

Attributes provide additional information about the elements. Attributes are embedded in the stat tag. An attribute consists of an attribute name and an attribute value. In the preceding sample XML code, the RESTAURANT element contains an attribute TYPE that specifies the cuisine that the restaurant specializes in.

Entities

Entities are used to specify an alias for test data that needs to be typed repeatedly. Entities must be declared before they are referenced in the XML document. An example of an entity is as follows:

```
<!ENTITY Poor "The restaurant has poor customer service">
```

This entity can be referenced as `&Poor`. For example,

```
<REMARKS> &Poor </REMARKS>
```

In an XML document, all entities are declared within a `DOCTYPE` declaration. The `<!DOCTYPE [...] >` declaration follows the XML declaration. For example,

```
<?xml version="1.0"?>
<!DOCTYPE RESTAURANT[
<!ENTITY Poor "The restaurant has poor customer service">
]>
```

Comments

The syntax to specify comments in an XML document is:

```
<!- Comments->
```

For example,

```
<?xml version="1.0"?>
<!-This is a comment ->
<RESTAURANT TYPE="CONTINENTAL">
      <NAME> Sensoi </NAME>
      <LOCATION TYPE="SOUTH" />
      <ADDRESS> West End, Wellingdon Street, New Delhi</ADDRESS>
      <PHONE>91-011-6854672</PHONE>
</RESTAURANT>
```

Applying Style Sheets to an XML Document

XML is used to organize and display data to Web users. The output of such a document is plain with different tags displayed in a tree structure and is not formatted. To format an XML document, you can apply a *style sheet*. Style sheets apply style to the XML documents and make them look attractive and user-friendly. Style sheets contain the rules that declare how an XML document must appear. There are many style sheets available in the market; two of these are:

- CSSs (*Cascading Style Sheets*). These help to manipulate the visibility, positioning and sizing of elements; colors; and background, font, text, and spacing of an element.

- XSL (*eXtensible Stylesheet Language*). XSL contains an XML vocabulary that specifies the formatting rules and a language to transform XML documents.

A CSS is included in an XML document using the following statement:

```
<? xml-stylesheet type="text/css" href="mycsssheet.css"?>
```

An XSL is included in an XML document using the following statement:

```
<? xml-stylesheet type="text/xsl" href="myxslsheet.xsl"?>
```

NOTE

An XSL sheet provides support for sorting operators and filtering.

The XML DOM

The XML DOM is used to access and manipulate the XML document programmatically. The DOM is an in-memory, cached tree representation of an XML document that enables the navigation and modification of a document including adding, updating, or deleting the content of elements. The DOM represents data as a hierarchy of object nodes.

Consider a sample XML document:

```
<book>
        <name> Gone with the Wind </name>
        <language> English </language>
</book>
```

According to the XML DOM, this document contains the following objects:

- **Document object.** This includes the entire document.
- **The book object.** This is a root node that has two child elements, name and language.
- **The name object.** This is a text object and has a sibling object, language.
- **Gone with the Wind.** This is a text object and a child of the name object.

- **The language object.** This is an object that has a sibling object name and a child text object.
- **English.** This is a child of the language object.

Table 26.2 lists some of the commonly used XML DOM objects.

Table 26.2 XML DOM Objects

Object	Description
DOMDocument	Represents the top node of the XML DOM tree
XMLDOMNode	Represents a single node in the DOM tree
XMLDOMAttribute	Represents an attribute object
XMLDOMCDATASection	Marks the text such that the text is not interpreted as markup language
XMLDOMDocumentType	Contains information associated with the document declaration
XMLDOMEntity	Represents an entity in the XML document
XMLDOMProcessingInstruction	Represents a processing instruction

NOTE

For information on using the XML DOM objects for scripting, refer to the section "Creating LotusScript Agents to Access XML."

Using XML in a Domino Application

Domino databases are well suited to handle XML data because their architecture is similar to those of XML in having separate data and presentation. Documents in Domino are created using forms. These forms can be compared to the DTDs that define the structure of the document. They also contain the presentation logic for the documents that represent the data. The same document can be displayed using multiple forms, thereby changing the presentation logic of the document. Thus forms can be compared to a style sheet that is applied to XML data.

The views in Domino can be used to display a collection of documents. Because a view does not contain the XML declaration and the root elements, it must be embedded on a page or a form before it can be viewed. The XML declaration and the root elements can then be inserted on this page to generate XML data.

Domino agents can be used to access XML data programmatically. You can use both LotusScript and Java agents to handle XML. In the following sections, you will learn to implement these Domino database elements to work with XML.

Designing a Form to Use XML

You can convert documents created in Notes into well-formed XML documents. These documents can then be used to export data to any platform. Perform the following steps to design a Restaurant form that describes details about the restaurants.

1. Create a new blank database named Restaurants in Domino Designer.
2. In the database, create a new form titled RDetails.
3. Place the cursor on the first line and enter the following XML declaration:

   ```
   <?xml version="1.0">
   ```

4. Place the cursor on the next line, and create the fields that you want to include in the form.
5. Enclose each field between a start and an end tag corresponding to the field enclosed. For example,

   ```
   <NAME> Name field </NAME>
   ```

6. Insert a line before the first field and enter the parent tag as `<RESTAURANT>`. Enter the end tag for this on the line after the last field.

   Figure 26.1 shows the form that you have just designed.

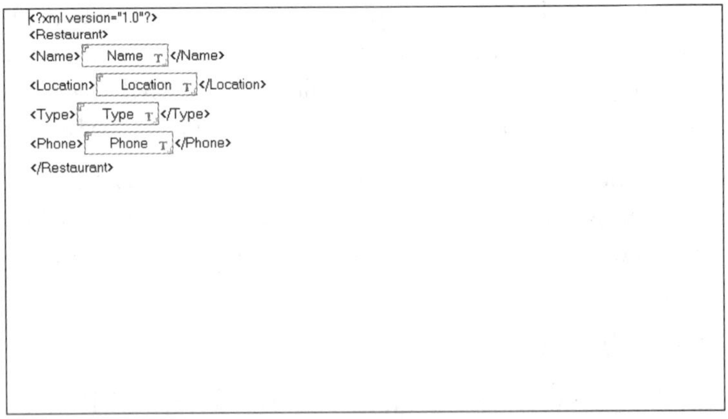

FIGURE 26.1 *The RDetails form*

7. In the form properties, select the Defaults tab, and in the On Web Access section, select the Content type as HTML. This ensures that the Domino Web sever passes the document as it is to the browser without converting it to HTML tags. Figure 26.2 shows the property on the Defaults tab of the form properties box.

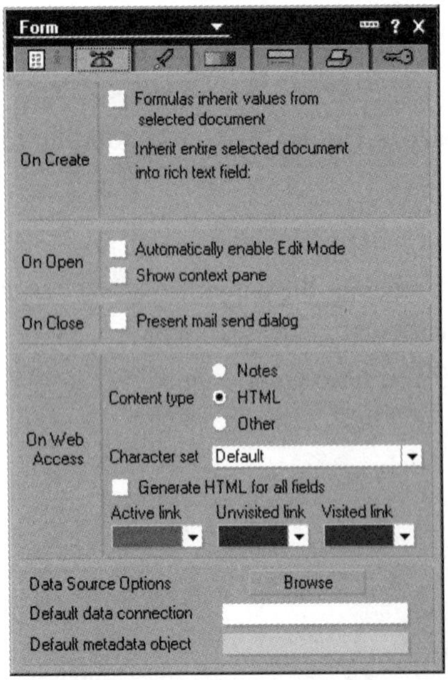

FIGURE 26.2 *The Defaults tab of the form properties dialog box*

8. Save and close the form.
9. Create a few documents using the RDetails form. To do so, choose Create/RDetails.

Designing a View for XML

To display the XML documents, you must create a view. To create the required view, perform the following steps:

1. In the Restaurant database, create a new shared view. Name the view **Restaurants**.
2. Choose Select By formula and enter the view selection formula as:

```
SELECT form="RDetails"
```

3. Click Save and Customize to close the Create view dialog box.
4. In the View dialog box, click the Advanced tab, and in the Web Access section, select the option Treat view contents as HTML to ensure that Domino does not create HTML tags for the view. Figure 26.3 displays the Advanced tab of the view properties box.

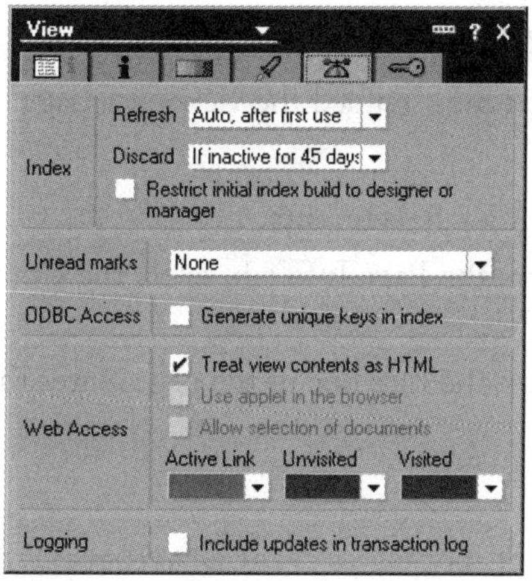

FIGURE 26.3 *The Advanced tab of the view properties dialog box*

5. Close the view properties dialog box. Add columns for each field in the RDetails form.
6. Select the first column. In the Column Value event in the Programmer's pane, choose to display Formula and enter the following formula:

```
"<Restaurant><Name>"+Name+"</Name>"
```

In this formula, `<Restaurant>` is the start tag for the parent element `Restaurant` and `<Name>` and `</Name>` are the start and end tags for the `Name` element. `Name` is the field.

7. Click the second column and enter the formula as:

```
"<Location>"+Location+"</Location>"
```

8. Repeat step 7 for the rest of the columns. For the last column, enter the formula as:

```
"<Phone>"+Phone+"</Phone></Restaurant>"
```

In this formula, `</Restaurant>` is the end tag for the parent element `<Restaurant>`.

9. Save and close the view.

Embedding the View on a Page

To add a root element to the XML, you must embed the view on a page. To do so, perform the following steps:

1. Create a new page and name it **ViewRestaurants**.
2. Open the page properties, and on the Page Info tab, select the Content type as HTML from the Web Access section.
3. Close the page properties, and on the first line of the page, enter the following XML declaration:

```
<?xml version="1.0"?>
```

4. On the next line, enter the parent root tag as `<RestaurantDetails>`.
5. Move the cursor to the next line and embed the Restaurant view.
6. Open the embedded view properties, and on the Info tab, select the option Display Using HTML from the Web Access section. Figure 26.4 displays the property in the Embedded View dialog box.

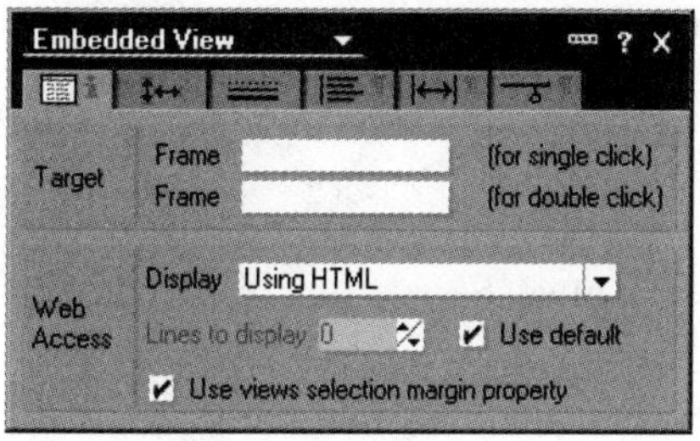

FIGURE 26.4 *The Embedded View dialog box*

7. On the line below the embedded view, enter the end root tag as:

```
</RestaurantDetails>
```

8. Save and close the page.

Preview the page in a browser. Figure 26.5 shows the output in Internet Explorer 5.0.

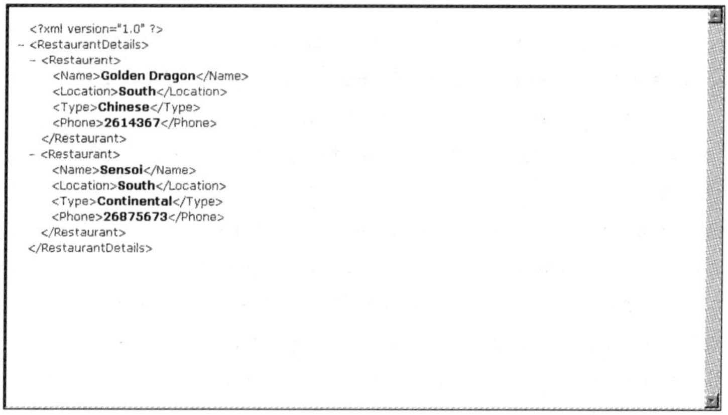

FIGURE 26.5 *XML generated on previewing the ViewRestaurants page in Internet Explorer 5.0*

Applying an XSL Style Sheet to Domino Data

To apply a style sheet to the Domino data, perform the following steps:

1. Create a new page in the Restaurants database and name it **StyleRestaurant.xsl**.
2. Open the page properties, and on the Page Info tab, select the Content type as HTML from the Web Access section.

3. Enter the style sheet text as shown below:

```
<?xml version="1.0"?>
<xsl:stylesheet xmlns:xsl="http://www.w3.org/TR/WD-xsl
<xsl:template match="/" >
<!--Set the table border to 3 pixels, inset, blue-->
<TABLE STYLE="border:3px inset blue">
    <!--Use the <TR> tag to create the first row of the table and
    set the  font of the text in this row to 10 point, boldface,
    Arial, and the background color of the row to cyan-->
    <TR STYLE="font-size:10pt; font-family:Arial;
    background-color: cyan;font-weight:bold">
        <!--Define text that'll appear in the first row of the table-->
        <TD>Name</TD>
        <TD>Location</TD>
        <TD>Type</TD>
        <TD>Phone</TD>
    </TR>
    <!--Apply the defined style to each element in the
    <restaurantdetails><restaurant> element and puts them in the
    table in order by the name tag in the document.-->
    <xsl:for-each select="RestaurantDetails/Restaurant"
    order-by="Name">
      <!--Create the second row and subsequent rows of the
      table and sets its font attributes to Arial, 10 point.
      It also sets the cell padding to 0 pixels and six pixels.-->
      <TR STYLE="font-family:Arial; font-size:10pt; padding:0px 6px">
      <!--Put the data contained by the various tags into the
      cells in the table-->
        <TD><xsl:value-of select="Name" /></TD>
        <TD><xsl:value-of select="Location" /></TD>
        <TD><xsl:value-of select="Type" /></TD>
        <TD><xsl:value-of select="Phone" /></TD
      </TR>
    </xsl:for-each>
</TABLE>
</xsl:template>
</xsl:stylesheet>
```

4. Save and close the page.
5. Open the ViewRestaurants page and below the line `<?xml version ="1.0"?>`, enter the following declaration:

```
<?xml:stylesheet type="text/xsl" href="restaurant.xsl ?OpenPage"?>
```

6. Save the page and preview it. The page gets formatted according to the style sheet applied. Figure 26.6 shows the XML document formatted according to the style sheet restaurant.xsl.

FIGURE 26.6 *XML page after applying a style sheet as previewed in Internet Explorer 5.0*

Creating LotusScript Agents to Access XML

You can programmatically access the XML data from Domino using a LotusScript agent. This agent can be executed from the Web using an outline entry, an action, or the `WebQuerySave` event of a form by writing the following formula:

@Command([ToolsRunMacro];"agent")

To create an agent that displays the ViewRestaurants page using a server-side LotusScript agent, perform the following steps:

1. Create a new agent in the Restaurants database.
2. In the Agent dialog box, enter the name of the agent as **View XML**.
3. In the Runtime options, the Trigger is selected as Action menu selection by default. Select the target as None.

4. Close the dialog box. Choose the option to run LotusScript and in the Script area enter the following code:

```
Dim xmldoc As Variant
sourceUrl="http://r6server/Retaurants.nsf/ViewRestaurants?OpenPage"
Set xmldoc = CreateObject("Microsoft.XMLDOM")
xmldoc.async = False
'This line loads the XML into the parser.
xmldoc.load(sourceUrl)
'This line prevents Domino from sending default headers.
Print "Content-type: text/xml"
'displays the resulting XML in the browser
Print xmldoc.xml
```

5. Save and close the agent.

Domino DTD

The Domino data can be exported to external databases or external data can be converted to Domino data by using XML. The representation of the Domino data in the XML format is known as DXL. DXL is used to define Domino-specific data and design elements. The structure of DXL is defined in the form of a DTD known as the Domino DTD. The Domino DTD contains the following components:

- Core entities
- Common entities
- Domino elements

Core Entities

The core entities are the data type definitions. Table 26.3 lists some of the core entities in Domino DTD.

Table 26.3 List of Core Entities in Domino DTD

Entity Name	Description
<!ENTITY % binary "#PCDATA">	Encoded Base64 data
<!ENTITY % boolean.choices "true|false">	Boolean (true or false) choice
<!ENTITY % dbid "CDATA">	Identifier for a database
<!ENTITY % float "CDATA">	Floating point value
<!ENTITY % noteid "CDATA">	Four to eight character hexadecimal identifier for a note
<!ENTITY % number "CDATA">	Number
<!ENTITY % replicaid "CDATA">	Identifier for a replicated database
<!ENTITY % string "CDATA">	String that can not be translated into another natural language
<!ENTITY % tstring "CDATA">	String that can be translated into another natural language
<!ENTITY % unid "CDATA">	32-character hexadecimal identifier for a document
<!ENTITY % uri "CDATA">	Uniform Resource Identifiers such as URLs

Common Entities

Common entities are the Domino DTD entities that are referenced in other entities or in more than one element. An example of a common entity is the `%acl.levels` entity. This entity defines the access levels allowed in a Domino database and can be used in the `<acl>` and `<aclentry>` elements. The `%acl.levels` entity is defined as follows:

```
<!ENTITY % acl.levels "noaccess ¦ depositor ¦ reader ¦ author ¦
 editor ¦ designer ¦ manager ">
```

Table 26.4 lists some of the common entities in the Domino DTD.

Table 26.4 List of Common Entities in Domino DTD

Entity Name	Description
%acl.levels	Lists the access levels allowed in a Domino database
%color	Defines colors
%field.kinds	Lists the options for defining whether a field is editable or computed
%formula.types	Defines the options for the formula type attributes in the <simpleaction> and <agent> elements
%imageformats	Defines the options for image formats
%item.complex.types	Defines the types of items allowed in a Domino database
%launch.all.whenopened	Lists the types of launch settings that can be applied to a Notes database
%launch.notes.whenopenend	Lists the launch settings that are specific to launching Notes databases in Lotus Notes
%note.attrs	Represents the attributes that are common to all notes, including design elements
%onopengoto.options	Lists the options for setting the focus when a view or folder opens
%onrefresh.options	Lists the options for refreshing a view or folder
%richtext.block	Lists the elements that appear at the paragraph level, such as the <block>, <richtext>, <section>, and <tablecell> elements
%richtext.links	Lists the types of links used in rich text elements
%root.attrs	Defines the attributes of root elements, such as <database>, <acl>, <profiledocument>, and <viewentries>
%send.value.types	Defines the data types that can make up the content of a mail message
%simple.types	Defines common data type elements
%view.and.folder.attrs	Defines the attributes of views and folders

Domino Elements

Domino elements include all the elements of a Notes database. Some of the Domino elements listed in the Domino DTD are listed in Table 26.5.

Table 26.5 List of Domino Elements in Domino DTD

List 1	List 2	List 3
<acl>	<keywords>	<sendmailaction>
<action>	<lastaccessed>	<sendto>
<agent>	<lotusscript>	<servlet>
<created>	<noteslaunch>	<sharedactions>
<database>	<number>	<sharedfield>
<databaseinfo>	<page>	<simpleaction>
<databaselink>	<profiledocument>	<subform>
<dataconnection>	<richtext>	<table>
<datamodified>	<role>	<text>
<datechoice>	<java>	<search>
<datetime>	<javascript>	<section>
<doclink>	<embeddedview>	<document>
<field>	<folder>	<form>
<formula>	<frame>	<fulltextsettings>
<java>	<javascript>	<updatedby>

Summary

This chapter discussed the basics of XML. It demonstrated the use of XML in Domino. You learned to create a form, a view, a page, and a LotusScript agent to access the page in order to create XML data from Domino. You also learned about the Domino DTD.

Chapter 27

Creating Help in a Notes Application

Help options provide assistance to an end user using an application. A Notes application has various methods to provide help information to end users. The "About Database" document in a database provides information about a database, such as its purpose, creator, and intended audience. The "Using Database" document specifies instructions to use a database. Refer to Chapter 2, "Basics of a Notes Application," to learn more about the "Using Database" and "About Database" documents.

This chapter introduces other help options available in Notes. It explains how to create field help in a form using options such as Help Description, Field Hint, and by creating a text pop-up. This chapter also describes how to configure context-sensitive help for a Notes database and how to display Notes, Designer, and Administration help databases programmatically.

Providing Help for a Field

A field is a container that helps capture information from an end user. A form contains labels for all fields. These labels describe the information that needs to be entered in a field. Notes offers the following options to provide additional help with a field:

- Field Help
- Field Hint
- Text pop-up

Field Help

The field help option displays help text in the Notes client when an end user fills out a document. It is one line of text that can contain a maximum of 70 characters. These characters can include letters, numbers, spaces, and punctuation. Figure 27.1 shows the field help at the bottom of the window, with the Complaint No. field.

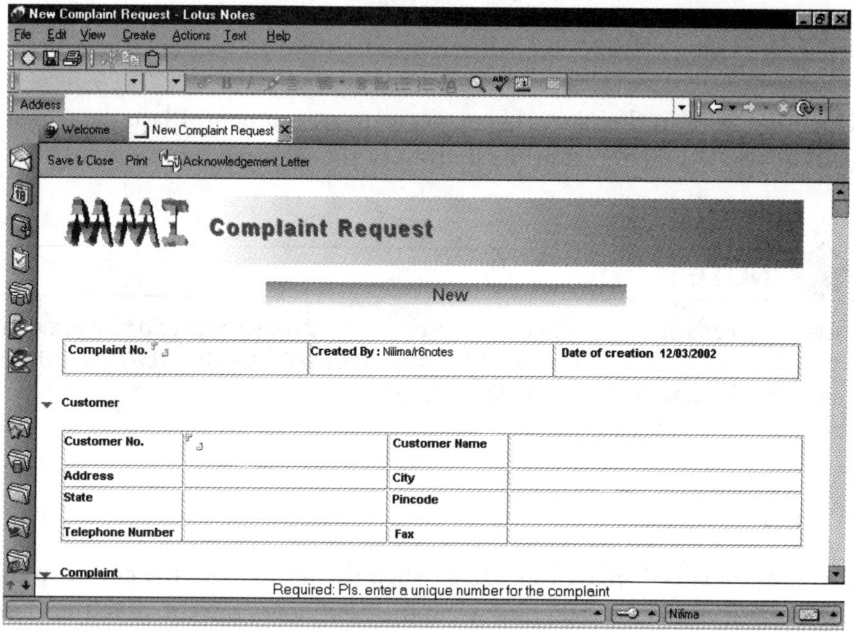

FIGURE 27.1 *Field help in the Notes client*

To add the field help option to any field:

1. Open the form that contains the field to which you want to add the help text in the Domino Designer.
2. Select the appropriate field and double-click to access field properties.
3. Select the Advanced tab and enter the help text in the Help Description field. Figure 27.2 shows the Advanced tab of field properties.

FIGURE 27.2 *The Advanced tab of field properties*

4. Close the Field dialog box.
5. Save and close the form.

Open the form in the Notes client to create a document. Place the cursor in the field to view the help text at the bottom of the window.

NOTE

Clear the menu option View/Show/Field Help to stop the display of field help in the Notes client. This option is selected by default. You can also use `@Command([ViewShowFieldHelp])` to hide or display the field help option for a field.

Field Hint

Field hint text is displayed in a field when the user moves the cursor to the field. Figure 27.3 shows the field hint when the user moves the cursor to the Complaint No. field. The hint text MMI-02-XXXX specifies the format of the Complaint No. This text disappears when the user clicks the field.

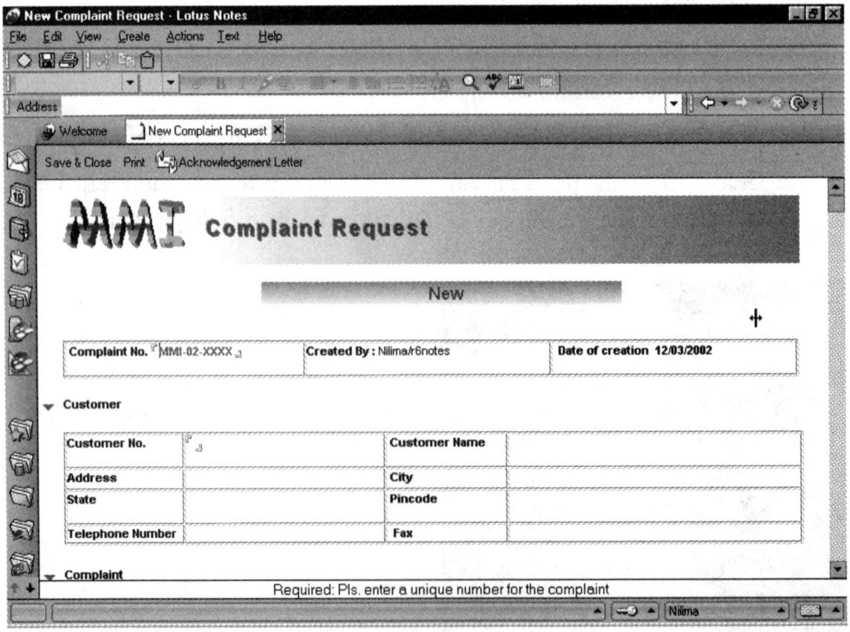

FIGURE 27.3 *A field hint in the Notes client*

To add field hint text to any field:

1. Open the form that contains the field in the Domino Designer.
2. Select the appropriate field and double-click to access field properties.
3. Select the Advanced tab. In the Field Hint field, enter the hint text that you want to display. Refer to Figure 27.2 to view the field hint text in the Advanced tab of field properties.
4. Close the Field dialog box.
5. Save and close the form.

Open the form in the Notes client to create a document. Move the cursor to the field to view the hint text.

Text Pop-Up

The text pop-up option is associated with a field label and is used to display multiline help text. Figure 27.4 shows a text pop-up that is displayed when the cursor is moved over the label Possible Claim in the form.

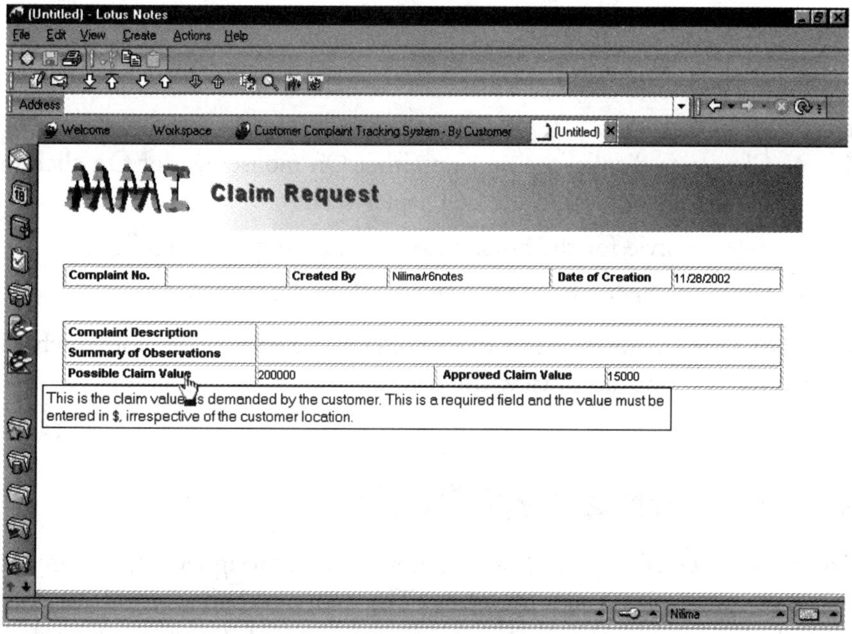

FIGURE 27.4 *A text pop-up attached to a field label*

To create a text pop-up for a field label:

1. Open the form in which you want to create the pop-up in Domino Designer.
2. Select the label on which you want to write the text pop-up. Select Create/Hotspot/Text Pop-up. The HotSpot Pop-up dialog box appears, as shown in Figure 27.5.

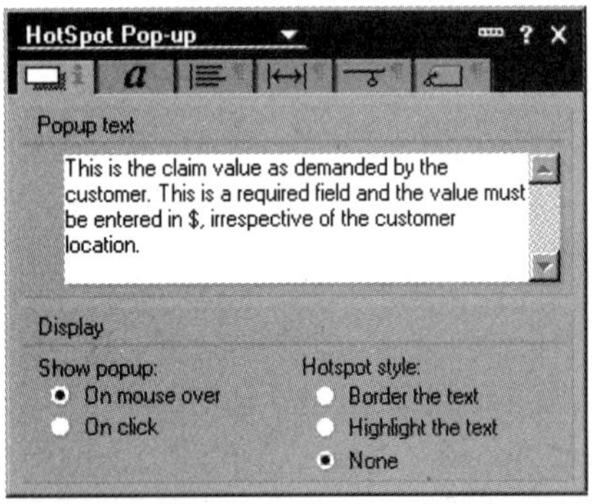

FIGURE 27.5 *The HotSpot Pop-up dialog box*

3. In the Popup text field, enter the help text that you want to attach to the label.
4. Choose to display the pop-up either On mouse over or On click in the Show pop-up option in the Display section.
5. Select a style for the hotspot to either border it or highlight it.
6. Close the dialog box and save and close the form.

Open the form in Notes client. Place the cursor over the label for which you have created the text pop-up to view the text.

Creating Detailed Help

To provide detailed help in an application, you can design a help document in the database and display it in a help view. The user can then access these documents from the help view in the database whenever required. To create a help document:

1. Open the database in which you want to create help documents in the Domino Designer.
2. Create a new form and name it **Help.**
3. Create fields on the form to define the field content. Figure 27.6 displays the layout of a sample help form.

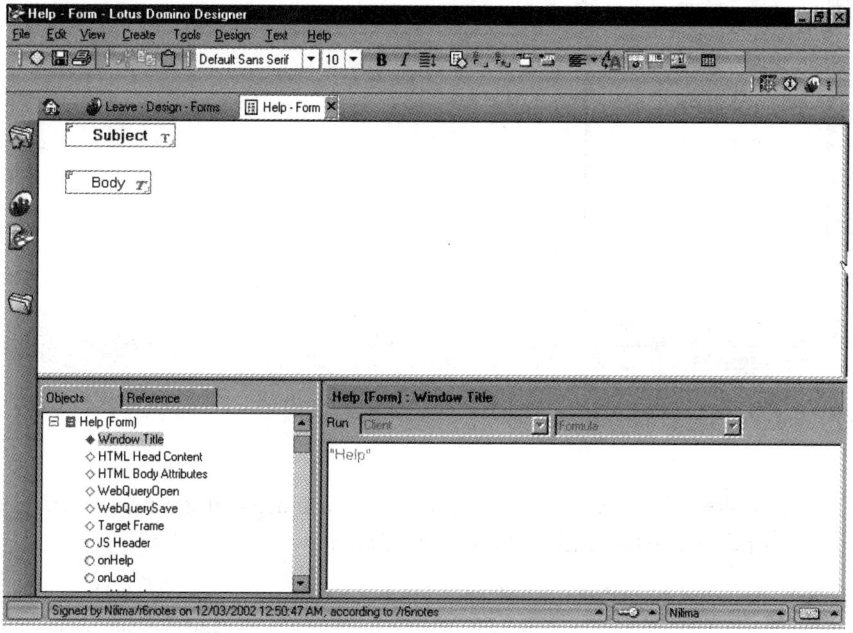

FIGURE 27.6 *A sample layout for a help form*

4. Enter the Window title as **Help**.
5. Save and close the form.
6. Use the menu option Create/Help in the Notes client to create help documents.
7. Open the help form in Domino Designer and from form properties, clear the option Include in Menu.
8. Save and close the form.
9. Create a help view to display this document. Figure 27.7 displays a sample help view.

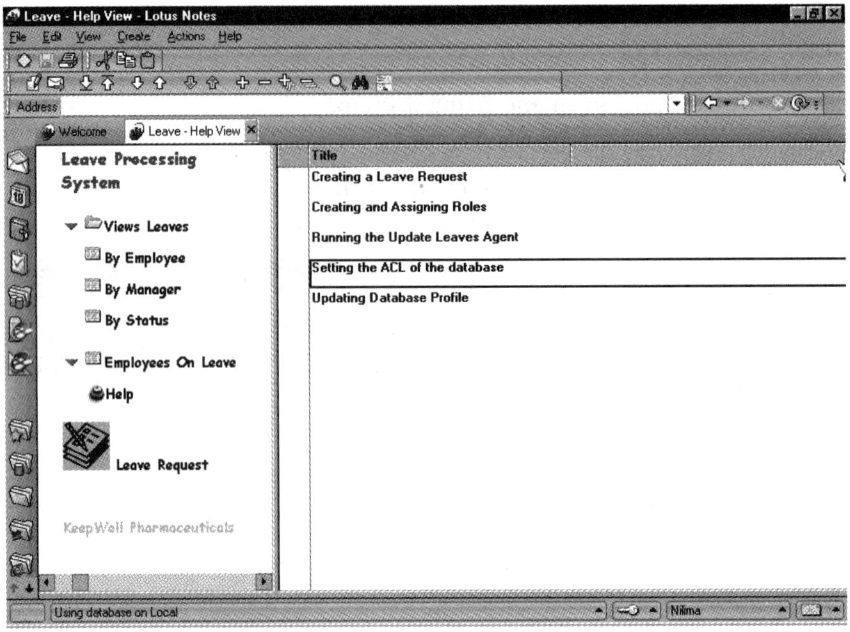

FIGURE 27.7 *A sample help view*

10. Make this view accessible to users. If you are using a navigator, create an option HELP and add a link to the view.

To get detailed help for any of the database features, users can click the HELP link or go to the help view directly and open a specific help document.

Providing Context-Sensitive Help

Context-sensitive help refers to the information displayed when a user clicks the F1 key. Notes has help databases for the Administration, Designer, and Notes clients. When you press the F1 key in any of the clients, help from the respective databases is displayed. For example, if you press the F1 key while working in a view in the Notes client, Help on views, folders, and panes from the Lotus Notes 6 Help database is displayed.

You can create your own help database and associate it with various design elements in the application to provide context-sensitive help to the users. If you associate a customized help document with any design element, it overrides the default Notes help.

Creating a Help Database

A help database contains a form used to create help documents. These documents are displayed in a view. To create a help database, perform the following steps:

1. Create a new database on the server. Name the database **MyHelp.**
2. Create a new form in the MyHelp Database. Name the form **HelpForm.** This form can have any layout and content, but it must have a field that can be used as a key to open the appropriate help documents from the application. Figure 27.8 shows the Help form with Title as the key field.

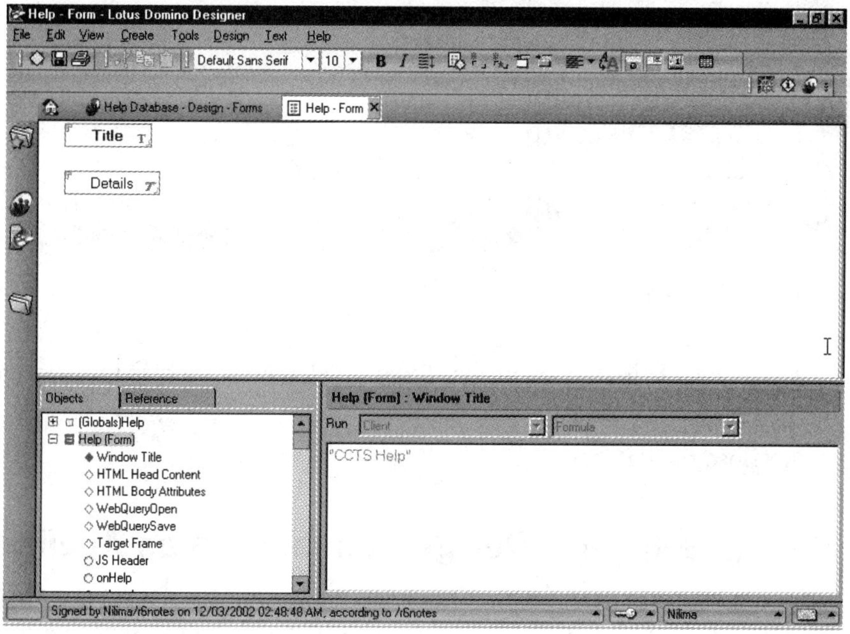

FIGURE 27.8 *A sample help form*

3. Create a view in the help database and assign a name to it. This must be a shared view and must contain help documents sorted by the key field. Figure 27.9 displays a sample help view.

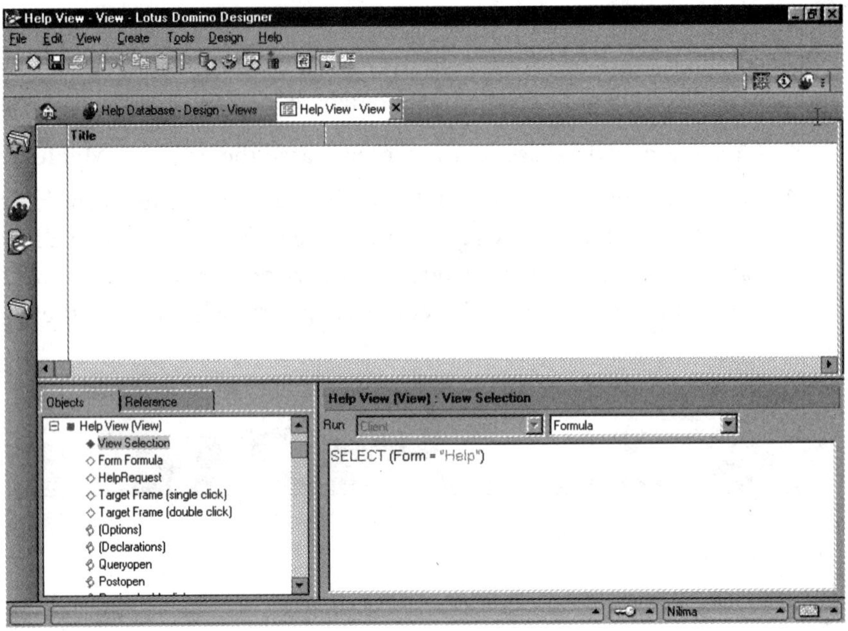

FIGURE 27.9 *A sample help view*

4. Create a help document for all design elements, such as forms, pages, views, and folders, in your application.
5. Close the database.

Associating Help with Design Elements in an Application

After designing the help database, you can associate help documents with individual design elements in the application to provide context-sensitive help. You can open a help document from a help database using the OpenHelpDocument @Command. The syntax of this @Command is as follows:

```
@Command([OpenHelpDocument];Server:Database;Viewname;Key)
```

In the preceding syntax:

- `Server` is the name of the server on which the database is located.
- `Database` is the path and the file name of the help database.
- `ViewName` is the name of the view in the help database that contains the help documents.

- `Key` is the value that is searched for in the first sorted column of the view. This corresponds to the key field created in the Help form.

You can also display documents from one of the Notes help databases using this @Command. To do this, replace the `Server:Database` parameter with one of the following options:

- `[ClientHelp]` to open Lotus Domino 6 Help.
- `[DesignerHelp]` to open Lotus Domino 6 Designer Help.
- `[AdminHelp]` to open Lotus 6 Administration Help.

For example, to display help when the user presses F1, you need to write this command on the `HelpRequest` or the `OnHelp` event of the specific design element. The `HelpRequest` event is available in a view and a folder, while the form and page have the event `OnHelp`.

Creating Context-Sensitive Help for the CCTS Application

To create context-sensitive help for the CCTS (*customer complaint tracking system*) that you created in Chapter 18, "Creating a Customer Complaint Tracking Application":

1. Create a database titled CCTSHelp on the server.
2. Create a form titled **HelpForm** and a view titled **Help View**, as described previously in this chapter, in the section "Creating a Help Database."
3. Use the HelpForm to create documents that describe the purpose and usage of various forms and views in the CCTS database. For each document, enter the name of the form or the view in the Title field.
4. Open the Claim Request form in the CCTS application. Click the OnHelp form event and select to run Formula in Client from the Run list. Enter the following code in the Script area:

```
@Command([OpenHelpDocument];"r6server/r6notes":"CCTSHelp";
"Help View";"ClaimRequest")
```

5. Preview the form and press the F1 key in the Notes client to test the document display. Figure 27.10 displays a sample help document that describes the Claim Request form in the CCTS application.

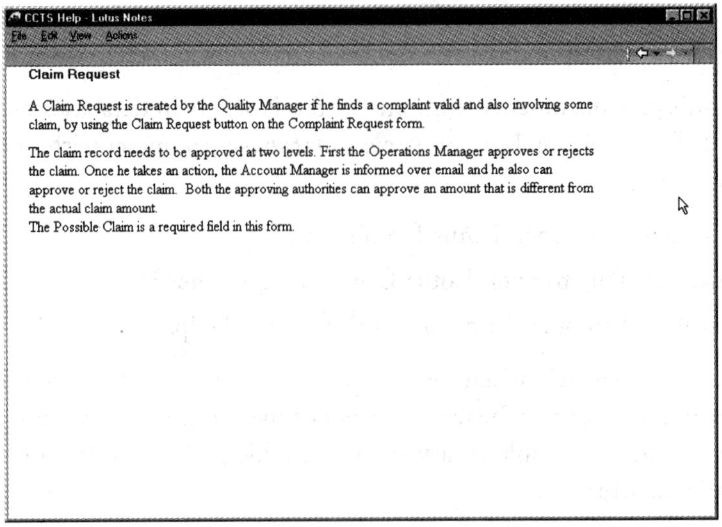

FIGURE 27.10 *A sample help document*

6. Repeat step 4 for all design elements for which you have created help documents in the CCTSHelp database. Specify the title of the help document as the last parameter to the @Command.
7. Close the database.

Summary

In a Notes application, you can create help using the "About Database" document, the "Using Database" document, the help description, the field hint, and the text pop-up. You can provide better help by creating a help document and a help view. It is also possible to create a help database to store help documents.

Chapter 28

Using Lists in Formula Language

A *list* is a collection of values of similar types grouped as an entity. Most often a list in Lotus Notes is used with a field that contains multiple values. For example, in an order form that contains orders for multiple products, the fields such as the product number, name, rate, and quantity are treated as lists because they hold multiple values.

In Lotus Notes formula language, you can create lists by concatenating values with a colon (:). In addition, some @Functions, such as `@UserRoles` and `@DbColumn`, return lists.

In this chapter, you'll be introduced to the basics of a list. You'll learn about the list operators and the @Functions used to work with lists. Finally, you'll look at some of the common applications of lists, list @Functions, and list operators in a Notes application.

Working with Lists

Lists are treated differently in Notes because when you perform any operation on a list, it acts on each of the list elements individually, rather than on a single element. For example, consider a list:

```
List:="pen":"pencil":"notebook"
```

To this list, you apply a standard string @Function as follows:

```
@UpperCase(List)
The resulting list will be "PEN":"PENCIL":"NOTEBOOK".
```

Similarly, if you perform a concatenation with a list as follows:

```
"I have a" + List
```

The result will be as follows:

```
"I have a pen": "I have a pencil": "I have a notebook"
```

NOTE

Lists are often used in the form of multivalue fields. In addition, they are used when you retrieve data from a view using the `@DbColumn` function.

List Operators

There are two commonly used list operators in formula language to work with lists:

- **List Concatenation operator.** A colon (:) is the list concatenation operator. It is used to create a list by combining two or more elements. For example, the following statement uses the concatenation operator to create a list named List1 with four elements:

  ```
  List1:="Apple":Mango":Grapes":Guava"
  ```

- **List Subscript operator.** A numeric value in square brackets ([]) is the list subscript operator. It is used to return one element from the list. It can be used with all types of lists, such as text, number, and date/time. The first element of a list is denoted with the subscript `1`. For example, consider a list List1 containing `"Apple":Mango":Grapes":Guava"`; the following statement will return `"Grapes"`:

List

CAUTION

A subscript less that 1 and greater than the number of elements in the list returns an error message Array index out of bounds.

You can perform arithmetic and comparison operations on lists in two ways, using pair-wise or permuted operators. For more information on these list operators, refer to the section " List Operators" in Chapter 4, "Working with Formulas in Domino Designer."

List Functions

Formula language has a rich collection of @Functions. Some of them are used exclusively with lists, whereas some can be used with lists as well as text type of data. The following sections explain some of the commonly used list functions:

- @Compare
- @IsNotMember

- @Member
- @Replace
- @Sort
- @Subset
- @Transform
- @Unique

To demonstrate these @Functions, the following two text lists have been used:

```
List1:="Apple":Mango":Grapes":Guava";
List2:="Apple":"Banana":"Watermelon":"Strawberries"
```

@Compare

The `@Compare` @Function is used to compare the alphabetical order (ASCII codes) of two lists, element by element. The syntax of this function is as follows:

```
@Compare(Textlist;Textlist;[options])
```

The options can be one of following:

- [CASESENSITIVE]
- [CASEINSENSITIVE]
- [ACCENTSENSITIVE]
- [ACCENTINSENSITIVE]
- [PITCHSENSITIVE]
- [PITCHINSENSITIVE]

This @Function returns a number list composed of one of the following values:

- `1` if the element in the first list is greater than the corresponding element in the second list.
- `0` if the element in the first list is equal to the corresponding element in the second list.
- `-1` if the element in the first list is less than the corresponding element in the second list.

For example,

```
@Compare(List1;List2)
will return 0:-1:1:1
```

The first element `"Apple"` is equal in both the lists; therefore, the result at the first position is `0`. The second element in the `List1` is `"Mango"`, whereas in `List2`, it is `"Banana"`. Because "M" is greater than "B," `-1` is returned at the second position. Similarly, the third and the fourth elements in `List1` are lesser than the corresponding elements in `List2`; therefore, the result is `1`.

@Count

The `@Count` @Function counts the number of elements in a list. This function returns `1` if the value in the list is `null` or is not a list.

The syntax of this function is as follows:

```
@Count(List )
```

where `list` can be a text, number, or date/time list.

For example, the following formula returns a value `4`:

```
@Count(List1)
```

@Elements

The `@Elements` @Function also returns the number of elements in a list. If the parameter passed is a null list or not a list, then `@Elements` returns `0`. The syntax of this function is:

```
@Elements(List)
```

where `list` can be a text, number, or date/time list.

The following statement returns a value `4`:

```
@Elements(List1)
```

The following example returns `0` if the user has not been assigned any roles in the ACL:

```
@Elements(@UserRoles))
```

@Explode

The `@Explode` @Function is used to convert a text string into a list with the specified separator. The syntax of this function is as follows:

```
@Explode(String;Separator;includeEmpties;newlineAsSeparator)
```

where

- `String` is the text string that you want to convert to a text list.
- `Separator` is the character separating the elements in the string. This is an optional parameter and Domino considers space, comma, and semicolon as the default separators.
- `includeEmpties` is an optional Boolean parameter used to specify whether or not an empty element should be added for a separator at the beginning or end of the string and also for two consecutive separators in the string.
- `newlineAsSeparator` is an optional parameter used to specify whether or not a new line should be considered as a separator. The value for this parameter is also specified as True or False.

For example, the following statement returns a list with three elements `user1`, `user2`, and `user3`.

```
@Explode("user1,user2,user2";",")
```

In the preceding example, comma (`,`) is the separator in the string.

A variation of the `@Explode` @Function is to create a list of dates by specifying a date range as follows:

```
@Explode(dateRange)
```

For example, `@Explode([01/01/02]-[01/05/02])` creates a list with date type elements as 01/01/02, 01/02/02, 01/03/02, 01/04/02, and 01/05/02.

@Implode

The `@Implode` @Function is used to convert a text list into a string. The default separator is a space. To use any other separator to join the elements of the list, you can specify the separator as the second argument to the list. The syntax for this function is as follows:

```
@Implode(TextList;Separator)
```

where `TextList` is the list to be joined to form the string and `Separator` is the character to be used between the elements in the string.

For example, the following statement converts `List1` to a text string:

```
@Implode(List1,",")
```

Consider another example,

```
"I Bought "+ @Implode(List1,",")
```

this returns the following string:

```
I Bought Apple, Mango, Grapes, Guava.
```

@IsMember

The `@IsMember` @Function checks whether or not the given string is part of a list. The syntax of this function is as follows:

```
@IsMember(String;List)
```

where `String` is the string to the searched in the `List`.

This function returns `1` or `true` if the string is found in the list. For example, the following statement returns `1`:

```
@IsMember("Watermelon";List2)
```

This function can also be used to search for one list in another list using the following syntax:

```
@IsMember(SList;List)
```

@IsNotMember

The `@IsNotMember` @Function is also used to search for a string or a list in another list. If the string is found, the function returns `0` (`false`); otherwise it returns `1` (`true`). The syntax is as follows:

```
@IsNotMember(String;List)
```

or

```
@IsNotMember(SList;List)
```

For example, the following statement returns `0`, because `Apple` is a member of `List1`:

```
@IsNotMember("Apple";List1)
```

@Member

The `@Member` @Function is used to find the position of a string in a text list. If the string is not found, then it returns 0. The syntax of this function is as follows:

```
@Member(String;List)
```

where `String` is searched in the `List`.

For example, the following statement returns `3`:

```
@Member("Grapes";List1)
```

@Replace

The `@Replace` @Function is used to find a value in a text list and replace it with another value. The syntax for this function is as follows:

```
@Replace(sourcelist;fromlist;tolist)
```

where `sourcelist` is the list in which the `@Replace` function is applied, `fromlist` is the list of values that you want to change, and `tolist` is the list of replacement values.

The following statement is used to replace `Apple` with `Mulberry` and `Watermelon` with `Blackberries`:

```
@Replace(List2;"Apple":"Watermelon";"Mulberry":Blackberries")
```

@Sort

The `@Sort` @Function is used to sort a list. The syntax for this function is as follows:

```
@Sort(List;[Order];customSortExpression)
```

where `List` is the list to be sorted.

An optional second parameter [Order] may be used to specify the order of the sort as one of the following:

- [ACCENTSENSITIVE]
- [ACCENTINSENSITIVE]
- [ASCENDING]
- [CASESENSITIVE]
- [CASEINSENSITIVE]
- [CUSTOMSORT]
- [DESCENDING]
- [PITCHSENSITIVE]
- [PITCHINSENSITIVE]

For example:

```
@Sort(List1;[ASCENDING])
```

The output of the preceding example is `"Apple":"Grapes":"Guava": "Mango"`.

A third parameter `customSortExpression` is used to specify the custom sort expression when the sort order is specified as `[CUSTOMSORT]`.

@Subset

The `@Subset` @Function is used to extract elements from a list. It searches the list from left to right and extracts the specified number of elements. The list can be searched from right to left by specifying a negative number. The syntax is as follows:

```
@Subset(List; Number)
```

where `List` can be a text, number, or date/time list and `Number` is the number of elements to be extracted from the list.

CAUTION

If you specify the second argument to the `@Subset` function as `0`, an error is returned.

For example, the following statement returns `Apple:Mango`.

```
@Subset(List1;2)
```

The following statement returns `Watermelon:Strawberries;`

```
@Subset(List2;-2)
```

@Transform

The `@Transform` @Function applies a formula to each element in a list and returns the result as a list. The syntax for this function is as follows:

```
@Transform(List;Variablename;Formula)
```

where `List` can be a text, number, or date/time. Each element of the list can be referenced in the formula by using `Variablename` and the `Formula` refers to the formula to be applied to the list.

For example, to concatenate "S_" before every element of a list and store the result in `NewList`, the following code can be used:

```
Nlist:="Rows":"Columns";
NewList:=@Transform(Nlist;"x";"S_"+x)
```

@Unique

The `@Unique` @Function is used to remove duplicate values from a text list. It returns the first occurrence of each element of the list. The syntax is as follows:

```
@Unique(TextList)
```

where `TextList` is the list from which duplicates have to be removed. For example, the following code returns `apple:mango:grapes`:

```
List1:="apple":"mango":"grapes":"mango";
@Unique(List1)
```

Moving ahead, you will learn how to manipulate a list.

Manipulating a List

When you work with lists, you need to perform various operations on them, such as adding to or removing elements from the list. These operations are performed using one or more of the list functions discussed in the preceding sections.

Adding Elements to a List

You can add elements to a list by using the list concatenation operator colon (:). The elements can be added to the beginning, middle, end, or at a specified position in the list. For example, to add an element `Orange` at the end of a list `List1`, where `List1` contains `"Red":"Blue":"Green"`, you must use the following statement:

```
List2:=List1:"Orange"
```

To add to the beginning of a list, you must use the following statement:

```
List2:="Orange":List1
```

To add an element in the middle of the list, you must either know the position in which you want to add the element or the element after which you want to add the new element. For example, to obtain a list `"Red":"Blue":"Orange":"Green"`, `"Orange"` can be added to `List1` either in the third position or after the element "Blue".

To add an element at a specified position, you must break the list into two, one containing the elements up to the element before the one to be deleted and the other containing the rest of the elements. Then you concatenate the first list, the new list, and the second list to obtain the final list.

For example, to add `Orange` in the third position, perform the following steps:

1. Obtain the first list containing two elements using the following code:

   ```
   FList:=@Subset(List1;2)
   ```

   This assigns `"Red":Blue"` to `FList`.

2. Obtain the second list containing the rest of the elements. To do this, first find the number of remaining elements and extract them starting from the end of the list, as shown below:

   ```
   Tot:=@Elements(List1);
   Rest:=Tot-2;
   SList:=@Subset(List1;-Rest)
   ```

   This assigns `Green` to `Rest`.

3. Concatenate the lists to obtain the final list using the following statements.

   ```
   NewList:=Flist:"Orange":Rest
   ```

   The NewList now contains `"Red":"Blue":"Orange":Green"`.

To add an element after a specified element, you must first find the position of the element in the list. You can do this by using the `@Member` function.

To find the position of `Blue` in `List1`, you can use the following statement:

```
@Member("Blue":List1)
```

After finding the position of the element, create two lists, one containing elements up to the chosen element and the other containing the rest of the elements. Finally, you concatenate the lists.

The complete code for this is shown below:

```
List1:="Red":"Blue":"Green";
Tot:=@Elements(List1);
Pos:= @Member("Blue":List1);
Flist:= :=@Subset(List1;Pos);
SList:=@Subset(List1;Pos-Tot)
NewList:=Flist:"Orange":Slist
```

Removing Elements from a List

To remove elements from a list, you must again break the list into two separate lists. The first list must contain the elements before the element to be deleted and the second list must contain the elements after the element to be deleted. This leaves out the specific element. These two lists can then be concatenated to obtain the final list.

Suppose `List1` contains `"Red":"Blue":"Green"`. To following statements delete the first element `Red` from the list:

```
List1:= "Red":"Blue":"Green"
Tot:=@Elements(List1);
Newlist:=@Subset(List1;1-Tot)
```

In the preceding code, `1-Tot` returns a negative number; therefore, the elements are extracted from the end leaving out the first element.

Now, to remove an element from the end—for example, to remove `Green` from the list—use the following statements:

```
List1:= "Red":"Blue":"Green"
Tot:=@Elements(List1);
Newlist:=@Subset(List1;Tot-1)
```

In the preceding code, `Tot-1` returns a positive number, thereby extracting elements from the beginning and leaving out the last element.

To extract `Blue` from `List1`, use the following code:

```
List1:="Red":"Blue":"Green";
Tot:=@Elements(List1);
Pos:= @Member("Blue":List1);
Flist:= :=@Subset(List1;Pos-1);
SList:=@Subset(List1;Pos-Tot)
NewList:=Flist:Slist
```

Using Lists in a Notes Application

As mentioned earlier, a list is used in multiple elements in a Notes application. A list can be used when you assign multiple values to a field. A list can also be used when you use @DbLookup to retrieve values from a view or you use other functions such as @UserRoles.

In the following sections, you'll learn how to use lists and list functions to perform the following tasks:

- Create a dynamic table
- Create choices for a keyword field
- Generate sequence numbers
- Check for unique value in a field

You will also create a view to display multivalue fields.

Creating a Dynamic Table

Often you create forms that contain tables, but the number of rows that the table must contain is not fixed. For example, say you have a bill form. The number of items that a customer buys can vary from 1 to 100 items. It is not practical to design a table with 100 rows and fields for each of the 100 items in advance. Instead, you can design a table that allows multiple entries without specifying the number of rows in advance. Consider a database titled Orders. This database contains two types of forms, a Product form that is used to add details about the new products and an Order form that is used to create orders for these products. The Order form must include details about the products that the customer wants to order. The details include Product Number, Product Name, Rate, and the Quantity Ordered. These details must be picked up from the existing Product documents. Table 28.1 lists the fields in the Product form.

Table 28.1 Details of Fields in the Product Form

FieldName	Type
ProductNo	Number, Editable
Pname	Text, Editable
Rate	Number, Editable

Table 28.2 lists the fields in the Order form.

Table 28.2 Details of Fields in the Order Form

FieldName	Type
OrderNo	Number, Editable
OrderDate	Date/Time, Computed when composed
CustomerName	Text, Editable
CustomerAddress	Text, Editable

To create the Order table as a dynamic table, first create a view that you will use to retrieve values from the Product documents, as demonstrated below:

1. Open the Orders database in Domino Designer.
2. Create a new shared view titled All Products For Lookup. In the view properties, enter an alias for the view as **PLU**.
3. Enter the View Selection condition as follows:

```
SELECT Form="Products"
```

4. Add columns to the view as specified in Table 28.3.

Table 28.3 Details of Columns in PLU View

Column Title	Column Value Type	Column Value
Product No.	Field	ProductNo
Product Name	Field	PName
Rate	Field	Rate

5. Select the properties of the Product No column, and in the Sorting tab, select Sort as Ascending.
6. Save and close the view.

A dynamic table contains fields that allow multiple values and have a multivalue separator set as a new line. This ensures that each entry into the field is displayed on a different line. In addition, to ensure that a user does not enter incorrect separators while entering data into the fields, these fields are made as Computed fields. The formula in these fields contains the field name itself so that fields can be assigned values programmatically. When assigning values to these fields, you must concatenate the new values with the existing ones to create a list and not assign them directly.

To create the dynamic table in the Order form, perform the following steps:

1. Open the Orders form in Domino Designer.
2. Create a 2-by-2 table.
3. In the columns of the first row, enter the field labels as Product Number, Product Name, Rate, Quantity, and Value.
4. In the second row, create fields corresponding to the labels in the first row. Table 28.4 describes the details about the fields to be created.

Table 28.4 Description of Fields for the Dynamic Table

Field Name	Type	Formula
ProductNo	Number, Computed	ProductNo
PName	Text, Computed	PName
Rate	Number, Computed	Rate
Quantity	Number, Computed	Quantity
Value	Number, Computed	Value

Figure 28.1 shows the layout of the table.

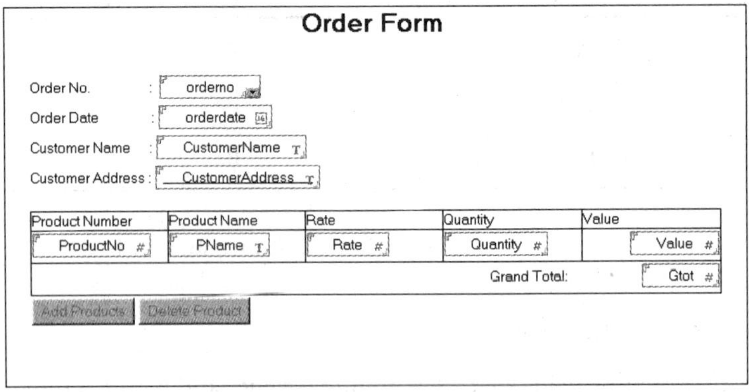

FIGURE 28.1 *The layout of the dynamic table*

5. Double-click the ProductNo field to access the field properties. On the Field Info tab, check the option Allow multiple values.
6. Select the Advanced tab and from the Multi-Value Options section, select Display separate values with NewLine. Figure 28.2 shows the Advanced tab of the field properties.

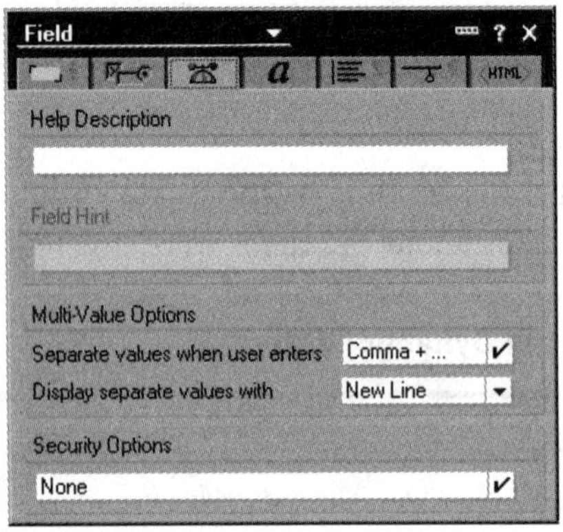

FIGURE 28.2 *Advanced tab of the field properties displaying the section Multi-Value Options*

7. Repeat steps 4 and 5 for all the fields in the table.
8. Create a hotspot button below the table. Enter the label as **Add Products.**

9. Select the Click event of the button and enter the following formula:

```
Rem "Retrieve a list of product numbers in the database";
plist:=@DbColumn("Notes":"Nocache";"":"";"PLU";1);

Rem "Display the list to the user in a dialog box";
tProductNo:=@TextToNumber(@Prompt([OkCancelList];

"Product Numbers";"Choose Product Number";null;@Text(plist)));
Rem "Retrieve the Product name and Rate using tProductNo as key";

tPName:=@DbLookup("Notes":"Nocache";"":"";"PLU";tProductNo;2);
tRate:=@DbLookup("Notes":"Nocache";"":"";"PLU";tProductNo;3);

Rem " Prompt the user to enter the quantity";
tQuantity:=@TextToNumber(@Prompt([OKCANCELEDIT];"Quantity";
"Enter Quantity";null));

Rem "Assign the value to the fields";
FIELD ProductNo:=@If(ProductNo=null;tProductNo;ProductNo:
tProductNo);
FIELD PName:=@If(PName=null;tPName;PName:tPName);
FIELD Rate:=@If(Rate=null;tRate;Rate:tRate);
FIELD Quantity:=@If(Quantity=null;tQuantity;Quantity:tQuantity);
FIELD Value:=Rate*Quantity;

Rem "Refresh the Document";
@Command([ViewRefreshFields])
```

10. To view a grand total at the bottom of the table, append a row to the table. Select all the columns and select Table/Merge Cells.
11. Enter the label **Grand Total** and create a new field named **gtot** of the type Number, Computed.
12. In the Value event of the gtot field, enter the following formula:

```
@If(Value=null;null;@Sum(Value))
```

13. Save the form and test it. Click the Add Product button multiple times to add multiple products to the order. Figure 28.3 displays a table after entering data.

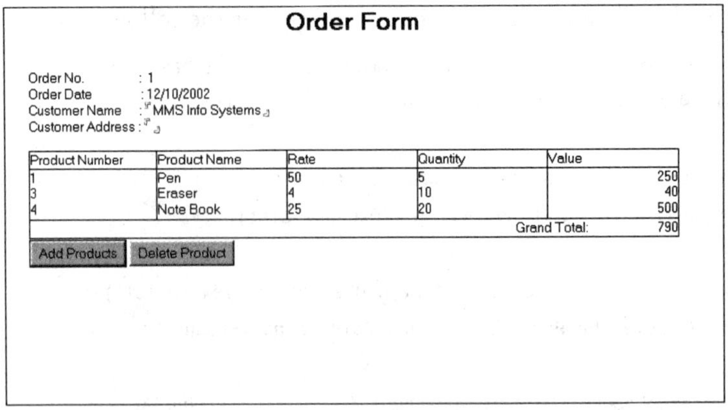

Order Form

Order No. : 1
Order Date : 12/10/2002
Customer Name : MMS Info Systems
Customer Address :

Product Number	Product Name	Rate	Quantity	Value
1	Pen	50	5	250
3	Eraser	4	10	40
4	Note Book	25	20	500
			Grand Total:	790

Add Products | Delete Product

FIGURE 28.3 *The dynamic table after entering data*

14. Create another button named **Delete** to delete entries from the table. In the Click event of the button, enter the following code:

```
plist:=@Text(ProductNo);
tProductNo:=@Prompt([OkCancelList];"Product Numbers";

"Choose Product Number to be deleted";null;plist);

Rem "Count the number of elements in the list";
len:=@Elements(plist);

Rem "Find the position in the list of the element to be deleted";
pos:=@Member(tProductNo;plist);
list1:=@If(pos=1;null;@Subset(plist;pos-1));
list2:=@If(pos=len;null;@Subset(plist;pos-len));
FIELD ProductNo:=@Trim(list1:list2);
list1:=@If(pos=1;null;@Subset(PName;pos-1));
list2:=@If(pos=len;null;@Subset(PName;pos-len));
FIELD PName:=@Trim(list1:list2);
Rlist:=@Text(Rate);
list1:=@If(pos=1;null;@Subset(Rlist;pos-1));
list2:=@If(pos=len;null;@Subset(Rlist;pos-len));
FIELD Rate:=@TextToNumber(@Trim(list1:list2));
Qlist:=@Text(Quantity);
list1:=@If(pos=1;null;@Subset(Qlist;pos-1));
```

```
list2:=@If(pos=len;null;@Subset(Qlist;pos-len));
FIELD Quantity:=@TextToNumber(@Trim(list1:list2));
FIELD Value:=@If(Rate!=null¦quantity!=null;rate*quantity;null);
@Command([ViewRefreshFields])
```

TIP

Similarly, you can add a button to update the entries in the dynamic table. You can also modify the existing code for the Add Products button so that if the user selects the same product number from the list twice, an entry is made to the table only the first time. The second time, the quantity in the existing entry is updated.

Creating a View to Display Multivalue Fields

The multivalue fields also need to be displayed in a view. A view can be created such that each entry in the multivalue field is displayed on a separate line. To create a view to display the order details, in the Orders database perform the following steps:

1. Create a new shared view named **All Orders** in the Orders database.
2. In the View Selection event, enter the following formula:

    ```
    SELECT form="Orders"
    ```

3. Create columns in the view as specified in Table 28.5.

Table 28.5 Details of Columns in All Orders View

Column Title	Column Value Type	Column Value
Order No.	Field	OrderNo
Order Date	Field	Odate
Product Name	Field	PName
Quantity	Field	Quantity

4. Double-click the Product Name column to access the column properties. On the Column Info tab, select the Multi-Value separator as New Line.

5. Repeat step 4 for the Quantity column.
6. Close the column properties and open the View properties box.
7. Select the Style tab. In the Rows section, select Height as 9 (lines).

NOTE

9 is the maximum height that you can select for a view column. If a multi-value field in a form has more than nine values, only the initial nine values can be displayed. If you want to display all the values, you can select the option show multiple values as separate entries on the Sorting tab of the column properties and also a sort option for the column. This displays all the value as separate rows in a view.

8. Select the option Shrink rows to content to ensure that the column height is adjusted according to the number of values in the order.
9. Save the view and preview it. Figure 28.4 shows the All Orders view.

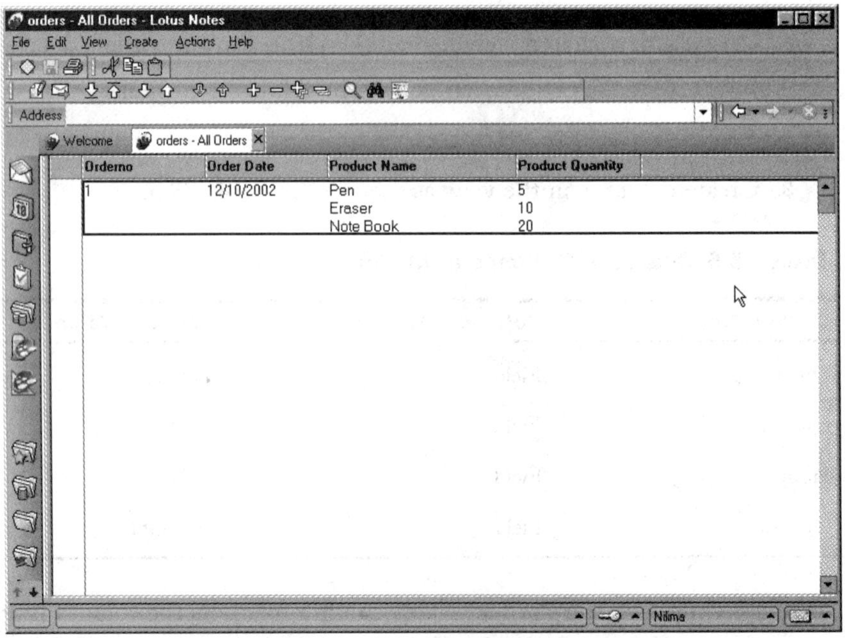

FIGURE 28.4 *The All Orders view displaying multivalue fields*

Generating Choices for a Keyword Field

A *keyword field* refers to a field that has predefined choices. A form in Domino Designer has the following types of keyword fields:

- Dialog list
- Check box
- Radio button
- List box
- Combo box

You have learned to enter choices for these fields by entering them directly in the field properties. Alternatively, you can use a formula to generate these choices. Make sure that this formula evaluates to a list. For example, the Order form in the Orders database contains a field CustomerName. This field can be designed as a dialog list type of field to display the values from the existing customer database. To do so, perform the following steps:

1. Open the Order form in Domino Designer.
2. Double-click the CustomerName field to access the field properties.
3. From the Type list, select Dialog list.
4. Select the Control tab and from the Choices list select Use formula for choices.
5. To retrieve values from the All Customers view in the Customer.nsf database on 6server/R6notes server, enter the following formula in the text box:

```
@DbColumn("Notes":"NoCache";"R6Server/R6Notes":"Customer.nsf";
"All Customers";1)
```

Figure 28.5 displays the Control tab of the CustomerName field:

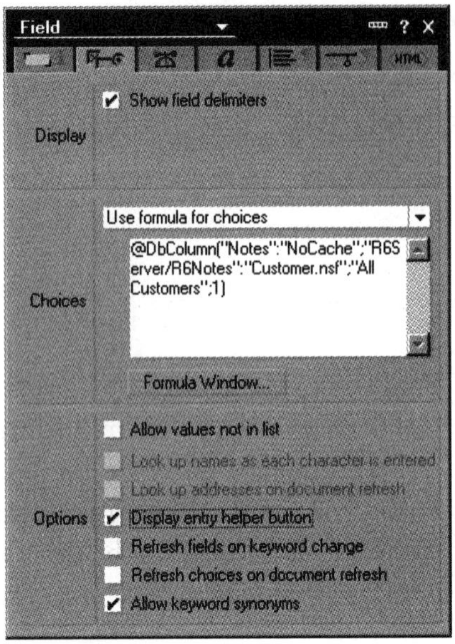

FIGURE 28.5 *The Control tab of the field properties for the CustomerName field*

6. Save the form and test it. When you click the entry helper button with the dialog list field, the names of all the existing customers from the customer database are displayed.

Generating Sequence Numbers

Most of the forms require a field that contains a unique code, such as customer code and product code. You can automatically generate sequences to assign unique running numbers to such fields.

As discussed in Chapter 24, "Developing an Order Processing System," to create a sequence number, you first create a view that contains a column to display the field to which the sequence number is to be assigned. This column displays the field in ascending order. In the field's Value event, use the `@DbColumn` @Function to retrieve all the values from the column in the view. Extract the last value, add one to it, and assign to the field.

The Product form contains a field ProductNumber that must be automatically generated as running numbers. To add this functionality to the Product form in the Orders database, perform the following steps:

1. Open the Orders database in Domino Designer.

2. Create a new shared, hidden view named **(All Products)**.
3. Enter the following as the view selection condition to ensure that only the Product documents are displayed in this view:

```
SELECT form="Product"
```

4. Double-click the first column and enter the title as **ProductNumber** in the column properties.
5. In the Column dialog box, under the Sorting tab, select Sort as Ascending. Close the properties box.
6. In the Programmer's pane, choose To display a field, and select ProductNo from the list of fields displayed.
7. Save and close the view.
8. Open the Product form to add the code to it.
9. Double-click the field ProductNo. Change the field type to Computed when composed.
10. Close the Field dialog box. In the Value event of the ProductNo field, enter the following code:

```
Rem "Retrieve list of Product numbers from the All Products view";
plist:=@DbColumn("Notes":"NoCache";"":"";"(All Products)";1);

Rem "Count the number of values in the list";
cnt:=@Elements(plist);

Rem "Get the value of the last Product number";
last:=@If(cnt=0;0;@Subset(plist;-1));

Rem " Add on to the last value and return to the current field";
Last+1
```

In the preceding code, the `@Dbcolumn` function is used to return the list or existing products from the All Products view. If no products are returned, a value `1` is assigned to the ProductNo field, otherwise, the last value plus 1 is returned.

TIP

If you want to start the sequence from a different number instead of 1, you can use an appropriate value in the last variable. For example, to start a sequence from `1001`, you can assign a value `1000` to the last variable.

You can also combine the number with text or date/time values to generate specific codes. For example, if the order number in the Order form is of the format `O/CurrentDate/SequenceNumber`, you can concatenate these values to the sequence number generated. If you use the order number in this format, you can retrieve the values from the view and count the number of values to generate the SequenceNumber part.

11. Save the form and preview it in the Notes previewer. A sequence number `1` should be displayed when you test the form the first time.

Validating a Field for Unique Values

Sometimes fields in a form must be validated for unique values. For example, in the Orders database, the Product form is used to capture details of products that can be ordered. In this case, the name of each product must be unique.

As you learned in Chapter 24, to validate a field for uniqueness, you must create a view containing the field that you want to validate for uniqueness.

CAUTION

Most often, you add code to check for uniqueness in the Input Validation event. However, in this approach, the validation fails when you open a document with a field for which you have added the validation code in the Input Validation event for editing. This is because the document you've opened for editing exists in the view and so does the value for the specific field.

To avoid this, you must add another column containing the Universal ID of the documents to the view. The Universal ID of the current document is compared against the Universal ID of the document that is found in the view. If the two Universal IDs are the same, it means that there is no duplication, but if the Universal IDs do not match, it would mean that the view contains another document with the same value and saving this document would lead to duplication.

To validate the PName field in the Product form for uniqueness, perform the following steps:

1. Open the Orders database in Domino Designer.
2. Create a shared, hidden view named **(Product Names)**.
3. Enter the view selection condition as follows:

   ```
   SELECT form="Product"
   ```

4. Double-click the first column and enter the title as **ProductName** in the column properties.
5. In the Column dialog box, under the Sorting tab, select Sort as Ascending. Close the properties box.
6. In the Programmer's pane, choose to display a field and select ProductName from the list of fields displayed.
7. Add a second column. Enter the column title as **UniqueID** and enter the following formula in the script area:

   ```
   @Text(@DocumentUniqueID)
   ```

NOTE

The `@DocumentUniqueID` @Function returns the Universal ID of a document that uniquely identifies the document across all replicas of a database. To display the Universal ID of a document, it must be converted to text.

8. Save and close the view.
9. Open the Product form and click the field ProductName.
10. Select the Input Validation event and enter the following code:

    ```
    Rem "Retrieve a list of Product names from the view";
    plist:=@DbColumn("Notes":"NoCache";"":"";"(Product Names)";1);

    Rem "Check if the product name in the current document
    exists in the list";
    @If(@IsNotMember(pname;plist);@Return(@Success);null);
    ```

```
Rem "Get the UNID of the document that has the same
product name as the current document";
docid:=@DbLookup("Notes":"Nocache";"";"(Product Names)";pname;2);

Rem "Get the UNID of the current document";
cdocid:=@Text(@DocumentUniqueID);

Rem "Check if the two documents are the same";
@If(docid=cdocid;@Success;@Failure("Duplicate Product Name"));
```

NOTE

To stop the execution of a formula and return the control and a specified value back to the document, you can use the `@Return` @Function. In the preceding code, `@If(@IsNotMember(pname;plist);@Return(@Success);Null)` ensures that if the product name in the current document is not found in the view, the code in the Input Validation event is terminated, without executing the following statements. `Null` takes the control to the next statement.

11. Save and test the form.

Summary

This chapter introduced you to the concepts of lists. It also discussed the various list functions, operators, and the methods to manipulate a list. You also explored some of the common application of lists in a Notes database.

Chapter 29

Using Calendaring Features in an Application

Domino has calendaring and scheduling features that allow users to check other users' free time, schedule meetings with them, and reserve rooms and resources such as laptops, projectors, and video equipment. This feature is handled by two tasks, Schedule Manager and Calendar Connector, that run on the Domino server. The Domino server has a database, busytime.nsf, to store the calendar information of users who have their mail databases on that server.

Each Notes user keeps a personal calendar in her mail database and creates a Calendar Profile. This profile contains information about who may access the user's free time information and specifies when the user is available for meetings. When any user is invited for a meeting, the busytime.nsf database is searched for information on the availability of the user and other resources. If the lookup involves searching different servers, the Calendar Connector sends out queries to the other server. When users schedule appointments in their calendars and reserve resources, the Schedule Manager task collects and updates that information in the Free Time database.

Domino Designer allows you to use the calendaring and scheduling features in a custom application. You can create a calendar-style view to record entries that are based on date and time. You can also create a group calendar in your application to monitor the schedules of people in your team.

In this chapter, you will be introduced to the various calendaring- and scheduling-related options available in Domino Designer. The chapter discusses how to create a calendar view and also discusses the *embedded scheduler* and the *embedded date picker*.

Creating a Calendaring Application

The Notes calendar is the default calendaring application of Domino. Domino provides you with a calendar view in the mail database. You use this view to keep track of your meetings, appointments, events, anniversaries, and reminders.

You can use the Notes calendar to schedule meetings at appropriate times by checking the free time of the invitees and the availability of resources. If you work with a team or have a group of people who work under you, you can create a group calendar to quickly check whether the people in the group are available at a specific time.

An example of a customized calendaring application is a project monitoring system. This system would allow a user to record new project details and also assign them to team members. This system should have a calendar view that allows a user to view all the projects in the database grouped by their start date. The system also would have a page with an embedded date picker to access a specific day from the calendar view.

Before you learn to implement various calendaring features in your project monitoring application, you must create a database and a form that you can use to create documents. Create the new database with the following options:

- Server: Local
- Title: Project Monitoring System
- File Name: Project.nsf
- Template: Blank

The users will use a Project Allotment form to assign a project to a team member. This form contains details about the project schedule as well as the people to whom it has been assigned. A project can also be assigned to a group. The form contains an embedded scheduler that will help check the schedules of a group of users before assigning a project to them.

Table 29.1 lists the fields of the Project Allotment form.

Table 29.1 Details of Fields on the Project Allotment Form

Label	Field Name	Type
ProjectCode	PCode	Text, Editable
Project Title	PTitle	Text, Editable
Description	Description	Text, Editable
Start Date	StartDate	Date/Time, Editable
End Date	EndDate	Date/Time, Editable
Assigned To	AssignedTo	Names, Editable
Assigned On	AssignDate	Date/Time, Computed when composed
Assigned By	AssignedBy	Names, Computed when composed

To design the layout for the Project Allotment form, perform the following steps:

1. Create a new form in the Projects database.
2. To specify a window title for the form, select the Window Title event from the Objects tab and enter the following code in the Script area:

```
"Project Allotment Form"
```

3. Create labels and fields on the form as specified in Table 29.1. Figure 29.1 displays the organization of these fields on the form.

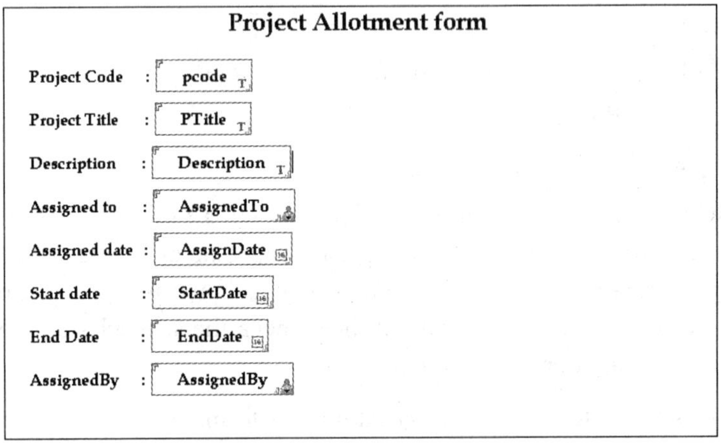

FIGURE 29.1 *The form layout for the Project Allotment form*

4. To allow display of both date and time in the StartDate field, select the Control tab and check Display Time. Note that Display Date is selected by default.
5. Repeat step 4 for the EndDate field.
6. To allow a user to pick up names from the address book for the AssignedTo field, select Use Address dialog for choices from the Choices section in the Control tab of the field properties. On the Field Info tab, check the option Allow multiple values.
7. Select the Value event of the AssignDate field and enter the following formula to assign the current date to the field:

```
@Today
```

8. Select the Value event of the AssignedBy field and enter the following formula to assign the current user's name to the field:

```
@UserName
```

9. Next, open the form properties and set the form properties as described below:
   - In the Name field, enter **Project Allotment|PA** as the name of the form.
   - In the Options section, check Automatically refresh fields.
10. Close the form properties and save the form layout.

Embedded Scheduler

An embedded scheduler is used to design forms that allow a user to check the schedules of a group of users. It helps users to schedule meetings and perform other group-related activities based on the free times available for each of the users.

An embedded scheduler can also be used to access the personal calendars of each of the users included in it by double-clicking the entry for the user in the embedded scheduler. The personal calendar of the user is displayed only if the user has granted permission to view his calendar entries to the person accessing the embedded scheduler.

Attributes of an Embedded Scheduler

An embedded scheduler has various attributes that need to be set in order for the scheduler to function. These attributes can be accessed from the Objects tab in the Programmer's pane by selecting the embedded scheduler. The values of these attributes are set by creating fields in the form and specifying the names of these fields as text or textlist. Table 29.2 describes the attributes for an embedded scheduler.

Table 29.2 Attributes of an Embedded Scheduler

Attribute Name	Attribute Description
Required People Items	Names of the people required for the activity being scheduled. This attribute must evaluate to the name or a list of names of the fields that contain the list of required people.
Optional People Items	Names of the people who are optional for the activity being scheduled. This attribute must evaluate to a name or a list of names of the fields that contain the list of optional people.
Room Items	Names of the rooms required for the activity being scheduled. This attribute must evaluate to name or a list of names of the fields that contain the list of rooms.
Resource Items	Names of the resources required for the activity being scheduled. This attribute must evaluate to name or a list of names of the fields that contain the list of resources.
Interval Start Time Item	Start date and time for the activity. This attribute must evaluate to the name of the field that contains the value for the start date and time.
Interval End Time Item	End date and time for the activity. This attribute must evaluate to the name of the field that contains the value for the end date and time.
Grid Start Time Item	The date and time from where the scheduler's busy time grid must begin. The default is current date and time. This attribute must evaluate to the name of the field that contains the required value.
Display Hours Per Day Item	The number of hours that the scheduler's busy time grid displays for each day. This attribute must evaluate to the name of the field that contains the value for the number of hours to be displayed in the grid.
Schedule Detail Item	When the scheduler retrieves scheduling data, detailed data is requested for these items. This attribute must evaluate to one or more names of fields containing the required information.

Properties of an Embedded Scheduler

You can customize an embedded scheduler by using the embedded scheduler properties. To access the properties of an embedded scheduler, click the embedded scheduler in the form and select Element/Scheduler Properties. This opens the Embedded Scheduler dialog box, as shown in Figure 29.2.

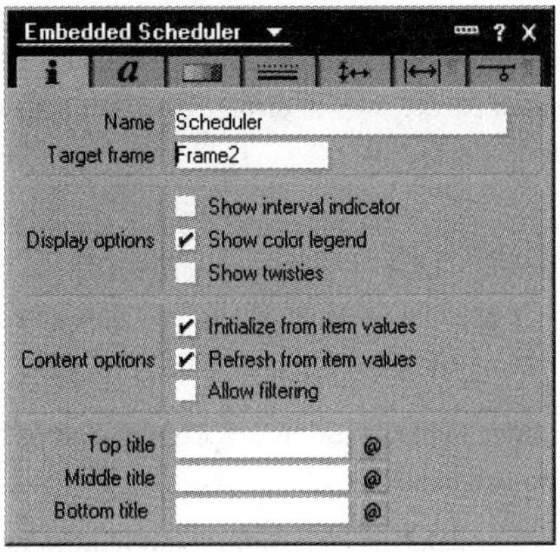

FIGURE 29.2 *The Embedded Scheduler dialog box*

Table 29.3 specifies the properties on the Info tab of the Embedded Scheduler dialog box, as seen in Figure 29.2.

Table 29.3 Properties on the Info Tab of the Embedded Scheduler Dialog Box

Property Name	Property Description
Name	Used to specify the Name of the scheduling element.
Target frame	Used to specify the frame in which you want to display the group members' calendar views and appointment documents when the name of a group member is clicked in the embedded scheduler.
Show interval indicator	Used to indicate whether or not to display the appointment indicator.
Show color legend	Used to indicate whether or not to display the busy time color legend.

(continues)

Table 29.3 Continued

Property Name	Property Description
Show twisties	Used to indicate whether or not to display twistie icons for required and optional people. Checking this option allows the user to collapse and expand the required and optional lists of people.
Initialize from item values	Used to specify that the scheduler control should initially determine which participants to display based on the values of the items previously specified.
Refresh from item values	Used to specify whether the scheduler control should refresh data from the values of the items by generating a new list of participants, the start and end times, and the hours to display or use the existing values.
Allow sorting	Used to indicate whether or not to display the sorting button above the attendee names.
Top, Middle, and Bottom titles	Used to enter a title for the top, middle, and bottom of the embedded scheduler.

The other tabs in the Embedded Scheduler dialog box are as follows:

- **Font tab.** This tab is used to specify the font, font size, style, and font color for the left header font, left font and the right header fonts. Figure 29.3 identifies the various regions on the embedded scheduler.

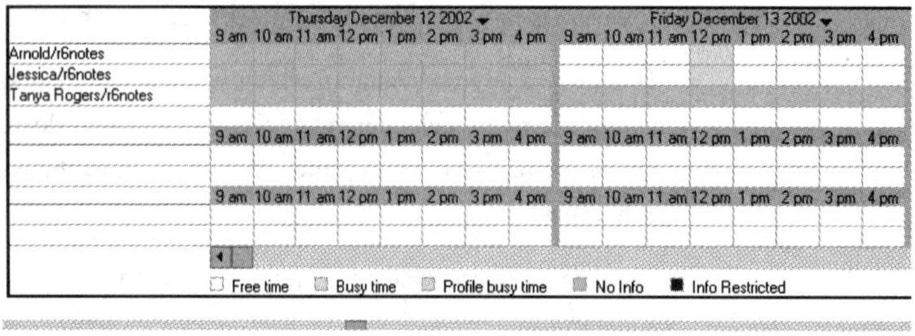

FIGURE 29.3 *Regions in an embedded scheduler*

- **Colors tab.** This tab is used to specify the background and the foreground colors for an embedded scheduler. Figure 29.4 displays the Color tab of the Embedded Scheduler dialog box.

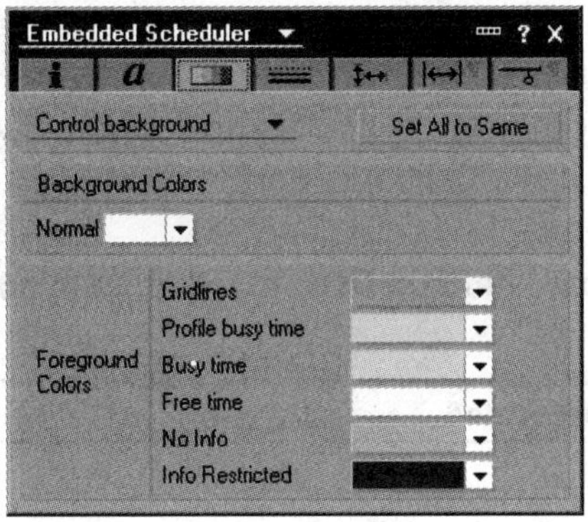

FIGURE 29.4 *The Color tab of the Embedded Scheduler dialog box*

You can set the background color for the following regions by clicking the down arrow next to the Control background option on the tab:

- Control
- Left header
- Left
- Right header
- Right
- Suggestions

The other tabs in the Embedded Scheduler dialog box are used to specify the border, layout, paragraph margins, and the paragraph Hide When options for the embedded scheduler.

Embedding a Scheduler on a Form

A scheduler embedded on a form requires the following information to display the schedules of the users:

- List of users whose schedules have to be displayed
- Week starting from which the schedule for the users should be displayed
- Number of hours per day of schedule information to be displayed

This information needs to be passed on to the corresponding attributes of the embedded scheduler as field names.

To embed a scheduler on the Project Allotment form, perform the following steps:

1. Identify the fields on the form that will be used to pass the required information to the embedded scheduler. Table 29.4 describes the fields on the Project Allotment form that will be used for this purpose.

Table 29.4 Fields on the Project Allotment Form Used for Programming the Embedded Scheduler

Field Name	Attribute Represented
AssignedTo	Requires People Item
StartDate	Interval Start Time Item

   The remaining piece of required information about the number of hours per day of the schedule information will be added through a hidden field.

2. Create a field on the top of the form named **Duration** of the type Number, Editable. Hide the field from all types of users and assign a default value 8 to the field.
3. Place the cursor at the location on the form where you want to embed the scheduler.
4. Select Create/Embedded Element/Scheduler. This embeds the scheduler on the form.
5. In the Object tab, select the attribute Required People Items and enter the following formula in the Script area:

```
"AssignedTo"
```

6. In the Objects tab, select the Interval Start Time Item attribute and enter the following formula:

```
"StartDate"
```

7. Select the attribute Display Hours Per Day Item and enter the following formula:

```
"Duration"
```

8. To specify a start time other than the default time for the schedule, create a new field named StartTime. Assign it a label **Schedule Start Time**. Select the field type as Date/Time, Editable. On the Control tab, clear Display Date and check Display Time to allow the user to enter only time in the field. On the Field Info tab, select Calendar/Time control to allow a user to select the time using a Time control. Figure 29.5 displays a Time control as displayed with the StartTime field.

FIGURE 29.5 *The Time control displayed with the StartTime field*

9. In the Objects tab, select the attribute Grid Start Time Item and enter the following formula in the Script area:

```
"StartTime"
```

10. Similarly, assign values to any other attributes for the embedded scheduler by creating fields for them.
11. Save the form and test it by creating a document using the Project Allotment form. Fill in the required details on the form and refresh. The embedded scheduler displays the schedules the users listed in the AssignedTo field, as shown in Figure 29.6.

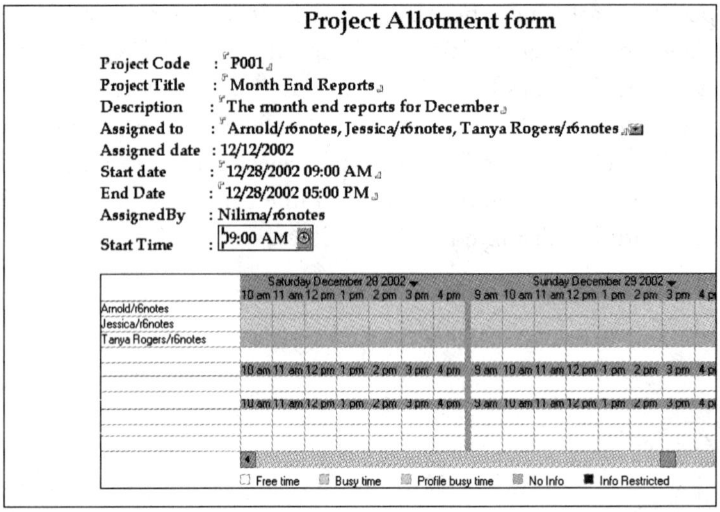

FIGURE 29.6 *The embedded scheduler displaying the schedules of selected users*

TIP

You can use the reserved field `$GroupScheduleshowLegend` with a value `0` to hide the color legend displayed at the bottom of the embedded scheduler.

NOTE

The embedded scheduler object in the Objects tab has an event `OnIntervalChange` that is triggered when the interval of the embedded scheduler changes.

Creating a Calendar View

A calendar view displays documents in a calendar format. Such a view can be used to record date- and time-based entries such as meetings, appointments, project schedules, and activity schedules. Figure 29.7 displays the default calendar view in a user's mail database.

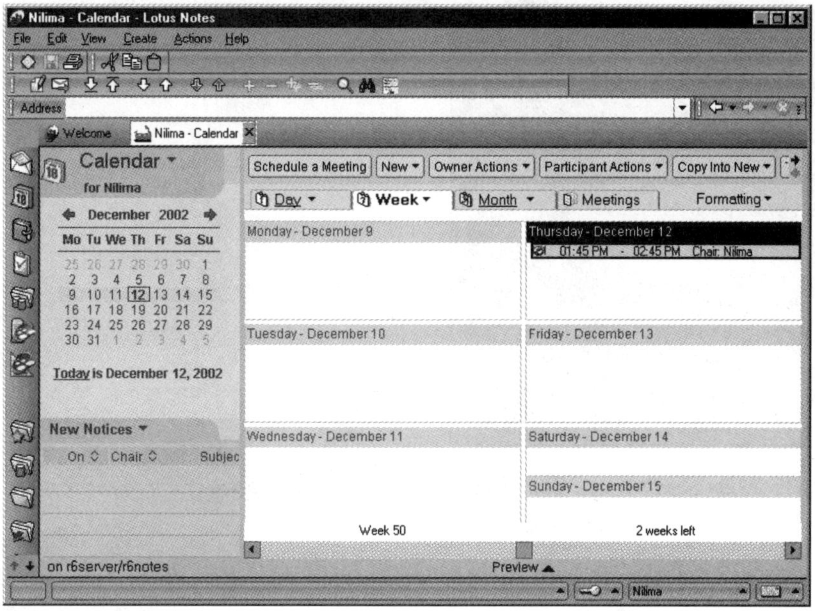

FIGURE 29.7 *The default calendar view in a user's mail database*

A calendar view requires at least two columns:

- The first column in a calendar view must evaluate to a date and time value, such as the start date for an activity or event. This column must be sorted in ascending order. It is usually hidden from users because the entry is displayed on the specified date in the calendar.
- The second column in a calendar view must contain a numeric value and must evaluate to the duration of the activity in minutes. This column must also be hidden.

You can include any other columns to include the information that you want to display in the calendar, such as the description of the activity.

When you create a calendar view, a Date and Time Format tab is added to the view the properties. This tab is used to format the Calendar view. Figure 29.8 displays the Date and Time Format tab of the view properties.

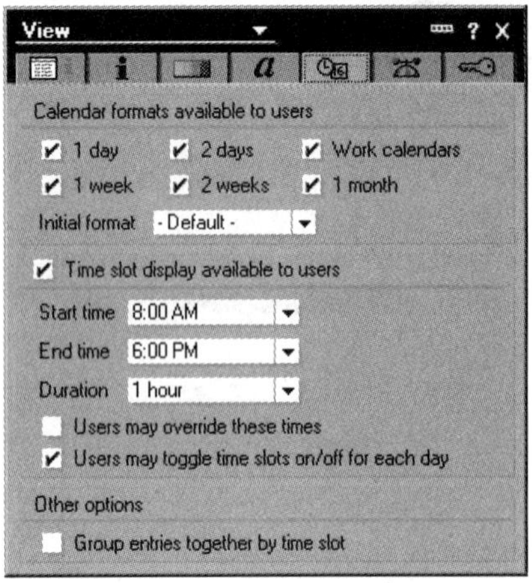

FIGURE 29.8 *The Date and Time Format tab of the view properties for a calendar view*

Following is a description of the properties seen in Figure 29.8.

- **Calendar formats available to users.** You can check one or more of the available formats depending on which options you want to assign the user. You can also select one of the formats as the Initial format, which will appear when a view first opens.
- **Time slot display available to users.** You can check this option to allow users to view the time slots in the calendar. Time slots display the time periods on the calendar view.

> **NOTE**
>
> A user can view or hide the time slots by using the Show Time Slots option under the Formatting action in the view.

- **Start time, End Time,** and **Duration.** If the Time slot display available to users option is checked, you can define these options.
- **Users may override these times.** Checking this option determines how time slots are displayed in the calendar from the user's Notes client calendar preference.

- **Users may toggle time slots on/off for each day.** Checking this option lets a user display and hide time slots for a selected day by using the clock icon on each day's calendar.
- **Group entries together by time slot.** Checking this option groups entries under time slots instead of listing entries for a day in the weekly and monthly views.

The Style tab of the calendar view also shows certain options that are specific to a calendar view. Figure 29.9 displays the Style tab of the calendar view.

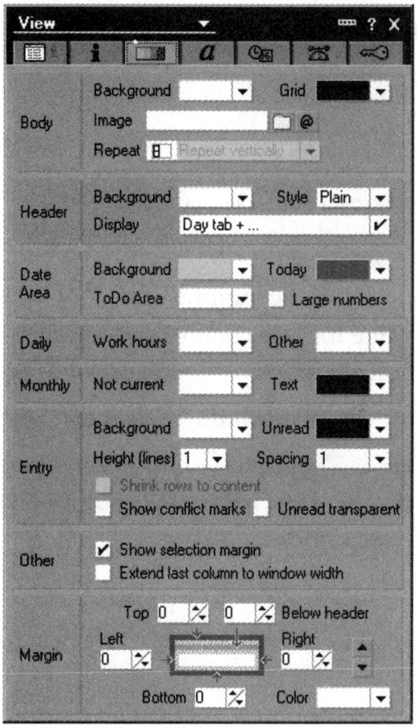

FIGURE 29.9 *The default calendar view in a user's mail database*

You can use this tab to set the colors of various elements of a calendar view. The Show conflict marks option is used to display a conflict bar for entries with schedule overlaps.

To create a calendar view in the Project database, which will enable a user to view the project documents organized by the start date of the project, perform the following steps:

1. Create a new shared view named All Project Schedules in the Projects database.
2. Enter the following view selection condition to ensure that only documents created using the Project Allotment form are displayed in the view:

```
SELECT Form="PA"
```

3. In the View info tab of the view properties, select Style as Calendar. This displays a dialog box as shown in Figure 29.10. Click Yes to continue.

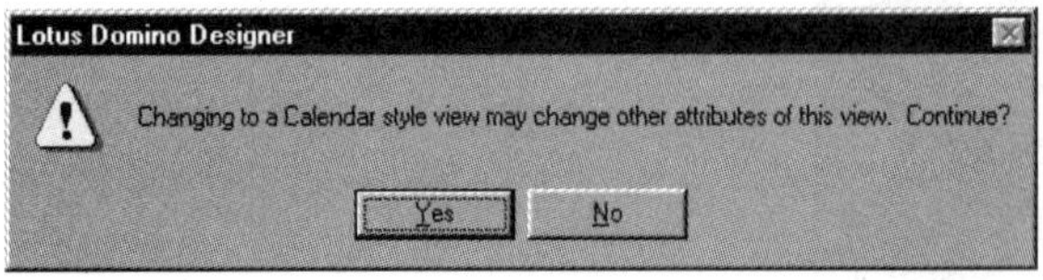

FIGURE 29.10 *The dialog box displayed on changing a view style to Calendar*

4. Close the View dialog box. Click the first column of the view. Choose to display a field for the Column Value for this column and select StartDate from the list of fields displayed.
5. Display the column properties for the first column. Select the Sorting tab and select Sort as Ascending.
6. Click the Date and Time Format tab of the column properties and check the Display Date and Display Time options.
7. Select the Advanced tab, and check Hide column.
8. Add a second column to the view. Choose to display a formula for the Column Value for this column.
9. In the Script area, enter the following formula to calculate the duration of the project:

```
(EndDate-StartDate)/60
```

   As mentioned earlier, the duration must be in minutes.
10. Select the Advanced tab from the column properties for this column and check Hide column.
11. Add a third column to the view. Select Field from the Display option in the Programmer's pane and select the field Description.

12. Access the view properties to format the calendar view.
13. Save the view and preview it in Notes. Figure 29.11 displays the calendar view as displayed in the Notes client.

> **NOTE**
>
> The view event Regiondoubleclick is triggered when a user double-clicks any region in the calendar view.

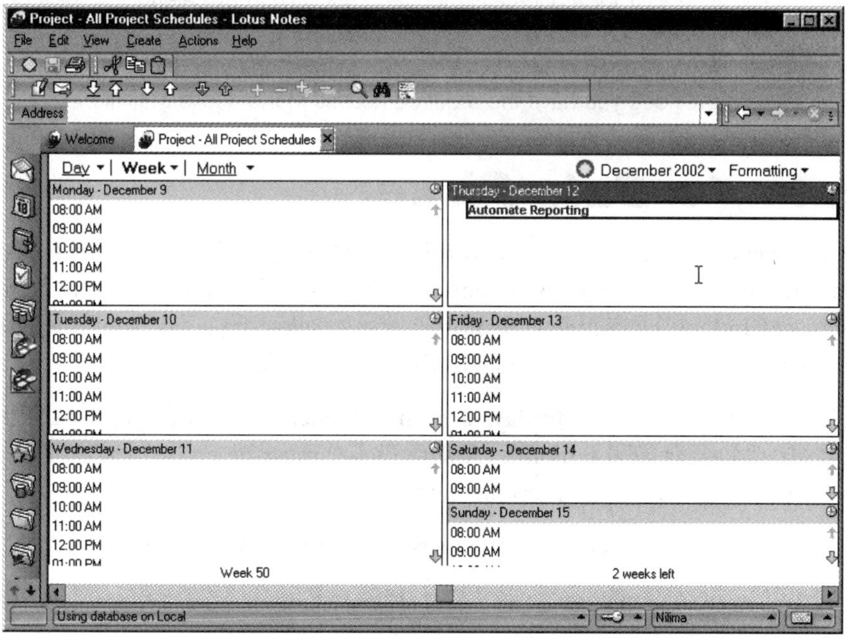

FIGURE 29.11 *The calendar view as displayed in a Notes client*

@COMMANDS FOR CALENDAR VIEWS

There are few @Commands that are used specifically with a calendar view. Some of these are listed below:

- `@Command([CalendarGoto];timedate)` takes the focus to a specified date in the calendar view
- `@Command([CheckCalendar];timedate)` pops up the specified date's calendar view from the current database in a dialog box. If you do not specify the `timedate` value, this @Command displays the current date's calendar view
- `@Command([CalendarFormat];number)` changes the calendar view display to the specified format. The `number` parameter refers to the format and can be specified as 1 for a one-day calendar, 2 for a two-day calendar, 7 for a one-week calendar, 14 for a two-week calendar, and 30 for a one-month calendar.
- `@Command([OpenView];username)` displays the calendar of the specified user provided you have the required access in the user's mail file.

Creating a Date Picker

An embedded date picker is a control used to select a date that works in coordination with a calendar view. When you display a date picker in one frame of a frameset and a calendar view in another frame, selecting a day from the date picker displays the corresponding day in the calendar view.

The date picker control displays a monthly calendar, and the user can choose a month and a day of the month. A date picker must be embedded on a page or a form to use it in a calendar application.

To embed a date picker on a page, perform the following steps:

1. Create a new page named **DatePicker Page** in the Projects database.
2. Place the cursor on the page at the location where you want to insert the date picker and select Create/Embedded Element/Date Picker. This embeds the date picker on the page.
3. Select the embedded date picker and choose Element/Date Picker Properties to display the properties of the embedded date picker. Figure 29.12 displays the Embedded Date Picker dialog box to set the properties of the date picker, such as horizontal and vertical size, font size and color, and the hide options.

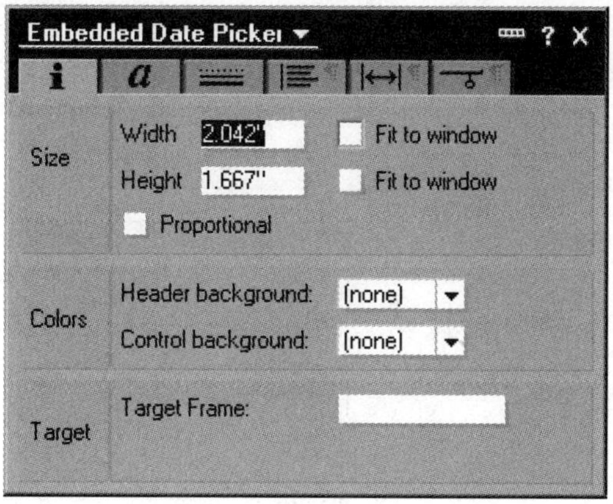

FIGURE 29.12 *The Embedded Date Picker dialog box*

4. On the Info tab, select a Target Frame as Frame2. This ensures that the date selected appears only in the calendar view in the specified target frame.
5. Embed other elements on the page, such as text and outlines, and save and close the page.

To use the DatePicker page and the calendar view perform the following steps:

1. Create a new frameset in the Projects database named Main containing two frames.
2. In the left frame, choose to display the page DatePicker page.
3. In the right frame, choose to display the calendar view, All Project Schedules. Name this frame **Frame2**.
4. Save and close the frameset.
5. Open the database properties and set the Main frameset as the launch option for the Projects database.
6. Open the database from the Notes client. Select any day from the date picker; the corresponding day in the calendar view must be displayed. Figure 29.13 displays the Main frameset as seen from a Notes client.

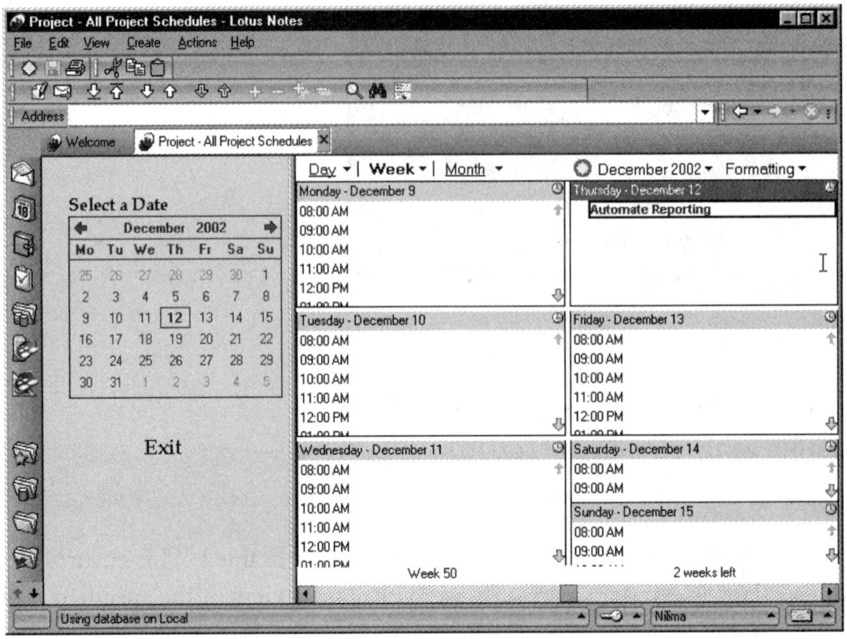

FIGURE 29.13 *The Main frameset as seen from a Notes client*

Summary

In this chapter, you learned about the various calendaring and scheduling options available in Domino Designer. You learned about an embedded scheduler and were introduced to a calendar view. You also learned to embed a date picker on a page and used the page in a frameset to navigate to a specific day in the calendar view.

PART VIII

Appendices

Appendix A

Domino LotusScript Classes

Domino LotusScript Classes

Domino LotusScript classes are classified into two categories, front-end and back-end classes. Front-end classes, also known as UI (*user interface*) classes, represent objects visible to the user on the screen, such as workspace, database, or navigator. Back-end classes, in contrast, are used to manipulate objects that are not visible to the user on the screen. For example, the `NotesDatabase` class represents a Notes database, which may or may not be the one on which the user is currently working.

Front-End Classes

As already mentioned, front-end classes represent objects visible to the user on the screen, with which a user can directly interact. The following sections comprise a list of front-end classes in LotusScript.

Button

The `Button` class is used to access the Click event associated with buttons, actions, and hotspots on forms and pages. This class does not contain any properties or methods.

Field

The `Field` class is used to access Entering and Exiting events for the fields in a form. This class does not contain any properties or methods.

Navigator

The `Navigator` class is used to access a navigator object in a database. This class also does not contain any properties or methods.

NotesUIDatabase

The `NotesUIDatabase` class, contained in the `NotesUIWorkspace` class, is used to access a database that is currently open in the Notes workspace. This class contains `NotesDatabase` and `NotesDocumentCollection` classes.

NotesUIDocument

The `NotesUIDocument` class, contained in the `NotesUIWorkspace` class, is used to access the currently opened document in the workspace. This class contains `NotesDocument` and `NotesUIScheduler` classes.

NotesUIScheduler

The `NotesUIScheduler` class, contained by the `NotesUIDocument` class, is used to access the embedded scheduler in a document. This class contains `NotesDateRange` and `NotesDateTime` classes.

NotesUIView

The `NotesUIView` class, contained in the `NotesUIWorkspace` class, is used to access the currently opened view in the Notes workspace. This class contains `NotesDocumentCollection` and `NotesUIView` classes.

NotesUIWorkspace

The `NotesUIWorkspace` class is used to access the current Notes workspace. This class contains `NotesUIDatabase`, `NotesUIDocument`, and `NotesUIView` classes.

Back-End Classes

Back-end classes are used to manipulate Domino objects that are not directly accessible to the user. These classes may be used to access any Domino object without user intervention.

NotesACL

The `NotesACL` class, contained in the `NotesDatabase` class, is used to access the ACL (*Access Control List*) of a database. This class contains the `NotesACLEntry` class.

NotesACLEntry

The NotesACLEntry class, contained in the NotesACL class, is used to access an individual entry in the ACL.

NotesAgent

The NotesAgent class is used to access an agent. This class is contained in NotesSession and NotesDatabase classes.

NotesColorObject

The NotesColorObject class represents a color and is used to dynamically set the color of objects, such as a view background or the font color of a view column. This class is contained in NotesSession, NotesRichTextSection, and NotesRichTextTable classes.

NotesDatabase

The NotesDatabase class, contained in NotesSession, NotesDbDirectory, and NotesUIDatabase classes, is used to access a Notes database.

The class contains the following classes:

- NotesACL
- NotesAgent
- NotesDocument
- NotesDocumentCollection
- NotesForm
- NotesOutline
- NotesReplication
- NotesView

NotesDateRange

The NotesDateRange class, contained in NotesSession and NotesUIScheduler classes, is used to access a range of date and time. The class contains the NotesDateTime class.

NotesDateTime

The `NotesDateTime` class, contained in `NotesDateRange` and `NotesSession` classes, is used to access date and time. This class is used to translate between the Domino date/time format and the LotusScript date/time format.

NotesDbDirectory

The `NotesDbDirectory` class, contained in the `NotesSession` class, is used to access the databases on a specific server or the local computer. This class contains the `NotesDatabase` class.

NotesDocument

The `NotesDocument` class is used to access a document within a database. This class contains `NotesEmbeddedObject`, `NotesItem`, `NotesMIMEEntity`, and `Notes-RichTextItem` classes and is contained in the following classes:

- `NotesDatabase`
- `NotesDocumentCollection`
- `NotesNewsletter`
- `NotesUIDocument`
- `NotesView`
- `NotesViewEntry`

NotesDocumentCollection

The `NotesDocumentCollection` class is used to access a set of documents that is selected on the basis of specified criteria.

This class contains the `NotesDocument` class and is contained in the following classes:

- `NotesDatabase`
- `NotesSession`
- `NotesUIDatabase`
- `NotesUIView`

NotesEmbeddedObject

The `NotesEmbeddedObject` class is used to access an embedded object, a linked object, or a file attachment in a document. The class is contained in the `NotesDocument` and `NotesRichTextItem` classes.

NotesForm

The `NotesForm` class is used to access a form in a database. The class is contained in the `NotesDatabase` class.

NotesInternational

The `NotesInternational` class is used to access the international settings (specified in the Control Panel) on a computer. For example, you can access the date and time format or the currency format for an individual computer's operating environment. This class is contained in the `NotesSession` class.

NotesItem

The `NotesItem` class is used to access a specific data item within a document. For example, this class can be used to access a field in a document displayed in the UI. This class is contained in the `NotesDocument` class and is the base class for the `NotesRichTextItem` class.

NotesLog

The `NotesLog` class, contained by the `NotesSession` class, is used to record information about the execution of a script, such as the actions performed or error messages. You can record this information in a database, a mail memo, a file, or an agent log.

NotesMIMEEntity

The `NotesMIMEEntity` class is used to access the MIME (*Multipurpose Internet Mail Extensions*) content of a document. This class is contained in `NotesItem` and is the base class for `NotesMIMEHeader`.

NotesMIMEHeader

The `NotesMIMEHeader` class represents the header in a MIME document. This class is contained in the `NotesMIMEEntity` class.

NotesName

The `NotesName` class is used to access a user or server name. This class is contained in the `NotesSession` class.

NotesNewsletter

The `NotesNewsletter` class is used to format a document that contains links to a set of documents that satisfy the specified criteria. The class is contained in `NotesSession` and is the base class for `NotesDocument`.

NotesNoteCollection

The `NotesNoteCollection` class represents a collection of data and design elements in a database. This class is contained in `NotesDatabase`.

NotesOutline

The `NotesOutline` class is used to access an outline. The class is contained in `NotesDatabase` and contains `NotesOutlineEntry`.

NotesOutlineEntry

The `NotesOutlineEntry` class is used to access one of the entries within an outline. The class is contained in the `NotesOutline` class.

NotesRegistration

The `NotesRegistration` class is used to create or administer an ID file. The class is contained in `NotesSession`.

NotesReplication

The `NotesReplication` class is used to access the replication settings for a database. The class is contained in `NotesDatabase`.

NotesRichTextItem

The `NotesRichTextItem` class, contained in the `NotesDocument` class, is used to access a rich text data type item in a Notes document. The class is derived from the `NotesItem` class and contains `NotesEmbeddedObject`.

NotesRichTextDocLink

The `NotesRichTextDocLink` class is used to access a doclink in a rich text item. This class is contained in `NotesRichTextItem` and `NotesRichTextNavigator` and contains `NotesRichTextStyle`.

NotesRichTextNavigator

The `NotesRichTextNavigator` class is used to navigate in a rich text item. This class is contained in `NotesRichTextItem` and contains `NotesRichTextSection`, `NotesRichTextTable`, and `NotesRichTextDocLink` classes.

NotesRichTextParagraphStyle

The `NotesRichTextParagraphStyle` class is used to access text paragraph attributes, such as spacing, margins, and the alignment of a rich text item. The class is contained in `NotesSession` and contains `NotesRichTextTab`.

NotesRichTextRange

The `NotesRichTextRange` class is used to access the elements in a rich text item sequentially. This class is contained in `NotesRichTextItem` and contains `Notes-RichTextStyle`.

NotesRichTextSection

The `NotesRichTextSection` class is used to access a collapsible section in a rich text item. This class is contained in `NotesRichTextNavigator` and contains `Notes-ColorObject` and `NotesRichTextStyle` classes.

NotesRichTextTab

The `NotesRichTextTab` class is used to access the tab attributes of a rich text item. This class is contained in `NotesRichTextParagraphStyle`.

NotesRichTextTable

The `NotesRichTextTable` class is used to access a table in a rich text item. This class is contained in `NotesRichTextItem` and `NotesRichTextNavigator` and contains `NotesColorObject`.

NotesRichTextStyle

The `NotesRichTextStyle` class is used to access the style attributes, such as font, font size, and font color, and effects of a rich text item.

This class is contained in the following classes:

- `NotesRichTextDocLink`
- `NotesRichTextNavigator`
- `NotesRichTextRange`
- `NotesRichTextSection`
- `NotesSession`

NotesSession

The `NotesSession` class is used to access the current environment, and it provides access to environment variables, information about the current user, information about the current Notes version and platform, and address books.

The `NotesSession` class contains the following classes:

- `NotesAgent`
- `NotesColorObject`
- `NotesDatabase`
- `NotesDateRange`
- `NotesDateTime`
- `NotesDbDirectory`
- `NotesDocument`
- `NotesDocumentCollection`
- `NotesInternational`
- `NotesName`
- `NotesLog`

- NotesNewsletter
- NotesRegistration
- NotesRichTextParagraphStyle
- NotesRichTextStyle
- NotesStream
- NotesTimer

NotesStream

The `NotesStream` class represents a stream of binary or character data. This class is contained in `NotesSession`.

NotesTimer

The `NotesTimer` class is used to trigger an event at a specific time. The class is contained in `NotesSession`.

NotesView

The `NotesView` class is used to access a view or folder in a database. The class is contained in `NotesDatabase` and `NotesUIView` classes and contains the following classes:

- NotesDocument
- NotesViewColumn
- NotesViewEntry
- NotesViewEntryCollection
- NotesViewNavigator

NotesViewColumn

The `NotesViewColumn` class is used to access a column in a view. This class is contained in `NotesView`.

NotesViewEntry

The `NotesViewEntry` class is used to access a specified row in a view. This class contains the `NotesDocument` class and is contained in the following classes:

- `NotesView`
- `NotesViewEntryCollection`
- `NotesViewNavigator`

NotesViewEntryCollection

The `NotesViewEntryCollection` class is used to access a collection of view entries selected according to specific criteria. The class is contained in `NotesView` and contains `NotesViewEntry`.

NotesViewNavigator

The `NotesViewNavigator` class is used to access all or a subset of the entries in a view. This class is contained in `NotesView` and `NotesViewEntry`.

Appendix B

Java Classes for Domino

Java Classes for Domino

Java has a set of built-in classes to access Domino objects. To access these classes, you need to import the `lotus.domino` package in your program as follows:

```
import lotus.domino.*
```

This package contains classes that represent all Domino objects, such as database, agent, and view. This package also contains classes that do not represent any specific Domino object. These classes are used to write Java code in Domino and are called *supporting classes*.

Domino Object Supporting Classes

Domino object supporting classes support the use of Java in Domino. They do not directly represent any Domino object; instead, they provide the framework for writing Java code in Domino and accessing Domino objects. Table B.1 lists the various supporting classes available in the `lotus.domino` package.

Table B.1 Domino Object Supporting Classes

Class	Description
`AgentBase`	Contains the `Session` object, which is the root class for all Domino objects in the containment hierarchy. A Java agent is created by extending the `AgentBase` class.
`AppletBase`	Used to define an applet that accesses Domino objects as a subclass.
`Base`	Defines methods that are common to all classes. All classes for Domino objects extend the `Base` class. This class cannot be accessed directly.
`NotesError`	Defines constants for Domino error codes.
`NotesException`	Used for exception handling in Domino and extends `java.lang.Exception`.
`NotesFactory`	Contains `createSession` methods and is used for creating the `Session` object by using different Java applications.

Class	Description
NotesThread	Used to run Java programs that make local calls to Lotus Notes/Domino classes. This class is created by extending `java.lang.Thread`, and it includes special initialization and termination code for Lotus Notes/Domino.

Java Classes for Domino Objects

Java classes for Domino objects extend the `Base` class and are used to access Domino objects, such as the database, the ACL (*Access Control List*), and the agent. These Java classes are similar to back-end LotusScript classes in functionality.

ACL

The `ACL` class is used to access the ACL of a database. This class is contained in the `Database` class and contains `ACLEntry`.

ACLEntry

The `ACLEntry` class is used to access an individual entry in the ACL. This class is contained in the `ACL` class and contains the `Name` class.

Agent

The `Agent` class is used to access an agent. This class is contained in `AgentContext` and `Database` classes.

AgentContext

The `AgentContext` class represents the environment where the agent is running. This class is contained in the `Session` class and contains the following classes:

- `Agent`
- `Database`
- `DateTime`
- `Document`
- `DocumentCollection`

Database

The `Database` class is used to access a database. The class is contained in `Session`, `DbDirectory`, and `AgentContext` classes and contains the following classes:

- `ACL`
- `Agent`
- `DateTime`
- `Document`
- `DocumentCollection`
- `Form`
- `Outline`
- `Replication`
- `View`

DateRange

The `DateRange` class is used to access a range of date and time values. This class is contained in the `Session` class and contains `DateTime`.

DateTime

The `DateTime` class represents date and time. This class is used to translate between the Domino date/time format and the Java date/time format. The class is contained in the following classes:

- `AgentContext`
- `Database`
- `DateRange`
- `Document`
- `View`
- `Session`

DbDirectory

The `DbDirectory` class is used to access the databases on a specific server or the local computer. The class is contained in the `Session` class and contains `Database`.

Document

The `Document` class is used to access a document within a database. The class is contained in `Database`, `DocumentCollection`, `Newsletter`, `View`, and `ViewEntry` classes and contains the following classes:

- `DateTime`
- `EmbeddedObject`
- `Item`
- `MIMEEntity`
- `RichTextItem`

DocumentCollection

The `DocumentCollection` class is used to access a set of documents selected on the basis of specified criteria. This class is contained in `Database`, `AgentContext`, and `View` classes and contains `Document`.

EmbeddedObject

The `EmbeddedObject` class is used to access an embedded object, a linked object, or a file attachment. The class is contained in the `Document` and `RichTextItem` classes.

Form

The `Form` class is used to access a form in a database. This class is contained in the `Database` class.

International

The `International` class is used to access the international settings (specified in the Control Panel) on a computer. You can access settings such as the date and time format or the currency format for an individual computer's operating environment. The class is contained in the `Session` class.

Item

The `Item` class is used to access a specific data item within a document. For example, an `Item` object is used to access a field in a document displayed in the UI. This class is contained in `Document` and contains `DateTime` and `MIMEEntity`. The `Item` class is the base class for `RichTextItem`.

Log

The `Log` class is used to record information about the execution of a script, such as the actions performed or error messages. You can record this information in a database, a mail memo, a file, or an agent log. This class is contained by the `Session` class.

MIMEEntity

The `MIMEEntity` class is used to access the MIME (*Multipurpose Internet Mail Extensions*) content of a document, and it represents an item of the type MIME. This class is contained in `Item` and contains `MIMEHeader`.

MIMEHeader

The `MIMEHeader` class represents the header in a MIME document. This class is contained in `MIMEEntity`.

Name

The `Name` class is used to access a user or server name. This class is contained in `AgentContext` and `Session` classes.

NewsLetter

The `NewsLetter` class is used to format a document that contains links to a set of documents that satisfy the specified criteria. The class is contained in `Session` and contains `Document`.

Outline

The `Outline` class is used to access an outline. This class is contained in `Database` and contains `OutlineEntry`.

OutlineEntry

The `OutlineEntry` class is used to access one of the entries within an outline. The class is contained in the `Outline` class.

Registration

The `Registration` class is used to create or administer an ID file. The class is contained in the `Session` class.

Replication

The `Replication` class is used to access the replication settings for a database. The class is contained in the `Database` class.

RichTextItem

The `RichTextItem` class is used to access a rich text data type item in a document. This class is contained in `Document` and contains `EmbeddedObject`. This class is derived from the `Item` class.

RichTextParagraphStyle

The `RichTextParagraphStyle` class is used to access the text paragraph attributes, such as spacing, margin, and alignment, of a rich text item. The class is contained in `Session` and contains `RichTextTab`.

RichTextStyle

The `RichTextStyle` class is used to access the style attributes, such as font, font size, font color, and effects, of a rich text item. This class is contained in `RichTextItem` and `Session`.

RichTextTab

The `RichTextTab` class is used to access the tab attributes, such as position and types of tabs, in a rich text item. This class is contained in the `RichTextParagraphStyle` class.

Session

The `Session` class is used to access the current Notes environment and to provide access to environment variables and information about the current user, the current version and platform, and address books. It contains all Domino objects in the containment hierarchy. The `Session` class is contained in `NotesFactory` and `AgentBase` and contains the following classes:

- `AgentContext`
- `Database`
- `DateRange`
- `DateTime`
- `DbDirectory`
- `International`
- `Name`
- `Log`
- `NewsLetter`
- `Registration`
- `RichTextParagraphStyle`
- `RichTextStyle`
- `Stream`

Stream

The `Stream` class represents a stream of binary or character data. This class is contained in `Session`.

View

The `View` class is used to access the documents in a view or folder in a database. The class is contained in `Database` and contains the following classes:

- `Document`
- `DateTime`
- `ViewColumn`
- `ViewEntry`

- `ViewEntryCollection`
- `ViewNavigator`

ViewColumn

The `ViewColumn` class is used to access a column in a view. This class is contained in the `View` class.

ViewEntry

The `ViewEntry` class is used to access a specified row in a view. This class is contained in `View`, `ViewEntryCollection`, and `ViewNavigator` classes and contains the `Document` class.

ViewEntryCollection

The `ViewEntryCollection` class is used to access a collection of view entries selected according to the specific criteria. The class is contained in `View` and contains `ViewEntry`.

ViewNavigator

The `ViewNavigator` class is used to access all or a subset of the entries in a view. This class is contained in `View` and `ViewEntry`.

Appendix C

Working with JavaScript

Fundamentals of JavaScript

JavaScript is an object-oriented scripting language created by Netscape. JavaScript is interpreted and executed by the browser. Therefore, it is used to perform actions such as field validation and calculation at the client side without submitting the form or performing a trip to the server. This enables a user to write code that can access and manipulate the client environment, such as the background color of a page in a browser.

JavaScript is a case-sensitive language and is most commonly written as part of an HTML document by including it in the `<Script>` tag. The following sections briefly describe the syntax of JavaScript.

Identifiers

Identifiers are names given to variables, methods, and objects. The name of an identifier must follow these guidelines.

- It must begin with an uppercase or lowercase letter or an underscore symbol (_).
- It can contain uppercase or lowercase letters, digits, or underscores for all subsequent characters.
- It cannot contain spaces.
- It cannot be the same as one of the reserved words in JavaScript.

Keywords

Keywords are identifiers used to perform predefined functions, such as declaring variables, defining loops, or checking conditions. Some keywords available in JavaScript are listed as follows:

- `Abstract`
- `else`
- `instanceof`

- `switch`
- `Boolean`
- `enum`
- `int`
- `synchronized`
- `break`
- `this`

Literals

Literals represent fixed values. The various types of literals are given below:

- **Integers.** An integer can be expressed in octal, decimal, or hexadecimal format. An octal integer is prefixed with a zero, and a hexadecimal integer is prefixed with 0x or 0X. For example, the decimal number 50 has the following representations in different formats:

  Decimal: 50

  Octal: 062

  Hexadecimal: 0x32
- **Floating points.** A floating-point number is a decimal integer with a fractional part. These numbers can be expressed in scientific notation by using the E or e symbol. For example, the following are floating-point numbers:

  50.2

  -35

  4.5e8
- **Boolean.** A Boolean literal represents one of the two values true or false. Boolean literals must be written in lowercase letters.
- **String.** A string literal represent zero or more characters enclosed in double or single quotes. For example, the following are string literals:

  "New York"

  '142, Wellingdon Crescent'

- **Special characters.** JavaScript literals include special characters for indicating a new line or backspace. These special characters are prefixed with a backslash. For example, the following are the special characters representing a backspace, a tab, and a new line, respectively:

  \b represents a backspace.

  \t represents a tab.

  \n represents a new line.

Operators

Operators are symbols used for manipulating data. Operators in JavaScript may be classified as follows:

- **Arithmetic operators.** These operators include addition (+), subtraction (-), multiplication (*), division (/), and modulus (%).
- **Assignment operator.** The assignment operator is the equal sign (=). JavaScript also has shorthand assignment operators as follows:

  +=: Used as `x+=y`; this statement is equivalent to `x=x+y`.

  -=: Used as `x-=y`; this statement is equivalent to `x=x-y`.

  *=: Used as `x*=y`; the statement is equivalent to `x=x*y`.

  /=: Used as `x/=y`; this statement is equivalent to `x=x/y`.

  %=: Used as `x%=y`; this statement is equivalent to `x=x%y`.
- **Unary operators.** These operators operate on a single value and include negation (-), increment (++), and decrement (--). The negation operator returns the negative value of a number. The increment and decrement operators respectively increase and decrease the value of a variable by one. For example, x++ increases the value of x by one and x-- decreases the value of x by one. The increment and decrement operators can be used as prefixes or suffixes.
- **Comparison operators.** Equal (= =), not equal (!=), less than (<), greater than (>), less than or equal (<=), and greater than or equal (>=) are comparison operators.
- **Logical operators.** AND, OR, and NOT are logical operators.

  The logical operator AND is represented as &&, OR is represented as `||`, and NOT is represented as `!`.

- **String operator.** The (+) operator is the string concatenation operator used to concatenate two strings.
- **typeof operator.** The typeof operator returns the type of data that its operand holds. For example,

  `typeof 50` returns number.

  `typeof true` returns Boolean.

  `typeof myvar` returns undefined if `myvar` is an undefined variable.

Variables

A *variable* is a named memory location that stores data. The name of a variable must be in accordance with the rules for naming an identifier. A variable is declared using the `var` keyword. For example, the following are variable declarations:

```
var uname;
var ctr;
var isover;
```

The data type of a variable is not determined at the time of declaration. Instead, the data type of a variable is based on the type of data assigned to it. A variable can be classified into one of the following data types:

- **number.** Used to store integer literals
- **boolean.** Used to store Boolean literals
- **string.** Used to store string literals
- **function.** Used to define functions that may be built-in JavaScript functions or user-defined functions (for example, `write()` is a built-in JavaScript function).
- **object.** Used to define JavaScript objects, such as window, document, or form

You can initialize a variable by assigning a value to it, as shown in the following example:

```
var=ctr;
ctr=0;
```

You can assign a value of a different data type to a variable that already has a value assigned to it. The following example declares a variable cost. First, a numeric value is assigned to it. Next, a string type value is assigned to the same variable.

```
var cost;
cost=200;
cost='Rs. 300';
```

A variable can be declared with a local or global scope. A *local variable* is defined inside a function and can only be accessed inside that function. A variable declared outside a function becomes a *global variable* and can be accessed from any function or other expressions.

Comments

A *comment* indicates statements that are not executed. Comments are used for documentation to enable programmers to easily understand the code.

Inline comments are start with `//`. For example,

```
var x; // the variable x is being declared
```

Comments that span multiple lines are enclosed between `/*` and `*/`. For example,

```
/* This complete line is a comment */
```

Control Structures and Loops

For conditional processing, JavaScript provides conditional statements, such as `if`, `if…else`, and `switch…case`. Additionally, JavaScript also provides a conditional operator, ?, whose syntax is as follows:

```
var result=(condition)?truevalue:falsevalue;
```

The variable `result` is assigned a value `truevalue` if the condition evaluates to true; otherwise, it is assigned the value `falsevalue`.

For performing tasks multiple times, JavaScript provides loops such as `while`, `do…while`, and `for`. The following sections explain the programming constructs in JavaScript.

Conditional Statements

Conditional statements are used to execute a set of statements based on certain conditions. The conditional statements available in JavaScript are `if`, `if…else`, and `switch…case`.

if

The `if` statement is used to check a condition using a logical expression and execute a set of statements based on the condition. The syntax of the `if` statement is as follows:

```
if (condition)
{
      [statements]
}
```

The following example displays the message "Please register yourself first" if the variable `user` contains the value `new`:

```
var user;
user=""Alex"
if (user = "new")
   {
         document.writeln("Please register yourself first");
   }
```

if...else

The `if...else` statement is used to execute a set of statements if a condition is true and another set of statements if the condition is false. The syntax of the `if...else` statement is as follows:

```
if (condition)
{
        [statements]
}
else
{
       [statements]
}
```

The following example displays the message "Please register yourself first" if the variable `user` contains a value `new`, otherwise, it displays the message "Welcome again!":

```
var user;
user="Alex"
```

```
if (user = "new")
{
    document.writeln("Please  register yourself first");
}
else
{
    document.writeln("Welcome again!");
}
```

switch...case

A `switch...case` block is used to compare a variable against multiple values. When a variable specified in a `switch` statement matches with the value specified in one of the `case` statements, all the statements in the remaining `case` statements are also executed. To prevent this, a `break` statement is used in each `case` statement. The following example illustrates the use of the `switch` statement:

```
var grade;
var leaves;
.
.
switch(grade)
{
case 'A':
    leaves=15;
    break;
case 'B':
    leaves=10;
    break;
case 'C':
    leaves=8;
    break;
default:
    leaves=0;
    break;
}
```

Loop Statements

A loop is used to perform iterations based on specific conditions. The `break` and `continue` keywords can be combined with any loop statement. The `break` keyword is used to exit a loop before its termination condition. The `continue` keyword is used to skip the remaining statements of the current loop and transfer the control to the condition evaluation.

for

The `for` statement consists of three expressions: initialization, condition checking, and loop expression, enclosed in parentheses. The syntax of the `for` loop is as follows:

```
for( [init_exp];[cond_expr];[loop_exp])
{
      [statements]
}
```

The following code displays numbers from 1 to 5:

```
for(var x=1; x<=5; x++)
{
   document.write(x);
   document.write("\n");
}
```

while

The `while` loop has the following syntax:

```
while(condition)
{
    [statements]
}
```

In the following code, numbers 1 to 5 are displayed using the `while` loop:

```
var x=0;
while(x<5)
{
    x=x+1;
    document.write(x);
}
```

do...while

In a `do...while` loop, the condition specified is checked after the execution of the statement block. Therefore, a `do...while` loop is executed at least once before checking the condition. The syntax of a `do...while` loop is specified below:

```
do
{
    [statements]
}
while(condition);
```

In the following code, the message "Hello" is displayed at least once, regardless of the value of `x`:

```
var x=6;
do
{
    document.writeln("Hello");
    x++;
}
while(x<5);
```

Label Statements

A label statement can be used to name a control structure. This allows you to break out of a conditional statement or a loop to a specific location. It is especially useful in the case of nested loops. In the following code, a `for` loop is nested inside another `for` loop. The inner loop contains a `break` statement. Without a label, the break statement will exit only out of the inner loop. The `break outerloop` statement makes the control exit from both the loops.

```
outerloop;
for(x=0 ;x<5; x++)
{
    for(y=0; y<5;y++)
    {
            document.write( "x is "+ x + "y is " + y);
            if(x==y)
            {
```

```
                break outerloop;
            }
        }
    }
```

with Statements

The `with` statement is used with object methods and properties. It is used to avoid repeatedly specifying reference to an object in a `with` block. For example, suppose you have to write multiple `document.write` statements in a program. You can simply enclose all these statements in a `with` block, as shown below:

```
var length=10;
var breadth=5;
var height=5;
with(document)
{
   write("length = "+ length);
   write("breadth = " + breadth);
   write("height = " + height);
   write("Volume = "+ length*breadth*height);
}
```

Functions

Functions are used to create named blocks that can be called from any place in a script. Using functions, you can define reusable code so that you do not have to write the same code multiple times. You can pass arguments to a function. The following code displays the creation and usage of a function named `calc_volume`:

```
//Declare a function calc_volume
function calc_volume(int1,int2,int3)
{
var volume=0;
volume=int1*int2*int3;
return(volume);
} //function ends
var volume=calc_volume(10,5,5); // call the function
document.write("Volume = "+ volume);
```

JavaScript Object Model

There are two types of DOMs (*Document Object Models*) available in JavaScript, Notes and Web. The Notes DOM can be used only in Notes, whereas the Web DOM is implemented on the Web. Some objects are available in both the DOMs, whereas some are available in only one of them. The following sections list JavaScript objects.

Area

The `Area` object is available only in the Web DOM. It defines an area on a document that is clickable, such as an image used as an image map, and creates a link to the hypertext reference loaded in the target window.

Array

The `Array` object is available in both Web and Notes DOMs. It is used to define arrays and contains methods and properties for manipulating an array. An *array* is used for holding a set of data elements that are represented by a single name but multiple subscripts. This object contains methods for sorting, slicing, and concatenating or joining an array.

Boolean

The `Boolean` object is available in both DOMs. It is used to convert a non-Boolean value into a Boolean value. It also contains a method to convert a Boolean value back to a string value.

Button

The `Button` object is available in the Web DOM. It represents the Domino hotspot buttons that are represented in HTML as `<INPUT TYPE=button>` tags.

A specialized button, Submit (available as the `Submit` object in the Web DOM), is used to submit an HTML form. You can also use the `Button` object to create a Submit button by calling the `Form.submit()` method.

Another specialized button, Reset (available as the `Reset` object in the Web DOM), is used to reset all form elements. The same reset functionality can be assigned to a button by using the method `form.reset()`.

Checkbox

The `Checkbox` object is available in the Web DOM. It is used to manipulate Domino fields of the type Checkbox. These fields are represented in HTML by using the `<INPUT Type=checkbox>` tag.

Date

The `Date` object is available in both DOMs. It is used to work with date and time values. It considers January 1, 1970, as the baseline date and does not work for dates prior to that. The date and time of a `Date` object reflect the client computer's date and time. This object contains methods to obtain the various components of a date, such as year, day, hour, minute, and second. It also contains methods to set the various components of a date.

Document

The `Document` object is available in both DOMs. This object is the subobject of the `Window` object and represents the actual content of the currently opened Domino form, page, or view. It contains all the UI elements of a Web application, such as text boxes, radio buttons, and check boxes. The `Document` object is used to display dynamic HTML pages.

FileUpload

The `FileUpload` object is available only in the Web DOM and is used to manipulate a file upload element. To create a FileUpload object, you can create a field and specify "INPUT TYPE=file" in the Other option on the Field extra HTML tab of the Field properties box.

Form

The `Form` object is available in both the DOMs. It consists of an array and is represented as `document.form[0]`. This array usually contains only one element, which can also be referred to as `_Dominoformname`. A form contains objects such as buttons, text areas, check boxes, or radio buttons. These objects are represented by their names as `document.forms[0].objectname`.

Frame

The `Frame` object is available only in the Web DOM and is used to manipulate the frames in a window. A frame can be accessed by its name, specified in the frames properties box.

Function

The `Function` object is available only in the Web DOM and is used to define the JavaScript code to be compiled into a function. A `Function` object is similar to a JavaScript function but is different because a `Function` object is considered as an object type variable. Additionally, a `Function` object is evaluated each time it is used and is slower in execution.

Hidden

The `Hidden` object is available only in the Web DOM and refers to Domino fields that have been hidden using the Hide paragraph options. These objects are represented in HTML by using the `<INPUT Type=hidden>` tag. A hidden field is accessible in the browser only if the Generate HTML for all fields option is selected in the Form properties box. A hidden object can be referenced by its Domino field name as `document.forms[0].fieldname`.

History

The `History` object represents an array of URLs that the client has visited in a window and applies to the currently opened window. This object is used to navigate forward and backward in the list of URLs that the user has visited and is equivalent to the history feature of a browser.

Image

The `Image` object is available in both Notes and Web DOMs. It is an array that represents the attachments, image resources, and pictures in a document. The

`Image` object is represented in HTML by the `<IMG>` tag. If an image is assigned a name in the HTML tab of the Picture properties, the image can be referred to as `document.picturename`.

Layer

The `Layer` object is available only in the Web DOM and represents a layer in an HTML document. This object contains methods to move a layer above or below another layer, resize a layer, or move a layer to a new position.

Link

The `Link` object is available in both the DOMs. It is an array that represents the actions, action hotspots, and link hotspots in documents. This object is represented using the `<A>` tag in HTML. If you have assigned a name to the action hotspot in the Hotspot Extra HTML tab of the Hotspot properties, you can refer to the hotspot as `document.hotspotname`.

Location

The `Location` object is available in both the DOMs and contains information about the current URL. It contains the origin of the page displayed in a window and can be used to access the URL programmatically. For example, you can use it to obtain information about the protocol used or the host name.

Math

The `Math` object is available in both the DOMs. It is a built-in object containing functions and properties for mathematical calculation and mathematical constants, such as pi. Since basic mathematical calculations can also be performed using operators, this object is used for advanced math functions. In addition to various trigonometric functions, it contains methods to find the maximum, minimum, rounded, ceiling, and floor values.

MimeType

The `MimeType` object is available in both the DOMs. It is a subobject of the `Navigator` object and represents a MIME (*Multipurpose Internet Mail Extension*) type supported by the client.

Navigator

The `Navigator` object is available in both the DOMs and contains information about the browser in use. You can use this object to retrieve information about the name and version of the browser. You can also obtain information about the platform on which the browser is running, the plug-ins installed on the browser, the MIME type objects that the browser supports, and the language of the browser.

Number

The `Number` object is available in both the DOMs and is used for manipulating number values. It is typically used to access certain constant values, such as the largest and smallest representable numbers and positive and negative infinity. It contains methods to convert a number to a string value or to return the primitive number value of a `Number` object.

Object

The `Object` object is available in both the DOMs. It is the base object for all other JavaScript objects.

Option

The `Option` object is available in both the DOMs and represents a choice in a selection list. Usually, this object is used in conjunction with the `Select` object. An `Option` object is used to reference a choice in a `Select` object.

Password

The `Password` object is available only in the Web DOM and refers to the Domino fields of the type Password. These objects are represented in HTML by using the `<INPUT Type=password>` tag. A `Password` object hides the text entered by the user with asterisks. A `Password` object can be referenced by its Domino field name as `document.forms[0].fieldname`.

Plugin

The `Plugin` object is available in both the DOMs and represents a software module installed on the client that the browser can invoke. This object represents an array of elements and MIME types handled by each plug-in. It contains a `refresh` method used to rebuild this array. It also contains properties to identify the description, names, and number of MIME types and the filename of the plug-in program in use.

In the Notes DOM, an additional `PluginArray` object is available that contains the `refresh` method.

Radio

The `Radio` object is available only in the Web DOM and refers to the Domino fields of the type radio button. These objects are represented in HTML by using the `<INPUT Type=radio>` tag. A `Radio` object can be referenced by its Domino field name as `document.forms[0].fieldname`.

Select

The `Select` object is available only in the Web DOM and refers to the Domino fields of any of the types Dialog list, Combo box, and List box. These objects are represented in HTML by using the `<INPUT Type=select>` tag. A `Select` object can be referenced by its Domino field name as `document.forms[0].fieldname`.

String

The `String` object is available in both DOMs and represents a set of alphanumeric characters that can be a literal string or a variable representing a string. This object contains methods to manipulate a string, such as concatenating strings, splitting strings, searching and replacing a string, or converting a string to uppercase letters.

A specialized object, RegExp, available in both Notes and Web DOMs, is used to represent the pattern of a regular expression. This object is used to find and replace matches in strings.

Text

The Text object is available only in the Web DOM and refers to Domino fields, such as Text, Number, Date/Time, Readers, Authors, and Names. These objects are represented in HTML by using the <INPUT> tag. A Text object can be referenced by its Domino field name as document.forms[0].fieldname.

Textarea

The Textarea object is available only in the Web DOM and is used to reference Domino fields of the type Rich Text. The HTML tag for this type of object is <TEXTAREA>. A Textarea object can be referenced by its Domino field name as document.forms[0].fieldname.

Window

The Window object is available in both DOMs and is used to access the currently opened page, form, view, and frame with the current focus in a frameset. This is the top-level object in JavaScript and contains four child objects: Document, Frame, Location, and History. A Window object is created whenever a browser window that contains every screen element is opened. In addition to the Window object, the Notes DOM contains the Screen object to describe the display screen.

Appendix D

Domino URL Reference

Domino URL Reference

Domino URLs are used to access Domino objects, such as databases, views, agents, or documents from a Web browser. A Domino URL consists of the following components:

- **Host name.** This is the DNS name or the IP address of the Domino server.
- **Domino object.** This is the Domino object that needs to be accessed. The Domino object can be specified using the name, alias, UNID (*Universal ID*), or NoteID of the object. The UNID uniquely identifies an element across all replicas of a database. A *NoteID* uniquely identifies an element within a particular database.
- **Action.** This is the action, such as open, save, or edit, that you want to perform on the object. An action is specified after a question mark (?). For example, `?OpenDatabase`.
- **Arguments.** These are the qualifiers specified with the action. A *qualifier* is preceded by an ampersand (&) sign. For example, to open a view in expanded mode, use the `&ExpandView` argument. The `&Login` argument can be appended to any Domino URL to force authentication with the server. When a URL is appended with the `&Login` argument, a user is prompted for a name and password regardless of the database ACL.

A sample Domino URL is as follows:

```
http://R6Server/Employee.nsf/All+Employees?OpenView&ExpandView
```

The components of this URL break down like so:

- `R6Server` is the DNS name of the Domino server.
- `Employee.nsf` is the Domino database that needs to be accessed.
- `All Employees` is the name of a view in the Employee database. A blank space in the object name must be replaced with a plus (+) symbol.
- `?OpenView` specifies the action to open the view.
- `&ExpandView` is the argument that expands all categories in the view.

The following sections explain the URLs to access various Domino objects.

Server

To access the home page of a Domino server, use the following syntax:

```
http://Host?OpenServer
```

For example, to open the home page of the server whose DNS name is `R6Server`, use the following URL:

```
http://R6Server?OpenServer
```

Database

To open a database on a server, use the following syntax:

```
http://Host/Database?OpenDatabase
```

You can specify either the name or the replica ID of the database to be accessed. A *replica ID* is a unique ID assigned to a database and is common for all replicas of the database. Therefore, even if the name of the database is modified; the database can be identified using its replica ID.

For example, the following URL opens the Employees database by specifying its name:

```
http://R6Server/Employees.nsf?OpenDatabase
```

You can also specify the replica ID of the database as follows:

```
http://R6Server/65256C620019448F?OpenDatabase
```

The "About Database" Document

To open the "About Database" document, use the following syntax:

```
http://Host/Database/$About?OpenAbout
```

For example, to open the "About Database" document of the Employees database, use the following URL:

```
http://R6Server/Employees.nsf/$about?OpenAbout
```

The "Using Database" Document

To open the "Using Database" document, use the following syntax:

```
http://Host/Database/$Help?OpenHelp
```

For example, to open the "Using Database" document of the Employees database, use the following URL:

```
http://R6Server/Employees.nsf/$help?OpenHelp
```

Icon

To access the database icon, use the following syntax:

```
http://Host/Database/$Icon?OpenIcon
```

For example, to open the database icon of the Employees database, use the following URL:

```
http://R6Server/Employees.nsf/$icon?OpenIcon
```

View

To open a view, use the following syntax:

```
http://Host/Database/View?OpenView
```

In the syntax, `View` can be replaced with the view name, alias, view UNID, view NoteID, or $defaultview.

For example, to open the All Employees view of the Employees database, use the following URL:

```
http://R6Server/Employees.nsf/All+Employees?OpenView
```

You can also open the All Employees view by specifying its UNID as follows:

```
http://R6server/Employees.nsf/0e914c60fa3f5dec65256c55001be462?OpenView
```

The following URL opens the default view of the Employees database:

```
http://R6Server/Employees.nsf/$defaultview?OpenView
```

When specifying a URL to open a view, you can use the following optional arguments with the `OpenView` command:

- **ExpandView.** Used to expand all categories of the view.
- **CollapseView.** Used to collapse all categories of the view.
- **Expand= n.** Used to display the nth row of the view in expanded form.
- **Collapse=n.** Used to display the nth row of the view in collapsed form.
- **Start=n.** Used to specify the row number of the document from where the view should start displaying.
- **Count=n.** Used to specify the number of rows of the view to be displayed. If you have used the Start argument, then the count starts from the row specified with the Start argument.
- **StartKey=String.** Used to specify a document key, at which the view starts displaying. A *document key* is used to retrieve a document based on the value of a field in the document. This value is searched in the first sorted column of the view.
- **RestrictToCategory=category.** Used to set the category to be displayed for a single category view. A *single category view* displays only one of the categories of a categorized view that is embedded on a page or a form.

Form

To open a form, use the following syntax:

```
http://Host/Database/Form?OpenForm
```

In this syntax, `Form` can be replaced by a form name, alias, form UNID, form NoteID, or `$defaultform`.

For example, the following URL opens the Employee details form with alias `emp`:

```
http://R6Server/Employees.nsf/emp?OpenForm
```

The following URL also opens the Employee details form by specifying its UNID:

```
http://r6server/Employees.nsf/545D330F9F4B8D9065256C55001970B4?Openform
```

To open the default form of the Employees database, use the following URL:

```
http://R6Server/Employees.nsf/$defaultform?OpenForm
```

When you open a form, you can use the optional argument `ParentUNID` with the `OpenForm` command. The `ParentUNID` argument is used to specify the UNID of the parent document, if the form is a response form. Additionally, if the form has the property "Formulas inherit values from selected document" enabled, the ParentUNID argument can be used.

For example, the following URL creates a response document to the form whose parent UNID is specified:

```
http://r6server/Employees.nsf/project?Openform&parentunid=1142886F0060856D65256C5E00
6A274B
```

Page

To open a page in a database, use the following syntax:

```
http://Host/Database/Page?OpenPage
```

In the syntax, `Page` can be replaced with the name, UNID, or NoteID of the page.

For example, the following URL opens the Company Policies page in the Employees database:

```
http://R6Server/Employees.nsf/Companyf+Policies?OpenPage
```

The following URL also opens the Company Policies page by specifying its UNID:

```
http://R6Server/Employees.nsf/214B1F361D08BC8F65256C580069BBE8?OpenPage
```

Frameset

To open a frameset, use the following syntax:

```
http://Host/Database/Frameset?OpenFrameset
```

In the syntax, `Frameset` can be replaced with the name, UNID, or NoteID of the frameset.

For example, the following URL opens the frameset named main in the Employees database:

```
http://R6Server/Employees.nsf/main?OpenFrameset.
```

The following URL specifies the UNID of the main frameset to open it:

```
http://R6Server/Employees.nsf/16FBF1ED30DF29C165256C5400672216?OpenFrameset
```

Document

You can perform various actions on a document, such as create, view, edit, or delete a document. The following sections explain the URLs for various actions.

Create a Document

To create a document based on a form, use the following syntax:

```
http://Host/Database/Form?CreateDocument
```

In the syntax, `Form` can be replaced with the form name, alias, form UNID, form NoteID, or `$defaultform`. For example, the following URL creates a document based on the Employee details form:

```
http://R6Server/Employees.nsf/emp?CreateDocument
```

In the URL, the alias `emp` is used instead of the form name.

Open a Document

To open a document based on a form, use the following syntax:

```
http://Host/Database/View/Document?OpenDocument
```

In the syntax, `Document` can be replaced with the document key, document UNID, document NoteID, or `$first`.

For example, the following URL opens the first document of the All Employees view:

```
http://R6server/Employees.nsf/All+Employees/$first?OpenDocument
```

The following URL opens the document whose department field contains IT, where department is the first sorted column of the By Department view.

```
http://R6Server/Employees.nsf/By+Department/IT?OpenDocument
```

The following URL opens the document with the specified UNID:

```
http://R6server/Employees.nsf/All+Employees/57f909de04a25dd665256c5e006a00e9?Open
Document
```

Edit a Document

To open a document in edit mode, use the following syntax:

```
http://Host/Database/View/Document?EditDocument
```

In the syntax, `Document` can be replaced with the document key, document UNID, document NoteID, or `$first`.

For example, to open the first document in the All Employees view for edit, use the following syntax:

```
http://R6Server/Employees.nsf/All+Employees/$first?EditDocument
```

The following URL opens the document with the specified UNID for edit:

```
http://R6server/Employees.nsf/All+Employees/57f909de04a25dd665256c5e006a00e9?Edit
Document
```

Delete a Document

To delete a document, use the following syntax:

```
http://Host/Database/View/Document?DeleteDocument
```

Similar to the `OpenDocument` and `EditDocument` commands, you can specify the document key, UNID, or the NoteID of the document to be deleted. For example, the following URL deletes the document with the specified UNID:

```
http://R6server/Employees.nsf/All+Employees/57f909de04a25dd665256c5e006a00e9?Delete
Document
```

Save a Document

Use the following syntax to save a document:

```
http://Host/Database/View/Document?SaveDocument
```

You can specify the UNID or the NoteID of the document to be saved. For example, the following URL saves the document with the specified UNID:

```
http://R6server/Employees.nsf/All+Employees/57f909de04a25dd665256c5e006a00e9?Save
Document
```

Agent

To run an agent, use the following syntax:

```
http://Host/Database/Agent?OpenAgent
```

In the syntax, `Agent` must be replaced with the agent name. You cannot use the UNID or the NoteID of the agent.

For example, the following URL runs the agent named sendmailagent in the Employees database:

```
http://R6Server/Employees.nsf/sendmailagent?openagent
```

Navigator

To open a navigator, use the following syntax:

```
http://Host/Database/Navigator?OpenNavigator
```

In the syntax, `Navigator` can be replaced with the name of the navigator, navigator UNID, navigator NoteID, or `$defaultnav`. If you use `$defaultnav`, it opens the default navigator, folders, in the database.

For example, the following URL opens the Main navigator in the Employees database:

```
http://R6Server/Employees.nsf/Main?OpenNavigator
```

The following URL also opens the Main navigator by specifying its UNID:

```
http://r6server/Employees.nsf/C35D51373C7CA44865256C570035C0F1?OpenNavigator
```

ImageResource

To open an image resource stored in a database, use the following syntax:

```
http://Host/Database/ImageResourceName?OpenImageResource
```

For example, the following URL opens the image resource named Companylogo stored in the Employees database:

```
http://R6Server/Employees.nsf/Companylogo?OpenImageResource
```

FileResource

To open a file stored as a file resource in a database, use the following syntax:

```
http://Host/Database/FileResourceName?OpenFileResource
```

For example, the following URL opens the Policy.pdf file stored as file resource in the Employees database:

```
http://R6Server/Employees.nsf/Policy.pdf?OpenFileResource
```

File Attachments

To open a file stored as an attachment in a document, use the following syntax:

```
http://Host/Database/View/Document/$File/Filename?OpenElement
```

For example, the following URL opens the file resume.txt attached to the document for the employee named Arnold:

```
http://R6Server/Employees.nsf/By+Name/Arnold/$File/resume.txt?OpenElement
```

Searching

You can search for text in a view, database, server, or domain. The common arguments that can be specified with the search commands are as follows:

- **Query=search string.** Specifies the string to be searched.
- **Count=n.** Specifies the number of search results to be displayed on each page.
- **SearchFuzzy=[TRUE, FALSE].** Specifies whether or not to use a fuzzy logic search. A fuzzy logic search looks for words with a slightly different spelling or arrangement.
- **SearchOrder=[1,2,3].** Specifies the sort order of the search result. Here 1 indicates sort by relevance, 2 indicates sort by date in ascending order, and 3 indicates sort by date in descending order.
- **SearchMax=n.** Specifies the maximum number of entries returned after search.

- **SearchWV=[TRUE,FALSE].** Specifies whether or not to include word variants in the search.
- **Start=n.** Specifies the document number starting from which the results should start displaying.
- **SearchThesaurus=[TRUE,FALSE].** Specifies whether or not to search for synonyms.

Searching a Domain

You can search for documents in the databases in a domain by using the `SearchDomain` command. To search for documents in a Domino domain, use the following syntax:

```
http://Host/Database/[templateform]?SearchDomain
```

You can create a search form that users can use to input the search conditions and the various search options. Then you can attach the preceding URL to the form to execute the search condition and display the results.

In the syntax, `templateform` is the form used to display the search result. If you do not specify this option, Domino looks for a default search form named `$$SearchDomainTemplate`.

Besides the common arguments for the search URLs, you can use the `SearchEntry = formname` argument with `SearchDomain` command. This argument displays the result of the domain search in the specified form.

Another argument is `Scope=[0,1,2]`, which is used to specify the scope of the search. In this argument, 1 indicates only Notes databases, 2 indicates only file system, and 0 indicates both.

Searching Multiple Databases

To enable users to search in multiple databases, you need to configure the SearchSite database. To search in multiple databases using the search form in the SearchSite database, you use the `SearchSite` command, as shown in the following URL:

```
http://Host/Database/[$SearchForm]?SearchSite
```

Searching a View

To search for documents in a view, use the following syntax:

```
http://Host/Database/View/[$searchForm]?Searchview
```

For example, the following URL searches for documents in the All Employees view that contain the text HR. Ten documents are displayed at a time and only 25 documents are returned.

```
http://R6Server/Employees.nsf/All+Employees?SearchView&Query=HR&Count=10&SearchMax=
25
```

Appendix E

Notes Features to Avoid When Developing Applications for the Web

Restricted @Functions

Not all @Functions are supported on the Web. The @Functions listed in Table E.1 are restricted on the Web.

Table E.1 @Functions Restricted on the Web

List 1	List 2	List 3
@Certificate	@DbCommand	@DDEExecute
@DDEInitiate	@DDEPoke	@DDETerminate
@DeleteDocument	@DialogBox	@DocChildren
@DocDescendants	@DocLevel	@DocLock
@DocMark	@DocNumber	@DocParentNumber
@DocSiblings	@Environment	@FontList
@GetFocusTable	@GetPortList	@HardDeleteDocument
@IsAgentEnabled	@IsCategory	@IsDocBeingMailed
@IsExpandable	@IsModalHelp	@MailDbName
@MailEncryptSaved Preference	@MailEncryptSent Preference	@MailSavePreference
@MailSend	@MailSignPreference	@Picklist
@Platform	@Prompt	@Responses
@SetEnvironment	@Unique	@UpdateFormulaContext
@URLGetHeader	@URLHistory	@UserPrivileges

NOTE

The `@DbCommand("Domino")` is allowed on the Web.

The `@DocChildren` @Function works only in view column formulas.

In the `@MailSend` @Function, the `[Encrypt]` and `[Sign]` flags do not work on the Web.

List of @Commands Supported on the Web

There are very few @Commands that are supported on the Web. The @Commands supported on the Web are listed in Table E.2.

Table E.2 @Commands Supported on the Web

List 1	List 2	List 3
CalendarFormat	CalendarGoto	Clear
CloseWindow	Compose	EditClear
EditDocument	EmptyTrash	FileCloseWindow
FileOpenDatabase	FileSave	Folder
FolderDocuments	MoveToTrash	NavigateNext
NavigateNextMain	NavigatePrev	NavigatePrevMain
NavNext	NavNextMain	NavPrev
NavPrevMain	OpenDocument	OpenFrameset
OpenHelpDocument	OpenNavigator	OpenPage
OpenView	RefreshFrame	RemoveFromFolder
RunAgent	SwitchView	ToolsRunMacro
ViewChange	ViewCollapse	ViewCollapseAll
ViewExpand	ViewExpandAll	ViewRefreshFields
ViewShowSearchBar		

Form Properties and Elements Not Supported on the Web

A form designed for use in Notes may not appear the same way when viewed on the Web. Some form elements and properties are not supported on the Web. This section lists such form properties and elements.

Form Properties

Table E.3 lists the form properties that are not supported on the Web.

Table E.3 Form Properties Not Supported on the Web

Property	Description
Versioning	Used to maintain a history of changes in a document by keeping both the old document and its new versions.
Anonymous Form	Used to create a form that does not record the names of authors or editors.
Conflict Handling	Used to handle conflicts arising because two users edit the same document in two different locations.
Store form in document	Used to store a form design along with every document. This property is supported only in read mode.
Disable Field Exchange	Used to exchange data between Notes and an OLE application on a field-by-field basis.
Automatically refresh fields	Used to refresh the calculations in a form automatically as soon as a field is modified.
On Create	Used to specify the default field values to be generated while creating a new document.
On Open	The Show context pane option is not supported.
Default Encryption Keys	Used to associate an encryption key with a form that must be used to encrypt all documents created using that form.
Disable printing/forwarding/copying to clipboard	Used to prevent a user from performing any specified operation.

Form Elements

Table E.4 lists the form elements that are not supported on the Web.

Table E.4 Form Elements Not Supported on the Web

Element	Description
Layout regions	Alternatively, you must use tables to align the elements in a form. You can also use layers to overlap elements.
Pop-up hotspots	Alternatively, you can display pop-ups using JavaScript. Check the term.
ActiveX components, OLE, and OCX objects	These are supported for Windows NT and 95 platforms, but the changes made to the objects cannot be saved. However, these objects are not supported for Macintosh, Unix, and OS/2 platforms.
Border controls for tables	If the top left cell of a Notes table has a border, the entire table is displayed with a border; otherwise, there is no border.

Field Properties Not Supported on the Web

Table E.5 lists the field properties that are not supported on the Web. Therefore, you must avoid using them while developing applications for the Web.

Table E.5 Field Properties Not Supported on the Web

Property	Description
Compute after Validation	Used to ensure that a field is computed only after all other fields have been validated
Give this field initial (default) focus	Used to set the initial focus on one of the fields
Display entry helper button option for keyword fields	Used to display a small arrow button for keywords fields, such as a dialog list, that display the pop-up list when users click on it

(continues)

Table E.5 Continued

Property	Description
Use Address dialog for choices for Names fields	Used to display the address dialog box to allow a user to select names from one of the directories
Use Access Control List for choices for Names fields	Used to display the entries in the ACL of a database to allow a user to select a name
Use View dialog for choices for Names field	Used to display a user-defined view to select a name
Help description	Used to display a help message at the bottom of a window when a user selects a field
Enable encryption for this field	Used to hide a field from selected users by encrypting it
Signed if mailed or saved in section	Used to attach a signature to a document

Notes View and Folder Properties Not Supported on the Web

Private views are not supported on the Web. Table E.6 lists the views and folder properties that are not supported on the Web.

Table E.6 View and Folder Properties Not Supported on the Web

Property	Description
Collapse all when database. is first opened	Used to display all view categories as collapsed.
Show in View menu.	A browser does not have access to the Notes menu; therefore, a view cannot be displayed in the menu.
On Open: Go To options	Used to specify options to indicate a document which must be selected when a view opens.
On Refresh options	Used to specify options to indicate how the documents should be refreshed in a view.

Property	Description
Unread rows	Used to assign a different font color to unread rows.
Alternate rows	Used to assign a different background color to alternate rows.
Show selection margin	Used to select a document in a view by clicking the left margin. This property is not supported for a view applet but is supported for a view rendered as HTML.
Beveled column headings	Used to specify a three-dimensional effect for the column heading in a view.
Refresh index options	Used to specify options for refreshing a view index. A view is reindexed by the Domino server.
Discard index options	Used to specify options related to when a view index must be discarded.
Show twistie when row is expandable	Twisties are always displayed with each row.

Notes Navigator Properties Not Supported on the Web

Table E.7 lists the navigator properties that are not supported on the Web.

Table E.7 Navigator Properties Not Supported on the Web

Property	Description
Auto adjust panes at run time	Used to allow a user to adjust the navigator pane in a client.
Polyline objects	Polyline objects display on the Web, but clicking them has no effect.
Highlight when options	Used to specify the highlight options for an object created in the navigator.

Notes Actions and Agent Properties Not Supported on the Web

When an application is accessed from the Web, the Notes menu is not available. Therefore, the features that require selection from a menu or related actions are not supported on the Web. The following subsections list the agent and action properties that are not supported on the Web.

Agents

The following agent properties do not work on the Web:

- **Manually from Actions Menu.** Web users do not have an Actions menu. Therefore, to run an agent, you must use actions or buttons that use `@Command([ToolsRunMacro]`. You can also use the `WebQuerySave` and `WebQueryOpen` form events.
- **"If Document Has Been Pasted" and the document selection option "Selected documents."** The concepts of pasted documents and selected documents don't apply to Web applications.

Form and View Actions

The following action properties are not supported on the Web:

- **Include action in Action menu.** Web users do not have an Actions menu. Therefore, you should use the Include action in button bar option.
- Default form and view actions that use system commands such as Edit Document, Categorize. You must use supported @Commands to create the equivalent actions.

Programs for Actions and Agents

Actions and agents are used to write code pieces to be executed when they are activated. The code can be written using simple actions, JavaScript, LotusScript, or formula language. The following types of code or programs are not supported on the Web:

- Simple actions
- LotusScript for forms, actions, and buttons

Domino Calendar Features Not Supported on the Web

The following calendar features are not supported on the Web:

- **Embedded Scheduler.** Used to embed a group calendar on a form. This is used to manage the schedule of a group.
- **Date Picker.** A date picker is a specialized calendar-type control that can be displayed with a field or added to a form or a page in order to allow a user to select a date.
- **Time Control.** Used to allow a user to select a time from a clock-type control and can be associated with a field that displays only time.
- **Duration Control.** Allows a user to select a time duration as the start and end time from a clock-type control. This control is associated with a field that displays only time and allows multiple values.

Domino Frame Properties Not Supported on the Web

The frame property Default target for links in frame should be avoided on the Web. This property is used to display a link from the source frame in a specified target frame.

The target frame can additionally be specified with each specific design element property. If the target frame is only specified in the frame properties box, when the element is replaced with another element, the links in the frame do not go to the target frame specified. To avoid this, the target frame must be specified in both the frame and the element properties box.

Domino Table Properties Not Supported on the Web

A table created in Domino Designer is displayed using the HTML <TABLE> tags. But all table features are not supported as they appear in Notes client. You can enhance tables by using HTML. Table E.8 list the table properties that are not supported on the Web.

Table E.8 Table Properties Not Supported on the Web

Property	Description
Column spacing	Used to adjust spaces for all cells between text and column borders.
Minimum height	Used to set the minimum height for all cells.
Row spacing	Used to adjust spaces for all cells between text and row borders.
Table width	The Fit to window option is not supported.
Color for cell borders	Used to specify the border color of the cells in a table.
Cell border style	The styles Ridge and Groove are not supported for cell borders.
Cell border thickness	A value greater than one is not supported.
Cell background	Only a solid background is supported. Gradients appear as the first color.
Table border style	Not supported for the entire table. The style for individual cell borders is applied.
Table border color	The border color for the entire table is not supported.
Table border effects	The border width is not supported.
Table thickness	The table thickness greater than one is not supported.
Table margin properties	Left and right margins are not supported. Table wrap and compatibility options are also not supported.
Table row property	Switch rows every n milliseconds and transitions for Show only one row at a time option is not supported on the Web.

Notes Text Styles Not Supported on the Web

The following text styles are not supported on the Web:

- Default fonts (Helvetica and Times Roman in Windows)
- Full Justification and No Wrap alignment styles
- Interline spacing that are not whole numbers are rounded off to the nearest whole number
- Formatting aids, such as tabs, indents, outdents, and extra spaces
- Shadow, Emboss, and Extrude text styles

Domino Formatting Features Not Supported on the Web

The following formatting options do not work on the Web:

- The color and size of a bullet in an ordered list
- The support for international characters (depends on the browser version and the fonts installed)
- The first line indent or outdent
- Full justification paragraph alignment
- Tabs

If you are developing an application for both a Notes client and a Web browser, the following formatting options should be avoided for a rich text field if the document is edited using both a Notes client and an editor applet in a Web browser.

- Images
- Ordered lists
- Tables
- Unordered lists

Features Not Supported by the Domino View Applet

A view embedded in a page or a form can be displayed in HTML or as a view applet. The following is the list of features that a view applet does not support:

- Pass-Thru HTML
- Calendar views
- On Refresh Options for the view
- Unread row color for a view
- Beveled headings or a view column
- Lines per heading view property
- Shrink rows to content view property
- Row spacing for a view
- Refresh Index options for the view
- Discard Index options for the view
- Unread marks for the view
- Options for ODBC access in a view
- Color of active links
- Color of visited and unvisited links
- Restrict initial index build to designer or manager view property
- View column fonts (limited to the fonts supported by Java)
- Column header fonts (limited to the fonts supported by Java)
- Show values in this column as links column property

Notes Horizontal Rule and Hotspot Properties Not Supported on the Web

The following horizontal rule and hotspot properties are not supported on the Web:

- **Horizontal rule.** Gradient color rules are not supported on the Web.
- **Hotspot.** Hotspot borders are not supported on the Web.

Appendix F

Performance-Tuning Domino Applications

Performance-Tuning Domino Applications

The performance of Domino applications can be defined in terms of two measures, application responsiveness and throughput. *Application responsiveness* refers to the time required for a particular operation that an application performs. Some of these operations are:

- Opening databases
- Opening views
- Opening documents
- Recalculation of documents
- Performing lookup operations against other databases
- Caching on the server side and the client side

Throughput is measured as data transfer rates, transactions performed per hour, and the associated resource utilization, such as CPU, memory, and storage capacity.

Improving the performance of Domino applications, therefore, involves improving the application responsiveness and throughput. Before delving into the details of how to improve application performance, first look at the factors that affect the application performance. The overall performance of your Domino applications depends on the following factors:

- Application architecture and design elements
- Application deployment factors
- Integration with external systems
- Configuration of Domino sever
- Network configuration
- Operating system configurations for server and client computers
- Various hardware configuration settings

Most of the time, application responsiveness is affected by the factors other than application architecture or design elements. Application responsiveness could be related to server load factors or response time for end user interactions. For example, server load is increased because of the following operations in a Domino application:

- View indexing
- Running agents

Leaving aside the factors regarding hardware and network configuration settings, you, as an application developer, need to take care of the application design elements as a measure to optimize application performance. The following sections discuss the various database design considerations to optimize application performance.

Application Design Factors

You can achieve better performance for your application by optimizing certain factors when designing the application. A Domino application can consist of a single database or multiple databases. You should consider splitting the application into several databases when:

- A single database is too large to incorporate the complete functionality.
- A single database is a mix of multiple features. In other words, a single database does not fit as a single logical unit.

Consider the first point. The number of documents stored and the size of the database affect the performance of an application. Therefore, splitting an application into several databases allows you to maintain the size of the databases and to distribute the load across several servers.

As for the second point, you can split an application based on database functionality or data elements. You should look at possibilities for compartmentalizing the functionality and associated data elements into different modules. Once you achieve the compartmentalization, you should split the modules into different databases.

There might be cases when an application cannot be split into several databases. In such cases, a single database represents the complete application. In such applications, you may use archival routines to move documents that meet certain criteria in to a different database. This helps to bring down the size of the of the online application database accessed by users most frequently. Based on the requirements, you may make the archived database online or keep it offline.

The next application-level design consideration is caching. In Domino, caching happens at the Domino server and at the Notes client workstation. While Notes client caches certain design elements locally on the workstation, Domino server caches design elements, lookups, and profile documents on the server. By making use of the caching mechanism to cache application design and data elements in your code, you can improve the application performance.

Forms and views are the major design elements in any database. While designing forms, consider the following points to improve application performance:

- Avoid the use of graphics
- Avoid the use of subforms
- Limit the number of tables
- Use sections and tabbed tables to improve Web access
- Limit the use of layout regions
- Avoid the use of `@Dblookup` and `@DbColumn` @Functions; instead use LotusScript
- Avoid using excessive and complex Hide When formulas

While creating views, consider the following points:

- Avoid using dynamic column sorting
- Avoid using too many columns in a view
- Avoid using complex calculations or formula in the view column
- Avoid using both ascending and descending sorting on columns; this occupies double the space and time for view indexing than single sorting
- Use categorization because it helps to improve response time, especially when documents contain reader names

Database Properties

There is a set of database properties that you can use to fine-tune the performance of your Domino application. However, note that disabling some of the properties may affect the functionality of your application. Following are some of these properties:

- **Allow use of stored form in this database.** Storing a form with every document uses system memory and may require as much as 20 times more disk space than not doing so. Disabling this property will improve the document opening time. Therefore, avoid using stored forms with documents.
- **Display images after loading.** Large image files may take more time to load, especially on slow connectivity links. Enabling this property will load all the text in the document first so that users can start reading the document while the images are getting loaded. Note that this property affects only how Notes clients load images and does not affect Web browser users.
- **Use JavaScript when generating pages.** This property controls how hotspot formulas are evaluated. If this property is enabled, hotspot formulas are not evaluated until the user clicks the hotspot. Enable this property to improve the display time for documents and navigators for your Web application.
- **Require SSL connection.** Enforcing SSL connection for your application allows you to achieve better security for your application on the Web. However, SSL requires encryption of the data that is passed back and forth between the browser and server. This adds overhead and slows down the response time. Disable this property for your Web applications if security is not of prime importance to your application.
- **Don't maintain unread marks.** Domino maintains unread marks for documents in the database on a per user basis. If you do not want this feature in your application, enable this property to improve the performance.
- **Optimize document table map.** Domino uses tables of document information when updating views. Domino searches each table for documents that appear in the view when the view is updated or rebuilt. Enabling this property will restrict Domino to search only the tables associated with the forms used by documents listed in the view. Domino uses the view selection formula for this purpose.
- **Don't overwrite free space.** To prevent unauthorized access, Domino overwrites the deleted data on a disk with a pattern, which affects the disk I/O. Enabling this property will inhibit this operation and improves performance.

- **Maintain Last Accessed property.** This controls whether the Accessed (In this file) property of the documents are updated when the documents are accessed for reading. Disabling this property decreases the disk I/O and improves the performance.
- **Disable transaction logging.** Transaction logging is used for faster recovery from server crashes. Enable this property to improve performance if you are not using transaction logging for your application.
- **Allow soft deletions.** When this property is enabled, Domino holds the documents marked for deletion based on the database property Soft delete expires time in hours. This allows you to restore deleted documents before the expiry time. Disable this property if you are not using this feature to improve performance.
- **Don't support specialized response hierarchy.** Domino maintains information in every document, which associates the documents with a parent document or response document, adding considerable overhead. Only the @Functions `@AllChildren` and `@AllDescendants` make use of this information. Enable this property to improve the performance of the database if you are not going to use the aforementioned @Functions in your application.
- **Don't allow headline monitoring.** This allows users to automatically monitor databases for information based on interest profile. To improve the performance, enable this property, which will restrict the users from monitoring the database.
- **Use LZ1 compression for attachments.** LZ1 compression uses an algorithm, which is quick and efficient compared to the Huffman method used in early releases of Domino. If you are not using a mixed environment of Domino Release 6 and earlier versions, enable this property to improve the performance.
- **Limit entries in $UpdatedBy fields.** With every document, Domino maintains the edit history in the special field $UpdatedBy. Maintaining this information occupies more disk space and slows the view updates. Limit this to a very small number to improve the performance of the database.
- **Limit entries in $Revision fields.** Similar to the edit history, Domino maintains the date and time of each document edit session. This is used for resolving replication or save conflicts. If the number of entries main-

tained is high, it occupies more disk space and slows down the view updates. Limiting the number of entries in this field will improve the performance of your application.

Database Size

As already mentioned, database size is one of the key factors that impacts application performance. A large database increases the application responsiveness, resulting in slow performance. Therefore, when designing an application, consider options to split the application into several databases.

After an application is deployed, you should control the database size to ensure that the application performance does not degrade. As a first step in maintaining control, you should constantly monitor the database size. You can monitor the database size in the Database property box. In the Info tab of the Database property box, click %Used to identify the percent of database that is currently in use, as shown in Figure F.1.

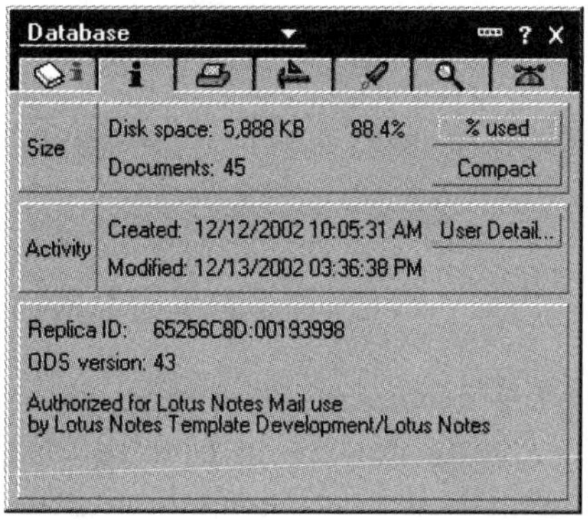

FIGURE F.1 *The Database property box displaying the database percent usage*

If this percent is high, you should consider compacting the database or archiving the documents in the database.

Compacting a Database

Most of the time, when you delete documents from a database, Domino does not immediately reduce the database file size. Instead, it tries to reuse the unused space. Therefore, even after the documents are deleted from a database, the database file size doesn't reduce, leading to poor performance. To reduce the database file size, you need to compact the database. Perform the following steps to compact a database:

1. Open the database.
2. Open the Database property box and activate the Info tab.
3. In the Info tab, click Compact. A message, "Your request to compact this database is now being carried out," appears, as shown in Figure F.2.
4. Click OK to proceed.

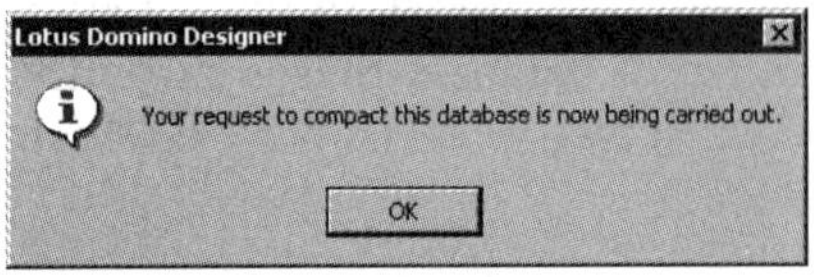

FIGURE F.2 *Compacting a database*

After compacting the database is complete, a message appears in the status bar to indicate the same.

Archiving Documents

Archiving documents involves copying the documents to a separate database, called the archive database, and then deleting the documents from the original or source database. You can archive documents based on the required criteria. For example, you can archive documents based on the number of days since the documents were last read or modified.

Documents can be archived on either the client or the server. When you archive documents, an archive database is created. By default, this database is stored in the data/archive directory on the client or server. The name of the archive database is the name of the database followed by the word *archive* in parentheses. For example, if you archive the documents of the Employees database, the archive database is named Employees (archive). The file name of the archive database is prefixed with a_ followed by the first six characters of the original database file name. You can modify the default location and file name of the archive database.

In addition to the archive database, an archive log database titled Archiving Log is created. This database stores the information about the archiving process. By default, this database is stored in the data\archive folder on the client or server. The file name of this database is prefixed with `l_` followed by the first six characters of the original database file name. Similar to the archive database, you can modify the default location and file name of the archiving log database. A single archiving log database can be used for multiple databases.

You can archive documents by using agents. These agents can be created using simple actions, formula language, LotusScript, or Java. Agents are discussed in detail in Chapter 2, "Basics of a Notes Application," and Chapter 7, "Working with Java."

You can also archive the documents by using the document archiving tool from the Database property box. Alternatively, you can archive the documents manually by choosing File/Database/Archive. Both of these methods are discussed in the following sections.

Document Archiving Tool

To run the document archiving tool, perform the following steps:

1. Open the database whose documents need to be archived.
2. Open the Database property box.
3. Click Archive Settings to open the Archive Settings dialog box, as shown in Figure F.3.

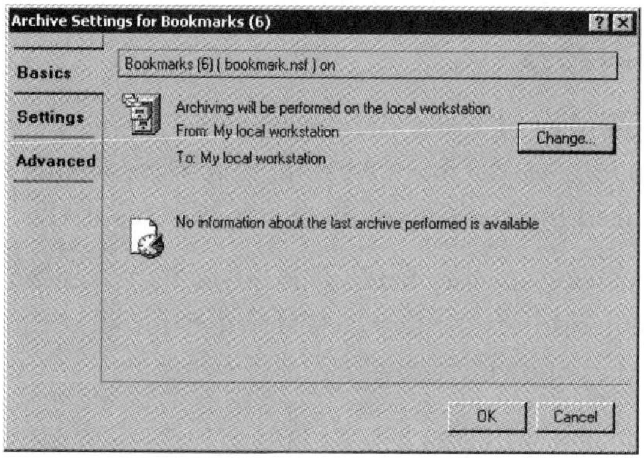

FIGURE F.3 *The Archive Settings dialog box*

4. In the Archive Settings dialog box, click the Change button to modify the destination for the archive database. It can be the local computer or the server. You can also specify whether the archiving is performed by Domino server or the Notes client manually on the local computer.

> **NOTE**
>
> To archive a database, you need to have one of the following access levels: for your mail database, at least Editor access with "delete documents" privilege; for any database other than your mail database, you need Manager access with "delete documents" privilege.

Manual Document Archiving

To archive documents manually from a client, perform the following steps:

1. Open the database to be archived.
2. Choose File/Database/Archive. A message box appears with the message "Do you want to archive documents from this database?"
3. Click Yes to proceed.

After the archiving is complete, Notes displays the number of documents archived and deleted.

Database Activities

Database activities, such as number of times the documents are read or written, impact the database performance. A database with high activities tends to perform slowly. Therefore, you need to monitor database activities regularly.

To monitor the database activities, a task, Statlog, runs on the Domino server every day at 5 A.M. This task identifies the database activities for all the databases on the server and reports the following activities:

- The total number of times users and servers accessed, read, or wrote to a database in the past 24 hours, one week, one month, and since the creation of the database
- The inactive views

- The user and server names who read or wrote documents; the list of user and server names is sorted by date

You can access the Statlog report using either the Database Activity Log entries in the log file database or the User Activity dialog box.

You can access the log file database (log.nsf) from the Domino Administrator. To view the Database Activity Log entries, perform the following steps:

1. Start Domino Administrator.
2. In the Server pane, select the server that stores the log file database.
3. Activate the Server/Analysis tab. In this tab, select the options Log/Database/Sizes and Log/Database/Usage. This tab is shown in Figure F.4.

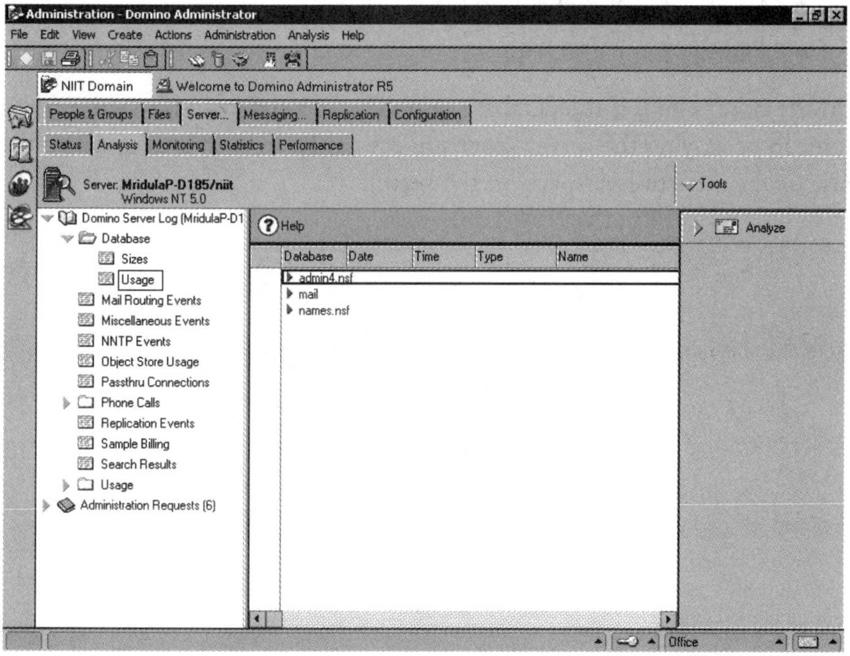

FIGURE F.4 *The Server/Analysis tab*

4. Double-click a Database Activity Log entry to view the activity details.

You can also open the log file database directly by selecting File/Database/Open from the Notes client if you do not have access to Domino Administrator.

You can access the User Activity dialog box from the Database property box. In the Database property box, activate the Info tab. In this tab, click User Details to view the User Activity dialog box.

If database activity is high, it leads to degradation of application performance. End users experience delays in accessing the database. Sometimes users may not even be able to access the database. To improve the application performance when database activity is high, set the database properties that optimize performance. Refer to the previous section, "Database Properties." If the performance does not improve even after setting the database properties, you should consider creating the database replica on another server.

Another alternative to improve the application performance is moving the database to one of the following:

- Another less heavily used disk on the same server
- Another more powerful server

On the other hand, if the database or a view in a database is inactive, there is no point in occupying the server space unnecessarily. In such a case, delete the database or the view to free space on the server.

Index

Symbols

A

B

C

D

E

F

M

N

O

P

T

W